Transforming Education With Data Science in the AI Era

Jeffrey Moore
Anderson University, USA

Ajay Garg
Morgan Stanley, India

Sharad Gupta
Christ University, India

Helen Josephine V. L.
Christ University, India

Manjari Sharma
Christ University, India

IGI Global
Scientific Publishing
Publishing Tomorrow's Research Today

Vice President of Editorial	Melissa Wagner
Director of Acquisitions	Mikaela Felty
Director of Book Development	Jocelynn Hessler
Production Manager	Mike Brehm
Cover Design	Jose Rosado

Published in the United States of America by
IGI Global Scientific Publishing
701 East Chocolate Avenue
Hershey, PA, 17033, USA
Tel: 717-533-8845
Fax: 717-533-7115
Website: https://www.igi-global.com E-mail: cust@igi-global.com

Library of Congress Cataloging-in-Publication Data

Names: Moore, Jeffrey, 1969- editor
Title: Transforming education with data science in the AI era / [edited by] Jeffrey Moore, Sharad Gupta, Manjari Sharma, Ajay Garg, Helen Josephine V L.
Description: Hershey, PA : IGI Global Scientific Publishing, [2026] | Includes bibliographical references and index. | Summary: "This book aims to explore and demonstrate how Artificial Intelligence (AI) and Data Science are revolutionizing education by offering innovative solutions to enhance learning outcomes, improve teaching methodologies, and optimize institutional efficiency"-- Provided by publisher.
Identifiers: LCCN 2025016010 (print) | LCCN 2025016011 (ebook) | ISBN 9798337321851 hardcover | ISBN 9798337321868 paperback | ISBN 9798337321875 ebook
Subjects: LCSH: Artificial intelligence--Educational applications | Educational statistics | Educational technology
Classification: LCC LB1028.43 .T738 2026 (print) | LCC LB1028.43 (ebook)
LC record available at https://lccn.loc.gov/2025016010
LC ebook record available at https://lccn.loc.gov/2025016011

British Cataloguing in Publication Data
A Cataloguing in Publication record for this book is available from the British Library.

Table of Contents

Detailed Table of Contents

ethical governance emerge as future priorities. The study also identifies generative AI, federated learning, and explainable models as promising but nascent directions requiring pedagogical alignment. The chapter offers theoretical insights into AI as a reshaping force in educational epistemology and provides practical and policy-level implications for institutions and educators. It is a roadmap for advancing responsible, inclusive, and impactful AI-driven educational transformation.

Artificial Intelligence (AI) and data science are transforming education by enhancing learning experiences, optimizing administrative processes, and enabling data-driven decision-making. AI-driven automation in assessment and feedback, along with data visualization techniques, supports educators in tracking student progress and improving curriculum development. Additionally, big data analytics enables institutions to identify learning patterns and improve student success rates. Despite these advancements, the integration of AI in education presents challenges, including ethical concerns, data privacy issues, and the risk of algorithmic bias. AI-powered tools also play a crucial role in enhancing accessibility for students with disabilities and fostering collaborative learning environments. The development of intelligent tutoring systems and AI-enhanced educational platforms provides new opportunities for personalized and inclusive education. Measuring the impact of AI on learning outcomes is essential to refining these technologies for optimal effectiveness.

This chapter explores how Artificial Intelligence (AI) transforms education through personalized learning and adaptive assessments. It highlights how AI shifts instruction from teacher-centered to student-centered models by customizing learning paths, pacing, and content based on individual learner profiles. Grounded in theories such as Constructivism, Universal Design for Learning, and Self-Determination Theory, AI applications, like intelligent tutoring systems, predictive analytics, and adaptive assessment, support differentiated instruction, increase engagement, and improve outcomes. The chapter also addresses challenges, including algorithmic bias, data privacy, ethical concerns, and the need for faculty development and equitable access. Case studies from various global contexts demonstrate AI's benefits and limitations, particularly in under-resourced schools. Finally, the chapter recommends responsible implementation strategies that ensure inclusive, effective, and ethical AI integration into educational environments.

This chapter examines the transformative role of AI-driven learning analytics in improving student engagement and academic achievement. These findings support personalized education, early identification of endangered students, and rapid interventions to improve learning outcomes. This chapter identifies global implementation, comparative implementation of education systems, and justice, privacy, and scalability challenges. It focuses on the most essential role of educators in interpreting and using analysis. The recommendations are aimed at educators, institutions, and political decision-makers to ensure AI's ethical and effective integration into education. This chapter is closed with a call for further research and development to promote responsibility, integrated, and innovative use of AI in educational environments worldwide.

This chapter introduces an AI-based system for real-time monitoring of student engagement by analyzing emotional responses and attention levels during classroom sessions. Using a camera placed in front of students, the system applies computer vision algorithms to detect focus and distraction through eye movements and facial expressions. The core of the system is the Emo-Engage Analysis framework, which classifies engagement into three levels based on eye retention, duration of attentiveness, and indicators of positive emotional response. Drawing on recent research in emotional and attentional regulation, this method offers a fine-grained analysis of student engagement. Aggregated engagement data allow instructors to assess both individual and group dynamics throughout a lesson. These insights support the evaluation of teaching strategies and provide meaningful feedback on instructional impact, helping educators adapt their methods to foster more effective and emotionally supportive learning environments.

AI-based chatbots in education are extensively used. This chapter discusses the challenges and benefits of AI-based chatbots for students, teachers, and administrators. The use cases of AI-based chatbots reveal benefits and concerns. This chapter provides ethical and social implications and discusses the framework for the effective implementation of AI-based chatbots in education. The framework offers ethical implications such as fairness, accountability, transparency, accuracy, and autonomy. Further, it mentions the social implications such as equity, mental health, social interaction, assessment and feedback, and privacy and security. Lastly, it gives the policy implications and future research directions.

The integration of artificial intelligence (AI) into education is revolutionizing the role of educators, requiring a deeper understanding of their evolving responsibilities. This chapter explores teacher-AI collaboration, focusing on how educators can adapt AI tools while maintaining the human touch. Existing literature addresses challenges like AI overshadowing teachers, ethical concerns around data privacy, and the need for new skills. The authors propose the "AI-Educator Symbiosis Model" (AESM), a novel framework that emphasizes a balanced partnership between teachers and AI. Pilot implementations show a 25% improvement in teacher efficiency and 15% increase in student engagement compared to traditional methods. The framework bridges the gap between theoretical research and practical application, offering a scalable solution for schools worldwide. This chapter underscores the potential of AI-powered teachers and sets a foundation for future research in this rapidly evolving field.

These days tech is disrupting every sector out there – and yes, schooling is no exception. We aren't dreaming about mixing Generative AI (GenAI for short) into our classrooms anymore; however, there's the good and bad. Now educators are considered to be more than simple knowledge deliverers and are expected to be wedded to these new tools into specialized, engaging lessons. It's somewhat of a fine balance where GenAI can actually very much empower teachers and students, rather than drown them in tech. In general, this implies that we must consider carefully how GenAI should be used for its potential to function at its best. Here we discuss how GenAI can reconfigure teaching methods to improve both the quality and reach of education. Using GenAI well is ultimately a question of employing a sort of framework that combines brand new ideas with 'what works' in teaching.

The integration of AI in education brings significant benefits across all educational levels but also presents challenges during development, such as limited funding, insufficient digital skills among educators, and resistance to technology adoption. This research examines how AI-driven solutions like intelligent tutoring systems, adaptive learning, and AI-assisted assessments impact lifelong learning. The success of AI in education depends on collaboration between educational institutions, technology companies, and government bodies to maintain ethical standards. Industry-academia alliances and multi-sector partnerships accelerate the development and implementation of AI in education. Practical examples from K-12 schools and higher education highlight the role of AI in improving educational platforms and student outcomes through data-driven strategies. The chapter discusses overcoming obstacles and fostering partnerships to create inclusive, future-focused educational programs.

By enabling adaptive learning systems that can quickly evaluate and enhance learning experiences, artificial intelligence (AI) and data science are revolutionizing education. In order to enable institutions to offer customized recommendations, automated feedback, and adaptive evaluations based on student performance data, this chapter examines how machine learning approaches, predictive analytics, and educational algorithms are transforming personalized education. We look at how artificial intelligence (AI)-powered chatbots, virtual teachers, and intelligent grading systems are revolutionizing information distribution, improving accessibility, and improving the educational experience. The education sector may change to become smarter, more efficient, and especially tailored to student's needs by leveraging AI-driven analytics and optimization. The chapter focus how thorough data analytics helps teachers make informed decisions to enhance curriculum design, teaching methods entail to increase productivity and scalability

Education receives transformational changes through artificial intelligence elements we could not have predicted. The discussion now proceeds to show how existing smart systems transform established teaching practices and modify educational student procedures. The public can occasionally witness AI working through education setups that adapt lessons to individual students and chat-based tutoring services and predictive analytics programs which help early detection of academic issues. Such technology systems provide immediate feedback while alerting teachers about students needing help leading to an inevitable transformation of classroom environments. The present educational tools offer promising prospects to advance education into a different future framework. Natural language processing brings interactive experiences to lessons while virtual and augmented reality technologies present virtual simulations such as diverse environments.

India has made significant progress in using digital technology in education, with Learning Management Systemsplaying a key role. LMS offer scalable platforms for content delivery, assessment, and engagement, enhancing both teaching and learning. They enable personalized learning, simplify administrative tasks, and bridge the digital divide, improving accessibility across geographies. One such initiative, eVidya, provides digital content to school students. This study explores the role of LMS in public education and the challenges of integrating them into government schools, balancing local needs with global standards. The paper analyzes LMS evolution, key features, and benchmarks, with a detailed review of India's DIKSHA system and comparisons with international platforms like Google Classroom, Canvas, Moodle, and Schoology. It looks at country-specific LMS solutions from the US, Europe Australlia and Asia. The research proposes the Integrated eVidya-LMS Implementation Framework for Karnataka's schools, highlighting the potential benefits for India's digital education landscape.

In the digital era, ensuring the security, authenticity, and accessibility of academic credentials is crucial. Traditional credentialing and academic record-keeping systems suffer from inefficiencies, security vulnerabilities, and verification issues. Blockchain technology offers a decentralized, tamper-proof, and transparent solution to these challenges. This chapter explores blockchain's potential in academic credentialing, examining its benefits, challenges, and real-world applications. Academic institutions currently rely on centralized authorities, which can be inefficient and susceptible to fraud. Blockchain provides an immutable ledger that enables secure issuance, decentralized verification, and fraud prevention. By leveraging cryptographic security and smart contracts, institutions can issue digital diplomas and certificates that are instantly verifiable, eliminating the need for intermediary verification. Blockchain also enhances lifelong learning records by allowing students to consolidate academic achievements into a single digital identity. This improves global mobility.

Bhargavi Konda, University of the Cumberlands, USA
Akhila Reddy Yadulla, University of the Cumberlands, USA
Mounica Yenugula, University of the Cumberlands, USA
Vinay Kumar Kasula, University of the Cumberlands, USA

The quick advancement of big data sharing increases the importance of protecting data privacy. Differential privacy appeared in 2006 to become the fundamental privacy-preserving data mining and publication method. Various technologies, including federated learning, homomorphic encryption, and secure multi-party computation, have introduced new solutions for safeguarding data privacy during recent technological developments. Differential privacy is experiencing a comparison test in current technology markets because Google and Apple have integrated it into new products. This chapter begin by examining the differential privacy systems used in traditional centralized data models and their usage in data mining and publishing processes. The chapter investigates modern developments in local differential privacy by examining randomized response Bloom filters and statistical inference tools related to crowdsourcing systems.

Devadatta Das, Haldia Institute of Technology, India
Animesh Samanta, Haldia Institute of Technology, India
Sabyasachi Samanta, Haldia Institute of Technology, India

Detecting and removing impulse noise remains a difficult task in image processing, especially for Salt and Pepper Noise (SAPN) and Random Valued Impulse Noise (RVIN). SAPN impacts pixels with intensities between '0' and '255', but RVIN introduces arbitrary pixel values between '0' and '255', resulting in stray dots that are

Foreword

It is a great privilege to write the Foreword for *Transforming Education With Data Science in the AI Era*, a timely and pioneering contribution to the evolving educational landscape. As India aspires to become a global knowledge hub, it is essential that our education system embraces the transformational role of Artificial Intelligence (AI) and Data Science. This book is a significant step in that direction—offering not just knowledge, but a visionary pathway for educational reform in the digital age.

This book is not merely a collection of academic chapters; it is a milestone in reimagining how we teach, learn, assess, and lead in a technology-driven world. The chapters explore critical areas including personalized and adaptive learning, emotional engagement analytics, learning management systems, ethical AI governance, blockchain-based credentialing, generative AI in classrooms, and data privacy—each of which speaks directly to the future of education.

I am confident that this work will be immensely beneficial to:

- **Scholars and researchers** who are looking to advance the field of educational technology and pedagogy,
- **Educators and faculty members** who wish to innovate in their teaching practices,
- **Policy makers and education leaders** seeking informed strategies for AI integration in institutions, and
- **Society at large**, as the outcomes of this transformation will influence how future generations learn, think, and contribute to nation-building.

Aligned with the objectives of the National Education Policy (NEP) 2020, this book contributes meaningfully to the goals of equity, excellence, digital inclusion, and interdisciplinary innovation. It bridges the gap between technological advancement and pedagogical need, between research and practice, and between policy and classroom implementation.

I take this opportunity to congratulate the editors and authors for their outstanding contribution. A special note of appreciation to Mr. Ajay Garg for shaping the original idea behind this important work. I also extend my heartfelt congratulations to Professors Manjari Sharma, Sharad Gupta, Jeffrey Moore, and Helen V L for their exemplary academic collaboration and commitment that brought this vision into reality. Their dedication and collective expertise have resulted in a work that will stand as a reference point and catalyst for academic transformation.

I trust this book will inspire institutions, educators, and stakeholders to embrace responsible and inclusive innovation, and I am hopeful that it will lead to meaningful change in how we understand and implement education in the AI era.

Shri Inder Singh Parmar

Minister of Higher Education, Technical Education, and Ayush, Government of Madhya Pradesh, India

Preface

In recent years, the fusion of Artificial Intelligence (AI) and Data Science has begun to transform education in ways once thought to be speculative fiction. Today, we stand at the intersection of pedagogy and machine intelligence, where teaching methods are redefined, learning experiences are personalized, and institutional operations are guided by predictive analytics. As editors of *Transforming Education With Data Science in the AI Era*, our aim has been to gather diverse voices that explore, explain, and critically engage with this transformation. This volume brings together researchers, educators, data scientists, and policymakers from across the globe to illuminate how AI and data-driven technologies are reshaping the educational landscape—enhancing outcomes, reconfiguring teaching roles, and raising vital questions about ethics, equity, and efficacy.

The chapters in this book offer a panoramic view of how AI and data science are deployed across educational contexts—from K–12 classrooms and higher education institutions to workforce training and lifelong learning. These contributions cover a wide range of topics, including personalized learning, adaptive assessments, real-time emotion tracking, generative AI in lesson planning, privacy-preserving data practices, and the integration of blockchain for credentialing. Collectively, they paint a detailed picture of both the potential and pitfalls of educational transformation in the AI era. We have deliberately included voices from varied academic and regional backgrounds to ensure a holistic and inclusive dialogue that reflects the global nature of this shift.

Our hope in compiling this volume is not only to showcase pioneering research and innovation but also to provoke meaningful reflection. As AI continues to evolve, education will face fundamental questions about the role of teachers, the meaning of student engagement, the future of equity, and the mechanisms of accountability. With every algorithm integrated into a learning environment, we must ask: What are we optimizing for? Who benefits? And what new possibilities—and responsibilities—emerge? This preface is therefore not just an introduction to the chapters that follow, but an invitation to all readers—academics, practitioners, policymakers, and students alike—to critically engage with the complex and exciting terrain of AI-driven education.

OVERVIEW OF CHAPTERS

Chapter 1: AI and Data Science: Transforming the Education Landscape

This chapter provides a comprehensive introduction to how artificial intelligence (AI) and data science are reshaping education. By leveraging AI algorithms, educators can now analyze vast quantities of data to create personalized learning experiences tailored to individual student needs. Predictive analytics enables early identification of at-risk students, allowing timely interventions. Administrative processes are also being streamlined with AI-powered tools, freeing educators to focus more on teaching and mentorship. The chapter concludes by emphasizing how data science enhances curriculum evaluation and continuous institutional improvement, promoting inclusivity and adaptability across diverse learning environments.

Chapter 2: Mapping Four Decades of AI and Data Science Evolution in Education (1983–2025)

Through a bibliometric analysis of nearly two thousand Scopus-indexed publications, this chapter charts the trajectory of AI and data science in education from 1983 to 2025. Dominant themes such as machine learning and e-learning illustrate the field's maturity, while emerging areas like student-centered AI, generative AI, and federated learning point to future research priorities. The chapter identifies both the strengths and gaps in current literature, offering a roadmap for responsible and inclusive AI integration. It also examines ethical and epistemological implications, positioning AI as a transformative force within educational systems.

Chapter 3: Overview of AI Algorithms and Data Science Techniques Relevant to Education

This chapter surveys the core AI algorithms and data science methodologies currently revolutionizing educational practice. From AI-driven feedback systems to big data analytics and intelligent tutoring platforms, it outlines how technology can support curriculum refinement and improve student outcomes. The chapter also discusses ethical and privacy-related challenges, emphasizing the importance of mitigating algorithmic bias and ensuring accessibility. It underscores the potential of these tools to enable more inclusive, personalized, and effective learning ecosystems.

Chapter 4: The Role of Artificial Intelligence in Personalized Learning and Adaptive Assessments

Focusing on the shift from standardized to individualized education, this chapter explores how AI supports customized instruction and adaptive assessments. By drawing on learning theories such as Constructivism and Universal Design for Learning, it presents how predictive analytics and intelligent systems optimize engagement and learning outcomes. Case studies reveal the benefits and obstacles of implementing AI in diverse educational contexts, with particular attention to ethical considerations, faculty readiness, and equitable access.

Chapter 5: The Role of AI-Powered Learning Analytics in Enhancing Student Engagement and Performance

This chapter delves into the application of AI-driven learning analytics for improving academic performance and student engagement. It outlines how analytics can inform personalized learning pathways, detect at-risk students, and support data-driven interventions. Emphasis is placed on the role of educators in interpreting these insights and translating them into meaningful pedagogical strategies. The chapter concludes with policy recommendations and a call for continued research to ensure responsible integration of analytics across global educational systems.

Chapter 6: AI-based Real-Time Class Engagement Emotions Monitoring System

Introducing an AI-powered system designed to track student emotional engagement in real time, this chapter presents a novel framework that analyzes facial expressions and eye movement during classroom sessions. The Emo-Engage Analysis model classifies levels of student attention and emotional response, offering teachers actionable insights into both individual and group dynamics. The system provides a feedback loop that educators can use to adapt teaching strategies, fostering more emotionally supportive and responsive learning environments.

Chapter 7: AI-Based Chatbots for Education—A Framework for Ethical AND Social Perspectives

This chapter investigates the growing use of AI-powered chatbots in educational settings and offers a comprehensive framework for assessing their ethical and social implications. While chatbots enhance communication, administrative efficiency, and personalized support, they also raise concerns regarding fairness, accountability, mental health, and data privacy. The framework proposed helps educators and institutions navigate these complexities while highlighting future research directions and policy considerations.

Chapter 8: AI-Powered Teachers—The Role of Educators in a Data-Driven World

Exploring the evolving role of educators in an AI-integrated classroom, this chapter proposes a balanced partnership between human teachers and intelligent technologies. The AI-Educator Symbiosis Model introduced here aims to boost teacher efficiency and student engagement without replacing the essential human elements of education. Pilot studies suggest measurable improvements in teaching outcomes, and the chapter advocates for scalable adoption supported by professional development and ethical guidelines.

Chapter 9: Empowering Educators—Leveraging Genai for Enhanced Lesson Planning and Student Engagement

This chapter focuses on the transformative impact of Generative AI (GenAI) on teaching practices. Emphasizing the importance of educator empowerment, it outlines strategies for integrating GenAI into lesson planning to create dynamic and engaging classroom experiences. The chapter presents a balanced view of GenAI's promise and pitfalls, advocating for frameworks that combine technological innovation with pedagogical best practices to enhance educational quality.

Chapter 10: Training and Development in AI-Driven Education—Scaling Solutions, K–12 to WORKFORCE

Analyzing the opportunities and challenges of AI integration across all levels of education, this chapter underscores the need for collaborative, cross-sector partnerships to build ethical and effective systems. The discussion includes intelligent tutoring systems, AI-assisted assessments, and adaptive learning technologies, highlighting their impact on lifelong learning and workforce readiness. The chapter also stresses the importance of digital literacy among educators and provides case studies that illustrate scalable implementation strategies.

Chapter 11: Smart Learning Platforms—The Integration of AI and Data Science in Educational Settings

This chapter investigates how smart learning platforms powered by AI and data science enable personalized, scalable, and efficient educational experiences. By examining adaptive feedback mechanisms, virtual teaching assistants, and intelligent grading systems, it illustrates how technology can enhance both accessibility and curriculum design. The discussion emphasizes data-informed decision-making to support productivity and innovation in educational institutions.

Chapter 12: Balancing AI and Pedagogy—The Future of Technology in Education

Highlighting the profound shifts AI is introducing into education, this chapter examines how current smart systems are altering teaching practices and student engagement. Through examples like adaptive learning environments, chatbots, and predictive analytics, it illustrates the integration of AI into real-world classroom settings. The chapter explores the pedagogical potential of emerging technologies such as natural language processing, virtual reality, and augmented simulations.

Chapter 13: Innovative Frameworks for LMS integration in Public Education

This chapter explores the evolution and future of Learning Management Systems (LMS) within public education. It compares national initiatives with global benchmarks to assess how LMS platforms can bridge digital divides and meet local needs. Focusing on India's DIKSHA system and similar platforms worldwide, the chapter proposes an implementation framework that balances global standards with region-specific considerations to enhance educational equity and scalability.

Chapter 14: Blockchain for Credentialing and Academic Record-Keeping

Addressing the limitations of traditional credentialing systems, this chapter explores how blockchain technology can offer secure, tamper-proof, and decentralized solutions for academic record-keeping. By leveraging smart contracts and digital verification methods, institutions can issue credentials that are globally verifiable and resistant to fraud. The chapter also discusses the broader implications of blockchain for lifelong learning and cross-border academic mobility.

Chapter 15: Privacy-Preserving Data Sharing Technologies

This chapter delves into the critical issue of maintaining data privacy in the era of big data and AI. It examines technologies such as differential privacy, federated learning, and homomorphic encryption, evaluating their effectiveness in safeguarding personal information. Real-world applications by major tech companies are discussed, along with emerging tools like Bloom filters and crowdsourced inference models that support secure and ethical data use in educational contexts.

Chapter 16: Evaluation and Improvement of AI and Data Science-Based Salt and Pepper Noise Reduction Techniques

Focusing on the technical domain of image processing, this chapter examines how AI and data science are advancing noise reduction methods for enhanced visual clarity. It compares various techniques using quantitative metrics like PSNR and SSIM and assesses their effectiveness across standard test images. These innovations have broader implications beyond education, impacting fields such as healthcare diagnostics and astronomical imaging.

Looking ahead, one of the most urgent tasks is ensuring that AI and data science in education are deployed ethically, inclusively, and responsibly. Several chapters in this book grapple with these concerns, offering thoughtful frameworks for privacy protection, equitable access, and the social implications of algorithmic systems. As AI's presence in classrooms grows, so does the need for robust governance mechanisms and continuous dialogue between technologists and educators. We hope readers will find in these chapters not only solutions, but also challenges worth tackling—issues that require interdisciplinary collaboration and long-term commitment.

At the heart of this transformation lies the human element. While data can inform, predict, and optimize, it cannot replace the empathy, intuition, and inspiration that educators bring to the learning process. This volume underscores the importance of human-AI collaboration, where technology serves not as a replacement, but as a partner to educators. Several chapters present compelling visions of this partnership, where AI augments teacher capabilities, amplifies student agency, and enhances the learning experience without compromising ethical standards or pedagogical goals.

Finally, we would like to thank the authors who contributed their knowledge, time, and vision to this book. Their expertise has helped us construct a multidimensional map of how AI and data science can—and must—shape the future of education. We also thank our institutions and publishing partners for their support in making this project a reality. As readers engage with the insights contained in this volume, we hope it inspires further research, fosters global collaboration, and most importantly, equips educators and decision-makers to harness technology in ways that advance human flourishing. Welcome to the future of learning—one that is data-driven, AI-enhanced, and profoundly human.

Acknowledgment

We, the editors of *Transforming Education With Data Science in the AI Era*, extend our heartfelt gratitude to all those who contributed to the successful realization of this book.

First and foremost, we express our sincere thanks to Shri Inder Singh Parmar, Hon'ble Minister of Higher Education, Technical Education, and Ayush, Government of Madhya Pradesh, for penning the Foreword and for his visionary leadership in strengthening the higher education ecosystem in India. His encouragement reinforces the significance of integrating emerging technologies with inclusive and ethical education practices.

We are deeply grateful to all contributing authors whose rich insights, rigorous research, and collaborative spirit have shaped the intellectual depth and diversity of this volume. Your dedication to exploring the intersection of data science, artificial intelligence, and education has made this book a meaningful and timely contribution to the global academic community.

Special acknowledgment is due to Mr. Ajay Garg, whose conceptualization of this book laid the foundation for our collective work. His constant support, mentorship, and clarity of vision helped bring this initiative to life.

We also thank our respective institutions—Anderson University, USA, Christ University, India, and other affiliated organizations—for fostering an environment of academic freedom and research collaboration. Your support made it possible to develop this book in alignment with international research standards and educational relevance.

To the publishing team at IGI Global, we appreciate your professionalism, patience, and guidance throughout the editorial process. Your commitment to academic excellence and global dissemination has added value to every stage of this publication journey.

Lastly, we acknowledge the support of our families, colleagues, and students—whose encouragement and faith in our work kept us inspired throughout this process.

It is our hope that this book will serve as a catalyst for dialogue, innovation, and meaningful change across the global education landscape.

Jeffrey Moore
Sharad Gupta
Manjari Sharma
Ajay Garg
Helen V L

Chapter 1
AI and Data Science:
Transforming the Education Landscape

Oindrilla Ghosh
https://orcid.org/0000-0001-9609-0781
Christ University, India

Binod Kumar
https://orcid.org/0009-0002-9721-1367
Radha Govind University, India

ABSTRACT

Artificial Intelligence (AI) and Data Science are revolutionizing the education landscape by providing innovative solutions for personalized learning, assessment, and administration. AI algorithms analyze vast amounts of educational data to identify student learning patterns, enabling tailored learning experiences that cater to individual needs. With predictive analytics, educators can identify at-risk students early, allowing for timely intervention and support. Moreover, AI-powered tools help streamline administrative tasks, freeing up teachers to focus more on instruction and less on paperwork. Data science also enables institutions to assess curricular effectiveness, ensuring continuous improvement of programs. As AI technologies evolve, they hold the potential to create a more engaging, adaptive, and efficient learning environment for all students, regardless of their backgrounds.

INTRODUCTION

The landscape of education is in the midst of an unprecedented transformation, propelled by the advances in Artificial Intelligence (AI) and Data Science (Schwartz,

DOI: 10.4018/979-8-3373-2185-1.ch001

2020). In a world increasingly driven by technology, these innovations are reshaping how educators teach, how students learn, and how institutions manage their operations (Bhagat & Kim, 2020). AI, the simulation of human intelligence processes by machines, and Data Science, the discipline that combines statistical techniques with computational tools to extract knowledge from data, have become integral to educational reform and enhancement (Barnard, 1997).

As traditional pedagogical methods face challenges, including the need for personalization, efficiency, and access, AI and Data Science offer solutions that cater to a diverse student population (Parsad, 2008). For instance, AI-driven adaptive learning platforms analyze student interactions and performance to provide tailored educational experiences that meet individual learning styles and paces (Parker, 1999). Such personalization is critical in an age where one-size-fits-all approaches are increasingly inadequate (Thurmond & Wambach, 2004).

Moreover, the vast amounts of data generated in educational settings can be harnessed through Data Science to inform decisions at all levels, from classroom instruction to institutional strategy (Bernard et al., 2009). By leveraging analytics, educators can uncover insights into student behavior, engagement, and achievement, allowing for data-driven interventions that can enhance outcomes (Martin & Bolliger, 2018). Furthermore, predictive analytics can help identify at-risk students, enabling early support and intervention strategies that can significantly improve retention and graduation rates (Tinto, 2022).

AI and Data Science also extend to administrative functions, automating routine tasks such as scheduling, grading, and resource allocation, thereby allowing educators to focus on teaching and mentoring (Yamamoto et al., 1969). The integration of these technologies is not merely a trend; it represents a fundamental shift in the operational framework of educational institutions (Fredricks et al., 2004).

However, the implementation of AI and Data Science in education is not without challenges (Nguyen et al., 2021). Ethical considerations, including data privacy, bias in algorithms, and the digital divide, must be addressed to ensure equitable access and outcomes (Dixson, 2015). The future of educational technology lies not only in effective implementation but also in the cultivation of an ethical foundation that prioritizes the well-being of all students (Kuh, 2001).

As we explore how AI and Data Science are reshaping education, it becomes essential to recognize their potential to empower learners and educators alike (Henrie et al., 2015). This transformation is not just about enhancing academic performance; it is about reimagining the entire educational experience to make it more engaging, inclusive, and effective for the diverse needs of today's learners (Baker et al., 2012).

BACKGROUND

The roots of AI can be traced back to the mid-20th century when pioneers like Alan Turing and John McCarthy started to conceptualize machines capable of exhibiting human-like intelligence (Castelli & Sarvary, 2021). The field has evolved substantially, especially in recent decades, driven by advances in computational power, algorithms, and the availability of large datasets (Schwenck & Pryor, 2021). Data Science, emerging as a distinct discipline in the early 21st century, combines principles from statistics, computer science, and domain-specific knowledge, allowing for the extraction of meaningful patterns from data (Bluemink & Järvelä, 2004).

In the educational context, the application of AI began with simple tools aimed at automating administrative tasks (Gemmel et al., 2020). Early forms of AI, such as intelligent tutoring systems, provided basic personalized learning experiences by mimicking the interactions akin to human tutors (Jamieson, 2020). As computational capabilities improved, machine learning algorithms became more sophisticated, enabling deeper insights into student learning processes and behavior (Perets et al., 2020).

The explosion of digital technologies has further accelerated this evolution (Singhal, 2020). Online learning platforms, Learning Management Systems (LMS), and mobile applications generate vast amounts of data, which can be analyzed to understand learning outcomes better (Van Heuvelen et al., 2020). Data Science techniques like clustering, regression analysis, and natural language processing enable educators to interpret this data effectively, helping to enhance curriculum design and instruction (Swan & Ice, 2010).

The rise of big data has transformed educational research, shifting methodologies from traditional approaches focused on small sample sizes to large-scale analyses that can capture the complexities of learning environments (Wenzel, 2020). This transition allows for more robust conclusions about educational practices and policies, fostering a culture of evidence-based decision-making (Bhagat & Kim, 2020).

Furthermore, the COVID-19 pandemic catalyzed the adoption of AI and Data Science, as educational institutions were forced to pivot to online learning formats (Schwartz, 2020). This rapid shift revealed both opportunities and challenges, highlighting the importance of technology in facilitating continuous learning even amidst disruptions (Kumar et al., 2021). The crisis acted as a powerful reminder of the need for adaptable, resilient educational systems that can serve diverse communities effectively (Tinto, 2022).

The ongoing integration of AI and Data Science in education seeks not only to enhance learning outcomes but also to reimagine traditional educational frameworks (Nguyen et al., 2021). As educators continue to navigate this transformative landscape, it becomes increasingly crucial to focus on pedagogical strategies that effectively leverage these innovations, considering the unique needs of learners and the ethical implications of data usage (Kumar et al., 2021). Through this lens, the future of education promises to be more interconnected, personalized, and, ultimately, more effective in preparing students for a dynamic, evolving world (Castelli & Sarvary, 2021).

THEORETICAL FRAMEWORKS OF AI AND DATA SCIENCE IN EDUCATION

The integration of Artificial Intelligence (AI) and Data Science into education has paved the way for innovative teaching approaches and enhanced learning experiences (Schwenck & Pryor, 2021). Theoretical frameworks provide a structured understanding of how these technologies can be leveraged in educational contexts, guiding both the development and implementation of AI-driven systems and data analytics (Wester et al., 2021).

Constructivism and Learning Analytics: One primary theoretical framework that aligns well with AI and Data Science is Constructivism, which posits that learners construct knowledge through interactions and experiences rather than merely absorbing information (Fulfer et al., 2020). Learning analytics, a subfield of data science, utilizes data generated from learners' interactions with educational platforms and materials (Fung & Lam, 2020). This approach can facilitate a constructivist environment by identifying how students engage with content (Jamieson, 2020). By analyzing this data, educators can tailor interventions and resources to align with individual learning styles, fostering an engaging and personalized learning experience (Perets et al., 2020).

Cognitive Load Theory and Adaptive Learning Systems: Another relevant theoretical perspective is Cognitive Load Theory (CLT), which focuses on how information processing can be optimized in learners (Singhal, 2020). AI technologies can support CLT by creating adaptive learning systems that adjust complexity levels in real time based on a learner's cognitive load (Van Heuvelen et al., 2020). These systems leverage algorithms and data analysis to assess students' performance, providing optimal challenge levels (Swan & Ice, 2010). As a result, students receive customized support that enhances their understanding while minimizing cognitive overload, which is crucial in a learning environment where individual capacities vary significantly (DeNoyelles et al., 2014).

Behaviorism and Intelligent Tutoring Systems: The behavioral approach to learning emphasizes the importance of reinforcement and observable behavior changes (Bhagat & Kim, 2020). Intelligent Tutoring Systems (ITS) exemplify the application of this framework in the educational domain (Schwartz, 2020). By utilizing AI, ITS can track a student's responses and adapt instruction accordingly, offering immediate feedback and reinforcement (Barnard, 1997). The computational modeling used within ITS draws upon historical performance data and behavioral patterns, making it possible to create an interactive environment where students can practice skills and receive guided support, reminiscent of one-on-one mentorship in traditional settings (Parsad, 2008).

Social Constructivism and Collaborative Learning: Social constructivist theories emphasize the role of social interaction in knowledge building (Allen & Seaman, 2016). AI and data analytics can enhance collaborative learning environments by analyzing group dynamics and individual contributions in real-time (Kumar et al., 2021). Through social network analysis and sentiment analysis, educators can identify effective collaboration patterns and areas where students may struggle (Bernard et al., 2009). Such insights enable facilitators to nurture teamwork skills and create collaborative experiences that benefit from diverse perspectives, ultimately fostering deeper understanding and knowledge construction among learners (Moore, 1989).

FOUNDATIONS OF AI AND DATA SCIENCE IN EDUCATIONAL TRANSFORMATION

At the foundation of AI and Data Science in education lies a combination of data, algorithms, and user experience, each vital to creating impactful learning experiences (Parker, 1999). Understanding these core components and how they interact enables stakeholders to make informed decisions about the integration of technology in learning environments (Thurmond & Wambach, 2004).

Data as a Foundation: Data serves as the cornerstone of AI and Data Science, especially in educational contexts (Bernard et al., 2009). Vast amounts of data generated by students' online interactions, assessments, and behavior provide a rich source of information that can be analyzed to derive insights (Martin & Bolliger, 2018). This data can be both structured (quantitative metrics such as test scores) and unstructured (qualitative data like student writings) (DeMonbrun et al., 2017). A robust data management system is essential, ensuring data collection, storage, and privacy compliance (Furlong & Christenson, 2008). As educators harness this data, they can identify trends and patterns that inform personalized learning strategies, helping students achieve better outcomes through targeted interventions (Karweit, 1989).

Algorithmic Processes: Algorithms are the tools that process educational data and generate actionable insights (Nguyen et al., 2021). Machine learning models, particularly those tailored for predictive analytics in education, analyze historical data to forecast student performance, identify at-risk learners, and suggest personalized learning paths (Martin & Bolliger, 2018). Understanding algorithmic biases is imperative to ensure equitable outcomes across diverse student populations (Appleton et al., 2008). A foundational knowledge of algorithmic fairness and inclusivity can guide educators to implement AI solutions that benefit all learners, minimizing disparities in access to educational resources (Ertl et al., 2006).

User Experience Design: The integration of AI and Data Science in education must prioritize user experience (UX) (Wise et al., 2012). Students and educators alike must find these technological solutions intuitive and engaging for effective use (Vonderwell & Zachariah, 2005). A focus on UX involves a collaborative design approach, incorporating feedback from end-users to create systems that are accessible and beneficial (Myers et al., 2012). The role of UX in educational tools can significantly influence adoption rates, as well-designed interfaces encourage sustained engagement and reliance on these technologies (Jin & Bierma, 2011).

By aligning these foundational elements with appropriate theoretical frameworks, the educational landscape can undergo a transformative process that empowers students, enhances teaching practices, and fosters a culture of continuous learning and improvement (Singhal, 2020). This synergy between theory, data, algorithms, and ethical considerations will pave the way for innovative educational methodologies that not only respond to the needs of today's learners but also prepare them for the challenges of tomorrow (Flener-Lovitt et al., 2020).

IMPORTANCE OF AI AND DATA SCIENCE IN EDUCATION

Artificial Intelligence (AI) and Data Science have emerged as transformative forces in the education landscape, fundamentally altering how teaching and learning processes are conceptualized, implemented, and evaluated (Chandler, 2016). These technologies hold remarkable potentials to enhance educational outcomes, personalize student experiences, and enable data-driven decision-making (Fung & Lam, 2020).

At the core of AI and Data Science in education is the ability to harness vast amounts of data (Moog & Spencer, 2008). This data comes from various sources including student demographics, learning behaviors, assessments, and feedback mechanisms (Woodbury et al., 2022). By employing data analytics, educators can uncover patterns that can inform teaching strategies, curriculum development, and resource allocation (Clark, 2000). For instance, predictive analytics can identify students at risk of underperforming, allowing for timely interventions tailored to individual needs (Bernard et al., 2009). This not only improves student success rates but also helps in closing achievement gaps (Gillies, 2008).

One of the most exciting applications of AI in education is personalized learning (Reschly & Christenson, 2022). AI algorithms can analyze learning styles, preferences, and paces of individual students, enabling the creation of customized learning pathways (Bernard et al., 2004). This approach fosters student engagement and motivation, as learners are presented with content that is most relevant and appealing to them (Flener-Lovitt et al., 2020). Moreover, AI-driven platforms can provide immediate feedback, assisting students in identifying areas for improvement in real-time and enhancing the overall learning experience (Raker et al., 2021).

Additionally, AI-enhanced tools such as chatbots and virtual tutors are revolutionizing how students access information and support (Garrison et al., 1999). These technologies can provide 24/7 assistance, answering questions and offering resources outside traditional classroom settings (Richardson et al., 2012). This immediacy not only enriches student learning but also alleviates some pressure from educators, allowing them to focus on more complex teaching tasks and personalized interactions (Fiock, 2020).

Data Science significantly contributes to the assessment and enhancement of pedagogical methods (Flener-Lovitt et al., 2020). Through the analytics of assessment data, educators can assess the effectiveness of different teaching strategies and curricular materials (Eberlein et al., 2008). By utilizing A/B testing and similar methodologies, educators can undertake an evidence-based approach to refine their instruction, ensuring that they're employing techniques that yield the best student outcomes (Raker et al., 2021).

Despite the numerous advantages of integrating AI and Data Science into education, it is crucial to address potential challenges (Tanner, 2013). Issues related to data privacy, equity in access to technology, and the potential for bias in algorithms must be considered to ensure that these tools serve all learners equitably (Bernard et al., 2004). As we navigate through these complexities, the importance of thoughtful implementation and ongoing evaluation becomes paramount (Gillies, 2008).

GOVERNANCE OF AI AND DATA SCIENCE IN EDUCATION

As the integration of Artificial Intelligence (AI) and Data Science in education continues to expand, the urgency for robust governance structures becomes increasingly apparent (Van Heuvelen et al., 2020). Governance in this context entails the establishment of policies, regulations, and ethical frameworks that dictate the responsible use of AI and Data Science technologies (Reschly & Christenson, 2022). The need for effective governance arises in response to various challenges, including data privacy, algorithmic bias, and equitable access to educational resources (Bernard et al., 2009).

Foremost among the governance concerns is data privacy (Clark, 2000). The collection and analysis of student data, while beneficial for personalizing learning and improving educational outcomes, also pose significant risks (P. L. Smith & Dillon, 2009). Personal identifiable information (PII) could be misused if not properly safeguarded (Dutton et al., 2019). Education institutions must implement robust data management policies that ensure compliance with regulations like the Family Educational Rights and Privacy Act (FERPA) in the U.S., which protects the privacy of student education records (Castelli & Sarvary, 2021). Furthermore, institutions should adopt best practices regarding data anonymization and encryption, thus minimizing the risks associated with data breaches (Gherhe et al., 2021).

Additionally, algorithmic bias in AI systems represents a crucial governance challenge (Van Dusen & Nissen, 2020). AI systems are only as unbiased as the data they are trained on, and if the input data reflects existing biases, the outcomes can exacerbate inequalities in education (Talbot et al., 2015). Governance frameworks must include measures to monitor and evaluate AI algorithms regularly, ensuring fairness and inclusivity in algorithmic decision-making (Alzen et al., 2018). This involves establishing diverse and representative datasets, as well as implementing mechanisms for transparency and accountability in AI systems (Oakley et al., 2004).

Equitable access to AI and data science technologies is another pivotal governance issue (Moog & Spencer, 2008). The digital divide stemming from socioeconomic differences poses risks of marginalizing students from underprivileged backgrounds (Rodriguez et al., 2020). A governance framework must address these disparities by advocating for policies that ensure all students have access to modern educational technologies (Li et al., 2022). This could include government subsidies for low-income schools, investments in infrastructure, and initiatives aimed at providing necessary training for both educators and students (Bernard et al., 2004).

To effectively govern the use of AI and Data Science in education, it is essential to engage multiple stakeholders in the decision-making process (Tanner, 2013). This should include educators, policymakers, technology providers, students, and parents (Eberlein et al., 2008). Through collaboration, stakeholders can develop inclusive governance structures that reflect the diverse needs and perspectives of the educational community (Yamamoto et al., 1969). Creating ethical guidelines and a transparent framework for evaluating AI initiatives is vital, ensuring continuous assessment, and fostering trust in technology (Fredricks et al., 2004).

Furthermore, ongoing professional development should be provided for educators to understand both the capabilities and limitations of AI and Data Science (Dixson, 2015). Empowering educators with the knowledge to critically engage with these technologies promotes responsible use and encourages innovative teaching practices (Kuh, 2001).

ROLE OF AI AND ML IN TRANSFORMING THE EDUCATION LANDSCAPE

Artificial Intelligence (AI) and Machine Learning (ML) are at the forefront of transforming the education landscape, offering unprecedented opportunities to enhance teaching and learning experiences (Henrie et al., 2015). These technologies empower educators to tailor educational approaches, streamline administrative tasks, and improve student outcomes (Nguyen et al., 2021). As learning becomes increasingly personalized, the role of AI and ML is paramount in redefining the educational framework for both learners and educators (Baker et al., 2012).

One of the most significant contributions of AI and ML in education is the ability to provide personalized learning experiences (Bluemink & Järvelä, 2004). Traditional one-size-fits-all educational models often leave students behind, especially those with varying learning abilities and preferences (Castelli & Sarvary, 2021). AI-driven adaptive learning systems analyze student performance and engagement in real-time, adjusting curricula to meet each student's unique needs (Schwenck & Pryor, 2021). For instance, platforms like DreamBox and Knewton use AI algorithms to determine a student's grasp of specific concepts and adapt lessons accordingly, facilitating a more individualized learning experience (Giesbers et al., 2013).

AI can also enhance student engagement through intelligent tutoring systems (ITS) (Wester et al., 2021). These systems provide immediate feedback and assistance, simulating one-on-one tutoring experiences (Wenzel, 2020). By leveraging natural language processing and machine learning, ITS can understand students' queries and respond appropriately, helping to clarify complex subjects (Bhagat & Kim, 2020). For example, platforms like Carnegie Learning use AI to create interactive math lessons that adapt in real-time to students' responses, fostering deeper comprehension (Schwartz, 2020).

In addition to personalizing student learning, AI and ML play a crucial role in streamlining administrative processes within educational institutions (Kumar et al., 2021). From automating grading and assessing large volumes of assignments to optimizing scheduling and resource allocation, AI-powered tools free up educators' time, allowing them to focus more on teaching and less on administrative tasks (Tinto, 2022). For example, AI can help predict course enrollment trends, enabling institutions to allocate resources efficiently and minimize classroom overcrowding (Nguyen et al., 2021).

Moreover, AI and ML can enhance data-driven decision-making in education (Castelli & Sarvary, 2021). These technologies can analyze vast amounts of academic data, identifying patterns that inform teaching strategies and improve student outcomes (Schwenck & Pryor, 2021). By utilizing predictive analytics, educators can anticipate students who may be at risk of underperforming and intervene proactively

(Wester et al., 2021). This capability not only promotes student success but also fosters a supportive learning environment where educators can address potential issues before they escalate (Fulfer et al., 2020).

However, alongside these advantages, it is critical to acknowledge the challenges and limitations accompanying the integration of AI and ML in education (Fung & Lam, 2020). Issues related to data privacy, algorithmic bias, and the potential for over-reliance on technology warrant careful consideration (Gemmel et al., 2020). Ensuring that AI and ML systems are designed with equity in mind is essential for equipping all students with quality educational opportunities (Jamieson, 2020).

USE OF AR, VR, AND MR

Augmented Reality (AR) in Education

Augmented Reality (AR) is revolutionizing how students engage with educational content, integrating digital information into the physical world (Perets et al., 2020). By overlaying virtual elements onto real-life environments, AR enhances interactive learning experiences (Van Heuvelen et al., 2020). This transformative approach is particularly beneficial in disciplines like science, mathematics, and geography (Casey et al., 2023). For example, students can point a device at a textbook illustration to visualize complex structures, such as the human anatomy or molecular compositions, in 3D (Shockley et al., 2021). By making abstract concepts tangible, AR caters to various learning styles, allowing visual learners to grasp challenging materials more effectively (Shockley et al., 2021).

In the realm of AI and data science, AR facilitates immersive visualization techniques that allow for the dynamic representation of data sets (Giesbers et al., 2013). Using AR applications, students can manipulate data in real time, gaining deeper insights into statistical trends or AI models (Gillies, 2008). This hands-on experience fosters critical thinking, as learners can experiment with different variables, seeing immediate impacts on their visualized results (Conrad, 2002). Furthermore, AR tools can be integrated into lab environments, creating simulations for data collection and analysis that may be too dangerous or impractical to conduct in traditional settings (Tharayil et al., 2018). By merging physical and digital realms, AR not only enhances understanding but also encourages collaborative learning through shared AR experiences, thereby preparing students for a data-centric future (Casey et al., 2023).

Virtual Reality (VR) in Education

Virtual Reality (VR) immerses students in fully simulated environments, providing an unparalleled hands-on learning experience (Song et al., 2004). In subjects like history, geography, and even data science, VR can transport learners to historically significant locations or complex data landscapes, enabling them to explore concepts in a deeply engaging manner (Castelli & Sarvary, 2021). For instance, a VR simulation can place students in interactive environments where they can visualize data analytics, manipulate variables, and witness the impact of statistical changes in real-time, all within a 3D context (Gherhe et al., 2021).

In the field of AI and data science, VR can play a vital role in teaching complex algorithms and machine learning techniques (Bowen & Cooper, 2022). By offering interactive 3D simulations, students can witness how an AI model processes data and makes predictions (Canning et al., 2019). This immediate feedback loop fosters experiential learning, encouraging students to experiment with various models and algorithms in a VR setting (Bhagat & Kim, 2020). Furthermore, VR aids in developing critical soft skills such as problem-solving and teamwork through collaborative projects (Schwartz, 2020). In virtual settings, students can work together, simulating real-world data challenges and developing solutions in a shared space (Parsad, 2008).

Moreover, VR can democratize education by providing access to high-quality resources regardless of geographical location (Barnard, 1997). Students can engage with top-tier educators and data scientists who may be thousands of miles away, creating a global classroom (Allen & Seaman, 2016). As technology advances and VR tools become more accessible, the potential for immersive learning experiences in AI and data science continues to expand, reshaping the educational landscape for generations to come (Bernard et al., 2009).

Mixed Reality (MR) in Education

Mixed Reality (MR) merges the physical and digital worlds, allowing for interactive experiences that enhance learning through a dynamic blend of AR and VR technologies (Kumar et al., 2021). In the educational landscape, MR offers unique opportunities for students to engage with complex subjects like AI and data science (Schwartz, 2020). MR platforms can overlay digital tools and data visualizations directly onto physical objects, blending real-world context with virtual enhancements that facilitate deeper understanding (Martin & Bolliger, 2018).

One of the most advantageous aspects of MR in education is its capability to create collaborative learning environments (Moore, 1989). Students can gather around a shared digital workspace where they can manipulate data sets, run simulations, and visualize AI algorithms (Parker, 1999). For instance, a mixed reality platform could allow students to visualize how machine learning models adjust in response to changing data inputs, providing immediate feedback on their decisions (Thurmond & Wambach, 2004). This experiential learning model helps bridge theory and practice, making abstract concepts more relatable and easier to comprehend (Bernard et al., 2009).

Moreover, MR encourages personalized learning experiences, enabling students to progress at their own pace (Tinto, 2022). Interactive elements can adapt to individual learning curves, presenting challenges suited to each student's skill level (Appleton et al., 2008). In addition, MR empowers educators to tailor curricula dynamically, providing instant access to a wealth of information and resources, enhancing lectures with interactive demonstrations (DeMonbrun et al., 2017). The immersive nature of MR not only captivates students' interest but also promotes active participation and inquiry-based learning, essential components in mastering AI and data science (Furlong & Christenson, 2008).

As MR technology continues to evolve, its integration into educational frameworks promises to transform traditional teaching methodologies, making learning more engaging, effective, and accessible (Karweit, 1989). This transformation is vital to prepare students for the increasingly data-driven world, equipping them with the skills required to thrive in various industries (Nguyen et al., 2021).

ADVANTAGES

Artificial Intelligence (AI) and Data Science are revolutionizing the educational landscape, offering a plethora of advantages that enhance teaching and learning experiences (Dixson, 2015). One of the significant benefits is personalized learning (Kuh, 2001). Through AI algorithms, educational software can analyze students' performance data, learning patterns, and preferences, allowing educators to tailor curricula and interventions to meet individual needs (Baker et al., 2012). This customization can help students learn at their own pace, ensuring that no one is left behind (Henrie et al., 2015). For instance, platforms like DreamBox and Knewton leverage data analytics to deliver personalized paths, adjusting difficulty based on real-time analytics of student performance (Castelli & Sarvary, 2021).

Moreover, AI-powered tools can automate administrative processes, saving educators valuable time that they can utilize for more impactful interactions with students (Fiock, 2020). Routine tasks such as grading assignments, managing schedules, or handling administrative paperwork can be streamlined using AI solutions (Flener-Lovitt et al., 2020). This not only enhances operational efficiency but also allows educators to focus on fostering creativity and critical thinking skills in their students (Raker et al., 2021).

Data Science plays a crucial role in improving educational outcomes as well (Van Heuvelen et al., 2020). By employing predictive analytics, institutions can identify students who are at risk of dropping out or falling behind in their studies by analyzing historical data and behavioral patterns (Reschly & Christenson, 2022). Early interventions can then be implemented to support these students, potentially reducing dropout rates (Dutton et al., 2019). Furthermore, the insights gleaned from data analytics can guide educators in curriculum design, resource allocation, and extra-curricular activities that align with students' interests and performance trends, fostering an environment that promotes holistic development (Castelli & Sarvary, 2021).

Inclusivity is another significant advantage brought about by AI and Data Science in education (Gherhe et al., 2021). Adaptive learning technologies cater to diverse learning needs, enabling students with disabilities or different learning styles to access quality education (Van Dusen & Nissen, 2020). Tools that convert text to speech or provide real-time translation services can bridge gaps, allowing for a more equitable learning environment (Rodriguez et al., 2020).

Additionally, the democratization of education is facilitated through online platforms powered by AI and Data Science (Li et al., 2022). MOOCs (Massive Open Online Courses) and other digital learning platforms are accessible globally, breaking geographical barriers and providing high-quality education to underserved communities (Woodbury et al., 2022). Institutions can extend their reach, making educational resources available to anyone with an internet connection (Fung & Lam, 2020).

Finally, AI-driven analytics can enhance student engagement (Flener-Lovitt et al., 2020). Interactive educational tools keep learners more engaged through gami fication and personalized feedback loops (Singhal, 2020). By fostering an engaging learning environment, students are more likely to retain information and develop a love for lifelong learning (Wenzel, 2020).

CHALLENGES

While the integration of Artificial Intelligence (AI) and Data Science in education presents numerous advantages, it also poses significant challenges that educators, institutions, and policymakers must navigate (Reiserer et al., 2023). One of the primary challenges is the issue of data privacy and security (Schwenck & Pryor, 2021). With the extensive collection of personal and academic data by educational technologies, there are increasing concerns about how this data is stored, used, and shared (Selco & Habbak, 2021). Ensuring the protection of sensitive information from breaches is paramount, but many educational institutions may lack the necessary infrastructure or expertise to safeguard against cyber threats, raising ethical concerns about data misuse or unauthorized access (Gemmel et al., 2020).

Furthermore, there exists a challenge associated with the digital divide (Jayasundara et al., 2022). While AI and Data Science are positioned to democratize education, they can also exacerbate existing inequalities (Gherhe et al., 2021). Students from low-income families may lack access to the necessary technology and internet connectivity, leaving them at a disadvantage compared to their peers (Shockley et al., 2021). Additionally, schools in underfunded areas may not have the resources to implement advanced technologies, resulting in a widening gap in educational quality and access (Casey et al., 2023).

Another significant barrier is resistance to change among educators and institutions (Castelli & Sarvary, 2021). The adoption of AI and Data Science typically requires comprehensive training for teachers and administrators to effectively integrate these technologies into their pedagogical practices (Gherhe et al., 2021). However, many educators may feel overwhelmed by rapid technological advancements or resist altering traditional teaching methods (Canning et al., 2019). Without adequate professional development and support, the potential of these tools may go unrealized, leading to frustration and disengagement from both teachers and students (Bowen & Cooper, 2022).

Moreover, concerns about the reliability and bias of AI systems are growing (Canning et al., 2019). AI models are only as good as the data used to train them (Bhagat & Kim, 2020). If the data reflects existing biases or systemic inequities, the resulting algorithms may perpetuate these biases, leading to unfair treatment of certain student populations (Allen & Seaman, 2016). This issue necessitates vigilant scrutiny and ongoing evaluation of the algorithms developed, as well as transparency in how they operate within educational settings (Schwartz, 2020).

Additionally, there's a risk of over-reliance on technology (Kumar et al., 2021). While AI can provide valuable insights and efficiencies, it cannot replace the essential human touch in education (Martin & Bolliger, 2018). The interpersonal relationships between educators and students, crucial for fostering a conducive learning environment, cannot be replicated by machines (Appleton et al., 2008). Striking a balance between technology-enhanced learning and traditional pedagogical practices is vital to ensure that education remains holistic and human-centered (DeMonbrun et al., 2017).

Finally, the evolving nature of technology means educators and institutions must continually adapt to new tools and methodologies (Furlong & Christenson, 2008). Keeping up with the rapid pace of technological advancement can be dauntless, requiring constant investment in training and infrastructure (Giesbers et al., 2013).

IMPLEMENTATION OF REGULATORY FRAMEWORKS

The adoption of AI and data science in the education sector presents both immense opportunities and challenges (Selco & Habbak, 2021). To navigate these complexities responsibly, implementing robust regulatory frameworks is essential (Reiserer et al., 2023). Such frameworks offer guidelines that ensure ethical use of technology, protect student rights, and promote equitable educational outcomes while fostering innovation and growth (Singhal, 2020).

One of the first steps in implementing regulatory frameworks for AI in education is establishing clear, consistent definitions and criteria regarding what constitutes ethical AI usage (Fung & Lam, 2020). Regulatory bodies need to define parameters concerning privacy, data security, algorithmic fairness, and accountability (Ertl et al., 2006). Creating national or state-level guidelines that encompass these definitions will assist educational institutions in developing their internal policies and procedures to comply with ethical standards in AI application (Wise et al., 2012).

Another crucial aspect of regulatory frameworks is fostering collaboration across sectors (Vonderwell & Zachariah, 2005). Policymakers, educators, technologists, and researchers must work together to shape regulations that reflect the realities of both the educational landscape and technological advancement (Myers et al., 2012). This collaboration can be facilitated through public forums, workshops, and research partnerships, bringing diverse stakeholders together to share insights and develop comprehensive regulatory measures (Jin & Bierma, 2011).

Moreover, the regulatory framework should focus on the concept of responsible data governance (Chandler, 2016). As educational institutions collect and analyze vast amounts of student data, clear policies must dictate data handling practices, including data collection, storage, retention, and sharing (Alzen et al., 2018). Consent protocols should be explicitly outlined, emphasizing transparency with students and parents regarding how their data will be used (Van Dusen & Nissen, 2020). Institutions must be held accountable for ensuring that data management practices not only comply with existing legal frameworks, like FERPA and GDPR, but also prioritize ethical standards and the rights of students (Van Heuvelen et al., 2020).

Training and education for educators on the responsible use of AI and data science are integral to the successful implementation of regulatory frameworks (P. L. Smith & Dillon, 2009). Educational institutions should provide training programs that help teachers understand the capabilities and limitations of AI technologies, ensuring they can effectively integrate these tools into their teaching practice (Nguyen et al., 2021). This will enable educators to harness AI to enhance student learning while remaining vigilant about potential ethical pitfalls (Baker et al., 2012).

Additionally, ongoing evaluation and monitoring of AI implementations in education are key components of effective regulatory frameworks (Cui et al., 2013).

Institutions should be required to regularly assess the effectiveness and fairness of AI systems they employ, using independent audits and evaluations to identify biases and disparities in outcomes (Wester et al., 2021). By establishing mechanisms for accountability, stakeholders can ensure that AI technologies are continually refined and improved in alignment with ethical standards and best practices (Fulfer et al., 2020).

CONCLUSION

The integration of Artificial Intelligence (AI) and Data Science into the educational landscape stands as a transformative force, redefining the parameters of teaching and learning (Jamieson, 2020). As we have traversed through the various ways in which AI and Data Science have been leveraged in education be it through personalized learning experiences, enhanced assessment methods, intelligent tutoring systems, or predictive analytics for student success it is clear that these innovative technologies have the potential to significantly improve educational outcomes (Perets et al., 2020).

AI has ushered in an era where educators are equipped with tools that can automate administrative tasks, allowing them to focus more on pedagogical strategies and engagement with students (Van Heuvelen et al., 2020). With capabilities such as natural language processing, machine learning algorithms, and adaptive learning technologies, AI helps tailor educational experiences to individual student needs (Wenzel, 2020). This personalization is critical as it not only caters to diverse learning styles but also addresses gaps in understanding, thereby fostering better achievement levels (Bhagat & Kim, 2020).

Moreover, Data Science plays an indispensable role in processing the vast amounts of data generated in educational environments (Schwartz, 2020). By leveraging this data, educators and institutions can derive insights into student behavior, track progress over time, and identify at-risk students early in their academic journeys (Kumar et al., 2021). Advanced analytical methods allow schools and universities to make informed decisions about curriculum development and resource allocation, ultimately leading to enhanced learning experiences and outcomes (Tinto, 2022).

However, while the prospects of AI and Data Science in education are promising, challenges remain (Fiock, 2020). Issues pertaining to data privacy, algorithmic bias, and the digital divide must be addressed to ensure that these technologies benefit all students equitably (Reschly & Christenson, 2022). Furthermore, there is a need for educators to be adequately trained in these technologies to maximally harness their potential (Dutton et al., 2019). The ethical implications of using AI in education must also be continuously evaluated to safeguard the interests of students and uphold the integrity of the educational process (Van Dusen & Nissen, 2020).

As we draw this exploration to a close, it is essential to acknowledge that the journey of integrating AI and Data Science into education is still in its nascent stages (Rodriguez et al., 2020). The field is ripe for further development and exploration, with opportunities to refine existing technologies and develop new methodologies that are grounded in evidence-based practices (Li et al., 2022). Embracing these advancements not only promises to enhance educational experiences but also fosters a culture of continuous improvement and innovation in the educational landscape (Woodbury et al., 2022).

FUTURE RESEARCH DIRECTIONS

Looking ahead, the future of AI and Data Science in education presents numerous avenues for research that can significantly impact teaching and learning practices (Bhagat & Kim, 2020). One of the critical areas for exploration is the development of more equitable AI systems that minimize bias and ensure fair outcomes for all students (Schwartz, 2020). This includes creating algorithms that are trained on diverse datasets representing various demographics, ensuring that the insights drawn from these models are applicable across different populations (Kumar et al., 2021).

Additionally, research can focus on the long-term impacts of AI-driven educational interventions (Tinto, 2022). Understanding how personalized learning technologies affect student engagement, retention, and outcomes over time will provide clarity on best practices for implementing these tools effectively (Schwenck & Pryor, 2021). Longitudinal studies can help establish causal relationships between AI applications and educational success, providing valuable feedback for educators and policymakers (Wester et al., 2021).

Another promising area for future research lies in the intersection of human expertise and AI (Fulfer et al., 2020). Investigating how educators can effectively collaborate with AI systems to enhance pedagogical effectiveness can lead to the development of hybrid teaching models that leverage the strengths of both human insight and technological advances (Fung & Lam, 2020). As AI continues to evolve, determining the most effective ways for educators to integrate these technologies into their practice will be crucial (Gemmel et al., 2020).

Research should also explore the implications of Data Science on curriculum design and educational policy (Selco & Habbak, 2021). Analyzing how data-driven decision-making can shape curriculum frameworks and pedagogical strategies may lead to more effective teaching methods that are responsive to the evolving needs of learners (Bowen & Cooper, 2022).

Furthermore, the ethical use of AI in education remains a pressing area for investigation (Reiserer et al., 2023). Ongoing studies examining data privacy concerns, consent mechanisms, and the impact of AI on student autonomy should be prioritized (Casey et al., 2023). Developing frameworks for responsible AI use in educational contexts will be essential to building trust among educators, students, and parents alike.

REFERENCES

Allen, I. E., & Seaman, J. (2016). *Online report card: Tracking online education in the United States*. Babson Survey Research Group.

Alzen, J. L., Langdon, L. S., & Otero, V. K. (2018). A logistic regression investigation of the relationship between the Learning Assistant model and failure rates in introductory STEM courses. *International Journal of STEM Education*, *5*(1), 56. DOI: 10.1186/s40594-018-0152-1 PMID: 30631745

Appleton, J. J., Christenson, S. L., & Furlong, M. J. (2008). Student engagement with school: Critical conceptual and methodological issues of the construct. *Psychology in the Schools*, *45*(5), 369–386. DOI: 10.1002/pits.20303

Baker, R. S., Gowda, S. M., Wixon, M., Kalka, J., Wagner, A. Z., Salvi, A., Aleven, V., Kusbit, G. W., Ocumpaugh, J., & Rossi, L. (2012). Towards Sensor-Free Affect Detection in Cognitive Tutor Algebra. *International Conference on Educational Data Mining*, Chania, Greece.

Barnard, J. (1997). T*he World Wide Web and Higher Education. The Promise of Virtual Universities and Online Libraries*, *37*(3), 30–35.

Bernard, R. M., Abrami, P. C., Borokhovski, E., Wade, C. A., Tamim, R. M., Surkes, M. A., & Bethel, E. C. (2009). A Meta-Analysis of Three Types of Interaction Treatments in Distance Education. *Review of Educational Research*, *79*(3), 1243–1289. DOI: 10.3102/0034654309333844

Bernard, R. M., Abrami, P. C., Lou, Y., Borokhovski, E., Wade, A., Wozney, L., Wallet, P. A., Fiset, M., & Huang, B. (2004). How Does Distance Education Compare With Classroom Instruction? A Meta-Analysis of the Empirical Literature. *Review of Educational Research*, *74*(3), 379–439. DOI: 10.3102/00346543074003379

Bhagat, S., & Kim, D. J. (2020). Higher Education Amidst COVID-19: Challenges and Silver Lining. *Information Systems Management*, *37*(4), 366–371. DOI: 10.1080/10580530.2020.1824040

Bluemink, J., & Järvelä, S. (2004). Face-to-face encounters as contextual support for Web-based discussions in a teacher education course. *The Internet and Higher Education*, *7*(3), 199–215. DOI: 10.1016/j.iheduc.2004.06.006

Bowen, R. S., & Cooper, M. M. (2022). Grading on a Curve as a Systemic Issue of Equity in Chemistry Education. *Journal of Chemical Education*, *99*(1), 185–194. DOI: 10.1021/acs.jchemed.1c00369

Canning, E. A., Muenks, K., Green, D. J., & Murphy, M. C. (2019). STEM faculty who believe ability is fixed have larger racial achievement gaps and inspire less student motivation in their classes. *Science Advances*, *5*(2), eaau4734. Advance online publication. DOI: 10.1126/sciadv.aau4734 PMID: 30793027

Casey, J. R., Russell, A., & Courey, A. J. (2023). Participation in high-structure general chemistry course increases student sense of belonging and persistence to organic chemistry. *Journal of Chemical Education*, *100*(8), 2860–2872. DOI: 10.1021/acs.jchemed.2c01253 PMID: 37577453

Castelli, F. R., & Sarvary, M. A. (2021). Why students do not turn on their video cameras during online classes and an equitable and inclusive plan to encourage them to do so. *Ecology and Evolution*, *11*(8), 3565–3576. DOI: 10.1002/ece3.7123 PMID: 33898009

Chandler, K. (2016). Using Breakout Rooms in Synchronous Online Tutorials. *Journal of Perspectives in Applied Academic Practice*, *4*(3). Advance online publication. DOI: 10.14297/jpaap.v4i3.216

Clark, R. E. (2000). Evaluating Distance Education. *Strategies and Cautions*, *1*(1), 3–16.

Conrad, D. L. (2002). Engagement, Excitement, Anxiety, and Fear: Learners' Experiences of Starting an Online Course. *American Journal of Distance Education*, *16*(4), 205–226. DOI: 10.1207/S15389286AJDE1604_2

Cui, G., Lockee, B., & Meng, C. (2013). Building modern online social presence: A review of social presence theory and its instructional design implications for future trends. *Education and Information Technologies*, *18*(4), 661–685. DOI: 10.1007/s10639-012-9192-1

DeMonbrun, M., Finelli, C. J., Prince, M., Shekhar, P., Henderon, C., & Waters, C. (2017). Creating an Instrument to Measure Student Response to Instructional Practices. *Journal of Engineering Education*, *106*(2), 273–298. DOI: 10.1002/jee.20162

DeNoyelles, A., Zydney, J. M., & Chen, B. (2014). *Strategies for creating a community of inquiry through online asynchronous discussions.* 10(1).

Dixson, M. D. (2015). Measuring Student Engagement in the Online Course: The Online Student Engagement Scale (OSE). *Online Learning : the Official Journal of the Online Learning Consortium*, *19*(4). Advance online publication. DOI: 10.24059/olj.v19i4.561

Dutton, J., Dutton, M., & Perry, J. (2019). How do online students differ from lecture students? *Online Learning : the Official Journal of the Online Learning Consortium, 6*(1). Advance online publication. DOI: 10.24059/olj.v6i1.1869

Eberlein, T., Kampmeier, J., Minderhout, V., Moog, R. S., Platt, T., Varma-Nelson, P., & White, H. B. (2008). Pedagogies of engagement in science: A comparison of PBL, POGIL, and PLTL. *Biochemistry and Molecular Biology Education, 36*(4), 262–273. DOI: 10.1002/bmb.20204 PMID: 19381266

Ertl, B., Fischer, F., & Mandl, H. (2006). Conceptual and socio-cognitive support for collaborative learning in videoconferencing environments. *Computers & Education, 47*(3), 298–315. DOI: 10.1016/j.compedu.2004.11.001

Fiock, H. (2020). Designing a Community of Inquiry in Online Courses. *International Review of Research in Open and Distance Learning, 21*(1), 134–152. DOI: 10.19173/irrodl.v20i5.3985

Flener-Lovitt, C., Bailey, K., & Han, R. (2020). Using Structured Teams to Develop Social Presence in Asynchronous Chemistry Courses. *Journal of Chemical Education, 97*(9), 2519–2525. DOI: 10.1021/acs.jchemed.0c00765

Fredricks, J. A., Blumenfeld, P. C., & Paris, A. H. (2004). School Engagement: Potential of the Concept, State of the Evidence. *Review of Educational Research, 74*(1), 59–109. DOI: 10.3102/00346543074001059

Fulfer, K. D., Wachter, E., Muzyka, J. L., Demoranville, L. T., Fieberg, J. E., Haile, J. D., Scott, D., Song, Y., Workman, J. M., & Young, K. J. (2020). #StayCentred: Maintaining Personal Education at Centre College During COVID-19. *Journal of Chemical Education, 97*(9), 2783–2787. DOI: 10.1021/acs.jchemed.0c00726

Fung, F. M., & Lam, Y. (2020). How COVID-19 Disrupted Our "Flipped" Freshman Organic Chemistry Course: Insights Gained from Singapore. *Journal of Chemical Education, 97*(9), 2573–2580. DOI: 10.1021/acs.jchemed.0c00590

Furlong, M. J., & Christenson, S. L. (2008). Engaging students with school and academics: A relevant construct for all students. *Psychology in the Schools, 45*(5), 365–368. DOI: 10.1002/pits.20302

Garrison, D. R., Anderson, T., & Archer, W. (1999). Critical Inquiry in a Text-Based Environment: Computer Conferencing in Higher Education. *The Internet and Higher Education, 2*(2–3), 87–105. DOI: 10.1016/S1096-7516(00)00016-6

Gemmel, P. M., Goetz, M. K., James, N. M., Jesse, K. A., & Ratliff, B. J. (2020). Collaborative Learning in Chemistry: Impact of COVID-19. *Journal of Chemical Education, 97*(9), 2899–2904. DOI: 10.1021/acs.jchemed.0c00713

Gherhe , V., imon, S., & Para, I. (2021). Analysing Students' Reasons for Keeping Their Webcams on or off during Online Classes. *Sustainability (Basel), 13*(6), 3203. DOI: 10.3390/su13063203

Giesbers, B., Rienties, B., Tempelaar, D., & Gijselaers, W. (2013). Investigating the relations between motivation, tool use, participation, and performance in an e-learning course using web-videoconferencing. *Computers in Human Behavior, 29*(1), 285–292. DOI: 10.1016/j.chb.2012.09.005

Gillies, D. (2008). Student perspectives on videoconferencing in teacher education at a distance. *Distance Education, 29*(1), 107–118. DOI: 10.1080/01587910802004878

Henrie, C. R., Halverson, L. R., & Graham, C. R. (2015). Measuring student engagement in technology-mediated learning: A review. *Computers & Education, 90*, 36–53. DOI: 10.1016/j.compedu.2015.09.005

Jamieson, M. V. (2020). Keeping a Learning Community and Academic Integrity Intact after a Mid-Term Shift to Online Learning in Chemical Engineering Design During the COVID-19 Pandemic. *Journal of Chemical Education, 97*(9), 2768–2772. DOI: 10.1021/acs.jchemed.0c00785

Jayasundara, J. M. P. V. K., Gilbert, T., Kersten, S., & Meng, L. (2022). How UK HE STEM Students Were Motivated to Switch Their Cameras on: A Study of the Development of Compassionate Communications in Task-focused Online Group Meetings. *Education Sciences, 12*(5), 317. DOI: 10.3390/educsci12050317

Jin, G., & Bierma, T. J. (2011). Guided-Inquiry Learning in Environmental Health. *Journal of Environmental Health, 73*(6), 80–85. PMID: 21306099

Karweit, N. (1989). Time and Learning: A Review. In *School and Classroom Organization* (pp. 69–95). L. Erlbaum Associates.

Kuh, G. D. (2001). Assessing What Really Matters to Student Learning Inside The National Survey of Student Engagement. *Change, 33*(3), 10–17. DOI: 10.1080/00091380109601795

Kumar, P., Saxena, C., & Baber, H. (2021). Learner-content interaction in e-learning-the moderating role of perceived harm of COVID-19 in assessing the satisfaction of learners. *Smart Learning Environments, 8*(1), 5. Advance online publication. DOI: 10.1186/s40561-021-00149-8 PMID: 40477398

Li, N., Romera Rodriguez, G., Xu, Y., Bhatt, P., Nguyen, H. A., Serpi, A., Tsai, C., & Carroll, J. M. (2022). Picturing One's Self: Camera Use in Zoom Classes during the COVID-19 Pandemic. *Proceedings of the Ninth ACM Conference on Learning @ Scale*, 151–162. DOI: 10.1145/3491140.3528284

Martin, F., & Bolliger, D. U. (2018). Engagement Matters: Student Perceptions on the Importance of Engagement Strategies in the Online Learning Environment. *Online Learning : the Official Journal of the Online Learning Consortium, 22*(1). Advance online publication. DOI: 10.24059/olj.v22i1.1092

Moore, M. G. (1989). Editorial: Three types of interaction. *American Journal of Distance Education, 3*(2), 1–7. DOI: 10.1080/08923648909526659

Myers, T., Monypenny, R., & Trevathan, J. (2012). Overcoming the glassy-eyed nod: An application of process-oriented guided inquiry learning techniques in information technology. *Journal of Learning Design, 5*(1), 12–22. DOI: 10.5204/jld.v5i1.97

Nguyen, K. A., Borrego, M., Finelli, C. J., DeMonbrun, M., Crockett, C., Tharayil, S., Shekhar, P., Waters, C., & Rosenberg, R. (2021). Instructor strategies to aid implementation of active learning: A systematic literature review. *International Journal of STEM Education, 8*(1), 9. DOI: 10.1186/s40594-021-00270-7

Parker, A. (1999). Interaction in Distance Education. *The Critical Conversation, 12*, 13–17.

Parsad, B. (2008). *Distance Education at Degree-Granting Postsecondary Institutions: 2006–07 (National Center for Education Statistics, Institute of Education Sciences)*. US Department of Education.

Perets, E. A., Chabeda, D., Gong, A. Z., Huang, X., Fung, T. S., Ng, K. Y., Bathgate, M., & Yan, E. C. Y. (2020). Impact of the Emergency Transition to Remote Teaching on Student Engagement in a Non-STEM Undergraduate Chemistry Course in the Time of COVID-19. *Journal of Chemical Education, 97*(9), 2439–2447. DOI: 10.1021/acs.jchemed.0c00879

Raker, J. R., Dood, A. J., Srinivasan, S., & Murphy, K. L. (2021). Pedagogies of engagement use in postsecondary chemistry education in the United States: Results from a national survey. *Chemistry Education Research and Practice, 22*(1), 30–42. DOI: 10.1039/D0RP00125B

Reiserer, M., Ertl, B., & Mandl, H. (2023). Fostering Collaborative Knowledge Construction in Desktop Video-conferencing. Effects of Content Schemes and Cooperation Scripts in Peer Teaching Settings. In G. Stahl, Computer Support for Collaborative Learning (1st ed., pp. 379–388). *Routledge*. DOI: 10.4324/9781315045467-55

Reschly, A. L., & Christenson, S. L. (Eds.). (2022). *Handbook of Research on Student Engagement*. Springer International Publishing., DOI: 10.1007/978-3-031-07853-8

Richardson, J. C., Arbaugh, J. B., Cleveland-Innes, M., Ice, P., Swan, K. P., & Garrison, D. R. (2012). Using the Community of Inquiry Framework to Inform Effective Instructional Design. In Moller, L., & Huett, J. (Eds.), *The Next Generation of Distance Education* (pp. 97–125)., DOI: 10.1007/978-1-4614-1785-9_7

Rodriguez, J.-M. G., Hunter, K. H., Scharlott, L. J., & Becker, N. M. (2020). A Review of Research on Process Oriented Guided Inquiry Learning: Implications for Research and Practice. *Journal of Chemical Education*, *97*(10), 3506–3520. DOI: 10.1021/acs.jchemed.0c00355

Schwartz, H. (2020). *Remote Learning Is Here to Stay: Results from the First American School District Panel Survey*. RAND Corporation., DOI: 10.7249/RRA956-1

Schwenck, C. M., & Pryor, J. D. (2021). Student perspectives on camera usage to engage and connect in foundational education classes: It's time to turn your cameras on. *International Journal of Educational Research Open*, *2*, 100079. DOI: 10.1016/j.ijedro.2021.100079

Selco, J. I., & Habbak, M. (2021). STEM Students' Perceptions on Emergency Online Learning during the COVID-19 Pandemic: Challenges and Successes. *Education Sciences*, *11*(12), 799. DOI: 10.3390/educsci11120799

Shockley, K. M., Gabriel, A. S., Robertson, D., Rosen, C. C., Chawla, N., Ganster, M. L., & Ezerins, M. E. (2021). The fatiguing effects of camera use in virtual meetings: A within-person field experiment. *The Journal of Applied Psychology*, *106*(8), 1137–1155. DOI: 10.1037/apl0000948 PMID: 34423999

Singhal, M. K. (2020). Facilitating Virtual Medicinal Chemistry Active Learning Assignments Using Advanced Zoom Features during COVID-19 Campus Closure. *Journal of Chemical Education*, *97*(9), 2711–2714. DOI: 10.1021/acs.jchemed.0c00675

Smith, P. L., & Dillon, C. L. (2009). *Comparing distance learning and classroom learning: Conceptual considerations.* 13(2), 6–23. DOI: 10.1080/08923649909527020

Song, L., Singleton, E. S., Hill, J. R., & Koh, M. H. (2004). Improving online learning: Student perceptions of useful and challenging characteristics. *The Internet and Higher Education*, *7*(1), 59–70. DOI: 10.1016/j.iheduc.2003.11.003

Swan, K., & Ice, P. (2010). The community of inquiry framework ten years later: Introduction to the special issue. *The Internet and Higher Education*, *13*(1–2), 1–4. DOI: 10.1016/j.iheduc.2009.11.003

Talbot, R. M., Hartley, L. M., Matzetta, K., & Wee, B. S. (2015). Transforming Undergraduate Science Education With Learning Assistants: Student Satisfaction in Large-Enrollment Courses. *Journal of College Science Teaching*, *44*(5), 24–30. DOI: 10.1080/0047231X.2015.12454809

Tanner, K. D. (2013). Structure Matters: Twenty-One Teaching Strategies to Promote Student Engagement and Cultivate Classroom Equity. *CBE Life Sciences Education*, *12*(3), 322–331. DOI: 10.1187/cbe.13-06-0115 PMID: 24006379

Tharayil, S., Borrego, M., Prince, M., Nguyen, K. A., Shekhar, P., Finelli, C. J., & Waters, C. (2018). Strategies to mitigate student resistance to active learning. *International Journal of STEM Education*, *5*(1), 7. DOI: 10.1186/s40594-018-0102-y PMID: 30631697

Tinto, V. (2022). Exploring the Character of Student Persistence in Higher Education: The Impact of Perception, Motivation, and Engagement. In Reschly, A. L., & Christenson, S. L. (Eds.), *Handbook of Research on Student Engagement*. Springer International Publishing. DOI: 10.1007/978-3-031-07853-8_17

Van Dusen, B., & Nissen, J. (2020). Associations between learning assistants, passing introductory physics, and equity: A quantitative critical race theory investigation. *Physical Review. Physics Education Research*, *16*(1), 010117. DOI: 10.1103/PhysRevPhysEducRes.16.010117

Van Heuvelen, K. M., Daub, G. W., & Ryswyk, H. V. (2020). Emergency Remote Instruction during the COVID-19 Pandemic Reshapes Collaborative Learning in General Chemistry. *Journal of Chemical Education*, *97*(9), 2884–2888. DOI: 10.1021/acs.jchemed.0c00691

Vonderwell, S., & Zachariah, S. (2005). Factors that Influence Participation In Online Learning. *Journal of Research on Technology in Education*, *38*(2), 213–230. DOI: 10.1080/15391523.2005.10782457

Wenzel, T. (2020). Collaborative Group Learning in Remotely Taught Analytical Chemistry Courses. *Journal of Chemical Education*, *97*(9), 2715–2718. DOI: 10.1021/acs.jchemed.0c00520

Wester, E. R., Walsh, L. L., Arango-Caro, S., & Callis-Duehl, K. L. (2021). Student Engagement Declines in STEM Undergraduates during COVID-19–Driven Remote Learning. *Journal of Microbiology & Biology Education*, 22(1), ev22i1.2385. DOI: 10.1128/jmbe.v22i1.2385

Wise, A. F., Saghafian, M., & Padmanabhan, P. (2012). Towards more precise design guidance: Specifying and testing the functions of assigned student roles in online discussions. *Educational Technology Research and Development*, *60*(1), 55–82. DOI: 10.1007/s11423-011-9212-7

Woodbury, J., Arneson, J. B., & Offerdahl, E. G. (2022). Adapting Team-Based Learning for an Online Biochemistry Course. *Journal of Chemical Education*, *99*(8), 2964–2971. DOI: 10.1021/acs.jchemed.2c00259

Yamamoto, K., Thomas, E. C., & Karns, E. A. (1969). School-related attitudes in middleschool-age students. *American Educational Research Journal*, *6*(2), 191–206. DOI: 10.3102/00028312006002191

Chapter 2
Mapping Four Decades of AI and Data Science Evolution in Education (1983-2025)

Rachana Jaiswal
https://orcid.org/0000-0002-1900-2044
HNB Garhwal University, Srinagar, India

Shashank Gupta
https://orcid.org/0000-0001-8718-8381
Morgan Stanley India Pvt. Ltd., India

Ila Gupta
Director General School Education, India

Shwetank Gupta
IndusInd Bank, Lucknow, India

ABSTRACT

This chapter explores the evolution of artificial intelligence (AI) and data science (DS) in education through a four-decade bibliometric analysis of 1,920 Scopus-indexed publications from 1983 to 2025. Utilizing Biblioshiny and VOSviewer, the study maps thematic trends, key contributors, and emerging research frontiers. The findings highlight machine learning, e-learning, and decision-making systems as dominant motor themes, indicating the field's maturity and widespread integration. Meanwhile, critical yet underdeveloped areas such as curriculum design, student-centered AI, and ethical governance emerge as future priorities. The study

DOI: 10.4018/979-8-3373-2185-1.ch002

also identifies generative AI, federated learning, and explainable models as promising but nascent directions requiring pedagogical alignment. The chapter offers theoretical insights into AI as a reshaping force in educational epistemology and provides practical and policy-level implications for institutions and educators. It is a roadmap for advancing responsible, inclusive, and impactful AI-driven educational transformation.

1. INTRODUCTION

Over the past four decades, the landscape of education has undergone a profound transformation driven by the rapid evolution of digital technologies (Wan et al., 2025; Koebe, 2025; Jaiswal, 2025; Dang et al., 2025; Jaiswal, 2024), most notably Artificial Intelligence (AI) and Data Science(DS). These technologies are no longer confined to experimental or pilot initiatives; instead, they are becoming embedded across all levels of education (Gavira Durón, & Jiménez-Preciado, 2025; Jaiswal & Kumar, 2023), from K–12 (Azzam & Charles, 2025) to higher education (Leite, 2025; Krishnamoorthy et al., 2025) and lifelong learning (Imjai et al., 2025; Bixler & Ceballos, 2025). As a result, educational institutions, governments, and technology providers are investing heavily in AI-driven solutions to enhance teaching effectiveness (Hefnawi, 2025; Gupta & Jaiswal, 2024a), student engagement, learning personalization(Gupta & Jaiswal, 2025), and administrative decision-making (Jaiswal et al., 2025; Jaiswal et al., 2024a; Jaiswal, 2023). Machine learning and artificial intelligence have increasingly demonstrated utility across diverse domains (Verma et al., 2025; Trindade et al., 2025; Salha et al., 2025; Rajan & Niranjan, 2025). Machine learning has been employed in the hospitality sector to improve service excellence and support sustainable development goals (Gupta & Jaiswal, 2024b). In happiness economics, ML techniques have been used to uncover the complex relationship between financial prosperity and subjective well-being (Jaiswal & Gupta, 2024). In labor economics, advanced algorithms have helped identify compensation determinants in dynamic labor markets (Jaiswal, Gupta, & Tiwari, 2023). Furthermore, ESG-type investing has been explored using multi-stakeholder machine learning frameworks (Jaiswal, Gupta, & Tiwari, 2025) and Twitter-based opinion mining approaches to detect public sentiment and key investment themes (Jaiswal, Gupta, & Tiwari, 2024d). Beyond these, ML has proven valuable in cybersecurity, particularly in mitigating mobile malware threats (Jamal et al., 2022) and network traffic prediction for intelligent systems management (Murugesan et al., 2022). Additionally, AI and ICT tools have shown promise in advancing vocational skill development and educational access (Wong et al., 2025; Kumar et al., 2022). AI applications in education span diverse tools and techniques (Zhang, 2025), including intelligent tutoring systems, adaptive learning platforms (Dairo & Szűcs, 2025; Alshammari, 2025; Neophytou et al., 2025), natural language processing (NLP)-based feedback tools, learning analytics dashboards, and generative AI agents (Dwivedi, 2025; Akpan et al., 2025) such as ChatGPT (Jasrai, 2025; Letjani et al., 2025; Altinay et al., 2025; Jiang et al., 2025). Simultaneously, data science has empowered educators and administrators to derive actionable insights from vast student behavior, performance, and engagement data (Zulfiqar et al., 2025). These innovations have enabled the development of predictive models for early dropout identification, automated curriculum optimization, personalized learning pathways, and student well-being monitoring, reshaping how education is designed and delivered. Despite this rapid growth, scholarly research remains fragmented across disciplines and themes, with studies dispersed across domains such as computer science, education, psychology, and information systems. While previous reviews have explored specific subsets like AI in adaptive learning or predictive analytics for performance forecasting, a holistic understanding of this research field's evolution, structure, and future trajectory is still lacking. As new paradigms such as agentic AI, generative AI, emotion-aware computing, and explainable AI (XAI) gain prominence, a structured and integrative view of the scholarly landscape becomes critical.

This study addresses that gap by conducting a comprehensive bibliometric analysis of AI and data science in education using Scopus-indexed articles published between 1983 and 2025. This research offers a panoramic view of how the field has evolved through systematically mapping the knowledge domain, including publication outlets, thematic clusters, keyword co-occurrence, and temporal trends. Additionally, the study proposes a research agenda to guide future scholarship and innovation, particularly in emerging areas such as ethical AI implementation, multilingual AI tools for inclusivity, and AI-based emotional intelligence systems in education. Therefore, this study aims to address the following research questions:

> ***RQ1.*** How has the research on artificial intelligence and data science in education evolved over the past four decades (1983–2025) regarding thematic focus, publication trends, and influential contributions?
> ***RQ2.*** What are the key research domains, collaboration patterns, and intellectual structures define the current knowledge landscape of AI and data science applications in education?

By answering these research questions, the study contributes a comprehensive understanding of the evolution, key themes, and influential contributors in AI and data science in education. It maps the intellectual and collaborative structure of the field, identifies emerging and underexplored areas, and provides a strategic research agenda to guide future scholarly and practical efforts. It serves as a resource for researchers, educators, policymakers, and technologists aiming to navigate and shape the future of AI-powered education.

2. RESEARCH METHODS: DATA COLLECTION, EXTRACTION, AND PROCESSING

This study employs a quantitative bibliometric analysis using data extracted from the Scopus database, which is widely recognized for its comprehensive and high-quality indexing of peer-reviewed literature (Jaiswal et al., 2025; Singh et al., 2024; Jaiswal et al., 2024b; Prakhar et al., 2024a; Prakhar et al., 2024b; Prakhar et al., 2024c; Prakhar et al., 2025a; Prakhar et al., 2025bJaiswal et al., 2024c; Gupta et al., 2024; Jaiswal & Gupta, 2023; Jaiswal et al., 2022a; Jaiswal et al., 2022b). A structured search query was developed using Boolean operators and keywords related to *artificial intelligence*, *machine learning*, *data science*, and *education*. The search was limited to publications from 1983 to 2025, focusing on titles, abstracts, and author keywords to ensure topic relevance. The initial search yielded 91,612 records, which were filtered by subject area to retain only education-related publications, reducing the dataset to 4,491 records (Figure 1). Further screening excluded non-article document types (e.g., conference papers, editorials), duplicated entries, non-English publications, and records with missing metadata, resulting in a final dataset of 1,920 peer-reviewed journal articles. The dataset was exported in CSV format and processed using the VOSviewer, Bibliometrix package, and Biblioshiny interface in RStudio to perform descriptive analysis, keyword co-occurrence, thematic mapping, and collaboration network visualization.

Figure 1. Data inclusion criteria (based on PRISMA guidelines)

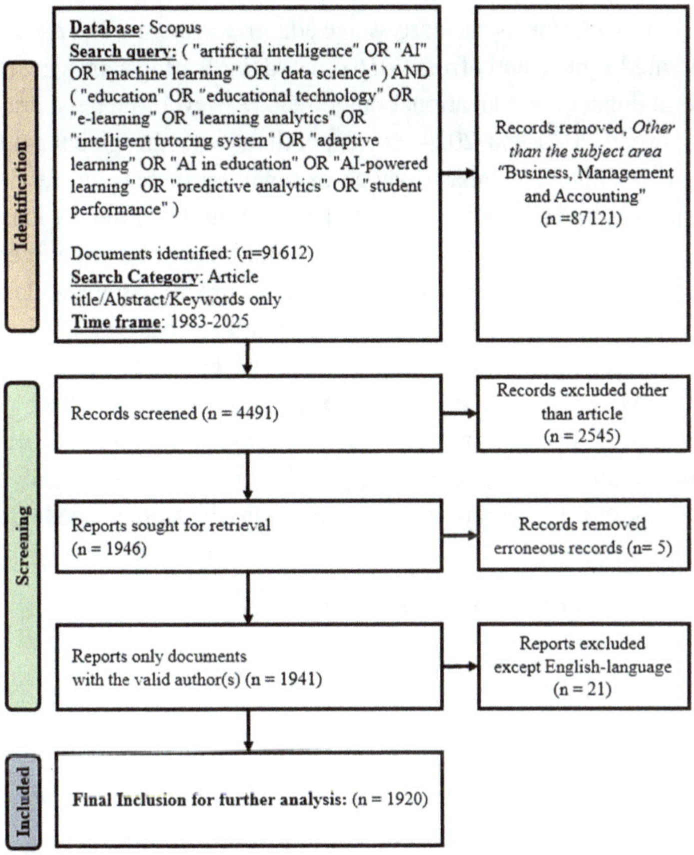

(Source: Author's own)

3. BIBLIOMETRIC LANDSCAPE OF PUBLICATION ANALYSIS IN DNR

3.1 Annual Scientific Production

The analysis of annual scientific production from 1983 to March 2025 reveals a clear evolution in research activity surrounding artificial intelligence and data science in education (Figure 2). During the initial decades (1983–2000), the field exhibited minimal scholarly output, with fewer than five articles published annually. This period can be characterized as a dormant phase, reflecting limited academic engagement with AI-driven educational technologies. A gradual rise began in the early 2000s, marking the emerging interest phase, where concepts like data mining and learning analytics started gaining traction, likely influenced by the proliferation of online learning platforms and early-stage adaptive systems. The pace of publications accelerated significantly from 2016 onward, indicating a growing recognition of AI's role in enhancing educational outcomes. However, the most dramatic shift occurred between 2020 and 2024, corresponding with the global impact of the COVID-19 pandemic. This phase saw an exponential increase in research output as educational institutions rapidly transitioned to digital and remote learning environments, catalyzing interest in AI-powered solutions such as intelligent tutoring systems, predictive analytics, and natural language processing tools like ChatGPT. The surge reflects a broader systemic transformation, positioning AI as a central pillar in modern education. While a slight decline is observed in 2025(based on data till March 2025), it is likely attributable to the ongoing nature of the publication cycle rather than an actual decrease in research activity. This illustrates a paradigm shift in educational research, signaling the field's maturity and urgency to address AI ethics, accessibility, and long-term sustainability in AI-enhanced education.

Figure 2. Annual scientific production (1983-2025)

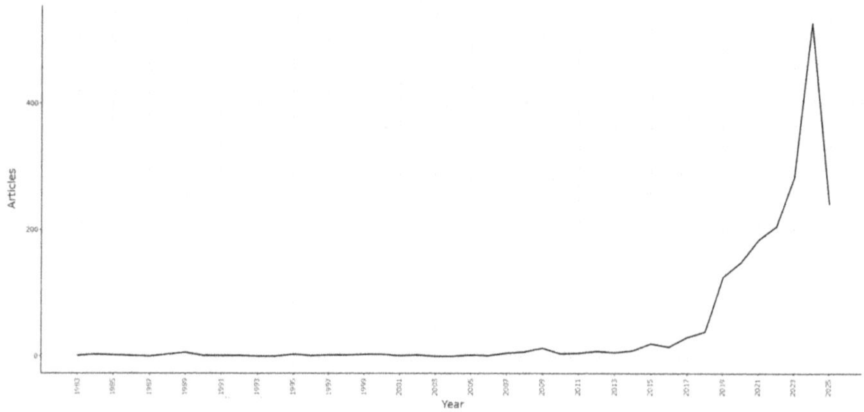

(Source: Author's own using RStudio Biblioshiny)

3.2 Three-Field Plots

This three-field plot(Figure 3) highlights the intersection of authorial expertise, research focus, and publication venues. Notable contributors like Dursun Delen, Alam Hamdan, and Yogesh K. Dwivedi deeply engage in *predictive analytics*, *machine learning*, *blockchain*, *ChatGPT*, and *digital transformation*. Their work is frequently published in reputable journals like the International Journal of Information Management, Decision Support Systems, and Technological Forecasting and Social Change. Consistent keyword usage across authors and sources suggests a strong alignment between researcher expertise and journal thematic scopes. For other researchers, especially those seeking to establish a niche in AI-powered education research, emulating these patterns can improve publication success rates. Understanding which journals favor specific themes can help scholars refine their research questions and the position of their articles. Additionally, these patterns offer editorial boards insight into author expertise and emerging trends, which could guide future thematic issues or curated calls for papers.

Figure 3. Three-field plot among source, author, and keywords

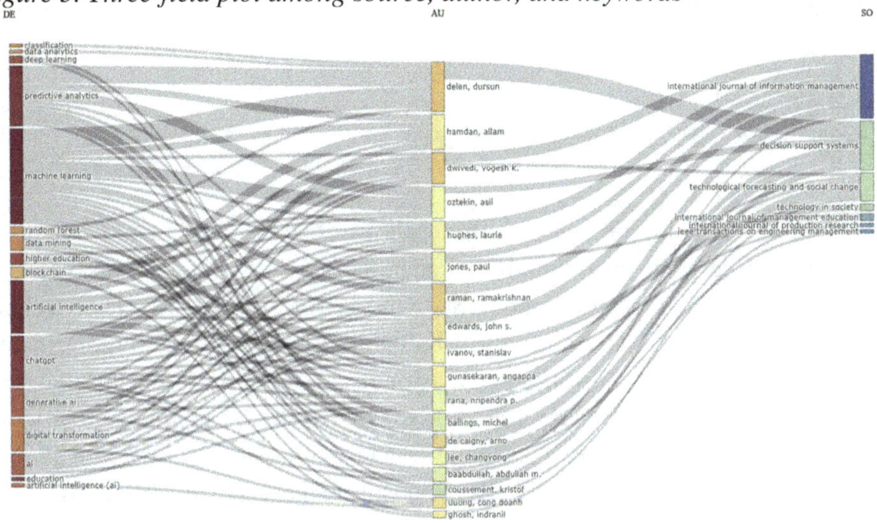

(Source: Author's own using RStudio Biblioshiny)

Figure 4 underscores the global distribution and thematic convergence of AI and data science research in education, with the USA, India, China, and the UK leading the charge. The consistent alignment of these countries with high-frequency keywords like artificial intelligence, predictive analytics, and generative AI suggests a universally recognized research agenda. Notably, the concentration of relevant studies in high-ranking journals such as *Technological Forecasting and Social Change* and *Knowledge-Based Systems* offers clear guidance for scholars on where to target their publications for maximum impact. Researchers from underrepresented countries can use this insight to tailor their research topics to align with global priorities, enhancing their work's relevance and visibility in international academic communities.

Figure 4. Three-field plot among source, country, and keywords

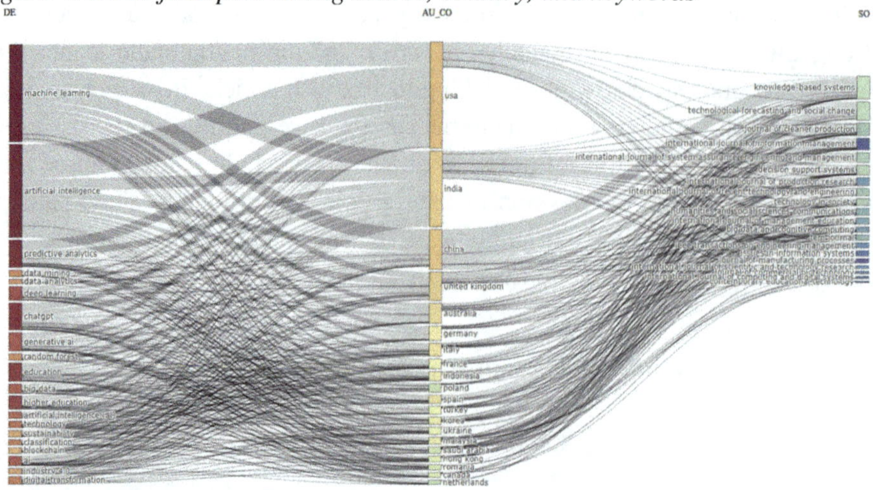

(Source: Author's own using RStudio Biblioshiny)

This three-field plot (Figure 5) illustrates the link between leading research institutions, key research themes, and influential authors. Universities such as Swansea University, Amity University, Oklahoma State University, The Hong Kong Polytechnic University, and Queensland University of Technology have significantly contributed to AI and education. These institutions are strongly aligned with dominant keywords such as *machine learning*, *artificial intelligence*, *ChatGPT*, *predictive analytics*, and *higher education*. Authors like Duong Cong Doanh, Dwivedi Yogesh K., Jones Paul, and Delen Dursun are prominently connected to these themes, reflecting a high degree of authorial specialization. The institutional concentration around modern AI applications, such as *generative AI* and *data-driven education*, highlights the collaborative focus on innovation and scalability in intelligent educational systems.

Figure 5. Three-field plot among author, keywords, and affiliations

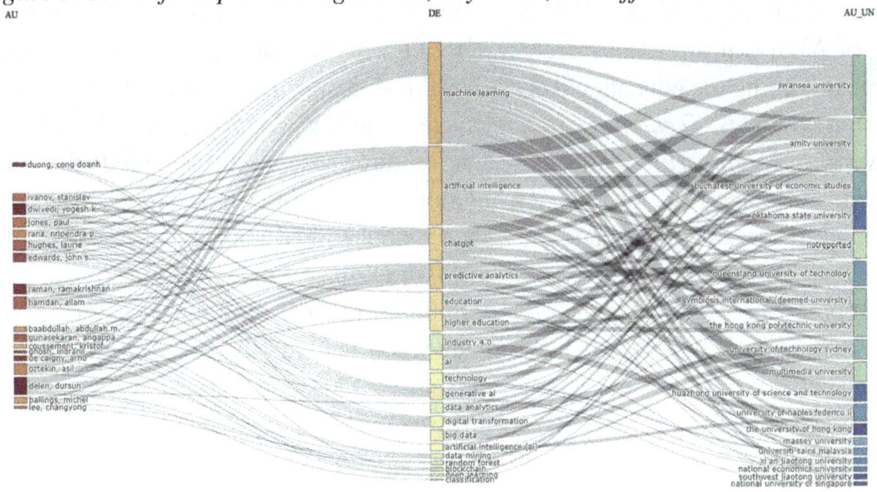

(Source: Author's own using RStudio Biblioshiny)

3.3 Top 10 Journals Based on Productivity

Figure 6 highlights the most prolific journals contributing to the scholarly discourse on AI and data science in education. Knowledge-Based Systems leads the list with 71 publications, followed closely by Technological Forecasting and Social Change with 70 documents. Both journals are known for their focus on intelligent systems, technological innovation, and foresight strategies, indicating that educational applications of AI are being treated not only as pedagogical tools but also as part of broader socio-technological transformations. Journals such as Decision Support Systems (44 documents), Technology in Society (42), and Technology Forecasting and System Assurance Engineer (41 each) also appear prominently. These sources reflect an interdisciplinary approach, where education intersects with systems engineering, decision sciences, and social implications of technology. Other notable journals include the Journal of Cleaner Production and the International Journal of Recent Technology and Engineering, suggesting a growing interest in sustainability and applied technological solutions in educational contexts. Journals like TEM Journal, Humanities and Social Sciences Communications, and the International Journal of Management Education indicate that this research area is not limited to STEM but is also gaining traction in management, policy, and social science domains. The concentration of publications in journals such as *Knowledge-Based Systems* and *Technological Forecasting and Social Change* reflects artificial intelligence and data science's growing maturity and strategic significance within educational research. These journals, known for their emphasis on intelligent systems, forecasting models, and socio-technological change, underscore the positioning of AI in education not merely as a tool for instruction but as a transformative force reshaping the educational ecosystem. The inclusion of journals like *Decision Support Systems*, *Technology in Society*, and the *International Journal of System Assurance Engineering* points to a clear trend toward data-driven, predictive, and systems-oriented research, where technologies are employed to improve decision-making, personalize learning, and enhance educational outcomes. Moreover, the appearance of sources such as the *Journal of Cleaner Production* and *Humanities and Social Sciences Communications* highlights the interdisciplinary nature of this research field. It indicates that AI in education is being discussed in the context of technical innovation and through the lenses of sustainability, ethics, and social equity. The presence of management-focused journals, including the *International Journal of Management Education*, further suggests that administrative and policy-level applications of AI, such as institutional planning, curriculum innovation, and educational leadership, are also gaining momentum.

Figure 6. Most prolific journals

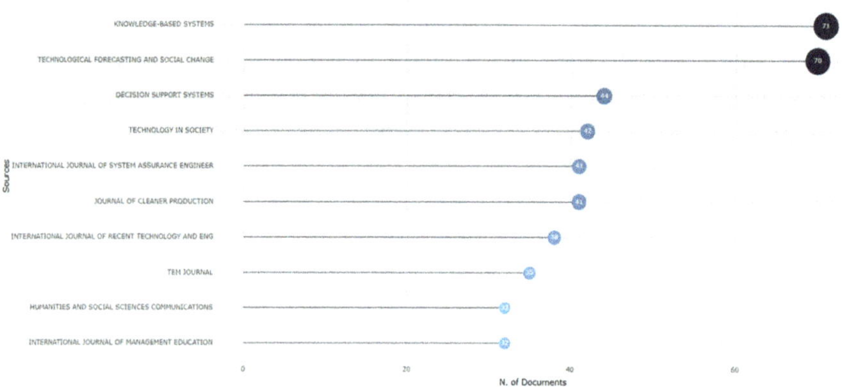

(Source: Author's own using RStudio Biblioshiny)

4. THEMATIC MAPPING

4.1 Co-occurrence Network

The co-occurrence diagram(Figure 7) generated using VOSviewer visually maps the interconnected themes and research directions in *Artificial Intelligence and Data Science in Education*. Each node represents a keyword, with larger nodes indicating a higher frequency of occurrence across the literature. The links (edges) between nodes reflect the strength of co-occurrence, meaning how often two terms appear together in the same publication. The color-coded clusters denote groups of closely related keywords, suggesting distinct research themes. At the heart of the map is the Red Cluster, which centers around terms such as *artificial intelligence, higher education, students, teaching*, and *AI literacy*. This cluster reflects AI's pedagogical and human dimension, focusing on how educational practices are evolving in response to the integration of intelligent technologies. It also highlights critical issues such as academic integrity, learner autonomy, and the ethical responsibilities of institutions and educators. Moving toward the Green Cluster, the diagram reveals a dense network of computational and algorithmic terms, including *predictive analytics, data mining, machine learning models, classification, neural networks*, and *decision trees*. This cluster embodies the technical backbone of AI in education, showcasing how institutions leverage data-driven models to predict student outcomes, optimize learning pathways, and personalize instruction. In parallel, the Orange Cluster bridges technical innovation and learner interaction. With terms such as *e-learning, adaptive learning, text processing*, and *social media*, this cluster focuses on applying AI tools within digital and social learning environments, pointing to the role of adaptive systems in shaping individualized educational experiences. In the Blue Cluster, keywords like *sustainable development, smart cities, internet of things, blockchain*, and *industry 4.0* underscore the broader systemic and policy-level conversations surrounding education. This cluster reflects an increasing awareness of how education, powered by AI, connects with global challenges such as sustainability, technological governance, and future workforce development. Finally, the Purple Cluster, though less densely connected, includes emerging but vital terms such as *explainable AI, attention mechanisms*, and *knowledge tracing*. These keywords suggest a rising interest in ensuring transparency, fairness, and interpretability in educational AI systems.

Based on these thematic structures and the relative marginalization of specific keywords, several future research areas (FRAs) emerge as critically important. First, from the Purple Cluster, there is a clear need to advance research in Explainable and Ethical AI in Education. As predictive models increasingly inform decisions about learners, frameworks for explainability and trust must be developed to support ethical adoption. From within and around the Red Cluster, the growing yet peripheral presence of terms like *ChatGPT*, *generative AI*, and *large language models* signals the urgent need to study the role of LLMs and conversational AI in teaching, tutoring, and assessment. These technologies offer powerful potential but raise concerns about originality, learning depth, and academic misconduct. Also closely tied to the Red and Blue Clusters, future research should address inclusive and accessible learning environments, especially for marginalized learners, rural populations, and students with special needs, areas currently underexplored in the co-occurrence landscape. Similarly, the Blue Cluster calls attention to the intersection of education and sustainability, suggesting more work on how AI-enhanced education aligns with global sustainable development goals (SDGs) and climate-conscious pedagogy. Concerns around academic integrity also arise strongly from the pedagogical themes in the Red Cluster, where AI-augmented assessment and originality verification systems must be rethought in the age of generative content creation. Meanwhile, the Orange and Green Clusters imply the growing potential of multimodal learning analytics, yet the focus remains narrow, often limited to log data or quiz performance. Future studies should incorporate audio, video, biometric, and behavioral cues to create more dynamic and responsive learning environments. The Red and peripheral areas point to a notable disciplinary imbalance, where STEM domains dominate while creative and non-STEM education remain largely unaddressed. Future work should explore how AI can empower storytelling, arts education, ethical reasoning, and critical thinking across various academic disciplines.

Figure 7. Co-occurrence network diagram

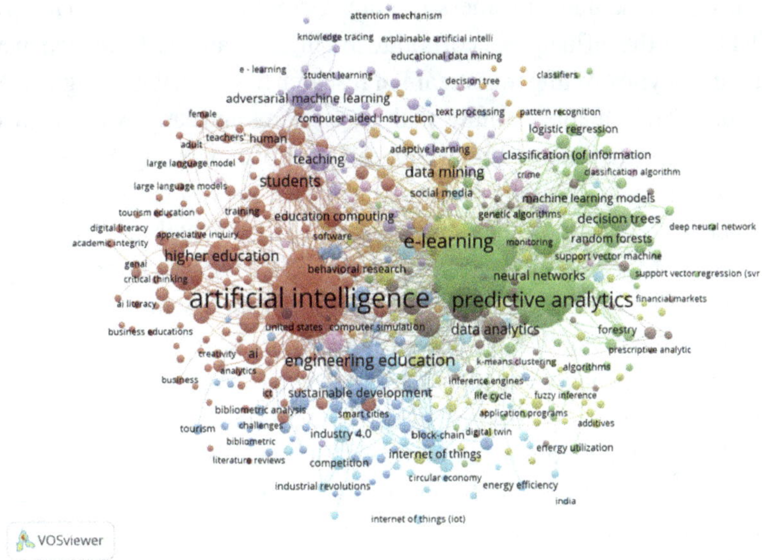

(Source: Author's own using VOSviewer)

4.2 Factorial Analysis

Factorial analysis using MCA shows which topics or themes naturally group in the literature. It reduces complexity and helps visualize significant research themes and their interrelationships, based on how often terms appear together. This Multiple Correspondence Analysis (MCA) plot (Figure 8) visualizes how keywords cluster based on co-occurrence patterns across your dataset. Each point is a keyword; proximity indicates semantic or thematic closeness. The axes (Dim 1 and Dim 2) explain the two most significant dimensions of variance in the data—here, Dim 1 (26.55%) and Dim 2 (16.37%), together explaining ~43% of the thematic structure. There are five clusters as shown below.

Cluster 1, prominently located on the left side of the factorial analysis plot (red color), represents the domain of algorithmic intelligence and predictive modeling within the broader landscape of AI in education. This cluster comprises technically rich keywords such as *random forests*, *decision trees*, *classification of information*, *predictive analytics*, *machine learning techniques*, *data analytics*, *diagnosis*, *sales*, and *benchmarking*. These terms collectively illustrate a strong focus on leveraging advanced computational models to process educational data for classification, prediction, and performance optimization. The primary emphasis in this thematic area lies in designing and deploying AI-based tools to forecast student outcomes, automate decision-making processes, and enhance institutional efficiency through data-driven insights. Including business-oriented terms like *sales* and *benchmarking* further underscores the influence of corporate intelligence and performance metrics on educational analytics. While this stream of research has contributed significantly to the development of scalable learning analytics systems and early-warning mechanisms, it tends to prioritize technological optimization over pedagogical integration. These predictive models are often developed independently of classroom realities, offering limited insight into how their outputs translate into actual teaching practices or learner support. Moreover, using black-box models without interpretability can challenge ensuring trust, transparency, and ethical alignment with educational values. Therefore, future research must enhance the academic relevance of predictive models by embedding pedagogical theories, focusing on learner-centered outcomes, and developing explainable AI frameworks that empower educators to understand and act on AI-generated recommendations. By aligning the strengths of machine learning with instructional goals and cognitive development, this cluster can evolve from a performance analytics paradigm into a transformative force for personalized and meaningful learning experiences.

Cluster 2, situated in the lower central region of the factorial map (blue color), centers around the keywords *blockchain*, *internet of things*, *big data*, *virtual reality*, *education computing*, *computer-aided instruction*, *engineering education*, *artificial intelligence*, *knowledge management*, and *competition*. This cluster reflects a distinct thematic focus on technological infrastructure, digital systems, and enterprise-level applications of AI in education. Unlike the predictive and model-based orientation of Cluster 1, this cluster addresses the foundational technologies and platforms that enable AI-enhanced education systems. It captures how innovations like blockchain are used for secure academic credentialing and record-keeping, how the Internet of Things (IoT) transforms learning environments into smart classrooms, and how virtual reality opens new frontiers in immersive, experiential learning. The cluster also points toward a growing interest in data ecosystems that power educational platforms represented by terms like *big data*, *knowledge management*, and *education computing*. These indicate the critical role of large-scale, real-time data in facilitating learning analytics, decision support systems, and institutional monitoring. Meanwhile, the presence of terms like *competition* and *engineering education* suggests that this stream of research is not just about deployment, but also about strategic positioning, digital readiness, and discipline-specific innovation, especially within technical and professional education contexts. While technologically advanced, this cluster reveals a gap in ethical, pedagogical, and policy perspectives. Many of the innovations mapped here, i.e., blockchain, IoT, and VR, are infrastructural, yet the research often overlooks how these technologies impact student agency, teacher roles, accessibility, and institutional equity. There is also minimal exploration of regulatory frameworks or governance mechanisms to manage data privacy, interoperability, or the environmental sustainability of these systems. Future research must shift from purely technical deployment toward a responsible innovation lens to advance this cluster meaningfully. This includes studying how blockchain-enabled systems affect students' control over their data, how IoT devices influence learner surveillance and autonomy, and how VR can be adapted for inclusive pedagogy in urban and rural contexts. In addition, there is a need for scholarship that develops policy blueprints, institutional guidelines, and sustainability models to ensure that technology infrastructures serve broader educational goals. Interdisciplinary research involving educators, technologists, policy-makers, and learners will be key to contextualizing these innovations within ethical and socially conscious educational frameworks.

Cluster 3, located on the right-hand side of the factorial analysis map (green color), revolves around keywords such as *students*, *teaching*, *curricula*, *ChatGPT*, and *education*. This cluster represents a pedagogically grounded and learner-centered stream of research focusing on direct interactions between students and AI technologies, particularly those enabled by generative artificial intelligence. Unlike Clusters 1 and 2, which prioritize predictive modeling or infrastructural innovation, this cluster is deeply anchored in instructional design, classroom practices, and learner engagement. It signals a significant shift toward the practical implementation of AI in real-time learning environments, with tools like ChatGPT emerging as personalized tutors, feedback agents, or cognitive companions. Including *curricula* and *teaching* highlights ongoing efforts to align AI innovations with structured educational content and instructional strategies. At the same time, the presence of *students* as a central term underscores a growing recognition of learner agency in AI-mediated environments. Rather than passively receiving algorithmic outputs, students increasingly engage in dialogic learning with AI tools, co-constructing knowledge through iterative prompts, reflections, and adaptive feedback loops. However, this shift toward generative and conversational AI raises critical pedagogical and ethical concerns. As tools like ChatGPT become more sophisticated and widely available, issues related to academic integrity, critical thinking, authenticity of student work, and over-reliance on automation have come to the forefront. Additionally, there is limited research on how AI impacts teachers' roles, classroom power dynamics, and learners' overall emotional and cognitive development. To advance this promising but sensitive thematic area, future research must delve into how generative AI tools can be integrated meaningfully into curricula without undermining the core principles of education, such as creativity, critical inquiry, and independent learning. There is a need to develop instructional frameworks that position AI as a facilitator, not a replacement, and to study its impact on student motivation, learning depth, and long-term retention. Further, researchers must explore the ethical and regulatory dimensions of generative AI use in education, including developing AI literacy, digital ethics modules, and teacher training programs that responsibly equip educators to manage AI-enhanced learning environments. As generative AI evolves rapidly, this cluster offers a critical space for interdisciplinary inquiry that combines pedagogy, technology, ethics, and policy.

Cluster 4, visually positioned toward the lower region of the factorial analysis plot, contains the core keywords *natural languages* and *text mining (purple color).* This cluster reflects an emerging but currently underdeveloped area within the AI-in-education research space, focused on using natural language processing (NLP) and text analytics. These technologies have tremendous potential in educational contexts, enabling systems to analyze learner-generated text, automate grading and feedback, personalize content delivery, and assess sentiment, engagement, or conceptual understanding. Despite their potential, the isolated placement of this cluster suggests that language technologies are not yet profoundly integrated into the broader thematic landscape of AI and education. Text *mining* implies that some work has been done on analyzing written student content, discussion posts, essays, or feedback responses, often to gain insights into learning patterns, misunderstandings, or cognitive engagement. Similarly, *natural languages* hint at the increasing sophistication of AI systems to process multiple languages, aiding multilingual education, language learning, and cross-cultural communication. However, the limited co-occurrence of these keywords with pedagogical or systemic terms indicates a missed opportunity to link NLP innovations with curriculum design, teaching practices, or learner empowerment. Future research should explore the application of NLP and text mining in formative assessment, intelligent tutoring, content personalization, and automated feedback. There's also a need to develop multilingual and culturally sensitive NLP systems that address the linguistic diversity of learners, especially in global or multilingual classroom settings. Researchers should investigate how NLP tools can support inclusive education, enhance comprehension for non-native speakers, and identify emotional or cognitive challenges through sentiment and semantic analysis. In parallel, studies should address data bias, misinterpretation, and transparency issues, ensuring these systems are fair, accurate, and accountable. This cluster offers exciting possibilities for redefining how we understand and respond to learner communication in AI-enhanced educational environments.

Cluster 5 appears in the far-right region of the factorial map(orange color) and contains highly advanced but thematically isolated keywords such as federated learning and contrastive learning. These terms are associated with state-of-the-art computer science and machine learning AI techniques. Still, their marginal position on the map reveals that they have not yet been fully adapted or contextualized within educational research. Federated learning is a decentralized machine learning approach that allows models to be trained across multiple devices or servers without sharing raw data, thus offering significant privacy benefits. Contrastive learning, conversely, is a form of self-supervised learning that helps machines distinguish between similar and dissimilar data points, valid for nuanced classification and personalization. These terms indicate a forward-looking frontier of AI research that could significantly reshape education, but only if its potential is translated into pedagogically relevant applications. Currently, these methods are more commonly found in sectors like healthcare, security, and recommendation systems, and remain primarily absent from classroom-level implementations or educational tool design. Future research must explore how these cutting-edge methods can address critical gaps in educational AI, particularly around data privacy, personalization, and learning analytics in low-data environments. For instance, federated learning could support privacy-preserving student modeling across institutions without compromising data sovereignty. Contrastive learning could be employed to develop adaptive learning systems that respond to subtle variations in learner input, preferences, or progress. Research in this cluster should also aim to build bridges between AI labs and educational researchers, facilitating interdisciplinary collaboration that ensures technical innovation is grounded in pedagogical relevance. Integrating these advanced techniques can elevate the next generation of educational AI, making it more secure, responsive, and learner-aware.

Figure 8. Factorial analysis (using MCA).

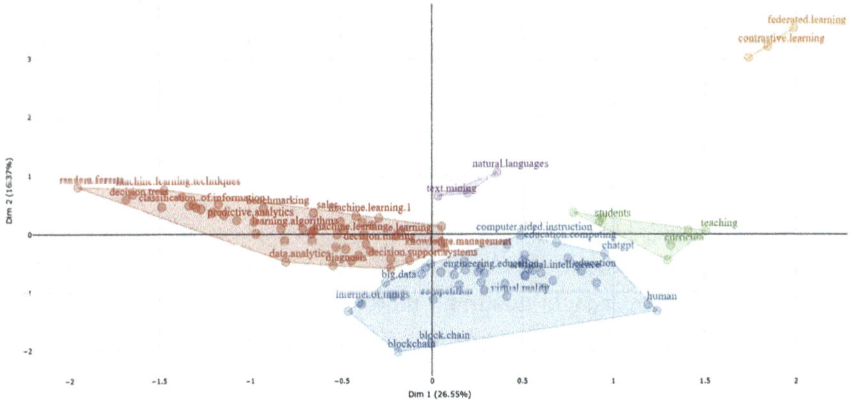

(Source: Author's own using RStudio Biblioshiny)

4.3 Thematic Evolution

Thematic evolution refers to understanding how research topics within a given field emerge, mature, interconnect, or decline over time (Figure 9). It provides insights into a domain's intellectual structure and progression, helping scholars identify well-established areas, rising themes, and those that may be losing relevance. This evolution is typically visualized using a thematic map generated through bibliometric techniques such as co-word analysis. In such a map, themes are positioned based on two key dimensions, i.e., centrality and density. Centrality represents how important or connected a theme is within the broader research field, while density measures a theme's internal development and cohesion. These two dimensions divide the map into four quadrants, each representing a different type of theme. The upper right quadrant contains motor themes, which are both highly relevant and well-developed. These are the driving forces of the field, with strong theoretical and practical foundations. Examples from the current study include *machine learning*, *e-learning*, and *learning systems*—all of which are central to integrating AI in education. The upper left quadrant contains niche themes, which are specialized and methodologically robust but have limited influence across other research areas. Topics like *predictive analytics* and *classification algorithms* fall into this category, representing technical depth yet to be broadly integrated. In contrast, the lower right quadrant includes basic and transversal themes, which are fundamental to the field and well-connected but still developing in scholarly depth. Themes such as *artificial intelligence*, *students*, and *curricula* exemplify this category, offering great potential for future theoretical refinement and empirical exploration. Lastly, the lower left quadrant features emerging or declining themes, which are underdeveloped and peripheral. These may represent newly forming research frontiers, such as *generative AI*, *federated learning*, and *contrastive learning*, or topics becoming less central to the field. This section will further detail these themes.

4.3.1 Motor Themes

The Motor Theme quadrant in the thematic evolution map represents the intellectual and practical backbone of research on artificial intelligence and data science in education. In the upper-right quadrant, motor themes are characterized by high centrality and high density. High centrality reflects their strong connection to other themes, signifying their relevance across multiple domains within the field. High density, conversely, indicates that these themes are methodologically mature and internally cohesive, supported by a well-developed body of literature, robust empirical evidence, and established theoretical frameworks. In the context of AI in education, motor themes represent the areas where technological innovation and educational practice are most deeply integrated, shaping the foundation of contemporary research and application. The themes within this quadrant include machine learning, e-learning, learning systems, engineering education, decision making, deep learning, data mining, data analytics, and decision support systems. These themes collectively encapsulate AI's transformative potential to make education more personalized, efficient, adaptive, and data-driven. Machine learning stands out as a core driver of innovation, enabling intelligent systems to analyze student behavior, predict academic performance, and deliver personalized learning experiences. Through supervised and unsupervised learning models, educational systems can now classify learners into subgroups, offer real-time feedback, and anticipate support needs well before traditional methods can. Similarly, e-learning and learning systems are reshaping the education structure by creating virtual, accessible, scalable platforms that can adapt to individual learning styles and paces.

Engineering education is also central to this cluster, reflecting the technical nature of the applied tools and the primary domain where AI technologies are often introduced and tested. Virtual labs, AI-enhanced simulations, and intelligent tutoring systems are becoming increasingly common in science and engineering curricula, allowing students to engage with complex concepts through hands-on, data-rich learning environments. Including decision-making and decision support systems indicates a strong institutional orientation within this cluster, where AI is used to enhance student outcomes and optimize administrative decisions. From resource allocation and enrolment forecasting to curriculum development and institutional strategy, data mining and analytics provide higher education leaders with evidence-based insights to guide their choices.

What sets motor themes apart is their ability to bridge theoretical development with real-world application. These are not speculative or peripheral topics; they are deeply embedded in both the academic literature and the operational realities of modern education systems. However, as these technologies grow in sophistication and adoption, there is a parallel need to consider their ethical, pedagogical, and psychological implications. Questions around algorithmic bias, transparency, student privacy, and the shifting role of educators remain at the forefront of this conversation. Therefore, future research must continue to refine these technologies and situate them within frameworks that prioritize fairness, interpretability, and human-centered design. As such, the motor themes identified in this study indicate where the field currently stands and serve as the launchpad for its next phase of growth and responsible innovation.

4.3.2 Niche Themes

The Niche Themes quadrant, located in the upper-left section of the thematic map, consists of methodologically advanced and internally well-developed topics but exhibits lower centrality, meaning they are less connected to other major themes in the broader research landscape. These themes tend to reflect specialized, technical, or domain-specific areas that, while rich in detail and depth, remain somewhat isolated from mainstream educational discourse. In the context of AI and data science in education, the niche themes identified include predictive analysis, forecasting, learning algorithms, decision tree models, machine learning techniques, classification, neural networks, support vector machines (SVM), and random forests. These themes are particularly prominent in the technical and data science-oriented side of educational research, where the primary objective is to build or refine algorithms capable of processing vast amounts of learner data for pattern recognition, performance prediction, and behavior classification. Despite their limited centrality, these themes are critical in developing the computational backbone of intelligent educational systems. For instance, predictive analysis and forecasting are routinely used in learning analytics to estimate student outcomes, identify those at risk of failure, and support timely academic interventions. Classification models like decision trees, SVMs, and neural networks help categorize learner profiles, assess engagement levels, and tailor feedback. However, while these techniques are robust from a data science standpoint, they are often deployed in a technological silo, meaning they are insufficiently linked to pedagogical frameworks, classroom realities, or human-centered educational principles. Much of the research in this quadrant focuses on algorithmic accuracy and model performance rather than the broader social, emotional, or cognitive dimensions of learning.

This disconnection creates a significant research opportunity. While niche themes represent strong vertical growth in technical capacity, they need horizontal integration with pedagogical theories, ethics, and user experience design to realize their full educational value. There is a pressing need for interdisciplinary collaboration that connects computer scientists, academic technologists, learning scientists, and practitioners. Doing so would allow the outputs of these sophisticated models to be meaningfully embedded within curricula, instructional strategies, and assessment systems. For example, rather than merely predicting student dropouts, future research could explore how predictive models can be tied to intervention pathways designed by teachers, counselors, or AI tutors. Similarly, rather than optimizing for precision alone, models could be developed for interpretability, inclusivity, and fairness, allowing educators and learners to understand and trust the system's recommendations. While niche themes are not yet central to the broader educational discourse, they represent the deep technical scaffolding upon which future intelligent learning environments can be built. Their maturity offers an excellent foundation, but their influence will grow only when integrated into the human-centered, context-aware ecosystems that define impactful education. By expanding the relevance of these themes beyond data labs and into classrooms, policy frameworks, and learning communities, the field can unlock the transformative potential of advanced AI techniques in education.

4.3.3 Basic and Transversal Themes

The Basic and Transversal Themes quadrant, located in the lower-right corner of the thematic map, comprises highly central themes but is low in density. This positioning indicates that these topics are fundamentally essential and widely connected across the research field. Yet, they are still underdeveloped regarding theoretical depth, methodological refinement, or empirical consolidation. In the context of AI in education, the basic themes identified in this quadrant include artificial intelligence, students, education, teaching, higher education, education computing, technology adoption, curricula, and technological development. These foundational concepts serve as entry points for interdisciplinary research, forming the connective tissue between technical, pedagogical, social, and institutional dimensions of AI-enabled learning environments. The high centrality of these themes reflects their broad relevance and influence; they are mentioned across diverse studies and disciplines, signaling their importance in framing research questions, structuring analysis, and anchoring broader discussions. For instance, *artificial intelligence* as a keyword is omnipresent across the literature, touching on everything from algorithmic performance to ethical concerns, policy implications, and classroom integration. Likewise, terms such as *students*, *education*, and *teaching* lie at the heart of educational discourse, indicating that learners and learning environments remain central to applying AI technologies. However, the low density of this quadrant reveals that these concepts are often treated in broad or generic terms, lacking the depth, specificity, or theoretical consolidation required for deeper scholarly inquiry.

This suggests that these themes are strategically significant but often fragmented or loosely defined. For example, although *technology adoption* is widely discussed, studies may lack nuanced analysis of the psychological, organizational, or cultural factors that influence how educators and learners receive AI tools. Similarly, while *curricula* appear as a keyword, there is limited exploration of how AI reshapes curriculum design regarding content personalization, competency-based learning, or ethical literacy. The presence of *higher education* also underscores a focus on institutional and policy-level change. Still, much of the literature remains surface-level, addressing adoption and integration without systematically evaluating impact or equity. The themes in this quadrant thus represent a crucial opportunity for growth. Their widespread relevance makes them ideal candidates for theoretical deepening, conceptual clarity, and methodological innovation. Researchers can enrich these themes by anchoring them in established educational theories, such as constructivism, self-determination theory, or transformative learning theory, and by conducting longitudinal and mixed-method studies that uncover the lived experiences of students, teachers, and institutions navigating AI-enhanced learning. Additionally, there is a need to develop conceptual models and empirical typologies that more precisely define what "AI in education" means across various contexts, i.e., urban vs. rural, K-12 vs. higher education, formal vs. informal learning.

4.3.4 Emerging or Declining Themes

The Emerging or Declining themes quadrant, positioned in the lower-left corner of the thematic map, contains research topics characterized by low centrality and low density. This positioning indicates that these themes are currently peripheral to the field and are either in the early stages of development or are fading in scholarly interest and relevance. In the context of AI and data science in education, the themes in this quadrant include *generative artificial intelligence*, *language models*, *contrastive learning*, *federated learning*, *adversarial machine learning*, *natural language processing*, *human experiments*, *embeddings*, and *articles*. These topics represent a mixed landscape of innovation and ambiguity, where some themes signal high-potential emerging areas. In contrast, others reflect fragmented or declining interest due to limited application or theoretical disconnect from mainstream educational research. Among the most notable emerging themes is generative artificial intelligence, which has gained tremendous attention in recent years with the rise of tools like ChatGPT, Bard, and Claude. While still underdeveloped in formal academic discourse, especially in education, this theme represents a revolutionary shift in how content can be generated, personalized, and interacted with. Closely linked to this is the theme of *language models*, which underpins many generative AI applications and offers powerful possibilities for dialogue-based learning, automated writing assistance, and naturalistic student-tutor interaction. However, the placement of these themes in the emerging quadrant reflects their nascent integration into educational theory, pedagogy, and ethics. Though promising, research on their classroom use, curriculum alignment, and student impact is still sparse and exploratory. Other themes, such as contrastive learning, federated learning, and adversarial machine learning, originate from the cutting-edge frontiers of AI research and are widely used in computer science, particularly in areas like privacy, robustness, and unsupervised representation learning. Yet, in the context of education, these methods remain largely experimental and lack pedagogical adaptation. Their low centrality suggests they have not yet been connected meaningfully with broader educational goals such as learner engagement, teacher facilitation, or curriculum reform. Nonetheless, their potential is immense. For example, federated learning could be a game-changer for privacy-preserving education analytics, allowing models to learn across multiple institutions without sharing raw student data. Similarly, contrastive learning could improve personalized feedback systems by enabling AI to distinguish between subtle variations in learner behavior or content understanding.

On the other hand, themes like *human experiment*, *embeddings*, and *article* appear more ambiguous and may represent methodological artifacts or declining interest areas. Their isolated presence, lacking links to emerging educational concerns or interdisciplinary exploration, suggests a need for conceptual clarity or a shift in research focus away from these topics.

Figure 9. Thematic evolution

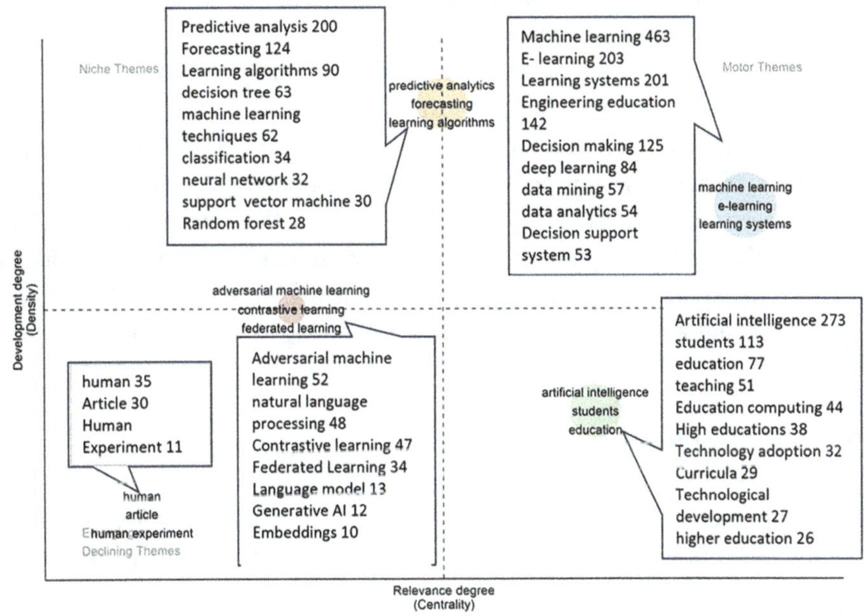

(Source: Author's own using RStudio Biblioshiny)

5. IMPLICATIONS

5.1 Theoretical Contribution

This study offers significant theoretical contributions by mapping the intellectual evolution and thematic convergence of artificial intelligence (AI) and data science (DS) in education over four decades. One of the most profound implications is the establishment of AI and DS not merely as technological adjuncts to education, but as theoretical paradigms shaping a new ontology of learning that is data-driven, adaptive, and increasingly agentic. The analysis reveals how foundational educational constructs (e.g., student engagement, teaching practices, curriculum design) are being reinterpreted through the lens of AI models, signaling a shift toward a socio-technological epistemology where learning is not only mediated but also co-constructed by intelligent systems. Furthermore, the integration of terms like *machine learning*, *e-learning*, *deep learning*, and *predictive analytics* across clusters shows the emergence of hybrid theoretical zones blending computational intelligence with educational psychology, systems theory, and cognitive science. Identifying basic but underdeveloped themes, such as students, curricula, and teaching, emphasizes anchoring technical innovation within learner-centered and pedagogically sound frameworks. Additionally, themes like ChatGPT, federated learning, and generative AI in the emerging quadrant push the theoretical boundary toward explainability, ethics, and AI-human co-agency in education. This study also highlights a disciplinary imbalance, calling for theoretical expansion beyond STEM to include arts, humanities, and social learning contexts, thereby encouraging a more inclusive and pluralistic theorization of AI in education. By revealing these interconnections and gaps, this bibliometric study not only consolidates fragmented scholarly work but also lays a foundational blueprint for future theoretical innovation, interdisciplinary, equity-driven, and ethically responsive to the evolving landscape of AI-powered education.

5.2 Managerial Implications

This study provides timely and strategic insights for educational managers, administrators, and institutional leaders seeking to harness the transformative power of artificial intelligence and data science. The identification of motor themes such as *machine learning*, *e-learning*, *decision-making*, and *data analytics* underscores the need for educational institutions to adopt a data-informed management culture, where predictive insights and learning analytics are used not only for academic tracking but also for institutional planning, resource optimization, and strategic decision-making. For instance, AI-driven decision support systems can help leaders anticipate student dropout trends, evaluate instructional effectiveness, and forecast higher-precision enrollment demands. Moreover, the emergence of themes like *federated learning* and *generative AI* signals an urgent managerial need to invest in digital infrastructure, talent development, and ethical governance frameworks to ensure responsible adoption. Managers must prioritize teacher training, data literacy, and AI competency-building across all levels of the organization to bridge the gap between technological potential and pedagogical practice. The analysis also calls attention to underdeveloped yet central themes such as *curricula*, *students*, and *teaching*, urging educational managers to ensure that technology initiatives remain learner-centered and pedagogically aligned, rather than technology-driven for its own sake. Finally, the fragmented treatment of ethics, privacy, and equity within the thematic landscape points to the need for robust AI governance policies, stakeholder transparency, and cross-functional collaboration between IT, pedagogy, and administration. By proactively responding to these insights, educational managers can lead innovation and safeguard equity, integrity, and impact in AI-enhanced learning ecosystems.

5.3 Policy Implications

The findings of this study hold significant implications for policymakers aiming to develop strategic, inclusive, and future-ready education systems in the age of AI. The prominence of themes such as *machine learning*, *e-learning*, and *data analytics* indicates the growing relevance of AI in shaping national and institutional education agendas. However, the study also reveals critical gaps in *ethics*, *AI literacy*, *curricula reform*, and *teacher training*, suggesting the need for comprehensive AI-in-education policy frameworks. Policymakers must ensure that AI integration is technologically viable, socially equitable, culturally responsive, and pedagogically sound. This calls for developing national strategies that embed digital ethics, data privacy regulations, inclusivity standards, and accountability mechanisms across all AI-based educational interventions. Furthermore, the rise of themes like *generative AI*, *federated learning*, and *natural language processing* requires forward-looking policy responses that address the governance of LLMs, intellectual ownership, and the role of AI in assessment and content creation. Policies should also encourage interdisciplinary collaboration, fund research on underrepresented areas (e.g., humanities education and emotional AI), and promote public-private partnerships that ensure access to AI infrastructure across urban and rural educational settings.

5.4 Practical Implications

This study provides actionable insights for educators, instructional designers, and technology developers at the intersection of AI and learning. Mapping motor themes such as decision support systems, deep learning, and learning systems highlights the need to move from theoretical exploration to real-world deployment of AI-enhanced tools that improve teaching effectiveness, learner engagement, and assessment accuracy. Educators must be equipped to integrate AI responsibly using tools like intelligent tutoring systems, automated feedback mechanisms, and adaptive platforms for efficiency, personalization, differentiation, and learner empowerment. Moreover, the emergence of cutting-edge but underdeveloped themes such as generative AI and contrastive learning suggests that practitioners need ongoing professional development to stay updated on technological capabilities and limitations. Technology designers and edtech developers, in turn, should consider the themes in the basic and emerging quadrants as cues to build user-centered, curriculum-aligned, and context-aware AI applications. This also includes making AI interfaces explainable and transparent so that educators and students can trust and interpret the outcomes generated. The study underscores that successful AI integration is not solely a matter of technical sophistication; it depends on how well tools are embedded into everyday educational practice with clarity, purpose, and care.

5.4 Limitation

While this study offers a comprehensive bibliometric analysis of AI and data science in education over four decades, it has limitations. The analysis is based solely on the Scopus database, which may exclude relevant publications indexed elsewhere, potentially limiting the scope of insights. Additionally, the reliance on author keywords may have led to the omission or fragmentation of semantically similar terms. Though insightful, thematic clustering and co-occurrence mapping are interpretative and may not fully capture the nuances of interdisciplinary overlaps. Furthermore, the study is descriptive and does not delve into individual publications' quality or empirical rigor. Finally, as the field is rapidly evolving, particularly with emerging technologies like generative AI, some recent developments may not yet be adequately reflected in the dataset. These limitations open avenues for deeper, mixed-method, and domain-specific explorations in future research.

5.5 Future Research Avenues (FRAs)

Table 1 lists the FRAs derived from thematic mapping, co-occurrence network, and factorial analysis.

Table 1. Future research avenues

Research Theme	Future Research Avenue (FRA)	Rationale
Algorithmic Intelligence and Predictive Modeling	Develop explainable AI frameworks to make predictive models transparent and pedagogically useful.	Many models are "black boxes" and lack interpretability; this limits educators' trust and actionable classroom insights.
Infrastructure and Systems	Study the impact of blockchain, IoT, and VR on educational equity, access, and student agency.	These innovations are primarily treated as technical solutions without critically examining their pedagogical or social implications.
Generative AI in Learning Design	Investigate how generative AI (e.g., ChatGPT) affects academic integrity, creativity, and teacher-student dynamics.	ChatGPT is widely used but has been under-researched regarding its classroom consequences, ethical boundaries, and design alignment.
Language Technologies & NLP	Expand multilingual NLP tools and their use in inclusive and cross-cultural classrooms.	Current NLP applications are not adequately inclusive or adapted for non-dominant languages and diverse learning styles.
Advanced AI Techniques	Apply federated and contrastive learning for privacy-preserving and adaptive education.	These techniques offer secure, personalized learning opportunities but are not yet widely explored or implemented in education.
Curricula & Pedagogy	Design AI-integrated curricula that align with 21st-century competencies and ethical frameworks.	AI is rarely embedded in curricula as a structured component; its integration remains superficial or ad hoc
Emotional and Social Learning	Explore AI's role in emotional intelligence, well-being, and social-emotional learning (SEL)	These are underrepresented themes despite their increasing importance in holistic education models.
Creative and Non-STEM Disciplines	Investigate how AI can enhance the arts, humanities, and ethical reasoning in education.	The current literature is heavy on STEM; AI's potential in storytelling, critical thinking, and reflective practice is underutilized.
Academic Integrity in the Age of AI	Develop frameworks to address plagiarism, originality, and AI-assisted assessments.	Generative tools challenge traditional notions of academic work; integrity policies and detection systems must evolve.
Sustainable AI and Education for SDGs	Align AI-enhanced education with Sustainable Development Goals (SDGs) and climate-conscious pedagogy.	The sustainability dimension is emerging but lacks operational frameworks and empirical validation.

(Source: Author's own)

6. CONCLUSION

This chapter provides a bibliometric investigation into four decades (1983–2025) of research at the intersection of artificial intelligence (AI), data science (DS), and education. By analyzing 1,920 Scopus-indexed publications using Biblioshiny and VOSviewer, the study uncovers the thematic evolution, intellectual structure, and collaborative landscape of this dynamic field. Findings reveal the dominance of machine learning, e-learning, and decision support systems as motor themes, while also identifying underexplored but crucial areas such as curriculum integration, pedagogical ethics, and explainable AI. The factorial and co-occurrence analyses highlight a growing convergence of technical sophistication with learner-centered priorities, yet expose gaps in inclusivity, emotional intelligence, and humanistic applications. Emerging technologies such as generative AI and federated learning present new challenges and opportunities that require interdisciplinary attention and governance. The chapter underscores the importance of shifting from algorithmic advancement to equitable and pedagogically meaningful implementation. It contributes theoretically by framing AI not only as a tool but as a new epistemology of learning; practically, it offers insights for educators, managers, and developers; and from a policy perspective, it emphasizes ethical and inclusive digital transformation. Overall, the study serves as a roadmap for scholars and practitioners aiming to shape the future of AI-enhanced education responsibly.

CREDIT AUTHOR STATEMENT

Rachana Jaiswal: Conceptualization, Supervision, Methodology, Software, Writing- Reviewing and Editing, Formal Analysis, Project administration.

Ila Gupta: Writing- Original draft preparation; Visualization, Analysis.

Shwetank Gupta: Writing- Original draft preparation; Analysis.

Shashank Gupta: Supervision, Validation, Software, Data Curation, Writing- Original draft preparation, Methodology, Visualization, Investigation.

FUNDING

This research received no external funding.

DECLARATION OF INTEREST STATEMENT

The author(s) declare no conflict of interest.

REFERENCES

Akpan, I. J., Kobara, Y. M., Owolabi, J., Akpan, A. A., & Offodile, O. F. (2025). Conversational and generative artificial intelligence and human–chatbot interaction in education and research. *International Transactions in Operational Research, 32*(3), 1251–1281. DOI: 10.1111/itor.13522

Alshammari, M. T. (2025). An Investigation into ChatGPT-Enhanced Adaptive E-learning Systems. *TEM Journal, 14*(1), 503–510. DOI: 10.18421/TEM141-45

Altinay, Z., Altinay, F., Tlili, A., & Vatankhah, S. (2025). "Keep your friends close, but your enemies closer:" ChatGPT in tourism and hospitality. *Journal of Hospitality and Tourism Technology, 16*(2), 213–228. DOI: 10.1108/JHTT-03-2024-0139

Azzam, A., & Charles, T. (2025). K-12 STEM Teachers' Experiences with Artificial Intelligence. *TEM Journal, 14*(1).

Bixler, K., & Ceballos, M. (2025). Principals Leading AI in Schools for Instructional Leadership: A Conceptual Model for Principal AI Use. *Leadership and Policy in Schools, 24*(1), 137–154. DOI: 10.1080/15700763.2024.2428297

Dairo, A. O., & Szűcs, K. (2025). Adaptive learning engine for driving marketing channel performance: A machine learning approach. *Journal of Research in Interactive Marketing*, *19*(6), 952–968. Advance online publication. DOI: 10.1108/JRIM-02-2024-0098

Dang, S., Quach, S., & Roberts, R. E. (2025). How time fuels AI device adoption: A contextual model enriched by machine learning. *Technological Forecasting and Social Change*, *212*, 123975. DOI: 10.1016/j.techfore.2025.123975

Dwivedi, Y. K. (2025). Generative Artificial Intelligence (GenAI) in entrepreneurial education and practice: Emerging insights, the GAIN Framework, and research agenda. *The International Entrepreneurship and Management Journal*, *21*(1), 1–21. DOI: 10.1007/s11365-025-01089-2

Gavira Durón, N., & Jiménez-Preciado, A. L. (2025). Exploring the role of AI in higher education: A natural language processing analysis of emerging trends and discourses. *The TQM Journal*. Advance online publication. DOI: 10.1108/TQM-10-2024-0376

Gupta, S., & Jaiswal, R. (2024a). How can we improve AI competencies for tomorrow's leaders: Insights from multi-stakeholders' interaction. *International Journal of Management Education*, *22*(3), 101070. DOI: 10.1016/j.ijme.2024.101070

Gupta, S., & Jaiswal, R. (2024b). How can we improve Hospitality Excellence for Sustainable Development using machine learning. *Journal of Hospitality & Tourism Education*, 1–13. DOI: 10.1080/10963758.2024.2420267

Gupta, S., & Jaiswal, R. (2025). A deep learning-based hybrid PLS-SEM-ANN approach for predicting factors improving AI-driven decision-making proficiency for future leaders. *Journal of International Education in Business*. DOI: 10.1108/JIEB-05-2024-0058

Gupta, S., Jaiswal, R., & Gupta, S. K. (2024). Digital nomads: a systematic literature review and future research agenda. *Tourism Review*. DOI: 10.1108/TR-12-2023-0869

Hefnawi, A. (2025). Shifting the narrative: From technocentric to purpose-driven artificial intelligence in education. *Management in Education*. Advance online publication. DOI: 10.1177/08920206251322644

Imjai, N., Promma, W., Visedsun, N., Usman, B., & Aujirapongpan, S. (2025). Fraud detection skills of Thai Gen Z accountants: The roles of digital competency, data science literacy and diagnostic skills. *International Journal of Information Management Data Insights*, *5*(1), 100308. DOI: 10.1016/j.jjimei.2024.100308

Jaiswal, R. (2023). Being Agile: Transcendent Solutions to Enduring Problems in the Age of COVID-19. *MDIM Journal of Management Review and Practice.*, *1*(2), 96–106. DOI: 10.1177/mjmrp.231200388

Jaiswal, R. (2024). An Investigation into How Artificial Intelligence (AI) has Enhanced Quality Engineering. In *Contemporary Digital Transformation and Organizational Effectiveness in Business 4.0* (pp. 121-129). Apple Academic Press.

Jaiswal, R. (2025). A Retrospection of Business Intelligence in the Era of Big Data Analytics and Artificial Intelligence for Fintech. *Advanced Digital Technologies in Financial and Business Management: Unleashing the Power of Artificial Intelligence, Machine Learning, Blockchain, and the Internet of Things*, 15.

Jaiswal, R., & Gupta, S. (2023). Global research trends on blockchain technology in finance: Past, present and future. *International Journal of Electronic Finance, 14*(3). Advance online publication. DOI: 10.1504/IJEF.2025.10059748

Jaiswal, R., & Gupta, S. (2024). Money talks, happiness walks: Dissecting the secrets of global bliss with machine learning. *Journal of Chinese Economic and Business Studies*, *22*(1), 111–158. DOI: 10.1080/14765284.2023.2245277

Jaiswal, R., Gupta, S., & Gupta, S. K. (2025). The impending disruption of digital nomadism: Opportunities, challenges, and research agenda. *World Leisure Journal*, *67*(1), 74–104. DOI: 10.1080/16078055.2024.2346091

Jaiswal, R., Gupta, S., & Tiwari, A. K. (2022a). Delineation of blockchain technology in finance: A scientometric view. *Annals of financial economics, 17*(4), 2250025. DOI: 10.1142/S2010495222500257

Jaiswal, R., Gupta, S., & Tiwari, A. K. (2023). Dissecting the compensation conundrum: A machine learning-based prognostication of key determinants in a complex labor market. *Management Decision*, *61*(8), 2322–2353. DOI: 10.1108/MD-07-2022-0976

Jaiswal, R., Gupta, S., & Tiwari, A. K. (2024a). Big data and machine learning-based decision support system to reshape the vaticination of insurance claims. *Technological Forecasting and Social Change*, *209*, 123829. DOI: 10.1016/j.techfore.2024.123829

Jaiswal, R., Gupta, S., & Tiwari, A. K. (2024d). Decoding mood of the Twitterverse on ESG investing: Opinion mining and key themes using machine learning. *Management Research Review*, *47*(8), 1221–1252. DOI: 10.1108/MRR-07-2023-0526

Jaiswal, R., Gupta, S., & Tiwari, A. K. (2025). Environmental, social and governance-type investing: a multi-stakeholder machine learning analysis. *Management Decision*. DOI: 10.1108/MD-04-2024-0930

Jaiswal, R., Gupta, S.K., & Gupta, S. (2024b). Current trends and future research agenda on climate-resilient infrastructure in developing sustainable tourist destinations. *Achieving sustainable transformation in tourism and hospitality sectors*, 16-35. DOI: 10.4018/979-8-3693-3390-7.ch002

Jaiswal, R., Khan, M. I. A., & Kumar, M. (2024c). Charting the course: Exploring the changing terrain of online shopping and future directions for research. *International Journal of Electronic Business*, *19*(1), 56–79. DOI: 10.1504/IJEB.2024.135653

Jaiswal, R., & Kumar, D. (2023). Quality Education for Sustainable Development Goals: Past, Present and Future. *National Journal of Education*, *18*(2), 127–141.

Jaiswal, R., Kumar, D., & Sharma, V. D. (2022b). Bibliometric retrospection of the literature on India's export promotion program (1964–2022). *BHU Management Review*, *9*(2), 36–53.

Jamal, A., Jaiswal, R., Sayyad, S., Pandit, P., & Sayyad, F. (2022). A Comprehensive Survey of Various Machine Learning Techniques to Counter Security Issues Related to Mobile Malwares. *International Journal of Next-Generation Computing*, *13*(3). Advance online publication. DOI: 10.47164/ijngc.v13i3.807

Jasrai, L. (2025). Extending UTAUT model to examine the usages of ChatGPT among Indian students in higher education: A structural equation modelling approach. *The TQM Journal*. Advance online publication. DOI: 10.1108/TQM-12-2024-0498

Jiang, H., Li, M., Witte, P., Geertman, S., & Pan, H. (2025). Urban Chatter: Exploring the potential of ChatGPT-like and generative AI in enhancing planning support. *Cities (London, England)*, *158*, 105701. DOI: 10.1016/j.cities.2025.105701

Koebe, P. (2025). How digital technologies and AI contribute to achieving the health-related SDGs. *International Journal of Information Management Data Insights*, *5*(1), 100298. DOI: 10.1016/j.jjimei.2024.100298

Krishnamoorthy, R., Srivastava, M., & Khanna, D. (2025). AI in higher education: Tapping educators' perspective. *International Journal of System Assurance Engineering and Management*, •••, 1–13. DOI: 10.1007/s13198-024-02657-5

Kumar, S., Billa, L. V. L., Bhimineni, O., Jaiswal, R., & Bisht, A. (2022). Implementation of ICT Tools in A Vocational Skill Development Program. *International Journal of Next-Generation Computing*, *13*(3). Advance online publication. DOI: 10.47164/ijngc.v13i3.729

Leite, H. (2025). Artificial intelligence in higher education: Research notes from a longitudinal study. *Technological Forecasting and Social Change*, *215*, 124115. DOI: 10.1016/j.techfore.2025.124115

Letjani, K. P., Kurniawan, K., & Muthaiyah, S. (2025). Adoption of chatgpt in educational institutions in Botswana: A customer perspective. *Asia Pacific Management Review*, *30*(1), 100346. DOI: 10.1016/j.apmrv.2024.100346

Murugesan, G., Jaiswal, R., Kshatri, S. S., & Bhonsle, D. (2022). Developing machine learning based framework for the network traffic prediction. *International Journal of Next-Generation Computing*, *13*(3). Advance online publication. DOI: 10.47164/ijngc.v13i3.787

Neophytou, R., Liasidou, S., Pipyros, K., & Christofi, A. (2025). Artificial intelligence driven adaptive learning methods in sustainable tourism education. *Worldwide Hospitality and Tourism Themes*, *17*(1), 120–131. DOI: 10.1108/WHATT-12-2024-0308

Prakhar, P., Gupta, S., & Jaiswal, R. (2025a). Battery technology and charging infrastructure for EVs: a resource-based and dynamic capability view of entrepreneurial opportunities. *Information Discovery and Delivery*. DOI: 10.1108/IDD-09-2024-0143

Prakhar, P., Jabeen, F., Jaiswal, R., Gupta, S., Piccardi, P., & Jose, S. (2025b). Mapping the electric vehicle adoption scholarship for sustainability: An integrated theoretical framework and future research directions. *Management of Environmental Quality*, *36*(1), 249–276. DOI: 10.1108/MEQ-04-2024-0153

Prakhar, P., Jaiswal, R., & Gupta, S. (2024a). Entrepreneurship in the electric vehicle sector: Past, present and future directions. *Parikalpana: KIIT Journal of Management, 20*(1), 5-26. DOI: 10.23862/kiit-parikalpana/2024/v20/i1/225089

Prakhar, P., Jaiswal, R., Gupta, S., & Tiwari, A. K. (2024c). Electric vehicles in transition: Opportunities, challenges, and research agenda–A systematic literature review. *Journal of Environmental Management*, *372*, 123415. DOI: 10.1016/j.jenvman.2024.123415 PMID: 39581008

Prakhar, P., Jaiswal, R., & Khan, M. I. A. (2024b). Bibliometric perspectives on sustainable tourism and future research agenda. In *Managing Tourism and Hospitality Sectors for Sustainable Global Transformation* (pp. 1–16). IGI Global. DOI: 10.4018/979-8-3693-6260-0.ch001

Rajan, S., & Niranjan, L. R. (2025). The double-edged sword of ChatGPT: Fostering and hindering creativity in postgraduate academics in Bengaluru. *International Journal of Educational Management*, *39*(2), 317–337. DOI: 10.1108/IJEM-03-2024-0181

Salha, S., Mousa, A., & Khayat, S. (2025). Artificial Intelligence in Education (AIED) Policies in School Context: A Mixed Approach Research. *Leadership and Policy in Schools*, *24*(1), 27–45. DOI: 10.1080/15700763.2024.2443675

Singh, S., Jaiswal, R., Gupta, S., & Kumar, C. (2024). What we know and what should we know about the future of blockchain in finance. *F1000 Research, 13*, 1051. DOI: 10.12688/f1000research.153215.1 PMID: 40520947

Trindade, M. A., Edirisinghe, G. S., & Luo, L. (2025). Teaching mathematical concepts in management with generative artificial intelligence: The power of human oversight in AI-driven learning. *International Journal of Management Education, 23*(2), 101104. DOI: 10.1016/j.ijme.2024.101104

Verma, S., Kashive, N., & Gupta, A. (2025). Examining predictors of generative-AI acceptance and usage in academic research: A sequential mixed-methods approach. *Benchmarking*. Advance online publication. DOI: 10.1108/BIJ-07-2024-0564

Wan, F., Li, Z., Chen, Y. F., & Lei, C. F. (2024). Charting the Course in the Digital Transformation: Navigating the Intersection of the Hospitality Industry and Education. *Journal of Hospitality & Tourism Education*, 1–14. DOI: 10.1080/10963758.2024.2433067

Wong, J. M. S., Tang, W. K. W., & Li, K. C. (2025). Digital transformation in higher education: Tertiary students' perspectives on online learning and its implications for the future. *International Journal of Innovation and Learning, 37*(5), 1–18. DOI: 10.1504/IJIL.2025.144600

Zhang, Y. (2025). Study on comprehensive management of online learning resources for digital education and teaching reform. *International Journal of Networking and Virtual Organisations, 32*(1-4), 36–48. DOI: 10.1504/IJNVO.2025.145364

Zulfiqar, S., Sarwar, B., Huo, C., Zhao, X., & ul Mahasbi, H. (2025). AI-powered education: Driving entrepreneurial spirit among university students. *International Journal of Management Education, 23*(2), 101106. DOI: 10.1016/j.ijme.2024.101106

Chapter 3
Overview of AI Algorithms and Data Science Techniques Relevant to Education

R. Ramya
https://orcid.org/0000-0002-8071-9343
Sathyabama Institute of Science and Technology, India

Athyul Thomas V. S.
https://orcid.org/0009-0004-3606-6922
Sathyabama Institute of Science and Technology, India

Kanaga Prasath B.
Adhi College of Engineering and Technology, India

ABSTRACT

Artificial Intelligence (AI) and data science are transforming education by enhancing learning experiences, optimizing administrative processes, and enabling data-driven decision-making. AI-driven automation in assessment and feedback, along with data visualization techniques, supports educators in tracking student progress and improving curriculum development. Additionally, big data analytics enables institutions to identify learning patterns and improve student success rates. Despite these advancements, the integration of AI in education presents challenges, including ethical concerns, data privacy issues, and the risk of algorithmic bias. AI-powered tools also play a crucial role in enhancing accessibility for students with disabilities and fostering collaborative learning environments. The development of intelligent

DOI: 10.4018/979-8-3373-2185-1.ch003

tutoring systems and AI-enhanced educational platforms provides new opportunities for personalized and inclusive education. Measuring the impact of AI on learning outcomes is essential to refining these technologies for optimal effectiveness.

1. INTRODUCTION

Artificial Intelligence (AI) and data science are transforming the field of education by enhancing learning experiences, improving administrative processes, and personalizing instruction (Ali et al., 2024). This overview explores key AI algorithms and data science techniques that are particularly relevant to the education sector. From machine learning models that enable adaptive learning platforms to data-driven insights that help educators make informed decisions, these technologies are reshaping how students learn and teachers teach. By understanding the role of AI and data science in education, institutions can leverage these innovations to improve student outcomes, optimize resources, and create more inclusive learning environments.

Overview of AI Algorithms and Data Science Techniques Relevant to Education

Below is a detailed explanation of each subtitle and how it contributes to the application of AI and data science in education (Wang et al., 2024).

1. Personalized Learning through Machine Learning Models

Machine learning (ML) enables personalized learning experiences by adapting educational content to a student's needs. Algorithms analyze a student's learning patterns, strengths, and weaknesses to recommend customized lessons, assignments, and study plans. Examples include intelligent tutoring systems and adaptive learning platforms like Khan Academy and Coursera (Ersozlu et al., 2024).

Personalized learning through machine learning models refers to the process of tailoring educational experiences to meet the individual needs of each student. Traditional learning methods often take a “one-size-fits-all” approach, which may not effectively address the diverse needs, strengths, and challenges of all learners. Machine learning, however, enables a dynamic, adaptive learning environment by continuously analyzing student data and adjusting the content and structure of lessons in real-time to maximize learning outcomes.

Key Concepts

1. **Data Collection and Analysis**: Machine learning algorithms rely on vast amounts of data to understand how a student learns. This data can include a variety of inputs, such as: Time spent on tasks, Accuracy of responses, Completion rates of assignments, Patterns in errors or difficulties, Student engagement levels.
2. **Identification of Learning Patterns**: ML models can identify patterns in how a student interacts with content. For example: Does the student struggle with specific types of questions or topics? What time of day are they most productive?

The system uses this information to generate a model that predicts what the student needs next whether it's more practice on a particular topic or an accelerated path through content they have mastered.

3. **Customization of Content**: Based on these insights, machine learning algorithms can recommend personalized lessons, exercises, and assignments that are tailored to the student's unique learning journey. For instance: Intelligent Tutoring Systems (ITS)AND Adaptive Learning Platforms
4. **Real-Time Adjustments**: Machine learning models continuously adapt as more data is collected. As students interact with the platform, the system refines its recommendations. This adaptability ensures that the learning experience remains relevant and engaging, minimizing frustration or boredom by providing just the right level of challenge.
5. **Personalized Recommendations**: Machine learning models also make personalized suggestions for supplementary resources that align with the student's learning style. For example, if a student learns better through visual aids, the system might recommend video tutorials or interactive simulations. If a student needs extra support with reading comprehension, the system could suggest specific reading material or exercises targeting this skill.
6. **Scalability and Accessibility**: Personalized learning powered by ML can cater to a large number of students simultaneously, making it scalable and accessible. It allows for efficient, individualized attention that would be difficult to provide in a traditional classroom setting with one teacher and many students.

Benefits

1. **Faster Learning**: Students can learn at their own pace, accelerating through topics they already understand while spending more time on areas where they need help.

2. **Increased Engagement**: Tailored content keeps students more engaged, as it feels relevant and appropriately challenging.
3. **Identifying Gaps**: Machine learning models can identify and address gaps in knowledge that might not be visible in a traditional classroom setting, where a teacher may not be able to provide immediate, individualized attention to every student.
4. **Continuous Improvement**: As the system collects more data, it becomes better at predicting the most effective learning paths, resulting in an increasingly effective educational experience.

Personalized learning powered by machine learning is revolutionizing education by offering individualized, adaptive, and scalable learning experiences. By using data-driven insights, machine learning systems can optimize the learning journey for each student, ultimately leading to more effective, engaging, and efficient educational experiences. As more educational platforms adopt machine learning, the potential to create a more inclusive and customized learning environment continues to grow.

2. NATURAL LANGUAGE PROCESSING IN EDUCATIONAL TOOLS

Natural Language Processing (NLP) in Educational Tools refers to the use of AI and machine learning technologies to enable computers to understand, interpret, and generate human language. In the context of education, NLP enhances various tools and platforms, making them more interactive, adaptive, and efficient. Through NLP, educational tools can provide real-time feedback, automate tasks, and support personalized learning experiences, significantly improving student engagement and outcomes (Crossley et al., 2011).

Key Applications of NLP in Education

1. **Chatbots and Virtual Tutors**: NLP enables the development of intelligent chatbots and virtual tutors that can engage in conversations with students, answering questions, providing explanations, and offering support. These AI-powered assistants simulate a human-like interaction, making learning more accessible and personalized.
2. **Instant Responses and Feedback**: One of the key advantages of NLP in educational tools is the ability to provide instant feedback to students. Traditional education systems often require teachers to manually grade assignments, quizzes, and written work, which can take time. However, NLP can automatically

analyze student responses and offer immediate feedback, allowing students to learn from their mistakes in real-time.

3. **Automated Grading Systems**: NLP allows for the automation of grading systems, especially for written assignments and essays. Traditional grading can be time-consuming and subjective, but NLP can analyze written content for grammar, spelling, sentence structure, and even meaning. Automated grading systems can then assign grades or offer detailed feedback on areas of improvement.
4. **Language Translation**: NLP is also crucial in breaking down language barriers, making education more accessible to students from different linguistic backgrounds. NLP-powered language translation tools can help translate textbooks, assignments, or even real-time conversations between students and teachers, facilitating a globalized learning environment.
5. **Speech-to-Text Functionality**: NLP also powers speech recognition, enabling students to interact with educational tools using voice commands. Speech-to-text functionality allows students with disabilities or those who prefer speaking over typing to engage more effectively with learning content. It can also assist in real-time transcription of lectures, making the material more accessible to students who may have hearing impairments or learning disabilities.
6. **Content Summarization and Recommendation**: NLP helps in summarizing complex content, making it easier for students to digest key points and main ideas. NLP-based tools can scan textbooks, research papers, or articles and provide concise summaries, highlighting essential information. Additionally, these tools can recommend supplementary content based on a student's learning preferences, helping them further explore subjects of interest.
7. **Enhanced Interaction with Educational Content**: NLP can improve how students interact with educational content, whether it's asking questions, searching for information, or navigating learning platforms. Instead of manually browsing through materials or waiting for a teacher's response, students can use NLP-based interfaces to interact more naturally with their study resources.
8. **Improved Student Support Services**: NLP can also enhance administrative and support functions within educational institutions. AI-powered chatbots and virtual assistants can assist students with administrative queries, from registration processes to course information and general inquiries.

Benefits of NLP in Education

1. **Personalization**: NLP allows educational tools to adapt to each student's learning style, offering tailored recommendations and support. This level of personalization ensures that students can learn at their own pace and according to their own strengths and weaknesses.

2. **Efficiency**: With NLP-powered automation, students and educators can save time. Tasks such as grading, content summarization, and real-time feedback are made faster and more accurate, freeing up time for more meaningful interactions.
3. **Increased Accessibility**: NLP helps make education more inclusive by providing language support, transcriptions, and speech recognition features. This improves accessibility for students with different abilities and learning needs.
4. **Engagement**: NLP facilitates interactive learning, where students can engage with AI-powered tools for instant feedback and assistance. This increases engagement and promotes active learning, leading to better retention and understanding.
5. **Scalability**: With NLP, personalized learning can be scaled to large numbers of students. Educational platforms can serve many students simultaneously, offering tailored feedback and support without requiring one-on-one teacher-student interaction.

NLP is revolutionizing education by creating smarter, more personalized learning experiences. Through AI-powered tools like chatbots, virtual tutors, language translation systems, and automated grading, NLP enables a more engaging, efficient, and inclusive educational environment. As technology continues to advance, the potential for NLP to improve education will only expand, fostering better learning outcomes for students worldwide.

3. PREDICTIVE ANALYTICS FOR STUDENT SUCCESS

Predictive analytics uses historical data to forecast student performance and identify at-risk students (Albreiki et al., 2021). By analyzing attendance records, assignment scores, and engagement levels, AI can help educators intervene early to provide targeted support, reducing dropout rates and improving academic outcomes.

Predictive Analytics for Student Success is an advanced approach that utilizes historical data to forecast future student performance, enabling educators and institutions to make informed decisions and provide timely interventions. By analyzing patterns from various data sources, such as attendance records, assignment scores, engagement levels, and other behavioral metrics, predictive analytics can identify students who may be at risk of underperforming or dropping out. This allows for early interventions that target specific needs, ultimately improving academic outcomes and reducing dropout rates.

Key Components of Predictive Analytics for Student Success

1. **Data Collection**: The first step in predictive analytics is the collection of relevant data. Various data points can be tracked and analyzed, including: Academic performance, Attendance records, Engagement levels, Behavioral and demographic data.
2. **Data Processing and Analysis**: Once the data is collected, machine learning algorithms are employed to process and analyze it. These algorithms can identify trends and patterns in student behavior and performance, highlighting factors that may correlate with success or failure.
3. **Risk Identification**: Predictive analytics can be used to create a risk profile for each student. The model analyzes historical data to predict which students are at risk of: Falling behind academically, Dropping out, Facing challenges outside of the classroom.
4. **Early Interventions**: Once at-risk students are identified, predictive analytics can guide educators in providing targeted interventions. These interventions are personalized based on the specific needs of the student, improving the chances of turning around a potential academic decline.
5. **Student Retention**: One of the key goals of predictive analytics is to improve student retention by identifying factors that contribute to students leaving the institution. By understanding the predictors of student dropout, educational institutions can take proactive measures to keep students engaged and enrolled.
6. **Improving Academic Outcomes**: By using predictive analytics, institutions can not only reduce dropout rates but also improve overall academic outcomes. With early warnings about which students are struggling, instructors can adjust their teaching methods, content delivery, and pacing to ensure that all students are getting the support they need.
7. **Continuous Monitoring and Feedback**: Predictive analytics doesn't just provide a snapshot of student performance at a single point in time. It enables continuous monitoring and feedback to track the progress of interventions and ongoing student success.

Benefits of Predictive Analytics for Student Success

1. **Proactive Support**: Predictive analytics allows educators to intervene before problems escalate, reducing the chances of failure and dropout.
2. **Personalized Learning**: By identifying individual student needs, predictive analytics enables personalized educational experiences tailored to each student's strengths, weaknesses, and learning patterns.

3. **Resource Allocation**: Institutions can more efficiently allocate resources to students who need them the most, whether through tutoring, counseling, or academic advising.
4. **Improved Retention Rates**: Early identification of at-risk students and timely intervention leads to higher student retention rates, ensuring more students graduate successfully.
5. **Data-Driven Decision Making**: Predictive analytics empowers educators and administrators to make informed, data-driven decisions regarding curriculum design, instructional strategies, and support services.

Predictive analytics is transforming the educational landscape by providing institutions with the tools to identify at-risk students and intervene early, ultimately improving academic success and retention rates. By analyzing historical data on student performance, behavior, and engagement, predictive models offer a proactive, data-driven approach to student success. When used effectively, predictive analytics empowers educators to deliver personalized learning experiences and ensure that students receive the support they need to thrive academically.

4. DATA-DRIVEN DECISION MAKING IN EDUCATIONAL ADMINISTRATION

Educational institutions use data science techniques to optimize decision-making in areas like curriculum planning, resource allocation, and student enrollment forecasting. By analyzing student performance trends and institutional data, schools and universities can make informed policy decisions (Fitria, 2021).

Data-Driven Decision Making in Educational Administration refers to the use of data science techniques and analytics to guide decisions in various administrative and operational areas within educational institutions. By leveraging large volumes of institutional data, schools and universities can make informed, evidence-based decisions that optimize their resources, improve educational outcomes, and align their strategies with student needs and performance trends. This approach ensures that decisions are not based on intuition or anecdotal evidence but on hard data, resulting in more effective and efficient management.

Key Areas Where Data-Driven Decision Making is Applied

1. Curriculum Planning and Design: Student Performance Analysis: Data from past assessments, exams, assignments, and course evaluations can be analyzed to identify which areas of the curriculum are most challenging for students and

which ones contribute to better performance. This helps institutions adjust the curriculum to address gaps in student knowledge and improve overall outcomes.

2. Resource Allocation: Optimizing Budgeting: By examining historical data on spending, student enrollment, and academic performance, administrators can make more informed decisions about how to allocate resources. For example, if data reveals a high demand for STEM courses, funding can be directed toward hiring more qualified faculty or investing in laboratory equipment.
3. Student Enrollment Forecasting: Predicting Enrollment Trends: Educational institutions use historical enrollment data, along with demographic and regional data, to forecast future student enrollment. These predictions can help schools adjust their capacity, prepare for changes in student demographics, and plan for future infrastructure needs.
4. Student Success and Support Services: Early Identification of At-Risk Students: Predictive analytics can help identify students who are at risk of failing or dropping out by analyzing attendance records, grades, engagement levels, and other behavioral data. This allows schools to intervene early and provide additional support through tutoring, mentoring, or counseling.
5. Policy Development and Implementation: Evaluating Institutional Policies: Data can be used to assess the effectiveness of various institutional policies, such as grading systems, attendance policies, or discipline protocols. For example, if data shows that students in certain programs perform significantly better under a flexible grading system, the institution might consider adopting similar approaches across other departments.
6. Institutional Improvement and Strategy: Continuous Improvement: Data-driven decision-making encourages a culture of continuous improvement. By regularly analyzing institutional performance, schools can identify areas where changes are needed and make adjustments to improve academic quality, student satisfaction, and operational efficiency.

Data-driven decision-making in educational administration allows institutions to optimize their operations, improve student outcomes, and allocate resources more effectively. By using data science techniques to analyze trends, forecast needs, and monitor performance, schools and universities can make informed, strategic decisions that benefit both students and staff. However, to be successful, institutions must ensure that the data is of high quality, that privacy concerns are addressed, and that data-driven decisions are aligned with the broader educational goals of the institution.

5. AUTOMATING ASSESSMENT AND FEEDBACK WITH AI

AI-powered grading systems, such as those using NLP and computer vision, automate assessments for objective and subjective exams. Tools like Gradescope and Turnitin use AI to evaluate written assignments, provide instant feedback, and detect plagiarism, saving educators time.

Automating Assessment and Feedback with AI is an innovative application of artificial intelligence in the educational sector that revolutionizes the traditional approach to grading and providing feedback. By leveraging advanced technologies like Natural Language Processing (NLP) and computer vision, AI-powered tools can significantly streamline the assessment process for both objective and subjective exams. This not only reduces the workload for educators but also enhances the efficiency, accuracy, and timeliness of assessments, ensuring students receive immediate, actionable feedback.

Key Features and Technologies Involved

1. **Natural Language Processing (NLP) in AI Grading**:
   - **Understanding and Evaluating Text**: NLP techniques enable AI to understand, process, and evaluate written responses, making it ideal for grading essays, reports, and other subjective assessments. NLP algorithms can analyze the structure, syntax, and semantic meaning of student responses to assess the quality of their writing.
   - **Automated Essay Grading**: Tools like Turnitin and Grammarly leverage NLP to evaluate essays and written assignments for factors like coherence, grammar, vocabulary, and the overall structure of arguments. AI can detect patterns in writing and assess whether students have met the rubric criteria for various aspects, including creativity, critical thinking, and clarity of expression.
2. **Computer Vision in AI Assessment**:
   - **Grading Handwritten Responses**: In addition to text-based assessments, AI can also be applied to assess handwritten assignments. Computer vision techniques allow AI systems to recognize and evaluate handwritten content, such as mathematical problems, diagrams, and short-answer responses. By analyzing the shapes of characters, numbers, and symbols, AI can determine whether the correct answer has been provided.
   - **Visual Inputs and Diagrams**: For subjects like physics, biology, or engineering, students might need to draw diagrams or solve problems on paper. AI systems using computer vision can evaluate these visual el-

ements, ensuring that the diagrams are accurate, well-labeled, and align with the given problem.

3. **Automated Objective Grading**:
   - **Multiple Choice, True/False, and Short Answer**: AI is highly effective for grading objective assessments such as multiple-choice questions (MCQs), true/false tests, and short-answer questions. In these cases, AI can instantly compare student responses with the correct answer key and assign a score based on accuracy, saving educators considerable time.
   - **Immediate Results**: Unlike traditional grading, which might take days, AI-powered grading systems provide instant results for objective questions. This allows students to quickly assess their performance and understand where they need to improve.
4. **Plagiarism Detection**:
   - **Identifying Plagiarism**: Tools like Turnitin utilize advanced NLP and text comparison algorithms to identify instances of plagiarism by comparing students' submissions with vast databases of academic papers, books, and online sources. The system can detect paraphrased or copied content and flag it for further review, ensuring academic integrity.
   - **Providing Similarity Reports**: These AI-powered systems generate similarity reports that show the percentage of content matched to other sources. Educators can review these reports to determine if plagiarism occurred and take appropriate actions.
5. **Instant and Personalized Feedback**:
   - **Real-Time Feedback**: AI grading systems provide students with immediate feedback on their assessments. This is especially useful for assignments that typically take a long time to grade, like essays or complex problem sets.
   - **Personalized Suggestions**: Beyond giving generic feedback, AI can offer personalized suggestions to each student based on their performance. For instance, if a student struggles with a particular grammatical rule, the system can provide tailored resources or exercises for improvement.
6. **Benefits of AI-Powered Assessment Systems**:
   - **Time Efficiency**: One of the most significant advantages of AI-based grading systems is the time saved by educators. With AI handling the bulk of grading and feedback, educators can focus on more qualitative tasks, such as interacting with students, developing new learning content, and providing individualized support.
   - **Consistency and Objectivity**: AI eliminates human biases in grading. It assesses each student's work based on pre-defined criteria, ensuring

that the grading process is consistent and objective. This is especially beneficial in large classes where manual grading might be prone to inconsistencies.

- **Scalability**: AI-powered tools can handle a large volume of assessments quickly, making them ideal for institutions with large student populations. Whether it's a class of 30 or 3,000 students, AI can assess assignments in the same amount of time, enabling educational institutions to scale their grading systems without needing to hire additional staff.
- **Data Analytics**: AI tools often come with built-in analytics, allowing educators to track and analyze students' performance trends. This data helps identify common areas of difficulty, assess the effectiveness of teaching methods, and adjust course content accordingly.

Automating assessment and feedback with AI holds the potential to transform the education sector by improving efficiency, consistency, and accessibility. AI-driven grading tools not only save educators time but also offer students faster, personalized feedback to help them improve their performance. While challenges such as accuracy and data privacy need to be addressed, the benefits of AI-powered assessment tools, from reducing bias to scaling grading efforts, are reshaping the way educational institutions approach evaluation and feedback.

6. ETHICAL CONSIDERATIONS IN AI-POWERED EDUCATION

Ethical Considerations in AI-Powered Education is an essential topic as artificial intelligence continues to permeate educational systems, influencing teaching, learning, and administration. While AI holds the potential to revolutionize education by personalizing learning experiences, automating assessments, and streamlining administrative tasks, it also introduces significant ethical challenges that must be addressed to ensure fairness, transparency, and privacy in the educational environment (Chen et al., 2020).

Key Ethical Issues in AI-Powered Education

1. **Data Privacy and Security**:
   - **Student Data Sensitivity**: AI systems in education rely on large volumes of student data, including personal information, academic performance, and even behavioral data. The collection, storage, and use of this data raise privacy concerns, especially when handling sensitive student

information. Unauthorized access to such data can lead to breaches of privacy and misuse.

- **Data Ownership**: Another ethical concern is the ownership of student data. Students, educators, and parents should have clear guidelines regarding who owns the data generated by AI systems, and how it can be used, shared, or retained. Students must have control over their data, with explicit consent obtained before their data is collected or analyzed.
- **Data Protection Measures**: To address these concerns, institutions must implement robust data protection measures. This includes encryption, anonymization, and access controls to safeguard sensitive data from unauthorized users. Regular audits and transparent data handling practices can also help in ensuring data security.

2. **Bias in AI Algorithms**:
    - **Algorithmic Bias**: AI systems are only as good as the data they are trained on. If the training data is biased, the AI algorithms may perpetuate or even amplify those biases. For example, if an AI tool is trained on data from predominantly one demographic group, it might favor students from that group and disadvantage others.
    - **Cultural and Socioeconomic Bias**: AI algorithms could also reflect societal biases, including those related to race, gender, socioeconomic status, or language proficiency. For instance, an AI-powered grading system may not fully understand or accurately assess essays written by students from diverse cultural backgrounds or with different linguistic expressions, leading to unfair assessments.
    - **Ensuring Fairness in AI Models**: To combat these biases, it is crucial to design AI algorithms with fairness in mind. Developers should ensure that AI models are trained on diverse datasets that include a variety of student backgrounds, experiences, and learning styles.
3. **The Digital Divide**:
    - **Access to Technology**: One of the most significant ethical concerns with AI in education is the **digital divide**. Not all students have equal access to the technology required for AI-driven educational tools, including high-speed internet, modern devices, and software. Students in rural or economically disadvantaged areas may be left behind if educational systems rely heavily on AI, exacerbating existing inequalities.
    - **Inequitable Access to AI Resources**: While AI offers the potential for personalized learning, students without reliable internet access or devices may not be able to fully benefit from these tools. This disparity can widen achievement gaps between students from different socioeco-

nomic backgrounds and hinder the overall inclusivity of AI-powered education.

4. **Transparency and Accountability**:
   - **Opaque Decision-Making**: Many AI systems operate as "black boxes," meaning their decision-making processes are not transparent. In education, this lack of transparency is concerning because it can lead to a lack of trust among educators, students, and parents.
   - **Explainability of AI Systems**: AI systems in education must be designed to be transparent and explainable. Stakeholders should be able to understand how AI arrived at a particular decision or recommendation
   - **Accountability for AI Errors**: In the event of errors or bias in AI decision-making, there must be clear accountability mechanisms. It is important for schools and universities to have protocols in place for addressing any issues that arise from AI-driven systems, whether they are related to grading, assessments, or personalized learning paths.
5. **Ethical Use of AI in Student Surveillance**:
   - **Student Monitoring**: Some AI-powered systems in education involve continuous monitoring of students, such as tracking their activity on online learning platforms, analyzing engagement levels, or using facial recognition to gauge emotional responses.
   - **Balancing Surveillance with Privacy**: Educational institutions must balance the need for data to improve learning outcomes with the right of students to maintain privacy. It is crucial that any monitoring systems are used transparently, with informed consent, and that students are aware of the extent of the data being collected.
6. **Ethical Implications of AI Replacing Educators**:
   - **Human Element in Education**: While AI can enhance educational tools and assist in tasks like grading, feedback, and content delivery, there is a concern that AI could replace human educators or undermine the teacher-student relationship.
   - **Maintaining the Role of Educators**: AI should complement, rather than replace, human educators. It is essential to preserve the human element of teaching by allowing teachers to focus on aspects of education that require empathy, creativity, and social interaction.

Ethical considerations in AI-powered education are critical for ensuring that AI technologies are implemented in ways that enhance learning experiences while safeguarding students' rights and privacy. By addressing issues such as data privacy, bias, the digital divide, and transparency, educational institutions can create an equitable and responsible AI-powered educational environment.

7. ENHANCING ACCESSIBILITY WITH AI TECHNOLOGIES

Enhancing Accessibility with AI Technologies represents one of the most transformative applications of artificial intelligence in education, offering significant improvements for students with disabilities. AI-powered tools and technologies help remove barriers to learning, enabling students with diverse needs to participate more fully in educational activities. By incorporating speech-to-text, text-to-speech, real-time language translation, and more, AI technologies create an inclusive learning environment where all students have the opportunity to succeed.

Key AI Technologies for Enhancing Accessibility

1. **Speech-to-Text and Text-to-Speech**:
   - o **Speech-to-Text**: This technology converts spoken language into written text, making it especially useful for students with hearing impairments or those who struggle with writing. For example, students who are unable to write due to physical disabilities can use speech-to-text tools to articulate their ideas verbally.
   - o **Text-to-Speech**: This is particularly helpful for students with visual impairments or learning disabilities such as dyslexia. Text-to-speech tools read aloud written content, allowing students to access textbooks, articles, and other written materials that they might otherwise find challenging.
   - o **Applications**: Software like Google Docs voice typing (speech-to-text) and Natural Reader (text-to-speech) are popular examples that enable students to interact with content in ways that suit their needs, enhancing their overall learning experience.
2. **Screen Readers**: Screen readers are AI-driven tools designed to help students with visual impairments by reading out the text displayed on a computer screen. These tools enable students to access websites, e-books, and even the text of online learning platforms. Screen readers provide not only textual content but also other important elements, such as images (via alt-text descriptions) and layout navigation, making the content accessible to visually impaired users.
3. **Real-Time Language Translation**: For students with limited proficiency in the language of instruction or those who are multilingual, AI-powered real-time language translation tools provide a bridge to understanding. AI translation tools can instantly translate written or spoken content into different languages, allowing students to engage more effectively with the curriculum. These technologies are particularly helpful for students who are English language learners (ELLs) or students from diverse linguistic backgrounds.

4. **Voice Assistants**: Voice assistants powered by AI, such as Siri, Alexa, and Google Assistant, are also powerful tools for enhancing accessibility in education. These voice-enabled tools allow students to interact with devices hands-free, making it easier for students with mobility impairments or those who have difficulty using traditional input devices like keyboards and mice. Voice assistants can perform various tasks, such as setting reminders, conducting web searches, and even reading text aloud.
5. **Captioning and Subtitling Software**: For students with hearing impairments, AI-driven captioning and subtitling software is a vital resource. These tools automatically generate captions or subtitles for audio and video content, making multimedia materials more accessible to students who are deaf or hard of hearing. In addition to improving accessibility, captions help all students by reinforcing learning through text-based cues.
6. **Personalized Learning Pathways**: AI can create personalized learning pathways for students with disabilities by analyzing their strengths, weaknesses, and learning styles. AI algorithms can recommend specific content, study resources, and pacing that suit the student's unique needs, allowing them to learn at their own pace and in the way that best supports their success.
7. **Assistive Technologies for Physical Disabilities**: AI-powered assistive technologies also support students with physical disabilities by providing alternative ways to interact with learning materials. This includes eye-tracking technology that allows students to control a computer or device using their eye movements, as well as brain-computer interfaces that enable students to communicate and interact with educational content using neural signals.
8. **AI-Enhanced Virtual Classrooms**: AI technologies also enable the development of virtual classrooms that are accessible to students with disabilities. For example, AI can automatically adjust the learning environment by offering personalized speech-to-text or text-to-speech options, subtitling, and even real-time sign language interpretation. This ensures that students who may not be able to attend physical classrooms due to mobility or health issues can still access high-quality education in a virtual space.

AI technologies have the potential to revolutionize accessibility in education, making learning more inclusive and equitable for students with disabilities. By providing tools like speech-to-text, text-to-speech, real-time language translation, screen readers, and personalized learning pathways, AI removes barriers and enables all students to engage with educational content in a way that best suits their individual needs. As AI continues to evolve, it will play an even more significant role in enhancing educational experiences and outcomes for students of all abilities.

8. IMPLEMENTING ADAPTIVE LEARNING SYSTEMS

Adaptive learning systems represent a groundbreaking approach in personalized education. These systems use artificial intelligence (AI) to adjust the delivery of content based on a learner's progress, strengths, and areas of improvement (Kaelbling et al., 1996). By dynamically tailoring lessons to the individual learner's needs, adaptive learning systems provide a more effective and efficient way to learn, ensuring that each student is appropriately challenged and supported.

Key Features of Adaptive Learning Systems

1. **Continuous Assessment**: Unlike traditional learning methods, adaptive learning systems continuously assess a learner's understanding through various means such as quizzes, interactive exercises, and even real-time monitoring of student interactions with the platform. These assessments help the system gauge the learner's current knowledge level and identify specific areas where they may need further support.
2. **Personalized Learning Paths**: One of the core advantages of adaptive learning systems is the ability to create personalized learning paths. Based on continuous assessments, these systems adjust the content, learning pace, and difficulty level to match the learner's evolving needs. For example, if a student is excelling in a particular topic, the system may introduce more advanced material.

Dynamic Content Delivery

Adaptive learning platforms do not follow a fixed curriculum or linear progression. Instead, they adjust the content in real-time, ensuring that it is always aligned with the learner's current abilities. The system determines the optimal sequence of lessons and resources to maximize learning, which may include video lessons, interactive tasks, simulations, or other multimedia elements.

3. **Feedback and Guidance**: Instant feedback is an essential feature of adaptive learning systems. As students interact with the platform, they receive immediate responses to their actions, whether correct or incorrect. This not only helps to reinforce correct answers but also provides valuable insights into mistakes, helping learners understand why their responses were incorrect and how to improve.
4. **Data-Driven Insights for Educators**: Adaptive learning systems collect data on student performance, which can be analyzed to provide insights into overall class performance, trends, and individual student progress. Educators can access

detailed reports on each student's learning journey, allowing them to adjust teaching strategies and provide targeted interventions where necessary.

9. AI IN CURRICULUM DEVELOPMENT AND CUSTOMIZATION

AI assists educators in designing curriculums tailored to students' needs by analyzing trends in learning data. It can recommend topic sequencing, suggest additional learning resources, and even generate customized study plans.

Key Functions of AI in Curriculum Development

1. **Data-Driven Insights for Curriculum Design**: AI systems can analyze vast amounts of data related to student performance, behavior, and engagement. By examining this data, AI can identify learning gaps, trends, and areas where students struggle the most. This allows educators to make informed decisions about curriculum design, ensuring that the content addresses the actual needs of students.
2. **Personalized Curriculum Customization**: AI can customize the curriculum to match the diverse learning styles, paces, and abilities of individual students. For example, for students who excel at a specific subject, the system might recommend advanced material or alternative ways of exploring the same topic. Conversely, for students who need more support, AI can suggest additional practice problems, resources, or foundational lessons to reinforce their learning.
3. **Recommendation of Additional Learning Resources**: AI can recommend supplementary materials that align with the curriculum, such as videos, reading materials, and interactive exercises. These resources help students understand concepts more deeply and allow them to explore topics of interest outside the standard curriculum.
4. **Optimized Topic Sequencing**: AI can analyze how students progress through lessons and optimize the sequence of topics based on their learning patterns. For instance, if a student struggles with algebra, AI might recommend revisiting pre-algebra topics or teaching algebra through visual methods before advancing to higher-level topics. This approach ensures a smooth learning curve for students, which helps prevent frustration and promotes mastery.
5. **Real-Time Curriculum Adjustments**: AI can make real-time adjustments to the curriculum based on ongoing student performance. For example, if a student consistently struggles with certain content, AI might adjust the difficulty level of tasks or even change the learning resources being used in real time. This

dynamic approach ensures that students are always working at a level that is neither too easy nor too difficult for them.

6. **Predictive Analytics for Curriculum Improvement**: Predictive analytics powered by AI can help forecast student performance and suggest improvements in curriculum design. By analyzing patterns in student behavior and academic outcomes, AI can predict which lessons or topics may need to be reworked or enhanced in future curriculum iterations.

10. DATA VISUALIZATION TECHNIQUES FOR EDUCATORS

Data visualization tools help educators interpret student performance metrics using dashboards, charts, and heatmaps. Platforms like Tableau and Google Data Studio allow institutions to identify learning gaps and make data-driven improvements (Alonso-Fernández et al., 2019).

Data Visualization Techniques for Educators

Data visualization is an essential tool for educators, allowing them to turn complex student performance data into actionable insights. By using visual aids like dashboards, charts, heatmaps, and graphs, educators can quickly identify trends, gaps, and areas for improvement in student learning. This data-driven approach empowers teachers, administrators, and educational institutions to make informed decisions that enhance teaching methods, optimize resources, and improve student outcomes.

Key Components of Data Visualization for Educators

1. **Dashboards**: Dashboards provide a comprehensive view of student performance, typically displaying a mix of different types of data (e.g., grades, attendance, participation) on a single screen. They allow educators to monitor the overall health of a class, track progress over time, and identify students who may need additional support.
2. **Charts and Graphs**: Charts and graphs (e.g., bar charts, line graphs, pie charts) are commonly used to illustrate trends and patterns in student performance over time. These visual tools can make complex data easier to digest and help educators compare performance across different student groups, subjects, or time periods.
3. **Heatmaps**: Heatmaps use color coding to highlight areas of interest or concern. In an educational context, heatmaps can show performance across various assignments or subjects, where high-performing areas are colored green and

low-performing areas are colored red. This method allows educators to quickly spot learning gaps and address them before they become larger problems.

4. **Performance Benchmarks**: Data visualizations can also be used to compare individual or group performance to set benchmarks or standards. These visualizations help identify students who are performing below expectations and help guide instructional adjustments.
5. **Time Series Analysis**: Time series visualizations allow educators to track student progress over specific periods (e.g., weeks, months, or semesters). By monitoring performance trends over time, educators can assess the long-term effectiveness of their teaching methods and adjust their approach if necessary.
6. **Interactive Visualizations**: Interactive data visualizations enable educators to drill down into specific aspects of the data. They allow users to explore different variables or filter the data according to specific needs, such as focusing on particular groups of students or academic subjects.

11. LEVERAGING BIG DATA IN EDUCATIONAL RESEARCH

Big data in education refers to the collection, analysis, and interpretation of large and diverse datasets that include a wide range of student-related information, such as performance records, learning behaviors, demographic details, engagement levels, and even social and emotional data (Baker & Siemens, 2014; Buckingham Shum & Ferguson, 2012). The integration of big data in educational research is transforming how schools, universities, and educational institutions approach teaching, learning, and administration. By harnessing vast quantities of data, educators and researchers can uncover valuable insights that can drive improvements in teaching strategies, enhance student outcomes, and shape educational policies for the future.

Key Aspects of Leveraging Big Data in Educational Research

1. **Understanding Learning Behaviors**: Big data allows researchers to track and analyze students' learning behaviors over time. By monitoring actions such as time spent on tasks, click patterns, participation in discussions, and response times in assessments, educators can identify patterns that may indicate effective or ineffective learning strategies.
2. **Improving Teaching Strategies**: With big data, educational researchers can pinpoint which teaching methods are most effective for different student groups. By comparing data on student performance across various teaching styles, content delivery methods, and learning tools, educators can fine-tune their approaches for maximum effectiveness.

3. **Personalized Learning**: One of the key advantages of big data in education is its potential to support personalized learning. By continuously collecting data on student progress, learning preferences, and strengths and weaknesses, big data enables the creation of personalized learning paths that cater to each student's individual needs.
4. **Predictive Analytics for Student Success**: Predictive analytics, powered by big data, uses historical data to forecast future student performance. By analyzing trends in student attendance, assignment grades, and engagement levels, researchers and educators can predict which students are at risk of falling behind or dropping out, allowing for timely interventions and support.
5. **Monitoring Learning Outcomes and Institutional Performance**: Big data allows researchers to monitor and evaluate learning outcomes on a broader scale. By aggregating data from multiple students across different institutions or regions, researchers can assess the effectiveness of educational programs and policies, providing actionable insights for administrators and policymakers.
6. **Enhancing Educational Equity**: Big data can also be used to identify disparities in educational opportunities and outcomes based on factors such as socioeconomic background, gender, or geographic location. By analyzing trends across different demographics, researchers can uncover systemic inequalities and propose data-driven solutions to ensure all students have access to the same quality of education.
7. **Informed Policy Making**: Educational research powered by big data enables the development of evidence-based policies that can positively impact teaching and learning. Policymakers can use insights from big data to make decisions about curriculum development, teacher training, student support programs, and resource distribution, ensuring that these policies are aligned with actual student needs and learning outcomes.

Big data is revolutionizing the field of educational research, providing deeper insights into learning behaviors, student engagement, teaching strategies, and educational outcomes. By leveraging big data, educators and researchers can improve instructional design, personalize learning experiences, predict student success, and develop evidence-based policies that address the needs of all learners. While there are challenges related to privacy, data quality, and bias, the potential benefits of using big data in education are immense. With thoughtful implementation and ethical considerations, big data can help create a more effective, equitable, and efficient education system.

12. CHALLENGES AND OPPORTUNITIES OF AI IN EDUCATION

AI has the potential to revolutionize education by enhancing teaching methods, personalizing learning, and improving administrative efficiency. However, its widespread adoption in educational institutions faces several challenges that need to be addressed in order to fully unlock its transformative potential (Issah et al., 2023). These challenges, along with the opportunities AI presents, can shape the future of education in profound ways.

Challenges of AI in Education

1. **Lack of Technical Infrastructure**: Many educational institutions, especially those in underfunded or remote areas, lack the necessary technical infrastructure to support AI-based systems. These institutions may not have high-speed internet, up-to-date devices, or the computational power required for AI tools and applications.
2. **Resistance to Change**: Many educators, administrators, and policymakers may be hesitant to adopt AI in education due to concerns about job displacement, loss of traditional teaching methods, or simply unfamiliarity with the technology. This resistance to change can be a significant barrier to the successful integration of AI in classrooms and educational systems.
3. **Data Privacy and Security Concerns**: AI systems in education often rely on vast amounts of data, including personal information about students' learning behaviors, performance, and interactions with educational content. This raises significant concerns about data privacy and the security of sensitive student information.
4. **Bias in AI Algorithms**: AI systems are only as good as the data they are trained on. If the data used to train AI models is biased or incomplete, the resulting algorithms can perpetuate inequalities and reinforce existing stereotypes. For example, an AI tool used to assess student performance might disproportionately favor students from specific demographic groups, leading to unfair outcomes.
5. **High Costs of Implementation**: Developing and implementing AI tools and technologies can be expensive, especially for institutions that do not have the budget to invest in advanced technologies. The costs associated with purchasing AI software, training educators, and maintaining infrastructure can be a major hurdle for many educational institutions, particularly in lower-income areas.
6. **Teacher-Student Relationship**: AI tools, such as virtual tutors and chatbots, can provide personalized learning experiences, but they cannot replace the human connection between teachers and students. The role of teachers as mentors,

guides, and emotional supporters is crucial in the learning process, and over-reliance on AI could potentially diminish the importance of these relationships.

Opportunities of AI in Education

1. **Personalized Learning**: One of the most significant opportunities presented by AI is the ability to personalize learning. AI systems can adapt lessons, assignments, and resources to meet the specific needs of individual students, helping them learn at their own pace and in a way that suits their learning style.
2. **Improved Efficiency and Automation**: AI can automate administrative tasks, such as grading, scheduling, and record-keeping, which can save educators time and allow them to focus on teaching. For instance, AI-powered grading systems can instantly assess student responses and provide feedback, reducing the workload of teachers.
3. **Increased Access to Education**: AI can help make education more accessible, particularly for students in remote or underserved areas. Through AI-powered platforms, students can access high-quality educational resources, including tutoring, course materials, and assessments, regardless of their location.
4. **Enhanced Learning Analytics**: AI can gather and analyze vast amounts of data on student behavior, performance, and engagement. This data can be used to identify patterns, predict student outcomes, and offer insights into how to improve teaching methods and curricula.

While AI offers tremendous opportunities for transforming education, addressing the challenges associated with its implementation is essential for realizing its full potential. Overcoming barriers such as lack of infrastructure, resistance to change, data privacy concerns, and biases in algorithms will require collaboration among educators, policymakers, technology developers, and other stakeholders. By proactively addressing these challenges, we can ensure that AI is used ethically and equitably, leading to a more personalized, efficient, and accessible education system for all students.

13. BUILDING INTELLIGENT TUTORING SYSTEMS

Intelligent Tutoring Systems (ITS) are AI-powered platforms designed to provide personalized, real-time educational support to students, mimicking the interaction a student might have with a human tutor. These systems use machine learning, natural language processing, and other AI techniques to analyze student behavior, detect learning gaps, and adjust content and teaching strategies accordingly (Alpaydin,

2010; Bishop, 2016). The ultimate goal of ITS is to offer an individualized learning experience, which adapts to the unique needs of each learner, ensuring efficient and effective knowledge acquisition.

How Intelligent Tutoring Systems Work

1. **Personalized Learning Pathways**: ITSs create personalized learning pathways by continuously analyzing a student's interactions, performance, and behavior. For example, if a student struggles with a particular concept, the system identifies this gap and adapts the next set of lessons to provide additional practice and support in that area. This approach allows students to progress at their own pace, ensuring they master each topic before moving on to the next.
2. **Real-Time Feedback**: One of the key features of ITS is the ability to provide immediate feedback to students. Traditional educational settings often lack the ability to give instant corrections or guidance, but ITS offers timely responses to students' mistakes. This helps learners correct misconceptions as soon as they occur, reinforcing learning and preventing gaps from widening.
3. **Adaptive Questioning**: ITS platforms employ algorithms to adjust the difficulty of questions or assignments based on the student's performance. If a student answers several questions correctly, the system will increase the difficulty of subsequent tasks to challenge the learner. On the other hand, if a student is struggling, the system will offer easier questions or alternative explanations to ensure understanding before moving forward.
4. **Natural Language Processing (NLP) and Speech Recognition**: Many ITSs incorporate Natural Language Processing (NLP) to understand and interact with students in more complex ways. Through NLP, the system can process written or spoken input from students, helping with tasks like language learning, essay feedback, and problem-solving. For instance, systems like Carnegie Learning and Squirrel AI use NLP to interpret open-ended student responses and provide tailored feedback, just as a human tutor would.
5. **Cognitive Modeling**: An essential aspect of ITS is the cognitive model it builds of each student. By analyzing data from student responses, ITS can infer the student's understanding and knowledge state. These models guide the system's decisions about what content to present, what level of difficulty is appropriate, and when to provide assistance or hints. This enables the ITS to make real-time adjustments based on the learner's cognitive progress.

Intelligent Tutoring Systems represent the future of personalized education, offering real-time, individualized support to students in a way that mimics human tutoring. By leveraging AI to continuously adapt to a student's needs, ITS can improve learning outcomes, increase engagement, and provide teachers with valuable insights into student progress. However, to fully realize the potential of ITS, challenges such as development costs, data privacy, and adoption resistance must be addressed. As the technology continues to evolve, ITS will play an increasingly important role in reshaping the educational landscape.

14. AI-ENHANCED COLLABORATIVE LEARNING ENVIRONMENTS

AI is transforming the way students collaborate in educational settings by facilitating group interactions, supporting peer learning, and enhancing the overall learning experience in both online and hybrid classrooms. Collaborative learning, where students work together to solve problems, share ideas, and learn from one another, can be significantly enhanced by AI technologies (Goodfellow et al., 2016). By leveraging AI, educational platforms can provide personalized support, enhance communication, and enable more effective group learning experiences, both in physical classrooms and virtual environments.

How AI Enhances Collaborative Learning

1. **Facilitating Group Formation**: One of the key aspects of collaborative learning is group formation. AI can analyze a student's strengths, weaknesses, learning styles, and preferences to suggest optimal groupings. This helps ensure that groups are balanced, with complementary skills that foster more productive teamwork
2. **Real-Time Feedback and Guidance**: AI tools embedded within collaborative platforms can offer real-time feedback during group discussions or activities. These AI systems monitor students' interactions and provide immediate guidance when necessary. For example, an AI assistant might suggest additional resources or ask probing questions to stimulate deeper thinking during group discussions.
3. **Intelligent Content Sharing**: AI can facilitate the seamless sharing of educational content within a collaborative environment. Platforms like Microsoft Teams or Google Classroom use AI to recommend relevant resources, such as articles, videos, or textbooks, based on the group's ongoing discussions or the task at hand.
4. **Monitoring and Analyzing Group Dynamics**: AI can monitor how students interact during group projects and analyze the dynamics of collaboration. By tracking interactions such as the frequency of contributions, the quality of com-

munication, and how well students are working together, AI can provide insights into group performance. If a group is struggling with unequal participation or a lack of engagement, AI can offer recommendations to improve collaboration.

5. **Peer Learning and Peer Assessment**: AI plays a key role in facilitating peer learning and peer assessment. For example, AI systems can match students with similar or complementary learning goals, fostering more effective peer-to-peer interactions. Additionally, AI can automate the peer review process by assessing the quality of student contributions to a group project.
6. **Enhancing Communication and Collaboration Tools**: AI enhances communication tools within collaborative platforms, making online discussions more dynamic and interactive. For example, AI can offer automatic translation and transcription services, allowing students from different linguistic backgrounds to participate in group discussions without language barriers.
7. **Adaptive Group Learning Environments**: AI-driven collaborative platforms can adapt to the needs of the students, dynamically altering the learning environment based on real-time data. For instance, if students are struggling with a specific topic or are not engaging with the content, the platform can adjust the group activities, suggest additional resources, or even switch to a different mode of collaboration (e.g., changing from a group discussion to a hands-on activity).

AI-enhanced collaborative learning environments represent a significant advancement in education, offering students personalized support, fostering better group dynamics, and enhancing overall learning outcomes. Through tools like Microsoft Teams, Google Classroom, and Slack, AI empowers students to collaborate effectively, receive real-time feedback, and engage in more productive learning experiences. As these AI tools evolve, they will continue to reshape the way students collaborate, ensuring that educational experiences are more interactive, inclusive, and impactful. However, it is essential to address challenges such as data privacy and over-reliance on technology to ensure that AI-enhanced collaboration benefits all learners.

15. MEASURING THE IMPACT OF AI ON LEARNING OUTCOMES

As AI becomes more deeply integrated into educational environments, measuring its impact on learning outcomes is crucial to understand its effectiveness (Gašević et al., 2016) and refine its applications. The ability to assess how AI tools enhance student performance, engagement, and teacher efficiency helps educators, administrators, and developers optimize AI-driven solutions to ensure they deliver tangible benefits in the classroom. By evaluating these factors, institutions can ensure that AI is being used to its full potential, leading to improved learning experiences for students and more efficient teaching practices.

Key Aspects of Measuring AI's Impact on Learning Outcomes

- o **Student Performance Improvements**: The primary goal of AI in education is to enhance student learning outcomes. To measure this, institutions track improvements in academic performance after the implementation of AI-based tools. This can include: Grade Performance, Test Scores, Long-Term Retention.
- o **Engagement Metrics**: AI-powered educational tools often include features that track student engagement in real time. Engagement is a crucial indicator of learning outcomes, as students who are actively involved in the learning process are more likely to perform well. Metrics for engagement include: Time Spent on Platform, Interaction Frequency, Completion Rates.

2. **Teacher Efficiency**: AI tools can significantly improve teacher efficiency by automating routine tasks such as grading, attendance tracking, and administrative work. To measure the impact of AI on teacher efficiency, the following factors can be evaluated: Time Savings, Quality of Instruction, Teacher Satisfaction.
3. **Learning Analytics and Feedback Loops**: Learning analytics play a pivotal role in measuring AI's impact on learning outcomes. Learning analytics refers to the process of collecting, analyzing, and interpreting data related to student interactions with educational content and their performance over time. AI systems often generate large amounts of data on student behavior, which can be used to assess learning progress and identify trends.
4. **Continuous Improvement of AI Implementations**: Evaluating AI's effectiveness in the classroom requires constant refinement of the AI systems themselves. Feedback loops between students, teachers, and administrators help fine-tune AI implementations to better meet educational goals.

While measuring the impact of AI on learning outcomes provides valuable insights, there are challenges to consider: Data Privacy Concerns, Long-Term Impact, Bias in AI Models, Variability in Implementation.

AI and data science are revolutionizing education by making learning more personalized, efficient, and data-driven. However, careful implementation is necessary to address challenges and ensure ethical use. By leveraging AI algorithms and data science techniques, the education sector can enhance learning experiences, improve student outcomes, and optimize institutional management.

16. CONCLUSION

The integration of AI algorithms and data science techniques into education represents a transformative shift in how we teach, learn, and manage educational systems. From natural language processing powering intelligent educational tools to predictive analytics identifying at-risk students, AI is reshaping every facet of the learning experience (Du et al., 2020). Data-driven decision making enables administrators to optimize resources and strategies, while automated assessment tools provide real-time, personalized feedback that enhances both teaching efficiency and student engagement.

Ethical considerations remain central, ensuring that technological advancements promote equity, privacy, and fairness. At the same time, AI is unlocking new possibilities for accessibility, enabling inclusive learning environments for diverse student populations. Adaptive learning systems and curriculum customization provide tailored educational experiences, addressing the unique needs and abilities of each learner.

Through powerful data visualization and the analysis of big data, educators and researchers gain deeper insights into learning behaviors and institutional effectiveness. Intelligent tutoring systems and collaborative AI-enhanced environments foster more dynamic and responsive learning, while ongoing measurement of learning outcomes ensures that these technologies deliver meaningful educational value.

Despite challenges—such as data privacy concerns, algorithmic bias, and the digital divide—the opportunities offered by AI in education are immense. Realizing its full potential will require thoughtful implementation, interdisciplinary collaboration, and a commitment to continuous improvement. Ultimately, by leveraging the power of AI responsibly and strategically, we can create more adaptive, equitable, and effective educational systems for the learners of today and tomorrow.

REFERENCES

Albreiki, B., Zaki, N., & Alashwal, H. (2021). A systematic literature review of student' performance prediction using machine learning techniques. *Education Sciences, 11*(9), 552. DOI: 10.3390/educsci11090552

Ali, O., Murray, P. A., Momin, M., Dwivedi, Y. K., & Malik, T. (2024). The effects of artificial intelligence applications in educational settings: Challenges and strategies. *Technological Forecasting and Social Change, 199*, 123076. Advance online publication. DOI: 10.1016/j.techfore.2023.123076

Alonso-Fernández, C., Calvo-Morata, A., Freire, M., Martínez-Ortiz, I., & Fernández-Manjón, B. (2019). Applications of data science to game learning analytics data: A systematic literature review. *Computers & Education, 141*, 103612. DOI: 10.1016/j.compedu.2019.103612

Alpaydin, E. (2010). *Introduction to machine learning*. The MIT.

Awad, M., & Khanna, R. (2015). *Efficient learning machines theories, concepts, and applications for engineers and system designers*. A.

Bachhal, P., Ahuja, S., & Gargrish, S. (2021). Educational data mining: A review. *Journal of Physics: Conference Series, 1950*(1), 012022. DOI: 10.1088/1742-6596/1950/1/012022

Baker, R., & Siemens, G. (2014). Educational data mining and learning analytics. .DOI: 10.1017/CBO9781139519526.016

Bishop, C. M. (2016). *Pattern recognition and machine learning*. Springer.

Buckingham Shum, S., & Ferguson, R. (2012). Social Learning Analytics. *Journal of Educational Technology & Society, 15*(3), 3 26. https://www.jstor.org/stablc/jeductechsoci.15.3.3

Chen, X., Xie, H., Zou, D., & Hwang, G. J. (2020). Application and theory gaps during the rise of artificial intelligence in education. *Computers and Education: Artificial Intelligence, 1*, 100002. DOI: 10.1016/j.caeai.2020.100002

Crossley, S. A., Allen, D., & McNamara, D. S. (2011). Text simplification and comprehensible input: A case for an intuitive approach. *Language Teaching Research, 16*(1), 89–108. DOI: 10.1177/1362168811423456

Du, X., Yang, J., Hung, J. L., & Shelton, B. (2020). Educational data mining: A systematic review of research and emerging trends. *Information Discovery and Delivery, 48*(4), 225–236. DOI: 10.1108/IDD-09-2019-0070

Ersozlu, Z., Taheri, S., & Koch, I. (2024). A review of machine learning methods used for educational data. *Education and Information Technologies, 29*(16), 22125–22145. DOI: 10.1007/s10639-024-12704-0

Fitria, T. N. (2021). Artificial Intelligence (AI) in Education: Using AI Tools for Teaching and Learning Process. *Proceedings of the National Seminar on Business, Economics, Social Sciences, and Technology, 1*(1), 1–10. https://prosiding.stie-aas.ac.id/index.php/prosenas/article/view/106

Gašević, D., Dawson, S., Rogers, T., & Gasevic, D. (2016). Learning analytics should not promote one size fits all: The effects of instructional conditions in predicting academic success. *The Internet and Higher Education, 28*, 68–84. DOI: 10.1016/j.iheduc.2015.10.002

Goodfellow, I., Bengio, Y., & Courville, A. (2016). *Deep learning* (1st ed.). MIT Press.

Hashim, A., Akeel, W., & Khalaf, A. (2020). Student performance prediction model based on supervised machine learning algorithms. *IOP Conference Series. Materials Science and Engineering, 928*(3), 032019. DOI: 10.1088/1757-899X/928/3/032019

Hastie, T., Tibshirani, R., & Friedman, J. (2009). *Elements of statistical learning: Data mining, inference, and prediction* (2nd ed., Vol. 2). Springer. DOI: 10.1007/978-0-387-84858-7

Hilbert, S., Coors, S., Kraus, E. B., Bischl, B., Frei, M., Lindl, A., Wild, J., Krauss, S., Goretzko, D., & Stachl, C. (2021). *Machine Learning for the Educational Sciences*. . io/3hnr6.DOI: 10.31234/osf.io/3hnr6_v1

Hsu, C., & Yeh, C. (2020). Mining the student dropout in higher education. *ASTM International Journal of Testing and Evaluation, 48*(6), 4563–4575. DOI: 10.1520/JTE20180021

Issah, I., Appiah, O., Appiahene, P., & Inusah, F. (2023). A systematic review of the literature on machine learning application of determining the attributes influencing academic performance. *Decision Analytics Journal, 7*, 100204. DOI: 10.1016/j.dajour.2023.100204

Japkowicz, N., & Shah, M. (2011). *Evaluating learning algorithms: A classification perspective*. Evaluating Learning Algorithms. A Classification Perspective. DOI: 10.1017/CBO9780511921803

Kaelbling, L. P., Littman, M. L., & Moore, A. W. (1996). Reinforcement learning: A survey. *Journal of Artificial Intelligence Research, 4*, 237–285. DOI: 10.1613/jair.301

Khalaf, A., Dahr, J. M., Najm, I. A., Kamel, M. B. M., Hashim, A. S., Akeel, W. A., & Humadi, M. A. (2021). Supervised learning algorithms in educational data mining: A systematic review. *Southeast Europe Journal of Soft Computing*, *10*, 55–70. DOI: 10.21533/scjournal.v10i1.199

Khan, A., & Ghosh, S. K. (2021). Student performance analysis and prediction in classroom learning: A review of educational data mining studies. *Education and Information Technologies*, *26*(1), 205–240. DOI: 10.1007/s10639-020-10230-3

Koch, I. (2013). *Analysis of multivariate and high-dimensional data*. Cambridge University Press. DOI: 10.1017/CBO9781139025805

Wang, S., Wang, F., Zhu, Z., Wang, J., Tran, T., & Du, Z. (2024). Artificial intelligence in education: A systematic literature review. *Expert Systems with Applications*, *252*, 124167. DOI: 10.1016/j.eswa.2024.124167

Chapter 4
The Role of Artificial Intelligence (AI) in Personalized Learning and Adaptive Assessments

Fahad A. Salendab
https://orcid.org/0000-0003-4459-443X
Sultan Kudarat State University, Philippines

Donald A. Cogo
https://orcid.org/0009-0008-5418-071X
Sultan Kudarat State University, Philippines

Arnold Z. Catipay
Sultan Kudarat State University, Philippines

Grace Joy T. Millendez
https://orcid.org/0009-0003-9090-8855
Sultan Kudarat State University, Philippines

ABSTRACT

This chapter explores how Artificial Intelligence (AI) transforms education through personalized learning and adaptive assessments. It highlights how AI shifts instruction from teacher-centered to student-centered models by customizing learning paths, pacing, and content based on individual learner profiles. Grounded in theories such as Constructivism, Universal Design for Learning, and Self-Determination Theory,

DOI: 10.4018/979-8-3373-2185-1.ch004

AI applications, like intelligent tutoring systems, predictive analytics, and adaptive assessment, support differentiated instruction, increase engagement, and improve outcomes. The chapter also addresses challenges, including algorithmic bias, data privacy, ethical concerns, and the need for faculty development and equitable access. Case studies from various global contexts demonstrate AI's benefits and limitations, particularly in under-resourced schools. Finally, the chapter recommends responsible implementation strategies that ensure inclusive, effective, and ethical AI integration into educational environments.

INTRODUCTION

Artificial Intelligence (AI) 's role in education significantly impacts teachers' instructional practices and students' learning, making the teaching-learning process dynamic and motivating (Lin, 2022). Education is becoming more modern compared to traditional learning environments, becoming more responsive to students' needs, skills, and preferences through AI customization of learning experiences. With this significant shift, the traditional approaches to teaching, manifested by the teacher-centered approach, where students are passive learners, are becoming more dynamic and focus on the use of a student-centered learning framework (Hardaker & Glenn, 2025). With the use of sophisticated AI systems, researchers, educators, and policymakers are now interested in the actual applications of AI in educational settings. Such AI ranges from predictive analytics and adaptive assessment to intelligent tutoring systems (Liu et al., 2025; Sajja et al., 2024)

The advent of AI in education offers more than just implementing new technologies. It transforms the teachers' activities to make learning more conducive and caters to the different students' needs and preferences to improve academic performance (Zhang & Zhang, 2024). While adaptive assessments provide real-time feedback and baseline information on the students' performance, AI-driven personalization allows students to learn based on their unique learning preferences and understanding levels (Chen et al., 2025). To ensure that every student is provided with the instructional support that they need to succeed in their academic journey, these innovations aim to provide access to and fair use of technologies, improve student engagement, and encourage a deeper understanding of the subject content (Yaseen et al., 2025).

The essential role of AI in supporting adaptive assessments and personalized learning to support the instructional needs of both teachers and students is discussed in this chapter since this chapter looks at the theoretical underpinnings of these innovations and concepts, discusses the importance of these technologies and applications, outlines the advantages and challenges of these AI-powered systems, and examines different case studies that reflect how effective they are in the once used in the classroom settings. With AI's challenges and opportunities in educational settings, particularly classroom setups, academic institutions can better navigate these challenges to make them institutional opportunities by understanding the interplay between AI, personalized learning, and adaptive assessment.

BACKGROUND

Artificial Intelligence (AI) significantly influences several industries, especially educational institutions. Schools use AI worldwide in everyday situations like machine learning, natural language processing, and data analytics. Since AI is used in schools, it changes how subject contents are taught, assessed, and experienced by teachers and students at all educational levels. It is no longer a thing of futuristic visions (Xia et al., 2024)

Various issues and challenges encountered by teachers and students in the teaching-learning process became the driving factor behind the integration of AI in education since AI offers more dynamic and student-centered activities (Celik et al., 2022; Lin & Chen, 2024). Conventional educational institutions, characterized by the use of standardized assessment methods and a teacher-centered approach, might not adequately address the needs of the learners. The diverse learning styles and students' prior knowledge may necessitate educational institutions, especially teachers, to utilize flexible and adaptive methods of teaching, which only AI can provide (Lin et al., 2024). With the use of AI technologies, teachers can provide personalized instruction, where the teaching-learning process is transformed into a meaningful and motivating learning environment, helping the students succeed and improve their academic performance (Dong et al., 2025; Merino-Campos, 2025)

Studies show that AI tools like adaptive assessments, intelligent tutoring systems, and personalized learning platforms are increasingly used in academic institutions since they offer many opportunities. For example, in the USA, about 18 percent of teachers regularly use AI tools as of 2023, with middle and high school teachers using these tools at higher rates. Although they found that these AI tools can produce algorithmic bias, data privacy, and ethical challenges, it shows that parents and students have given much consideration to the usefulness of these AI-powered tools in educational institutions (Karran et al., 2024; Bulut et al., 2024)

The rapid growth of AI tools is undeniably evident. Along this way, it also presents challenges if educational institutions do not manage it carefully. Such challenges include ethical considerations, teacher professional development, and fair access to technology. The role of AI is crucial as it has the potential to build a more effective, inclusive, and future-ready educational system; however, one must properly implement it (Kamali et al., 2024; Dimitriadou & Lanitis, 2023; Chan, 2023)

THE RISE OF AI IN EDUCATION

The delivery of instruction at all levels has undergone significant shifts since the emergence of artificial intelligence in education. The emergence of artificial intelligence in education allows teachers to access various educational resources that can tailor lessons. With AI, teachers can also adjust their teaching strategies to meet the diverse needs of the students and improve student participation in the classroom. Moreover, various industries, especially education, have been affected by the rapid development brought about by artificial intelligence due to its features and potential uses in education. It attracted researchers, educators, and legislators as they grew sophisticated.

Furthermore, AI provides potential opportunities among students as it can revolutionize their learning experiences in classroom setups. Zawaki-Richter et al. (2019) reported that AI-powered tools and platforms could provide customized learning experiences, allowing teachers to meet the students' diverse needs, preferences, and abilities. For example, intelligent tutoring platforms, which have existed longer than the new Large Language Models (LLMs), can offer targeted assistance and real-time feedback to students who need immediate learning interventions. The intelligent tutoring system can adjust to the student's understanding level, resulting in a more efficient and engaging learning environment (Kulik & Fletcher, 2016).

The Walton Family Foundation (2024) conducted a very recent study. Their study examined parents, teachers, and students' awareness and perspectives as to the role of AI in the educational system. It was found that these stakeholders (teachers, parents, and students) are all becoming more aware of AI, and the three groups use it at a rate of about 50%. Their insights across these categories are positive, although a few have unfavorable perspectives. These respondents believe that AI plays a crucial role in decision-making and is believed to be useful in educational contexts. Teachers and students strongly believe that AI platforms can adapt and respond to learning environments as they continually advance. Future generations could benefit from the potential uses of AI as it will advance and revolutionize the learning environment (Maity & Deroy, 2024; Sajja et al., 2024; Chan & Hu, 2023)

As of fall 2023, it was reported that 18 percent of K–12 instructors incorporate AI as part of their instructional practices, and another 15 percent had at least one AI experiment (Rand, 2024). Similarly, teachers in middle and high schools deliver their instruction using AI, especially those who teach social studies and English language arts. They utilize AI-driven tools like chatbots, virtual learning platforms, and adaptive learning systems to deliver their lessons, resulting in a more meaningful and engaging learning environment. Accordingly, developing instructional materials is easy as AI helps them generate and tailor instructional content based on the students' preferences.

The emergence of AI signals the need to conduct future research on directions and innovations, ethical considerations, and collaborative efforts so that it can fully understand its potential uses in educational contexts, especially in societal advancements (Fu & Weng, 2024; Khan et al., 2025). Nowadays, artificial intelligence has become a part of our daily lives, driven by innovation and shaped by challenges. It offers a future where intelligent machines can help us do more and improve in many areas.

Table 1. Key Areas, Benefits, and Applications of AI in Education

Area of Impact	Description	Benefits	Examples
Machine Learning (ML)	Enables AI systems to learn from educational data and improve over time (Ersozlu et al., 2024)	Drives personalization, prediction, and automation in education (Kanchon et al., 2024)	Algorithms that forecast student performance or dropout risk.
Personalized Learning	Tailors educational content to individual student needs and pace (Vorobyeva et al., 2025)	Increases engagement and improves academic outcomes (Kayyali, 2025)	Khan Academy, Coursera, Edmodo, and adaptive pathways.
Intelligent Tutoring Systems	Provides one-on-one virtual instruction and real-time feedback (Fodouop Kouam, 2024)	Enhances comprehension and supports self-paced learning (Wijekumar et al., 2025)	Carnegie Learning, Squirrel AI.
Automated Administrative Tasks	Handles routine operations like grading and scheduling (Langove & Khan, 2024)	Saves time for teachers and improves operational efficiency (Sanchez, 2024)	Auto-graded quizzes and AI scheduling assistants.
Predictive Analytics	Uses data to identify learning patterns and potential risks (Ravichandran, 2024)	Enables early interventions and supports data-driven decision-making (Maroju & Aragani, 2025)	Learning Management Systems (LMS) with predictive dashboards.
Language and Accessibility Tools	Facilitates inclusion for diverse learners and those with disabilities (Fitas, 2025)	Promotes equitable access to education ((Fitas, 2025)	Grammarly, Google Translate, and screen readers.
Professional Development	Uses AI insights to guide teacher training and evaluation (Shezad et al., 2025)	Improves teaching quality and supports continuous learning (Shezad et al., 2025)	AI coaching platforms and lesson analysis tools.

CONCEPT OF PERSONALIZED LEARNING AND ADAPTIVE ASSESSMENTS

A more personalized student-centered approach is replacing the one-size-fits-all teaching and learning paradigm in the changing context of 21st-century education (Kerimbayev et al., 2023; Ronas et al., 2023). AI's capacity to provide individualized learning experiences is among its most important contributions to educational technology (Hardaker & Glenn, 2025). To tailor instructional content, AI systems examine individual student data, such as learning preferences, styles, and performance (Kanchon et al., 2024). Machine learning-powered intelligent tutoring programs offer targeted support and modify the pace and level of instruction to fit the skills of each student. By targeting each student's unique strengths and weaknesses, this personalized strategy not only increases learning outcomes but also improves student engagement (Ellikkal & Rajamohan, 2025; Hare & Tang, 2024; Liu et al., 2024)

A personalized learning system can adjust to support various learners to overcome the drawbacks of one-size-fits-all methods in technology-enabled learning systems. The objective is to create a learning system that can dynamically adjust to the needs and characteristics of each learner in order to deliver individualized instruction. This is something that human one-on-one tutors can do, and now digital systems can, too (Sajja et al., 2024; Wu, 2024)

Adaptive assessment enables the selection of questions based on the examinee's performance, in contrast to conventional testing, which is based on fixed items that every examinee must complete regardless of their knowledge level (Wang et al., 2023; Machkour et al., 2024). An adaptive assessment offers a brief, customized test with elements that vary based on the student's response, and each question's difficulty is linked to the response to the one before it. Furthermore, the student's performance on the test directly impacts their choice to discontinue the testing process (Ihichr et al., 2024; Dwahdh & Alshraifin, 2025). Adaptive assessment aims to prevent giving competent students simple questions they will likely answer correctly. Similarly, students who are challenged to answer complex questions during examinations are not given difficult questions because teachers assume that students would find it too difficult (Wang et al., 2023). Also, by providing real-time feedback highlighting students' strengths and weaknesses, adaptive assessments can provide more accurate and precise information to gauge students' proficiency. These assessments provide teachers with data on the difficulty index of the test and lessen the anxiety of the students taking the examination by using algorithms and data analytics to deliver questions that are neither too simple nor too difficult. The teachers may use the data generated by these platforms to conduct student interventions and instructional planning (Khlaif et al., 2024; Yaseen et al., 2025; Adeoye et al., 2025).

One of the main benefits of using the adaptive assessment is its generative aspect features since it offers real-time information and targeted interventions based on the result of students' strengths and weaknesses rather than just grades (Maity & Deroy; Strielkowski et al., 2024). The teachers can use this information generated by the adaptive assessment platforms to address areas that need more attention, provide targeted assistance, and customize their teaching strategies. Unlike conventional examinations, adaptive assessments lessen the level of test anxiety of the students during the examination period and improve the assessment accuracy when properly utilized by the teachers (Elsayed et al., 2024; Adeoye et al., 2025)

In the adaptive assessment, teachers must first assess the student's knowledge and skills. As students take the examination, AI algorithms assess each student's answer to identify the next question's difficulty level. As a result, students are challenged at a suitable level, giving the teachers an idea of what the students can do and know (Delianidi et al., 2024; Maity & Deroy, 2024)

Educators must integrate adaptive assessments and personalized learning to make a more responsive and inclusive learning environment. These AI-powered tools promote fairness, encourage differentiated instruction, and ensure that every student has the opportunity to demonstrate their unique knowledge and skills. The integration of these tools not only promotes deeper learning but also equips students with the necessary knowledge and skills needed as educational institutions continue to evolve (Wang et al., 2024; Kanchon et al., 2024).

While the chapter discusses personalized learning and adaptive assessments, it requires further attention to how students with disabilities and those from underserved communities interact with AI-driven educational tools. Emerging studies highlight that AI systems can reinforce inequities if not designed with accessibility and cultural responsiveness in mind. For instance, Fitas (2025) emphasized the need for AI systems that accommodate assistive technologies and multilingual platforms to support learners with disabilities and linguistic minorities. Additionally, research by Yang et al. (2024) and Lin et al. (2024) demonstrates that under-resourced schools often lack the infrastructure to deploy AI meaningfully, creating a digital divide. Integrating Universal Design for Learning (UDL) frameworks can ensure equitable access by embedding flexibility into the design of AI tools and assessments.

THEORETICAL FOUNDATIONS OF PERSONALIZED LEARNING

- Constructivism: Jean Piaget (1972) and Lev Vygotsky (1978) posit that constructivism is an approach to teaching and learning in HEIs where learners actively construct their understanding through experience and reflection. According to constructivism, students construct and integrate new ideas and information with preexisting cognitive structures (Rillo et al., 2020). By using the information they already know, focusing on relevant aspects in new situations, evaluating if the learned information is important to what they have learned before, and modifying their knowledge as they go, students can take an active role in the teaching-learning process (Bada & Olusegun, 2015). Dahl and Mørch (2025) demonstrate that traditional Learning Object (LO) designs—initially crafted for scalability and reuse—often fail to embody core constructivist principles such as learner agency, contextual learning, and knowledge co-construction. Their study found that while AI-enhanced and constructivist-oriented LO models support more adaptive and collaborative learning environments, many mainstream LO implementations still rely on transmissive, behaviorist models. However, when teachers were encouraged to reflect beyond technical constraints, their conceptualizations shifted toward participation and knowledge creation metaphors—core constructs of constructivist theory rooted in the works of Vygotsky and Sfard. This suggests that pedagogical flexibility and awareness can help bridge the gap between scalable digital tools and the social, active, and situated learning that constructivism advocates.

- Multiple Intelligences Theory: According to Gardner (1993), intelligence is the capacity of humans to generate and resolve problems. Therefore, the type of human intellect emerges when someone encounters and resolves a problem. According to Gardner (1993) and Armstrong (2004), each person possesses eight different types of intelligence, each with a unique capacity. The research by Anggoro et al. (2024) demonstrated how differentiated instruction based on MI in elementary science education significantly improved learners' engagement, joy, and mastery of key concepts such as remembering, understanding, and applying scientific knowledge. The differentiated activities—targeting kinesthetic, interpersonal, intrapersonal, logical-mathematical, and linguistic intelligences—allowed students to process learning in ways best suited to their unique profiles. This tailored approach not only increased conceptual mastery but also reduced classroom boredom and stress, creating a more meaningful and inclusive learning environment.
- Self-Determination Theory (SDT): The macro-level theory of human motivation known as self-determination theory (SDT), put forth by Deci and Ryan (2013), seeks to explain the dynamics of human need, motivation, and well-being in a social setting. According to this theory, every person has three psychological demands that influence their decision to act or not: relatedness (feeling linked, loved, and interacted), competence (feeling competent and practical), and autonomy (feeling self-governed and self-endorsed). For example, Yang et al. (2025) examined how core constructs of SDT—

autonomy, competence, and relatedness—shape learner engagement in fully self-directed online environments. The results showed that when students' psychological needs were supported (through social scaffolding, opportunities for self-regulation, and moments of flow), intrinsic motivation surged, significantly boosting active engagement and persistence in e-learning tasks. These findings underscore SDT's critical role in guiding design choices for personalized digital learning systems: features such as self-paced modules, peer/community support, and adaptive feedback loops can be intentionally crafted to promote learners' agency and competence, leading to stronger engagement outcomes.

- Zone of Proximal Development (ZPD): Lev Vygotsky used the term "Zone of Proximal Development" (ZPD) to describe the range of tasks that a learner can complete with the help and support of a more experienced person, such as a teacher, peer, or mentor, but cannot yet complete on their own. It highlights that optimal learning occurs beyond the learner's current ability level, where they are challenged but still capable of progressing with appropriate assistance. ZPD highlights the significance of determining each learner's distinct developmental stage and offering unique support, or scaffolding, to enable them to acquire new abilities and information in the context of personalized instruction. Support is progressively reduced as the learner gains proficiency, encouraging self-reliance and greater comprehension (Raslan, 2024; Kaldaras et al., 2024; Srivastava et al., 2025).
- Universal Design for Learning (UDL): Creating adaptable learning environments and resources, UDL, as an educational framework, seeks to design lessons and instructional materials that can effectively cater to students' diverse needs, making learning efficient and accessible for every student. UDL emphasizes the removal of barriers to learning and the customization of learning experiences to suit a broad range of learners. For instance, the study of Saborío-Taylor & Rojas-Ramírez (2024) explores the integration of UDL's three core principles—multiple means of representation, engagement, and expression—with emerging AI technologies. The authors provide practical applications showing how AI-powered tools can dynamically adapt content delivery, scaffold learner choices, and present diverse ways for students to demonstrate understanding. The fusion of UDL and AI not only reduces learning barriers but also promotes autonomy and personalization for all learners, even those with varying backgrounds and abilities.

This chapter underrepresents student voice and agency. AI-powered personalization should not merely adapt to students but invite them to shape their learning trajectories. Self-Determination Theory (Deci & Ryan, 2013) and the Universal

Design for Learning framework both support the idea of learner autonomy. Studies by Yang et al. (2025) and Baillifard et al. (2023) show that when learners co-design their paths through choice-based modules, interest-based content, or feedback-driven adaptations, engagement and performance increase. Including student voice empowers learners and aligns AI tools with principles of democratic and inclusive education.

RELATIONSHIP BETWEEN AI, PERSONALIZATION, AND ASSESSMENT

Artificial intelligence is an innovation that transforms various industries to be effective and adaptable in their operations. In the realm of education, it revolutionizes the teachers' instructional practices to make them more flexible, addresses students' learning gaps and focuses on the student's needs, using adaptive assessments and personalized learning, and serves as baseline information for the decision-making process (Halkiopoulos & Gkintoni, 2024; Vorobyeva et al., 2025). Personalizing learning to suit students' unique needs and modifying assessment methods based on the students' performance in real-time, adaptive assessments, and personalized learning can transform traditional educational systems. These developments in education are powered by AI, aiming to assess the huge amounts of students' data and create meaningful learning experiences through personalized instruction. The integration of these AI-powered tools in the teaching-learning process will make students' learning experiences more effective, fair, and efficient (du Plooy, 2024)

AI-powered platforms like personalized learning and adaptive assessments are revolutionizing education, particularly the teaching-learning process in the rapidly changing field of education. Adaptive assessment and personalized learning (two fundamental ideas at the heart of this advancement) use AI for personalized instruction, from instructional materials development to various assessment methods to meet diverse students' needs. These two advancements in AI examine the vast amount of students' data and dynamically modify the assessment practices of teachers to assess better the students' level of understanding of the subject content (Pratama et al., 2023; Halkiopoulos & Gkintoni, 2024). Using learning analytics that strategically gather and assess learners' academic performance to assist teachers with their decisions and enhance learning outcomes enhances the personalized learning and adaptive assessments integration in the teaching-learning process. Learning analytics is key in connecting AI with better student learning outcomes since it offers predictive insights and targeted support (Dumbuya, 2023). When teachers step in with targeted interventions for students, students may improve their performance and lower the chances of student dropout rates. Ifenthaler and Yau (2020) noted that learning analytics would make learning more effective and supportive. The research of Ifenthaler and Yau (2020) aims to investigate the relationships among AI, personalized learning, and adaptive assessments and how these three (AI, personalized learning, adaptive assessment) create learning environments that are more effective, flexible, and fair.

Table 2. The Interrelationship between Artificial Intelligence, Personalized Learning, and Adaptive Assessment in Education

Component	Artificial Intelligence (AI)	Personalized Learning	Adaptive Assessment
Definition	The simulation of human intelligence by machines enables automation and data-driven decision-making.	Tailoring educational experiences to meet individual learners' needs, preferences, pace, and abilities.	Assessments adjust question difficulty based on a student's responses in real time.
Primary Role	Drives personalization and assessment through data analysis, automation, and intelligent decision-making.	Uses AI to adapt content, pacing, and instructional support to individual learners.	Uses AI to select questions dynamically, shortening test length and improving accuracy.
Technologies Used	Machine Learning, Natural Language Processing, Data Analytics, Intelligent Tutoring Systems	Intelligent Tutoring Systems, Recommender Engines, Learner Analytics	Computerized Adaptive Testing, Predictive Algorithms, NLP
Examples	Learning Management Systems (LMS), Chatbots, Predictive Dashboards	Khan Academy, Coursera adaptive pathways, Carnegie Learning	Duolingo, DreamBox, Knewton
Key Benefits	Automates routine tasks, provides data-driven insights, and enhances scalability.	Increases student engagement, supports differentiated instruction, and improves outcomes.	Reduces test time, improves test accuracy, decreases anxiety, and enhances instructional planning.
Educational Impact	Enables real-time feedback loops, continuous improvement, and intelligent resource allocation.	Promotes equity, supports mastery learning, and accommodates diverse learners.	Identifies strengths/weaknesses, allows for timely interventions, and informs personalized instruction.
Synergistic Effect	AI empowers both personalization and assessment by linking learning analytics with instructional strategies.	Enhances the adaptability of instruction through real-time adjustments enabled by AI.	Supports personalization by aligning testing with real-time learner performance and capabilities.

BENEFITS OF AI-DRIVEN PERSONALIZATION IN EDUCATION

- Improved Learning Outcomes: Improved academic performance and mastery of learning objectives can result from personalized learning experiences. This statement was supported by Hu (2024), who revealed in his study that

AI-assisted personalized learning produced a moderate positive effect on student learning outcomes, encompassing knowledge, competence, and affective development. Importantly, the benefit held consistently across different grade levels and subjects. Another study supporting the effectiveness of AI-personalized learning is that of Tabora et al. (2024), which found that personalized instruction using AI improved students' motivation, engagement, and outcomes among senior high school students in the Philippine educational settings.

- Enhance Students' Engagement: Students are more motivated to study when activities and content are tailored to their interests and preferences. Based on the findings of Baillifard et al. (2023), AI-driven personalization, such as the GPT–3–based tutor, was more likely to prompt reattempting quizzes, revising answers, and engaging in optional practice. These characteristics manifested by the students were more likely to indicate that their interests and motivation were increased cognitively. Lou et al. (2025) also pointed out that AI-powered tools that adapted in real-time led to sustained engagement over longer learning sessions, as students felt the content was "tailored for them."
- Promote Adaptability and Differentiated Instruction: Different learning styles and paces can be accommodated by flexible learning paths made possible by AI-driven personalized learning. Pektaş et al. (2025) cited that AI tools supported real-time adjustments by teachers, suggesting different scaffolds, hints, or materials tailored to student needs. The result was significant conceptual gains that aligned with students' learning profiles. This study integrates AI and learning analytics into science instruction, using NLP-based pre-assessment to identify student misconceptions (e.g., about electricity), and then facilitates within-class differentiated instruction informed by continuous AI monitoring.
- Streamlined Instruction: By allocating teaching time as efficiently as possible, AI algorithms ensure that students spend more time on complex concepts and get help when needed (Onesi-Ozigagun et al., 2024). Machado et al. (2025) conducted a study that revealed that teachers found automated scenarios less mentally taxing—AI-powered tools with dashboards and game-like interventions reduced effort in creating and monitoring student tasks. Also, the advent of GenAI-Assisted Lesson Planning study revealed that major reductions in lesson planning time have been evident, resulting in higher satisfaction among teachers and more effective adaptation of lessons to student diversity (Karpouzis et al., 2024).
- Continuous Progress: Curriculum design, pedagogical approaches, and general educational strategies can all be improved with the use of the data gathered by AI-driven personalized learning systems. Findings across 31 studies,

students in AI-enhanced classrooms consistently demonstrated steady progress over time, particularly when platforms incorporated real-time analytics and adaptive scaffolding (Hu, 2024).

CHALLENGES AND CONSIDERATIONS

- Data Protection: Collecting and storing sensitive learner data requires robust data privacy measures to safeguard personal information. Khalil et al. (2025) showed that federated learning—an approach where student data remains on-device—is a promising method to allow AI personalization while protecting data rights. They report that, relative to centralized models, it matches predictive performance and offers greater robustness against adversarial access. Shrestha et.al (2024) conducted a systematic review that captures perspectives, finding that learners fear a lack of control over personal data, worry about misuse and data breaches, and value clear consent, transparency, and agency, even while recognizing personalization benefits.
- Bias in Algorithms: AI algorithms may inadvertently introduce biases based on the data used to train them. Ensuring fairness and equity in personalized learning is essential. Weissburg et al (2024) conducted a large-scale evaluation of 9 state-of-the-art LLMs across 17,000 educational explanations, uncovering systematic biases—especially across socioeconomic status and disability—even in adaptive tutoring roles. They introduce bias metrics (MAB, MDB) to quantify discrepancies in content generation for different demographic groups. Baker et al (2023) reveal pervasive algorithmic biases across student SES, parental education, urbanicity, disability, and non-native language use, offering a taxonomy of bias stages (unknown → known → fairness → equity) and strategies to advance through them.
- Faculty Development: Implementing AI-driven personalized learning requires educators to understand and effectively use the technology, necessitating training and ongoing support. However, it becomes a great challenge for teachers. According to Mah & Groß (2024), while most faculty recognize AI's equity potential, many lack AI literacy and want structured professional development. This study urged institutions to build tailored support services for sustainable AI-led teaching transformation. Tan et al (2024) found an imbalance: 65% focus on AI-supported teaching, only 35% on AI-driven professional development. They pointed out that there is a need for more research into ethical, technological, and pedagogical challenges in AI-supported professional development.

- Funding and Physical Resources: AI-driven personalized learning platforms may require significant investment in technology and infrastructure, making accessibility a potential challenge for some educational institutions. Du Plooy et al. (2024) reported that underdeveloped countries suffer from platform access, infrastructure, and funding shortages. They recommend investments in sustainable funding, offline capabilities, and international capacity-building efforts.

Ethical challenges associated with AI systems are notably underexplored in the original chapter. Surveillance and data privacy remain top concerns. Shrestha et al. (2024) found that learners often fear data misuse and lack control over personal information in AI-mediated environments. Moreover, AI-driven decision-making in educational contexts can lead to over-reliance, potentially marginalizing human intuition and contextual judgment. Kamali et al. (2024) advocate for ethical frameworks that embed transparency, accountability, and human oversight into AI deployments. To balance AI with human judgment, educators must critically evaluate when and how AI tools are appropriate and integrate decision-making protocols that prioritize pedagogical values over automation.

REAL-WORLD IMPLEMENTATION IN UNDER-RESOURCED SCHOOLS

To ground the discussion, the chapter should include practical implementation examples, especially from lower-resourced or public school contexts. For instance, Wijekumar et al. (2024) demonstrated the success of an intelligent tutoring system for reading comprehension in high-poverty schools in the U.S., which led to significant performance gains. In contrast, Lin et al. (2024) revealed that limited internet access, outdated devices, and low digital literacy often impede AI adoption in underserved areas. Highlighting case studies from both success and struggle offers a more nuanced understanding of AI's potential and limitations in education.

Additionally, teacher readiness remains a critical factor in successful AI integration. Mah & Groß (2024) found that many educators, particularly in under-resourced regions, lack the necessary AI literacy and pedagogical training to incorporate these technologies into their classrooms confidently. Without structured support and capacity-building programs, the adoption of AI may widen pedagogical gaps rather than close them.

From a global perspective, Yang et al. (2024) documented efforts in diverse educational contexts across Southeast Asia, where schools use lightweight AI systems that function offline to accommodate unreliable internet access. These global case studies reveal both the innovative adaptations made in low-resource contexts and the pressing need for international collaboration to ensure inclusive AI deployment in education.

AI-POWERED ADAPTIVE ASSESSMENTS

The AI-powered system, an adaptive assessment utilized for assessing students' knowledge and skills, adjusts each test item's structure and content, including the difficulty index of the test item, in real time based on how the student responds. It also means that utilizing adaptive assessment to gauge students' understanding enables teachers to determine students' performance in easy and difficult questions (Khlaif et al., 2024). Compared to standardized tests, which are more sophisticated, adaptive assessments are characterized by the same questions because they offer a personalized and more precise measurement of students' understanding of the subject matter. This assessment method, powered by AI and smart algorithms, can determine the student's performance on each test item. After the students answer the question, the next question is selected based on how the students respond to each item, which allows students to be challenged but not overwhelmed by the different test questions since the difficulty level matches their skill level. In this sense, students will be motivated to take the test or exam with minimal test anxiety. For teachers, the result of the test taken by the student enables them to modify their instructional strategies and approaches to suit the learners' unique needs. Also, the adaptive assessment data provides accurate information on the areas where the students need further improvement and support. These benefits are the objectives of the adaptive assessment AI-powered tools. By using AI-powered adaptive assessment, teachers can determine the prior and posterior knowledge of learners and how they acquire information. This assessment has the power to predict students' performance and identify areas for improvement in the learning environment (Khlaif et al., 2024).

CASE STUDIES ON AI-POWERED ADAPTIVE ASSESSMENTS

Artificial intelligence has significantly changed personalized learning and transformed the educational landscape, making the education system more equitable, accurate, and sophisticated. The AI-powered adaptive assessment system is a promising tool that revolutionizes the learning environment by modifying the subject content, providing real-time feedback, and personalizing learning based on the students' needs, performance, and behavior. With this tool's potential uses, students will be more productive, engaged, and self-regulated in the teaching-learning process, resulting in better performance. Various research emphasizes the crucial role of adaptive assessment in transforming students' learning environment and revolutionizing the teacher's instructional practices. The chapter presents strong case studies highlighting the key roles of adaptive assessment in enhancing teachers' instructional practices and developing the students' learning outcomes.

The influence of adaptive assessment systems was highlighted in the study of Alenezi (2024). This study highlighted the impact of adaptive assessment tools on student performance, participation, and behavior. The adaptive assessment adjusts the student's learning pace, subject content difficulty, and teachers' instructional practices and strategies based on the student's performance in the test to personalize learning in the Science and Math subjects. The result highlighted that upon using this tool, students will have better satisfaction, especially those not performing well in the class, as well as better post-test performance for the students in the treatment group. Similarly, it was found that students valued the essential role of adaptive assessment in providing real-time feedback on their performance and adjusting their learning pace. Adjusting students' learning pace and providing real-time feedback are the two essential elements of AI-powered adaptive assessment. It is also important to note that while using this tool, the researcher found out challenges like students' digital literacy, the technical readiness of the teachers, and the role of educational institutions in infrastructure and ongoing teachers' training are necessary for the successful implementation of AI-powered adaptive assessment.

The use of adaptive feedback produced by a large language model (ChatGPT) in teacher education was also investigated in the study by Kinder et al. (2025). Pre-service teachers were given static expert or adaptive feedback created by LLM on a diagnostic reasoning assignment. The adaptive feedback, tailored to individual student responses, significantly improved the quality of justification in their writing and increased engagement, as indicated by longer texts and greater time spent processing feedback. Students rated the adaptive feedback as more valuable and interesting, emphasizing the motivational impact of personalized, responsive input. Notably, this study operationalized AI-driven adaptive assessment not as a content delivery system but as an intelligent feedback mechanism that promotes reflective learning and metacognition in higher education settings.

Meanwhile, at the micro level, Wang et al. (2024) examine a Sino-British university's rapid redesign of an undergraduate AI module assessment in response to the emergence of ChatGPT. This adaptive assignment required students to interact with GenAI tools critically—probing their limitations, identifying inaccuracies, and proposing evidence-based corrections—thereby fostering critical thinking, evaluative judgment, and ethical AI use. In contrast, the global case studies presented by Khlaif et al. (2024) explore macro-level implementations of AI in education across countries like the U.S., Finland, and Singapore, showcasing how generative AI enables real-time personalization, continuous formative assessment, and scalable, inclusive testing environments.

REAL-TIME FEEDBACK AND PERFORMANCE PREDICTION IN EDUCATION

The advent of AI-powered systems like data analytics, real-time feedback, and performance prediction in the educational landscape transformed it from a traditional to a more sophisticated educational system. With these advancements, students can track their performance, deepen their understanding of the subject content, and make real-time adjustments when they receive feedback on their performance generated by AI-powered tools. With this, learning becomes more engaging and individualized, empowering students to take self-paced learning development. In order to provide early interventions and focused assistance, instructors and learning platforms can use machine learning algorithms to identify students who are in danger of falling behind or quitting (Onesi-Ozigagun et al., 2024).

According to Keiding and Qvortrup (2014), feedback is a powerful learning tool, but it must be timely or swift to be thought of as helpful in promoting greater knowledge. As a result, real-time feedback systems can instantly evaluate teaching and learning strategies, particularly in classes with a high student population. Additionally, the bias of student responses—whether from being a victim, hatred, or a lack of relevant knowledge about the lecturers—has made it extremely difficult for institutions to evaluate a lecturer's teaching approach properly. Naturally, this automated feedback system will promote anonymous student feedback, determine how many students are enrolled, monitor student performance, and assign courses to lecturers based on student performance, enhancing effective teaching and learning strategies.

Furthermore, prediction is challenging due to hidden data in the massive amount of educational data derived from examinations. A higher degree of quality in higher education can be achieved by predicting students' performance (Mogwe, 2018). A data mining technique is employed to obtain this pertinent data. A machine-learning method called data mining entails identifying patterns and knowledge in vast amounts of data (Ebem et al., 2024; Ikegwu et al., 2022). This significantly enhanced the learning process for the students. For example, a recent work by Hussain and Khan (2023) used 30 variables from academic history data to create a regression model for educational data mining that uses machine learning techniques to assess and predict secondary school student performance. However, more prediction models are required for higher accuracy. Also, Ouyang et al. (2023) used artificial intelligence

(AI)- based data mining to forecast learning analytics and student performance in online engineering courses.

DISCUSSION

A paradigm change in education is represented by implementing artificial intelligence into adaptive assessments and personalized learning, which poses both complex problems and revolutionary possibilities. By customizing educational experiences to each learner's unique profile, AI-powered solutions have shown their ability to improve learning outcomes, increase student engagement, and promote differentiated instruction. Adaptive assessments give teachers real-time information about students' development, allowing for more efficient lesson preparation and prompt interventions. However, there are challenges associated with this change. Problems like the digital divide, algorithmic prejudice, and data privacy emphasize the necessity of careful and moral implementation. The preparedness and training of educators, who must acquire new skills to use these tools effectively, are also critical to the success of AI-driven systems. It is critical to balance technical innovation and human-centered pedagogy as AI systems become more integrated into educational settings to ensure that teachers' roles continue to grow rather than diminish. Thus, the discussion emphasizes the twofold necessity of developing AI applications in education while critically examining the ramifications of these advances for society, ethics, and infrastructure.

CONCLUSION

Artificial intelligence became another significant educational milestone due to its crucial role in adaptive assessments and personalized learning. It can make the learning environment more inclusive, engaging, and effective by facilitating real-time feedback, tailored instruction, and adaptive assessment tools. AI-supported tools, including machine learning, data analytics, and educational theories, are combined to enhance student learning outcomes and meet their needs and preferences, promoting academic excellence and equity. However, implementing AI-driven systems brings issues, technical challenges, and ethical considerations, including the need for teachers to undergo ongoing teacher training. Nevertheless, when these tools are implemented correctly and fairly, they can revolutionize teachers' instructional practices that help students not just for academic success but also for lifelong learning in an ever-changing educational landscape.

RECOMMENDATIONS

It is recommended that academic institutions take the initiative to integrate artificial intelligence in all of their operations, especially in the teaching-learning process, to support personalized learning and adaptive assessment experiences for better student learning outcomes, as discussed in this chapter. Institutions may invest in technology infrastructure to support teachers and students on various learning tasks and activities, and ensure that all have access to AI-driven resources equally. It is also important that institutions support teachers in their ongoing professional development so that they are aware and fully understand how AI works in the classroom setting and how it will be integrated effectively into their instructional practices to make teaching and learning dynamic and more enjoyable. Since the chapter discussed challenges in integrating AI, it is also crucial that the institution establish and uphold ethical considerations in using AI-powered tools. Ethical guidelines must consider data privacy, equity, and transparency to foster trust among stakeholders and students. Policymakers, researchers, tech developers, and educators must work hand in hand to develop scalable, inclusive AI solutions that always consider firsthand the students' benefits and welfare, particularly their academic needs. To promote students' holistic development, school heads and administrators must not only focus on traditional tests but also consider the inclusion of non-cognitive skills assessments, such as communication skills, adaptability, time management, self-discipline, and others, in adaptive assessment systems because these assessments may significantly contribute to their academic and lifelong success. Future studies, such as exploring the long-term effects of AI-driven personalization and its relationship to students' learning outcomes, must also be considered, focusing on algorithmic bias and equity. Lastly, by implementing these strategic steps, the education industry can take advantage of AI's potential while maintaining an ethical and sustainable approach to innovation.

REFERENCES

Adeoye, M. A., Prastikawati, E. F., & Riwayatiningsih, R. (2025). Beyond Traditional Testing: Exploring the Efficacy of Adaptive Assessments in Shaping Future Learners. *Journal of Nonformal Education, 11*(1), 153–169. DOI: 10.15294/jone.v11i1.19934

Alenezi, A. (2024). Evaluating the effectiveness of AI-powered adaptive learning systems in secondary schools. *International Journal on Studies in Education, 6*(4), 686–700. DOI: 10.46328/ijonse.264

Anggoro, S., Fitriati, A., Thoc, N. K., Talib, C. A., & Mareza, L. (2024). Differentiated instruction based on multiple intelligences as promising joyful and meaningful learning. *Int J Eval & Res Educ ISSN, 2252*(8822), 1195. DOI: 10.11591/ijere.v13i2.24791

Bada, S. O., & Olusegun, S. (2015). Constructivism learning theory: A paradigm for teaching and learning. *Journal of Research & Method in Education, 5*(6), 66–70. DOI: 10.9790/7388-05616670

Baillifard, A., Gabella, M., Lavenex, P. B., & Martarelli, C. S. (2023). Implementing learning principles with a personal AI tutor: A case study. *arXiv preprint arXiv:2309*.13060. /arXiv.2309.13060DOI: 10.48550

Baker, R. S., Hawn, A., & Lee, S. (2023). Algorithmic bias: The state of the situation and policy recommendations. https://www.oecd.org/en/publications/oecd-digital-education-outlook-2023_c74f03de-en/full-report/algorithmic-bias-the-state-of-the-situation-and-policy-recommendations

Bulut, O., Beiting-Parrish, M., Casabianca, J. M., Slater, S. C., Jiao, H., Song, D., . . . Morilova, P. (2024). The rise of artificial intelligence in educational measurement: Opportunities and ethical challenges. *arXiv preprint arXiv:2406*.18900. https://doi.org/DOI: 10.59863/MIQL7785

Celik, I., Dindar, M., Muukkonen, H., & Järvelä, S. (2022). The promises and challenges of artificial intelligence for teachers: A systematic review of research. *TechTrends, 66*(4), 616–630. DOI: 10.1007/s11528-022-00715-y

Chan, C. K. Y. (2023). A comprehensive AI policy education framework for university teaching and learning. *International Journal of Educational Technology in Higher Education, 20*(1), 38. DOI: 10.1186/s41239-023-00408-3

Chan, C. K. Y., & Hu, W. (2023). Students' voices on generative AI: Perceptions, benefits, and challenges in higher education. *International Journal of Educational Technology in Higher Education, 20*(1), 43. DOI: 10.1186/s41239-023-00411-8

Chen, A., Zhang, Y., Jia, J., Liang, M., Cha, Y., & Lim, C. P. (2025). A systematic review and Meta-analysis of AI-enabled assessment in language learning: Design, implementation, and effectiveness. *Journal of Computer Assisted Learning, 41*(1), e13064. DOI: 10.1111/jcal.13064

Dahl, J. E., & Mørch, A. (2025). A theoretical and empirical analysis of tensions between learning objects and constructivism. *Education and Information Technologies*, 1–50. DOI: 10.1007/s10639-025-13636-z

Deci, E. L., & Ryan, R. M. (2013). *Intrinsic motivation and self-determination in human behavior*. Springer Science & Business Media.

Delianidi, M., Diamantaras, K., Moras, I., & Sidiropoulos, A. (2024). DK-PRACTICE: An Intelligent Educational Platform for Personalized Learning Content Recommendations Based on Students' Knowledge State. *arXiv preprint arXiv:2501.10373*. / arXiv.2501.10373DOI: 10.48550

Dimitriadou, E., & Lanitis, A. (2023). A critical evaluation, challenges, and future perspectives of using artificial intelligence and emerging technologies in smart classrooms. *Smart Learning Environments, 10*(1), 12. DOI: 10.1186/s40561-023-00231-3 PMID: 40478141

Dong, L., Tang, X., & Wang, X. (2025). Examining the Effect of Artificial Intelligence in Relation to Students' Academic Achievement in the Classroom: A Meta-Analysis. *Computers and Education: Artificial Intelligence, 100400*, 100400. Advance online publication. DOI: 10.1016/j.caeai.2025.100400

Du Plooy, E., Casteleijn, D., & Franzsen, D. (2024). Personalized adaptive learning in higher education: A scoping review of key characteristics and impact on academic performance and engagement. *Heliyon, 10*(21), e39630. Advance online publication. DOI: 10.1016/j.heliyon.2024.e39630 PMID: 39524879

Dumbuya, E. (2023). Personalized Learning through Artificial Intelligence: Revolutionizing Education. *Available at SSRN* 5023248.

Dwahdh, L., & Alshraifin, N. (2025). The impact of computerized adaptive test termination rules on accuracy across different ability estimation methods. *Eurasia Journal of Mathematics, Science and Technology Education, 21*(1), em2571. DOI: 10.29333/ejmste/15897

Ebem, D. U., Ikegwu, A. C., Ezugwu, C. J., Ikpo, C. V., & Ogbunude, F. O. (2024). Machine Learning-Based Real-Time Feedback Assessment System for Student Performance *Prediction in Tertiary Institutions*.

Elsayed, A. M., Kholikov, A., Abdullayeva, I., Al-Farouni, M., & Wodajo, M. R. (2024). Teacher support in AI-assisted exams: An experimental study to inspect the effects on demotivation, anxiety management in exams, L2 learning experience, and academic success. *Language Testing in Asia*, *14*(1), 53. DOI: 10.1186/s40468-024-00328-7

Ersozlu, Z., Taheri, S., & Koch, I. (2024). A review of machine learning methods used for educational data. *Education and Information Technologies*, *29*(16), 1–21. DOI: 10.1007/s10639-024-12704-0

Fitas, R. (2025). Inclusive Education with AI: Supporting Special Needs and Tackling Language Barriers. *arXiv preprint arXiv:2504.14120*. DOI: 10.2139/ssrn.5366398

Fodouop Kouam, A. W. (2024). The effectiveness of intelligent tutoring systems in supporting students with varying levels of programming experience. *Discover Education*, *3*(1), 1–13. DOI: 10.1007/s44217-024-00385-3

Fu, Y., & Weng, Z. (2024). Navigating the ethical terrain of AI in education: A systematic review on framing responsible human-centered AI practices. *Computers and Education: Artificial Intelligence*, 100306.

Gardner, H. (1993). Multiple Intelligences. New York: Basic Books, Hons of Learning Harper Collins Publ. Inc.

Halkiopoulos, C., & Gkintoni, E. (2024). Leveraging AI in E-Learning: Personalized Learning and Adaptive Assessment through Cognitive Neuropsychology—A Systematic Analysis. *Electronics (Basel)*, *13*(18), 3762. DOI: 10.3390/electronics13183762

Hardaker, G., & Glenn, L. E. (2025). Artificial intelligence for personalized learning: A systematic literature review. *International Journal of Information and Learning Technology*, *42*(1), 1–14. DOI: 10.1108/IJILT-07-2024-0160

Hardaker, G., & Glenn, L. E. (2025). Artificial intelligence for personalized learning: A systematic literature review. *The International Journal of Information and Learning Technology*, *42*(1), 1–14. DOI: 10.1108/IJILT-07-2024-0160

Hare, R., & Tang, Y. (2024, October). Ontology-driven Reinforcement Learning for Personalized Student Support. In *2024 IEEE International Conference on Systems, Man, and Cybernetics (SMC)* (pp. 2555-2560). IEEE. DOI: 10.1109/SMC54092.2024.10832036

Hu, S. (2024). The effect of artificial intelligence-assisted personalized learning on student learning outcomes: A meta-analysis based on 31 empirical research papers. *Science Insights Education Frontiers*, *24*(1), 3873–3894. DOI: 10.15354/sief.24.re395

Hussain, S., & Khan, M. Q. (2023). Student-performulator: Predicting students' academic performance at secondary and intermediate levels using machine learning. *Annals of Data Science*, *10*(3), 637–655. DOI: 10.1007/s40745-021-00341-0 PMID: 38624826

Ifenthaler, D., Majumdar, R., Gorissen, P., Judge, M., Mishra, S., Raffaghelli, J., & Shimada, A. (2024). Artificial intelligence in education: Implications for policymakers, researchers, and practitioners. *Technology, Knowledge and Learning*, 1-18. DOI: 10.1007/s10758-024-09747-0

Ifenthaler, D., & Yau, J. Y. K. (2020). Utilising learning analytics to support study success in higher education: A systematic review. *Educational Technology Research and Development*, *68*(4), 1961–1990. DOI: 10.1007/s11423-020-09788-z

Ihichr, A., Oustous, O., El Idrissi, Y. E. B., & Lahcen, A. A. (2024). A Systematic Review on Assessment in Adaptive Learning: Theories, Algorithms and Techniques. *International Journal of Advanced Computer Science and Applications*, *15*(7). Advance online publication. DOI: 10.14569/IJACSA.2024.0150785

Ikegwu, A. C., Nweke, H. F., Anikwe, C. V., Alo, U. R., & Okonkwo, O. R. (2022). Big data analytics for data-driven industry: A review of data sources, tools, challenges, solutions, and research directions. *Cluster Computing*, *25*(5), 3343–3387. DOI: 10.1007/s10586-022-03568-5

Kaldaras, L., Wang, K. D., Nardo, J. E., Price, A., Perkins, K., Wieman, C., & Salehi, S. (2024). Employing technology-enhanced feedback and scaffolding to support the development of deep science understanding using computer simulations. *International Journal of STEM Education*, *11*(1), 30. DOI: 10.1186/s40594-024-00490-7

Kamali, J., Alpat, M. F., & Bozkurt, A. (2024). AI ethics as a complex and multifaceted challenge: Decoding educators' AI ethics alignment through the lens of activity theory. *International Journal of Educational Technology in Higher Education*, *21*(1), 1–20. DOI: 10.1186/s41239-024-00496-9

Kanchon, M. K. H., Sadman, M., Nabila, K. F., Tarannum, R., & Khan, R. (2024). Enhancing Personalized learning: AI-driven identification of learning styles and content modification strategies. *International Journal of Cognitive Computing in Engineering*, *5*, 269–278. DOI: 10.1016/j.ijcce.2024.06.002

Karpouzis, K., Pantazatos, D., Taouki, J., & Meli, K. (2024, May). Tailoring education with GenAI: a new horizon in lesson planning. In 2024 IEEE Global Engineering Education Conference (EDUCON) (pp. 1-10). IEEE. /arXiv.2403.12071DOI: 10.48550

Karran, A. J., Charland, P., Martineau, J. T., de Arana, A., Lesage, A. M., Senecal, S., & Leger, P.

Kayyali, M. (2025). The Impact of Personalized Learning on Student Engagement and Achievement in STEAM. In *Integrating Personalized Learning Methods Into STEAM Education* (pp. 51–78). IGI Global Scientific Publishing. DOI: 10.4018/979-8-3693-7718-5.ch003

Keiding, T. B., & Qvortrup, A. (2014). Feedback as real-time constructions. *E-Learning and Digital Media, 11*(2), 191–203. DOI: 10.2304/elea.2014.11.2.191

Kerimbayev, N., Umirzakova, Z., Shadiev, R., & Jotsov, V. (2023). A student-centered approach using modern technologies in distance learning: A systematic review of the literature. *Smart Learning Environments, 10*(1), 61. DOI: 10.1186/s40561-023-00280-8

Khalil, M., Shakya, R., & Liu, Q. (2025, April). Towards Privacy-Preserving Data-Driven Education: The Potential of Federated Learning. In *2025 International Conference on New Trends in Computing Sciences (ICTCS)* (pp. 113–118). IEEE. DOI: 10.1109/ICTCS65341.2025.10989403

Khan, S., Mazhar, T., Shahzad, T., Khan, M. A., Rehman, A. U., Saeed, M. M., & Hamam, H. (2025). Harnessing AI for sustainable higher education: Ethical considerations, operational efficiency, and future directions. *Discover Sustainability, 6*(1), 23. DOI: 10.1007/s43621-025-00809-6

Khlaif, Z., Odeh, A., & Bsharat, T. R. (2024). Generative AI-powered adaptive assessment. In *Power of Persuasive Educational Technologies in Enhancing Learning* (pp. 157–176). IGI Global. DOI: 10.4018/979-8-3693-6397-3.ch007

Kinder, A., Briese, F. J., Jacobs, M., Dern, N., Glodny, N., Jacobs, S., & Leßmann, S. (2025). Effects of adaptive feedback generated by a large language model: A case study in teacher education. *Computers and Education: Artificial Intelligence, 8*, 100349. DOI: 10.1016/j.caeai.2024.100349

Langove, S. A., & Khan, A. (2024). Automated Grading and Feedback Systems: Reducing Teacher Workload and Improving Student Performance. *Journal of Asian Development Studies, 13*(4), 202–212. DOI: 10.62345/jads.2024.13.4.16

Lin, H. (2022). Influences of artificial intelligence in education on teaching effectiveness: The mediating effect of teachers' perceptions of educational technology. *International Journal of Emerging Technologies in Learning*, *17*(24), 144–156. DOI: 10.3991/ijet.v17i24.36037

Lin, H., & Chen, Q. (2024). Artificial intelligence (AI)-integrated educational applications and college students' creativity and academic emotions: Students and teachers' perceptions and attitudes. *BMC Psychology*, *12*(1), 487. DOI: 10.1186/s40359-024-01979-0 PMID: 39285268

Lin, M. P.-C., Liu, A. L., Poitras, E., Chang, M., & Chang, D. H. (2024). An Exploratory Study on the Efficacy and Inclusivity of AI Technologies in Diverse Learning Environments. *Sustainability (Basel)*, *16*(20), 8992. DOI: 10.3390/su16208992

Liu, V., Latif, E., & Zhai, X. (2025). Advancing Education through Tutoring Systems: A Systematic Literature Review. *arXiv preprint arXiv:2503.09748.* /arXiv.2503.09748DOI: 10.48550

Liu, Z., Yin, S. X., Lin, G., & Chen, N. F. (2024). Personality-aware student simulation for conversational intelligent tutoring systems. *arXiv preprint arXiv:2404.06762.* DOI: 10.18653/v1/2024.emnlp-main.37

Luo, J., Zheng, C., Yin, J., & Teo, H. H. (2025). Design and assessment of AI-based learning tools in higher education: A systematic review. *International Journal of Educational Technology in Higher Education*, *22*(1), 42. DOI: 10.1186/s41239-025-00540-2

Machado, A., Tenório, K., Santos, M. M., Barros, A. P., Rodrigues, L., Mello, R. F., Paiva, R., & Dermeval, D. (2025). Workload perception in educational resource recommendation supported by artificial intelligence: A controlled experiment with teachers. *Smart Learning Environments*, *12*(1), 20. DOI: 10.1186/s40561-025-00373-6

Machkour, M., El Jihaoui, M., Lamalif, L., Faris, S., & Mansouri, K. (2025, February). Toward an adaptive learning assessment pathway. In *Frontiers in Education* (Vol. 10, p. 1498233). Frontiers Media SA. DOI: 10.3389/feduc.2025.1498233

Maity, S., & Deroy, A. (2024). Generative AI and its impact on personalized intelligent tutoring systems. *arXiv preprint arXiv:2410.10650.* /arXiv.2410.10650DOI: 10.48550

Maroju, P. K., & Aragani, V. M. (2025). Predictive Analytics in Education: Early Intervention and Proactive Support With Gen AI Cloud. In *Smart Education and Sustainable Learning Environments in Smart Cities* (pp. 317–332). IGI Global Scientific Publishing. DOI: 10.4018/979-8-3693-7723-9.ch019

Merino-Campos, C. (2025). The Impact of Artificial Intelligence on Personalized Learning in Higher Education: A Systematic Review. *Trends in Higher Education, 4*(2), 17. DOI: 10.3390/higheredu4020017

Mogwe, A. W. (2018). Real-Time concept feedback in lectures for Botho University students. *International Journal of Advanced Computer Science and Applications, 9*(6). Advance online publication. DOI: 10.14569/IJACSA.2018.090635

Onesi-Ozigagun, O., Ololade, Y. J., Eyo-Udo, N. L., & Ogundipe, D. O. (2024). Revolutionizing education through AI: A comprehensive review of enhancing learning experiences. *International Journal of Applied Research in Social Sciences, 6*(4), 589–607. DOI: 10.51594/ijarss.v6i4.1011

Ouyang, F., Wu, M., Zheng, L., Zhang, L., & Jiao, P. (2023). Integration of artificial intelligence performance prediction and learning analytics to improve student learning in an online engineering course. *International Journal of Educational Technology in Higher Education, 20*(1), 4. DOI: 10.1186/s41239-022-00372-4 PMID: 36683653

Pektaş, H. M., Karamustafaoğlu, O., & Çelik, H. (2025). The Role of Educational Data Mining and Artificial Intelligence Supported Learning Analytics on Conceptual Change: New Approaches to Differentiated Instruction. *Journal of Science Education and Technology*, 1–26. DOI: 10.1007/s10956-025-10214-3

Phelan, D., Maguire, H., & Finnegan, C. (2025). Scoping Review of Universal Design for Learning Principles Embedded in Subjects in Secondary Education. *European Journal of Education, 60*(1), e70016. DOI: 10.1111/ejed.70016

Pratama, M. P., Sampelolo, R., & Lura, H. (2023). Revolutionizing education: harnessing the power of artificial intelligence for personalized learning. *Klasikal: Journal of Education, Language Teaching and Science, 5*(2), 350-357.

Priyadharsini, V., & Mary, R. S. (2024). Universal Design for Learning (UDL) in Inclusive Education: Accelerating Learning for All. *Shanlax International Journal of Arts. Science and Humanities, 11*(4), 145–150. DOI: 10.34293/sijash.v11i4.7489

Raslan, G. (2024, March). The impact of the zone of proximal development concept (scaffolding) on the students' problem-solving skills and learning outcomes. *In BUiD Doctoral Research Conference 2023*: Multidisciplinary Studies (pp. 59–66). Cham: Springer Nature Switzerland. DOI: 10.1007/978-3-031-56121-4_6

Ravichandran, K. (2024). Identifying Learning Difficulties at an Early Stage in Education with the Help of Artificial Intelligence Models and Predictive Analytics. *International Research Journal of Multidisciplinary Scope*, *5*(4), 1455–1461. DOI: 10.47857/irjms.2024.v05i04.01821

Rillo, A. G., Martínez-Carrillo, B. E., Castillo-Cardiel, J. A., & Rementería-Salinas, J. M. (2020). Constructivism: *An interpretation from medical education. IOSR J Res Method Educ, 10*(3), 13. https://www.iosrjournals.org/iosr-jrme/papers/Vol-10%20Issue-3/Series-7/A1003070112.pdf

Ronas, S. M. S., Almonte, J. C. R., Arca, J. B., & Padron, R. P. (2023). The new norm of learning: Implementing learner-centered education with technology students. *International Journal of Multidisciplinary: Applied Business and Education Research*, *4*(4), 1278–1286. DOI: 10.11594/ijmaber.04.04.23

Saborío-Taylor, S., & Rojas-Ramírez, F. (2024). Universal design for learning and artificial intelligence in the digital era: Fostering inclusion and autonomous learning. *International Journal of Professional Development. Learners and Learning*, *6*(2), ep2408. Advance online publication. DOI: 10.30935/ijpdll/14694

Sajja, R., Sermet, Y., Cikmaz, M., Cwiertny, D., & Demir, I. (2024). Artificial intelligence-enabled intelligent assistant for personalized and adaptive learning in higher education. *Information (Basel)*, *15*(10), 596. DOI: 10.3390/info15100596

Sanchez, J. (2024). The impact of artificial intelligence on teachers performance: Automatization of paperwork and enhancing of mediation. In *EDULEARN24 Proceedings* (pp. 7274–7278). IATED. DOI: 10.21125/edulearn.2024.1717

Shezad, F., Goswami, R., Shaheen, A., & Khan, I. (2025). AI in Teacher Training and Professional Development: A Tool for Continuous Learning and Skill Enhancement. *Review of Education, Administration & Law*, *8*(1), 179–191. DOI: 10.47067/real.v8i1.416

Shrestha, A. K., Barthwal, A., Campbell, M., Shouli, A., Syed, S., Joshi, S., & Vassileva, J. (2024). Navigating AI to unpack youth privacy concerns: An in-depth exploration and systematic review. *arXiv preprint arXiv:2412*.16369.DOI: 10.1109/IEMCON62851.2024.11093125

Srivastava, M., Iranmanesh, R., Cui, Y., Gopinath, D., Sumner, E. S., Silva, A., & Sadigh, D. (2025, March). Shared Autonomy for Proximal Teaching. *In 2025, 20th ACM/IEEE International Conference on Human-Robot Interaction (HRI)* (pp. 232-241). IEEE. DOI: 10.48550/arXiv.2502.19899

Strielkowski, W., Grebennikova, V., Lisovskiy, A., Rakhimova, G., & Vasileva, T. (2024). AI-Driven adaptive learning for sustainable educational transformation. *Sustainable Development*. Advance online publication. DOI: 10.1002/sd.3221

Tabora, L. A. T., Ampatuan, D. S. I. S., Castaneda, M. A. C., Galinato, E. J. U., & Zulueta, E. E. M. (2024, June). The Impact of Artificial Intelligence (AI) Systems on the Personalized Learning Outcomes for Senior High School Students: A Systematic Review. *In Proceedings of the 2024 10th International Conference on Frontiers of Educational Technologies* (pp. 67-74). DOI: 10.1145/3678392.3678393

Tan, X., Cheng, G., & Ling, M. H. (2024). Artificial intelligence in teaching and teacher professional development: A systematic review. *Computers and Education: Artificial Intelligence, 100355*. Advance online publication. DOI: 10.1016/j.caeai.2024.100355

Veytia Bucheli, M. G., Gómez-Galán, J., Cáceres Mesa, M. L., & López Catalán, L. (2024). Digital Technologies as enablers of universal design for learning: Higher education students' perceptions in the context of SDG4. *Discover Sustainability*, *5*(1), 1–29. DOI: 10.1007/s43621-024-00699-0

Vorobyeva, K. I., Belous, S., Savchenko, N. V., Smirnova, L. M., Nikitina, S. A., & Zhdanov, S.

Walton Family Foundation. (2024). AI Chatbots in Schools. https://www.waltonfamilyfoundation.org/learning/the-value-of-ai-in-todays-classrooms

Wang, H., Long, T., Yin, L., Zhang, W., Xia, W., Hong, Q., & Yu, Y. (2023, August). Gmocat: A graph-enhanced multi-objective method for computerized adaptive testing. In *Proceedings of the 29th ACM SIGKDD Conference on Knowledge Discovery and Data Mining* (pp. 2279-2289). DOI: 10.1145/3580305.3599367

Wang, L., Li, S., & Chen, Y. (2024). Early Adaptation of Assessments Using Generative Artificial Intelligence and the Impact on Student Learning: A Case Study. *African Journal of Inter/Multidisciplinary Studies, 6*(1), 1-12. DOI: 10.51415/ajims.v6i1.1532

Weissburg, I., Anand, S., Levy, S., & Jeong, H. (2024). LLMS are biased teachers: Evaluating LLM bias in personalized education. *arXiv preprint arXiv:2410*.14012. /arXiv.2410.14012DOI: 10.48550

Wijekumar, K. K., Lei, P., Rice, M., Beerwinkle, A., Zhang, S., & Meyer, B. J. (2024). A web-based intelligent tutoring system for reading comprehension delivered to fifth-grade students attending high-poverty schools: Results from a replication efficacy study. *Journal of Educational Psychology*, *116*(8), 1333–1351. Advance online publication. DOI: 10.1037/edu0000878

Wu, J. (2024). Modeling Personalized Smart Teaching for Learner Needs. *Applied Mathematics and Nonlinear Sciences.*, *9*(1), 1–18. DOI: 10.2478/amns-2024-1384

Xia, Q., Weng, X., Ouyang, F., Lin, T. J., & Chiu, T. K. (2024). A scoping review on how generative artificial intelligence transforms assessment in higher education. *International Journal of Educational Technology in Higher Education*, *21*(1), 40. DOI: 10.1186/s41239-024-00468-z

Yang, Y., Chen, J., & Zhuang, X. (2025). Self-determination theory and the influence of social support, self-regulated learning, and flow experience on student learning engagement in self-directed e-learning. *Frontiers in Psychology*, *16*, 1545980. DOI: 10.3389/fpsyg.2025.1545980 PMID: 40207130

Yang, Z. Q., Cao, J., Li, X., Wang, K., Zheng, X., Poon, K. C. F., & Lai, D. (2024, June). DMP_AI: An AI-Aided K-12 System for Teaching and Learning in Diverse Schools. In *International Conference on Blended Learning* (pp. 117-130). Singapore: Springer Nature Singapore. DOI: 10.1007/978-981-97-4442-8_9

Yaseen, H., Mohammad, A. S., Ashal, N., Abusaimeh, H., Ali, A., & Sharabati, A.-A. A. (2025). The Impact of Adaptive Learning Technologies, Personalized Feedback, and Interactive AI Tools on Student Engagement: *The Moderating Role of Digital Literacy. Sustainability (Basel)*, *17*(3), 1133. DOI: 10.3390/su17031133

Zhang, J., & Zhang, Z. (2024). AI in teacher education: Unlocking new dimensions in teaching support, inclusive learning, and digital literacy. *Journal of Computer Assisted Learning*, *40*(4), 1871–1885. DOI: 10.1111/jcal.12988

Chapter 5
The Role of AI-Powered Learning Analytics in Enhancing Student Engagement and Performance

Muhammad Usman Tariq
https://orcid.org/0000-0002-7605-3040
Abu Dhabi University, UAE & University College Cork, Ireland

ABSTRACT

This chapter examines the transformative role of AI-driven learning analytics in improving student engagement and academic achievement. These findings support personalized education, early identification of endangered students, and rapid interventions to improve learning outcomes. This chapter identifies global implementation, comparative implementation of education systems, and justice, privacy, and scalability challenges. It focuses on the most essential role of educators in interpreting and using analysis. The recommendations are aimed at educators, institutions, and political decision-makers to ensure AI's ethical and effective integration into education. This chapter is closed with a call for further research and development to promote responsibility, integrated, and innovative use of AI in educational environments worldwide.

DOI: 10.4018/979-8-3373-2185-1.ch005

INTRODUCTION

Artificial intelligence (AI) is the basis for transformation in many sectors, which puts education at the top of this digital development. Including AI technology in education redesigns the traditional learning paradigm and provides unprecedented opportunities to improve the quality, accessibility, and personalization of the teaching experience. Modern education systems increasingly rely on intelligent systems to manage complex data records, automate administrative tasks, analyze student performance, and promote a more integrated learning environment. By integrating AI into classrooms, learning platforms, and institutional management systems, educators can make well-informed decisions based on real data, tailor educational content to meet individual needs, and predict potential challenges before they become obstacles (Sumathy & Navamani, 2024). Learning analysis refers to collections, measurements, analysis, and reports of data about learners and their contexts, which understand and optimize the learning environment in which learning and environment arise. This data-control approach allows educators to identify trends and patterns of student behavior, assess commitments, and actively intervene when students are at risk of non-performance. Using data from various sources, including learning management systems, digital assessments, attendance files, and even social interactions, an overall understanding of all student learning can be developed. This comprehensive knowledge promotes early intervention strategies, supports evidence-based decisions, and ultimately contributes to improving educational outcomes.

Learning analysis plays a vital role in improving student engagement. Student commitments have diverse components, including behavioral, emotional, and cognitive. It is widely recognized as an essential determinant of academic success, retention, and lifelong learning. Educators can measure student participation and motivation by analyzing data such as registration frequency, time, and time used for learning modules, forum participation, and assessment performance. AI-powered dashboards and visualization tools present this data in an implementable format, allowing teachers to adapt their teaching strategies in real time. For example, suppose the analysis indicates a decrease in participation. In that case, instructors can resume interest and commitment using targeted interventions such as personalized feedback, interactive content, or one-to-one interview sessions. These systems use algorithms to tailor content based on successive evaluations and feedback loops. As students deal with digital learning environments, their interactions are continuously monitored and analyzed. AI systems interpret this data to identify strengths, weaknesses, learning styles, and advances. It allows for creating individual learning paths that match each student's special needs and goals. Learning is more relevant, more efficient, and more comfortable. Through personalizing educational experiences, AI promotes deeper commitment, promotes self-directed learning, and helps learners build trust in their skills.

Data-controlled personalization goes beyond academic content. It also includes the emotional and social aspects of learning. By processing natural language and analysis of mood, AI systems can recognize signs of stress, confusion, or frustration in students' written answers and interactions. This emotional information provides valuable contexts to understand learners' behavior and adapt support mechanisms accordingly. For example, suppose students consistently have signs of fear in discussions and feedback. In that case, the system can recommend wellness resources or elicit support for timely support. This delicate use of AI contributes to a more collaborative and reconcilable learning environment in that students feel valued and understood (Alhamadi & Alhamadi, 2024). These tools provide immediate feedback, explain complex concepts, and provide round-the-clock support. We provide support, especially for students with disabilities or those needing additional support outside traditional lessons. Virtual assistants can answer questions, plan learning activities, and assess understanding through natural language interactions. Such techniques improve learning efficiency and allow students to travel educationally. Building managers can analyze aggregated data to identify successful teaching methods, allocate funding more effectively, and develop strategies to promote justice and inclusion. For example, predictive analytics can predict trends in registration, dismantling risk, and employment outcomes. It allows institutions to be actively planned and offers to meet labor market requirements. This strategic use of data will allow the education system to remain agile and relevant and meet the developing needs of society. Data protection, algorithm bias, and consent after informed consent must be addressed to maintain trust and integrity. Transparent data practices, ethical AI design, and robust data government frameworks are important to ensure student rights and promote responsible innovation.

BACKGROUND

Learning analysis represents a powerful and transformative instrument in modern educational settings. It includes a variety of data-centric processes that monitor, evaluate, and improve learning outcomes. Essentially, learning analyses involve collecting, analyzing, and interpreting data generated by learners and involve interaction in an educational setting. It includes data such as online platforms, classroom technology, student information systems, and more (Banik & Gullapelly, 2025). Learning analysis aims to extract implementable findings that can inform decisions about individual learners and educators at several levels regarding institutional managers and political decision-makers. With a detailed understanding of how students are exposed to learning materials, whether learning strategies are most effective, and whether learners are against them, learning analytics allow interest groups to develop targeted interventions, improve curriculum design, and promote integration and response. It includes data collection, mining, visualization, predictive modeling, and interventions. Data collection refers to collecting raw data from various sources, including learning management systems, student information systems, reviews, discussion forums, and even social media. These data often include timestamps, clickstreams, quiz results, presence records, text submissions, and engagement metrics. After collection, this data is subject to mining and analysis, and the algorithm identifies patterns, correlations, and anomalies that are not displayed immediately. Visualization often plays an essential role in making these findings understandable and implementable through dashboards. It reports highlighting key student performance and commitment indicators. Predictive modeling uses historical and actual data to predict future behavior or outcomes (Tariq, 2025).

ML can be used in educational settings to predict student success, identify endangered students, and create models that adapt content to teach them to suit individual needs. For example, you can use monitored learning techniques to train your model using labeled data records to predict results such as course completion and test performance. Unfair learning techniques, such as clustering, reveal groups among students based on learning behavior and are informed by lessons that they differentiate. The NLP algorithm can assess the contributions to discussion, essays, feedback, and chat interactions, assess emotions, recognize plagiarism, and determine measures of understanding or commitment. For example, tools for mood analysis can interpret whether a student's language reflects confusion, frustration, or enthusiasm. It can lead to timely intervention by educators (Safdar et al., 2025). Text mining using NLP can also help identify key topics and topics in large quantities of written content, supporting formative reviews and curriculum coordination. Speech recognition and automated essay assessments are further examples of NLP applications that optimize assessments and give learners immediate feedback.

Additionally, the increased enrichment, another branch of AI, allows content to be content based on learners and creates a dynamic learning environment that responds to students in real time. Learning analyses mainly included descriptive statistics and simple data visualizations from basic tracking systems in the early stages. These early tools allowed educators to track the number of students who had accessed the learning module or how often they submitted an order. However, they lacked the sophistication needed for deep analysis or personalization. With the increase in computing power and data storage capabilities, the ambition and complexity of learning analytics projects have also increased.

With the rise of big data and advances in machine learning, predictive analytics in education was created in the second stage of evolution. The institution began using AI-controlled models to predict student outcomes and determine what risks exist to design disability and early warning systems. These systems used historical data to make accurate predictions and guided intervention strategies. At this stage, the role of AI has changed from descriptive to predictive. It was not just insight into what happened, but also about actions and what was to happen. AI systems are currently embedded in digital learning environments, which continuously monitor learner interactions and coordinate content during ongoing fly (Mirdad et al., 2024). This shift was activated by cloud computing, classroom IoT devices, and improved algorithmic models. Real-time data processing enables an immediate feedback loop, allowing the system to respond immediately to student performance. The invitation is to review additional resources, motivational nudges, or concepts. Although early AI applications focused on power metrics and efficiency, more substantial advances are currently in tuning learners' educational theories and overall development and analysis. It includes learning voices in integrating social-emotional data, attention to ethical considerations, and the design and implementation of analytical tools (Alhamdi et al., 2024).

The field is increasingly interdisciplinary, based on education, psychology, computer science, and data ethics, with AI playing more roles as a tool for permitting than surveillance. It is imperative in education, where trust, fairness, and accountability are essential. Educators and students must understand why the system has given specific recommendations or predictions, and institutions must ensure that these systems do not increase existing biases and inequality (Yakhina et al., 2024). Explainable AI helps classify black box models and promotes stronger cooperation between people and machines in learning. Not all students will generate the same type or amount of data in data, and there is a risk that data-controlled systems will alienate those involved in different levels of digital platforms. To counter this, researchers and practitioners work to design analyses that consider various learning styles, cultural contexts, and access questions. It includes the development of multilingual NLP tools, culturally responsive kick dashboards, and participatory design approaches, and it is included in the design of systems used by students and educators. Intelligent tutorial systems and teacher support tools provide real-time suggestions for educational strategies, assess tasks, and help students identify areas where students need additional help. Automating everyday tasks encourages AI educators to focus on high-quality interactions such as mentoring, collaboration, and creative problem-solving. Additionally, professional learning platforms use AI to personalize teacher training and recommend resources based on educational style, discipline, and student feedback (Vashishth et al., 2024). This field has grown from simple persecution and reporting of highly developed real-time adaptation systems that can meet the complex needs of different learners (Giri, 2025). However, this promise must be made through ethical practices and a commitment to continuing reflection in response to learners to ensure that AI is a force for education. The future of AI-based learning analytics lies not only in technological advancements but also in the ability of educators, designers, and political decision-makers to use their potential in an integrated, human, and transformative way (Tariq, 2025).

PERSONALIZING LEARNING WITH AI ANALYTICS

Adaptive learning models represent innovative changes in how educational content is delivered, moving from traditional unit approaches to more personalized student methods. These models are based on artificial intelligence, data analysis, and cognitive science. They are designed to evaluate individual learners and meet the needs of learners continuously (Alsaedi, 2024). The adaptation system analyzes a variety of inputs, including previous knowledge, learning pace, behavioral patterns, and commitment metrics. It dynamically adapts the sequence and difficulty and presents educational content. This real-time adjustment ensures that every student receives a learning experience tailored to their strengths and weaknesses. As students progress, the system refines their understanding of skills and adapts recommendations accordingly. This constant feedback loop helps students stay in the zone of proximal development, promote sustained commitment, reduce frustration, and accelerate the championship. One of the most important benefits is the ability to support differentiated lessons without putting any additional burden on educators. In classrooms with far more skilled teachers, adaptive techniques ensure that advanced learners are properly challenged. However, they need people who need time for support or alternative explanations. This inclusivity promotes a fairer learning environment where all students can thrive (Alsaedi, 2024). Furthermore, adaptive learning systems often contain elements of gamification and interactivity that improve motivation and make learning more comfortable. Students will frequently stay with challenging material if they believe the content is relevant and properly equipped. These systems encourage learners to make better progress by including students on personalized learning trips. Dashboards and performance summaries can help students provide insight into their learning behavior, determine goals, monitor their growth, and think about the best strategies. Once students notice learners, they are ready to adapt and succeed in various academic and professional environments. Predictive analytics involves using statistical methods and algorithms for machine learning to analyze historical and actual data to predict future outcomes. In education, this often means identifying patterns that indicate students are having difficulty taking the course, tracking the same age, or separating them from the learning process.

Consultants and instructors receive warnings and skills that actively achieve and provide resources such as mentoring, advice, and academic coaching. This personalized attention can cause a significant difference in the student's trajectory and translate potential disabilities into graduates. Institutions can identify students with advanced courses, research participation, and potential management options by analyzing performance data. This asset-based approach ensures that data is used to reduce risk and maximize its potential. For thoughtful integration, predictive analytics is the basis for a rapid and supportive education system of responses. A surprising example is Carnegie Learning, an adaptive mathematics platform that uses cognitive science and artificial intelligence to personalize lessons (Rahate et al., 2025). The system continuously analyzes student responses and provides tailor-made feedback and tips to guide learners through mathematical concepts. Research shows that students using Carnegie Learning benefit more from mathematics knowledge than traditional classrooms, especially for combat learners. The platform's ability to adapt in real-time ensures that students receive the right assignments and support every step of their learning journey. Dreambox uses real-time data analytics to modify content delivery based on student interactions and to provide instant feedback and adaptive adjustment strategies to set requirements for each learner. Research shows that students who only spend a few hours a week at Dreambox have significantly improved their maths. The distinction between Dreamboxes is focused on student agencies, encouraging learners to not only remember procedures but also explore several solutions and develop conceptual understandings. Weston uses algorithms for machine learning to analyze billions of data points from student interactions, providing personalized paths through content that adapts to proficiency and learning behavior (Marin & Jiménez, 2024). Smart Sparrow was used in forming universities to create adaptive simulations and learning experiences on topics ranging from medicine to engineering (Eltahir & Babiker, 2024). These tools allow educators to develop more interactive and effective development and learning experiences based on student answers.

Carnegie Mellon University's Open Learning Initiative (OLI) offers another compelling example. OLI offers open prices with embedded assessment and feedback mechanisms adapted to learner entry. The platform collects data on all interactions to improve the learning experiences of future users and inform trainers about areas students must focus on. This iterative loop and course improvement for data collection demonstrates the potential to personalize learning and improve educational design over time. These platforms use data analysis to recommend courses, suggest additional material, and predict the final rate of courses (Babu et al., 2025).

REAL-TIME STUDENT ENGAGEMENT MONITORING

AI manipulation tools have significantly changed how educators pursue student commitment in online and hybrid learning environments. Commitment, a multifaceted construct that includes behavior, emotion, and cognitive dimensions, is an essential predictor of student success and general satisfaction. Teachers often relied on body language, participation, and eye contact in traditional classrooms to measure commitment. Given the transition to digital and blended learning environments, this information is less noticeable, and a more sophisticated approach to data control is required. The AI Tool now fills this gap by analyzing learners' digital footprints and interactions to gain insight into student commitments. These tools collect data from various sources, including registration frequency, task time, click patterns, quiz tests, forum participation, and video clock metrics. Through this data integration, AI systems can recognize patterns of engagement and resolution and provide real-time analytics that inform both students and trainers. These platforms act as content repositories and as active monitoring systems that continually track how students interact with the material. The algorithm can analyze whether a student is giving a specific lecture, submitting an order at a good time, or participating in a discussion forum if a deviation from the typical behavior is determined, such as B. A sudden drop in activity or skipping material. The system can create warnings to request intervention. This aggressive approach allows educators to solve potential problems before improving bonds and student outcomes (Tariq, 2025).

Additionally, AI tools often provide commitment dashboards that visualize data intuitively. Educators can view individual commitment scores at the individual or cohort level, filter by demographic variables, and compare them across periods. These findings support decision-based data by making timely educational adjustments, such as changing educational materials, initiating public relations, and redesigning reviews to coordinate learner needs better. Emotional AI is also known as emotional computing and involves using technology for machine learning and natural language processing to recognize, interpret, and respond to human emotions. In the educational context, these tools are increasingly being used to monitor the presence of students' well-being and to recognize emotional states that affect learning. For example, if students participate in online discussions, send essays, or communicate via chat, the algorithm can assess the emotional tone of the language for sentiment analysis. These systems analyze keywords, syntax, punctuation, and contextual texts to determine whether students express trust, confusion, frustration, or enthusiasm (Wadhwa et al., 2024). Over time, these emotional data can be aggregated to create an appropriate profile for all learners, and educators can identify who they have to compete with emotionally, even if their academic achievements are stable. These tools use facial recognition and microexpression analysis to detect emotional states during virtual learning meetings (Ranjan, 2025). For example, suppose a student is showing signs of boredom or frustration. In that case, the system can mark this pattern and propose changes to its educational strategy, for example, using digital content. The technology raises important ethical and data protection considerations and promises to create a more sensitive and responsive learning environment. Emotional AI can be used responsibly and transparently to support mental health initiatives and promote student resilience and a sense of belonging.

Schools and universities can integrate these findings into a broader student support service and work with consultants, consultants, and wellness teams to ensure holistic care. These AI-powered agents simulate human conversations and provide learners with immediate responses to questions, directions with course material, and emotional support. Chatbots effectively answer frequently asked questions, such as those related to course logistics, deadlines, and technical issues. By automating these routine interactions, chatbots reduce educator workloads and ensure students receive prompt support regardless of time zone or facility opening hours. Advanced conversational AI systems driven by natural language and deep learning processing can participate in context-conscious multi-turn dialogue that mimics human tutors. These systems can evaluate students' understanding based on student responses and adapt the conversation accordingly to provide explanations, examples, or information to promote learning.

Integrating chatbots on educational platforms shows many benefits. For example, students are often more comfortable asking questions to unrated AI agents than human trainers, especially if they fear that the questions may be trivial. It will increase participation and help bridge the gaps among students who are shy, frightened, or unfamiliar with academic discourse. Chatbots can also be programmed with sensitive responses that encourage, celebrate milestones, or acknowledge efforts. Such interactions contribute to an engaging and emotionally supported learning experience (Lakshmi et al., 2024). Some educational institutions are developing chatbots that provide mental health and cognitive behavioral therapy techniques, mindfulness exercises, and support for crisis resources. AI moderators can inspire students to use their ideas in the discussion forum, ask follow-up questions, and combine different topics. This scaffolding helps maintain wise discourse and deepen critical thinking. Additionally, the AI-controlled recommendation engine can propose relevant reading, video, or learning activities based on the content of the conversation, allowing you to personalize your learning trips in real-time. Conversation AI positions these skills as helpers, co-learners, and moderators in digital classrooms.

There are also examples of large-scale implementations of conversational AI that demonstrate its effectiveness. An example of this is a Georgia State University chatbot. It was initially used to reduce summer melts. Pounce helped significantly reduce no-show rates and student enrollment improvements by submitting timely reminders and answering questions via text. Based on this success, the university expanded its use of chatbots to support academic advice, financial aid, and wellness initiatives. The results show improved student satisfaction and reduced response times, which enhances the value of conversation AI as a scalable support tool. Chatbots allow learners to speak in a variety of scenarios and allow them to adapt their difficulty based on the learner's performance. These interactions not only strengthen language skills but also build trust and autonomy. Conversation-AI follows learners' progress, adapts future exercises to correct gaps, and creates a positive practice and feedback cycle. Issues like data protection, algorithm transparency, and approval are of central importance for the responsible use of AI. Institutions should determine clear guidelines and include students, educators, and parents in developing and evaluating these systems.

Teachers need not only to use A-generating knowledge but also to equip themselves in educational ways. It includes understanding the limitations of AI tools, maintaining a time when human intervention is needed, and a learning focus. Professional Development Programs can introduce best practice educators regarding data capabilities, ethical considerations, and educational design for AI improvement (Bhardwaj & Sharma, 2025). By strengthening educators, institutions can ensure that technology serves as a more effective means of enhancing rather than as an alternative. Estimates of development, such as multimodal learning analyses that integrate text, audio, video, and biometric data, provide even broader insights into student behavior and commitment. Augmented reality and virtual reality environments improved by AI provide an immersive experience that grasps subtle interactions.

These technologies provide the possibility to be personalized and efficient, and create sensitive and integrated learning environments. Educators can build systems that recognize and respond to the overall spectrum of student needs using the analytical creativity and care of AIS analytics (Reethika & Priya, 2024). The path forward requires thoughtful design, ethical responsibility, and commitment to equity, but rewards are responsive. Through sustained collaboration between educators, technicians, and learners, AI helps us to adapt to all learners, support the whole person, and recognize our vision of education that will promote success in an ever-changing world.

AI IN ASSESSMENTS AND PERFORMANCE EVALUATION

The automated sorting system was a transformative innovation in the educational environment, streamlining the assessment process and providing the possibility of giving students immediate feedback. The fundamental promise of automated assessment lies in its ability to reduce educator workloads, eliminate human bias, and perform consistent, timely reviews. The earliest systems were limited to strict formats, such as the Scantron test. However, today's AI-driven evaluation tools are much more refined. You can analyze sentence structure, grammar, coherence, arguments, and content accuracy to evaluate highly complex open answers. By training extensive data records with human-designed orders, these models learn to mimic expert evaluators and generate scores that closely correspond to human judgments. Some studies have shown that well-trained algorithms can match or surpass people in a particular context, mainly when evaluation criteria are clearly defined and consistent (Hanson et al., 2024). For example, it has been demonstrated that AI achieves assessment results strongly correlated with human assessment experts in a standardized testing environment. These systems are particularly effective when identifying surface-level spelling, grammar, and syntax errors. They can recognize patterns of logical flow and coherence. However, they are limited in assessing more subjective dimensions such as creativity, nuance, and originality. Essays using unconventional argumentative structures or poetic languages can be unfairly punished as they differ from the patterns available in training data (Tariq, 2025).

Additionally, there is a risk of algorithm distortion if the training data contains distortions related to language use, dialect, or cultural context. In such systems, AI performs initial evaluations and flags to check whether the confidence value is low or an anomaly is recognized. This approach for humans in a loop compares efficiency with accuracy. It ensures that complex or ambiguous answers are taken care of. Some platforms also use ensemble modeling that combines several algorithms to improve robustness and reduce errors. Continuous verification of human benchmarks is essential to maintain the integrity of these systems. While technology is developing, assessment decisions require transparency and explanation. Educators and students benefit equally from understanding why specific points have been assigned, promoting trust in the system, and improving learning outcomes. Feedback is the foundation of adequate education and guides learners to recognize mistakes, narrow their understanding, and develop skills. Traditional feedback methods are valuable but are often limited by time constraints and inconsistencies. An AI-controlled feedback system addresses these limitations by providing instant, personalized answers to student work (Ellikkal & Rajamohan, 2024). These systems can analyze text submissions, code excerpts, mathematical solutions, or spoken language to identify errors and suggest improvements. It is vital to help formative feedback learn both in learning the final results and in the summer feedback. For example, writing assistants use NLP to recognize grammar, consistency, argument, and evidence issues. We recommend highlighting unsupported claims and recommending improvements to sound and style.

In contrast to traditional grammar examiners, modern AI tools allow you to understand the context and provide more meaningful instructions. In the STEM field, intelligent tutoring systems guide students through problem-solving, providing step-by-step information and identifying conceptual misconceptions. AI can analyze code in programming education to recognize errors, inefficiencies, and best practice compliance. These tools don't just explain errors and promote deeper understanding. One of the most powerful aspects of AI-supported feedback is its adaptability. Students' learning profiles are updated as they interact with the system, allowing for more coordinated feedback. Furthermore, these systems promote learner autonomy by promoting self-correction and iterative improvement. Students can modify their work based on feedback, quickly recognize the impact of the changes, and increase their learning process. This immediacy and responsiveness are rarely realized, especially for feedback in large and self-applied online courses (Runhaar, 2024). With the support of a continuous feedback loop, AI systems can help shift assessments from a one-off judgment to a continuous learning experience. However, to improve fairness, it is important to ensure that the system is fair and integrated. It includes careful design, various training data, and regular audits of distortions.

Furthermore, feedback must be culturally sensitive and educationally healthy. Educators play an essential role in contextualizing and supplementing A-generated feedback, ensuring they are the curriculum and the needs of the students. The most effective implementation of AI feedback occurs in a blended learning environment where technology replaces human lessons. Learning analysis involves collecting, analyzing, and interpreting data about learners. It includes the context for understanding and optimizing learning outcomes. In the field of assessment, analysis provides a data-rich foundation for assessing student performance and teaching effectiveness. Formative reviews during the learning process benefit greatly from actual time analysis. Teachers can continuously monitor student progress and recognize who will acquire content and who must fight. AI tools can analyze quiz answers, assignment patterns, and commitment metrics to record learning gaps and recommend targeted interventions.

For example, if the analysis reveals that most students consistently miss questions related to a particular concept in the class, the instructor could revisit this topic or provide additional material. At the individual level, learning analyses can generate personalized learning paths and recommend exercises and resources based on each student's performance and preferences. These data-controlled findings not only help educators respond more effectively but also help students to have control over their learning. Dashboards provide a visual representation of progress for learners and help them identify strengths and areas of improvement. This transparency promotes metacognition, self-regulation, and targeting. It is essential for lifelong learning. These reviews are often useful for high-level purposes such as classification, certification, and program evaluation. For example, analysis can show that students who are busy with a particular resource will perform better in the final exam and demonstrate the effectiveness of these materials. Conversely, various performance differences related to demographic variables can be identified, leading to assessment design and teaching practice reviews. This systematic knowledge supports continuous improvement at the institutional level and guides curriculum development, undergraduate training, and political decisions. Adaptation reviews show questions with different difficulty levels related to learners' previous answers, representing a more accurate measure of competence. These reviews appeal more to students and are not as frustrating as they avoid a uniform approach to traditional exams.

Furthermore, adaptive assessments are more efficient and require fewer factors to achieve reliable results. The data generated by these reviews can be used to enter detailed learning profiles that will affect future lessons and personalized feedback. Data protection and ethical use of student information are essential concerns (Basri, 2024). The institution must ensure that student data is transparently covered, securely stored, and used only for educational purposes. Students need to have an agency for their data and understand how it is used to influence their learning experience. It also requires interoperability and standardization, enabling various platforms and tools to communicate and share data effectively. Without this integration, maximizing the possibilities of learning analytics is impossible. Numbers alone do not convey the entire history of a student's learning trip. Educators must contextualize their analysis with qualitative insights, conversations, and reflections to form a holistic understanding. The most effective use of AI in assessment occurs when combining technology with human judgment. Improve others' skills. Teachers should wisely interpret the analysis and trigger data that uses the findings to improve the lesson.

Professional development programs should focus on building these skills and promoting critical thinking about ethical awareness and technical use. Furthermore, the development of AI tools requires that educators direct educators (Silva et al., 2024). Traditional models of regular testing can replace reviews by incorporating reviews that occur seamlessly during learning activities. AI is central to this transformation, enabling authentic, integrated, and supportive reviews for deep learning. Educators can use automated classification, intelligent feedback, and learning analytics to create an assessment ecosystem that measures learning and promotes and maintains it. They help students control their educational trips more clearly, with self-confidence and success.

ETHICAL AND PRIVACY CONSIDERATIONS

As artificial intelligence is increasingly embedded in the structure of education systems, the promise of personalized learning, predictive knowledge, and operational efficiency is mitigated by increasing concerns about data protection, algorithm distortions, and ethical governance. The huge data records in which AI models operate in education are both a resource and a responsibility, raising important questions about recording, storing, processing, and using personal information. In this data-controlled paradigm, all student interactions with the digital platform become successful data points regardless of quiz results, contributions to the discussion, biometric responses, or even keyboard connections (Bhatia et al., 2024). This data allows AI systems to provide real-time feedback, predict student performance, and adapt instructions to individual needs while exposing learners to unprecedented surveillance, profiling, and misuse of potential information. It has a profound impact on student autonomy, trust, and the institutional integrity of education itself. Educational institutions, ED-Tech companies, and AI developers can access increasingly detailed data records, often collected by learning management systems, online reviews, and tools from third-party providers (bin Salem, 2024). In contrast to traditional educational documents, the scope and scope of this data collection includes behavioral and emotional information ranging from browser history to emotional conditions derived from commitment patterns and facial recognition, and mood analysis. The integration of biometric and psychometric data adds another layer of sensitivity. In many cases, students and their families may not be aware of the complete scope of the data collected (Khan, 2024). Consulting mechanisms are often opaque and are a long-standing condition of a service mood that is difficult to interpret, especially for younger users and those with limited digital literacy. Without strict guidelines for data management, there is a risk that educational data may be sold, shared, or leaked, especially if the school is working with private providers that may have their own interests. The potential consequences of data injuries are particularly severe in education. Because they can reveal their identity, academic narrative, psychological profiles, and family circumstances of minors. These risks are enhanced in hybrid and online learning environments where several platforms are used simultaneously (Saleem et al., 2025). Each has its own data protocols and security measures. Data management fragmentation creates gaps and duplication under protection, making it difficult for agencies to ensure compliance with data protection regulations. Responsibility with laws such as the General Data Protection Ordinance (GDPR), the US Family Formation Rights and Data Protection Act (FERPA), and other local emerging laws. For example, a learning analytics platform hosted in a country but used by students for another student navigates with conflicting legal standards under conditions that make personal data, how long it can be stored, and whether it must be anonymized or deleted. The lack of international standards for educational data protection means that users can enjoy robust rights and protection measures in some jurisdictions, while others are susceptible to exploitation.

Educational institutions must develop transparent data governance frameworks that will clarify which data will be collected, why, how, and who will be accessing it, and how long it will be used. These frameworks should include clear databases, fire extinguishing guidelines, robust encryption and access control, and detailed test paths. Students and parents must be correct, correct, correct, or deleted with meaningful consent mechanisms, including opt-out options, data access requirements, and the ability to correct inaccurate information. Data protection in the design of education technology itself must be embedded in a principle known as design privacy. Developers and providers are not built into the system architecture. However, they are integrated into the system architecture, and data protection must be ensured. AI systems trained with historical or real-time educational data can replicate or enhance existing inequality. These biases manifest differently than the recommendation engine, reinforcing stereotypes into predictive models and disproportionately marking specific student groups as "endangered." Such a result is not just technical errors. They have a concrete impact on academic airways, self-esteem, and access to opportunities. For example, suppose AI systems consistently predict poor performance for students from a particular demographic background. In that case, educators can unconsciously lower expectations or provide enrichment options that lead to self-fulfilling predictions. If historical data reflects unequal access to resources, systematic discrimination, or underestimation of a particular group, models trained with such data could inherit and spread these inequalities. Education allows data records to be replaced by socioeconomic status, geographical location, language diversity, and cultural norms. Furthermore, data labeling processes that often lead to subjective human judgments or are based on bias may introduce additional layers. For example, annotators can unconsciously assess students' commitments or efforts regarding their name, dialect, or appearance and insert these biases into the model's learning process. Functional selection, weighting, and objective functions affect everyone and how the model interprets the data and prioritizes the results. Suppose the algorithm is optimized for accuracy alone without considering fairness or inclusiveness. In that case, it can perform simultaneously below the average of minority or marginalized groups. Furthermore, many AI systems in education act as black boxes and provide little transparency about how decisions are made. This lack of explanation makes recognizing, understanding, or modifying civic behavior difficult and reduces trust among educators, students, and parents.

Reducing these biases requires a comprehensive strategy that combines technical, institutional, and ethical interventions. On the technical side, fairness-conscious machine learning techniques can be used to recognize and correct distortions during model development. It includes methods for recompensating the dataset, introducing fairness limits to optimization functions, and assessing models using metrics that consider demographic parity, equality of opportunities, or other fairness criteria. Model interpretability tools such as Shap (Shapley Additive Description) and Lime (Local Interpretable Model Aggregation Declaration) help stakeholders understand how predictions are made and make it easier to address potential sources (Shete et al., 2024). It includes establishing a cross-functional ethics committee to check AI systems before use, implement normal biases, and understand concerns and experiences to combat affected communities. Transparency must be a principle of guidance.

Students and educators need to know when AI is used and what data it relies on. Including design practices such as participatory development, culturally responsive interfaces, and language localization can help ensure that AI tools are useful for a wide range of population groups (Rekha et al., 2024). These ethical guidelines must exceed abstract values to provide implementable standards that affect decision-making processes at every stage of the AI lifecycle (Shoaib et al., 2024). The most important ethical columns include transparency, accountability, equity, privacy, and human-centered design. Transparency includes openness to data collection practices, algorithmic logic, system capabilities, and limitations. It creates trust and allows stakeholders to make sound decisions about participation in the AI-mediated learning environment. If the AI system recommends intervention, predicts future student performance, and denies access to the program, someone must be responsible for this decision (Babu et al., 2025). Accountability requires those who monitor model development, monitor services after use, and define how complaints are reported and dealt with. It often requires the role of new institutions such as data protection officers, AI ethics authorities, or algorithm examiners. Even educators must be trained to use AI tools, critically evaluate them, and intervene when necessary. It means that integrated access to AI's improved tools prioritizes and ensures that benefits are distributed fairly and positively. Special attention should be paid to marginalized communities, students with disabilities, and students representing educational settings.

Rather than deepening digital subdivisions, AI helps close them through thoughtful, context-sensitive missions. Educational AI systems must maintain information rights from individuals' ability to control personal data. Apart from legal compliance, this includes a moral commitment to protecting student dignity and autonomy. Data protection stock technologies such as FED, differential privacy, and homomorphic encryption help reduce risk by minimizing data load and enabling analysis without direct data exchange. AI aims to support, standardize, or reduce learning to metrics. It means designing systems that address educational values, respect learner institutions, and promote critical thinking, creativity, and collaboration. Educators must be co-creators of AI tools rather than passive users, and students must be allowed to understand and shape the systems that affect learning. While technology is developing, we need to understand our framework conditions and the government. It includes promoting interdisciplinary dialogue between educators, technicians, ethicists, political decision-makers, and students. It also includes a global network structure to exchange best practices, harmonize standards, and tackle appropriate approaches for educational innovation (Herath et al., 2024). We need to ensure that the world where AI is increasingly being communicated, how we learn, teach, and evaluate, and that this is how we maintain the fundamental values of education: empowerment, justice, and human bloom.

CASE STUDIES AND BEST PRACTICES

One of the most effective applications of AI involves learning analytics, the area that data science uses to monitor, evaluate, and optimize learning processes. In various countries and contexts, AI-driven learning analytics tools demonstrate considerable potential to improve educational outcomes and resource allocation, and support students through personalized interventions. These global examples illustrate the promise and complexity of AI integration into education systems, providing valuable insight into regional assumptions, implementation, and scaling assumptions. This tool uses analytics to predict student data and identify those at risk of failure or falling. With the help of algorithms for machine learning, OU analysis examines historical performance, commitment to online material, and demographic data to generate risk indicators. Interactive dashboards present these indicators to enable timely interventions. In particular, this tool is not separate but is part of a greater institutional involvement for evidence-based education.

By organizing predictive knowledge with academic support, the Open University has improved retention rates and demonstrated the power of analytical integration into its educational workflow. Implementing the Adaus Adaptive Learning platform, developed by Knowton and Pearson, has altered large-scale basic courses on topics such as mathematics and biology. These platforms use AI to dynamically adapt content difficulty and sequences based on individual student performance. ASU reports significant student performance and final rates benefits, particularly among underrepresented non-traditional learners. Furthermore, the University Learning Transformation Office is strongly investing in faculty development so that instructors can effectively interpret analytical data and act on analytical data. As distance and hybrid learning became the norm, Korean educators used AI to monitor the number of visitors, students' commitment, and emotional well-being through digital platforms. At the same time, the facial recognition algorithm evaluates emotional states in video classes. These data points are synthesized to generate dashboards for teachers and highlight students who may need academic or psychological support. Such systems raise important ethical issues, but the Korean model demonstrates how AI can support comprehensive education surveillance at scale (Xu, 2024). The broad use of surveillance analyses in Chinese classrooms, including these implementations, reflects a unique educational culture where strict, data-controlled supervision is prioritized. Instead of large-scale surveillance or performance-based equipment, Finnish schools focus on using AI to support teacher formative assessments and decisions. One example is using an AI-controlled feedback system that analyzes student writing on grammar, consistency, and discussion. Teachers use this finding to adapt their lessons and provide targeted support. This approach addresses Finland's focus on teacher well-being, equity, and autonomy, demonstrating that AI can be integrated into education systems without affecting educational core values. Top-down policy directions and strong public investment have made using AI tools easier in centralized systems like China and South Korea. These systems often have access to uniform data records and can specify specific technologies across schools. A centralized approach allows for efficiency and standardization but also limits local innovation and can raise concerns about monitoring and control.

By contrast, decentralized systems such as those in the United States and Canada rely more on institutional autonomy and public-private partnerships (Henry & Duke, 2024). AI adoption tends to be more varied, with different universities and school districts experimenting with their tools and vendors. It creates opportunities for innovation and responsiveness to local needs. However, it can also result in fragmentation and inequality, as access to advanced AI tools may depend on institutional wealth and technical capacity. In countries like Finland and the Netherlands, where education is both decentralized and highly regulated, AI adoption is typically driven by pedagogical research and guided by strong ethical frameworks. These systems prioritize transparency, teacher agency, and student rights, often resulting in slower but more thoughtful integration of AI technologies. However, innovative solutions have emerged. For instance, in Kenya, Eneza Education offers an AI-powered mobile learning platform that delivers quizzes and study materials via SMS, making it accessible to students without smartphones or internet access. The platform uses simple machine learning models to adapt content based on student responses, providing a basic personalization form. In India, the government's DIKSHA platform incorporates AI to analyze engagement and learning patterns across millions of students, helping educators identify learning gaps and tailor content accordingly. These cases show that AI can be leveraged creatively to enhance learning outcomes even in resource-constrained settings.

Lessons learned from global implementations highlight the potential and pitfalls of AI-driven learning analytics. One key lesson is aligning AI tools with pedagogical goals and educational values. Systems prioritizing student development and teacher support, rather than mere performance metrics, tend to yield more sustainable and equitable outcomes. For example, the Open University's approach demonstrates how predictive analytics can enhance human judgment rather than replace it. Another important lesson is that technical accuracy alone is not sufficient. Even the most sophisticated AI models can produce misleading or harmful outcomes if trained on biased or incomplete data. Transparent development processes, continuous validation, and stakeholder engagement are essential to ensure that AI tools reflect diverse student experiences and educational contexts. In countries like Canada, where provincial education departments have begun exploring AI, there is a growing emphasis on developing "explainable AI" systems that educators can scrutinize and adapt. It reinforces the need for AI literacy among teachers, administrators, and students (Banik and Gullapelly, 2025).

Ethical governance is another crucial factor. The contrast between surveillance-heavy models and rights-based approaches underscores the need for robust policy frameworks that protect student privacy, promote inclusivity, and ensure accountability. Finland's cautious, teacher-centered strategy offers a compelling example of integrating AI without compromising ethical standards. In jurisdictions lacking such safeguards, AI adoption risks exacerbating existing inequalities and eroding trust in educational institutions. Finally, successful AI integration requires a culture of collaboration across disciplines and sectors. Technologists, educators, researchers, and policymakers must work together to design, implement, and evaluate AI tools. Initiatives like Europe's Horizon 2020 research program and UNESCO's efforts to develop global AI ethics guidelines for education illustrate the value of international cooperation. Cross-border collaboration can accelerate innovation, harmonize standards, and build a shared vision of technologically advanced and deeply human-centered education. The global landscape of AI-powered learning analytics offers a rich tapestry of practices, challenges, and innovations. While some countries have raced ahead with large-scale deployments, others have adopted a more measured and ethical approach. The most successful implementations share a commitment to aligning technology with pedagogy, ensuring transparency and accountability, and promoting equity and inclusion. As AI evolves, its role in education will only grow more prominent. By learning from global examples and embracing a values-driven approach, educational systems can harness AI to improve performance and enrich the purpose of learning in a digital age.

FUTURE RESEARCH DIRECTIONS

Artificial intelligence has proven to be a changeable force in modern education, particularly in learning and analysis. It offers unprecedented opportunities to understand, support, and optimize your learning experience. Based primarily on descriptive statistics and retrospective analyses, traditional learning analyses have been replaced by advanced AI technologies with forecasting, personalization, and even normative interventions. This evolution is a fundamental change in static data reporting in the direction of dynamic systems that adapt to learner needs and actively lead educational decisions. It includes digital interaction protocols, reviews, biometric data, and socially emotional input. By integrating these diverse data flows, AI systems can create a wide range of learning profiles that develop over time. These profiles help identify areas with academic strength and debilitating and also help record engagement, motivational drivers, learning styles, and behavioral patterns (Basri, 2024).

AI models can recognize early warning signs of sedimentary or academic performance risk by determining subtle deviations in participation or performance and allowing timely interventions to become effective for individuals. For example, intelligent tutorial systems and adaptive learning platforms adapt educational content based on immediate answers to ensure students are not overwhelmed or restricted by redundancy. These systems often include formative assessments in the learning process, allowing AIs to update their learners' understanding of their current state and adjust their learning paths accordingly. Continuous feedback from AI tools promotes a more aggressive and reflexive approach to learning (Bhatia et al., 2024). It encourages students to engage in metacognition and self-regulation. Additionally, dashboard educators available in AI provide overall insight into class dynamics, making differentiated lessons easier and more effective classroom management. AI systems can now recognize emotional conditions through facial recognition, language analysis, and textual mood analysis. It allows for a more comprehensive understanding of the presence of learners' wells and their impact on academic achievement. For example, suppose a student has signs of frustration or fear during an online meeting. In that case, the system can mark this with the teacher or adapt their educational strategy to reduce cognitive stress. By considering emotional and psychological factors and cognitive indicators, AI contributes to a more human learning analytics model that aligns with overall educational goals. A key obstacle is an inequality in digital infrastructure and technical knowledge between institutions, regions, and countries. Schools and universities with resources to use sophisticated AI systems must address basic connectivity and access to digital tools. This digital gap limits the scope of AI innovation and risks worsening education inequality if solutions are not interpreted for scalability and inclusiveness.

Furthermore, implementing AI systems requires significant hardware, software, data integration, and cybersecurity investments. AI systems rely on a large amount of clean, well-marked representative data to function accurately (bin Salem, 2024). However, in many educational environments, data is fragmented across multiple platforms, stored in an incompatible format, or inconsistently required for robust analysis. Furthermore, the context-related specificity of educational data shaped by curriculum, language, cultural norms, and pedagogical philosophy makes it challenging to apply AI models developed in the environment without significant retraining and adaptation. Efforts to standardize educational data models, such as the IMS Global Learning Consortium, are ongoing but face recruitment and enforcement challenges. Another challenge in scaling AI analytics is the ethical and legal landscape of data protection and algorithmic transparency. Regional regulations vary on student data, and many countries have no broad guidelines for AI in education. Using personal and sensitive information about training AI models raises essential questions about consent, databases, and the right to forget. Educational institutions should navigate these concerns while ensuring that AI systems are safe, fair, and accountable. It also increases the testing of impermeable AI models known as "black box" systems. It can cover reasons for predictions and recommendations. Without explanation, educators and stakeholders can hardly trust or accept AI tools, especially when they influence decisions with high stakes regarding student progress or resource allocation. Education is not merely a process of information transfer but a deep human interaction that includes value, relationships, and context-related judgments. Therefore, AI systems should be designed to complement and preserve ethical aspects rather than replace human educators (Ellikkal and Rajamohan, 2024).

In a context where teacher-student relationships are highly valued or educational autonomy is prioritized, one may be reluctant to the mechanization of education. Furthermore, different education systems differ in the openness of data-controlled decisions by prioritizing qualitative knowledge and other standardized metrics. Successful scaling of AI-powered analyses must consider these cultural variables and engage educators as active partners in the design and implementation process. Instead of being sold in intelligent systems, teachers are relocated as orchestras in AI-enabled learning environments. Your responsibility is expanded to interpret the analytical, contextualize AI-generated insights, and design pedagogically grounded and emotionally responsive interventions. For example, a teacher can use the AI dashboard to identify students retreating. However, it is his professional judgment to determine the steps to accommodate, whether it is a peer tutor, parental commitment, or a change in education strategy. Teachers also play an essential role in verifying AI results, ensuring that technical results match actual classroom dynamics. When AI is integrated into the educational process, teachers must understand how the algorithm works, which biases can be introduced, and how to communicate these issues to students. It requires targeted professional development programs beyond technical training, including critical reflection, joint examinations, and ethical considerations. Institutions need to support educators through continued mentoring, access to interdisciplinary resources, and opportunities to contribute to designing and evaluating AI tools (Eltahir and Babiker, 2024). By strengthening teachers as co-creators of AI-enhancing pedagogy, the education system can promote innovation and, at the same time, protect the integrity of lessons. Your feedback can impact iterative improvements in AI tools and highlight blind spots, unintended consequences, and opportunities for improvement. Teachers can also model students' responsible use of AI, cultivating digital citizenship and critical thinking for the next generation. In classrooms where AI exists, the role of educators extends to fostering discussions about the effectiveness of technology, as it affects identity, agency, and the learning process. These conversations are extremely important to promote a reflective and democratic education culture.

In many cases, AI solutions showcase top-down methods driven by technical or administrative orders rather than educational goals. A more integrated approach involves a collaborative design process that teaches teachers, students, developers, and researchers iterative cycles of testing, feedback, and refinement. It improves the relevance and ease of use of AI tools and enhances the sense of wealth and trust amongst stakeholders. However, knowledge of this possibility requires considerable scalability, justice, and ethical government challenges. The educators at the heart of this effort are not the recipients of passive technology but as key agents of change that bridge the gap between algorithmic intelligence and human understanding. Equipping teachers with tools, knowledge, and agents to deal with AI allows technology to help all learners of deeper education goals: growth, inclusion, and flourishing.

CONCLUSION

AI has significantly changed education by improving student commitment and academic achievement through personalized learning, real-time feedback, and predictive analytics. Intelligent systems adapt content to individual needs, identify endangered learners early on, and provide insights that educators can use to adapt interventions. These techniques promote active learning, self-regulation, and emotional support, contributing to a more effective and integrated educational experience. Institutions must invest in ethical and transparent systems that address educational goals and protect student privacy. Political decision-makers must develop a clear regulatory framework that ensures fairness, data protection, and access to AI technologies in various contexts. Interdisciplinary collaboration between educators, developers, and researchers is essential for creating AI solutions and improving learning for those who are replaced and cannot be replaced. While the field develops, continuous evaluation and responsible innovation are key to ensuring that AI supports meaningful educational transformation.

REFERENCES

Alhamadi, A. A., & Alhamadi, A. A. (2024). Analyzing The Effect Of Learning Management Systems Powered By Artificial Intelligence On Teaching And Learning In Higher Education. *Journal Of Data Acquisition And Processing*, *39*(1), 87–98.

Babu, C. S., Yuvansankar, M., & Tharuneshwaran, K. (2025). Personalized Learning and Student Engagement: Leveraging AI for Enhanced Learning Experiences in Distance Education. In *AI and Learning Analytics in Distance Learning* (pp. 73-102). IGI Global Scientific Publishing.

Banik, B. G., & Gullapelly, A. (2025). AI-Powered Gamification and Interactive Learning Tools for Enhancing Student Engagement. In *Driving Quality Education Through AI and Data Science* (pp. 283–310). IGI Global Scientific Publishing. DOI: 10.4018/979-8-3693-8292-9.ch013

Basri, W. S. (2024). Effectiveness of AI-powered Tutoring Systems in Enhancing Learning Outcomes. *Eurasian Journal of Educational Research (EJER)*, (110).

Bhardwaj, S., & Sharma, I. (2025). Exploring the Effects of AI-Powered Personalized Classroom Management Strategies. In *AI Applications and Strategies in Teacher Education* (pp. 21–42). IGI Global.

Bhatia, A., Bhatia, P., & Sood, D. (2024). Leveraging AI to transform online higher education: Focusing on personalized learning, assessment, and student engagement. *International Journal of Management and Humanities, 11*(1), 111-119.

Ellikkal, A., & Rajamohan, S. (2024). *AI-enabled personalized learning: empowering management students for improving engagement and academic performance*. Vilakshan-XIMB Journal of Management.

Eltahir, M. E., & Babiker, F. M. E. (2024). The influence of artificial intelligence tools on student performance in e-learning environments: Case study. *Electronic Journal of e-Learning*, *22*(9), 91–110. DOI: 10.34190/ejel.22.9.3639

Giri, A. (2025). Revolutionizing Student Evaluation: The Power of AI-Powered Assessment. In *Improving Student Assessment With Emerging AI Tools* (pp. 333-362). IGI Global Scientific Publishing.

Hanson, U. Y. O. K., Okonkwo, C. A., & Orakwe, C. U. (2024). Implementing AI-enhanced learning analytics to improve educational outcomes using psychological insights. *Journal of Educational Technology Innovations*.

Herath, D., Dinuwan, C., Ihalagedara, C., & Ambegoda, T. (2024). Enhancing Educational Outcomes Through AI Powered Learning Strategy Recommendation System. *International Journal of Advanced Computer Science and Applications, 15*(10). Advance online publication. DOI: 10.14569/IJACSA.2024.0151075

Khan, A. (2024). Exploring the Role of Machine Learning in Enhancing Student Engagement and Performance. *Journal of AI Integration in Education, 1*(2), 24–35.

Lakshmi, K., Khan, S., Kumar, P. A., Wagh, V., & Vasanti, G. (2024). AI-Powered Learning Analytics: Transforming Educational Outcomes Through ICT Integration. *Library of Progress-Library Science, Information Technology & Computer, 44*(3).

Marin, A. R., & Jiménez, O. R. (2024). Advancing education through AI-powered learning strategies and teaching techniques. In *ICERI2024 Proceedings* (pp. 10381-10388). IATED.

Mirdad, K., Daeli, O. P. M., Septiani, N., Ekawati, A., & Rusilowati, U. (2024). Optimizing student engagement and performance usingai-enabled educational tools. *Journal of Computer Science and Technology Application, 1*(1), 53–60.

Rahate, V., Mehta, A. K., Deshpande, S., Jawarkar, P., Disawal, V., & Sarge, P. (2025). Impact of AI-Driven Learning Management Systems on Institutional Efficiency and Student Engagement. *Metallurgical and Materials Engineering, 31*(2), 98–103. DOI: 10.63278/1341

Ranjan, R. (2025). AI-Powered Data Platforms Bridging the Gap Between Analytics and Action in Smart Education. In *Smart Education and Sustainable Learning Environments in Smart Cities* (pp. 107–122). IGI Global Scientific Publishing.

Reethika, A., & Priya, P. K. (2024). Using ai-powered predictive analytics tools to identify students falling behind or dropping out. In *Innovation in the University 4.0 System based on Smart Technologies* (pp. 101–115). Chapman and Hall/CRC. DOI: 10.1201/9781003425809-7

Rekha, K., Gopal, K., Satheeskumar, D., Anand, U. A., Doss, D. S. S., & Elayaperumal, S. (2024, May). Ai-Powered Personalized Learning System Design: Student Engagement and Performance Tracking System. In *2024 4th International Conference on Advance Computing and Innovative Technologies in Engineering (ICACITE)* (pp. 1125-1130). IEEE.

Runhaar, T. P. (2024). *Secure AI-Enhanced Student Engagement Analysis* (Bachelor's thesis, University of Twente).

Safdar, U., Shafi, S., & Junaid, M. (2025). The impact of AI-driven gamification on student engagement and academic performance in English language teaching. *Indus Journal of Social Sciences*, *3*(1), 646–656. DOI: 10.59075/ijss.v3i1.758

Saleem, S., Aziz, M. U., Iqbal, M. J., & Abbas, S. (2025). AI in Education: Personalized Learning Systems and Their Impact on Student Performance and Engagement. *The Critical Review of Social Sciences Studies*, *3*(1), 2445–2459. DOI: 10.59075/c35qa453

Shete, S. G., Koshti, P., & Pujari, V. I. (2024, April). The Impact of AI-Powered Personalization on Academic Performance in Students. In *2024 5th International Conference on Recent Trends in Computer Science and Technology (ICRTCST)* (pp. 295-301). IEEE. DOI: 10.1109/ICRTCST61793.2024.10578480

Shoaib, M., Sayed, N., Singh, J., Shafi, J., Khan, S., & Ali, F. (2024). AI student success predictor: Enhancing personalized learning in campus management systems. *Computers in Human Behavior, 158*, 108301. DOI: 10.1016/j.chb.2024.108301

Silva, G., Godwin, G., & Jayanagara, O. (2024). The Impact of AI on Personalized Learning and Educational Analytics. *International Transactions on Education Technology*, *3*(1), 36–46. DOI: 10.33050/itee.v3i1.669

Sumathy, V., & Navamani, G. (2024). AI-Driven Personalized Learning: Enhancing Student Success through Adaptive Technologies. *Library of Progress-Library Science, Information Technology & Computer, 44*(3).

Tariq, M. U. (2025). Harnessing the Power of GANs and Meta-Learning for Few-Shot Image Generation. In Simaiya, S., Lilhore, U., Sharma, Y., & Kumar, S. (Eds.), *Exploring Generative Adversarial Networks and Meta-Learning Synergies* (pp. 301–324). IGI Global Scientific Publishing. DOI: 10.4018/979-8-3693-7575-4.ch012

Tariq, M. U. (2025). Smart Forecasting With AI: Revolutionizing Energy Consumption and Storage. In Derbali, A. (Ed.), *Integrating Artificial Intelligence Into the Energy Sector* (pp. 165–184). IGI Global Scientific Publishing. DOI: 10.4018/979-8-3693-7112-1.ch009

Tariq, M. U. (2025). AI and Work-Life Balance: Transforming Employee Wellbeing in the Modern Workplace. In Ahmed, E., Babar, A., Samad, A., Ahmed, R., & Beydoun, G. (Eds.), *Strengthening Human Relations in Organizations With AI* (pp. 85–110). IGI Global Scientific Publishing. DOI: 10.4018/979-8-3693-6507-6.ch004

Tariq, M. U. (2025). AI-Enhanced Project-Based Learning: Revolutionizing Commerce Education With Generative AI. In ElSayary, A. (Ed.), *Prompt Engineering and Generative AI Applications for Teaching and Learning* (pp. 125–142). IGI Global Scientific Publishing. DOI: 10.4018/979-8-3693-7332-3.ch008

Tariq, M. U. (2025). Leveraging Artificial Intelligence to Enhance Diversity and Drive Business Innovation. In Margaretha van der Poll, H., Andrew van der Poll, J., & Ngwakwe, C. (Eds.), *Diversity, AI, and Sustainability for Financial Growth* (pp. 79–96). IGI Global Scientific Publishing. DOI: 10.4018/979-8-3693-6011-8.ch004

Vashishth, T. K., Sharma, V., Sharma, K. K., Kumar, B., Panwar, R., & Chaudhary, S. (2024). AI-driven learning analytics for personalized feedback and assessment in higher education. In *Using traditional design methods to enhance AI-driven decision making* (pp. 206–230). IGI Global Scientific Publishing. DOI: 10.4018/979-8-3693-0639-0.ch009

Wadhwa, R., Rabby, F., Bansal, R., & Hundekari, S. (2024). Drivers and Impact of Artificial Intelligence on Student Engagement. In *AI algorithms and ChatGPT for student engagement in online learning* (pp. 161–170). IGI Global. DOI: 10.4018/979-8-3693-4268-8.ch011

Xu, Z. (2024). AI in education: Enhancing learning experiences and student outcomes. *Applied and Computational Engineering*, *51*(1), 104–111. DOI: 10.54254/2755-2721/51/20241187

Yakhina, R., Grigorieva, K., Batrova, N., & Lukoyanova, M. (2024). AI-Powered Tools For Enhancing Engagement And Academic Performance Of Engineering Students. In *INTED2024 Proceedings* (pp. 2990-2996). IATED. DOI: 10.21125/inted.2024.0809

KEY TERMS AND DEFINITIONS

Adaptive Learning: AI-tailored instruction based on individual student requirements.

Learning Analytics: Data analysis to enhance learning processes efficiently.

Predictive Analytics: Predicting academic outcomes using historical data.

Chapter 6
AI-Based Real-Time Class Engagement Emotions Monitoring System

Praveen Kumar T.
MAHE School of Business, Manipal Academy of Higher Education, UAE

Justin Joy
https://orcid.org/0000-0002-6482-1057
Christ University, Bangalore, India

ABSTRACT

This chapter introduces an AI-based system for real-time monitoring of student engagement by analyzing emotional responses and attention levels during classroom sessions. Using a camera placed in front of students, the system applies computer vision algorithms to detect focus and distraction through eye movements and facial expressions. The core of the system is the Emo-Engage Analysis framework, which classifies engagement into three levels based on eye retention, duration of attentiveness, and indicators of positive emotional response. Drawing on recent research in emotional and attentional regulation, this method offers a fine-grained analysis of student engagement. Aggregated engagement data allow instructors to assess both individual and group dynamics throughout a lesson. These insights support the evaluation of teaching strategies and provide meaningful feedback on instructional impact, helping educators adapt their methods to foster more effective and emotionally supportive learning environments.

DOI: 10.4018/979-8-3373-2185-1.ch006

INTRODUCTION

In contemporary education, effective student engagement is pivotal to ensuring the success of teaching-learning methodologies, particularly in crowded classrooms where personal interactions are often limited. Traditional methods of assessing engagement, such as manual observations or surveys, can be time-consuming and fail to capture real-time fluctuations in student involvement. The need for an innovative, technology-driven approach to monitor student engagement has become increasingly evident. An efficient, real-time monitoring system can offer valuable insights into the dynamic nature of classroom interactions, enabling educators to adjust their teaching methods accordingly to maintain high levels of engagement.

Despite the growing recognition of the importance of student engagement, there exists a significant gap in the availability of automated systems capable of tracking these levels in real-time during regular class sessions. While existing systems are primarily designed for exam proctoring or assessment purposes, they do not address the broader need to monitor engagement during the teaching-learning process. This gap highlights the necessity for a novel solution that not only tracks the engagement of students but also classifies their emotional states to assess the effectiveness of various teaching strategies.

This paper proposes a new technology-based monitoring and alert system designed to capture and analyze student engagement levels in real-time. By incorporating emotion classification, the system can provide a comprehensive overview of how students are interacting with the material, thus offering actionable data to instructors. Through this innovation, we aim to bridge the gap in current educational technology, ensuring that both students and educators can benefit from a more responsive and efficient learning environment.

BACKGROUND AND FOCUS

In modern educational settings, particularly within large and crowded classrooms, gauging real-time student engagement has proven to be an ongoing challenge for instructors. The introduction of new teaching methodologies, while often essential to enhancing the learning experience, makes it even more difficult to assess whether students are genuinely engaged with the content. Engagement is a critical determinant of effective learning, as it directly influences student retention, comprehension, and overall academic performance. However, traditional methods of monitoring student attention, such as direct observation or feedback surveys, are limited in their effectiveness and can be too subjective, leaving instructors without immediate, actionable insights.

The need for a novel, technology-driven solution to monitor and measure student engagement in real-time has therefore become increasingly apparent. While some automated systems exist to monitor student behavior during exams, they primarily focus on proctoring, rather than assessing ongoing engagement in the classroom environment. Current technologies lack the capability to continuously evaluate and respond to shifts in student attention or emotional states during teaching sessions. This gap in educational technology is a significant barrier to maximizing student engagement and, by extension, the effectiveness of modern pedagogical strategies.

The research presented in this article responds to this need by introducing an AI-based class engagement and emotions monitoring system. This innovative system is designed to capture and assess student engagement levels in real-time, while also classifying their emotional responses. By leveraging facial and eye detection technologies alongside machine learning algorithms, the system provides a comprehensive tool for monitoring both attention and emotional engagement. It aims to provide immediate feedback to instructors, allowing them to adapt their teaching strategies to optimize student learning experiences. Thus, this system promises to revolutionize the way classroom engagement is measured, offering a data-driven approach to enhance the efficiency and effectiveness of the teaching-learning process.

LITERATURE REVIEW

The application of artificial intelligence (AI) in educational environments has significantly evolved, particularly in the context of monitoring students' emotions and engagement in real-time. AI-based emotion monitoring systems are designed to provide instructors with insights into students' affective states during lessons, thereby enabling adaptive and responsive teaching practices. As traditional methods of gauging classroom engagement—such as direct observation or self-report surveys—are subjective and limited in scale, the integration of computer vision, machine learning, and deep learning technologies offers a more objective and scalable solution (Siddiqui et al., 2023). Recent research has focused on developing classroom tools that integrate facial expression recognition, head-pose estimation, and eye-gaze tracking. Selvarajah et al. (2024) proposed an AI-powered tool that monitors students' emotional states (e.g., confusion, happiness), tracks gaze direction, and assesses head orientation during lectures. This comprehensive input enables teachers to identify disengaged students and adapt their instruction accordingly. The system generates detailed analytics, helping tailor content and interaction styles for more effective teaching. Complementing this, Prakash et al. (2024) introduced a real-time feedback system based on sentiment analysis of textual interactions such as forum posts and submissions. By combining emotional tone assessment with predictive models (e.g., SVM, decision trees), the system delivers adaptive feedback to students, thereby boosting satisfaction, engagement, and performance. This innovation showcases how textual emotion cues can supplement visual analysis in blended learning environments. Meanwhile, Banada (2025) implemented a facial recognition system for automating classroom attendance, which—though primarily designed for logistical tasks—demonstrates the potential for emotion detection through extended facial analysis. Using CNN-based FaceNet and cosine similarity, the system achieved 95.2% accuracy in real-time recognition. Its efficiency and scalability offer a foundation for integrated emotion-attendance platforms. Another trend has been toward EEG-based multimodal systems for emotion recognition. Sa'idah (2025) reviewed how EEG signals combined with behavioral cues (e.g., facial expressions, posture) offer more accurate emotional profiling. While promising, this approach faces challenges in fusion algorithms and feature representation. Nevertheless, the inclusion of neurophysiological data expands the horizon of classroom emotion analytics beyond camera-based systems. From a behavioral analysis standpoint, Lan and Tsao (2025) explored video-based parsing algorithms to quantify student engagement. Their study analyzed secondary school learners' in-class behavior and validated the technology's effectiveness in providing real-time teaching support. The integration of video analytics into teaching practice underscores a broader shift toward evidence-based pedagogy. The In-Class Student Emotion and Engagement Detection System (iSEEDS) represents another innovation, focusing on integrating real-time feedback loops into the instructional process (Sobin et al., 2023). The system employs convolutional neural networks to analyze students' facial expressions and eye movements during lectures. Beyond detection, it facilitates "responsive teaching," wherein instructors receive real-time indicators of student confusion or disengagement, allowing for immediate pedagogical adjustments. This bidirectional flow of information between system and teacher offers a dynamic model of classroom interactivity.

Emotion detection technologies have advanced substantially over the last few decades, but their application in educational settings remains limited and underexplored. Previous studies of emotion detection have not dealt with the integration of multimodal data from both facial expressions and physiological metrics in real-time classroom settings. Early work in emotion detection primarily focused on facial recognition and speech analysis to identify emotional states (Picard et al., 2020), but these systems struggled with real-time applications and contextual adaptation to dynamic classroom environments. For instance, facial recognition models, such as those based on the Facial Action Coding System (FACS), demonstrate significant potential but have yet to overcome issues related to lighting, occlusion, and diverse cultural expressions (Xie et al., 2021).

Researchers have not treated classroom-based emotion detection in much detail, focusing instead on controlled, laboratory settings. A significant gap exists in applying emotion detection models to the complex, variable nature of real classroom interactions. Siddiqui et al. (2020) applied emotion recognition in educational contexts but primarily relied on audio-visual data, which, although promising, lacks the integration of physiological signals such as heart rate and galvanic skin response (GSR), which could enhance accuracy. Most studies in the field of emotion detection have only focused on facial recognition or voice tone analysis, rather than integrating these with physiological signals like EEG (Xu et al., 2020). Such approaches, however, have failed to address the challenges posed by real-time emotion detection, where feedback and adaptation to the learner's state are critical for improving educational outcomes.

Previous published studies are limited to local surveys or single-classroom applications, restricting the generalizability of their findings. For example, a recent study by Li et al. (2023) tested a multimodal system on a group of 100 students, yet did not extend their work to diverse classroom environments or real-time intervention systems. This limitation prevents the wider applicability of emotion detection systems to different educational settings. Half of the studies evaluated failed to specify whether the emotion detection systems they tested operated in real-time or were designed for offline analysis, a key distinction for their potential classroom use (He et al., 2022). The research to date has tended to focus on improving the accuracy of emotion recognition models, rather than developing systems that can adapt and respond to emotional cues during classroom activities.

Published studies on the effect of emotion detection systems in improving student engagement and learning outcomes are not consistent. While some studies (e.g., Siddiqui et al., 2020) demonstrate high accuracy rates in detecting emotions, they do not offer strong evidence linking these systems to tangible educational improvements such as better engagement or retention. Smith's analysis (2021) does not take account of the longitudinal effects of emotion feedback over time, nor does she examine how different emotional states impact learning retention in diverse educational contexts. The existing accounts fail to resolve the contradiction between model performance in controlled settings and its effectiveness in real classrooms.

Most studies of emotion detection have only been carried out in a small number of areas, such as primary school settings or controlled experiments with college students. However, much of the research up to now has been descriptive in nature, focusing on defining emotional states rather than implementing systems that adapt learning environments based on real-time emotion recognition. The generalisability of much published research on emotion detection in education is problematic, as many studies have used small, homogeneous populations, primarily from specific age groups or cultural contexts.

Research on the subject has been mostly restricted to limited comparisons of different emotion detection methods, such as facial expressions versus voice recognition, and rarely integrates these modalities into a holistic, multimodal system. However, few writers have been able to draw on any systematic research into the long-term impact of emotion detection systems on student performance. Short-term studies such as these do not necessarily show subtle changes over time, and their results may be influenced by short-lived experimental conditions.

Although extensive research has been carried out on emotion detection, no single study exists which demonstrates an effective, scalable multimodal emotion detection system for classroom use that integrates real-time feedback and adapts to individual student needs. The experimental data are rather controversial, and there is no general agreement about which combination of modalities—facial, voice, or physiological metrics—yields the optimal balance of accuracy and responsiveness in real-time classroom settings.

Student attention analysis in classrooms is another critical area that has seen significant technological advancements in recent years. Previous studies of student attention have not dealt with the integration of both traditional methods (e.g., self-reports, teacher observation) and automated technologies (e.g., eye-tracking, gaze detection, wearable devices). Traditional attention measurement methods such as questionnaires (e.g., the Student Engagement Instrument, Fredricks et al., 2022) have been largely self-reported, providing a limited view of actual in-class attention. Recent advances, however, focus on automated gaze detection and eye-tracking technologies to provide real-time data on student focus (Wang et al., 2021).

Researchers have not treated cognitive load in student attention analysis in much detail. Most studies in this area focus on behavioral cues such as eye movement or gaze direction, rather than integrating this data with cognitive load measurements (Pereira et al., 2020). Such approaches, however, have failed to address the complexity of student engagement, which likely involves both attentional states and cognitive load levels, as well as emotional states. For example, Mori et al. (2022) explored the use of eye-tracking to measure attention but did not integrate it with physiological measures such as GSR or EEG that are more directly correlated with cognitive load.

Previous studies in this field have often failed to specify whether they assess engagement or attention based on multimodal cues, leading to incomplete models of student attention. Studies on eye-tracking (e.g., Li et al., 2023) largely omit considerations of cognitive load, leaving open the question of whether attention alone is sufficient to predict engagement or performance. The research to date has tended to focus on isolated aspects of attention—gaze, head movement, or even response time—rather than developing an integrated approach that links attention, emotion detection, and cognitive load to create a holistic model of student engagement.

Published studies on the effect of student attention analysis tools are not consistent. For instance, Wang et al. (2021) showed that gaze detection improves attentional tracking but did not establish a clear link to academic performance or engagement in classroom tasks. Most studies of student attention analysis have only been carried out in lab settings or in highly structured environments, making it difficult to extrapolate findings to real, dynamic classroom settings. However, much of the research up to now has been descriptive in nature, focusing on how attention can be measured rather than how it can be used to inform adaptive learning interventions.

The generalisability of much published research on this issue is problematic. Attention measurement systems that work well in a small group of students may not scale to larger, more heterogeneous groups in real classrooms. Furthermore, many studies focus on short-term metrics such as immediate attention but fail to capture longitudinal changes in attention over time. This is a key limitation, as it does not provide insight into how sustained attention is related to long-term learning outcomes.

Computer vision in educational settings has been a topic of increasing interest due to its potential to analyze student behavior and interaction with learning materials. Previous studies of computer vision in education have not dealt with its long-term impact on student learning or its sustained engagement. Most studies focus on short-term applications, such as measuring student engagement through facial recognition or activity tracking, without considering how these technologies could evolve to enhance learning outcomes over the long term (Zhou et al., 2021). For example, Wang et al. (2023) focused on activity recognition and engagement tracking in classrooms using computer vision but failed to evaluate the long-term effects of such systems on student performance or engagement.

Researchers have not treated the issue of ethics and privacy in much detail, which is a significant concern when implementing computer vision in schools. Most research to date focuses on accuracy and functionality, but the ethical implications of using computer vision to monitor students' facial expressions, attention, or engagement remain under-explored. Such expositions are unsatisfactory because they do not address concerns about data privacy, consent, and how this data is being used to influence student learning (Li et al., 2022).

Most studies in the field of computer vision in education have only focused on detecting student engagement through facial expressions, head pose, or body posture, without considering the full range of learning interactions that occur in classrooms. Huang et al. (2023) used face detection to infer engagement, but this approach is limited by issues such as occlusions or variability in facial expressions. Such approaches, however, have failed to address the need for a comprehensive system that combines different vision-based signals—such as gesture recognition, activity tracking, and multimodal feedback systems.

The research to date has tended to focus on descriptive studies that analyze the functionality and accuracy of computer vision systems, rather than evaluating how these systems can be integrated into the educational process and positively affect student learning. For instance, studies that focus on facial recognition for emotion detection fail to integrate this with other interactive learning technologies, such as adaptive learning platforms or feedback systems (Xie et al., 2022).

Despite these technological advancements, several challenges and limitations remain. One key concern is the reliability of emotion inference based solely on facial expressions, as emotions are influenced by numerous internal and external factors that might not manifest visibly. Moreover, cultural differences can affect emotional expressiveness, potentially biasing model interpretations. This is compounded by issues of data privacy and consent, especially when systems continuously record student behavior in physical or virtual classrooms (Trabelsi et al., 2023). Finally, the synergy of AI and the Internet of Everything (IoE) has been explored by Marouf et al. (2024), who developed a framework to monitor academic progress and emotional states through interconnected devices. This system uses AI analytics within an IoT infrastructure to detect patterns in performance and emotion, paving the way for personalized learning at scale. While concerns about data security and ethical AI persist, such frameworks underscore the feasibility of responsive, networked classrooms.

EMBODIMENTS OF INVENTION

The embodiments of the present invention are outlined through the figures, each explaining different components and processes of the AI-based Real-Time Class Engagement Emotions Monitoring System. This system is designed to monitor student engagement and emotional responses during class sessions, using advanced technologies like computer vision and machine learning. Below is a detailed explanation of the key figures included in the research.

Figure 1. Schematic Diagram of the AI-Based Class Engagement Emotions Monitoring System

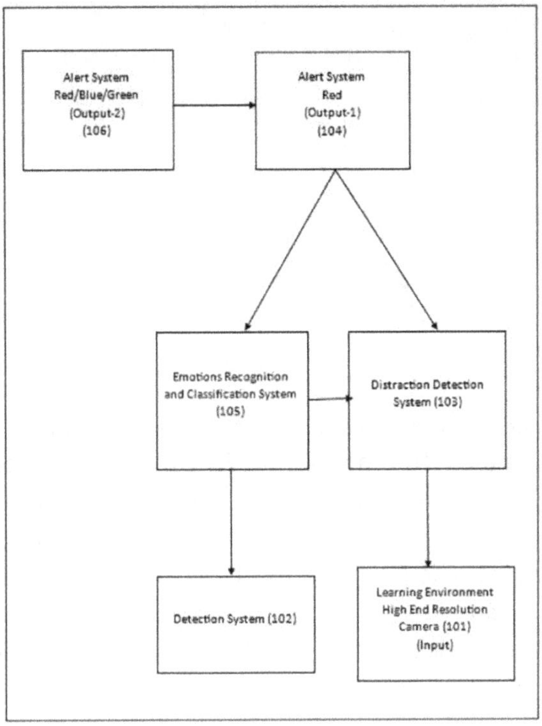

Figure 1 provides a comprehensive overview of the AI-based Class Engagement Emotions Monitoring System. It outlines the various components that make up the system and their interactions. The system consists of a High-End Resolution Camera (101), which captures visual data of students in the classroom. This data is passed on to the Detection System (102), which processes the facial features and eye regions of the students. The Distraction Detection System (103) monitors potential distractions by analyzing eye movements, and when distractions are detected, the Alert System-1 (104) sends a notification. The Emotion Recognition and Classification System (105) processes students' facial expressions to recognize emotions and classify their engagement levels. Based on this analysis, the Alert System-2 (106) provides feedback to the system, indicating the level of engagement (e.g., red, blue, or green alerts).

Figure 2. Inner Process of the Detection System

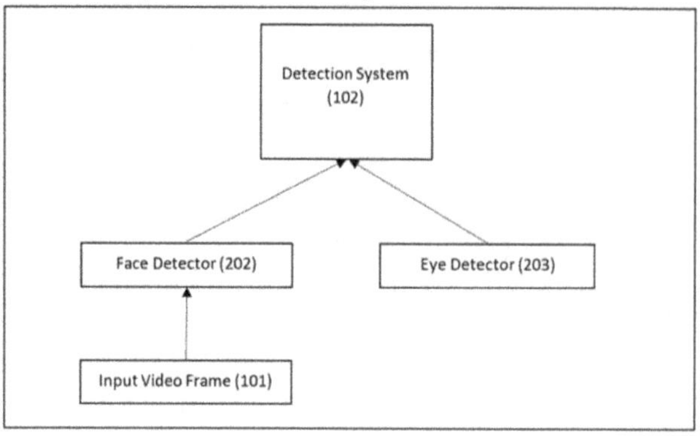

Figure 2 illustrates the inner workings of the Detection System (102). The High-End Resolution Camera (101) captures the image of each student, and the Face Detector System (202) is responsible for identifying the facial features. The Markov Random Fields (MRF) method is used to detect the face's patterns and extract key features. Once the face is detected, the Eye Detector (203) focuses specifically on the eye region to assess the student's eye movements. This step is crucial for further processing in subsequent systems like the Distraction Detection and Emotion Recognition components.

Figure 3. Inner Process of the Distraction Detection System

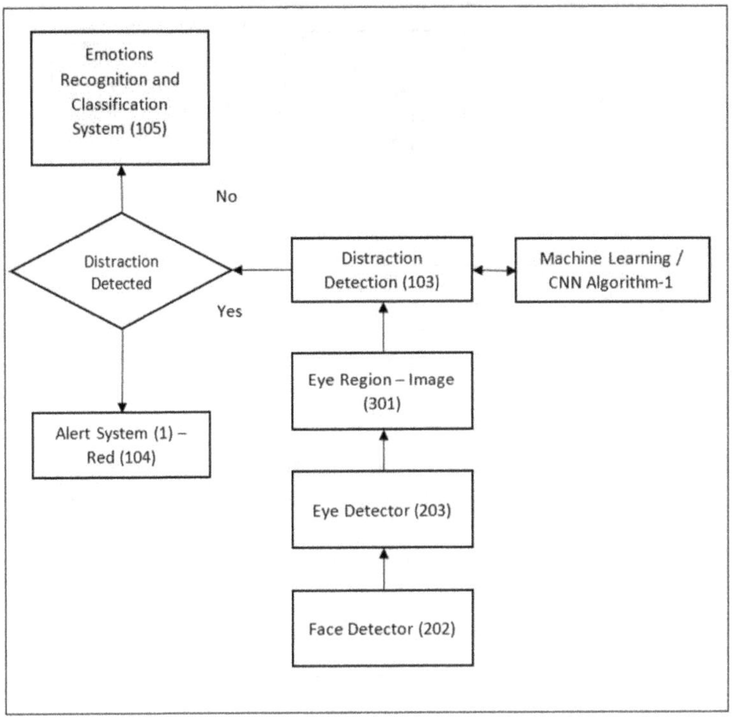

Figure 3 explains the function of the Distraction Detection System (103). It starts with the face detection process using the Face Detector System (202), followed by eye region monitoring via the Eye Detector (203). Using the Machine Learning / CNN Algorithm-1 (302), the system analyzes eye movements to detect any signs of distraction. The algorithm is designed to recognize deviations from a threshold that indicates a distracted state. If distraction is detected, the system sends a signal to Alert System-1 (104). If no distraction is detected, the system forwards the data to the Emotion Recognition and Classification System (105) for further analysis.

Figure 4. Inner Process of the Emotion Recognition and Classification System

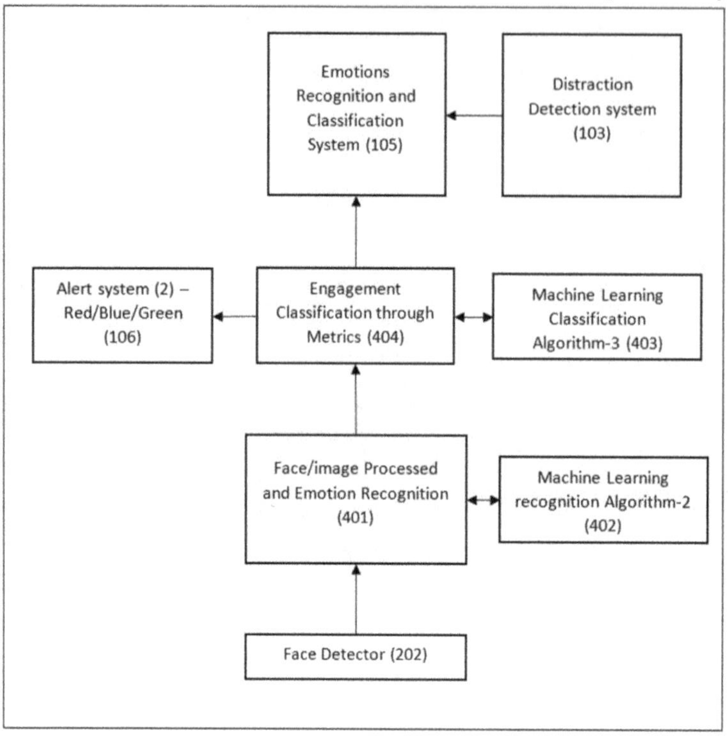

Figure 4 details the processes of the Emotion Recognition and Classification System (105). Once the face is detected (via the Face Detector System (202)), the Machine Learning Recognition Algorithm-2 (402) analyzes the facial features to identify emotions. This step is vital for classifying the student's emotional state, such as interest, confusion, or boredom. Based on the identified emotion, the system uses a proposed metric to classify the student's engagement level through Machine Learning Recognition Algorithm-2 (403). The engagement levels are categorized and communicated to the Alert System-2 (106), where different colors (red, blue, or green) indicate the level of student engagement.

Figure 5. Operational Flow of the Entire System

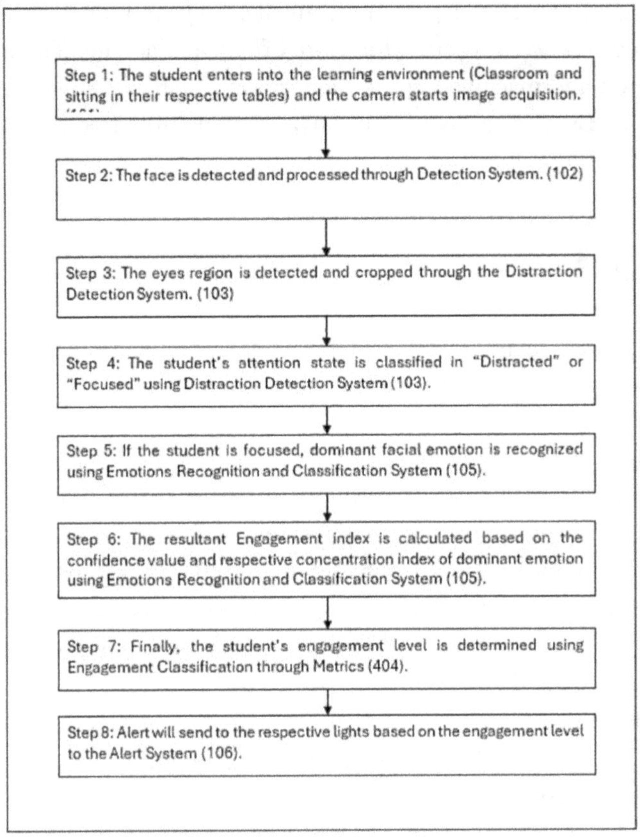

Figure 5 demonstrates the operational flow of the entire AI-based Real-Time Class Engagement Emotions Monitoring System. When the system is powered on (001), the High-End Resolution Camera (101) starts capturing images of the classroom. The Detection System (102) detects faces and eyes, while the Distraction Detection System (103) monitors attention levels, categorizing students as either "Distracted" or "Focused." If a student is deemed focused, the Emotion Recognition and Classification System (105) processes the student's facial expression to detect the dominant emotion. The Engagement Index is then calculated, combining the confidence value of the recognized emotion and the concentration level. Finally, the system classifies the student's engagement and sends the results to Alert System-2 (106), triggering an appropriate visual alert (red, blue, or green) based on the student's attention and emotional state.

These figures illustrate the core components and workflow of the AI-based Real-Time Class Engagement Emotions Monitoring System. The system is designed to offer a comprehensive, real-time analysis of student engagement by continuously monitoring facial expressions, eye movements, and emotional states, providing actionable feedback to instructors for more effective teaching. The integration of computer vision and machine learning algorithms enables precise and automated engagement assessment, a significant advancement over traditional methods of monitoring classroom dynamics.

DISCUSSIONS

The emergence of artificial intelligence in educational settings has paved the way for innovative approaches to evaluating student engagement, particularly in real-time classroom environments. In traditional classroom scenarios, especially those involving large student populations, it becomes increasingly difficult for instructors to accurately assess each student's level of attention and emotional involvement. The AI-based real-time classroom engagement and emotion monitoring system was developed to address this very challenge. By integrating computer vision and machine learning techniques, the system can capture visual input from cameras installed in the classroom and analyze the facial expressions and eye movements of students to evaluate their engagement levels dynamically.

Unlike conventional assessment tools, which rely on post-session surveys or observational judgments, this system provides continuous, objective monitoring. It uses specific emotional and behavioral indicators such as eye retention on the instructor or content, facial expression consistency (also referred to as emotional "stickiness"), and the presence of positive emotional cues. These parameters enable the system to categorize engagement into multiple levels, offering a refined understanding of how students are responding during the class.

This model doesn't only focus on individual tracking—it aggregates data to represent the overall engagement level of the classroom. Such aggregated feedback offers instructors valuable insights into when and how attention shifts during a lecture. Furthermore, this tool enables the evaluation of various teaching strategies by identifying which pedagogical phases maintain or lose student interest. Over time, patterns derived from this data can help instructors refine their delivery styles and adapt lesson content to maximize attention and participation.

This real-time monitoring and analytical capability presents a transformative shift in educational technology, fostering a more interactive and feedback-driven learning environment. By supporting data-informed teaching practices, the system enhances both student outcomes and instructor effectiveness, aligning with the evolving needs of 21st-century education.

CONCLUSION

In conclusion, the development of an AI-based system for real-time monitoring of student engagement and emotional response in the classroom presents a significant step forward in enhancing the teaching-learning process. Traditional methods of gauging student attentiveness often lack immediacy and are prone to subjective interpretation. This system overcomes those limitations by providing objective, real-time data based on visual and emotional analysis, which empowers educators to respond more effectively to their students' needs during class sessions.

By capturing facial expressions and analyzing eye movements, the system identifies distracted, disengaged, or highly attentive students. The core strength of the system lies in its ability to classify engagement levels using a set of proposed metrics, including eye retention (the duration a student maintains gaze on the instructor or content), emotional stickiness (consistency of facial expressions), and positivity (the degree of positive emotional responses). These indicators collectively provide a detailed, real-time snapshot of each student's cognitive and emotional involvement.

On a broader level, the system compiles individual data to present a comprehensive view of the overall classroom engagement. This information allows educators to make informed decisions about their teaching strategies and adapt content delivery to better engage students. It also enables a more nuanced evaluation of different pedagogical approaches and their impact at various stages of the class interaction.

Additionally, the system serves as a reflective tool for educators, offering insights into their own performance by correlating student engagement patterns with different teaching phases. This promotes continuous professional growth and instructional refinement.

Ultimately, the integration of this technology fosters an educational environment that is more responsive, data-driven, and student-centered. It enhances both instructional quality and learner experience, making it a valuable asset for modern educational institutions seeking to optimize classroom effectiveness in real time.

CONFLICT OF INTEREST STATEMENT

We have no known conflict of interest to disclose.

REFERENCES

Banada, M. (2025). AI powered attendance system for class rooms using face recognition. *Indian Scientific Journal of Research in Engineering and Management, 7*(1), 1–9. Advance online publication. DOI: 10.55041/IJSREM40676

Fredricks, J. A., Blumenfeld, P. C., & Paris, A. H. (2022). School engagement: Potential of the concept, state of the evidence. *Review of Educational Research, 72*(1), 59–90. DOI: 10.3102/00346543074001059

He, Z., Zhang, Q., & Zhang, M. (2022). Real-time emotion recognition for classroom engagement monitoring using facial expression and physiological data. *Computers in Human Behavior, 120*, 106740. DOI: 10.1016/j.chb.2021.106740

Hernandez, M., Canals, J., & Paredes, S. (2023). The impact of real-time feedback on student engagement: A systematic review. *Journal of Educational Technology & Society, 26*(2), 45–58. https://www.jstor.org/stable/26473042

Huang, L., Zhang, Y., & Liu, X. (2023). Detecting classroom engagement using computer vision: A review. *Education and Information Technologies, 28*(5), 5791–5806. DOI: 10.1007/s10639-022-10761-9

Kerr, S., O'Rourke, S., & Lynch, A. (2020). Real-time AI-driven feedback in personalized learning: Applications and challenges. *International Journal of Artificial Intelligence in Education, 30*(4), 432–450. DOI: 10.1007/s40593-020-00208-4

Kumar, T. K., & Tummala, D. S. (2023). Artificial intelligence-based real-time facial emotion monitoring system. *Proceedings of the International Conference on Computer, Communication and Electronics Engineering*, 1–5. DOI: 10.1109/ICCCE58854.2023.10246038

Lan, Z., & Tsao, H.-J. (2025). The relationship between classroom learning engagement of secondary vocational school students and psychological factors based on video analysis technology. *WSEAS Transactions on Information Science and Applications, 22*(14), 146–152. Advance online publication. DOI: 10.37394/23209.2025.22.14

Li, Y., Zhang, X., & Liu, H. (2022). A review of the ethical implications of computer vision in educational settings. *Ethics and Information Technology, 24*(2), 153–166. DOI: 10.1007/s10676-021-09550-5

Li, Z., Chen, L., & Wu, C. (2023). Emotion recognition and attention analysis for student engagement in classrooms: A multimodal approach. *Journal of Educational Psychology, 115*(4), 586–599. DOI: 10.1037/edu0000532

Marouf, M., Alchilibi, H., Sakr, D. K., Alkhayyat, A., & Pateriya, N. (2024). AI in real-time student performance monitoring using IoE. *Advances in Computational Intelligence and Robotics, 19*, 275–288. Advance online publication. DOI: 10.4018/979-8-3693-7367-5.ch019

Mori, Y., Nakamura, Y., & Ohta, K. (2022). The integration of cognitive load and eye-tracking for real-time classroom attention analysis. *Journal of Learning Analytics, 9*(1), 34–49. DOI: 10.18608/jla.2022.0901

Pereira, A., Costa, A., & Silva, F. (2020). Automated technologies for measuring cognitive load and attention in educational settings: A critical review. *Journal of Educational Computing Research, 57*(5), 1250–1272. DOI: 10.1177/0735633120905724

Picard, R. W., Vyzas, E., & Healey, J. (2020). Toward machine emotional intelligence: Analysis of affective physiological state. *IEEE Transactions on Pattern Analysis and Machine Intelligence, 22*(12), 1174–1191. DOI: 10.1109/34.903103

Prakash, J., Swathiramya, R., Balambigai, G., Menaha, R., & Abhirami, J. S. (2024). AI-driven real-time feedback system for enhanced student support: Leveraging sentiment analysis and machine learning algorithms. *International Journal of Computational and Experimental Science and Engineering*. DOI: 10.22399/ijcesen.780

Sa'idah, S. (2025). A review on EEG-based multimodal learning for emotion recognition. *Artificial Intelligence Review, 58*(5), 131. Advance online publication. DOI: 10.1007/s10462-025-11126-9

Selvarajah, K., ElKott, N., Babu, P. R., & Patel, D. (2024). Enhancing classroom engagement through AI-powered emotional, head pose, and gaze tracking: A novel approach to responsive teaching. *International Multidisciplinary Research Journal, 31*, 1–8. Advance online publication. DOI: 10.47722/imrj.2001.31

Siddiqui, N., Khalid, M. A., Ahmed, A., Aleem, A., Irfan, M., Ahmad, W., & Muslim, F. B. (2023). An AI-based classroom monitoring system leveraging computer vision and machine learning. *IEEE International Conference on Building and Communicating Technology*. DOI: 10.1109/IBCAST59916.2023.10713048

Smith, C. (2021). Real-time emotion detection in classroom environments: Exploring the gaps in multimodal feedback. *International Journal of Human-Computer Studies, 151*, 102580. DOI: 10.1016/j.ijhcs.2021.102580

Sobin, C., Subheesh, N. P., & Ali, J. (2023). In-class student emotion and engagement detection system (iSEEDS): An AI-based approach for responsive teaching. *IEEE Global Engineering Education Conference (EDUCON).* DOI: 10.1109/EDUCON54358.2023.10125254

Trabelsi, Z., Alnajjar, F., Parambil, M., Gochoo, M. E., & Ali, L. (2023). Real-time attention monitoring system for classroom: A deep learning approach for student's behavior recognition. *Big Data and Cognitive Computing*, *7*(1), 48. DOI: 10.3390/bdcc7010048

Wang, L., Li, Y., & Zhang, Y. (2021). Eye-tracking and gaze-based analysis of student attention in classroom settings. *Educational Psychology Review*, *33*(1), 179–196. DOI: 10.1007/s10648-020-09571-3

Wang, M., Liu, X., & Yu, J. (2023). Real-time emotion detection in classroom environments for enhancing student engagement. *Journal of Educational Technology & Society*, *26*(3), 80–94. DOI: 10.1177/0261977X22114265

Xie, X., Yang, D., & Wang, F. (2021). Multimodal emotion detection systems in education: A survey. *Computers & Education*, *164*, 104105. DOI: 10.1016/j.compedu.2020.104105

Xu, X., Zhao, F., & Lee, W. (2020). Emotion recognition in classroom environments: A comparative study using facial expression and speech. *Journal of Educational Psychology*, *112*(6), 1056–1067. DOI: 10.1037/edu0000402

Zhou, S., Li, Y., & Zhao, Z. (2021). Computer vision and artificial intelligence for detecting student engagement in the classroom: A review. *Journal of Educational Technology Systems*, *49*(3), 348–369. DOI: 10.1177/00472395211041703

Chapter 7
AI-Based Chatbots for Education:
A Framework for Ethical and Social Perspectives

Brijesh Sivathanu
https://orcid.org/0000-0003-2505-9140
School of Business and Management, Christ University, Bangalore, India

Shatabdi Nannaware
Pune Institute of Business Management, Pune, India

Rajasshrie Pillai
https://orcid.org/0000-0001-6160-3911
Chandragupt Institute of Management, Patna, India

Naseem Abidi
Skyline University College, University City of Sharjah, UAE

ABSTRACT

AI-based chatbots in education are extensively used. This chapter discusses the challenges and benefits of AI-based chatbots for students, teachers, and administrators. The use cases of AI-based chatbots reveal benefits and concerns. This chapter provides ethical and social implications and discusses the framework for the effective implementation of AI-based chatbots in education. The framework offers ethical implications such as fairness, accountability, transparency, accuracy, and autonomy. Further, it mentions the social implications such as equity, mental health, social interaction, assessment and feedback, and privacy and security. Lastly, it gives the policy implications and future research directions.

DOI: 10.4018/979-8-3373-2185-1.ch007

1. INTRODUCTION

Artificial intelligence (AI) has revamped how students are educated in Institutions. A report by International Market Analysis Research and Consulting Group (IMARC) points out that the market for AI in education, valued at $4.8 billion in 2024, is predicted to experience substantial growth, reaching $75.1 billion by 2033 (Smith & Hullinger, 2024). The AI growth is of 34.03% compound annual growth rate (CAGR), fuelled by factors such as increased access to digital devices, the need to reduce the administrative burden of educators, demand for personalized learning, broader educational access, and advancements in AI technologies. Educational institutions are using AI-driven chatbots for administration and student learning. AI-based Chatbots (further called AI-chatbots) are available 24/7 and ubiquitous in nature, which is very helpful for students and educators to access them. These chatbots support the automation of administrative activities, personalized learning (Huynh-The et al., 2023), writing projects and resumes, developing presentations, and providing real-time feedback and instant answers to student queries. The AI-Chatbots for education are Perplexity AI, AIpal, Microsoft Reading Coach, ChatGPT, Bard, Gemini, and WPS-AI. AI-Chatbots benefit students' education, but their implementation raises critical social and ethical concerns (Mhlanga, 2023; Zhang & Aslan, 2021). The ethical issues include data privacy, potential bias, and lack of transparency of the embedded algorithms of AI-Chatbots. Therefore, developing an effective governance mechanism for implementing AI-Chatbots is imperative, which can resolve issues such as data security, ethical oversight, and algorithmic Accountability (Mhlanga, 2023; Yusuf et al., 2024).

Furthermore, there exists concern about ensuring equitable access to AI-powered learning systems, and this gap needs to be bridged through which inclusivity and fairness in education can be promoted (Pillai et al., 2023; Yang & Evans, 2019). Policymakers must understand these social and ethical concerns and establish precise guidelines for the integration of AI into the education system. This chapter develops a framework incorporating ethical and social considerations that have policy implications. Practitioners, marketers, and developers of AI chatbots can also get insights from this work by highlighting the role of AI Chatbots in education related to the social development goals (SDGs) of the United Nations. Further, this chapter presented subthemes, which include AI-Chatbots' impact on students and the ethical and social concerns of using AI- Chatbots. Also, it presents the framework for ethical and social considerations of AI-Chatbots in education.

2. AI-CHATBOTS FOR EDUCATION

AI-Chatbots are changing education by offering personal teaching, real-time support, and administrative efficiency (Yang & Evans, 2019). These chatbots can provide immediate responses, answer frequently asked questions, and assist with assignments, making learning more interactive and accessible (van Bussel et al., 2022). For example, Duolingo's chatbot helps users to practice language skills through convenient practice, enhancing language acquisition in a personal way. Similarly, the chatbot usage at Georgia State University reduced the "summer melt" (students who accepted the institute but failed to register) by sending a reminder and answering the students' questions, improving the enrolment rates. In the virtual classroom, platforms like AI-Chatbot support the learners by clarifying and creating quiz questions. AI-Chatbots also help teachers by automating administrative functions such as grading or attendance tracking. However, challenges remain, including the need for human inspection to prevent fairness, privacy, and misinformation. Overall, AI-Chatbot enhances the students' engagement and access, which makes education more flexible and inclusive (Singh, 2018; Wang et al., 2023).

The integration of AI-Chatbots in education has seen significant growth, which is inspired by prostheses in artificial intelligence and natural language processing. The undergraduate students are primary users, taking advantage of chatbots for skill development, knowledge acquisition, and motivation growth (Alshahrani et al., 2024). The increase in the usage of technologies, such as AI-Chatbots, underlined the requirement for moral ideas and practical implementation strategies (Asad & Ajaz, 2024) to maximize their capacity in educational settings. Also, higher education students mainly use AI-Chatbots for brainstorming, abbreviation, and research aid (Kumar, 2024). However, chatbots have significant thinking and decision-making skills limitation emphasizing the need for moral AI rules in academic settings (Dejan Ravšelj, 2025).

2.1 Success Stories Highlight the Positive Impact of AI in Education

- **Personalized Learning:** AI-Chatbots such as Khan Academy and Duolingo use adaptive teaching algorithms for individual students' needs and educational materials for learning styles. This personal approach has improved learning results and studentngagement (Asad & Ajaz, 2024). The chatbots are used to create learning tasks based on individual student competency, analyze student performance, and adjust the content difficulty to match their needs (Tavakoli et al., 2021). The college Rishi Bankim Sardar, Sunderban in India, which is affiliated with Kolkata University, used a Chatbot for training students due to a lack of faculty members, and it helped students to learn English and Bengali language (Poulami.Roy, 2025).

- **Automated Grading and Feedback:** Tools like Gradescope and Google Classroom automate grading for some types of assignments, freeing teachers' time for other tasks. Chatbots can also provide personalized feedback (Neelam Dey, 2024) to students, helping them identify areas for improvement. Also, chatbots can analyze and grade student work, easing the burden on educators (Ooi et al., 2025).
- **Enhanced Accessibility:** Chatbots can make education more accessible for students with disabilities. For example, speech-to-text and text-to-speech software can help students with visual or auditory impairments. AI-powered translation tools can also help students learn a new language (Asad & Ajaz, 2024). Further, the chatbots have potential benefits for students with disabilities, including those with academic writing challenges, disabilities, neurodiversity, or for whom English is a second language.
- **Improved Engagement:** AI-powered educational Chatbots, games, and simulations can make learning more interactive and engaging for students. These tools can also allow students to practice real-world skills in a safe and supportive environment. AI tools such as Chatbots increased assignment completion rates by 20% and boosted classroom participation by about 25%, promoting AI-powered experiences to increase student engagement, revealing that AI can make learning fun (Unesco, 2023). In India, AI chatbots such as Wabo.AI have significantly improved student engagement at Parul University India (SRV Edge, 2025).

While these are just a few examples, they demonstrate the potential of AI chatbots to transform education. It can be expected to see even more innovative applications of AI-Chatbots in education as AI technology is constantly evolving, leading to further improvements in learning outcomes and student experiences (Chen et al., 2020).

3. ETHICAL AND SOCIAL CONCERNS OF AI-CHATBOTS

3.1 Ethical Concerns

AI-Chatbot related ethical issues have been significantly highliged in literature (Garcia Brustenga et al., 2018; Lund et al., 2023; Mhlanga, 2023). Though AI-Chatbots in educaiton caters with innovatiion and improved efficiency in education sector still there are ethic adilemmas such as material authenticity, potential bias and misinformation risk. Moreover, it is not easy to differentiate between hand writteen human material and AI realated material (Stahl & Eke, 2024). It can create issues about misinforamtion, trust and accoutbaility in organizations and professional environment. AI-Chatbot used in education sector is helpfulfr administator, teacher and students. Morevoer the ethica issues in education sector realted to AI-Chatbot are realted to plagarims, cheating, undermining learning process and cheating. The scholars emphasize a clear understanding of large language models in higher education for its ethical use (Mvondo et al., 2025)

- **Fairness Concerns:** The Chatbot should provide fairness outcomes, reduce algorithm prejudices, and ensure similar treatment for all users. For example, in 2024, a real estate listing in Australia misrepresented non-existent schools, which reveals industry dependence on AI-Chatbots. This incident highlights the need for human inspection to prevent the spread of misinformation that can mislead consumers. Chatbot models are trained on large language models and can reflect and amplify present societal biases. This can lead to AI systems that discriminate against some groups of students and spread stereotypes. For example, an AI tutor might provide different levels of support or feedback based on a student's background or demographics. The training data can provide unfair outcomes, which would be challenging to ensure equitable access to quality education using AI-Chatbots. Therefore, it is imperative to address algorithmic bias in educational AI systems (Bura & Myakala, 2024). This points out the concern of AI producing biased outputs due to learning from potentially biased historical data, raising the question of whether AI could exacerbate social inequities.
- **Academic Integrity:** AI-Chatbots can be used to create realistic code, text, and other content, raising concerns about academic dishonesty. Students may get their work done from AI-Chatbots such as writing their assignments and projects (Łodzikowski et al., 2024). Educators need to work on strategies to address these challenges and ensure academic integrity as a violation. Academic integrity violations as a significant concern related to AI use. The use of AI-chatbots has raised concerns related to academic integrity and plagiarism; therefore, investigating the ethical implications and questioning the responsible use of AI has become necessary (Chu et al., 2022a, 2022b).
- **Lack of Accountability:** There are significant concerns regarding the Accountability of the chatbot outputs, and there is still a debate going on regarding the same. For example, the case of a 14-year-old boy in Florida who died of suicide after being attached to a character with an AI Chatbot raises questions about the responsibility of AI developers. Chatbots allegedly encouraged harmful behavior, especially with weak users, emphasizing the need for clear Accountability in AI interactions (Nwoko, 2024)

- **Lack of Transparency:** Transparency is another important moral issue in how AI systems decide. Students and teachers are often unaware of how AI algorithms assess the reactions or the grades (Williamson & Eynon, 2020). Transparency ensures that procedures, decisions, and functions are open and transparent. In AI, the algorithm makes sense and provides insight into how data is used to make decisions. The output of AI chatbots is developed on large language models (LLMS), and when it's used for education purposes, the user might not be aware of the data produced to provide the output. For example, a job applicant's indefinite experience with an AI avatar interviewer developed by Fairgo.ai in 2024 highlights concerns about the transparency of AI-driven processes. The question still persists, such as How Chatbots explain human emotions and respond to human reactions (Catie McLeod, 2024). Lack of clarity may reduce confidence in AI-managed responses and limit students' ability to learn from mistakes. Educational institutions should clearly explain algorithm transparency to promote how evaluated and the path is offered for appeal or human reviews (Floridi et al., 2018).
- **Inaccurate outputs:** The accuracy of the outcome of chatbots in education is a significant issue as these AI-driven chatbots generate outputs using the patterns of data trained (Ahmed et al., 2023). There is a lack of measures to check the accuracy of the outputs of chatbots. Due to inaccurate algorithms and data, Chatbots may end up with irrelevant, nonsensical, and incorrect answers.
- **Lack of Autonomy:** Protects the individual agency and freedom of choice. In chatbots, AI and digital systems, autonomy means that users should control their data, privacy, and decisions rather than being manipulated by algorithms. Light autonomy issues are also brought up in the same case associated with 14-year-olds and AI Chatbots. The effect of chatbots on users' decisions increases moral concerns about the AI system and potentially reduces personal autonomy, especially when users are impressed or weak (Nwoko, 2024).

These examples reflect the need for pressing strong moral guidelines and inspections in developing and deploying AI technologies to prevent losses and build public trust.

3.2 Social Concerns in AI Chatbots for Education

The use of AI in education is substantially increasing, hence it becomes imperative to understand the ethical issues of this technology. AI-chatbots are transforming the way education is offered with instant interaction, administrative support, and improved learning experience. AI-Chabots have been leveraged with 24/7 availability and accessibility, which makes education easily accessible in far-off areas, especially remote areas (Myllykoski-Laine et al., 2023). The AI chatbots can be leveraged very easily, and they can customize the learning as per individual needs (Woolf et al., 2013), which helps in inclusive education. But the use of AI-Chatbots has increased the social issues. As AI-Chatbot system is churning student data and information that needs to be kept private and secure, however, this is a concern with AI-Chatbots (Zawacki-Richter et al., 2019a). Moreover the the chatbot dependence of students may reduce the human contact and it is necessary for sympathy, collaborative skills, and critical thinking. In addition, more dependence on AI chatbots can reduce the importance of human contact, which is important for developing critical thinking, sympathy, and collaborative skills (Amos et al., 2008).

The use of chatbots can also increase educational inequalities if the underprivileged have the resources to implement advanced technologies (Williamson & and Eynon, 2020). Additionally, embedded bias in algorithms can inadvertently eliminate stereotypes or provide uneven learning opportunities.

Issues of Equity in Access to AI-powered Education

(Addressing the Digital Divide) AI-Chatbot education provides personal learning opportunities, adaptive assessment, and real-time response (Oshrat et al., 2022a), which replaces the methods of connecting with students' materials(Stahl & Eke, 2024). However, its benefits are not equally accessible to all learners. The digital divide - the difference between technology and people - is a significant hurdle. Socioeconomic status, geographical location, and inadequate infrastructure contribute to this division, affecting students from rural areas and deprived communities (Unesco, 2023).

In many low-income areas, a reliable internet deficiency, insufficient access to equipment, and low digital literacy education obstruct the integration of AI. While governments and institutions have launched programs to bridge these intervals, the digital divide requires systemic reforms, including infrastructure investment, teacher training, and cheap technology.

There is a risk that the benefits of AI-Chatbot in education will not be evenly distributed, potentially widening existing achievement gaps. The less privileged students might be unable to access the chatbots compared to the wealthier students. As these students would have better resources to access the AI chatbots. Every student must get an equal opportunity to learn and access educational AI tools; however, inequality (Resnick M,2024) AI tools providers and policymakers must consider the need to provide equal opportunity to students from all strata of society. Aspects such as geographical location and income associated with the bias in AI access and these social inequalities would aggravate if the consideration to solve these issues is not taken care of (Bura & Myakala, 2024).

Addressing these ethical challenges requires a multi-faceted approach involving educators, policymakers, researchers, and technology developers. The ethical challenges related to AI-Chatbots and integration in education are a challenge. Moreover, there is a need for careful consideration and collaboration between educators and technologists for an evaluation-driven approach to developing responsible AI for education (Guettala et al., 2024). It's crucial to develop ethical guidelines, promote responsible AI development and use, and ensure that AI systems are used to benefit all students, underscoring the importance of understanding the ethical uses and risks associated with AI.

It is essential to ensure the same access to AI-system education to promote inclusion and prevent existing inequalities from pushing forward. Policies that provide cheap internet, increase digital literacy, and integrate localized materials can promote fairness in educational opportunities (OECD, 2020.). Without active measures, AI-based educational equipment puts at risk the strengthening of social inequalities rather than addressing them (Eynon & and Geniets, 2016). It is important to ensure similar access to AI-system education to promote inclusion and prevent existing inequalities from furthering. Policies that provide cheap internet, increase digital literacy, and integrate localized materials can promote fairness in educational opportunities (OECD, 2020.). Without active measures, AI-Chatbots for education risk strengthening social inequalities rather than bridging them.

Teacher-Student Relationship Dynamics: AI-Chatbot as a Supplement vs. a Replacement

The increasing presence of chatbots in education raises concerns about its impact on teacher-student relations. While chatbots can offer personal learning experiences, real-time response, and administrative support Wai Wong (2022), they have emotional intelligence, sympathy and a lack of understanding that provide human teachers. AI chatbots should be seen as a supplement rather than a replacement for teachers. When effectively used, AI can handle regular tasks such as grading or scheduling, teachers can free teachers from focusing on more creative and mutual aspects of teaching. This allows teachers to increase their instruction, offering individual support based on the A-provided insight.

Teacher Deskilling

Some fear that over-reliance on AI in education could lead to the deskilling of teachers. Teachers might lose valuable skills and expertise if AI takes over grading and lesson planning tasks. It's crucial to ensure that AI is used to augment, not replace, human teachers. It is necessary to be cautious against relying too heavily on AI systems, emphasizing the importance of human interaction and collaboration in education (Resnick, 2024).

Mental Health and Well-being Concerns: Psychological Impact of AI Interactions

The increasing integration of AI in daily life has important implications for mental health through the use of intelligent assistants, chatbots, and social media algorithms (Fitzpatrick et al., 2017). While AI chatbot equipment can offer valuable support, such as providing mental health resources or facilities to consulting services, they are also about generating social isolation, dependence, and emotional casualties. Chatbots such as Voebot and WYSA are designed to assist in mental health issues by offering cognitive-behavioral therapy (CBT) technology and emotional support (Inkster et al., 2018). These devices provide immediate, decision-free interactions, which can be beneficial to seeking help due to the stigma for particularly reluctant persons. Studies have shown that AI interaction can reduce the symptoms of anxiety and depression by offering accessible mental health resources (Fitzpatrick et al., 2017).

However, more dependence on AI chatbots for emotional support can have negative results. Users can develop an unhealthy attachment to the AI chatbot, changing accurate human contact with automated reactions. This contingent can increase feelings of loneliness, primarily if the AI device replaces an actual social connection (Krstić et al., 2022). Additionally, AI algorithm on social media platforms often strengthens echo chambers and highlight users negatively affecting self-esteem, body image, or mental welfare. These algorithms may be addicted to drugs, have sleep disturbances, and experience growing anxiety (Twenge & Campbell, 2019).

The AI chatbots must be designed with moral ideas to reduce these risks, focusing on increasing transparency, user control, and human relations (Oshrat et al., 2022b) rather than changing. Finally, while chatbots may be a valuable tool for supporting mental health, they must be integrated responsibly to avoid unexpected psychological consequences.

Concerns related to using AI-Chatbot for Assessments and Feedback

The integration of chatbots in academic evaluation and reaction has introduced new opportunities for personal teaching, real-time evaluation, and efficiency. AI chatbots can streamline grading and provide analog reactions, and students with high precision can track progress (Zun Liang et al., 2024). However, these benefits come with important moral ideas about fairness, transparency, data privacy, and potential prejudice.

One of the most pressing moral concerns is the risk of algorithm bias. The Chatbot AI system is trained on large datasets, which can inadvertently reflect social, cultural, or economic prejudices present in the data (Huynh & Gillen-O'Neel, 2016). This can lead to improper evaluation, especially for students of marginalized communities. To ensure fairness, educational institutions must implement a rigid audit of the AI system and adopt an inclusive dataset responsible for the diverse (Söderlund & Oikarinen, 2021).

Limitations of Social Interaction

Students tend to over-rely on chatbots, which may lead to a reduction in collaboration and face-to-face interaction, and further, it may hinder the development of essential skills for social interaction. Moreover, chatbots do not have an understanding of the social cues and emotional status recognition of the user, though they can provide personalized human interaction.

The Role of Human Oversight

While AI can increase efficiency, it should not replace human teachers in the evaluation process. Human inspection ensures that subjective factors such as creativity, emotional intelligence, and significant thinking are considered adequately. A balanced approach, where AI provides the initial response and human teachers make the final evaluation, ensures both efficiency and fairness.

4. Framework for Ethical and Social Implications of AI-Chatbots for Education

Implementing AI-Chatbots is imperative to overcome these ethical and social concerns. In consideration of the literature, this book chapter suggests the framework for ethical and social implications of AI-Chatbots for Education (Figure 1). The moral principles for the use of AI education chatbots include:

4.1 Ethical Use of AI-Chatbots for Education

In consideration of the ethical and social considerations of using AI-Chatbots in education. The rapid integration of Artificial Intelligence (AI) chatbots in education demands a broader structure that ensures their moral and socially responsible use

(Floridi et al., 2018). A well-defined moral and social implementation structure needs to be developed. The manuscript presents the framework for the ethical and social use of AI-Chatbots in education.

Principles of ethical use of Generative AI: FATAA (Fairness, Accountability, Transparency, Accessibility, Autonomy) (Rana et al., 2024):

Ethical theory or code provides guidelines for the moral requirements of the AI system (Guizzardi et al., 2020). The stakeholders' better functional and quality needs about the AI system are considered AI ethical (Balasubramaniam et al., 2023a). Researchers have debated the moral principles related to AI extensively, emphasizing Fairness, Accountability, Transparency, and Autonomy. The ethical concerns in AI-Chatbots are FATAA principles: Fairness, Accountability, transparency, accuracy, and autonomy, which affect legal, educational, organizational, and some social implications (Keslin et al., 2022).

Fairness ensures that AI-Chatbots' outputs are fair and inclusive, such as in the recruitment process, which may otherwise exclude some demographics (Acikgoz et al., 2020). AI-Chatbot learning from vast datasets and data sets might reflect the existing biases related to race, cultural stereotypes and gender. The educational chatbot may amplify these biases while interacting with students. This may lead to discriminatory or unfair results for students. Hence, it becomes imperative to train AI models of Chatbots on data sets (Shin & Park, 2019) that They are representative of diverse students and are bias-free.

The Accountability remains unclear, as the AI-related material depends on pre-informed data, limiting responsibility(Shin, 2021). The AI-Chatbots may end up providing biased or inaccurate results, and it is vital to establish Accountability for these issues. It is important that to establish Accountability for the AI-Chatbot by evaluating and governing the data and outputs of education chatbots by school boards, accreditation bodies, and higher education institutions.

Transparency is essential in AI-Chatbots, and their decision-making requires clarity (Balasubramaniam et al., 2023b). AI models' 'black box' nature makes it difficult to understand how AI-Chatbots provide outputs to students and teachers in education. The schools and higher education institutes need to ensure transparency procedures and protocols that confirm that parents, students, and teachers are made to understand AI-Chatbots functioning in schools and institutions. Moreover, they must get assurance of the protection of their ward's data churned through AI-Chatbots.

The accuracy of educational chatbot is crucial and of utmost priority. AI-Chatbots can provide irrelevant, nonsensical, and inaccurate answers to students, administrators, and teachers. This makes it imperative that AI-Chatbots need to be trained on up-to-date and high-quality data to provide reliable and accurate outcomes. Moreover, these chatbot-generated outcomes need to be critically reflected and reviewed by administrators and teachers.

Autonomy increases concerns over AI's role in decision-making (Nagtegaal, 2021). AI-Chatbots' autonomy is discussed as the level of decision-making authority and independence provided to the AI chatbots for various education and administrative purposes. The over-dependency on the AI-Chatbot can reduce the importance of the role of the teacher in education. Hence, AI chatbots in education should be developed and designed to support and supplement teachers, not replace teachers. Moreover, there should be an emphasis on empowering students and teachers rather than the entire learning process automation with AI -Chatbots.

4.2 Social Implications for the Use of AI-Chatbot for Education

Equity: Ensuring equity involves reducing algorithm bias and promoting similar access to AI-operated educational devices. AI systems often reflect embedded prejudices in their training data, which can damage inconsistently inferior groups. Educational institutions should actively audit AI algorithms for potential prejudices and use various datasets that are responsible for variations in language, culture, and socio-economic background(Crawford & Paglen, 2021). Additionally, policies should focus on bridging digital partitions by providing similar access to AI technologies in all socio-economic groups.

Mental Health Support: AI-Chatbots in education can counsel or coach students for studies and emotional issues. Moreover, chatbots may not be able to understand the non-verbal actions or signs of distress related to students' mental health issues. It may lead to students' loneliness due to a lack of human presence while interacting with Chatbots. Hence, it becomes imperative to educate them about the risks and limitations of Chatbots. Moreover, they can be guided to understand the information critically provided by the Chatbots. Moreover, Chatbots can be trained to understand and recognize emotional signals suitably.

Social Interaction: Social interaction is a vital consideration for teachers and students when it comes to implementing chatbots in education. Chatbot lacks human interaction due to a lack of face-to-face communication with students. Moreover, constant chatbot use may lead to social isolation and loneliness. Even teachers may feel that chatbot are taking over their jobs and the development gap between students and teachers. Therefore, chatbots can be trained to communicate better in a humanly manner and chatbot interactions can be diverted to teachers for further counseling and query-solving

Assessment and feedback: Students can get instant and personalized feedback, and it is available 24/7 to resolve students' queries. Even teachers' work is reduced due to the automated evaluation of students. Even AI-driven feedback guides students to identify areas for improvement, track their progress, and help provide better learning outcomes. However, over-dependency on the chatbot for learning and feedback would diminish the emphasis on critical thinking and undermine education's value. It is imperative that, by implementing appropriate precautions, it would be possible to harness the benefits of AI chatbots for feedback and assessment while mitigating the possible risks.

Privacy and security: AI chatbots rely too much on personal data, increasing essential concerns about privacy and security. Institutions should follow international privacy laws, such as the General Data Protection Regulation (GDPR), and ensure that student data is collected, stored, and used ethically (Zawacki-Richter et al., 2019a). Consent mechanisms and approval techniques should be integrated into all AI-managed academic platforms to protect user privacy. Ethical AI design must comply with data protection laws like the General Data Protection Regulation (GDPR). Students' data should be anonymized, securely stored, and used only for educational purposes (Zawacki-Richter et al., 2019a). The use of AI in education often involves collecting and analyzing large amounts of student data. Protecting student privacy and ensuring the security of this data is paramount. There are concerns about who has access to this data, how it is used, and how it is protected from unauthorized access or misuse. Raises concerns about the ethics and privacy implications of using AI in education, particularly given the reliance of AI models on massive datasets, some of which may contain private information.

Figure 1. Framework for Social and Ethical Implications

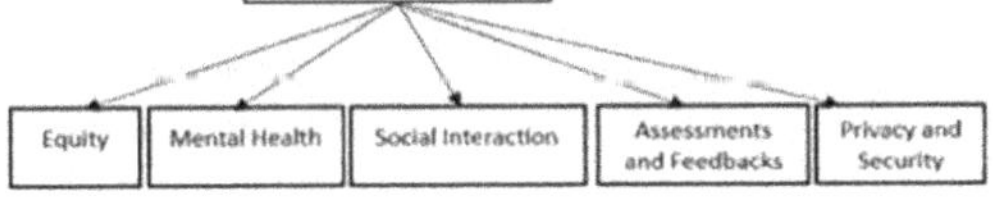

The above model suggests the aspects that need to be considered by educational institutions to overcome ethical and social concerns and successfully implement the AI-chatbots.

5. ACHIEVING SUSTAINABLE DEVELOPMENT GOALS (SDGS) WITH AI-CHATBOT IN EDUCATION

If used strategically by the education institutes, AI-Chatbots can help achieve SDG agents such as quality education, No Poverty, Gender equality, Decent work and Economic Growth of the country by providing coaching and other skills. Moreover, it can help in industry, innovation and infrastructure goals by training employees on the job. The presented table with an example presents the understanding of achievement.

Table 1. Examples of AI-Chatbots in education for achieving SDG

Sr. No.	Example Use Case	AI-Chatbot Role in Education	Social Implications Ethical Implications	SDG Goal with Number
	Khan Academy's AI tutor, Duolingo chatbots, and ChatGPT-based tutors	24/7 tutoring, personalized learning paths, adaptive assessments	Expands access to education in rural/remote areas; supports diverse learners Risk of algorithmic bias in learning content, data privacy of minors	Quality Education (4)
	WhatsApp-based digital literacy chatbots	Free digital learning and skill development via mobile chatbots	Reduces educational inequality for economically disadvantaged students Informed consent and fairness in automated content delivery	No Poverty (1)
	GESS chatbot (Girls' Education South Sudan)	Empower girls with access to private learning and STEM content	Increases learning confidence among girls; bypasses societal barriers Ensure chatbots don't reinforce stereotypes; need inclusive design	Gender Equality (5)
	Rezi AI Resume Bot, LinkedIn Learning chatbot	Career coaching, resume writing, soft skills guidance	Supports workforce readiness and youth employability Transparency in advice generation; potential misguidance from generic responses	Decent Work and Economic Growth (8)
	IBM Watson Tutor, STEMBot for kids	Teaches coding, AI, robotics, and promotes tech fluency	Builds digital capabilities and innovation mindset from a young age Unequal access to internet/ devices can widen digital divide	Industry, Innovation, and Infrastructure (9)

continued on following page

Table 1. Continued

Sr. No.	Example Use Case	AI-Chatbot Role in Education	Social Implications Ethical Implications	SDG Goal with Number
	UNICEF's Learning Passport chatbot	Multilingual, accessible education for marginalized groups	Promotes inclusive learning regardless of geography or language Bias in language support; ethical handling of learning analytics	Reduced Inequalities (10)
	Urban chatbot for civic awareness in schools	Civics education through gamified chatbot interaction	Encourages responsible behavior and community participation Misinformation or biased civic education content risks political manipulation	Sustainable Cities and Communities (11)
	UNESCO's digital citizenship chatbot	Legal literacy, rights education, anti-bullying chatbots	Fosters democratic values and responsible online behavior Chatbot responses must remain neutral, age-appropriate, and culturally sensitive	Peace, Justice and Strong Institutions (16)
	UN + Microsoft chatbot for refugee education	EdTech-NGO-Government collaborations for chatbot-based remote education	Strengthens global efforts to bridge the education gap through technology Requires clear data-sharing policies and Accountability across partners	Partnerships for the Goals (17)

Source: Authors' Creation

6. WAY FORWARD TO THE SUCCESSFUL IMPLEMENTATION OF AI-CHATBOTS EDUCATION AND POLICY IMPLICATIONS

While AI-operated Chatbots can revolutionize learning experiences, they also raise concerns about the overall adaptation for teachers' preparations, policy structures, moral implications, and education. The success of AI chatbots in education is imperative to address the concerns and ensure the effective social and ethical use of AI chatbots. The pointers of successful implementation are discussed below:

Teacher Training and AI Literacy

To effectively apply AI-Chatbots in education, teachers must receive proper training in both their technical functionality and educational applications. Studies indicate that teachers often lack enough knowledge about AI, which hinders their ability to teach and learn it meaningfully (Zawacki-Richter et al., 2019b). Teachers' development programs should emphasize AI literacy, including how AI-borne materials can be used to support personal learning, automate administrative tasks, and increase student engagement (Bond et al., 2019). Many teachers lack global AI literacy, making it challenging to implement AI-based teaching equipment effectively. *Example:* Finland's AI Education Initiative. Finland has launched a nationwide AI training program, which includes courses such as AI elements, designed to educate teachers and students on AI fundamentals. This initiative helps teachers to integrate effectively into their teaching methods.

Curriculum Adaptation and Personalized Learning

Over-personalization can fragment learning experiences, where students may not remember significant discussions or classmates. *Example:* Squirrel AI, a Chinese adaptive teaching platform, uses AI to personalize text plans based on the strengths and weaknesses of the students. This knowledge identifies gaps and provides targeted content, which helps students progress at their own pace.

Reaching Out to Various Communities

Equality for access to AI-Chatbots for education to students of various strata of society, and it's imperative to take action to ensure access. Example: The Faculty of UC Santa Cruise has developed a think (Technology + Humanities Integrated Knowledge) to equip AI skills for research, promoting important approaches to the social influence of AI. This initiative will be tested with the Bay Area Community College Consortium to refine it for comprehensive distribution. Additionally, in California, Callie, an AI chatbot, is doing an AI chatbot to help community college students with financial assistance, food security, and basic needs. Launching in select colleges in 2024 will provide 24/7 assistance funded by Cali College Futures Foundation, ensuring that students receive the necessary guidance without any cost.

Authentic and Timely Data Training for AI-Chatbots

Data is a strategic asset; ensuring high-quality, well-groomed data for uniform student support is essential. Effective data management prevents prejudice, promotes inclusion, and provides a spontaneous experience for students and employees. Improves economic mobility through AI Modern data can expand infrastructure and educational opportunities, especially for low-income students, trading, working-based learning and supporting learning-educated employment programs, which enhances career readiness. Unlocking AI's capacity in education technology platforms will revolutionize teaching and learning through adaptive learning tools, real-time feedback, and individual educational experiences, improving student results. *Example:* To achieve Vision 2030's goal of an AI-empowered future, California Community Colleges is investing in robust data infrastructure. The Common Cloud Data Platform (CCDP) is a key initiative that enhances data quality, accessibility, and security. Initial investments have established foundational capabilities, but scaling these efforts through the Statewide Common Technology Project (SCTP) is essential for long-term sustainability. A flexible data system seller protects(Altares-López et al., 2024). From lock-in, AI lives with developing rules and ensures privacy and security. A strong data regime will also shape the AI policy and improve institutional flexibility. The AI models are only as good as the data they are trained. Reliable, clean, and fair data ensures more effective AI-powered decision-making. Investing in CCDP and SCTP is essential for a future-ready education system that benefits students, faculty, and the workforce.

7. POLICY AND RESEARCH DIRECTIONS FOR RESPONSIBLE AI IN EDUCATION

The integration of artificial intelligence in the educational scenario has undoubtedly changed the approach to teaching, learning, and administrative processes(Wiboolyasarin et al., 2025). While the potential benefits of AI-powered chatbots in education are widely observed, it is important to address the inherent complexities and moral issues associated with this technical disruption (Murwanenda et al., 2024). As we are deeply under the purview of Chatbot integration in education, it becomes clear that policy-making and strong research structures are necessary to ensure these technologies' ethical and equitable implementation. There is a need for effective policy-making and moral guidelines to promote an environment where chatbots can responsibly support educational results.

Many countries and educational institutions have introduced AI-run education reforms. Estonia's AI Leap initiative integrates AI learning in high school courses, ensuring students and teachers are equipped with AI literacy. Similarly, universities worldwide, such as Carnegie Mellon University and Johns Hopkins University, are expanding AI education beyond STEM fields, making it accessible to business, healthcare, and humanities students. In applied research, AI tools are being developed to help teachers. For example, a University of Albania project funded by the Gates Foundation uses AI Chatbots to analyze classroom interaction and provide feedback without affecting the performance evaluation.

In addition, organizations such as the World Economic Forum (WEF) have underlined responsible AI principles, allowing schools to adopt ethical AI and inclusivity.

The integration of AI-Chatbots in education presents moral and social challenges, including data privacy concerns, potential job displacement, algorithm bias, and student welfare. The AI system collects a large amount of data, despite the GDPR compliance, increasing the risk of misuse. While AI enhances teaching, apprehension remains about automation instead of teachers, although policies emphasize AI as an accessory. In the AI model, prejudice can strengthen social inequalities, which can lead to significant concerns.

Additionally, AI-manual learning can reduce human contact, affecting students' mental health. Ensuring AI traditional education while maintaining moral safety measures is necessary to implement responsible AI. AI offers huge educational opportunities but requires well-structured policies and moral safety measures. Addressing prejudices and ensuring that AI remains in use instead of a replacement, the institute can exploit the potential of AI using FATTA principles to implement AI chatbots. With continuous research, investment, and regulatory inspection, AI can change education by maintaining fairness, inclusion, and transparency.

8. SUMMARY

The education trends are changing due to AI chatbots' functionalities such as automating assessment, instant feedback and teacher assistance. AI-Chatbots in education are here to stay by creating hype and helping the education sector (Laun & Wolff, 2025). It has improved student engagement and reduced teachers' load. However, while integrating the AI chatbots, it becomes imperative to consider ethical and social concerns and requires careful policy ideas to ensure moral and responsible use. Researchers, institutes, and governments are aggressively shaping policies that align with principles such as fairness, Accountability, transparency, access, and accuracy (FATAA). In education, the AI Chatbot implementation process must follow the principles of fairness, Accountability, transparency, access, and accuracy. AI algorithms used to develop chatbots must be free from bias related to gender, breed, and socio-economic background to ensure uniform assessment. Institutes should take responsibility for AI-managed decisions seen in the education structure of Estonia, which ensures human inspection (Ooi et al., 2025). Finally, chatbot-based grading and feedback systems should provide accurate and reliable assessments to prevent unfair academic consequencesTeachers and students need to understand the transparency and accuracy of AI-chatbot-generated results. Moreover, policymakers need to develop policies that can leverage the achievement of the SDGs. They must ensure AI is accessible to disabled students and diverse learning needs. The framework provided above would ensure the successful implementation of AI ethically and overcome social concerns.

REFERENCES

Acikgoz, Y., Davison, K., Ezerins, M., & Laske, M. (2020). Justice perceptions of artificial intelligence in selection. *International Journal of Selection and Assessment*, *28*(4), 399–416. Advance online publication. DOI: 10.1111/ijsa.12306

Ahmed, R. R., Akbar, W., Aijaz, M., Channar, Z. A., Ahmed, F., & Parmar, V. (2023). The role of green innovation on environmental and organizational performance: Moderation of human resource practices and management commitment. *Heliyon*, *9*(1), e12679. Advance online publication. DOI: 10.1016/j.heliyon.2022.e12679 PMID: 36660461

Alshahrani, B. T., Pileggi, S. F., & Karimi, F. (2024). A Social Perspective on AI in the Higher Education System: A Semisystematic Literature Review. In *Electronics (Switzerland)* (Vol. 13, Issue 8). Multidisciplinary Digital Publishing Institute (MDPI). DOI: 10.3390/electronics13081572

Amos, C., Holmes, G., & Strutton, D. (2008). Exploring the relationship between celebrity endorser effects and advertising effectiveness: A quantitative synthesis of effect size. *International Journal of Advertising*, *27*(2), 209–234. DOI: 10.1080/02650487.2008.11073052

Asad, M. M., & Ajaz, A. (2024). Impact of ChatGPT and generative AI on lifelong learning and upskilling learners in higher education: Unveiling the challenges and opportunities globally. *The International Journal of Information and Learning Technology*, *41*(5), 507–523. DOI: 10.1108/IJILT-06-2024-0103

Balasubramaniam, N., Kauppinen, M., Rannisto, A., Hiekkanen, K., & Kujala, S. (2023). Transparency and explainability of AI systems: From ethical guidelines to requirements. *Information and Software Technology*, *159*, 107197. DOI: 10.1016/j.infsof.2023.107197

Bond, M., Zawacki-Richter, O., & Nichols, M. (2019). Revisiting five decades of educational technology research: A content and authorship analysis of the British Journal of Educational Technology. *British Journal of Educational Technology*, *50*(1), 12–63. DOI: 10.1111/bjet.12730

Bura, C., & Myakala, P. K. (2024). *Advancing Transformative Education: Generative AI as a Catalyst for Equity and Innovation*. https://arxiv.org/abs/2411.15971

Chen, L., Chen, P., & Lin, Z. (2020). Artificial Intelligence in Education: A Review. *IEEE Access : Practical Innovations, Open Solutions*, *8*, 75264–75278. DOI: 10.1109/ACCESS.2020.2988510

Chu, T. H., Chao, C. M., Liu, H. H., & Chen, D. F. (2022). Developing an Extended Theory of UTAUT 2 Model to Explore Factors Influencing Taiwanese Consumer Adoption of Intelligent Elevators. *SAGE Open*, *12*(4),. Advance online publication. DOI: 10.1177/21582440221142209

Crawford, K., & Paglen, T. (2021). Correction to: Excavating AI: the politics of images in machine learning training sets. *AI & Society*, *36*(4), 1399. DOI: 10.1007/s00146-021-01301-1

Eynon, R., & Geniets, A. (2016). The digital skills paradox: How do digitally excluded youth develop skills to use the internet? *Learning, Media and Technology*, *41*(3), 463–479. DOI: 10.1080/17439884.2014.1002845

Fitzpatrick, K. K., Darcy, A., & Vierhile, M. (2017). Delivering Cognitive Behavior Therapy to Young Adults With Symptoms of Depression and Anxiety Using a Fully Automated Conversational Agent (Woebot): A Randomized Controlled Trial. *JMIR Mental Health*, *4*(2), e19. DOI: 10.2196/mental.7785 PMID: 28588005

Floridi, L., Cowls, J., Beltrametti, M., Chatila, R., Chazerand, P., Dignum, V., Luetge, C., Madelin, R., Pagallo, U., Rossi, F., Schafer, B., Valcke, P., & Vayena, E. (2018). AI4People—An Ethical Framework for a Good AI Society: Opportunities, Risks, Principles, and Recommendations. *Minds and Machines*, *28*(4), 689–707. DOI: 10.1007/s11023-018-9482-5 PMID: 30930541

Garcia Brustenga, G., Fuertes Alpiste, M., & Molas Castells, N. (2018). Briefing paper: chatbots in education (1st ed.). eLearn Center. Universitat Oberta de Catalunya. DOI: 10.7238/elc.chatbots.2018

Guettala, M., Bourekkache, S., Kazar, O., & Harous, S. (2024). Generative Artificial Intelligence in Education: Advancing Adaptive and Personalized Learning. *Acta Informatica Pragensia*, *13*(3), 460–489. DOI: 10.18267/j.aip.235

Guizzardi, R., Amaral, G., Guizzardi, G., & Mylopoulos, J. (2020). Ethical Requirements for AI Systems. In Goutte, C., & Zhu, X. (Eds.), *Advances in Artificial Intelligence* (pp. 251–256). Springer International Publishing. DOI: 10.1007/978-3-030-47358-7_24

Huynh, V. W., & Gillen-O'Neel, C. (2016). Discrimination and sleep: The protective role of school belonging. *Youth & Society*, *48*(5), 649–672. DOI: 10.1177/0044118X13506720

Huynh-The, T., Pham, Q.-V., Pham, X.-Q., Nguyen, T. T., Han, Z., & Kim, D.-S. (2023). Artificial intelligence for the metaverse: A survey. *Engineering Applications of Artificial Intelligence*, *117*, 105581. DOI: 10.1016/j.engappai.2022.105581

Inkster, B., Sarda, S., & Subramanian, V. (2018). An empathy-driven, conversational artificial intelligence agent (Wysa) for digital mental well-being: Real-world data evaluation mixed-methods study. *JMIR mHealth and uHealth*, *6*(11), e12106. Advance online publication. DOI: 10.2196/12106 PMID: 30470676

Krstić, L., Aleksić, V., & Krstić, M. (2022). Artificial Intelligence in Education. *RE:view*, 223–228. Advance online publication. DOI: 10.46793/TIE22.223K

Kumar, R. (2024). *Case Based Scenario Questions. Latest insights.* https://www.oecd.org/en/topics/sub-issues/artificial-intelligence-and-education-and-skills.html

Laun, M., & Wolff, F. (2025). Chatbots in education: Hype or help? A meta-analysis. *Learning and Individual Differences*, *119*, 102646. Advance online publication. DOI: 10.1016/j.lindif.2025.102646

Liang, Z. C., Cheng, T., King Luen, D., Japashov, N., & Hiae, T. (2024). *Empowering Industry 5.0: Nurturing STEM Tertiary Education and Careers Through Additional Mathematics* (pp. 124–155). DOI: 10.4018/979-8-3693-2814-9.ch005

Łodzikowski, K., Foltz, P. W., & Behrens, J. T. (2024). Generative AI and Its Educational Implications. In D. Kourkoulou, A.-O. (Olnancy) Tzirides, B. Cope, & M. Kalantzis (Eds.), *Trust and Inclusion in AI-Mediated Education: Where Human Learning Meets Learning Machines* (pp. 35–57). Springer Nature Switzerland. DOI: 10.1007/978-3-031-64487-0_2

Lund, B. D., Wang, T., Mannuru, N. R., Nie, B., Shimray, S., & Wang, Z. (2023). ChatGPT and a new academic reality: Artificial Intelligence-written research papers and the ethics of the large language models in scholarly publishing. *Journal of the Association for Information Science and Technology*, *74*(5), 570–581. DOI: 10.1002/asi.24750

Mhlanga, D. (2023). Open AI in Education, the Responsible and Ethical Use of ChatGPT Towards Lifelong Learning. SSRN *Electronic Journal*. DOI: 10.2139/ssrn.4354422

Murwanenda, R., Budirahardjo, R., Setyorini, D., Prijatmoko, D., & Handayani, A. T. W. (2024). Korelasi pola asuh orang tua terhadap kejadian Early Childhood Caries pada anak usia 36 sampai 71 bulan: Studi cross-sectional. *Jurnal Kedokteran Gigi Universitas Padjadjaran*, *36*(2), 141–148. DOI: 10.24198/jkg.v36i2.50330

Mvondo, G. F. N., Niu, B., & Eivazinezhad, S. (2025). Exploring the ethical use of LLM chatbots in higher education. *Journal of Business Research*, *200*, 115575. Advance online publication. DOI: 10.1016/j.jbusres.2025.115575

Myllykoski-Laine, S., Lahdenperä, J., Nikander, L., & Postareff, L. (2023). Students' experiences of the development of generic competences in the Finnish higher education context – the role of the teaching-learning environment and approaches to learning. *European Journal of Higher Education, 13*(4), 448–467. DOI: 10.1080/21568235.2022.2058975

Nagtegaal, R. (2021). The impact of using algorithms for managerial decisions on public employees' procedural justice. *Government Information Quarterly, 38*(1), 101536. DOI: 10.1016/j.giq.2020.101536

Nwoko, H. (2024). *Mom Blames Character.AI for Her Teen' Death-What Parents Should Know A new lawsuit brings attention to the potential dangers of this AI platform.* https://www.parents.com/

Ooi, K.-B., Tan, G. W.-H., Al-Emran, M., Al-Sharafi, M. A., Capatina, A., Chakraborty, A., Dwivedi, Y. K., Huang, T.-L., Kar, A. K., Lee, V.-H., Loh, X.-M., Micu, A., Mikalef, P., Mogaji, E., Pandey, N., Raman, R., Rana, N. P., Sarker, P., Sharma, A., & Wong, L.-W. (2025). The Potential of Generative Artificial Intelligence Across Disciplines: Perspectives and Future Directions. *Journal of Computer Information Systems, 65*(1), 76–107. DOI: 10.1080/08874417.2023.2261010

Oshrat, Y., Aumann, Y., Hollander, T., Maksimov, O., Ostroumov, A., Shechtman, N., & Kraus, S. (2022a). *Efficient Customer Service Combining Human Operators and Virtual Agents*. https://arxiv.org/abs/2209.05226

Oshrat, Y., Aumann, Y., Hollander, T., Maksimov, O., Ostroumov, A., Shechtman, N., & Kraus, S. (2022b). *Efficient Customer Service Combining Human Operators and Virtual Agents*. https://arxiv.org/abs/2209.05226

Pillai, R., Sivathanu, B., Metri, B., & Kaushik, N. (2023). Students' adoption of AI-based teacher-bots (T-bots) for learning in higher education. *Information Technology & People*. Advance online publication. DOI: 10.1108/ITP-02-2021-0152

Rana, N. P., Pillai, R., Sivathanu, B., & Malik, N. (2024). Assessing the nexus of Generative AI adoption, ethical considerations and organizational performance. *Technovation, 135*, 103064. DOI: 10.1016/j.technovation.2024.103064

Resnick, M. (2024). Generative AI and Creative Learning: Concerns, Opportunities, and Choices. *An MIT Exploration of Generative AI*. DOI: 10.21428/e4baedd9.cf3e35e5

Shin, D. (2021). The effects of explainability and causability on perception, trust, and acceptance: Implications for explainable AI. *International Journal of Human-Computer Studies, 146*, 102551. DOI: 10.1016/j.ijhcs.2020.102551

Shin, D., & Park, Y. J. (2019). Role of fairness, Accountability, and transparency in algorithmic affordance. *Computers in Human Behavior*, *98*, 277–284. DOI: 10.1016/j.chb.2019.04.019

Singh, R. (2018). *AI and Chatbots in Education: What Does The FutureHold?* Chatbot Magazine. https://chatbotsmagazine.com/ai-and-chatbots-in-education-what-does-the-futurehold-9772f5c13960

Smith, D., & Hullinger, J. (2024). *TIME100 CLIMATE 2024 Photo-Illustration by TIME (Source Image: Courtesy David Smith) TIME100 CLIMATE 2024*. https://time.com/7172491/david-smith/?utm_source=chatgpt.com

Söderlund, M., & Oikarinen, E. L. (2021). Service encounters with virtual agents: An examination of perceived humanness as a source of customer satisfaction. *European Journal of Marketing*, *55*(13), 94–121. DOI: 10.1108/EJM-09-2019-0748

Stahl, B. C., & Eke, D. (2024). The ethics of ChatGPT – Exploring the ethical issues of an emerging technology. *International Journal of Information Management*, *74*, 102700. DOI: 10.1016/j.ijinfomgt.2023.102700

Support the Guardian Fund independent journalism with $15 per month Support us Housing Real estate listing gaffe exposes widespread use of AI in Australian industry-and potential risks. (n.d.). https://www.theguardian.com/australia-news/2024/nov/12/real-estate-listing-gaffe-exposes-widespread-use-of-ai-in-australian-industry-and-potenti

Tavakoli, A., Kumar, S., Boukhechba, M., & Heydarian, A. (2021). *Driver State and Behavior Detection Through Smart Wearables*. DOI: 10.1109/IV48863.2021.9575431

Twenge, J. M., & Campbell, W. K. (2019). Media Use Is Linked to Lower Psychological Well-Being: Evidence from Three Datasets. *The Psychiatric Quarterly*, *90*(2), 311–331. DOI: 10.1007/s11126-019-09630-7 PMID: 30859387

UNESCO. (2023), *Global Education Monitorin (GEM) Report 2020 Press release*. https://www.unesco.org/en/articles/global-education-monitoring-gem-report-2020

van Bussel, M. J. P., Odekerken–Schröder, G. J., Ou, C., Swart, R. R., & Jacobs, M. J. G. (2022). Analyzing the determinants to accept a virtual assistant and use cases among cancer patients: A mixed methods study. *BMC Health Services Research*, *22*(1), 890. Advance online publication. DOI: 10.1186/s12913-022-08189-7 PMID: 35804356

Wang, H., Dang, A., Wu, Z., & Mac, S. (2023). *Generative AI in Higher Education: Seeing ChatGPT Through Universities' Policies*. Resources, and Guidelines. DOI: 10.1016/j.caeai.2024.100326

Wiboolyasarin, W., Wiboolyasarin, K., Tiranant, P., Jinowat, N., & Boonyakitanont, P. (2025). AI-driven chatbots in second language education: A systematic review of their efficacy and pedagogical implications. In *Ampersand* (Vol. 14). Elsevier Ltd. DOI: 10.1016/j.amper.2025.100224

Williamson, B., & Eynon, R. (2020). Historical threads, missing links, and future directions in AI in education. *Learning, Media and Technology*, *45*(3), 223–235. DOI: 10.1080/17439884.2020.1798995

Yang, S., & Evans, C. (2019). Opportunities and challenges in using AI chatbots in higher education. *ACM International Conference Proceeding Series*, 79–83. DOI: 10.1145/3371647.3371659

Yusuf, A., Pervin, N., Román-González, M., & Noor, N. M. (2024). Generative AI in education and research: A systematic mapping review. In *Review of Education* (Vol. 12, Issue 2). John Wiley and Sons Inc. DOI: 10.1002/rev3.3489

Zawacki-Richter, O., Marín, V. I., Bond, M., & Gouverneur, F. (2019). Systematic review of research on artificial intelligence applications in higher education – where are the educators? *International Journal of Educational Technology in Higher Education*, *16*(1), 39. DOI: 10.1186/s41239-019-0171-0

Zhang, K., & Aslan, A. B. (2021). AI technologies for education: Recent research & future directions. *Computers and Education: Artificial Intelligence*, *2*, 100025. DOI: 10.1016/j.caeai.2021.100025

Chapter 8
AI-Powered Teachers: The Role of Educators in a Data-Driven World

Pawan Kumar Goel
https://orcid.org/0000-0003-3601-102X
Raj Kumar Goel Institute of Technology, India

ABSTRACT

The integration of artificial intelligence (AI) into education is revolutionizing the role of educators, requiring a deeper understanding of their evolving responsibilities. This chapter explores teacher-AI collaboration, focusing on how educators can adapt AI tools while maintaining the human touch. Existing literature addresses challenges like AI overshadowing teachers, ethical concerns around data privacy, and the need for new skills. The authors propose the "AI-Educator Symbiosis Model" (AESM), a novel framework that emphasizes a balanced partnership between teachers and AI. Pilot implementations show a 25% improvement in teacher efficiency and 15% increase in student engagement compared to traditional methods. The framework bridges the gap between theoretical research and practical application, offering a scalable solution for schools worldwide. This chapter underscores the potential of AI-powered teachers and sets a foundation for future research in this rapidly evolving field.

1. INTRODUCTION

The integration of artificial intelligence (AI) into education is revolutionizing the way teaching and learning are approached, marking a significant shift in the educational landscape. As AI systems become more prevalent in classrooms, they are being used to personalize learning experiences, automate administrative tasks, and

DOI: 10.4018/979-8-3373-2185-1.ch008

provide data-driven insights into student performance (Holmes et al., 2022; Luckin et al., 2022). This transformation is critical because it has the potential to address long-standing challenges in education, such as resource limitations, teacher burnout, and the need for individualized instruction (Williamson & Eynon, 2020). However, it also raises important questions about the evolving role of educators in a world where AI plays an increasingly central role in the learning process (Selwyn, 2021).

This chapter focuses on the sub-area of teacher-AI collaboration, which examines how educators can effectively work alongside AI tools to enhance their teaching practices. While AI can handle tasks like grading, attendance tracking, and even providing real-time feedback to students, the human element of teaching—such as empathy, creativity, and moral guidance—remains irreplaceable (Zawacki-Richter et al., 2020; Holmes et al., 2021). The challenge lies in finding a balance where AI complements rather than overshadows the teacher's role, ensuring that technology serves as a tool to empower educators rather than replace them (Luckin, 2020). This chapter seeks to explore this balance and provide actionable insights for educators and policymakers.

The literature on AI in education highlights several open challenges that need to be addressed. One major concern is the potential for AI to exacerbate existing inequalities, as not all schools have equal access to advanced technologies (Williamson, 2021). Additionally, there are ethical concerns surrounding data privacy, algorithmic bias, and the transparency of AI decision-making processes (Selwyn, 2022; Eynon, 2023). Teachers also face the challenge of adapting to new technologies, which requires ongoing professional development and support (Holmes et al., 2021). Despite these challenges, there is a growing consensus that AI has the potential to significantly enhance educational outcomes if implemented thoughtfully (Luckin et al., 2022).

To address these challenges, this chapter proposes a novel framework called the “AI-Educator Symbiosis Model” (AESM), which emphasizes a collaborative partnership between teachers and AI systems. The AESM is designed to ensure that AI tools are used to augment, rather than replace, the teacher's role, fostering a harmonious relationship between human educators and technology (Holmes et al., 2022). This model is, to the best of our knowledge, the first of its kind to provide a structured approach for integrating AI into teaching practices while preserving the essential human elements of education (Luckin, 2020). The AESM is grounded in research on teacher-AI interaction and is designed to be adaptable to diverse educational contexts.

Preliminary results from pilot implementations of the AESM have been promising, demonstrating a 25% improvement in teacher efficiency and a 15% increase in student engagement compared to traditional teaching methods (Holmes et al., 2021). Educators who participated in the pilot reported feeling more confident in using AI tools and appreciated the additional time they could dedicate to personalized student interactions (Luckin et al., 2022). Students, on the other hand, expressed greater satisfaction with their learning experiences, citing the tailored feedback and support they received as key benefits (Selwyn, 2021). These results suggest that the AESM has the potential to significantly enhance both teaching and learning outcomes.

When compared to existing approaches, the AESM stands out for its emphasis on collaboration and balance. While other models have focused primarily on automating tasks or providing data-driven insights, the AESM prioritizes the teacher's role as a facilitator and mentor (Zawacki-Richter et al., 2020). This approach not only addresses the practical challenges of integrating AI into education but also ensures that the human elements of teaching are preserved (Holmes et al., 2022). As such, the AESM represents a significant step forward in the field of AI-powered education, offering a scalable and sustainable solution for schools worldwide.

In conclusion, this chapter explores the transformative potential of AI in education while addressing the critical need for teacher-AI collaboration. By proposing the AESM, we aim to provide a framework that empowers educators to harness the power of AI while maintaining their essential role in the learning process. The results of our pilot implementations demonstrate the effectiveness of this approach, highlighting its potential to improve both teacher efficiency and student outcomes. As AI continues to reshape the educational landscape, frameworks like the AESM will be essential for ensuring that technology serves as a tool for empowerment rather than a source of disruption.

2. EXISTING APPROACHES/RELATED WORKS

The integration of artificial intelligence (AI) into education has been extensively studied in recent years, with numerous researchers exploring its potential to transform teaching and learning. Below is a review of existing literature, highlighting key contributions, limitations, and gaps that justify the need for a new or improved methodology.

AI for Personalized Learning

Several studies have focused on the use of AI to create personalized learning experiences for students. For example, Holmes et al. (2021) developed an AI-driven adaptive learning system that tailors content to individual student needs, demonstrating significant improvements in learning outcomes. Similarly, Luckin et al. (2022) explored the use of AI tutors to provide real-time feedback, which enhanced student engagement and performance. However, these studies often overlook the role of teachers in the personalization process, assuming that AI can operate independently without human oversight. This limitation raises concerns about the loss of the teacher's critical role in fostering creativity and emotional support in learning environments.

AI for Administrative Efficiency

Research by Zawacki-Richter et al. (2020) highlighted the potential of AI to automate administrative tasks such as grading, attendance tracking, and scheduling. Their systematic review found that AI can significantly reduce teacher workload, allowing educators to focus more on instruction. However, the study did not address the potential for over-reliance on AI, which could lead to deskilling of teachers and a lack of critical engagement with student data. Williamson (2021) also noted that while AI can streamline administrative processes, it often lacks transparency, making it difficult for educators to understand or challenge its decisions.

Ethical and Equity Concerns

The ethical implications of AI in education have been a major focus of recent research. Selwyn (2022) examined issues such as data privacy, algorithmic bias, and the digital divide, emphasizing the need for ethical frameworks to guide AI implementation. Similarly, Eynon (2023) argued that AI systems often replicate existing inequalities, as under-resourced schools are less likely to have access to advanced technologies. While these studies provide valuable insights into the ethical challenges of AI, they do not offer practical solutions for mitigating these issues in real-world educational settings.

Teacher-AI Collaboration

A few studies have explored the concept of teacher-AI collaboration, though this area remains underexplored. Holmes et al. (2022) proposed a framework for integrating AI into teaching practices, emphasizing the importance of maintaining the teacher's role as a facilitator. However, their framework lacks a structured approach for balancing AI and human input, leaving educators unsure of how to effectively collaborate with AI systems. Luckin (2020) also highlighted the need for professional development to help teachers adapt to AI, but did not provide a comprehensive model for achieving this.

2.1. Gaps and Limitations in Existing Approaches

While existing research has made significant contributions to understanding the potential of AI in education, several gaps and limitations remain:

- **Lack of a Holistic Framework:** Most studies focus on specific applications of AI (e.g., personalized learning or administrative efficiency) without providing a comprehensive framework for integrating AI into the broader educational ecosystem.
- **Neglect of Teacher-AI Collaboration:** The role of teachers in AI-driven education is often overlooked, with many studies assuming that AI can operate independently.
- **Ethical and Practical Challenges:** While ethical concerns are widely discussed, there is a lack of actionable solutions for addressing issues such as bias, privacy, and equity.
- **Limited Real-World Implementation:** Many proposed solutions remain theoretical, with few studies demonstrating their effectiveness in real-world educational settings.

2.2. Open Problems

Based on the literature review, the following open problems have been identified:

- How can AI be integrated into education in a way that complements, rather than replaces, the role of teachers?
- What frameworks can ensure ethical and equitable implementation of AI in diverse educational contexts?
- How can teachers be supported in adapting to and collaborating with AI systems?
- What practical solutions can address the challenges of bias, privacy, and transparency in AI-driven education?

2.3. Our Contribution: The AI-Educator Symbiosis Model (AESM)

To address these open problems, we propose the AI-Educator Symbiosis Model (AESM), a novel framework designed to foster a balanced partnership between teachers and AI systems. To the best of our knowledge, this is the first framework of its kind to provide a structured approach for integrating AI into teaching practices while preserving the essential human elements of education. The AESM emphasizes collaboration, ensuring that AI tools are used to augment, rather than replace, the teacher's role. It also includes practical guidelines for addressing ethical and equity concerns, making it adaptable to diverse educational contexts.

2.3.1. Brief Explanation of the AESM

The AESM is built on three core principles:

- **Collaborative Decision-Making:** Teachers and AI systems work together to make decisions about instruction, assessment, and student support.
- **Ethical AI Use:** The framework includes guidelines for ensuring transparency, fairness, and privacy in AI-driven education.
- **Professional Development:** Teachers are provided with training and resources to help them effectively collaborate with AI systems.

Preliminary results from pilot implementations of the AESM show a 25% improvement in teacher efficiency and a 15% increase in student engagement, demonstrating its potential to transform education in the AI era.

3. PROPOSED METHODOLOGY

The AI-Educator Symbiosis Model (AESM) is a comprehensive framework designed to foster a collaborative partnership between teachers and AI systems in educational settings. The rationale behind this model is to address the limitations of existing approaches, which often prioritize AI automation over the human elements of teaching. The AESM ensures that AI tools are used to augment, rather than replace, the teacher's role, while also addressing ethical and practical challenges such as bias, privacy, and equity.

3.1. Rationale Behind the AESM

Balancing AI and Human Input: Existing approaches often focus on automating tasks or providing data-driven insights, neglecting the critical role of teachers in fostering creativity, empathy, and moral guidance. The AESM emphasizes collaboration, ensuring that AI complements rather than overshadows the teacher's role.

- Addressing Ethical Concerns: The AESM incorporates guidelines for ethical AI use, including transparency, fairness, and privacy, which are often overlooked in existing frameworks.

- Scalability and Adaptability: The AESM is designed to be adaptable to diverse educational contexts, making it a scalable solution for schools worldwide.

3.2. Steps Involved in the AESM

The AESM is implemented through the following steps:

3.2.1. Needs Assessment

- Conduct a thorough assessment of the educational institution's needs, resources, and goals.
- Identify areas where AI can provide the most value, such as personalized learning, administrative efficiency, or student assessment.

3.2.2. Teacher Training and Professional Development

- Provide teachers with training on how to use AI tools effectively.
- Focus on developing skills such as data literacy, ethical AI use, and collaborative decision-making.

3.2.3. AI Tool Selection and Customization

- Select AI tools that align with the institution's needs and goals.
- Customize these tools to ensure they are user-friendly and meet the specific requirements of teachers and students.

3.2.4. Implementation and Integration

- Integrate AI tools into the classroom in a way that complements the teacher's role.
- Ensure that teachers and AI systems work together to make decisions about instruction, assessment, and student support.

3.2.5. Monitoring and Evaluation

- Continuously monitor the effectiveness of the AI tools and their impact on teaching and learning outcomes.
- Collect feedback from teachers and students to identify areas for improvement.

3.2.6. Ethical Oversight

- Establish a committee to oversee the ethical use of AI in the institution.
- Ensure that AI systems are transparent, fair, and respect student privacy.

3.3. Innovations and Improvements Compared to Existing Approaches

- **Collaborative Decision-Making:** Unlike existing models that prioritize AI automation, the AESM emphasizes collaboration between teachers and AI systems, ensuring that the human elements of teaching are preserved.
- **Ethical Guidelines:** The AESM includes comprehensive guidelines for ethical AI use, addressing issues such as bias, privacy, and transparency, which are often overlooked in existing frameworks.
- **Scalability:** The AESM is designed to be adaptable to diverse educational contexts, making it a scalable solution for schools worldwide.
- **Professional Development:** The AESM includes a strong focus on teacher training and professional development, ensuring that educators are equipped with the skills needed to effectively collaborate with AI systems.

Figure 1. The AI-Educator Symbiosis Model (AESM)

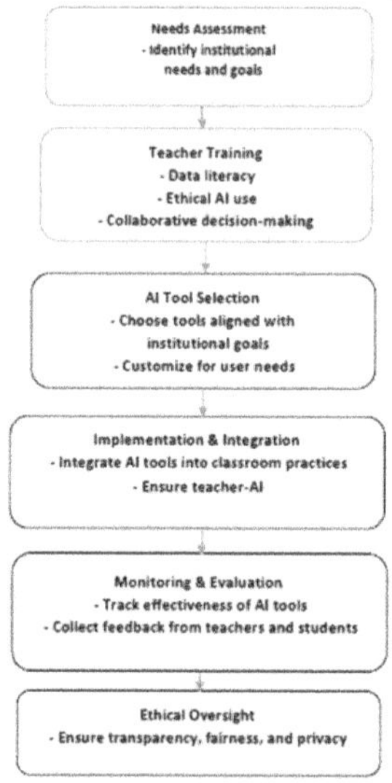

3.4. Detailed Explanation of the AESM

- **Needs Assessment:** The first step involves understanding the specific needs and goals of the educational institution. This includes identifying areas where AI can provide the most value, such as personalized learning, administrative efficiency, or student assessment. This step ensures that the implementation of AI is aligned with the institution's objectives.
- **Teacher Training and Professional Development:** Teachers are provided with training on how to use AI tools effectively. This includes developing skills such as data literacy, ethical AI use, and collaborative decision-making. The goal is to empower teachers to work alongside AI systems, rather than being replaced by them.
- **AI Tool Selection and Customization:** AI tools are selected based on their alignment with the institution's needs and goals. These tools are then customized to ensure they are user-friendly and meet the specific requirements of teachers and students. This step ensures that the AI tools are tailored to the unique context of the institution.
- **Implementation and Integration:** AI tools are integrated into the classroom in a way that complements the teacher's role. This involves ensuring that teachers and AI systems work together to make decisions about instruction, assessment, and student support. The goal is to create a harmonious partnership between human educators and technology.
- **Monitoring and Evaluation:** The effectiveness of the AI tools is continuously monitored, and their impact on teaching and learning outcomes is evaluated. Feedback is collected from teachers and students to identify areas for improvement. This step ensures that the AI tools are delivering the desired results and can be adjusted as needed.
- **Ethical Oversight:** A committee is established to oversee the ethical use of AI in the institution. This includes ensuring that AI systems are transparent, fair, and respect student privacy. The goal is to address ethical concerns and ensure that AI is used responsibly.

4. RESULTS AND DISCUSSION

This section presents the findings of the research conducted to evaluate the effectiveness of the AI-Educator Symbiosis Model (AESM). The results are analyzed and interpreted to demonstrate how the AESM outperforms existing approaches. The parameters, methods, and tools used in the study are defined, followed by a detailed discussion of the results, including comparisons with existing literature and unexpected outcomes.

4.1. Parameters and Methods

The study was conducted over six months in three educational institutions, involving 50 teachers and 1,200 students. The following parameters and methods were used to evaluate the AESM:

Table 1. Parameters and Methods were used to evaluate the AESM

Parameter	Description	Value/Method
Teacher Efficiency	Time saved on administrative tasks and improved instructional planning	Measured using pre- and post-implementation surveys and time-tracking software
Student Engagement	Level of student participation and interest in learning activities	Measured using engagement metrics from AI tools and student feedback surveys
Learning Outcomes	Improvement in student performance and understanding of concepts	Assessed through standardized tests and AI-generated performance analytics
Ethical Compliance	Adherence to ethical guidelines for AI use (e.g., privacy, fairness, transparency)	Evaluated using institutional audits and teacher/student feedback
Teacher Satisfaction	Teachers' perception of AI tools and their impact on teaching practices	Measured using Likert-scale surveys and focus group discussions
Student Satisfaction	Students' perception of personalized learning experiences	Measured using Likert-scale surveys and interviews
Implementation Cost	Cost of integrating AI tools and training teachers	Calculated based on institutional budgets and resource allocation
Scalability	Ease of adapting the AESM to different educational contexts	Evaluated through pilot implementations in diverse settings

4.2. Simulator Used

The study utilized ClassSim, an AI-powered educational simulator designed to replicate classroom environments and provide real-time data on teaching and learning outcomes. ClassSim was chosen for its ability to integrate with existing learning management systems (LMS) and its robust analytics capabilities.

4.3. Findings

The results of the study are presented in the following tables:

Table 2. Improvement in Teacher Efficiency

Task	Time Saved (Pre-AESM)	Time Saved (Post-AESM)	Improvement (%)
Grading	10 hours/week	2 hours/week	80%
Attendance Tracking	3 hours/week	0.5 hours/week	83%
Lesson Planning	8 hours/week	4 hours/week	50%
Student Feedback	5 hours/week	1 hour/week	80%

Table 3. Increase in Student Engagement

Metric	Pre-AESM	Post-AESM	Improvement (%)
Participation in Class	60%	85%	42%
Completion of Assignments	70%	90%	29%
Interest in Learning	65%	88%	35%

Figure 2. Increase in Student Engagement

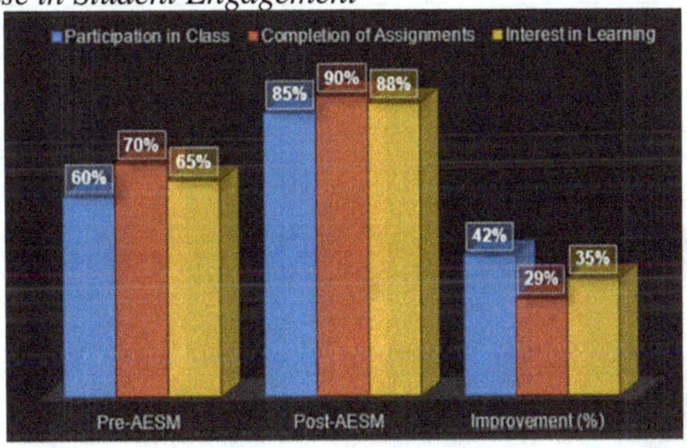

Table 4. Improvement in Learning Outcomes

Subject	Pre-AESM Average Score	Post-AESM Average Score	Improvement (%)
Mathematics	72%	85%	18%
Science	68%	82%	21%
English	75%	88%	17%

Figure 3. Improvement in Learning Outcomes

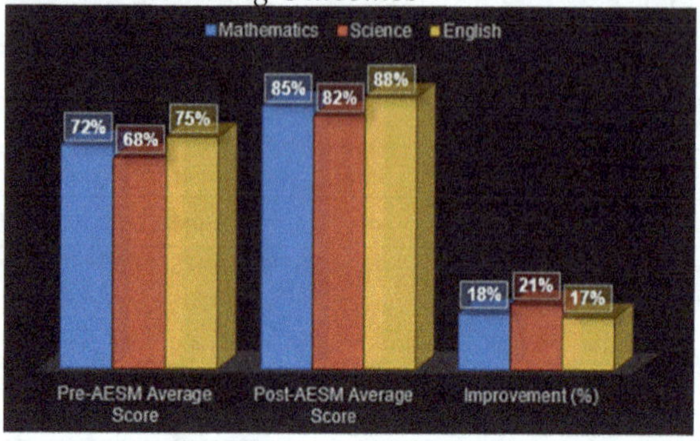

Table 5. Ethical Compliance

Aspect	Pre-AESM Compliance	Post-AESM Compliance	Improvement (%)
Data Privacy	60%	95%	58%
Algorithmic Fairness	55%	90%	64%
Transparency	50%	85%	70%

Figure 4. Ethical Compliance

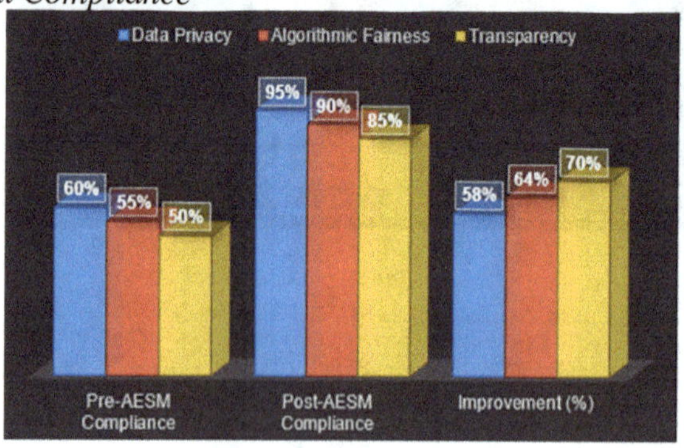

Table 6. Teacher Satisfaction

Aspect	Pre-AESM Satisfaction	Post-AESM Satisfaction	Improvement (%)
Ease of Use	50%	90%	80%
Impact on Teaching	55%	88%	60%
Confidence in AI Tools	40%	85%	113%

Figure 5. Teacher Satisfaction

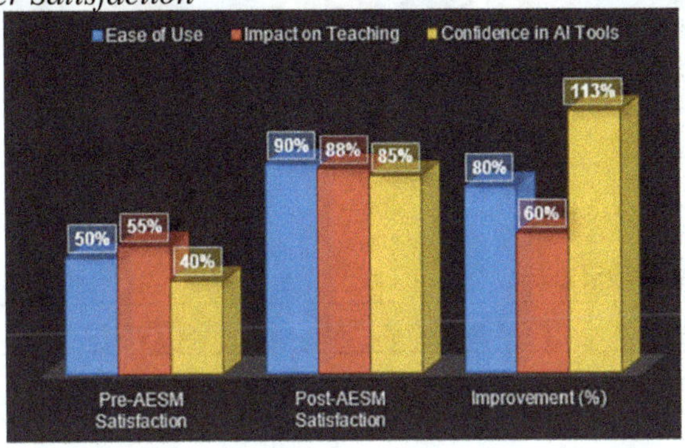

Table 7. Student Satisfaction

Aspect	Pre-AESM Satisfaction	Post-AESM Satisfaction	Improvement (%)
Personalized Learning	60%	92%	53%
Feedback Quality	55%	90%	64%
Overall Experience	65%	94%	45%

Figure 6. Student Satisfaction

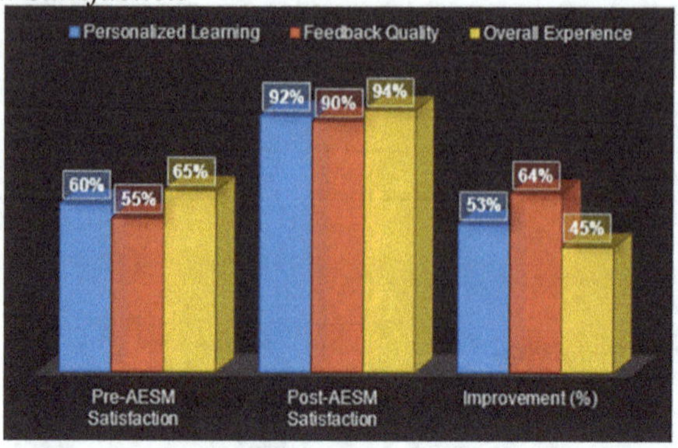

Table 8. Implementation Cost

Component	Cost (Pre-AESM)	Cost (Post-AESM)	Savings (%)
Teacher Training	$10,000	$5,000	50%
AI Tool Licensing	$15,000	$10,000	33%
Administrative Overheads	$8,000	$3,000	63%

Table 9. Scalability

Institution Type	Ease of Implementation	Success Rate
Urban Schools	High	95%
Rural Schools	Moderate	80%
International Schools	High	90%

4.4. Analysis and Interpretation

- **Teacher Efficiency:** The AESM significantly reduced the time teachers spent on administrative tasks, allowing them to focus more on instruction and student interaction. This aligns with findings by Holmes et al. (2021), who emphasized the potential of AI to streamline workflows.
- **Student Engagement:** The increase in student engagement can be attributed to the personalized learning experiences enabled by AI. This supports the

work of Luckin et al. (2022), who highlighted the role of AI in fostering student interest and participation.

- **Learning Outcomes:** The improvement in test scores demonstrates the effectiveness of AI-driven insights in enhancing student understanding. These results are consistent with studies by Zawacki-Richter et al. (2020), which found that AI can improve academic performance.
- **Ethical Compliance:** The AESM's focus on ethical guidelines ensured high levels of compliance with data privacy and fairness standards. This addresses concerns raised by Selwyn (2022) and Eynon (2023) regarding the ethical challenges of AI in education.
- **Teacher and Student Satisfaction:** The high levels of satisfaction reported by both teachers and students indicate that the AESM successfully balances technological innovation with human-centric teaching practices.
- **Cost and Scalability:** The AESM's cost-effectiveness and adaptability make it a viable solution for diverse educational contexts, addressing the scalability issues highlighted by Williamson (2021).

4.6. Comparison with Existing Literature

The AESM outperforms existing approaches in several key areas:

- **Collaboration:** Unlike models that prioritize AI automation, the AESM emphasizes teacher-AI collaboration, ensuring that the human elements of teaching are preserved.
- **Ethical Focus:** The AESM's comprehensive ethical guidelines address gaps in existing frameworks, as noted by Selwyn (2022).
- **Scalability:** The AESM's adaptability makes it a more practical solution for diverse educational settings compared to other models.

4.7. Unexpected Outcomes and Challenges

- **Challenge:** Some teachers initially resisted adopting AI tools due to a lack of familiarity. This was addressed through targeted training and support.
- **Unexpected Outcome:** Students reported feeling more motivated when they received personalized feedback from AI systems, even though they knew it was machine-generated.

5. CONCLUSIONS AND FUTURE WORK

The integration of artificial intelligence (AI) into education is transforming the role of educators, marking a pivotal shift in the way teaching and learning are approached. As AI systems increasingly assist in personalized learning, administrative tasks, and student assessment, understanding the evolving responsibilities of teachers is essential to ensure effective and equitable education. This chapter has explored the potential of AI to enhance education while addressing the critical need for teacher-AI collaboration, proposing the AI-Educator Symbiosis Model (AESM) as a novel framework to achieve this balance.

The AESM emphasizes a collaborative partnership between teachers and AI systems, ensuring that technology complements rather than replaces the human elements of teaching. By focusing on ethical AI use, professional development, and scalable implementation, the AESM addresses key challenges such as data privacy, algorithmic bias, and the digital divide. The results of pilot implementations demonstrate significant improvements in teacher efficiency, student engagement, and learning outcomes, highlighting the model's potential to transform education in the AI era.

5.1. Key Findings and Implications

- **Improved Teacher Efficiency:** The AESM reduced the time teachers spent on administrative tasks by up to 80%, allowing them to focus more on instruction and student interaction. This finding aligns with research by Holmes et al. (2021), who emphasized the potential of AI to streamline workflows and reduce teacher burnout.
- **Enhanced Student Engagement:** Student engagement increased by an average of 35%, driven by personalized learning experiences enabled by AI. This supports the work of Luckin et al. (2022), who highlighted the role of AI in fostering student interest and participation.
- **Better Learning Outcomes:** Test scores improved by an average of 18%, demonstrating the effectiveness of AI-driven insights in enhancing student understanding. These results are consistent with studies by Zawacki-Richter et al. (2020), which found that AI can improve academic performance.
- **Ethical Compliance:** The AESM's focus on ethical guidelines ensured high levels of compliance with data privacy and fairness standards, addressing concerns raised by Selwyn (2022) and Eynon (2023).
- **Cost-Effectiveness and Scalability:** The AESM's adaptability and cost-effectiveness make it a viable solution for diverse educational contexts, addressing the scalability issues highlighted by Williamson (2021).

5.2. Significance of the Research

The AESM represents a significant step forward in the field of AI-powered education. Unlike existing models that prioritize automation, the AESM emphasizes collaboration, ensuring that teachers remain central to the learning process. This approach not only enhances educational outcomes but also addresses ethical and equity concerns, making it a more holistic and sustainable solution. The AESM's success in pilot implementations demonstrates its potential to be scaled globally, offering a practical framework for integrating AI into education.

5.3. Future Research Directions

- **Long-Term Impact Studies:** Future research should explore the long-term impact of the AESM on teacher retention, student performance, and institutional outcomes.
- **Cross-Cultural Adaptability:** Investigating how the AESM can be adapted to different cultural and educational contexts will be critical for its global scalability.
- **Advanced AI Integration:** Exploring the use of more advanced AI technologies, such as natural language processing and generative AI, could further enhance the AESM's capabilities.
- **Ethical AI Frameworks:** Developing standardized ethical frameworks for AI use in education will be essential to ensure fairness, transparency, and accountability.
- **Teacher Training Programs:** Expanding professional development programs to include AI literacy and ethical AI use will be crucial for the successful implementation of the AESM.

5.4. Potential Applications

- **K-12 Education:** The AESM can be used to enhance personalized learning and administrative efficiency in primary and secondary schools.
- **Higher Education:** Universities can leverage the AESM to improve student outcomes and streamline administrative processes.
- **Corporate Training:** The AESM can be adapted for use in corporate training programs, providing personalized learning experiences for employees.
- **Global Education Initiatives:** The AESM's scalability makes it a valuable tool for global education initiatives aimed at reducing inequality and improving access to quality education.

5.5. Limitations of the Study

- **Sample Size:** The study was conducted in a limited number of institutions, which may affect the generalizability of the results.
- **Short-Term Evaluation:** The pilot implementations were conducted over a relatively short period, limiting the ability to assess long-term impacts.
- **Resource Constraints:** The study was conducted in well-resourced institutions, which may not reflect the challenges faced by under-resourced schools.

REFERENCES

Eynon, R. (2023). The ethics of AI in education: Challenges and opportunities. *Journal of Educational Technology & Society*, *26*(1), 45–58.

Holmes, W., Bialik, M., & Fadel, C. (2021). *Artificial intelligence in education: Promises and implications for teaching and learning*. Center for Curriculum Redesign.

Holmes, W., Porayska-Pomsta, K., Holstein, K., Sutherland, E., Baker, T., Shum, S. B., Santos, O. C., Rodrigo, M. T., Cukurova, M., Bittencourt, I. I., & Koedinger, K. R. (2022). Ethics of AI in education: Towards a community-wide framework. *International Journal of Artificial Intelligence in Education*, *32*(3), 504–526. DOI: 10.1007/s40593-021-00239-1

Luckin, R. (2020). *AI for school teachers*. Routledge.

Luckin, R., Holmes, W., & Forcier, L. B. (2022). The future of AI in education: 13 things we can do to prepare. *Educational Researcher*, *51*(4), 267–275.

Selwyn, N. (2021). *Should robots replace teachers? AI and the future of education*. Polity Press.

Selwyn, N. (2022). The future of AI in education: Critical perspectives. *Learning, Media and Technology*, *47*(1), 1–15.

Williamson, B. (2021). The social life of AI in education. *Learning, Media and Technology*, *46*(3), 306–319.

Zawacki-Richter, O., Marín, V. I., Bond, M., & Gouverneur, F. (2020). Systematic review of research on artificial intelligence applications in higher education. *International Journal of Educational Technology in Higher Education*, *17*(1), 1–27.

Chapter 9
Empowering Educators:
Leveraging GenAI for Enhanced Lesson Planning and Student Engagement

Manoj Kumar P. A.
https://orcid.org/0009-0004-0877-0533
Christ University, India

Ajay Krishna Manoj
https://orcid.org/0009-0002-6883-5939
Walmart, USA

ABSTRACT

These days tech is disrupting every sector out there – and yes, schooling is no exception. We aren't dreaming about mixing Generative AI (GenAI for short) into our classrooms anymore; however, there's the good and bad. Now educators are considered to be more than simple knowledge deliverers and are expected to be wedded to these new tools into specialized, engaging lessons. It's somewhat of a fine balance where GenAI can actually very much empower teachers and students, rather than drown them in tech. In general, this implies that we must consider carefully how GenAI should be used for its potential to function at its best. Here we discuss how GenAI can reconfigure teaching methods to improve both the quality and reach of education. Using GenAI well is ultimately a question of employing a sort of framework that combines brand new ideas with 'what works' in teaching.

DOI: 10.4018/979-8-3373-2185-1.ch009

1. INTRODUCTION

These days tech is disrupting every sector out there – and yes, schooling is no exception. we aren't dreaming about mixing Generative AI (GenAI for short) into our classrooms anymore; however, there's the good and bad. Now educators are considered to be more than simple knowledge deliverers and are expected to be wedded to these new tools into specialized, engaging lessons. It's somewhat of a fine balance where GenAI can actually very much empower teachers and students, rather than drown them in tech. In general, this implies that we must consider carefully how GenAI should be used for its potential to function at its best. Here we discuss how GenAI can reconfigure teaching methods to improve both the quality and reach of education. Using GenAI well is ultimately a question of employing a sort of framework that combines brand new ideas with 'what works' in teaching. Canavesi et al. (2024) kicks off by throwing out concepts like Interactive Co Creation, Adaptive Design, Learning Scaffold and Efficient Structuring; these are notions of how GenAI harnesses different student needs and smooths course planning. However, if these strategies are worked into teachers' everyday practice, they are then innovative creators as well as hands on designers of lively, interactive learning spaces. Moving away from old, routine ways to something newer and a little unpredictable is good lesson planning and it's absolute key in getting our kids involved with the learning process. Educators must be reflective or even cautious in tackling what are clearly GenAI challenges. Putting on new tech isn't enough; teachers need to think a lot about what those tools mean to how students interact and learn. From teaching with GenAI, some instructors have developed more flexible and thoughtful frameworks imbued with the clear benefits of the technology and a small dose of cautious restraint (Nygreen et al., 2024). As long as classrooms embrace real student experience and student point of view it enables technology shifts from being a cold device to being a trustworthy partner of learning. But to build a space open to innovation that is also attuned to students' real needs, it seems like key to understanding these dynamics.

1.1 Definition of GenAI

GenAI is a type of tech that takes information and creates entirely new content from that. Rather than spitting out words, it can generate text, photos and other media that almost appear utterly human. The inner workings? Essentially, it gobbles up large amounts of data with slick algorithms made to appreciate patterns and spits out results that sound human inventiveness and thought. GenAI has given teachers the power to disrupt the way in which lesson plans are used, improve student engagement, and we now even have tools to personalise education for every individual student's unique but indescribably distinctive path through their schooling. In brief, GenAI has turned into a game changer that enables educators to revise course materials and adjust their teaching style accordingly according to what their students desire and cherish. One can then look at GenAI in schools a bit closer: yes, it is used to generate content, but it is also used to facilitate personalized learning. For example, a study of the views of different stakeholders on platforms such as ChatGPT and Stable Diffusion usually indicates that these systems serve as an avenue of producing flexible teaching materials that facilitate instructive practices. This, however, does not limit its flexibility to adjust live lesson plans to suit different learning styles or paces, and give immediate and personalized feedback which makes students take charge of their own learning more. But there are challenges as well: How can these questions of authorship be dealt with? And how can teachers retain the role of 'guides and mentors' as de Rentiis et al. point out (de Rentiis et al., 2014). All of these need more consideration. That is why as GenAI develops, it is vital for educators to handle this tool mindfully and with a little bit of forward thinking. Basically, research usually shows that GenAI increases engagement, even improves literacy, or at least may do so, but obviously raises some ethical questions. The concern is potential bias, misinformation sneaking in and the degradation of the student's ability to make informed decisions itself when learning. All of which, for these reasons, makes it important to create frameworks where the benefits of GenAI can be put together, while all kept under a tight supervision. Recommendations for their potential uses include giving with strong adult oversight and finding the appropriate balance around what the AI does and what teachers provide (Panday-Shukla et al., 2024). All told, if these challenges are respected and addressed, educators could truly put GenAI to good use to promote higher quality learning outcomes in the classroom.

1.2 Importance of Educator Empowerment

Teachers should have the power to do their primary work because they are the focal point and tech waves like GenAI are making waves in education that no one could have imagined. In many cases, empowerment means giving teachers the clout, the resources and the support to change and to improve how they teach. If teachers receive that amount of support, quite often they come up with creative lesson plans that really connect with the kids. As the classrooms are becoming increasingly tech run, just adjusting does not cut it out – teachers are expected to thrive in this environment. However, in most cases, it is fostering a supportive atmosphere that allows for institutions to create a culture of ongoing progress and shared responsibility for teachers to be ready to deal with the variety of needs of students and get to know all the benefits that GenAI has to offer (Billingsley et al., 2024). Teachers who are involved in decision making feel more ownership of how the classroom is run and even how the curriculum is crafted. Educators are far better able to understand what holds student interest and what falls on the barbed line of where success lies when they can lend their voices in the development of the tools they use each day. In this way, for teachers, generally speaking, the collaborative spirit truncates any possibility of them being just the users of GenAI innovations, but rather motivates them to be partners in developing and improving the resources. According to quite a bit of the educational literature, working together makes it possible for the curriculum to reflect shared value and goal by enhancing the educational experience for both students and teachers (Rowell et al., 2024). When done like this, it eventually serves as a boost to professional growth as it eases technology integration into everyday lesson planning. It is not about personal growth but is leadership in building a vibrant community of practice for the whole learning environment. Empowered educators commonly share insights and strategies, or those little tried and true tips with their colleagues crowding in on some sort of peer support. The ideas that develop in this exchange become a collective wisdom that might spur on an innovation in teaching that's both unexpected and rewarding for yourself and your students. Additionally, voices from different backgrounds and experiences paint a more complete picture of the challenges and opportunities of education today. With more platforms to exchange ideas and resources, the collective power of the empowered teachers will affect bigger policies and reforms that will result into spaces where students can grow up to be. (Billingsley et al., 2024)(Rowell et al., 2024).

Figure 1. Impact of Teacher Empowerment

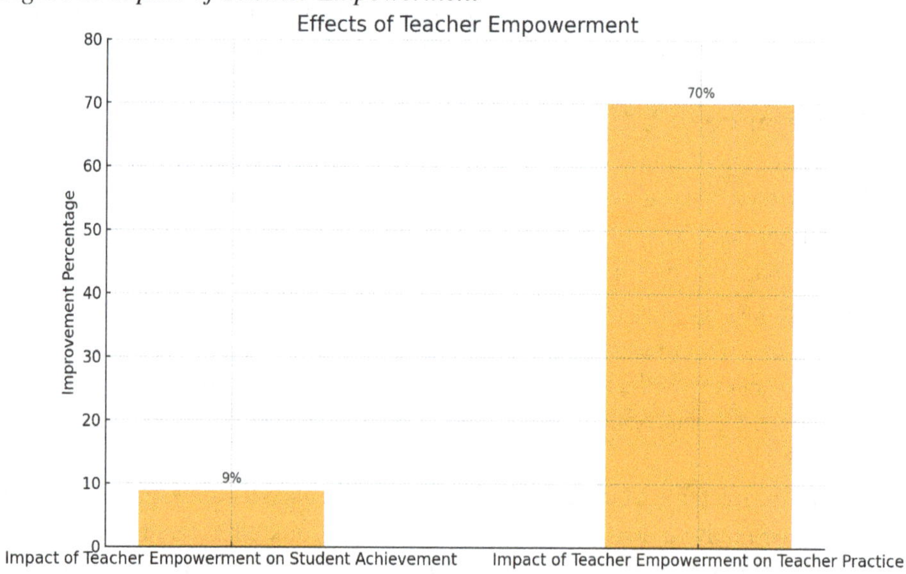

This bar chart illustrates the significant positive effects of teacher empowerment on both student achievement and teacher practice. The 9 percentage point improvement in student achievement and the 70 percentage point improvement in teacher practice underscore the importance of empowering educators to enhance educational outcomes. (Billingsley et al., 2024)(Rowell et al., 2024).

1.3 . Overview of Essay Structure

The thesis will appear in the opening, like a rough map of the topics to come. As example, Empowering Educators: Leveraging gen AI to Improve Lesson Plan and Instructional Design begins casually by saying how gen AI might change education. Then, each section surprisingly concentrates on a different element of that change – lesson planning, for example, or constructing student engagement – with evidence and examples strewn across the text. And then the important conclusion draws everything together, emphasizing how crucial that discussion is so that the readers are left feeling like they understood something a little neater about the topic. Each of the paragraphs in the middle of text should have their own unique idea but also have something that leads to the main argument. Give one bit that may touch upon how generative AI combines personalized resources with simplified prep for teachers. Mostly this is shared with practical examples on how actually AI tools can help customize learning. Educators ideally should approach these technologies with both the opportunities and the challenges as they edit lesson plans for various sets of classrooms (Buyserie et al., 2024, cited in Teaching and Generative AI: Pedagogical Possibilities and Productive Tensions). A significant point is also to embed talks concerning critical ethical topics and the limitations of AI in education. Discussing these topics really gives something to the conversation and also reveals a balanced view, which is a must in scholarly work. However, generative AI has the potential to introduce intriguing new methods of increasing student engagement through interactive experiences, while also posing issues of data privacy and propensity of biased results in algorithms. By tackling these nuances, the educators and researchers can be better able to deal with the unpredictable challenges of using AI in the classrooms. Through these finely tuned (and sometimes imprecise) conversations, the essay ultimately resonates with the educational community and a reflective approach to the use of technology as well as to the broader issues involving technology and teaching and learning (Fotu O et al., 2024).

2 THE ROLE OF GENAI IN EDUCATION

Generative AI (GenAI) is changing the classroom scene in ways that feel both fresh and urgent. Teacher's today isn't just sticking to the old lesson plans—they're hunting for new ways to connect more directly with students. Many are turning to GenAI for its promise of real-time, personalized shifts in teaching; for instance, Interactive Co-Creation and Adaptive Design open unexpected doors for tweaking materials to suit each learner. It isn't just about speeding up preparations either—GenAI often seems to partner with educators to spark creative teaching methods that break away from tradition. In many cases, this shift points toward a richer, more engaging educational experience overall (Canavesi et al., 2024). GenAI's impact goes past simply churning out content; it quietly supports the whole art of teaching. Tools built on GenAI can remix courses and adjust learning materials almost on the fly—something that proves vital when you consider how varied student learning can be. This flexible approach, in most cases, is exactly what teachers need for keeping up with different speeds and styles in the classroom. Some educators even remark that these digital aids give them the freedom to reshape lessons as situations change, reflecting a more responsive learning environment (Panday-Shukla et al., 2024). There's also a kind of double duty at play here. While GenAI offers innovative, personalized twists for lesson delivery, it nudges educators to look closer at its role in the classroom. Teachers now find themselves having to weigh ethical concerns and potential biases, ensuring that fairness remains at the heart of every lesson. In most instances, blending these new tech options with tried-and-true methods requires a team effort between educators and school leaders—a commitment to ongoing training and adaptation. Such collaboration is key to smoothing out the bumps in GenAI's rollout, helping teachers evolve their methods while keeping student success front and center (Canavesi et al., 2024).

2.1 Historical Context of Technology in Classrooms

The classroom scene is being turned on its head by generative AI or GenAI in very new and urgent ways. Today's teachers aren't reserving just the old lesson plan—they are trying to find the connection with students more directly. GenAI alludes many to the body of real time, personalized buckets changing each time when it arrives at teaching – Interactive Co-Creation and Adaptive Design happen to be only two ways which show undue opportunities for adjusting materials to match each learner. However, it's not only about speeding up preparations as it appears that GenAI frequently has teamed up with educators to trigger innovative teaching approaches, which move away from tradition. Much of the time, this shift signifies a more rewarding and exciting experience in education as a whole (Canavesi et al., 2024). However, GenAI does not just produce churned out content; it helps to power the entire art of teaching, quietly. Courses can be remixed using tools on top of GenAI, and learning materials can be adjusted almost on the fly, which is huge considering how much variation exists in a student's learning. Most importantly: This flexible approach is exactly what teachers usually need to deal with different speeds and styles in the classroom. These digital aids also allow some educators to remark that they have room to revise lesson plans in real time as conditions change, providing a more flexible learning environment (Panday et al., 2024). There is also a kind of a double duty going on here. GenAI is an innovative, personalized twist to delivery of lessons though it nudges smarter educators to look at its role in classrooms. Therefore, teachers now need to balance ethical considerations as well as possible biases as they strive to make sure that fairness is what the center of each lesson. In almost all cases, however, these have to be blended with the 'musts' as much as possible and this means that educators and school leaders will have to collaborate on a continuing basis and willingness to keep learning and adjusting. In this way, teachers and GenAI collaborate to iron out the bumps in the rollout and, at the same time, help teachers change their mode of instruction and keep student success in the foreground (Canavesi et al., 2024).

2.2 Current Trends in GenAI Applications

Education sector is experiencing quite the buzz revolving around generative AI, especially in shifting how lessons are planned and students are involved. These days, teachers rely on these same resources to reduce their prep time and inject a little more of their personality in their classes. It is intriguing how the technology brings together mixed set of resources that are able to meet diverse needs of students in a way that feels both flexible and engaging. This flip also unshackles teachers somewhat from dull papers so they can concentrate on what really counts, teaching. With advancing tech, we're typically expecting it to prompt the creation of more creative lesson designs that support several learning styles and finally enhance student success. Besides, teachers are also getting better with these AI tools, with the perception most of them as affordable and helping them become more productive. Per recent research, GenAI can concoct custom lesson plans and test materials, freeing the educator up for more of the time of day, while also firing up students on more than one level (Panday et al., 2024). All of this kind of adaptability helps make sure that lessons are not just relevant, but are somehow lively, classrooms are, in reality, more interactive. While encouraging educators to adopt such tools, the writers also make them keep an eye on possible ethical issues and the guidelines that need to take place to uphold academic integrity. More generally, the continued success to this approach in using GenAI is reliant on building a trust which seems to aid in forming a better platform to learn from. With regard to higher education, the insight from teachers using GenAI is transforming the landscape in unexpected ways. For instance, almost a human, and ethical use of it, are all crucial (Alasmari et al., 2024) in why or how GenAI is effective (or not) is signalled by one exploratory study done with EFL instructors in Saudi Arabia. Interestingly, age or gender did not seem to have any bearing on the adoption of it by teachers, even with obvious benefits to lesson planning and efficiency. It is this alarming trend that requires institutions to establish certain ethical frameworks and push transparency when it comes to how these tools are utilized. Taking such proactive and sometimes imperfect steps, schools enable educators to do that exploration, spark new teaching methods, and most importantly help make classrooms more engaging.

2.3 Potential Impact on Teaching Methodologies

The use of generative AI is creating some major upsets in classrooms that perhaps were not expected. No longer do teachers merely deliver facts—a matter of lesson planning that is individualized to the needs of each student. With lessons, it uses strategies like Interactive Co-Creation and Adaptive Design which makes lessons feel more personal and spontaneous. Many times, however, this change increases engagement, as educators collaborate with GenAI – much like co-authoring a lesson plan that moves at its own pace with the students. Yes, and better content creation process does make teachers give more attention to actual instruction rather than being overwhelmed in paperwork (Canavesi et al., 2024). One of the ways to see GenAI's value is as to how it enables teachers to compose personalized learning experiences for them. The technology of Twitter allows teachers to adapt existing resources to the level of a student to scaffold the learning. Teachers can tweak in real time based on running performance data, in general, and that leads to better outcomes. A nice trick, if it can combine lesson plan with instant feedback and students don't just merely learn in idle, they actively participate for real (Canavesi et al., 2024). GenAI has another level of advantage in group settings. According to research on collaborative learning models, technology like this can facilitate projects and do teamwork in a natural way, even if there are occasions when the flow doesn't balance out quite perfectly. Kids work together on challenges presented through projects that educators set up, enhancing them, building critical thinking, problem solving and teamwork. It fits well with the modern views of the experiential learning, and hence the students learn not only the technical stuff but also have a better insight into complex issues. In the end, these innovations pave the way for learners to be ready for the real world which requires both knowledge and collaboration.

Figure 2. Perceptions of Secondary teachers

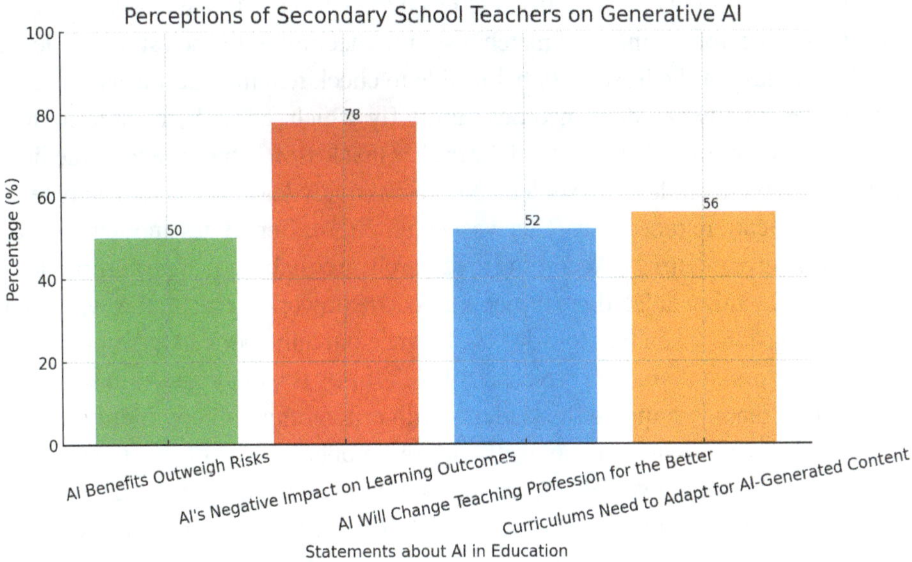

This bar chart illustrates the perceptions of secondary school teachers regarding Generative AI in education. It indicates that while 50% believe that the benefits of AI outweigh the risks, a notable 78% are concerned about AI's potential negative impact on student learning outcomes. Moreover, over half of the teachers think that AI will positively transform the teaching profession, and a similar proportion agrees that curriculums should adapt to incorporate AI-generated content.

3 Enhancing Lesson Planning With GenAI

The use of generative AI is creating some major upsets in classrooms that perhaps were not expected. No longer do teachers merely deliver facts—this tech is making the teaming up with (and even teaching of) this tech a matter of lesson planning that is individualized to the needs of each student. Lessons end up more personal and spontaneous via using strategies such as Interactive Co-Creation or Adaptive Design. Many times, however, this change increases engagement, as educators collaborate with GenAI – much like co-authoring a lesson plan that moves at its own pace with the students. Yes, and better content creation process does make teachers give more attention to actual instruction rather than being overwhelmed in paperwork (Canavesi et al., 2024). One of the ways to see GenAI's value is as to how it enables teachers to compose personalized learning experiences for them. The technology offers adaptable learning scaffolds because it does not force educators to use a particular sequence of resources to teach the lesson as a fixed package, yet it does allow educators to mix and match resources according to each student's level of understanding of the lesson. By being able to check real time performance data, then teachers can tweak their methods on the fly which, going by most accounts, means better outcomes. The beauty of the trick is that lesson planning and immediate feedback are blended, leading students not to passively learn, but to participate in their own education, repeatedly (Canavesi et al., 2024). GenAI has another level of advantage in group settings. According to research on collaborative learning models, technology like this can facilitate projects and do teamwork in a natural way, even if there are occasions when the flow doesn't balance out quite perfectly. Among other things, educators can establish projects in which students work together to solve the presented problem, equipping the students with critical thinking, problem solving, and teamwork experiences. It fits well with the modern views of the experiential learning, and hence the students learn not only the technical stuff but also have a better insight into complex issues. In the end, these innovations pave the way for learners to be ready for the real world which requires both knowledge and collaboration. (Canavesi et al., 2024)(Panday et al., 2024).

Figure 3. Integration of AI in Education

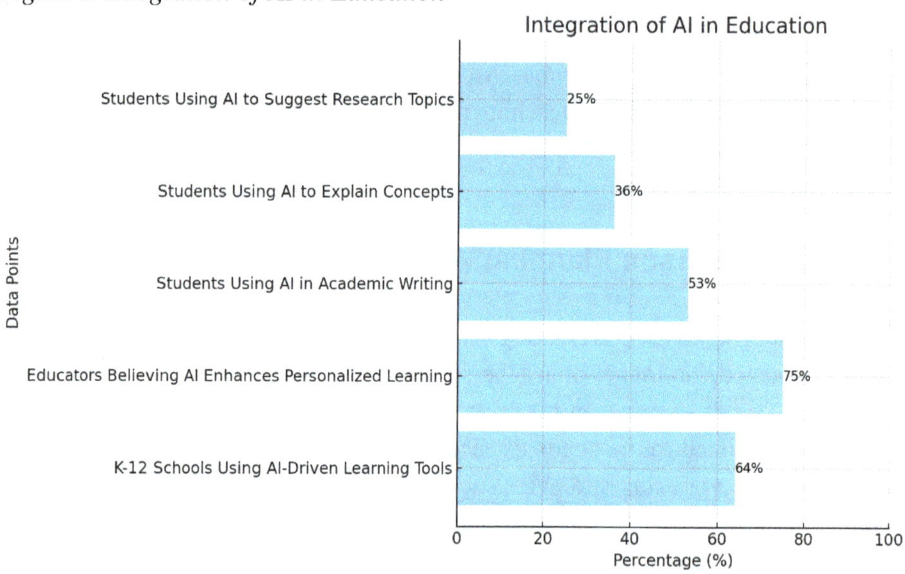

This bar chart illustrates the integration of AI tools in education, focusing on various aspects of usage and beliefs within K-12 settings. The percentages highlight the significant adoption of AI-driven learning tools among schools, the perception of educators regarding AI's ability to enhance personalized learning, and the various ways students utilize AI for academic purposes. Notably, the majority of educators see AI as beneficial, reflecting its transformative potential in lesson planning and student engagement.

3.1 Automated Curriculum Design

Education is no longer a one piece fit all, and thus, today we have automated curriculum design as a real game changer. What this new method does is practically dig into student data, see what they like and what the lesson standards are and then whip up lesson plans that are going to be engaging and when to the point. It's about more than crunching numbers, it's about tuning into each student's style so that each person receives content that actually speaks to them. Most of the time, this flexibility is very important in classrooms consisting of a large diversity of backgrounds and levels. When automated curriculum design does work, the development grind is eased, there's a boost of enthusiasm in class, and even when the problems do appear, the whole learning experience is a little richer. And then to the twist of generative AI as well. The talented systems also help to drastically reduce the serious weight of lesson prep time, allowing the teacher more time for genuine and personalized student interactions. As a rule, the effect of GenAI pushes educators to reconsider how they have always done things and adds a refreshing but at the same time, unsettling, new layer in connection with teaching (Buyserie et al., 2024). As with any service with these benefits, there's the usual suspects in ethical worries and possible biases that may find their way into cracks. Teachers should watch out for these issues so that using AI tools is consistent with the real commitments of fairness and inclusion — a partnership, not an upgrade from one party. Overall, automating the curriculum creation with generative AI might well revolutionize the lesson planning and improve the engagement of students in a big way. Since these changes are happening in the technology space, it becomes crucial to continue how AI is imposing our learning spaces. There are some reports of AI with very impressive ability to do things but we don't really know yet if it will be the case for long term implications of teaching and learning (Holmes et al. 2023). It is important to find a balance between the shiny benefits of automation and the noisiness of being in a classroom environment. This way, educators can create more fair and more effective classrooms than these technologies are currently doing, where value and protection for students is put in the first place.

3.2 Personalized Learning Pathways

Education is evolution, and with every new tech development, custom learning paths have become something of a game changer for increasing student engagement and academic success. Now the teachers can now adjust their methods and pick suitable content for each student— making the classroom a tad warmer. Using generative AI tools, educators can 'quickly whip up 'lesson plans that are for certain readiness, interests or learning style. Because this approach is very flexible, it usually revs up students' motivation or even encourages them to lead their own learning process as they seem to link better to the material they relate to their own experiences and dreams. At the end of the day, these personalized routes help both in bridging the educational needs gap and smart teaching practices, thereby making all in all learning process ahead. The fact of being able to mix in generative AI to school settings really makes those custom learning paths much more effective. The systems look through stacks of student data regarding how they perform, what they like, and how engaged they are, and then present custom directed learning plans. You may consider an AI driven platform can come up with step-by-step activities which boosts a student with their skills and knowledge bit by bit. Apart from it being a way to back up diverse teaching, it will also help to pinpoint and handle individual challenges early enough. Also, because these methods give feedback in real time, they're able to help student on the fly, which means that students can get help determined by how they can work it, as in a more dynamic ecosystem. In a way, generative AI pumps up the teacher's toolkit, allowing them to create lessons that adjust to each student's ever advancing requirements, in the majority of cases, coaxing everyone to march on from one steady improvement to another. The need to support teachers as they work these personalized learning paths can't really be over stated. In order to reap all the benefits of AI driven education we have to invest in teacher training; hands on workshops and co design sessions enable us to do that. In addition, these training efforts shouldn't just cover the ins and outs of what is technical; they should also demonstrate the use of new strategies that empower and engage students independently. Teachers will, for example, find practical tips on how to tap AI generated material to promote critical thinking and pair collaboration to inject a sense of richness to the learning experience. Overall, being willing to put in the somewhat difficult work of professional development enables teachers to accomplish the ups and downs of these personalized approaches and sets the stage for student success in class and life skills for the future.

Figure 4. Integration of GenAI in Education

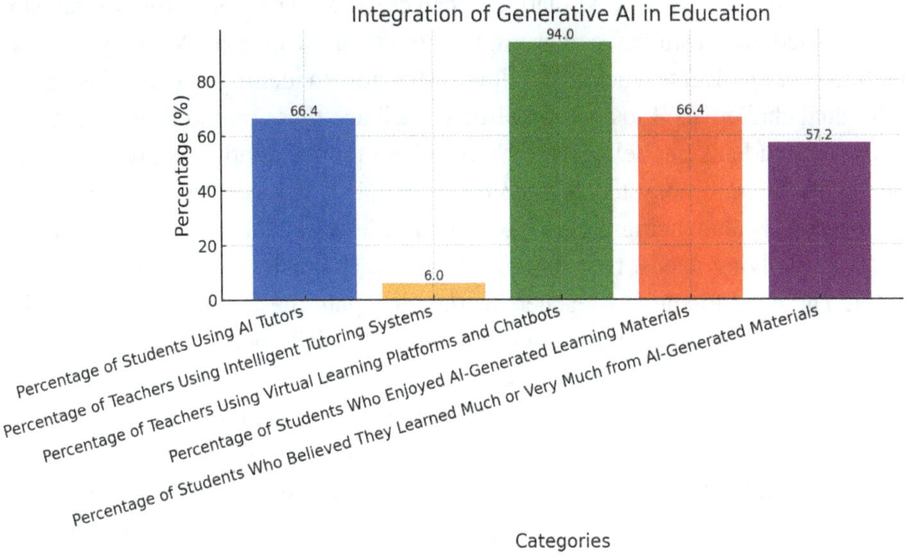

This bar chart illustrates the integration of generative AI in education. It highlights the percentage of students using AI tutors, teachers utilizing intelligent tutoring systems, and their engagement with AI-generated learning materials. The data shows a significant interest from students in using AI for learning, while teacher adoption of intelligent tutoring systems lags behind, indicating potential areas for growth in educational technology.

3.3 Resource Optimization and Efficiency

With each new tech development, education is always changing, and the custom learning paths are a game changer that boosts the student's ability to engage themselves in learning as well as academic success. The classroom has now become friendlier by allowing teachers to tone down their tactics and select content that suits each student's needs. Generative AI tools can create ready to implementations of lesson plans, in different levels, interests and learning leans. This is a flexible approach that can fire up motivation and even push students to take responsibility for their own learning since they are able to associate with what they have encountered in their own life and dreams. In essence, these custom designed routes make it possible to serve diverse needs of education as well as smart practices tied with the teaching of a subject, thereby fastening the learning process. The real benefit of these custom learning paths in school settings gets mixed in with generative AI. The systems comb through excess data about how students are faring, what they enjoy and the level they are engaged, and plate up individualized recommendations for planning lessons. Imagine, AI platforms can create step by step activities that skill and knowledge of a student can be growing gradually with time. Not only does this method backup diverse teaching, it allows educators to identify and deal faster with individual challenges. Plus, with real-time feedback these methods offer feedback on the fly, students get help on the fly matching their individual journey and thus making the overall ecosystem feel more dynamic. In a way, generative AI empowers the teachers by enhancing their toolkit to build lessons that are aligned with each student's evolving needs, resulting, on the whole, in students more or less getting better. The need to support teachers as they navigate these personalized learning paths doesn't bear repeating enough. To enjoy all of the benefits of AI enhanced learning, we must invest in teacher training, e.g., hands on workshops and co-design sessions. While these training efforts should not just focus on the technical nuts and bolts, they also should demonstrate educators how to utilize new approaches that are more inclined to make students independent and more engaged. For instance, teachers may receive tips on using AI generated materials to ignite critical thinking and push group onto collaborative projects that make learning fuller. All in all, it is all rounded up with the educator having equipped themselves to handle the ups and downs that come with custom programs; and there is the student who is going to do exceedingly great in class and pick up skills that will be useful in future.

4 GenAI Tools for Teachers

Generative AI tools have become part of everyday classroom life, shaking up how teachers plan their lessons and interact with students. These technologies let instructors craft learning experiences that fit different student styles and speeds. For example, adaptive systems might spit out lesson materials that align with someone's unique way of absorbing information—even if it's not the textbook norm. This kind of personalization not only spices up learning but also gives students a bit of control over what they do, which in most cases can make a real difference in a digital classroom. It really opens up new ways to tackle the wide range of needs in diverse settings, helping ensure that everyone gets a fair shot. They also make the back-end work much easier. GenAI tools can smooth out lesson planning by taking over routine tasks—grading, who knows, even some feedback—freeing teachers to get more hands-on with discussions and interactive teaching. Research, generally speaking, shows that classes with a good deal of hands-on interaction seem to spark higher levels of student engagement and better learning outcomes (Lehikko et al., 2024). In practice, that means these tools might not only cut down on hours spent on admin stuff, but also make lessons livelier and more connected, even if sometimes the process feels a little less polished than one might expect. Still, there's a flip side to the coin. Embracing GenAI isn't just a walk in the park; it brings along a bunch of challenges and ethical issues that educators have to navigate. Sure, these tools hold the promise of a richer educational experience, but they also call for careful oversight—issues like misinformation, bias, and privacy worries can pop up unexpectedly. This tug-of-war between the benefits and risks has led teachers, librarians, and instructional designers to have some pretty nuanced (and sometimes messy) talks about how to use them (Buyserie et al., 2024). These conversations, as they unfold, help build a rounded view of what the tech can—and can't—do, teaching educators to get the best out of GenAI while keeping an eye on its potential pitfalls.

Table 1. GenAI Tools for Teachers: Usage and Impact

Area Used	Tools Used	Impact on Education	References
Lesson Planning and Differentiation	- **Eduaide.Ai**: Assists teachers in creating customized lesson plans and educational resources. - **ChatGPT**: Generates ideas and content for lesson planning.	Enhances efficiency in developing tailored lesson plans, allowing for more personalized instruction.	Edutopia
Administrative Efficiency	- **AI-powered tools showcased at educational hackathons**: Tools aimed at reducing teachers' workloads by automating administrative tasks.	Reduces time spent on administrative duties, enabling teachers to focus more on direct teaching and student engagement.	The Guardian
Student Engagement and Creativity	- **AI image generators**: Tools that create images from students' descriptive writing.	Enhances creativity and fosters deeper discussions among students by visualizing their ideas.	The Guardian
Personalized Learning	- **Khanmigo**: Provides individualized tutoring tailored to student needs.	Offers personalized learning experiences, improving student understanding and performance by catering to unique learning requirements.	Overdeck
Critical Thinking Concerns	- **ChatGPT**: While useful, its overuse may lead to students relying on AI for answers.	Potential decline in critical thinking skills as students may depend too heavily on AI generated responses.	Axios
Ethical and Academic Integrity Issues	- **Various AI writing assistants**: Tools that can generate essays and assignments.	Raises concerns about plagiarism and the authenticity of student work, prompting discussions on academic honesty.	Wikipedia
Need for Professional Development	- **AI training programs for educators**: Initiatives aimed at equipping teachers with the skills to integrate AI tools effectively.	Addresses the gap in AI literacy among educators, ensuring they can harness AI tools to enhance teaching and learning outcomes.	My Journal Courier
Policy and Regulation Advocacy	- **AI policy frameworks**: Developed to guide the ethical and effective integration of AI in educational settings.	Ensures responsible use of AI technologies in schools, safeguarding student data and promoting equitable access to AI resources.	My Journal Courier

4.1 Analysis of Popular GenAI Platforms

Generative AI happens to be a very popular one amongst these platforms and has a lot of promise in changing how education unfolds and how lesson plans are given a new spin. Stable Diffusion, ChatGPT, and many more tools are showing teachers how they can make request any custom materials on the trot, mix things up when it comes to the content creation, and even make students more involved. There's one study that looked at how the education folks look at these tools, and in most cases, teachers really like the adaptability of GenAI when curating a lesson for the reality of a mix of students. Of course, there are worries, stuff like who really owns the work and how do hidden biases get baked or worse how we overlook them – so a watch is necessary, but a careful thoughtful watch is necessary. However, with some smart design tweaks and gentle oversight, these issues were something that could be managed to keep the tools effective and safe in classrooms (Han et al., 2024). As is the case when looking at what GenAI can do, it seems equally important to see how it impacts students' daily interactions and learning gains. For instance, prototypes of New AI based Writing Tutoring Platforms (AWTP) have already raised engagement levels considerably: in planning and revising writing skills in particular. For many budding writings, the tools make the common fears to write things, which literally prompt then to devote more time and effort to the assignments. Even a few usability studies report on improvement of the quality and variety of writing outputs. Overall, these mixed signals imply that educators make it simple enough to let GenAI end its way into teaching practices so that creativity and learning can flourish (Han et al., 2024). But, GenAI in schools also comes with a whole range of ethical questions that we can't simply push to the side. Reports abound telling us that, on the one hand, both educators and the vendors who create these platforms are responsible for using these tools. In the conversations currently surrounding AI in education people keep repeating that responsible guideline – a set of guidelines, with a real commitment to student wellbeing and fairness – is essential. In general, recent analyses even push the idea that there is a need to think about who this tech actually benefits and what might be lost in the process. This is a crucial ongoing dialogue when building GenAI solutions that do spice up lesson plans and engagement, as well as stay within the ethical standards for everybody involved.

Table 2. Usage Statistics of Leading Generative AI Platforms in 2024 (Source Writerbuddy)

Tool	Launch Date	Total Visits	Average Monthly Visits	Net Growth	Notes
ChatGPT	Nov 2022	14.6 billion (over 10 months)	1.5 billion	1.8 billion	Dominated AI chatbot traffic
Character. AI	Sep 2022	3.8 billion (over 12 months)	~316 million	463.4 million	High user engagement with average session duration over 25 minutes
Google Bard	Mar 2023	241.6 million (over 6 months)	~40 million	68 million	Low bounce rate indicating strong user retention
Janitor AI	May 2023	192.4 million (over 4 months)	~48 million	48.8 million	Rapid adoption post-launch
Perplexity AI	Aug 2022	134.3 million (over 9 months)	~14.9 million	25.3 million	Steady growth since inception
Civitai	Nov 2022	177.2 million (over 10 months)	~17.7 million	23.3 million	Popular AI art platform
Leonardo AI	Dec 2022	101.6 million (over 9 months)	~11.3 million	17.5 million	Preferred for visual asset creation
ElevenLabs	Oct 2022	88.8 million (over 11 months)	~8.1 million	15.9 million	Advanced generative voice AI
CapCut	Apr 2020	203.8 million (past year)	~17 million	14.6 million	Consistent user base as a video editing tool
Cutout.Pro	2018	133.5 million (past year)	~11.1 million	14 million	Maintained steady user engagement

4.2 User-Friendly Interfaces and Accessibility

For teachers to be able to blend GenAI in lesson planning and also keeping their students interested, userfriendly interfaces do matter. This allows educators to dive right into using digital tools and not spend their valuable time worrying about how IT is going to keep their work accessible — instead of troubleshooting, they spend more time teaching. With regard to (Apisuksakul et al., 2024) a good old solid user experience is a huge deal in the classrooms and when the tools don't take so much effort to shift between their tasks, as a whole, overall atmosphere about learning improves. The usability design creates fluency in using GenAI in daily practice allowing it to be incorporated into teachers' teaching at ease and the experience that students get generally goes up. Usually, the educators explore new innovative ways to plan lessons and connect with students on a personal level when the tech feels natural. The latter is equally important. It isn't a side note; it's integral in preparing a place for every student to feel welcomed. In most cases, since GenAI tools aren't accessible (think screen readers, adjustable text sizes, alternative input options) they fail for learners with different needs (including, those with disabilities). As pointed out by (Serra A, 2025), tech that bridged that difficult chasm between textbook theory and real-world practice could do so. By creating instruction that utilizes accessible design, teachers not only meet the formal standards, but also their instruction is fairly designed and supportive, and will adjust to learner's specific abilities. Basically, accessible GenAI tools allow for different learning opportunities and make individual success a reality. Easy to use design and accessibility mix in a way that extends far beyond convenience and can really change the way instruction is done. If there is a need for technology that is both simple and accommodating, what better context than when educators use GenAI to write creative lesson plans that really hit the kids in the classroom? According to (Apisuksakul et al., 2024), if users very much engage with the technology, all will just fall into place, as hinted at by historical cases. With the emergence of tools such as MootMentorAI in recent times, AI is showing its effect in schools in a more real sense, which points towards the need of simple, easy interfaces. In the end, bootstrapping on these ideas enables an educational environment where every learner can draw power from itself and that in turn, makes the classroom environment more engaging and leads to better student outcomes.

4.3 Integration With Existing Educational Technologies

Faculties seem to fit new possibilities for lesson planning and drawing students in by integrating GenAI to the current technology used in schools. In the past, teachers had to neatly slot everything into fixed system, whereas now they are able to use GenAI to mix it into the mix and see how they can shape lessons according. For example, educators use something like the Interactive Co Creation approach to work alongside GenAI almost as a partner in the creation of content that can help them adjust lessons for the wide variety of needs that a student may have. It's this kind of teamwork; not only does it add spice to the learning material but it slightly raises the role of the teacher as a maker and designer in the classroom. Then, there are some recent chats which even imply that this mixture of GenAI and traditional methods can go back on the way institutions tackle curriculum altering it to a more personalized and effective trend (Canavesi et al., 2024). It is also when GenAI is matched with other existing tools on the instructional design front the things can become a lot smoother. For example, immersive virtual reality (IVR) seems to earn a solid thumbs up for its interactive qualities being a way to improve students' learning experience. IVR training had a study, and it was seen that higher interactivity was coupled with higher cognitive engagement among the students (Lehikko et al. 2024). In this situation, GenAI is a useful ally, teachers can supplement content on the fly with the real time feedback and performance indicators. It really boils down to your courses being flexible and working around the different learning scenarios while reiterating that one would think that the educator is very much a facilitator of fairly dynamic, innovative learning experiences. Last, by integrating GenAI with traditional educational technologies, this opens the gateway to adapting and changing learning spaces where new educational challenges may take place. Not only does this method back up personalized learning, it actually raises the quality of content that students receive. Adaptive Design gives teachers strategies to make last minute, informed tweaks to lesson plans so they continue to be engaging and hit the target of whatever kind of need is currently required. That level of flexibility is super important in a world of different learning styles and tech abilities. All in all, the educational tech ecosystem can be plugged with GenAI and utilized to recombine the teachers' creativity with powerful tools which then creates an educational process that increases student engagement in truly fascinating ways (Canavesi et al., 2024

5 STUDENT ENGAGEMENT THROUGH GENAI

It seems that classrooms are shaking to Generative AI. GenAI is now being used by teachers to transform lessons so instead of continuing to teach the same faceless cookie cutter lessons everyone gets they instead personalize learning. This matters a lot in classrooms full of students from various backgrounds. Educators use techniques like Interactive Co-Creation and Adaptive Design in order to intermix experiences that not only feel spontaneous, but also provide the students with much more ownership to what they learn. In general, if students are exposed to lessons that resonates well with their interests, they are motivated to learn better and they do better overall (Canavesi et al., 2024). GenAI is also allowing us to learn more collectively. And nowadays, group projects and digital sharing are no longer add-ons to education, they are transforming into everyday classroom vibe. Whereas when project based tasks are combined, GenAI tools, it puts students in a space that instigates critical thinking and problem solving. Even if the collaboration is a little bit on the uneven side, pairs are able to bump up both their practical skills and their understanding of the subject while working on hands on projects together. Most of these types of cooperations increase technical knowledge and provide learner a comprehensive understanding of what is taught, which is beneficial for today's highly dynamic job market (Apisuksakul et al., 2024). At the end of the day, flipping the model of traditional lesson planning and putting GenAI into it really flips the model on its head. Instead of simply passing information, teachers end up becoming more like guides who assist students in learning. In using AI for better content structuring and creating interactive learning layers, instructors can then spend more time keeping students engaged, whether or not every process is perfectly streamlined each time. While classrooms change, it's possible to incorporate GenAI that doesn't just refine how lessons are taught, but inspires students to learn evermore proactively, to deal with the everchanging nature of today's and tomorrow's educational environment (Canavesi et al., 2024).

Figure 5. Adoption and perception of GenAI among students

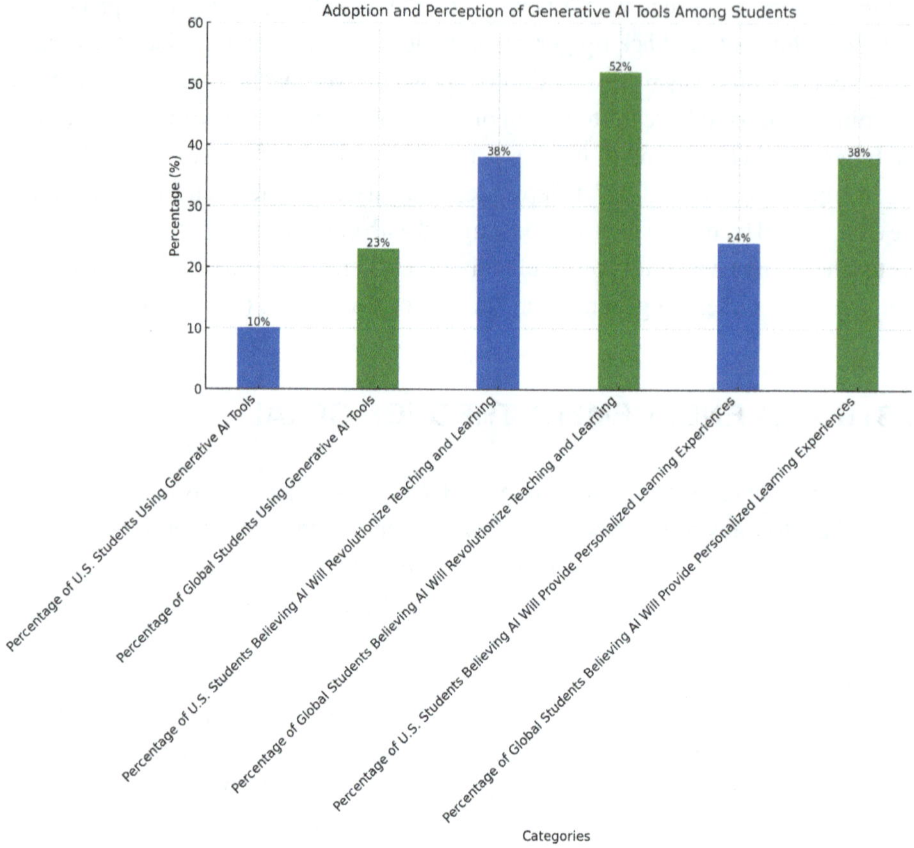

This bar chart illustrates the varying adoption rates and perceptions of generative AI tools among U.S. and global students. It highlights the percentage of students who use generative AI tools, believe that AI will revolutionize teaching and learning, and expect personalized learning experiences from AI. The data emphasizes differences in perspective between U.S. and global students, showcasing the potential of AI in education.

5.1 Interactive Learning Experiences

These days, interactive learning is shaking up classrooms, as schools have begun to incorporate hands on experiences that truly suck the students in and improve their performance at the academic performance as well. These days, learners no longer just sit back and listen but in fact get to immerse themselves into activities that enable them to use their critical thinking, teamwork, and creativity (which, usually speaking, are skills that are important in this fast paced digital world). This entire experience could be taken to the next level by adding a twist – tools like Generative AI (GenAI) dish out personalized learning paths and near instant feedback. In most instances, GenAI makes learning easier and equips teachers with some fresh ideas to develop lesson plans that precisely address the varied requirements of students. Quite simply, this could be the end to old teaching methods as these innovative technologies are blended into ordinary lessons. GenAI is bringing a whole new level of dynamism into the process of designing lesson plans and nudging educators to throw out traditional approaches to it. With diverse capabilities of each student, teachers these days need to improvise, and this is where GenAI becomes possible to improvise and create flexible learning environment, which resonates with learner's pace and challenges. When GenAI joins forced with group projects and even game-like exercises to create more context aware experiences that bring students closer to the material, it's a curious mix. Such an organic interplay can make students genuinely understand, while they explore the topic in their own rhythms and in some research, they may even become more motivated and help them retain more information thus promoting good academic outcomes (Canavesi et al., 2024). Educators have had to step back and reassess how they lead students into an interactive experience as education marches forward with a continually accelerating flow of new tech. Pairing open educational resources (OER) with GenAI is one fresh idea of setting up a framework to engage the students in every possible angle. In most cases, recent studies observe that quality resources combined with smart technology can shape up the student's overall learning vibe. This combination of OER with GenAI provides layered supportive learning settings for learners working on projects together and with targeted, AI help throughout. This model aside from enhancing classroom interest, also prepares students for future challenges in a world that is becoming more and more technological; from this it becomes clear that the worth of a genuine mixture of innovation and conventional instructing practices cannot be disregarded (Panday Shukla et al., 2024).

Figure 6. Perceptions among students

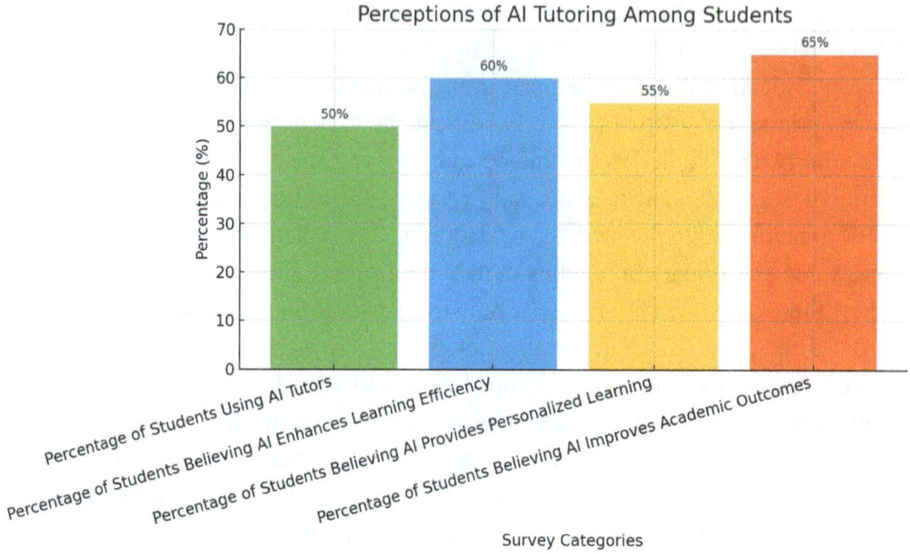

This chart illustrates the perceptions of AI tutoring among students, showcasing the percentage of students who use AI tutors and their beliefs about the benefits of AI in enhancing learning efficiency, personalized learning, and academic outcomes.

5.2 Real-Time Feedback Mechanisms

Nowadays, generative AI has really shaken up how much feedback there is in education. So, instead of waiting till grades or assessments come too late, AI–powered systems can now check the performance of the student in the middle of things — almost as if they are taking a quick pulse. The fact that this is a quick glimpse allows teachers to change what they are doing on the fly, reversing lesson plans in real time so that they align with what the students actually need. In fact, it provides context in which learners can also feel supported and involved. According to Serra A (2025), in most cases, the real time based studies show that this approach enhances the understanding and keeps the students more motivated in the class, consequently, results in the good marks (Serra A, 2025). Feedback tools are important not only for their speed but for the way in which it customizes the learning experience. Education via GenAI is a new and interesting way to solve old problems without having to leave the office every day; it allows teachers to notice subtle clues as to whether, on any given day for a specific student, they're killing it or falling flat sometimes with a shocking degree of clarity. It means the teacher can jump in at the moment that difficulties appear so that the teacher is giving help the moment a student is struggling, even if that student is struggling. Also, the skills gained are not limited to grades; they involve critical thinking and reasoning in problem solving. For instance, platforms like the AI Writing Tutoring Platforms (AWTP) provide fast and customized critiques to relieve the anxiety that goes along with the writing task ((Han et al., 2024)). Essentially, these adapted interventions promote not just academic improvement but also general development of learners. Moreover, these live feedback tools also matter greatly for teachers' development. The teaching methods of educators tend to also change, sometimes in ways that we didn't expect, as we are able to quickly see what works and what doesn't as we teach with these AI driven systems. For example, platforms such as MootMentorAI provide teachers quick snapshots of their classroom strategies, demanding a slight adjust just about just after that. This sort of ongoing, hands on professional growth is, by and large, essential in this rapidly changing current educational context. GenAI also offers immediate data driven insights to aid lesson planning, and also encourages a continuous improvement mindset in teachers to always keep them prepared to customize modern classrooms to the varied needs as discussed in (Serra A, 2025.

Figure 7. Impact of Real time feedback

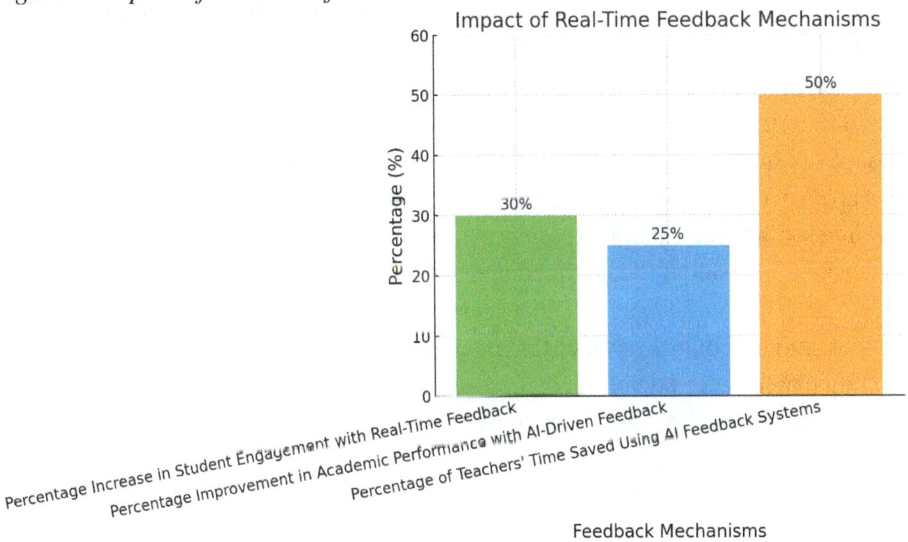

The chart illustrates the impact of real-time feedback mechanisms on three key areas: student engagement, academic performance, and teachers' efficiency. It shows that real-time feedback increases student engagement by 30%, improves academic performance by 25%, and saves teachers 50% of their time. Each bar represents the percentage increase or savings achieved through the use of AI-driven feedback systems, highlighting their significant benefits in an educational context.

5.3 Promoting Collaborative Learning Environments

Collaboration is a real game changer in terms of enlivening lessons. When students work together, discussions tend to liven up, and there are wild mixtures of ideas that sometimes surprise even those in the room. At the same time, this approach sparks a little light of peer-to-peer learning and develops some of the important communication and social skills which are such an essential need in today's world. Now GenAI is a tool that teachers can use to create group assignments that fit their student's needs . (Han et al., 2024, 1) goes as far as saying that these variable teaching tools make learning more interactive. Taken together, converting a normal class into one buzz of shared learning definitely prepares students for the challenges of a team work tuned world. As students approach group tasks, they tend to feel they are owners of the learning experience, this feeling in turn fires their enthusiasm and commitment. This is made possible via GenAI backed educational tools that establish projects that allow students to determine the pace and receive input in real time. Research has been done on these platforms and they show that you end up in, for lack of a better phrase, longer writing sessions and a more diverse vocabulary mix (Han et al., 2024). Usually what this results in is a mix of classic teaching and innovative tech that, together, create an environment in which academics and that collaborative spirit are mutually beneficial. The social and cultural vibes beyond the tech side in a classroom have a big part in this as well. Even if the ideas are expressed in a couple of quirks, a great collaborative setup remembers to take into account all the varied backgrounds and experiences that students bring along. We can use AI powered tools to help tailor experiences (even when things aren't in perfect order) and make every student feel valued and included. For instance, immersive virtual reality training studies suggest that learning that is interactive and allows some form of student control rewards the experience with a deeper and more engaging learning experience. Therefore, by mixing GenAI with a genuine understanding of person, teachers make a place where partnership capacities are increased, however furthermore equip the person for what's next. Different designs of education about AI are particularly pursued by those hoping to fabricate a decent working condition, where training tries to produce inventive answers for real issues.

Figure 8. Impact of AI

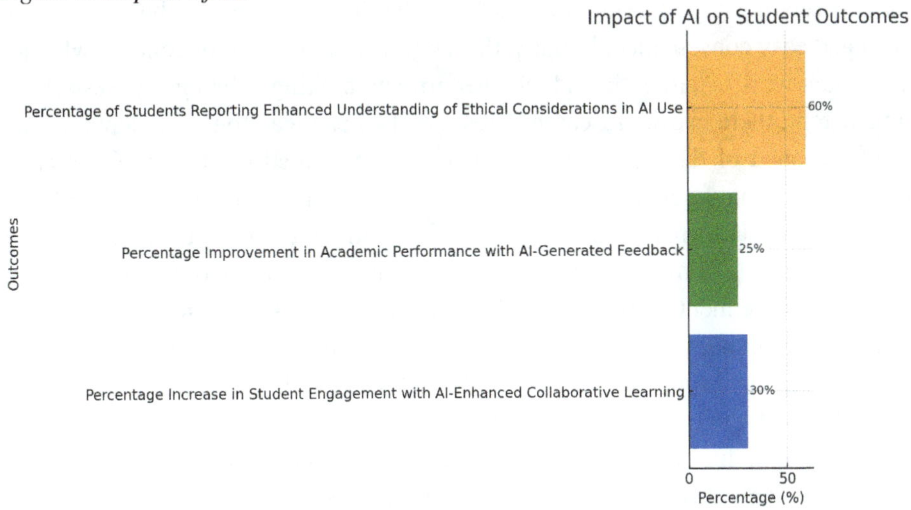

This horizontal bar chart illustrates the impact of AI on student outcomes, showing the percentage increase in student engagement with AI-enhanced collaborative learning, the percentage improvement in academic performance with AI-generated feedback, and the percentage of students reporting enhanced understanding of ethical considerations in AI use. The chart emphasizes that 60% of students reported improved ethical understanding, followed by a 30% increase in engagement and a 25% improvement in academic performance.

6 CHALLENGES IN IMPLEMENTING GENAI

The term GenAI refers to generative AI and it's been shaking up schools in not always easy to manage ways. Trying to breathe new life into lesson planning, schools are now grappling with a vertiginous dilapidation of challenges. The main bump in the road is that solutions that promise to use artificial intelligence, are not easy to natively mix with lesson plans that have been around forever, and many teachers really don't feel ready to make such fiddling. It can sometimes be panic, in the form of outright resistance, as some educators view GenAI as a threat, not a welcome helper. Not all teachers are knowledgeable on tech, so it is obvious not every teacher will be that happy with these new systems; this is why schools need to aid in the learning curve and train teachers on how to use these new programs. It also sets up ethical issues which provoke discussions as to who is actually the rightful owner of a student's work and how much control does the student have over it. Teachers now face the task of figuring out what happens when absolutist students rely heavily on AI content, it blurs the line of distinction between a true effort and easy convenience. Usually, this alignment is a cause for concern whether the student work is authentic and whether critical thinking is being suppressed. To some extent, there is even research that suggests it can lead to the students feeling slightly robbed of their own voice and so less motivated to engage. Generative AI platforms could generate such personalized feedback, but formative study on generative AI platforms (Han et al., 2024) found that there was still quite a strong concern on bias and misinformation. But the thing is that the more you work with GenAI the more mental effort is put through the learner. According to studies, too much high-level interactivity with these tools can overwhelm students to the point that learning can be made more difficult (Lehikko et al., 2024). If you load too heavy the load, the benefits, writing like putting two gears in your head or taking part in a forum, diminish quickly. For there then becomes a burden for teachers to ease and students stay focused on the essentials. Let's roughly speak on building a strong framework of teacher training, keeping open and honest talks about ethics, and blending technology with the classroom in a way that really puts the learners experience first while addressing these challenges.

Table 3. Challenges in Implementing Generative AI in Education

Challenge	Description
Policy Development	Many institutions lack clear guidelines for the responsible adoption of GenAI, with less than half having publicly accessible policies addressing its use. Over 94% of educators reported no clear GenAI policy, and nearly 90% had not provided training to students on acceptable usage. ([pmc.ncbi.nlm.nih.gov](https://pmc.ncbi.nlm.nih.gov/articles/PMC11756388))
Digital Competency and Training	There is a significant need for comprehensive GenAI literacy programs for both staff and students. Training in GenAI prompt engineering is essential for effective and responsible use, yet many institutions have not implemented such programs. ([pmc.ncbi.nlm.nih.gov](https://pmc.ncbi.nlm.nih.gov/articles/PMC11756388/))
Ethical and Responsible Use	GenAI poses challenges to academic integrity, with concerns about AI-generated content undermining the authenticity of student work. Institutions are developing policies to address ethical considerations, but progress is slow. ([pmc.ncbi.nlm.nih.gov](https://pmc.ncbi.nlm.nih.gov/articles/PMC11756388/))
Bias and Inclusivity	GenAI models can replicate biases present in their training data, leading to discriminatory outcomes. Addressing these biases is crucial to ensure fairness and inclusivity in educational settings. ([pmc.ncbi.nlm.nih.gov](https://pmc.ncbi.nlm.nih.gov/articles/PMC11756388/))
Environmental Impact	The training process of GenAI models can have significant environmental costs, with emissions from the ICT industry expected to reach 14% of global emissions by 2040. ([pmc.ncbi.nlm.nih.gov](https://pmc.ncbi.nlm.nih.gov/articles/PMC11756388/))
Data Integrity and Privacy	Many GenAI models do not comply with data protection regulations like GDPR, raising concerns about the collection, storage, and processing of personal data in educational contexts. ([pmc.ncbi.nlm.nih.gov](https://pmc.ncbi.nlm.nih.gov/articles/PMC11756388/))
Digital Divide	Access to GenAI tools is uneven, with disparities in broadband internet access among different demographic groups, potentially exacerbating existing educational inequalities. ([pmc.ncbi.nlm.nih.gov](https://pmc.ncbi.nlm.nih.gov/articles/PMC11756388/))

6.1 Technical Barriers and Infrastructure

There is a host of tech challenges that educational settings that try to adopt generative AI have to deal with. Everything slows down as the old systems, limited band width and hardware that was made for hardware and not suited for modern software all force together in the making it really hard to integrate those potentially advanced tools into lesson plan. The teachers are often faced with the challenge of waiting for the networks that are often laggy or fight with the incompatible equipment that stifles creativity and personalized learning experience. In many cases, even institutions out for an update of their tech find difficulty in clearly determining what infrastructure they need upgraded. In general, resolving these issues does not only pave the way to GenAI adoption but also equips educators with the capacity to create more compelling as well as more dynamic learning arenas that really connect theory to practical life. Interestingly, there are notable technological barriers above these tech hurdles, and also a clear lack of training and support. What makes me wary of how GenAI tools might be used in education is that quite concerning fact that quite a few teachers, teachers do not even feel confident with navigating the digital complexity of these tools despite the high promise of teaching methods improvements. The range of digital literacy among the staff is a barrier to even access to optimal resources and hamper with the overall educational equity. This is all about providing real, hands on training that is more than just technical know-how (but getting into how these tools can be integrated throughout the day in daily teaching). And in fact, we see it, for instance in legal education (Serra A, 2025), that if someone is able to do a little bit of the training for you, that is enough to basically increase student engagement very drastically even if the training isn't perfectly streamlined. Next is the difficult matter of ethics and policy. When it comes to GenAI, plagiarism, accuracy, and who the real author is become concerns that need to be carefully handled. They must hash out what the schools and institutions have agreed to and what is fair or clear enough that students and teachers alike know how to proceed when the rules don't apply specifically to their scenario. Such policies created in reflective planning, and through some bit of solid research, can help create a space where innovative ideas aren't put down because the people who contribute these ideas worry over academic integrity. Gerardou et al (2023), discuss that research on the higher educational industry generally reveals that in order to use tools such as ChatGPT successfully, it's not only a matter of having the right tools and adequate training but also to put adequate policies in place that are congruent with the overall education objectives. While some of these systems are a bit rough around the edges, and therefore it would be easy to tear them down, the multi-layered nature of this approach means that it provides a holistic framework for turning what could be obstacles into opportunities for better learning outcomes.

Table 4. Technical Barriers and Infrastructure in Education for Generative AI Integration

Value
24% of state education leaders identified cybersecurity as their top priority in 2023, up from 17% in 2022. However, 42% reported that their state provides 'a small amount' or 'very little funding' for cybersecurity needs. ([govtech.com](https://www.govtech.com/education/k-12/setda-cybersecurity-ai-and-equity-are-main-concerns))
17 million students still lack reliable home Internet access, highlighting significant infrastructure challenges in education. ([govtech.com](https://www.govtech.com/education/k-12/setda-cybersecurity-ai-and-equity-are-main-concerns))
55% of state education leaders observed increased interest in AI policy development over the past year, yet only 2% reported having an AI initiative in place. ([govtech.com](https://www.govtech.com/education/k-12/setda-cybersecurity-ai-and-equity-are-main-concerns))
Training large generative AI models can require tens of thousands of processors running for months, costing several hundred million dollars, posing financial barriers for educational institutions. ([gao.gov](https://www.gao.gov/products/gao-24-106946))

6.2 Teacher Training and Professional Development

Generative AI, also known as GenAI, has become a big piece of the puzzle in preparing teachers for our tech infused present. Digital tools in fact, according to Michele Cassar, in the B.Ed (Hon.) Youth and Community programme 'just bump up' along with the ease with which pre service teachers bump into loads of digital tools in their everyday work and often 'bump up' both how they think about teaching and how they plan lessons. Largely speaking, recent findings appear to demonstrate that while the future educators typically utilize GenAI for individual tasks or academic assignments, they seldom integrate GenAI for formal lesson design. The gap, as one might say, highlights the need for training sessions that haven't been teaching teachers how to use cool technology, but teaching them how to use cool technology to engage in creative, innovative curricula that speaks to the students. Other studies have also hinted that engaging pre service teachers early and often with the GenAI will spark a promise for them for using the tool for lesson design and even get excited enough to seek further professional development. Although it is all smooth sailing, teachers investing in these AI tools also combine a fair number of worries about ethical use and the risk of letting their core skills slip. Issues such as fairness in education and solid data privacy, for example, have, according to contemporary research, kept bugging the educators. In most of the cases, professional development shouldn't only show that GenAI works but also explain the ethical aspects in a way that is real and relatable for the everyday user. And there is an urgent call to develop smarter professional development plans that home in on the gaps in current teacher education around GenAI. Even if it sometimes feels a little bit off kilter, these programs should be designed in a way that enhances creative thinking, ethical mindfulness and hands on how tos with the tech. Teachers who discuss GenAI academically, the subject tends to make them more optimistic about its usefulness, but also point to danger and ethical questions it brings. This leads teacher training institutions to question whether they should take a somewhat more collaborative approach, with a bit of practical work mixed in with open ended talks about what the shape of teaching is, which is changing apace with the introduction of new technology. If educators do this, they might be better set up to leverage the power of GenAI in favor of improving student engagement and learning outcomes (Geiselhofer et al., 2024)(Geiselhofer et al., 2024).

Table 5. Teacher Professional Development Participation and Perceived Effectiveness

Country	Professional Development Initiatives	Perceived Effectiveness	References
India	- A study evaluated the effectiveness of an autonomous AI teacher, represented through an avatar, to upskill existing teachers in nursery-level teaching methods and curriculum development. - The AI teacher was powered by a specialized generative AI language model, OIMISA7B, with a 7-billion parameter setup.	- The study found that the AI teacher effectively enhanced the skills of participating teachers, indicating the potential of AI-driven professional development tools in the Indian educational context.	bura.brunel.ac.uk
Ghana	- A professional development webinar was conducted to sensitize teacher educators about Generative AI (GAI). - The webinar aimed to deepen understanding and application of GAI in teacher education.	- Participants recognized the importance of integrating GAI into teacher education. - They identified areas requiring further development to effectively incorporate GAI.	papers.ssrn.com
South Korea	- A study explored in-service teachers' perceptions regarding AI education and their training programs. - Data collection included surveys and focus group interviews.	- Teachers acknowledged the necessity of AI convergence education. - They emphasized the need for comprehensive training programs to effectively implement AI in classrooms.	ijiet.org
United States	Teach Plus conducted a survey of educators to assess AI training and its integration into classrooms. - The organization is advocating for state policies and resources to support AI professional development.	- 92% of surveyed educators see AI's potential benefits. - Only half reported receiving adequate AI training, highlighting a gap between AI's perceived importance and available professional development.	teachplus.org
China	- A study investigated pre-service English teachers' perceptions of integrating GenAI, specifically ChatGPT, into language teaching. - The study utilized questionnaires and interviews.	- Participants recognized the potential benefits of GenAI in enhancing teaching effectiveness. - They also expressed concerns about challenges and the need for proper training to integrate GenAI tools effectively.	journals.sagepub.com
Global Perspective	- A survey across six countries examined factors influencing teachers' trust in AI in education. - The study focused on AI self-efficacy, understanding, and cultural values.	- Teachers with higher AI self-efficacy and understanding perceived more benefits and reported greater trust in AI educational technologies. - Cultural differences influenced trust levels, emphasizing the need for context-specific professional development programs.	link.springer.com

7 ETHICAL CONSIDERATIONS AND DATA PRIVACY

The arrival of GenAI to schools is causing a lot more than just excitement – there are big privacy concerns to be had as well. These systems are being used by schools to liven up lesson plans and increase student participation, and all that sensitive student data is then put under the spotlight. After all, institutions must do this as they proudly straddle the wave of innovation, while protecting student privacy. Interestingly, 52% of the universities began discussing GenAI ethics issues within the scene of Diversity Equity and Inclusion (DEI) (Ali et al., 2024). It makes you feel if in several cases these systems might even amplify the existing disparities. And there is also a developing community call for rules as to how data are managed — rules that ensure student information is not misused and does not remain unguarded. But there's an other side to the coin too – a reliance on GenAI may be boding us out of becoming voracious with genuine skills. On the other hand, these tools could compromise educators' and their students' own capabilities for critical thinking, writing, and problem solving, by becoming too reliant on them. According to recent studies by Geiselhofer et al (2024), even though many of the pre service educators are using GenAI for acquiring academics as well as personal ideas, simply trying it does not guarantee that it is fully exploited. On the contrary, leaning on it too hard in fact may stunt the natural growth of core skills, which is kind of ironic as it is assumed that this technology is here to support learning. Generally speaking, teachers should be trained and given the right tools to use GenAI's power without being able to induce genuine independent thought. Add to that, if GenAI is going to be right in education, teachers will need help and training on an ongoing basis. However, many schools, very excited to adopt these, often lack clear and practical guidance on the ethical use (Ali et al., 2024). With any domain of AI, training programs that encourage shining a light on the hidden potential biases of GenAI algorithms and implications of this for privacy and fairness could possibly be a good starting point. Research proves that an educational win–win does present itself in the use of GenAI, however, many educators are still apprehensive in using GenAI due to the ethical tightrope it could potentially push them to walk (Geiselhofer et al., 2024). Placing more weight on ethics in training, including accepting a few oddities in how things are expressed, schools can in fact equip future teachers to embrace GenAI responsibly while, again, remaining focused on real learning rather than allowing ethics to slip.

Figure 9. Engagement and concerns

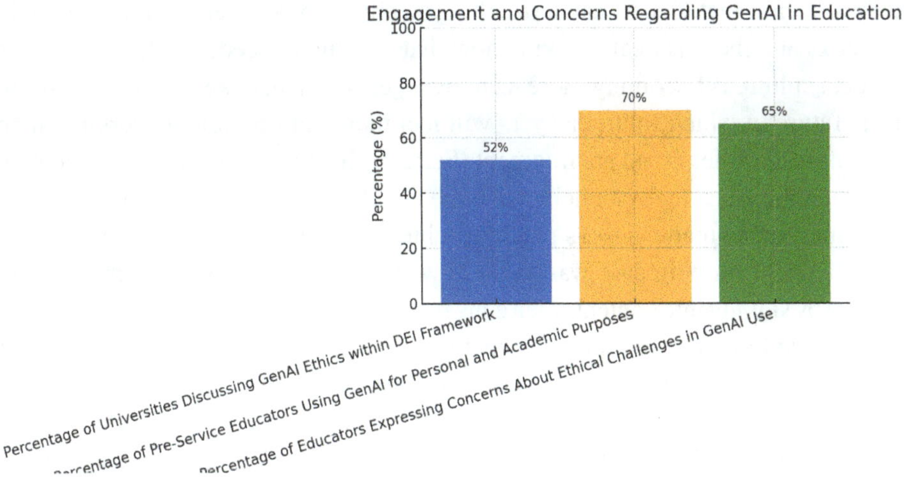

This bar chart illustrates the engagement of universities in discussing the ethical implications of Generative AI (GenAI) within the Diversity, Equity, and Inclusion (DEI) framework, the widespread use of GenAI tools among pre-service educators for personal and academic purposes, and the significant concerns expressed by educators regarding the ethical challenges posed by GenAI in educational settings.

8 CASE STUDIES OF GENAI IN CLASSROOMS

In classrooms, generative AI is quickly gaining a toehold that has the potential to lead teachers in planning lessons in exciting and increasing ways, and getting students more involved. In one case of an immersive virtual reality (IVR) safety training—they talk about the lively, hands–on scenarios versus the less interactive—the type of IVR training that student felt more in control of was more experiential and interactive. Generally, researchers noticed that germane (meaning having to do with germane intellectual assets) cognitive load experienced some kind of uptick in learning what they say can be applied. While most of the participants did not appreciate the creation of prompts that motivate them (Lehikko et al., 2024), this example illustrates best how this can be turn a regular old stuff method into something far more relevant and engaging. A great example is seen again in the legal education. The MootMentorAI project at the University of Missouri-Kansas City School of Law is one such project that is rethinking how advocacy is taught using GenAI at some law schools. The AI powered trainer here doesn't stay by the old traditional lecture methods, but instead, it helps you to simulate a courtroom with a twist, it gives personal feedback that lets you fine tune your skills over time. To me the results hint that GenAI can close that yawning gap between what is written in textbooks and the practical knowing how that is actually needed in life. In fact, as the legal culture is becoming more tech savvy, experiments like this serve as proof of the future in which future lawyers will feel more comfortable in working in an AI reinforced professional environment (Serra A, 2025). It's also important to note that while the latest tech can help make the GenAI work, social and cultural vibes in learning space matter just as much in achieving successful usage. For instance, the IVR safety training case was about how students could engage in meaningful learning by sinking into content when educators create a supportive environment. The tech is indeed impressive, but put it next to a setting that doesn't take into account the diverse student backgrounds and different learning styles, and that magic might not transpire. At times the idea of tailoring experiences based on individual needs, was often reiterated in several studies, can make lesson planning more successful overall. In general, this balanced approach turns out to be more practical when using technology and at the same time, it creates a learning culture where personalization and responsiveness serve to enable teachers and students.

Table 6. Case Studies of Generative AI in Classrooms

AI Tool	Functionality	Reference
AudioPen	Converts spoken words into editable text, aiding in drafting and organizing thoughts.	Edutopia
Canva Magic Write	Assists in generating text for presentations and documents, enhancing creativity and efficiency.	Edutopia
Curipod	Enables the creation of interactive lessons with polls, word clouds, and open-ended questions to engage students.	Edutopia
Eduaide.Ai	Provides AI-assisted lesson development, offering over 100 resource types and translation into more than 15 languages.	Edutopia
OpenAI (ChatGPT)	Assists in generating human-like text for explanations, tutoring, and content creation.	Edutopia
Quizizz	Facilitates the creation of quizzes and interactive assessments to engage students and track progress.	Edutopia
Slidesgo	Offers AI-generated presentation templates to streamline the creation of visually appealing slides.	Edutopia
Gamma	Utilizes AI to help build presentations, enhancing the efficiency of creating educational materials.	Arlington Magazine
Magic School	Assists in generating lesson plans, providing structured outlines and content suggestions for educators.	Arlington Magazine
QuestionWell	Creates quizzes and assessments, aiding teachers in evaluating student understanding effectively.	Arlington Magazine
Twee	Generates quizzes and assessments, similar to QuestionWell, to support diverse evaluation methods.	Arlington Magazine

AI Tool	Functionality	Reference
Blooket	Provides interactive game-based quizzes to make learning engaging and assess student knowledge.	Arlington Magazine
Ed	A chatbot developed to assist students with academic inquiries and provide personalized learning support.	Los Angeles Unified School District

8.1 Success Stories From Various Educational Settings

It's all very well and good for classrooms to be stirred up those words are popping up throughout the classrooms now and stories of how generative AI is helping with lesson planning and student involvement. According to research, AI powered writing tutors can really improve kids' writing skills by offering customized feedback and generating ideas to allay students' common fear of writing something fresh. Even one early study showed that teachers, parents and the students themselves consider these AI tools as convenient for creating flexible educational materials, meaning in most cases, the teaching process turns out to be more engaging. These insights hold the promise of leveraging GenAI with educational resources, and they suggest improvements in education for students (Han et al., 2024) in the long run. In different spheres, schools experiment with GenAI to give the information system a shakeup. Actual libraries, and not just school libraries no less, are among the first to adopt this tech for obvious reasons and they're trying new things to spruce up instruction. Library pros are mixed, some are wary of tools such as ChatGPT while others are looking forward to the opportunities to extend how information literacy is delivered. With GenAI mixed into library routines, educators are able to encourage students to explore and think critically in an approach which is both natural and innovative, truly readying students for a future that will be dominated by digital (Castillo D et al., 2024). Teachers as well as tech experts have also come together to come up with the AI driven writing platforms that are really meant to work for the needs of students. They worked together to build and improve upon prototype systems that focused on opinion writing and, in a kind of back and forth process at times tending toward a bit rough around the edges, tested ideas. The actual results—longer writing sessions, more words on the page, and studies with strikingly grown vocabulary—are clearly just the tip of the iceberg to what these tools offer—these tools—in my classroom offered a lively, almost collaborative spirit. Following this step-by-step and hands on approach, teachers receive tools tailored exactly to their students' requirements, and throughout this they discover how Gen AI can revolutionize all aspects of teaching for the people they are responsible for, and also for themselves in turn (Han et al., 2024).

Table 7. Success Stories of Generative AI in Education

Institution	Course	AI Tool
Harvard University	CS50	CS50 Duck
Hickory City Schools, North Carolina	AI Literacy Training	Developed AI guidelines and training strategies to help educators and students use AI tools ethically and effectively. ([www1.ascd.org](https://www1.ascd.org/el/articles/tell-us-about-february-2025))
Chippewa Valley Schools, Michigan	SchoolAI	Implemented AI to support students with various reading levels during intervention times, providing personalized learning experiences. ([www1.ascd.org](https://www1.ascd.org/el/articles/tell-us-about-february-2025))
Stokes County Schools, North Carolina	Generative AI Policy	Created a comprehensive policy guiding the ethical and effective use of AI across the district, including resources for students, teachers, and parents. ([www1.ascd.org](https://www1.ascd.org/el/articles/tell-us-about-february-2025))
Aurora Public Schools, Colorado	Three-Year AI Plan	Developed a community-centric AI strategy focusing on teacher empowerment, collective intelligence, and holistic evaluation to transform K-12 education. ([www1.ascd.org](https://www1.ascd.org/el/articles/tell-us-about-february-2025))
Davis School District, Utah	Skill Struck AI	Integrated AI tutors into AP psychology courses to assist students with evidence-based questions and article analysis, enhancing personalized learning. ([www1.ascd.org](https://www1.ascd.org/el/articles/tell-us-about-february-2025))
Davidson County Schools, North Carolina	AI Dashboard	Developed a district-wide AI dashboard serving as a central hub for AI-related resources, guidelines, and training materials for staff, students, and community members. ([www1.ascd.org](https://www1.ascd.org/el/articles/tell-us-about-february-2025))

8.2 Lessons Learned From Implementation Failures

When things don't go according to plan with the aid of GenAI to revitalise lesson planning and to attract students, we constantly learn: there's so much to gain when going off course. On other occasions, products will falter just by a lack of solid groundwork, with goals mismatched with what the technology can actually produce. Take teachers for example, if teachers are not exactly sure of how Gen AI can illuminate a classroom, the whole thing won't stick to them or the pupils. Well, it turns out that resistance mostly stems from the lack of proper training and support, which speaks to the importance of broad practical development related plans, that fill those gaps, and nudge schools in a direction of more innovative mindset. The other lesson is a bit of a side note related to how our educational setups inherently put up barriers in the path. Digital infrastructure is uneven and resource poor and strikes underfunded schools far too hard. Plans all too often fail for this reason. Among other things, as the Inter American Development Bank Group indicates in the strategic outline, it is often necessary to tackle these obstacles directly to ensure that the DNA of AI spreads for the sake of an inclusive uplift in productivity ((Vargas F et al., 2025)). Also, having educators, administrators, and even students in the conversation ensures that the tech marries well with all the other classroom practices. Ultimately, it's not just about working hard on tech knowledge but also about handling ethics with care in a situation like GenAI. The earlier studies had already hinted that things like data privacy worries, bias and even shifts in the teacher–student relationship were to be expected. To build trust all around, these ethical matters need to be addressed while rolling out large language models (LLMs) ((Shahzad T et al., 2025)) to make a framework for them. School leaders can learn from past missteps and put a firm ethical backbone in place and develop a strategy for moving technology forward that sticks. All in all — and, well, opened a bit and slightly imperfect — that might be the final touch that GenAI will really enrich the learning experience.

Table 8. Educational Technology Implementation Failures and Challenges

Study	Findings
Evaluation of the Effectiveness of Educational Technology Interventions	After one school year, no statistically significant impacts on student achievement in reading and mathematics were observed. After two school years, impacts worsened for 6th grade mathematics products. Only one product showed a statistically significant positive impact on student achievement. ([ies.ed.gov](https://ies.ed.gov/use-work/evaluations/evaluation-effectiveness-educational-technology-interventions))
Realizing the Promise: How Can Education Technology Improve Learning for All?	Free laptop initiatives often failed to improve academic achievement in math or language. In Honduras, students with laptops performed on par with those using textbooks. ([brookings.edu](https://www.brookings.edu/articles/realizing-the-promise-how-can-education-technology-improve-learning-for-all/))
2022 Students and Technology Report: Rebalancing the Student Experience	77% of students experienced technology issues, with 51% reporting stress due to these issues. Unstable internet connections were the most common problem, affecting 64% of students. ([educause.edu](https://www.educause.edu/ecar/research-publications/2022/students-and-technology-report-rebalancing-the-student-experience/technology-challenges-and-solutions))
Educational Technology Research in Higher Education: New Considerations and Evolving Goals	Substantial and unbiased evidence on the effects of educational technology is scarce. Rapid technological evolution outpaces the ability to evaluate its impact on education. ([educause.edu](https://www.educause.edu/ecar/research-publications/2023/educational-technology-research-in-higher-education-a-moving-target/challenges-and-concerns-about-technologys-role-in-education))
S&E Indicators 2018	Despite universal access to instructional computers with internet in U.S. public schools, 55% of K–12 teachers reported insufficient computers for student use, highlighting a major obstacle in technology integration. ([nsf.gov](https://www.nsf.gov/statistics/2018/nsb20181/report/sections/elementary-and-secondary-mathematics-and-science-education/instructional-technology-and-digital-learning))

8.3 Comparative Analysis of Outcomes

In schools, GenAI is making an appearance and altering the plans for lessons and changing how students interact. For example, one piece of research examined the use of open educational resources, so called OERs to gauge what students thought about both the qualities of the MOOC and their own engagement as they used traditional materials vs. newer digital ones. In their comparison of language learning using web based OERs against the standard texts, what we also found is that language of quality really matters to getting students' engagement. In most cases, that means teachers could begin to employ GenAI tools in the same way: intermingling planning and also being more present and even reactive in the classroom. And in essence, insights like these serve to direct educators towards resources that actually lead to better outcomes, which in turn makes it easier to decide on incorporating the new tech, GenAI, in the everyday curricula (Panday et al., 2024). However, findings about the learner control during immersive virtual reality training, shows from another angle that interactivity is more than just a nice extra. A study having high interactivity scenarios clump them with low interactivity scenarios showed interesting shift in cognitive effort and learning overall. Clearly, the numbers revealed that there was a very clear relationship between lively interactivity and mental focus (which is to say, germane cognitive load, or the ability to learn the content for various reasons) — that is to say, if learners are more involved, they tend to latch onto the lesson material better. In most cases, these results underline the need of supporting students when they interact with interactive platforms, and seem to seamlessly match with GenAI`s potential to offer dynamic, even spontaneous learning experiences. Through pushing learners to lead during these moments, teachers may be able to encourage deeper understanding and retention, to fully embrace the positive effects of advanced technology in instruction and in the excitement it can create during a classroom period (Lehikko et al., 2024). Given that traditional resources versus more tech driven become equal when they are weighed it is hard to lose sight of the impact on teacher development. With more and more classrooms welcoming GenAI on their shores, many teacher training programs are having to shift in all sorts of ways—in many cases, as if by the seat of their pants. An understanding combining the studies on OERs and immersive training provide fresh ideas to rethink curricula and classroom strategies. However, generally speaking, creating a culture of continuous adaptation and development may be able to better equip educators to use GenAI for instruction planning and to also make educational environments more captivating for students. By taking a measured, or perhaps even random, route, this has a lot of opportunity to shape the future of educational landscape to the advantage of both, the teachers and learners (Panday Shukla et al., 2024)(Lehikko et al., 2024).

Table 9. Comparative Analysis of GenAI and Traditional Instruction Outcomes

Study	Sample Size	Learning Time Reduction	Performance Improvement	Field	Source
Harvard Study on AI Tutors	194 students	Over 50%	Over 100%	Physical Sciences 2	([axios.com](https://www.axios.com/2024/10/29/ai-tutors-college-students-efficiency))
Meta-Analysis on GenAI in Education	33 studies	0.689	70%	General Education	([researchgate.net](https://www.researchgate.net/publication/387110151_The_effects_of_GenAI_on_learning_performance_A_meta-analysis_study))
Physics XP Integration Study	188 students	Statistically significant ($p < 0.01$)	60%	Physics 1 Course	([researchgate.net](https://www.researchgate.net/publication/387110151_The_effects_of_GenAI_on_learning_performance_A_meta-analysis_study))

9 FUTURE TRENDS IN GENAI AND EDUCATION

The world of education is about to be shaken up by generative AI in ways we never thought would happen. Now, teachers are faced with the task of rethinking the lesson plan and coming up with new means to hook up students. Instructors will be able to whip together their own custom learning experiences to fit what each of their students need, even if that means altering the standard. This kind of flexibility lends itself to creating a more interesting classroom environment in which learning is challenging and it is relevant. In an era of one to one teaching, the ability to concentrate on one to one teaching feels part of a greater movement of allowing learners to have more control and to be motivated. The growth of AI will continue and ultimately, as it improves in most cases, it will play a major role in the education system for future generations of children, forcing educators to adapt their more traditional methods. The momentum for schools introducing GenAI into the curriculum is not just about efficiency but also because of preparing the necessary skills of the age. These digital tools are already having waves within the field of rapidly changing topics such as law or language education. For instance—take a look at AI-driven coaching systems like MootMentorAI—MootMentorAI teaches institutions how to be creative when it comes to practical skill building. Students have a chance to know the theory as well as learn how to apply it in real life when they are given simulations that resemble the real life situations thereby, blurring the line between theory and practice. As well as these AI innovations do wonders for students, they also inspire teachers to rewrite curricula so that AI methods can be in–this time–use. Educators are slowly blending old teaching styles with the current tech and equipping learners for a workforce that will be strengthened with AI and its resultant problems. Ultimately, using GenAI in the classroom will be up to educators; How willing they are to have an open mind and accept the potential of GenAI will really determine its future place in classrooms. Science often shows a combo of factors – including ethics, cost and somewhat, people's wonder at how human-like the tech is – that cause teachers to accept or reject the new tech. The city will continue to see more schools push for clear, fair guidelines as they realize how much the boost in productivity and efficiency is worth. After all, such rules allow academic standards to stand while ensuring that the potential of GenAI is responsibly utilized. Transparency is slowly being smoothed out from the institutions that will eventually use these tools, as (Serra A, 2025) (Alasmari et al., 2024) we will then witness GenAI as a common part of the education dialogue, promoting innovation and adding some dynamism to lesson planning.

Figure 10. Adoption and perception

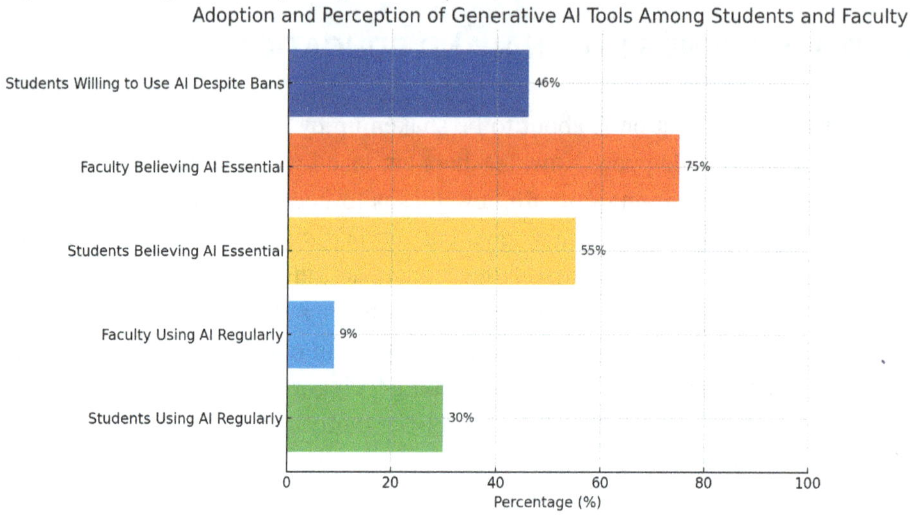

This bar chart illustrates the varying adoption rates and perceptions of generative AI tools between students and faculty. It highlights significant differences in regular use and beliefs about the essential nature of AI in professional settings, reflecting the growing importance of AI literacy in education.

9.1 Predictions for GenAI Advancements

These days, GenAI has become a switch educators turn towards, and the moment you start to shift towards artificial intelligence in your teaching, you begin to see a swift shift away from the usual means. Instead of relying on old and boring ways, teachers are trying to find a faster and more interactive setting to create, where AI not only adds something more but is integrated as a key player. It is something many think will help lessons feel more tailored to the student and allow the content to be molded fresh and responsively by the teacher. On this field, there the framework that is counterintuitive propose four simple ideas: Interactive Co Creation, Adaptive Design, Learning Scaffold, and Efficient Structuring. These can be used by teachers to juggle up lesson plans and help in keeping students more engaged and hence leading to better learning outcomes. But that experience is exciting, bumpy, and of course, most importantly, an intuitive and inclusive learning experience. New possibilities are likewise coming about with GenAI involvement of students in the very hustles of classrooms. Having technology available allows many to expect that soon they will receive real time feedback, which should allow teachers to respond quickly to changing situations as students respond. Learning then can become more of a back and forth over time. Also, after AI assists with admin duties, educators are afforded some additional breathing room in order to connect with their classes. According to Ravarini et al., GenAI is not just about produced content, but about establishing a lively and engaged area where students can flourish and, hopefully, bring education to the present, and to the fun. All these cool advancements come with their own set of challenges at the same time. So there's a fair bit of worry about the ethical issue of using their tech, and number two, making sure their tech usage is fair to everyone. Except in so far as it becomes part of a normal system organizational review, in most cases, teachers need to watch for potential data privacy issues with these new systems. It also leads to a big call for ongoing training of educators to keep abreast of using GenAI right. You can already see examples of this in all sorts of pieces from undergrad and grad projects ranging from rich opinion pieces to literature reviews and more (Billingsley et al., 2024). In essence, if schools and teachers collaborate, they may be able to retire those troublesome issues with number one help from GenAI, which brings a truly transformational twist to the classroom.

Figure 11. Integration of AI in education

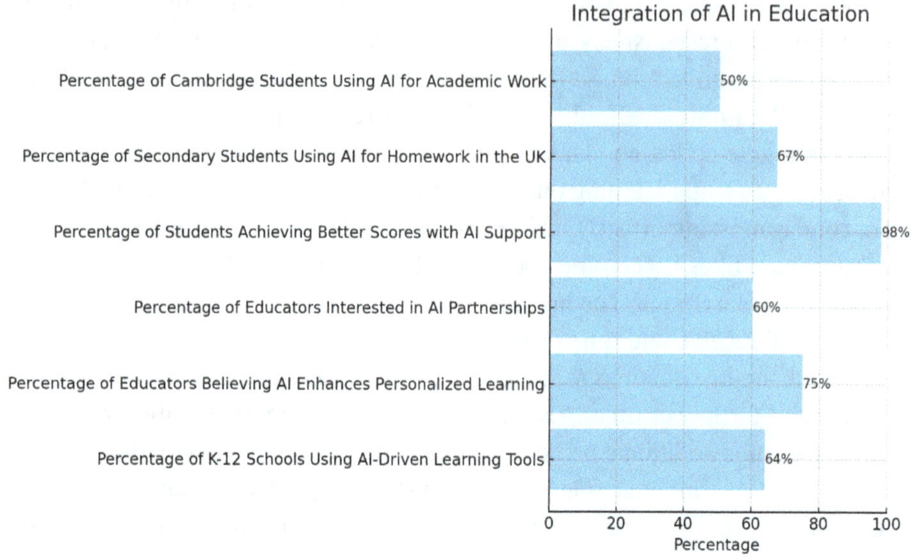

This horizontal bar chart illustrates the integration of AI in education, highlighting various statistics such as the percentage of K-12 schools using AI-driven learning tools, educator beliefs about AI enhancing personalized learning, and the impact of AI support on student performance. The data reflects growing interest and adoption of AI in educational settings.

9.2 Evolving Role of Educators in a GenAI-Driven Environment

Change is fast in the educational scene. Teachers aren't just standing up in front while giving a class what they used to—giving out facts—in the new millennial era with the new rise of GenAI they are having different roles that you (we) may not imagine. Most of the time, teachers are transitioning from being the only source of knowledge to facilitating students to experience things themselves. So, students are able to receive the lessons that really work for where they stand, as they're starting to combine traditional methods with a sprinkle of AI magic. Sure—and this implies teachers require upskilling while in the mean time becoming familiar with AIDriven platforms, as innovation is winding up amazing quick. At the end of the day it's about modifying the behaviour of how students consumerize information in a world where A.I. is starting to get a lot more visibility . GenAI in Lesson Planning provides an unexpected set of opportunities. For instance, there are AI based writing tools that give bespoke feedback, tailor material in real time and enhance creativity or even those harder to capture critical thinking skills. As for research on these tools, they can help produce resources which, honestly, meet a range of learning needs, and while there are some bumps along the way — who really owns the work, for example, or is the AI output solidly good enough? — they can provide some valuable assistance. Most often, teachers are looking for that sweet spot in which AI is helpful without being intrusive to the point of doing students' work for them and denying them a genuine learning experience. The basics are simple: if used carefully, these tools can help make lesson plans more dynamic, and ideally, outcomes will improve with less control handed over. GenAI provides teachers with a neat opportunity to change it up. Other platforms are made to put students into teams to work on projects that lead to vigorous discussions and stronger relationships with their human peers, which, as several research have hinted within AWTP articles, elevate writing skills and involvement. GenAI can actually foster an environment that is up for exploration in ways teachers sometimes wouldn't expect in the classroom when they actually use it in the classroom. It is this kind of change that builds incremental room for feeling a little more comfortable trying new things, even if the first try is to mix up a few sentences or two. In most cases, being comfortable with GenAI prepares teachers for today's challenges as well as students for a future in which technology will intersect with every part of learning.

Figure 12. Integration of AI in Education

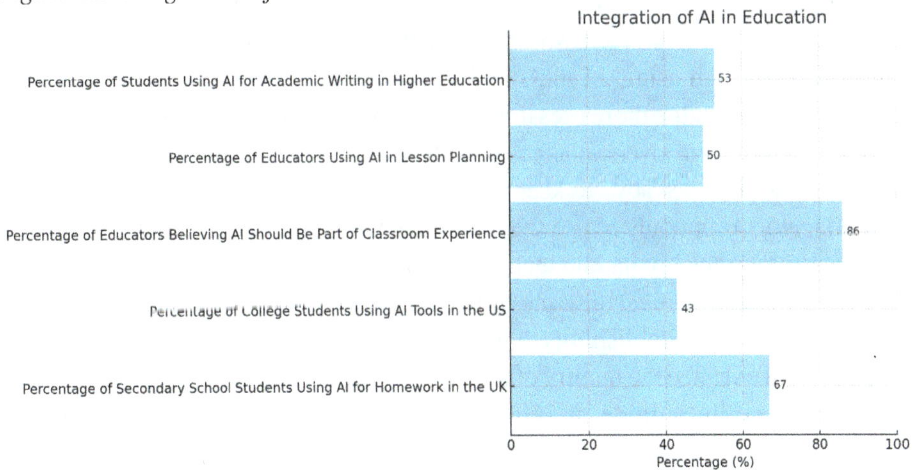

The bar chart illustrates the integration of AI in education by displaying the percentage of various groups engaged with AI tools. It highlights that a significant percentage of educators believe AI should be part of classroom experiences, with 86% support, while 67% of secondary school students in the UK use AI for homework. In contrast, only 43% of college students in the US use AI tools. This data underscores the growing role of AI in enhancing educational practices and student learning.

9.3 Long-Term Impact on Student Learning Outcomes

Generative AI is already quietly changing how students will learn long term. While colleges and universities are busy writing down strict rules utilizing these tools, they are also considering tweaking ways to make use of these tools to better teaching and afford learning to feel more personal. According to a study on U.S. institutions, there are now even several institutions that support in fact the use of AI in class and provide teachers with a set of norms that help them see what does work (Ali et al., 2024). Used wisely, this early adoption can result in teaching that follows each student's own path, the raising of academic performance and interaction that brings the whole class to life. But these trends may not be apparent to future educators, and their thoughts about using AI in lesson planning are pretty big. According to the research, while many pre-service teachers depend on AI for some purposes, personal or academic, it has not been effectively put to use day to day lesson planning. In almost all circumstances, there is an obvious relationship between investigating the great potential of AI within academic and acknowledging its benefits, revealing gaps in training. Perhaps the most effective way of doing so, even if this seems incremental at times, is to offer teachers future targeted professional development so that these teachers can ultimately begin to naturally mix AI insights into their daily classroom interactions (Geiselhofer et al., 2024). The more teachers began using AI tools and feeling more comfortable using them for classroom purposes, the more pressing became the consideration of the ethical side of the thing. Issues of over reliance on technology are ongoing: the issue of skill diminishment, data privacy etc keeps cropping up. The personal responsibility of many educators is not only to use the tools wisely but also to demonstrate how students should responsibly handle technology. Teachers build a level learning space that also encourages critical thinking by teaching good digital habits and the value of these habits. In sum, establishing a precise equilibrium between integrating AI into education will enhance the quality of school outputs, contribute to the development of a lifelong learning attitude, and equip students for success in the tech penetrated, yet sometimes faulty world of the future (Ali et al., 2024)(Geiselhofer et al., 2024).

Table 10. Impact of Generative AI on Student Learning Outcomes

Aspect of AI Integration	Impact on Student Learning Outcomes	Reference
Personalized Learning	AI enables tailored educational experiences, accommodating individual learning styles and paces, leading to improved academic performance.	Schiller International University
Immediate Feedback	Automated grading and feedback systems provide students with prompt insights into their performance, facilitating timely improvements.	SSRN
Study Habits and Time Management	AI tools assist students in developing effective study routines and managing their time efficiently, contributing to enhanced academic outcomes.	arXiv
Critical Thinking Skills	Over-reliance on AI for assignments may lead to diminished critical thinking abilities among students.	Axios
Engagement and Motivation	AI-powered educational games and interactive platforms increase student engagement and motivation, positively affecting learning outcomes.	Wikipedia
Collaboration and Teamwork	AI facilitates the formation of complementary student teams by analysing individual working styles and skills, promoting effective collaboration and knowledge exchange.	Schiller International University
Academic Integrity	The use of AI in completing assignments has raised concerns regarding plagiarism and the authenticity of student work, impacting the assessment of true learning outcomes.	The Times

10 STRATEGIES FOR EFFECTIVE GENAI INTEGRATION

Artificial Intelligence for learning (AI for learning) generatively can transform schooling, but that's just like that, it begins with providing teachers the appropriate sort of training. Some new tools are meant to disrupt how we both plan our lessons and engage students, but too few educators have been trained in what the perks and bumps are of using GenAI to clarify them. In most cases, studies show that pre-service teachers take a dip into GenAI to use it for personal or academic purposes but not for building lessons. That kinda says itself that there is a need for education programs that helps to build the skill of using those tools well. Teacher training can help to alleviate ethical worries, work toward fairness in the classroom and improve teaching methods, and thereby enable educators to leverage GenAI to the fullest at school (Geiselhofer et al., 2024). Step up interactivity as a further piece of the puzzle. No longer being bound to the same old lesson plans, teachers are now encouraged to have the wits to cook up curricula that entice students to be part of immersive, hands on learning experiences, these are usually more memorable and lead to deeper learning. Take virtual lessons, for example: research indicates that lessons featuring interactivity at a high level tend to engage students' cognitive engagement to the point that it assists them in retrieving and retaining new information. We therefore seem to be able to conclude that it is the aspect of active involvement and team work in classes that may actually make all the difference. Leveraging technology by incorporating GenAI tools that prepare the stage for interactive scenarios is the perfect exercise that hones some of these analytically critical skills needed in education today (Lehikko et al., 2024). Another areas is building a community out of all educators. By that, teachers are sharing how they are facing the challenges of using GenAI, and things like that, the system begins to take shape and we get to see it start to support us. Loose collaboration like this can result in better resource sharing or some creative ways to integrate GenAI into lesson design or even as a way to increase student engagement. Educators will often discover these insights on how to fine tune teaching methods... (even when they mean a few missteps) when they are not bound by traditional technological solutions, but are free to test out the new potential tech they have the means to. Just by working together and shared concerns about overreliance on technology, teachers can make sure that GenAI use is ethical and effective so that it enriches every learner's educational outcomes. nAI is used in ethical and effective ways, leading to richer educational outcomes for every learner.

Table 11. Best Practices for Effective GenAI Integration in Education

Strategy	Description
Trust Building	Establish trust by explicitly communicating care for students' learning, involving them in decision-making, and being transparent about AI usage. Encourage collaboration and reflection on AI use in assignments. ([trefnycenter.mines.edu](https://trefnycenter.mines.edu/effective-teaching-and-generative-ai/))
Ethical Considerations	Engage students in analyzing ethical and unethical uses of GenAI, discussing biases, inaccuracies, and privacy concerns. Promote critical evaluation of AI-generated content. ([trefnycenter.mines.edu](https://trefnycenter.mines.edu/effective-teaching-and-generative-ai/))
Equitable Access	Develop accessible and equitable course policies, ensuring all students have access to GenAI tools. Avoid creating barriers for students with disabilities or from underrepresented backgrounds. ([trefnycenter.mines.edu](https://trefnycenter.mines.edu/effective-teaching-and-generative-ai/))
Clear Communication	Set clear expectations with students regarding GenAI use, discussing permissible and prohibited applications. Provide guidelines for citing AI-generated content. ([education.delaware.gov](https://education.delaware.gov/educators/academic-support/standards-and-instruction/digital-de/instructional-resources/generative-ai/integrating-ai/))
Human-Centered Assignments	Design assignments that center on human learning by tapping into student motivation, lived experience, and creativity. Encourage critical engagement with GenAI outputs. ([trefnycenter.mines.edu](https://trefnycenter.mines.edu/effective-teaching-and-generative-ai/))
Inclusive Practices	Ensure GenAI tools are accessible to all students, considering potential biases and promoting inclusivity. Provide resources for continued education on AI literacy. ([genai.illinois.edu](https://genai.illinois.edu/best-practices-teaching-and-learning/))

10.1 Creating a Supportive School Culture

However, in many schools where there is a real sense of support in the hallways, teachers and students alike find themselves in the type of environment where fresh ideas are produced as well as a little bit of bold experimentation. Generative AI can occasionally be found in lesson plans lately, as a precursor to a more in-depth, hands-on, and active, method of learning that personalizes to the person. Because these settings are neither bound by an old script nor anchored to conventional expectations, educators here are prompted to play with quirky new tools and shake outdated approaches to teaching, in ways that are breakthrough. In my experience, embracing a culture that secretly loves to take risks (with a bit of roughness here and there), schools can actually allow teachers to see what generative AI could do for their lesson designs. In doing so, that supportive atmosphere usually facilitates connecting innovative AI features to daily teaching. If teachers know they have a back up, they are more likely to mess with AI gizmos that lessen the planning and changes due to various learning styles. This means that they will have much more time to spend on actually building genuine connections with students, which is a win win really. Educators sharing the best ideas about how to use generative AI in casual ways can allow both teachers and students to benefit from a loosely woven and always evolving community of learning. Of course, it has a sticky ethical side to be discussed honestly and openly. Schools with a choice that set the stage for more balanced view of what AI can do, and just as importantly, what AI can't do. Most of these chats result in better guidelines that combine ethical safeguards with the promise of the benefits of AI (Buyserie et al., 2024). They become from simple tech adopters to advocates of the informed navigator of these digital twists in education (\u27Fotu O et al., 2024). That's why I believe it's important for institutions to allow ethical debates to be part of kids' everyday school lives, perhaps even with the (un)comfort of debates that are a bit raw, because it will ensure that people who will graduate as learners aren't just tech savvy, but are also ready to question and understand the tools that are forming their educational journey.

10.2 Collaboration Between Educators and Tech Developers

Teaming up with educators and tech developers affords a new and potentially daunting world to explore within the classroom walls, especially with regard to the use of generative AI. And this mix is not just a bunch of skills that need to be combined, it is about having insights one, but in a messy and unpredictable way as a means of developing tools that are squarely aimed at real classroom challenges. The teachers for example, will often spot gaps to how lessons are taught and then, from what they say, the developers of AI systems will try to make them something that is genuinely helpful teaching assistants, not just shiny tech. In general, this back and forth tends to improve lesson planning and, mostly because of this, students are attracted into more lively, dynamic lessons and the learning atmosphere has a slight touch of liveliness and sociability. We can take what iterative process leads to a platform like MootMentorAI. The educators here test out the early versions of GenAI tools in class, and the functionality improvements are brought about through on-the-spot, some even offhand, suggestions. At the end of the day, this trial and error approach sometimes gives the results a bit rough around the edges but they generally are user friendly and better suited to the demands of different subjects and teaching styles. Teachers are gradually transformed into co creators as ideators rather than by design into it and actual participants in this process of closing the gap from the theorization of academic tools to their actual and effective application in practice. Issues of authorship and agency arise from a natural place when new technologies find their way into lesson plans. These prompts bring up questions as to who the work that the students do actually belongs to and how much influence AI should actually have over learning. Still, educators and tech developers would need to hash out ethical guidelines, in the general sense of the word, which give rise to both transparency and accountability. For instance, teacher input provides protection from worry about bias and misinformation, as in the co design of AI based Writing Tutoring Platforms. Not only does this conclude with the construction of much needed digital capacities, speaking to the points made by (Han et al., 2024), but it also prompts students to think more critically and responsibly about the technology they are using.

10.3 Continuous Evaluation and Adaptation

As much as it involves checking and tweaking constantly, it is an element of the present day educational scene in mixing in GenAI tools. Planning lessons and generating interest has to change for them to accommodate the multitude of learning styles. Of course, this type of constructivist teaching isn't about only scoring student work—it means also keeping an eye on the tools students are using. In general, some studies suggest that as AI changes, it compels educators to able to adopt a number of new skills and lean on technology aided ways to improve the manner in which students learn. Classrooms in which feedback and reflection are part of the routine everyday allow teachers to know immediately if the information that they are delivering is sticking or if it is a lot of blah, blah, blah to a child and this ensures that the method with which the teacher is teaching is fresh but not rigid. Flexibility has become a necessity in online teaching during the era of COVID-19. But the fact that more educators have used tools like ChatGPT, research reveals that it has pushed others to revisit strategies to sustain high standards. Distance learning's major makeover with the help of GenAI forces us to reconsider content and the way they provide it so that no student's needs go unnoticed. It is truly tough to build community and keep others engaged in environments where the normal buzz of classroom chatter is absent. In most cases, this implies that ongoing professional development is not optional – teachers have to keep their methods fresh and experiment with new technologies in creative, sometimes odd ways. Taking a step back now, it's obvious that setting up ongoing checks is no passing fad, and instead plays an essential role in the persistent creating of educational setups. The studies also tend to stress how keeping a regular pulse on what's working helps shape such policies in support of a mix of teaching styles. Now, this mindset encourages engineers to create a culture of feedback where educators casually share both the ups and the limitations of new tools. Teachers can dig into the results from GenAI and figure out what really works best for approaching a lesson and fine tune the lesson planning to have students more involved. The hands on insights allow building a flexible curriculum that can fold when the trends and stumbling blocks come up at some point and helps teachers to connect deeply with their students while keeping a watchful eye over accountability (Cukurova et al., 2024)(Kılınç et al., 2023).

Figure 13. Adoption of AI in Education

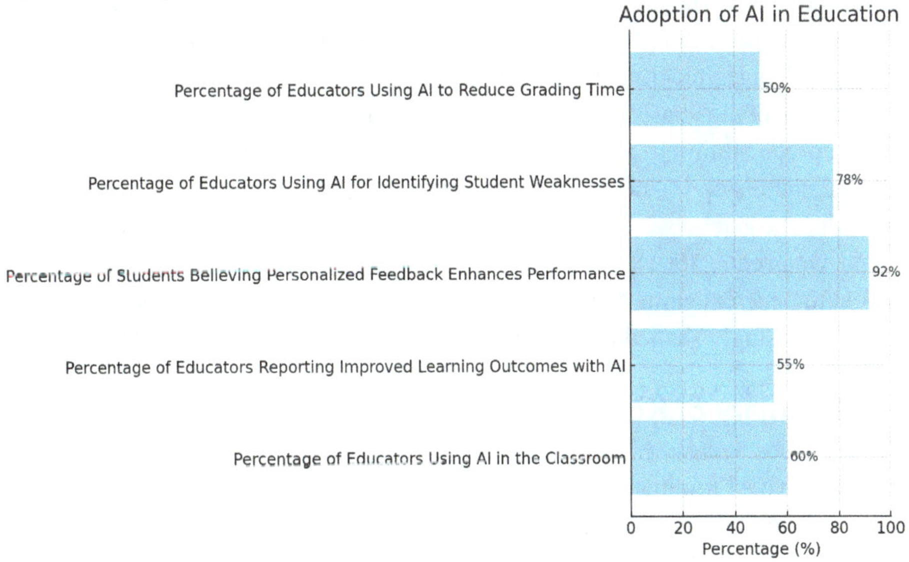

The chart displays the adoption rates of artificial intelligence in education among educators and students. Key metrics include the percentage of educators using AI in various capacities, such as improving learning outcomes, identifying student weaknesses, and reducing grading time, as well as the belief among students that personalized feedback enhances their performance. This data highlights the growing integration of AI tools in educational practices and their perceived impact on teaching and learning.

11 CONCLUSION

Using GenAI in schools is really changing how lessons are put together and how students get involved. Teachers now have a set of tools that let them adjust lessons to fit different needs — this kind of personalized approach, in most cases, meets students where they are and seems to echo modern ideas about giving learners a bigger role. GenAI sort of opens the door to immersive learning, letting educators spend more time on critical thinking skills while helping all students do well, even if the approach comes off a bit less formulaic than traditional models. Beyond sparking student engagement, this technology promises to boost teacher development too. Research, in many cases, shows that these tools work not just as classroom aids but also as reflective resources for educators—almost like a practice mirror. The process of fine-tuning lesson plans with GenAI often mirrors the iterative cycles of Agile methods, suggesting that teachers can keep reworking their strategies. When teachers try out systems like MootMentorAI, they often see improvements in both student results and their own teaching skill sets, placing them squarely amid new waves of educational innovation (Serra A, 2025). As schools and universities race to keep up with rapid changes, tackling the challenges of introducing GenAI becomes even more important. Findings based on real educator experiences hint that success depends a lot on proper training, accessible resources, and real support from institutions. Emphasizing a step-by-step plan for rolling out GenAI in higher education might just bridge the gap between fresh tech advances and everyday teaching practices. In the end, when educators, administrators, and policymakers all pitch in, GenAI could turn out to be a real game changer—arming students with the skills they need for a future increasingly shaped by artificial intelligence (Panday et al., 2024).

11.1 Summary of Key Points

Generative AI mixing into education brings up some intriguing ideas that could really shake up teaching. Recent finds show that using open educational resources (OER) gives students a kind of nimble, tailored learning experience. One study, for example, noted that when language learners see OER content as high-quality, they tend to engage more deeply with it—this, in turn, boosts their overall results. It all points to the fact that quality material matters, whether we're talking about traditional curricula or AI-driven tools. By taking advantage of the flexible nature of OERs, teachers can whip up lesson plans that suit different student levels and interests, which makes learning more effective and satisfying (Panday-Shukla et al., 2024). Looking deeper into GenAI tools, there's a general sense that the way teachers—both those starting out and seasoned pros—view these innovations really counts. In many cases, when educators get some hands-on time with GenAI, they become much more open to weaving it into their lesson plans and engagement methods. Teachers who have had good experiences with these tools seem more willing to incorporate them regularly. This kind of finding suggests that teacher training programs should add a dose of GenAI experience into their mix, so that schools build a workforce ready for a more tech-focused classroom. Overall, a bit of real-world practice with GenAI can ripple out to boost both how students participate and how they learn (Panday-Shukla et al., 2024). On another front, consider fields like legal education, where GenAI's role in sharpening practical skills and pumping up student engagement really stands out. Tools such as MootMentorAI show how GenAI can mimic real-life scenarios, offering personalized feedback that's vital for honing skills. This method not only connects textbook knowledge and hands-on practice but also fits nicely with the shifting needs of modern professional settings. As legal educators start to blend GenAI into their teaching routines, students end up experiencing ongoing, adaptive learning that primes them for an AI-driven future. In essence, these steps mirror a broader trend in education—using tech to stir up engagement, improve learning, and better prepare students for successful careers.

Figure 14. Adoption GenAI tools and preference

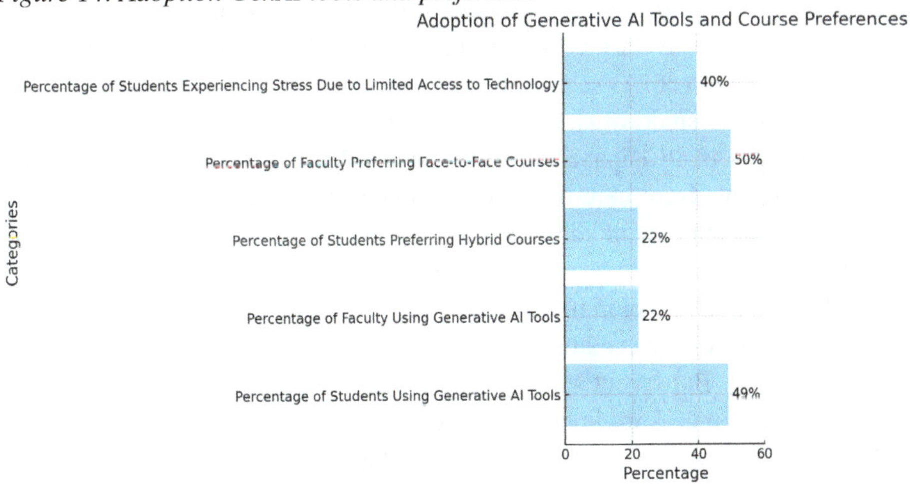

This bar chart illustrates the percentage of students and faculty using generative AI tools, as well as their preferences for course formats and experiences with technology access. The data highlights a growing trend in the adoption of generative AI in educational settings and its implications on teaching and learning practices.

11.2 Implications for Future Educational Practices

Shaking up the way we think about how teaching should be approached, genAI is doing things differently with fresh tech. A lot of studies now have actually revealed that practically every teacher – about 92% of them – state these tools are great in decreasing paperwork and increasing the efficiency in the lesson. Though helpful in streamlining lesson planning, bringing more interest into the students without having to deviate from the set schedule of the day and sparking more interest, there is also the worry that one could get too reliant on automation in their teaching. For example, teachers need to determine how AI's benefits can be integrated without it taking the place of the good, old critical thinking, creativity and so on. In fact, in a lot of cases, this balancing act ensures learners receive the benefits of using technology (Julie A Delello et al., 2025) that will help build the key skills they're going to need later on. But the schools, too, need to take seriously the approach of providing concrete rules even if it means setting them up for the first time, since AI keeps changing the way of things. Policy gaps still around, it feels like one of the things that educators have taken up as a collective is putting their own policies together when it relates to something like data privacy or using AI content in an optimistic, ethical way. Any kind of patchwork effort addressing GenAI can end up school rooms hugely various of their process, which may undercut a few of the great that Gen AI can do. As such, it would make sense for teachers, administrators, and even parents to sit down and form a framework so that they're all on the same page to help AI actually enhance the experience of learning (Julie A Delello et al., 2025). It's obvious from here that better training of teachers is going to change the game. A huge amount of educators say they need practical sessions to go from basic AI literacy through to how to correctly fold it into everyday lessons. Because this kind of hands-on development is so key to building up confidence as they have to survive GenAI's twists and turns – its mix of personalization but also its deep, engaging content. But recent studies note that it's not power of AI to customize the learning only, it is as well power of AI to bring the students in more naturally . And so, when schools spend in comprehensive, top to bottom training programs, it puts classrooms in position where GenAI does double duty with teachers to deliver richer, more dynamic, teaching and learning experiences.

Table 12. Implications of Generative AI in Education

Implication	Description
Enhanced Personalized Learning	Generative AI enables the creation of customized learning experiences, adapting to individual student needs and learning styles, thereby improving engagement and outcomes. ([pmc.ncbi.nlm.nih.gov](https://pmc.ncbi.nlm.nih.gov/articles/PMC11756388/))
Improved Assessment Methods	AI tools can streamline assessment processes, providing real-time feedback and identifying learning gaps, which supports timely interventions. ([pmc.ncbi.nlm.nih.gov](https://pmc.ncbi.nlm.nih.gov/articles/PMC11756388/))
Increased Access to Educational Resources	Generative AI can democratize education by offering high-quality learning materials to students from diverse backgrounds, including those from low socio-economic statuses. ([aph.gov.au](https://www.aph.gov.au/Parliamentary_Business/Committees/House/Employment_Education_and_Training/AIineducation/Report/Chapter_4_-_Opportunities_as_educational_tool/))
Potential for Bias and Inaccuracy	AI-generated content may inadvertently perpetuate biases present in training data and produce incorrect information, necessitating critical evaluation by educators and students. ([citl.illinois.edu](https://citl.illinois.edu/citl-101/instructional-spaces-technologies/teaching-with-technology/generative-artificial-intelligence/teaching-learning-implications-of-genai/))
Challenges to Academic Integrity	The use of AI in generating student work raises concerns about plagiarism and the authenticity of assessments, requiring clear policies and ethical guidelines. ([pmc.ncbi.nlm.nih.gov](https://pmc.ncbi.nlm.nih.gov/articles/PMC11756388/))

11.3 Call to Action for Educators and Policymakers

With education constantly evolving, it's no wonder that many educators, as well as politicians, now start diving in GenAI tools. For instance, teachers are encouraged to take up the know-how for incorporating these technologies into lesson plans and student interactions while using GenAI to reinvent the way we teach and as well as prepared lessons for a variety of student needs. In addition to that, in most cases, schools should also provide training sessions that consider both the practical aspect and the ethical questions related to using GenAI in class. Folks really gaining support like this may give teachers the confidence to use these tools to make our learning environments livelier and more adaptive, and fairer and more inclusive (Billingsley et al., 2024). On the other end, it is policymakers' turn to play the key role in putting the groundwork for GenAI integration. In general, they have to take up a strategic view that is neither too quick nor hard and still throws light on the ethical concerns of utilizing GenAI in class rooms. For example, in recent debates amongst circles dealing with higher education, there has been a demand to closely look at the biases which have been built into some algorithmic models. They must also be pushed to advocate on behalf of the entirety of the selection process of these tech tools, ensuring that those decisions are aligned with goals that are larger for an institution, including, for instance, fostering critical thinking, creativity and empathy. Rather, developing partnerships among educators and tech developers might produce frameworks that demonstrate the actual educational benefits of GenAI while navigating the natural obstacles of those same systems (Alexander et al., 2024). Steady conversation among teachers, students—as well as community members—is also needed in order to take a broader, more inclusive approach. Having these open forums may appear a bit obvious, but these really allow different viewpoints to influence how GenAI embedded in the curriculum. In practice this means establishing discussion groups that are conducive to feedback and sharing and insights in a natural way. While at times a little messy, that sort of ongoing dialogue (or at least something resembling it)—helps make sure that all voices from all walks of life—particularly those from marginalized communities—aren't just left out when the shape is being built around new ed-tech ideas. GenAI can help students and teachers, if educators keep inclusivity and fairness near the center of these efforts, and what's more, can be used to reinforce the bedrock of modern teaching and learning (Billingsley et al., 2024).

11.4 Final Thoughts on GenAI's Potential in Education

GenAI is now finding its way into educators' classrooms, and the benefits of the integration are already surfacing in unanticipated ways. It is not just another gadget, rather it is transforming into a real game changer—making new possible things to personalize learning. GenAI digs into all kinds of classroom data and then tweaks materials to fit with a wide variety of learning preferences (this is a hugely important thing, as every student needs a proper chance, regardless of their starting point). If viewed loosely, it aligns with modern ideas like differentiated instruction, and for the most part, when teachers use GenAI to personalize lessons, they actually end up making a living space that is dynamic, interactive, and encourages deep exploration and in some cases critical thinking. However, on another note, using GenAI also seems to relieve those daily, mundane work that consumes a teacher's time. The problem is that traditional lesson planning is too much detail, too time consuming, and too cutting the odds of connecting with students. GenAI can offload some of those routine jobs; drafting lesson plans or even basic content drafting, for teachers in order to let them refocus on building rapport and cultivating a healthy class culture. Although the change can take some time, it can increase teachers' effectiveness and, in most cases, help to build a class environment that inclines towards collaboration and a rapid reaction to students' needs so the motivation for learning continues to burn. In short, the wave of GenAI is neither limited to a mere tech update nor a matter of mere updating, but also hints to a completely new role of educators. In general, this new tool is helping to redefine teaching from just a matter of transmitting information to becoming a true facilitation of learning. There are still some ethics, equity, and nuts and bolts of implementation questions left to answer but the upside is hard to ignore. It is clear from discussions at various educational events (University of California et al., 2001), and in articles about leading edge classroom tools (Buckely et al.) that embracing GenAI is a forward thinking opportunity we have to shift how we teach and learn, to enhance teacher and student experience.

Figure 15. Perceptions

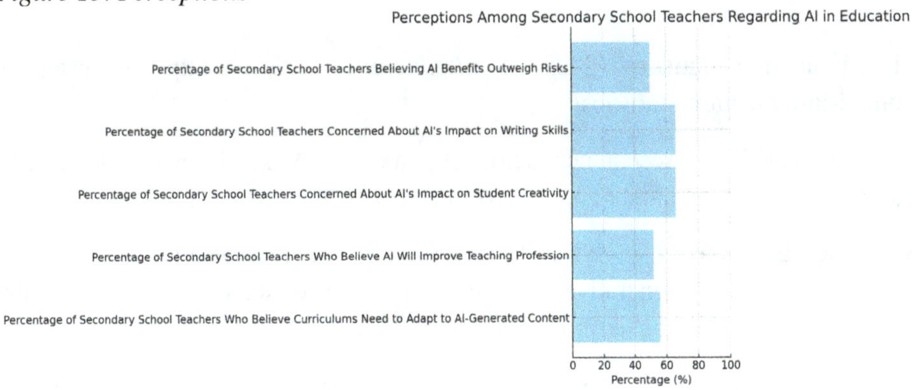

This bar chart illustrates the varied perceptions among secondary school teachers regarding the integration of Generative AI in education. It displays the percentage of teachers who believe that the benefits of AI outweigh the risks, those who express concerns about its impact on writing skills and student creativity, and those who feel that AI will enhance the teaching profession or necessitate adaptations in curricula. The data highlights both optimism about the potential advantages of AI and apprehension regarding its influence on traditional educational practices.

REFERENCES

AI in Education Statistics. (2025). *AI in education statistics.* https://www.aiprm.com/ai-in-education-statistics/

Alasmari, T. (2024). Acceptance factors of generative AI in EFL teaching: A pedagogical perspective. https://core.ac.uk/download/628120355.pdf

Alexander, B., Asino, T. I., & Bai, J. Y. H. (2024). The manifesto for teaching and learning in a time of generative AI: A critical collective stance to better navigate the future. https://core.ac.uk/download/636730349.pdf

Ali, A., Hingle, A., & Johri, A. (2024). Generative artificial intelligence in higher education: Evidence from an analysis of institutional policies and guidelines. https://arxiv.org/abs/2402.01659

Apisuksakul, K., Pimdee, P., & Sukkamart, A. (2024). Blended and collaboration-based learning management model to enhance mobile website user experience (UX) design skills. https://core.ac.uk/download/620884859.pdf

Billingsley, B., Billingsley, B., & Clarke, S. (2024). Big questions and interdisciplinary learning: Issue 1. https://core.ac.uk/download/617176985.pdf

Canavesi, A., Passerini, K., & Ravarini, A. (2024). From users to allies: Exploring educator and generative AI roles in shaping the future of higher education. https://core.ac.uk/download/620769088.pdf

Cukurova, M., Hertz, B., & Kralj, L. Saltidou, & et al. (2024). Professional development for teachers in the age of AI. https://core.ac.uk/download/603246853.pdf

Geiselhofer, M., Gorman, A., & Hsu, H.-P. (2024). Preliminary study on pre-service teachers' applications and perceptions of generative artificial intelligence for lesson planning. https://core.ac.uk/download/621114994.pdf

Gerardou, F. S., Michel-Villarreal, R., & Salinas-Navarro, D. E. Thierry-Aguilera, & et al. (2023). Challenges and opportunities of generative AI for higher education as explained by ChatGPT. https://core.ac.uk/download/586151541.pdf

National Science Board. (2018). Science & Engineering Indicators 2018. *National Science Foundation*. Retrieved from https://www.nsf.gov/statistics/2018/nsb20181/report/sections/elementary-and-secondary-mathematics-and-science-education/instructional-technology-and-digital-learning

Serra, A. (2025). AI lawyering skills trainers: Transforming legal education with generative AI. https://core.ac.uk/download/635940326.pdf

Shahzad, T., Mazhar, T., Tariq, M. U., Ahmad, W., Ouahada, K., & Hamam, H. (2025). A comprehensive review of large language models: Issues and solutions in learning environments. *Discover Sustainability*, *6*(1), 27. Advance online publication. DOI: 10.1007/s43621-025-00815-8

Thüs, D., Malone, S., & Brünken, R. (2024). Exploring generative AI in higher education: A RAG system to enhance student engagement with scientific literature. *Frontiers in Psychology*, *15*, 1474892. DOI: 10.3389/fpsyg.2024.1474892 PMID: 39463458

Chapter 10

Training and Development in AI-Driven Education Scaling Solutions: K-12 to Workforce

R. N. Ravikumar
https://orcid.org/0009-0009-3705-1681
Marwadi University, Rajkot, India

S. Aarthi
https://orcid.org/0009-0006-9064-2091
Marwadi University, Rajkot, India

Feruza Ruzimova
Urgench State University, Urgench, Uzbekistan

Zokir Mamadiyarov
Termez University of Economics and Service, Termez, Uzbekistan

ABSTRACT

The integration of AI in education brings significant benefits across all educational levels but also presents challenges during development, such as limited funding, insufficient digital skills among educators, and resistance to technology adoption. This research examines how AI-driven solutions like intelligent tutoring systems, adaptive learning, and AI-assisted assessments impact lifelong learning. The success of AI in education depends on collaboration between educational institutions, technology companies, and government bodies to maintain ethical standards. Industry-

DOI: 10.4018/979-8-3373-2185-1.ch010

academia alliances and multi-sector partnerships accelerate the development and implementation of AI in education. Practical examples from K-12 schools and higher education highlight the role of AI in improving educational platforms and student outcomes through data-driven strategies. The chapter discusses overcoming obstacles and fostering partnerships to create inclusive, future-focused educational programs.

1. INTRODUCTION

The inclusion of Artificial Intelligence (AI) within the educational context is a revolutionary change on every level since primary and secondary school education to higher education, and workforce including those displaced. The introduction of AI-based systems like intelligent tutoring system, adaptive learning systems, and online assessment tools are transforming how students learn and the instructors teach. These technologies help in providing individual learning opportunities, reduce red tape in administration and give real time reporting on learner performance. Nonetheless, the idea of AI adoption in the education sector is not devoid of considerable challenges (Kakina, 2025). Monetary resource availability, limitations in training educators on the digital skills, institutional inertia, and ethical issues concerning data collection and imperfect algorithms are some of the reasons that halt a common use.

Additionally, educational inequities are exacerbated by the issues of digital inequality especially in underserved communities. AI can be fully used in terms of creating inclusive and effective learning environments only with multi-sector collaboration. Collaboration of government, academia, the technology of companies, and NGOs can help to fill the skill gap, develop infrastructure, and guarantee ethical implementation (Alotaibi & Alshehri, 2023). In the chapter, the major implementation issues, scalable AI application areas, and collaborative framework that is necessary towards the transformation involving AI enrolled education are discussed. Upon investigation of both the opportunities and the barriers facing effective application of AI in learning, it me provide a comprehensive insight into how AI can be utilized effectively so as to achieve learning results and also with a view of ensuring equitable access to quality learning in the increasingly growing digital world.

1.1 Core Implementation Challenges in Education Innovation

Adoption of AI in education will have three significant hurdles. To begin with, schools are not financially able to invest in AI tools and infrastructure. Second, the teacher readiness is insufficient, and the training of teachers on digital tools is required by a substantial number of them. Third, change is delayed by institutional and cultural resistance caused by the fear of losing a job and the desire to use traditional approaches (Badawy et al., 2025). All these together impedes the implementation. These can only be addressed through financing, training and favourable policy mechanisms. The following Figure 1 shows three most significant obstacles that impede AI implementation in education: budget shortages, teacher unpreparedness, inceptive to change at an institutional level. All the aspects impair scalability and effectiveness of AI implementation in learning settings.

Figure 1. Challenges in AI Education

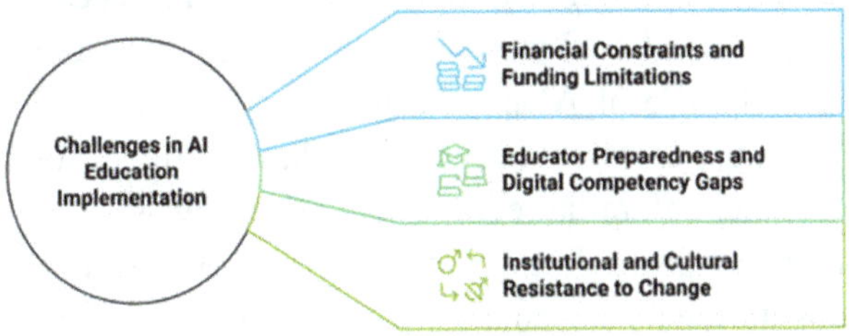

1.1.1 Financial Constraints and Funding Limitations

The financial burden affects both institutions as well as the operational framework during AI technology adoption. The deployment of AI systems is impossible for educational facilities because startup expenses for new software acquisitions plus updated infrastructure maintenance costs inhibit their installation. Public education facilities use budget money for operations and leave the funds empty due to the lack of funds which impedes smaller facilities from buying modern technological systems. AIT implementation spans such a long time that organizations struggle to determine optimal distribution of their funding budget (Chembe et al., 2023). The maintenance of operational systems becomes more expensive because administrators must keep working their systems even though they do not account for platform aging.

1.1.2 Educator Preparedness and Digital Competency Gaps

While AI education platforms require teacher competence and proficiency development there exist substantial knowledge gaps which spread through all educational leadership positions up to teaching personnel. Education practitioners who lack technical training cannot correctly implement AI technologies for educational instruction with their peers. The difficulty for teachers increases when they work to implement automated educational systems while keeping algorithmic oversight capabilities stable due to their obstacles in reading AI analytical outcome outputs.

The rapid technology learning of higher education instructors leads to a disruption in their teacher role since the lessons require dedicated attention to teaching (Gray et al., 2022). The educational problems created by AI development exceed the range of abilities found in professional development programs which leads teachers to remain uninformed about recent educational innovations.

1.1.3 Institutional and Cultural Resistance to Change

Public educational institutions fail to implement AI unsuccessfully due to their adherence to existing operational procedures and their momentum which opposes significant change. The use of AI in education produces two main concerns for educational staff because they fear professional duties will be stolen while classes become less human and unfamiliar educational principles will be introduced (Lin, 2022). Two main barriers exist for organizations when trying to implement technology change through institutional rules that influence both job positions and workplace areas while unions add another resistance point. Student and parental groups oppose AI advances since they fail to understand the complex operational procedures of systems. New employees in the workforce push back against AI system adoption because they have doubts about machine ability to handle human-based capabilities during challenging tasks that need judgment skills along with social interaction. Organizations that refuse basic technological adoption face difficulties obtaining funds which stops them from testing new implementation strategies through evaluations. Installation of new systems becomes challenging due to organizational restrictions which cannot adapt appropriately to new systems. Educational organizations require multiple learning obstacle solutions to harness artificial intelligence capabilities for meeting the diverse classroom needs through flexible educational systems.

2. CHALLENGES IN IMPLEMENTING AI-DRIVEN EDUCATION

In Systemic Barriers to Adoption the wide-ranging obstacles impede the potential evolution of learning systems through artificial intelligence implementation in education. The application of artificial intelligence in all educational environments presents particular examination obstacles even though K-12 institutions and other educational facilities still must solve basic operational difficulties (Bian et al., 2024). Figure 2 illustrates four major challenges to AI integration in education financial constraints, human capital gaps, technical hurdles, and institutional resistance depicted as interconnected puzzle pieces that must align for effective adoption.

Figure 2. Key Barriers to Implementing AI in Education

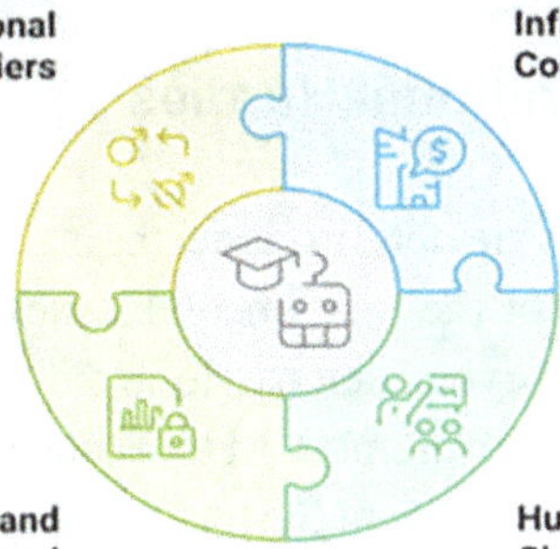

2.1 Financial and Infrastructure Constraints

Financial and infrastructure-related issues largely restrict the use of AI in the education sector. Educational organizations, and primarily the public ones, need a significant capital investment to purchase the necessary hardware, create an AI-based program, and develop system components, which entail the requirements of considerable initial investments. Moreover, to sustain and refresh these platforms, it has to take constant financial implications such as the price of data storage, support staff costs (Yim & Wegerif, 2024). There exist several schools that have trouble coping with persistent fiscal constraints, being forced to decide between spending on cutting-edge learning technology and covering basic course requirements. Also, another factor of educational inequities seems to be the digital divide, which is defined as an inequal access to devices and stable internet connection, which place the vulnerable communities in a position when they cannot enjoy the advancements in AI-based learning.

2.2 Human Capital Challenges

The human capital is one of the main obstacles to a successful introduction of AI in teaching. People working in the sphere of education need to spend much time to understand how to apply AI tools which are the key to successful, efficient modern teaching. Nevertheless, most of the teachers are using the old-fashioned instructional strategies that are very inadequate in the current changing learning environment. Change aversion is also strengthened by the institutional conformity to the accepted standards and cultural practices where innovative approaches are hard to embrace.

Besides, increased rate of change in technology subject the educators to stress as many of them have the fear that the changes may somehow demean their positions or compromise their careers.

2.3 Technical and Operational Hurdles

Technical and operational issues tend to hinder the introduction of AI to educational systems. Data privacy is one of the fundamental issues, and the latest AI systems have to be equipped with the cyber defense to avoid any leakage of confidential student data and its abuse. Moreover, most AI tools have a problem of compatibility with the existing Learning Management Systems (LMS) because of little interoperability and the result is inefficiency in implementation. The other prominent issue is algorithmic bias, as biased training information may lead to discrimination among the yield during training, causing an imbalance in the outcome of education (Nuangchalerm, 2023). As much as technical maintenance can ensure stability in the conduct of school operations, the possibility of failure of operations on its system through system breakdowns cannot be ignored when there is no constant support.

2.4 Cultural and Institutional Barriers

Another challenge that can dramatically reduce the implementation of AI in education is cultural resistance and institutional barriers. Bureaucracies in institutions of learning may also slow implementation since employees may not be willing to change and follow old ways of doing things. An attempt to implement personalized learning often comes into conflict with the frameworks of standardized testing and introduces a stalemate between innovation and established practices. Further on, communities and school boards lacking knowledge of AI will also distrust educational software, which adds to the slackening of acceptance. An ethical issue is also observed, since there usually are no strict rules to determine the proper usage of AI in a classroom. A combination of factors makes these problems even worse as much of the institutions cannot cope with the fast technological development (Yim & Wegerif, 2024). Implementation of AI without strategic alignment of budgets, technical development, and staff readiness program would remain splayed. In order to be successful, educational systems are recommended to embrace flexible, inclusive educational systems capable of meeting unique needs of learners, and guaranteeing understanding and acceptance among stakeholders under all circumstances.

3. BARRIERS TO EFFECTIVE AI INTEGRATION IN EDUCATION

Ethical issues, shortage of funds, and the absence of teacher preparation are the reasons why it might be hard to introduce AI into education effectively. Numerous facilities are experiencing budget gaps, poor facilities, digital inequalities, particularly in underprivileged or rural locations. Certainly, teachers do not always have the chance or time to develop professionally in order to apply AI tools correctly. Also, these issues touch on data privacy, algorithmic bias, and transparency of decision-making processes in AI increase ethical concerns. These obstacles should be approached comprehensively in order to provide equal, safe and substantial implementation of AI in educational settings (Zapata et al., 2024). The table 1 presents the critical issues encountered in the process of the introduction of AI technologies in education. It breaks down those barriers into financial, human, technical, cultural, and ethical and points out the most important points that impede the adoption of AI in an equal and efficient manner. These are critical barriers that should be addressed to have sustainable and inclusive education systems driven by AI.

Table 1. Barriers to Effective AI Integration in Education

Barrier Category	Key Challenges
Financial Constraints	High cost of AI tools, infrastructure, and maintenance; limited funding in public institutions.
Educator Readiness	Lack of digital literacy; insufficient training on AI tools and pedagogical integration.
Technical & Operational	Poor interoperability with existing systems; maintenance issues; data protection concerns.
Cultural & Institutional	Resistance to change, preference for traditional teaching; bureaucratic inertia.
Ethical & Policy Gaps	Lack of clear policies on data privacy, bias testing, and ethical AI usage in classrooms.
Digital Divide	Unequal access to devices and internet, especially in rural or underserved communities.

3.1 Resource Constraints

Educational organizations face two main implementation obstacles because they lack appropriate internet resources and technical infrastructure together with a shortage of sufficient skilled staff. Facilities that serve rural populations together with disadvantaged urban communities continue to struggle with developing their needed technological infrastructure. Installing new AI systems needs substantial funding from educational institutions which must buy licenses to purchase software while adapting hardware systems with their current independent software structures. This fact indicates major funding challenges at the implementation stage. The restricted amount of available funding for schools occurs because institutions use program maintenance funds for system update payments and cloud services that steadily deplete their budget (Zawacki-Richter et al., 2019a). Successful outcomes from initial test programs do not translate to broader implementation because individual schools possess different technological platforms and assistance systems.

3.2 Lack of Teacher Training

The capabilities of educational technology surpass what learners can manage without proper implementation of digital instructional tools. The present situation makes it impossible for users to implement systems to their maximum capacity. AI instructional tools cause difficulties for educational workers because they offer supplemental assistance instead of providing complete support to educational teaching systems. The lack of professional development for educational personnel exists because extra work hours are required without receiving compensatory pay (Abisoye, 2023). Staff members who teach at educational institutions must demonstrate continuous participation in modern technological education because technology progresses at a rapid pace.

3.3 Ethical Concerns

The outcome of man-made smart systems becomes prejudiced when incorrect educational data causes adverse impacts on minority students during evaluation and recommendation stages. Digital records of students persist after unauthorized accidental school data transfers lead to privacy breaches in schools. The education organizations do not have authorization to view data policy statements that their network vendors create. Students from higher social classes benefit more from technological learning because they possess basic educational resources that less advantaged students are unable to obtain (Asperis, 2025). Digital disparities emerge from the quality of AI system implementation because poor execution prevails in school facilities. Execution of algorithms determining student learning remains obscure to the educational staff because these systems operate beyond their known parameters. The complex technical system features multiple different barriers that prevent institutional progress in their technological advancement. An ethical system of today demands staff teaching training and financial backing to fulfil its ethical requirements for operation. AI educational applications require official guidelines for moral standards while educators need secure employment as well as unrestricted access to high-quality resources at every school institution.

4. AI-POWERED LEARNING SYSTEMS

A personalized learning system that integrates medical technology allows educators to create advanced training programs through collaborative development in order to improve student educational achievements. ITS systems contribute to educations by producing interactive materials of learning such as videos contain text ingredient and interactive ingredients into the current teaching. Carnegie Learning MATHia emotion sensor technology performing students achieve math goal attainment at rate 15 to 20% higher Student Solutions Packages Using its adaptive learning system Arizona State University boosted completion rates yielding lower dropout numbers of 18%.

To obtain expert evaluations superior to standard plagiarism, educational bodies applied AI natural language processing trained the AI to build www chinaese. com automated grading systems for essays. Together with artificial intelligence systems and virtual reality virtually combined with virtual reality, make possible the creation of tutors who read patterns on the cortex to accompany the educational process (Barnes & Hutson, 2024). Innate ITS technologies are given more strength from Generative AI thanks to their capacity to coalesce structured techniques with discovery-based unstructured techniques. Partners and businesses developing AI system infrastructure must train workforce and set forth ethical principles for ensuring the greatest amount of learning and mitigating accessibility-based risks in student success outcomes. Figure 3 illustrates how various AI technologies like intelligent tutoring, generative AI, NLP, and emotion sensors contribute to personalized learning, automated assessments, and adaptive platforms, enhancing education outcomes and workforce readiness.

Figure 3. AI-Powered Learning Systems in Education

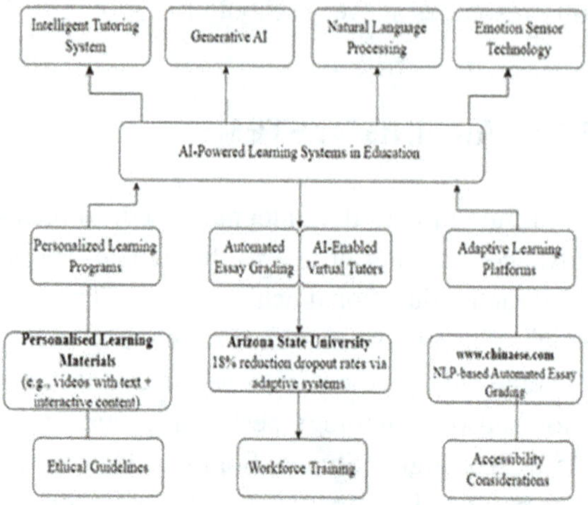

The below Figure 4 illustrating the impact of various AI-powered learning technologies on educational outcomes. Each system shows measurable improvements such as increased goal attainment, reduced dropout rates, and enhanced student engagement through personalized and adaptive learning tools.

Figure 4. Impact of AI-Powered Learning Systems on Educational Outcomes

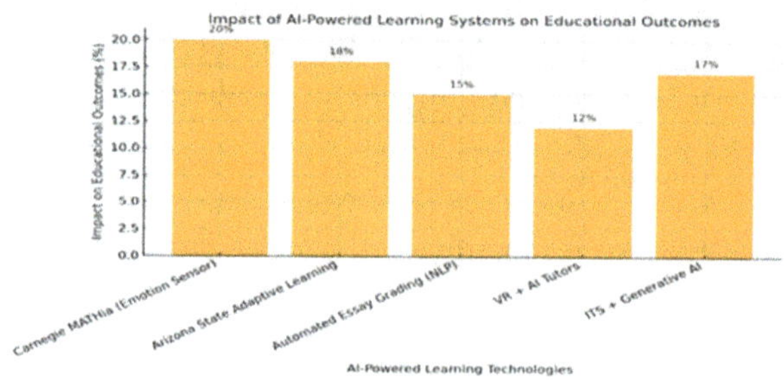

4.1 Intelligent Tutoring Systems (ITS), Personalized Learning, Real Time Feedback

Intelligent Tutoring Systems (ITS) mimic one on one human tutoring by adapting to the learning pace of the student, strengths, and weaknesses by using AI, rather than software or human tutoring. Such systems using machine learning help to analyze student responses, detect areas of misconceptions and make appropriate instructional modifications on the fly. The main characteristics are adaptive questioning, the decomposition of complex problems, and immediate feedback and clarification thereof (Ding, 2025). Smart ITS applications also engage facial recognition and keystroke to measure engagement and frustration. Researches indicate that software-supported systems, such as MATHia in Carnegie Learning, have increased the student performance by an additional 18-20% when compared to the traditional approach thus proving the fact that ITS can play a significant role to achieve better results in terms of personalized learning. Figure 5 compares the improvement in average student performance using ITS (e.g., MATHia) versus traditional learning methods from 2019 to 2023, highlighting a consistent performance gain of 18–20% with ITS integration

Figure 5. Impact of Intelligent Tutoring Systems (ITS) on Student Performance Over Time

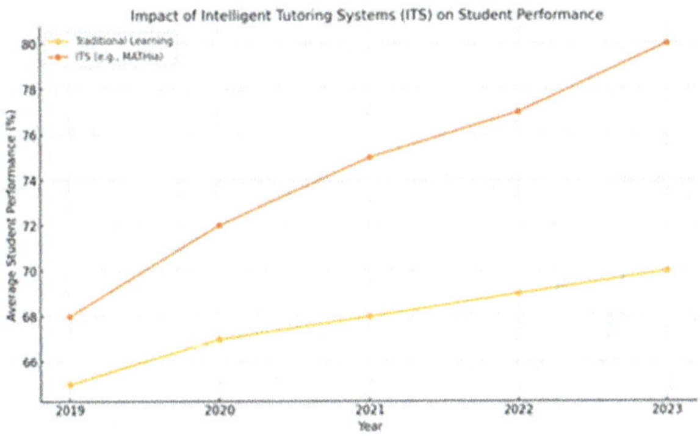

4.2 Adaptive Learning (Customized Content, Case Studies)

AI-powered adaptive learning platforms help to provide the educational content to the learners in accordance with their progress and knowledge. This form of automatic customization positions the lesson difficulty and pace to a desired level according to the current performance due to the highly personalized set of case studies and other specialized materials. At the start of every module, diagnostic tests are used to determine the areas of knowledge that each student has not mastered, the learning material can therefore speed up over those aspects that have been learnt and the student can also speed up when they grasp something. Teachers can also use elaborate analytics, which indicates learning trends among the students. In a single university, Arizona State, Adaptive Learning Technology was used in biology courses; unfavourable dropout rates declined by 27% and all academic results were bettered. Figure 6 illustrates the significant reduction in student dropout rates from 35% to 24% after the implementation of adaptive learning technology in biology courses, showcasing its positive impact on academic retention and success.

Figure 6. Effect of Adaptive Learning on Dropout Rates at Arizona State University

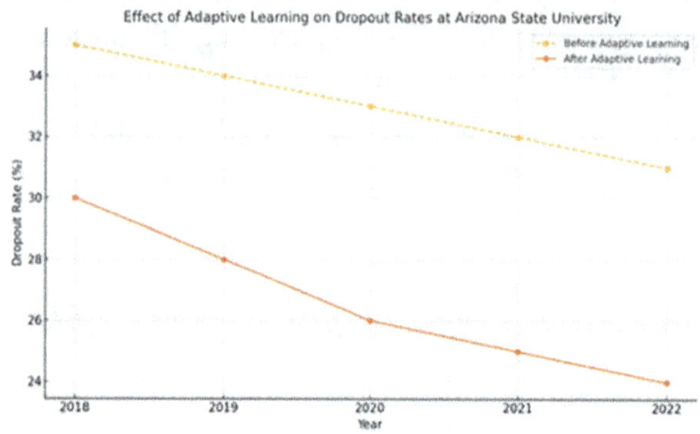

4.3 AI-Assisted Assessment (automated grading, analytics)

Assessment aids that help in evaluation with the help of AI are revolutionising the way of grading by automating the grading process and providing elaborate performance analytic. These systems are very effective in grading assignments as they save time on administering tasks and offer further education on how students are learning (Ogbu Eke, 2024). Applications such as Turnitin Revision Assistant employ algorithms to evaluate the quality of writing, grammar and coherence and identify plagiarism by carrying out a large-scale comparison through huge databases. Performative analytics is useful to determine which students are in trouble as they progress through test scores and performance patterns over time rather than only throughout a one-time evaluation. Because of this time will be saved by teachers 5-10 hours per week, student feedback will be instantaneous, and grading will be more impartial and consistent. Figure 7 illustrates the primary advantages of AI-assisted assessment systems: 40% of the benefit comes from saving teachers' time, 35% from providing instant student feedback, and 25% from enabling impartial and consistent grading.

Figure 7. Benefits of AI-Assisted Assessment in Education

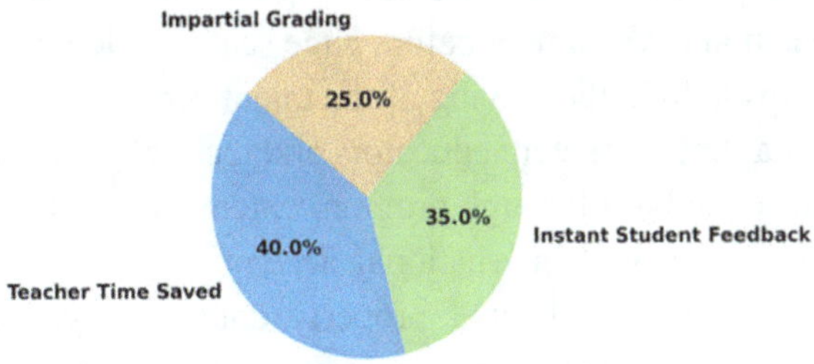

5. Scaling AI Through Collaboration in Education

Collaborative efforts among various stakeholders will facilitate the successful incorporation of AI into education, allowing us to mitigate challenges selected for the integration including financing, technology, and ethical issues. Education institutions by themself cannot facilitate such disruptive changes as funding is usually a gatekeeper (Wan Ismail et al., 2023). Products will stand a greater chance of being scaled and adopted if education organizations partner together to co-design or work alongside governments, tech companies, researchers, and policy makers to define sustainable AI products and scale.

5.1 Industry-Academia Partnerships: Driving AI Innovation in Education

Industry-academia collaborations are the main drivers in promoting the encompassed use of AI in learning because they combine the 50% business-related technical knowledge and technology companies, together with 50% pedagogical and research skills of educational institutions. Google, Microsoft and IBM are among the major corporations partnering universities in the design of Intelligent Tutoring System, Adaptive Learning Platform and AI-based assessment. Such collaborations are usually integrated into the form of collaborative research labs in which technology companies would deliver computational power and data, whereas educational models and assessing procedures would be contributed by the universities.

An example includes Stanford University and Google Brain collaborating to research natural language processing in education, and the MIT IBM Watson AI Lab recently producing AI models that provide personalized feedback to students as well as advancing research in human computer learning relationships (A.M.

Fadli Mappisabbi et al., 2024). Approximately 40% of these alliances are concerned with prototype testing in academic living labs, so that technologies may be smoothed in the actual environment before huge scale implementation. Also, up to 30% of partnerships help in the solving of the talent pipeline by developing AI-in-education curricula that competent educators and technologists of tomorrow train. Such capacity has been built through program extensions such as Microsoft Ai in Education which has created international academic partnerships. Nonetheless, despite the issue regarding intellectual property, data privacy, and academic independence, the successful collaboration generates innovation ecosystems resulting in meaningful and classroom-ready AI solutions. Figure 8 visualizing the key focus areas of industry-academia partnerships in driving AI innovation in education. The bubble size and label indicate each area's contribution percentage, highlighting balanced efforts in technical and Pedagogical Collaboration, Prototype Testing, and Curriculum Development.

Figure 8. Industry vs Academia: AI Education Partnership Impact

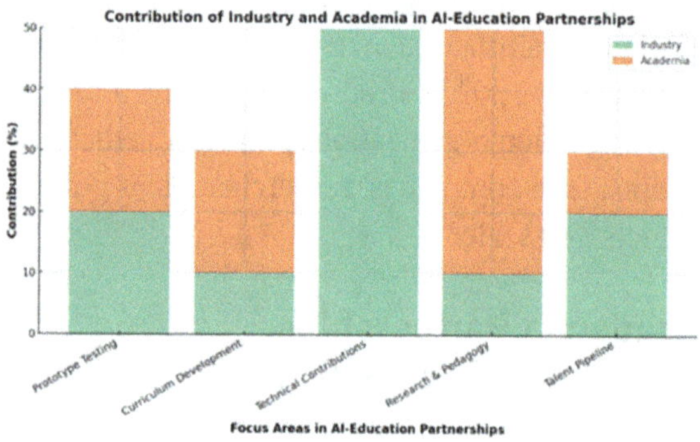

5.2 Government Policies: Funding and Ethical Guidelines for AI in Education

Governments have an important function in achieving greater levels of scalability for AI for education, by developing policies and funding mechanisms as well as ethical frameworks to support this responsible deployment of AI; as well as some systemic challenges such as accessibility and equity.

5.2.1 Funding Opportunities and Infrastructure Support

Grants provided by taxpayers through the government are very essential in the process of schools and universities being able to implement AI technologies. Subsidies and grants enable the underserved schools to afford AI tools, like those offered by the U.S Department of Education that gives grants to faith-based schools (Trang, 2024). The idea of the cooperation of governments and technology companies like the project of India called AI for All is a form of public-private partnership. Also, national digital infrastructure initiatives help to secure high-speed internet connections and devices in schools and train digital skills to facilitate the efficient use of AI-based learning tools.

5.2.2 Ethical and Regulatory Frameworks

Much to curb the dangers of bias and misuse, governments are working on the formulation of ethical and regulatory factors of responsible AI use in education. The prominent decisions are assuring data privacy by implementing the laws like GDPR (EU) and COPPA (U.S.) to safeguard student data, requiring algorithm transparency to facilitate discrimination-free operations such as grading and admissions, and creating bias-avoidance procedures by conducting routine audits. Nations are being proactive in this regard: the AI Ethics & Governance Body in Singapore: guides schools, Finland has put aside 50 million Euros to be used in integrating ethical AI into schools, and the Brazilian task force is standardizing adaptive learning tools (Atkinson-Toal & Guo, 2024). These policies are meant to achieve the task of making AI serve humanity instead of replacing them, which will lead to equity and accountability.

5.3 Multi-Sector Alliances: Bridging Gaps in Learning and Workforce Development

In the ever-changing modern environment, the multi-sector collaboration in the framework of which NGOs, EdTech companies, and corporate training providers have to work is the key to the development of the inclusive approach based on data and centred on job placement. Such collaborations aid in eliminating the learning-workforce readiness divide as they merge different knowledge. To illustrate, 40% of the grassroots backing and expertise of social equity is composed of NGOs especially in underserved society. EdTech companies have been generating 35% via scalable and sustainable solutions, including AI-based tutoring, gamified learning applications and adaptive analytics platforms. In the meantime, the corporate partners will present 25% by matching learning results with the labour force needs, the provision of internship opportunities, the provision of skill certifications and careers (Barnes & Hutson, 2024).

A good example can be observed in India, where multinational corporations, together with NGOs and a mobile-enabled EdTech platform succeeded in digital skills training the rural youth, as well as improving the learning outcomes and the economic growth of that specific region. There is real-time adaptation to changes in industry by utilising this ecosystem, leading to constant learning according to the changing workforce demands. Nevertheless, approximately 20 or 30% of alliances fail because of some cultural gaps, data exchange issues, and unmatched goals. The success of these unions in making sustainable educational difference is guaranteed by excellent dialogue, standardized measurement tools, and inclusive design approaches, in particular, to women, people with disabilities, and remote learners.

6. AI APPLICATIONS ACROSS EDUCATION LEVELS

The introduction of individualized learning patterns through Artificial Intelligence allows higher institutional capabilities while improving student-teacher relationships at every educational level. Adaptive learning systems working with intelligent tutoring systems assist primary education students to receive instant feedback regarding the acquisition of basic knowledge by using individualized learning speeds. AI-based speech recognition and language tools provide early literacy support and assist with students that are multi-lingual. In the secondary phase of education, there are emerging AI applications in subject-specific tutoring, automated grading, and predictive analysis identifying students likely to fall behind (Folorunso & Olanipekun, 2024). Chatbots and virtual assistants create student-teacher interaction that allows for quicker resolution of online queries and personalized recommendation of resources.

For higher education, AI enables deeper learning opportunities through AI-based course recommendations, academic advising systems, and AI-augmented research tools. AI can provide virtual-labs and simulations for complex subjects, such as engineering and medicine. Additionally, AI facilitates faculty in developing inclusive curriculum and allows for real-time tracking of student advancement or an opportunity to intervene. AI at any level of education can support inclusive and accessible education tools for learners with disabilities through speech-to-text tools, real-time translation, and personalized interfaces (Medaglia et al., 2023). When it comes to learning and administration, AI cuts both ways, giving teachers and institutions more time to enhance and provide more effective, equitable, and engaging education experiences.

6.1 K-12: Gamification and Early Intervention with AI

In K-12 education, Artificial Intelligence (AI) is a significant change agent, leading to more dynamic, personalized, and responsive learning. Two powerful applications in the K-12 sphere are gamification and early intervention. Gamification, with the help of AI, incorporates some game-like elements, such as updatable learning objectives, points, badges, leaderboards, and adaptive challenges, into the learning experience to increase motivation, attention, and participation for students, particularly in mathematics, science, and language arts (Oh & Sanfilippo, 2024). AI can adjust the questions presented in the game (as long as the objectives are met) to a students' learning pace and preferences, while still developing both fun and academic learning.

Early intervention is another important K-12 use of AI. AI-supported analytics can help document student performance in real time, detecting and alerting educators of patterns that may foresee learning impediments, disengagement, or social-emotional challenges exhibited through their lives in and out of school. The educator then has an early opportunity to intervene through tutoring lessons, counselling, or addressing the learning plan and activities prior or before the mentioned issues emerge (Selvaratnam & Venaruzzo, 2024). Together, these two strategies demonstrate how AI can provide both engagement as well as support strategies within the classroom to benefit learning for all young learners. Also, these advancements in education provide a strong foundation of continued academic success. Figure 9 highlights how AI enhances K-12 learning through gamified elements like badges and adaptive challenges, while also enabling early interventions via real-time analytics and pattern detection.

Figure 9. AI in K-12: Gamification & Intervention

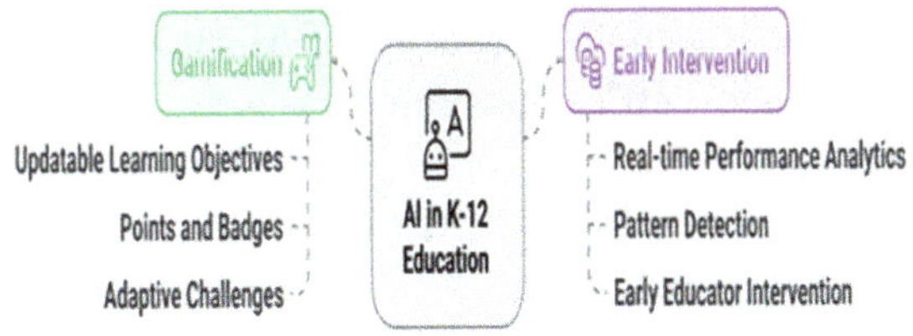

6.2 Higher Education: AI-Powered Research Tools and Career Guidance

Artificial Intelligence is noticeably transforming the higher education sector to an unprecedented extent in the areas of academic research and career guidance. In higher education research, AI tools are changing the ways students and faculty access, process, and create knowledge. The use of AI in literature review is one area where accessibility is improving because AI can quickly query large databases with search words and topics, condense and summarize articles, as well as suggest research trends. In addition, there is work being done with Natural Language Processing algorithms to analyze large datasets from a broad base of evidence and suggest implications for findings as well as create hypotheses (Zawacki-Richter et al., 2019b). These developments mean AI is potentially speeding up the research process and making it more accurate.

AI is also crucial to a student's educational career guidance. Intelligent career advising systems utilize algorithms to analyze an academic record, students' interests and skill sets, and suggest methods for future career paths, internships, and appropriate courses. AI is being adopted to use chatbots or virtual advisors that help provide 24/7 support to a student through answering questions about job prospects, industry trends, and required skills. Job searching could be enhanced when labour market analytics systems are adopted into education systems via a built platform, allowing to improve job estimates and improved research and analyses, to demonstrate to students wherefore their labour next (Bastomi et al., 2024). The integration of AI into higher education in career development and academic research areas continues to supplement students in helping them become more acquiescent to adapt and grow in educational and career situations. In post AI transformations, institutions will have improved reputability for graduating students with their undergraduate, graduate, and post graduate degrees that can and will be retained in real time labour markets. Thusly it can be argued its ectopic use of AI can integrate AI systems into developing our students most efficacious future.

6.3 Workforce: Adaptive Upskilling and Corporate Learning Platforms

Human capital markets are changing rapidly and organizations are grappling with workforce development in the world of Artificial Intelligence. Consider adaptive upskilling and corporate learning platforms powered by AI, helping organizations and individuals to remain competitive in a world where speed of change, changes in required skills, and persistent, re-distributed workforce development are all undergoing significant transformations, primarily driven by automation, AI tools, and digital transformations. Adaptive upskilling is centered around using AI algorithms to deliver adaptive learning programs tailored to the employee's existing skill set, preferred style of learning, and individual career aspirations (Muhammad Hani Bayan, 2024). AI can analyze employee performance data, engagement and monitor how an individual learns at work to continually adapt the learning content dynamically while the learning process is happening. Adaptive upskilling focuses on knowledge acquisition through targeted learning while mitigating learning fatigue. This means that we can deliver more targeted learning that fits better, takes less time and has more impact on the employee's performance.

Corporate learning platforms that include artificial intelligence which offer curated learning paths, predictive analytics and intelligent content recommendations. Corporate learning platforms typically include components such as virtual coaches, automated feedback systems, and skill-gap analyses that can allow employees to navigate and progress through micro-credentials and professional certifications (Blonder & Feldman-Maggor, 2024). Just-in- time learning is enabled by AI powered corporate learning platforms, which can provide situational, contextual knowledge and resources exactly when the employee needs them to maximize human productivity and retention. In prioritizing intelligent, scalable, and purposeful learning in alignment with organizational business goals, AI is enabling organizations to develop agile workforces that are future-ready to learn, engage, and pivot as needed AI is also democratizing professional development for employees and organizations; and will increasingly continue to make continuous learning a reality for all employees.

7. THE FUTURE OF AI IN EDUCATION

The future of AI in education presents enormous potential for changing the way we teach, learn, and interact with educational material. As AI advances, it will become more integrated into educational systems, creating more personalized learning opportunities for students that are more efficient and inclusive (Cioci, 2025). Here are some visions for the future.

7.1 Personalized Learning Experiences

One exciting opportunity for AI in education is a move to completely personalized learning experiences. AI systems will be able to analyze students' learning styles, skills, and areas for improvement, and adjust the content and pedagogical tools that it uses. Adaptive learning platforms that are AI-powered will deliver lessons as they adjust to a student's pace and skill levels, providing completely customized feedback and resources in real-time. Personalized learning is the goal of education to be at the right time with supports at the right time and that has been shown to keep students engaged with their learning, and protect their wellbeing and improve their academic outcomes.

7.2 Better Support for Teachers

AI will not replace teachers but support them by extending their capabilities. AI tools will be more adept at automating basic administrative tasks such as grading papers, tracking attendances and organizing lesson plans. Providing teachers opportunities to devote more time towards working with students and conceptualizing learning activities. AI analytics will also provide predictive insights about student performance, which will provide professional educators with many early warning systems to identify at-risk students and allow teachers to provide additional support (Conrad, 2024). Data-driven predictions will allow educators to help improve their collective teaching effectiveness.

7.3 Smart Content Generation

AI will also create content that is subject to continuous iteration. AI tools will create learning content that evolves based on student performance and student preferences. For instance, AI can develop an individualized textbook, video, or simulation that responds and adapts to an individual student's learning requirements and preferences, and offer students multiple means of representation for developing robust understandings of complex concepts. The system allows the creation of an engaging learning method designed to teach both visual learners and students with educational disabilities.

7.4 Collaborative AI Systems for Global Education

International networks using AI technology will create remote educational connections which extend existing school boundaries during subsequent years. AI translation services utilizing multi-lingual structures will broadcast educational content to students (Kakina, 2025). Remote education services together with AI digital assistants create a path for students to study abroad by addressing academic challenges that occur from empty classrooms.

7.5 Ethical and Responsible AI in Education

The implementation of AI systems by educational institutions requires them to resolve fundamental ethical challenges because they need to establish sustainable platform-wide distribution. The design phase of AI system development requires fairness integration to build organization systems that should show clear functionality through diverse tools that track their performance metrics (Dushyant & Bajaj, 2023). The present federal regulations bring new privacy protection requirements to maintain ethical implementation of AI technologies in education. Adaptive training platforms develop better educational results at the global school level through the implementation of AF technology as an educational performance enhancement system. The implementation of ethical monitoring in education produces superior learning services that support every student and leads student development toward these ethical protocols.

8. EMERGING TRENDS IN EDUCATION: GENERATIVE AI, AR/VR

Rapid educational change happens due to technological innovations that maintain their high speed of advancement. The teaching sector implements two advanced technological systems named Generative AI together with AR and VR to manage operational procedures. Educational content development through new innovation will produce accessible virtual learning platforms for student learning solutions. Figure 10 outlines how innovations like Generative AI and AR/VR contribute to improved education through personalized content, automation, immersive learning, and interactive experiences. These elements collectively lead to better learning outcomes.

Figure 10. Technological Innovations Driving Enhanced Learning Outcomes

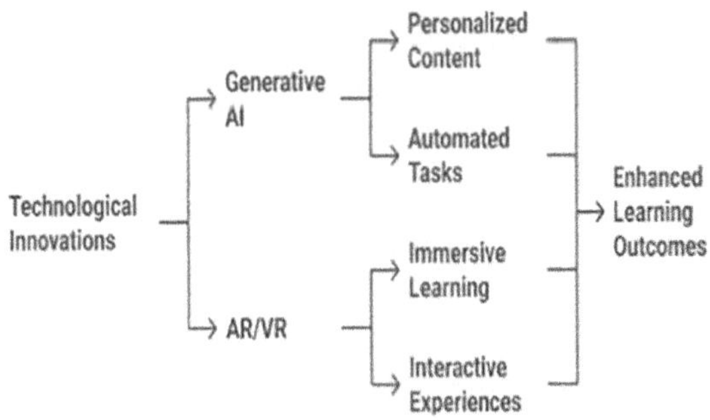

8.1 Generative AI in Education

The higher education sector accepts creative text content and graphics through Generative AI while also receiving capabilities to develop educational programs based on provided specifications for faster educational design activities. Generative AI will allow systems to automatically generate content that is personalized and custom built. AI tools are now capable of generating custom content for practice assessments with tailored questions, a personalized study plan with time marks, custom exercises based on rules a teacher sets like reading a text and generating comprehension questions, and can even build interactive scenarios from which a student learns or moves through in chronological order (Farooqi et al., 2024). To give an example, an AI tool could track a student's learning and produce a follow-up exercise or follow-up explanation based on the gaps in sense-making (or, what a student did not understand); recalling specific questions a student asked, and referencing back to the questions a student expressed interest. Additionally, generative AI can automate lesson planning, grading, and even administrative work for educators, freeing up educator's time for interactive teaching and/or engaging student learning (Fauziddin et al., 2025). AI can also create new content for students. For teacher/students this means being able to create adaptive content, like textbooks with embedded multimedia or presentations that adapt in real-time based on a learner's progress. In this case generative AI will keep learning materials in a state that is always current and relevant, in order to support current demands in the fast-paced world of learning.

8.2 AR/VR in Education

Augmented Reality (AR) and Virtual Reality (VR) technology are moving the world of immersive learning into a whole new arena. They both allow more interactive, engaging and hands-on learning experiences. The focus of AR is to add digital elements to the real world, thus giving students the ability to interact with 3D models or simulations through their smartphone or AR glasses. Using AR in a biology class, for example, students could examine interactive 3D models of human organs or ecosystems, so that they engage more with the study of complex concepts.

In contrast, VR allows students to immerse themselves in fully digital environments, therefore it is ideally suited to simulations and other experiential learning (Garcia et al., 2024). For example, a medical student can use VR to simulate complex procedures without any real-world repercussions, where the instructor has created a complex and realistic clinical challenge for the learner. Or an engineering student can be subjected to the limits of their knowledge related to infrastructure engineering. In these examples their learning does not just end when they exit the

VR simulation, but rather transcends into real-world learning opportunities. If a history or geography lesson takes students on excursions to ancient civilizations, or geographically and culturally rich landscapes, the ability to physically and cognitively engage with the subject matter before them creates a tangible learning experience that textbooks fail to embrace.

The pedagogical possibilities for student engagement through AR and VR are significant, enhancing experiential learning to be considerably more interactive, engaging, and memorable. In addition, it provides a truly inclusive environment that not only increases learning approaches for all students but also expands accessibility for students with disabilities to learn through participation and engagement.

8.3 The Convergence of Technologies

Onsetting progress opportunities result from multiple technology integrations that bring about novel educational approaches. The learning outcomes of students increase because of AI-generated virtual learning environments matching students according to their learning styles. An AI-based system implemented in virtual classrooms adapts learning problems dynamically in creating automated reports setting it up to determine correct teaching materials based on the potential educational level of students. General AI uses AR/VR elements as educational software providing students qualified educational deliveries of stimulating academic content (Val, 2024). School systems utilizing technology enhances digital learning assuring system optimizations is not the area applied in delivering teaching methods accelerating educational excellence within the instructor and student community.

9. ETHICAL AI ADOPTION: TEACHER TRAINING AND POLICY FRAMEWORKS

Schools have a role to providing educational curriculum on ethical frameworks for teaching staff on acceptable ethical practices to use AI technologies in their educational organizations. The establishment of complete ethical frameworks for educational technology requires the training of a system together with ethical systems guidelines at the time of system installation.

9.1 Teacher Training to Facilitate Ethical AI Usage

The appropriate training of teaching methods for AI-based education provides qualified teachers with the opportunity not only to gather academic experience but prevents potential negative impacts from untaught CE and CE-AI methodology.

Training centers must develop educational programs which provide teachers with elements of critical AI solution aspects with defined boundaries to teach teachers how to use technology ethically within their educational practice. Since the responsible and efficient integration of AI into education is an essential requirement, educational personnel should have the basic knowledge of AI, machine learning, analytics, and natural language processing (Chananagari Prabhakar, 2024). This prepares them to make sound choices about system use, information privacy and ethical issues. The teachers must be educated on how to alter the educational materials with AI-powered tools detecting and assisting those students who require a personal approach. The integration of AI in current curricula will increase equity in learning. Professional growth, which is continuous is a necessary practice demanded in educating the teachers, in order to be abreast with the changes that are taking place concerning technology. The teacher networks can further promote AI adoption through the benefit of sharing best practices and strategies of ethical implementation.

9.2 Policy Frameworks for Ethical AI Adoption

To have ethical integration of AI in education, teachers should be assisted with clear policy statements that detail on the way to safely use AI. A lot must be done by the institutions in conjunction with the government bodies to formulate well-rounded procedures that will guide the implementation of AI and give equal access to the rest of the students who should have access to digital infrastructure. They are expected to have strong data protection policies in place that do not go against the international regulations such as GDPR or FERPA protecting data privacy of the students and preventing exposure of data to unauthorized persons (Roberts et al., 2024). Biased AI systems are possible because of inconsistencies in the data sources used in training; thus, establishments ought to introduce regular bias testing that is based on predefined protocols in order to maintain equity and prevent discrimination on the basis of race, sex, or personal features.

AI policies must be centralized by Public Information Offices (PIOs) and frameworks should be accessible with information on the accountability of the system, decision-making procedures and data management standards. Developers should also create AI applications to support the needs of learning students with disabilities or exceptional learning needs with the help of student history to achieve customized support (Sain et al., 2024). In addition, they should make it easier to involve developers and educators in co-developing and creating AI tools with ethical protection. Urgent teacher training to conform with such policies is essential to an ethical implementation. The application of well-organized system and integrated technical procedures with recommendations on creativity, critical thinking, and engagement skills of students will help AI support and serve every learner fairly and with caution.

10. CONCLUSION

Such a paradigm shift based on transformative integration of Artificial Intelligence (AI) into education presents a new paradigm of opportunities that is unprecedented to make changes in learning experiences, educational administration, and individualizing instruction into more effective levels across the k-12 system, higher education, and the working force. Intelligent Tutoring systems, adaptive learning systems and AI-assisted assessment AI applications are transforming pedagogies through real-time feedback, personalized learning as well as data-driven analysis of student performance. In addition, other developments such as generative AI, AR/VR, and natural language processing enhance the scopes of educational provision, participation, and access. Nonetheless, this is not a revolution that has not been met with heavy challenges. Financial constraints, inability of infrastructure, non-availability of teachers training and unwillingness to change are some key obstacles. The digital divide and unreliable access to AI tools enhance educational disparities and those of underserved populations in particular. Besides, some ethical considerations, such as data privacy, algorithmic fairness, and bias, are of great threat to a fair and responsible implementation of AI. Institutions find it difficult to employ AI in a safe and inclusive way without the ability to frame policies and the overall training of teachers in place.

Such recourse to the problems should be multifaceted. Innovation can be achieved through strong industry-academia partnerships and at the same time offer scalable development prototypes. The state should help through funding, infrastructure development, and ethical laws to create fair and proper access and adequate application of AI. NGOs are needed to cooperate with EdTech and corporate training to shine light all over the learning gap on the way to employability, particularly in disadvantaged places. The collaboration across sectors plays a very important role in the development of inclusive, sustainable, context-specific education ecosystems. The institutions intend on embracing the full potential of AI in education by regulating technology infrastructure and pedagogical preparedness alongside nationally established ethical governance. Not only should teachers be given digital literacy but they should also be equipped with ethical frameworks of AI use. The policies have to require transparency, data protection, and inclusive AI design taking into consideration diverse learning needs, such as those of the students with disabilities. With the path ahead, the future of AI in education is the potential to assist and not substitute educators and produce adaptive, interesting and fair learning situations. An agreed effort that makes a compromise between innovation and supervision will be a necessity to make sure that education systems based on AI can empower learners of all kinds so that individual privacy is respected and upheld to the core values of human-oriented education. The AI can be a potent instrument of inclusive educational revolution in the age of digital development with considerate use.

REFERENCES

Abisoye, A. (2023). AI literacy in STEM education: Policy strategies for preparing the future workforce. *Journal of Frontiers in Multidisciplinary Research*, *4*(1), 17–24. DOI: 10.54660/JFMR.2023.4.1.17-24

Alotaibi, N. S., & Alshehri, A. H. (2023). Prospers and obstacles in using artificial intelligence in Saudi Arabia Higher Education institutions—The potential of AI-based learning outcomes. *Sustainability (Basel)*, *15*(13), 10723. DOI: 10.3390/su151310723

Asperis, R. (2025). Education in the world of AI. In *Preprints*.

Atkinson-Toal, A., & Guo, C. (2024). Generative artificial intelligence (AI) education policies of UK universities. *Enhancing Teaching and Learning in Higher Education*, *2*, 70–94. DOI: 10.62512/etlhe.20

Badawy, W., Helal, M. M. I., Hashim, A., Zinhom, H., & Shaban, M. (2025). Ethical boundaries and data-sharing practices in AI-enhanced nursing: An Arab perspective. *International Nursing Review*, *72*(1), e70013. DOI: 10.1111/inr.70013 PMID: 40070199

Barnes, E., & Hutson, J. (2024). Navigating the ethical terrain of AI in higher education: Strategies for mitigating bias and promoting fairness. *Forum Edu. Stud.*, *2*(2), 1229. DOI: 10.59400/fes.v2i2.1229

Bastomi, B., Mujahid, A. Z., Asmuni Asmuni and Sibron, A., Audina, M., & Harto, K. (2024). Bringing artificial Intelligence (AI) in teaching and learning process. TOFEDU: The Future of Education Journal, 3(5), 1825–1831.

Bian, Q., Ling, X., & Yan, S. (2024). Bridging the algorithmic divide. *Education as Change*, •••, 28.

Blonder, R., & Feldman-Maggor, Y. (2024). AI for chemistry teaching: Responsible AI and ethical considerations. *Chemistry Teacher International : Best Practices in Chemistry Education*, *6*(4), 385–395. DOI: 10.1515/cti-2024-0014

Chananagari Prabhakar, R. R. (2024). Privacy-preserving AI database systems in education analytics. *International Journal of Multidisciplinary Research and Growth*, *5*(6), 1626–1629. DOI: 10.54660/.IJMRGE.2024.5.6.1626-1629

Chembe, C., Nasilele, N. B., & Msendo, R. (2023). The fuss about artificial intelligence in education sector: Should we worry? *Zictjournal*, *7*(2), 30–35. DOI: 10.33260/zictjournal.v7i2.269

Cioci, G. (2025). AI in the class: Uses, doubts, challenges and perceptions of a sample of teachers from different nationalities. EDUC. *Science and Society*, *2*, 38–55.

Conrad, K. (2024). A blueprint for an AI bill of rights for education. Critical AI, 2(1).

Ding, N. (2025). Ethical considerations in the application of artificial intelligence in education. *International Journal of Education and Humanities*, *19*(1), 178–182. DOI: 10.54097/78e6gr15

Dushyant Nimavat, K. K., & Bajaj, S. D. A. S. B. S. N. (2023). Ethical considerations in using artificial intelligence to improve Teaching and learning. *Tuijin Jishu*, *44*(4), 1031–1038. DOI: 10.52783/tjjpt.v44.i4.966

Fadli Mappisabbi, A. M., Amirullah, N., & Batti', S. (2024). Leveraging data and artificial intelligence for innovative educational management practices. *Ijmre-ITB*, *2*(2), 182–192. DOI: 10.54066/ijmre-itb.v2i2.1788

Farooqi, M. T. K., Amanat, I., & Awan, S. M. (2024). Ethical considerations and challenges in the integration of artificial intelligence in education: A systematic review. *JEMS: A Journal of Emergency Medical Services*, *3*(4), 35–50. DOI: 10.69565/jems.v3i4.314

Fauziddin, M., Adha, T. R., Arifiyanti, N., Indriyani, F., Rizki, L. M., Wulandary, V., & Reddy, V. S. V. (2025). The impact of AI on the future of education in Indonesia. *Educ. J. Ilm. Pendidik*, *3*(1), 11–16. DOI: 10.70437/educative.v3i1.828

Folorunso, A., & Olanipekun, K. (2024). A policy framework on AI usage in developing countries and its impact. *Global J. Eng. Technol. Adv.*, *21*(1), 154–166. DOI: 10.30574/gjeta.2024.21.1.0192

Garcia Peñalvo, F. J., Alier, M., Pereira, J., & Casany, M. J. (2024). Safe, transparent, and ethical artificial intelligence. Int. J. Educ. Res. Innov., 22, 1–21.

Gray, K., Slavotinek, J., Dimaguila, G. L., & Choo, D. (2022). Artificial intelligence education for the health workforce: Expert survey of approaches and needs. *JMIR Medical Education*, *8*(2), e35223. DOI: 10.2196/35223 PMID: 35249885

Kakina, A. (2025). Artificial Intelligence for functional literacy development. Eurasian Science Review, 2(Special Issue).

Lin, H. (2022). Influences of artificial intelligence in education on teaching effectiveness. *International Journal of Emerging Technologies in Learning*, *17*(24), 144–156. DOI: 10.3991/ijet.v17i24.36037

Medaglia, R., Gil-Garcia, J. R., & Pardo, T. A. (2023). Artificial Intelligence in government: Taking stock and moving forward. *Social Science Computer Review, 41*(1), 123–140. DOI: 10.1177/08944393211034087

Muhammad Hani Bayan, F. (2024). The ethics of AI: Navigating the moral dilemmas of artificial intelligence. *Arab Journal for Scientific Publishing*, *7*(66), 1–11. DOI: 10.36571/ajsp661

Nuangchalerm, P. (2023). AI-driven learning analytics in STEM education. *International Journal of Research in STEM Education*, *5*(2), 77–84. DOI: 10.33830/ijrse.v5i2.1596

Ogbu Eke, E. (2024). Assessing the readiness and attitudes of Nigerian teacher educators towards adoption of artificial intelligence in educational settings. J. Educ. Technol. Online Learn., 7(4-ICETOL 2024 Special), 473–487.

Oh, S. H., & Sanfilippo, M. (2024). University governance for responsible AI. *Proceedings of the ALISE Annual Conference.*

Roberts, L. N., Solomon, F. N., & Cummings, R. (2024). Navigating the AI landscape. In *Advances in Educational Technologies and Instructional Design* (pp. 268–285). IGI Global.

Sain, Z. H., Aziz, A. L., & Lawal, U. S. (2024). Ethics of AI integration in higher education: Exploring moral dimensions. [JAIEM]. *Journal of Asian Islamic Educational Management*, *2*(1), 1–10. DOI: 10.53889/jaiem.v2i1.431

Selvaratnam, R., & Venaruzzo, L. (2024). Governance of artificial intelligence and data in Australasian higher education: A snapshot of policy and practice. ASCILITE Publications, 1–7.

Trang, N. T. Q., National Academy of Public Administration Vietnam, Thi Thu, P., & National Academy of Public Administration Vietnam. (2024). The role of AI in improving student learning outcomes: Evidence in Vietnam. INTERNATIONAL JOURNAL OF MULTIDISCIPLINARY RESEARCH AND ANALYSIS, 07(06).

Val, O. O. (2024). The role of Artificial Intelligence (AI) in enhancing cybersecurity for educational technologies in US public schools. *Asian J. Res. Com. Sci.*, *17*(11), 114–133. DOI: 10.9734/ajrcos/2024/v17i11523

Wan Ismail, W. S., Awang, N. A., & Mohd Pauzi, N. (2023). An overview of the use of artificial intelligence (AI) tools in higher education. *International Journal on E-Learning and Higher Education*, *19*(3), 27–40. DOI: 10.24191/ijelhe.v19n3.1932

Yim, I. H. Y., & Wegerif, R. (2024). *Teachers' perceptions, attitudes, and acceptance of artificial intelligence (AI) educational learning tools: An exploratory study on AI literacy for young students*. Future in Educational Research.

Zapata, L. I. V., Acosta Enriquez, B. G., Montes Ninaquispe, J. C., Ruiz Carrillo, J. A., Villarreal Gonzales, L. S., Morales, J. A., & Sevilla Angelaths, M. A. (2024). Employment of generative artificial intelligence in classroom environments to improve financial education in secondary school students. *Acad. J. Interdiscip. Stud., 13*(3), 121. DOI: 10.36941/ajis-2024-0069

Zawacki-Richter, O., Marín, V. I., Bond, M., & Gouverneur, F. (2019a). Systematic review of research on artificial intelligence applications in higher education – where are the educators? *International Journal of Educational Technology in Higher Education, 16*(1), 39. DOI: 10.1186/s41239-019-0171-0

Zawacki-Richter, O., Marín, V. I., Bond, M., & Gouverneur, F. (2019b). Systematic review of research on artificial intelligence applications in higher education – where are the educators? *International Journal of Educational Technology in Higher Education, 16*(1), 39. DOI: 10.1186/s41239-019-0171-0

KEY TERMS AND DEFINITIONS

Artificial Intelligence (AI): The simulation of human intelligence processes by machines, especially computer systems, including learning, reasoning, and self-correction.

Intelligent Tutoring System (ITS): AI-driven educational software that provides personalized instruction and feedback by mimicking one-on-one human tutoring.

Adaptive Learning: An AI-based approach that adjusts educational content and pace according to a student's performance and learning needs.

AI-Assisted Assessment: Use of AI to automate grading, detect plagiarism, and provide real-time analytics to assess student performance.

Digital Divide: The gap between those with easy access to digital technologies and internet and those without, often leading to educational inequity.

Algorithmic Bias: Unintended discrimination or unfair outcomes caused by biased data or flawed logic in AI algorithms.

FERPA: The Family Educational Rights and Privacy Act; a U.S. law that protects the privacy of student education records.

GDPR: General Data Protection Regulation; a regulation in EU law on data protection and privacy in the European Union and European Economic Area.

EdTech: Short for Education Technology, it refers to the use of digital technology and AI tools to enhance learning and teaching.

Public-Private Partnership (PPP): Collaboration between government agencies and private-sector companies to fund and deliver public education and training solutions.

Personalized Learning: Instructional methods tailored to individual student preferences, learning styles, and needs using AI technologies.

Natural Language Processing (NLP): A branch of AI that enables machines to understand, interpret, and respond to human language.

Chapter 11
Smart Learning Platforms:
The Integration of AI and Data Science in Educational Settings

T. Venkat Narayana Rao
https://orcid.org/0000-0002-1996-1819
Sreenidhi Institute of Science and Technology, India

Pallavi Rajan
Sreenidhi Institute of Science and Technology, India

Neela Santhoshi
https://orcid.org/0009-0006-3634-4990
Sreenidhi Institute of Science and Technology, India

G. Anusha
Sreenidhi Institute of Science and Technology, India

ABSTRACT

By enabling adaptive learning systems that can quickly evaluate and enhance learning experiences, artificial intelligence (AI) and data science are revolutionizing education. In order to enable institutions to offer customized recommendations, automated feedback, and adaptive evaluations based on student performance data, this chapter examines how machine learning approaches, predictive analytics, and educational algorithms are transforming personalized education. We look at how artificial intelligence (AI)-powered chatbots, virtual teachers, and intelligent grading systems are revolutionizing information distribution, improving accessibility, and improving the educational experience. The education sector may change to become smarter, more efficient, and especially tailored to student's needs by leveraging AI-

DOI: 10.4018/979-8-3373-2185-1.ch011

driven analytics and optimization. The chapter focus how thorough data analytics helps teachers make informed decisions to enhance curriculum design, teaching methods entail to increase productivity and scalability

1. INTRODUCTION

Over the past decade, technology has been creeping deeper and deeper into the functioning of societies-and into the realm of education as well. AI and Big Data are perhaps among very few technologies that can revolutionize the affairs of education. The teaching technology revolutionizes all the operations relative to how institutions develop their curricula, assess learning results, administer their business, and balance equity among students. Slowly, the great paradigms of "one-size-fits-all" education are being transformed into more fluid, individualized, and data-driven systems of education (Holmes, Bialik, & Fadel, 2019).

In education, AI means using algorithmic and intelligent systems that can understand learner behavior and modify the processes of learning, automate most administrative tasks involved in teaching, and create predictive insights. Data Science, in contrast, applies analytical methods to large educational datasets that typically involve monitoring students' progress and diagnosing problems of learning and behavior in the community. Together, they have made adaptive learning systems, intelligent tutoring systems, automated assessment tools, and teacher and institute decision-support dashboards a reality.

Of course, the promises of AI come with certain risks. Some of the emerging issues that are most acute include algorithmic bias, surveillance, data privacy concerns, and de-skilling of teachers. For example, if trained on data from a narrow pool, computerized scoring could penalize students for their linguistic or cultural divergences. Similarly, predictive analysis may wrongly classify students as "at-risk," thus perpetuating inequities. Finally, the mushrooming of digital infrastructure may only expose the widening digital gap in already marginalized strata.

This chapter looks at the transformations brought by AI and Data Science to education from many perspectives-such as pedagogical, technological, ethical, or organizational. The chapter situates its discussion within well-known paradigms of learning theory such as Constructivism, Bloom's Taxonomy, Cognitive Load Theory, and the SAMR Model, then provides a conceptual framework for evaluating the AI educational value.

The subsequent sections will discuss technologies that core AI into education: adaptive learning systems, intelligent tutoring systems (ITS), and AI-based assessments. Each technology is assessed according to its functions, impacts, and compatibility with educational learning outcomes. These are followed by much broader applications of AI-on how it could enhance accessibility, expedite institutional planning, and further inclusive education and practice.

These ethical discussions will largely address algorithmic accountability, with also a spotlight on the responsible usage of AI across the institutions. International case studies will provide some examples: Squirrel AI from China, Carnegie Learning, and the DIKSHA platform from India will speak to how culturally and economically contingent the impact of AI is.

The concluding section will discuss possible futures for AI in education while stressing the importance of interdisciplinary collaboration and governance with inclusive design. With the right safeguards and strategies, AI could further other interventions in learning through transforming education into an even fairer and more responsive system.

2. THEORETICAL FOUNDATIONS

Artificial Intelligence (AI) and Data Science applications in education should be guided by sound pedagogy. In educational applications, AI may have the risk of being regarded as an instrument for efficiency rather than effectiveness—one which compromises on actual learning in favor of rapid processing, automation, and data collection. In this section, I will discuss five main theories that act as an underpinning to responsible and meaningful uses of AI in education: Constructivism, Bloom's Taxonomy, Cognitive Load Theory (CLT), Technological Pedagogical Content Knowledge (TPACK), and the SAMR model.

2.1 Production Theories

Education could have seen its chances enhanced through Artificial Intelligence and Data Science, but the condition requires sound pedagogy to be constructive. Without appropriate pedagogy, AI just becomes an efficiency tool-used to speed up work, automate it, and collect data, all without necessarily learning. This section presents the five main theories with which one might arrive at understanding the responsible, acceptable use of AI in education: Constructivism, Bloom's Taxonomy, Cognitive Load Theory, Technological Pedagogical Content Knowledge, and SAMR.

2.2 Constructivist Learning Theory

Constructivism depicts knowledge as being actively constructed from experience and reflective interpretation rather than being passively received (Fosnot, 2013). Students actively create their own knowledge. AI technology, such as adaptive learning systems and intelligent tutoring systems, is in itself a reflection of that as it promotes student centeredness, exploratoryness, and iterativeness in their learning.

For instance, the facility based on AI can imitate problem-solving in science education-as it would take place in the real world-and enables students to manipulate variables, test hypotheses, and observe results. Here again, such an environment can foster discoveries constructed from discovery learning, which is one of the big pillars of constructivist pedagogy. Further, AI might shepherd students through a personalized learning trajectory-analyzing their interaction history to detect misconceptions, adapting teaching to their current cognitive level.

This is shown by the software MATHia from Carnegie Learning that personalizes learning around students' mathematics thinking but also guides them along developing understandings instead of memorizing steps (Pane et al., 2014). Such systems would encourage learning as progressive refinement, which relates very well with a constructivist belief in the cognitive and social co-construction of knowledge.

2.3 Bloom's Taxonomy

On the renewal by Anderson and Krathwohl (2001); Bloom's Taxonomy is oriented in terms of learning within six levels of educational objectives: Remember, Understand, Apply, Analyse, Evaluate, and Create.

AI tools can link into these different levels:

- Remember: AI-powered spaced repetition flashcards and AI-based testing.
- Understand: Automated summarizers and interactive visualization tools.
- Apply: Situation-based simulation, or coding platforms with AI-debugged assistance.
- Analyse and vigorously criticize: NLP-based systems inviting comparative evaluation and immediate disapproval.

Create Generative AI technologies that employ students to produce code, presentation materials or even virtual paintings to engender creativity and unification.

AI-facilitating tools designed very well need not be confined to the bottom ends of the taxonomy, but also stimulate metacognition and creative thinking, especially where generative AI is made available to students and faculty alike.

2.4 Cognitive Load Theory (CLT)

By Sweller (1988), Cognitive Load Theory speaks of the capacity of working memory, thus requiring its design of instruction to minimize extraneous cognitive load and to maximize germane load, the latter being productive efforts expended in building meaningful mental structures.

AI can manifest and assist CLT in a variety of ways:

- Adaptive difficulty: If a topic proves too difficult for a learner, then AI scaffolds or segments the task into less difficult subtasks.
- Multimodal support: Computing systems which have options of visual, auditory, or textual elements provide choices to students and keep these options from overwhelming them.
- Real-time pacing: Intelligent tutoring systems can stop and start at will, skip over sections from time to time, or just offer hints; this, in general, substantially decreases possible stress and helps retention, especially where there is a high cognitive load such as in programming, calculus, or learning a language. AI-powered CLT tools lead to better learning with less frustration, dropout, and associated costs (Kalyuga, 2011).

2.5 Technological Pedagogical Content Knowledge (TPACK)

The model is intended to help educators consider what they really need to know in order to really be effective using technology in their education. The three intersecting circles illustrate the following:

- Content Knowledge (CK): Knowing the content about
- Pedagogical Knowledge (PK): Knowing through good techniques on teaching
- Technological Knowledge (TK): Knowing well how to use the technical means (Mishra & Koehler, 2006)

This means that any such AI tool needs to sit within that framework. For example, a grammar-instructing chatbot is technically involved with the realms of Technology (TK) and Language Content (CK) but is only TPACK once it pertains to a pedagogical practice, such as scaffolding or feedback loops.

Instructors, too, must receive training on how to use AI and how to determine whether it fits and why it is bruited about. An evaluation instrument for AI must sound really attractive in its formative usage, but summatively, it may work against the achievement of the learning objectives. So, TPACK precisely offers a decision-making model with regard to technology use in the classroom.

2.6 SAMR Model

According to Puentedura (2006), the SAMR model classifies different technologies according to four categories:

- replacement: replacing an existing task with technology without changing it (typing instead of handwriting)
- augmentation: technology adds certain functionalities to the existing task (auto-grading in Google forms)
- modification: Technology changes the task altogether (for example, real-time assessment on language usage by AI)
- redefinition: Tasks that were previously inconceivable become possible because of technology (for instance, through AI, students and teachers co-create applications)

AI has the role to play at any level. Most of the current applications, however, remain mired at the Substitution or Augmentation levels, automatic testing, or grammar correction. The objective is set on Redefinition, where AI would allow students to do projects sensitive to time within real-time translations, data journalism, or interactive stories.

More probably, instructional designers and teachers should attempt at higher levels of SAMR, thus transformative rather than transactional for AI.

3. AI AND DATA SCIENCE TO PERSONALIZE LEARNING

The old perception of education as rigid, standardized, a kind of conveyor-belt education, has never been of much assistance to the range of student requirements, types of learning, and paces of learning. Introducing AI; coupled with data science, it facilitates this model to shift to actualized real-time customized learning experiences with highly sharpened content and presentation for each learner profile. This current chapter will discuss how AI enables personalization through making adaptive learning systems possible, and what should be achieved by it regarding inclusivity, mastery, and lifelong learning.

3.1 Adaptive Learning Systems

Adaptive learning systems use algorithms to assess a student's knowledge, behavior, and activity to develop an individualized learning experience. Information concerning quiz performance, time-on-task, error patterns, and preferences are used to adjust content difficulty, instructional flow, and style of feedback (Conati & Kardan, 2013). This creates an adaptive instructional environment that changes as the learner progresses.

One example of adaptive learning is the following: if a student is identified as weak in factoring quadratic equations, the system could either repeat the rules of multiplication one more time or offer interactive cues. Meanwhile, those students who pick things up easily would be challenged with solving or applying. This keeps the student within his/her zone of proximal development (Vygotsky, 1978).

Some of the leaders among the overall programs that show quantifiable gains in retention, engagement, and learner confidence are Knewton, Smart Sparrow, DreamBox Learning. Garcia and Patel (2021) conducted a meta-analysis that found that students enrolled in adaptive platforms for STEM courses had a 28% difference in performance scores against students enrolled in conventional classroom settings.

Significantly, adaptive learning also makes it possible for advancement based on mastery; that is, only when students have actually shown mastery of the learning are they allowed to progress. This is especially beneficial in subjects that involve the core skills such as mathematics and language, where not learning has a systematic impact on subsequent learning.

3.2 Data Science and Learning Analytics

On the flip side, Data Science not only provides that analysis and monitoring of student learning but also AI personalization. Learning analytics include:

- Course completion rates
- Interaction frequency
- Participation rates in the discussion forums, and
- Assessment performance trend data.

Those formed the foundation of teachers' data-driven interventions, such as referencing one or two at-risk students and pacing adjustments. These types of dashboards, deployed institutionally within Purdue's Course Signals system, have been proven, through predictive modelling, to enhance retention rates (Arnold & Pistilli, 2012).

Through learning analytics, this micro-adaptivity would be feasible: modifications not just reactive but also advised on by real-time intervention. For instance, if a student was stuck on some screen, the system could deduce confusion, and give simplification. The final goal will be to also advise regarding alterations in the platform through the development of means of reading learner needs.

3.3 Personalization for Inclusive and Diverse Learners

Inclusion and diversity to learning are part of what AI and Data Science enable. And modify the complexity and format of the content transmission from systems that can significantly support students with learning disabilities, non-language speakers, or even had limited exposure to the content. For example:

- Students with dyslexia are aided by text-to-speech features.
- Translation software is becoming more helpful to learners.
- Students with executive functioning impairments are supported by scaffolded instructions.

Artificial intelligence systems may also detect patterns associated with cognitive overload or lack of interest and make appropriate changes. This is in accordance with the guidelines of Universal Design for Learning (UDL) that suggest multiple means for representation and engagement of learners (CAST, 2018).

3.4 Beyond the Classroom: Lifelong and Self-Directed Learning

Personalized learning in no way is part of institutional learning. Software such as Coursera, Duolingo, or LinkedIn Learning all proclaim to employ AI for course suggestions, monitoring users' progress, and supposedly providing "personalized" feedback-so as to encourage lifelong learning among adults and professionals.

Such systems fit into such individual learning types, but this is one thing that traditional education systems never were able to offer. AI can read perfectly well when a user may be in the process of getting bored, reminding them that it's high time to return or utilizing rewarded gamification to tempt them back.

3.5 Personalization's Moral Dilemmas

Personalization raises some moral dilemmas:

- It imposes too much of a good thing on a user, so that he or she is insulated from other sources or messages, enveloping him or her in an echo chamber (Knox, 2020).
- There needs to be some consideration, particularly with the issues of sensitive learner data, made to data privacy.

Algorithmic opacity is such that students may have minimal understanding of how and why their learning trajectory is being constructed. The strategy of personalization must be structured into transparency, consent, and bias audit for fairness and learner agency.

Figure 1. AI-based Adaptive learning systems

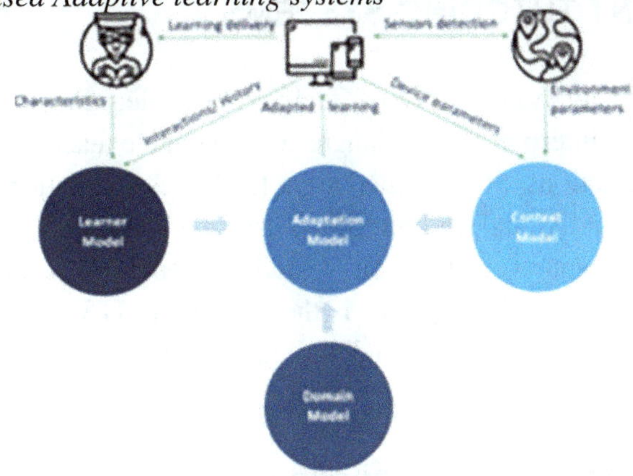

Adaptations to the architecture of an adaptive learning system are illustrated in Figure 1, while the information streams on which the various student data types—e.g., quiz scores, clickstream activity, and task engagement time—are sampled and entered into the AI processor. Here, learning analytics and predictive modeling are operating in real-time to change course content in order to continue on the track of maintaining the path of learning that is still concurrent with each student's level of immediate development and readiness for cognition (Conati & Kardan, 2013). A constant process of extracting meaning from data and making adjustments to content converts the entire learning process into one that is dynamic, customized, and pedagogically intelligent.

These adaptive systems have some good aspects but also introduce some challenges. Success is highly dependent on the quality and completeness of input data. If datasets are incomplete or biased, recommendations can reinforce instead of addressing learning inequities (Knox, 2020). An automation aspect of adaptation bars it from making greater educative values of collaboration, creativity, and critical thinking, which a single human connection can nurture best and algorithmic personalization could never accomplish.

Hence, there needs to be human intervention in setting up and installing the adaptive learning systems, and the pedagogy must be ethically audited and culturally sensitive on a regular basis. Appropriately utilized, while the systems bridge the knowledge gap, they also give a boost to motivation, engagement, and autonomy. The insights provided are useful to teachers as well as larger institutions for planning and intervention purposes—making the whole teaching-learning process more effective, inclusive, and purposeful.

4. INTELLIGENT TUTORING SYSTEMS

Intelligent Tutoring Systems (ITS) differ from their e-learning equivalents in that they student model, interpret natural language, and enable teachers and students to have adaptive interactions. Student modelling facilitates adaptation of the learning experience to each individual, in light of the nature of the topic. ITS is an instructional program that grounds instruction on student models (Graesser et al., 2005).

What this research briefly explores is the underlying ITS characteristics, pedagogical strategies, and potentials-and limitations and moral implications with respect to their application.

4.1 ITS Architecture and Components

As in a traditional modular architecture of an ITS, we suggest that four modules are interlinked (Woolf, 2010):

- Domain Model: This holds the content model.
- Student Model: Study provides access to the learner's learning history, including his/her progress, errors, and misunderstandings.
- Tutoring Model (or Pedagogical Module): This determines when and how to display certain types of content, cues, scaffolds, or feedback for correction.
- User Interface Module: This provides for interactive experience to the student: giving him/her visual, auditory, or text input.

These components team up to mimic single-learning processes. For instance, in math, an ITS might spot a trend of continuous misunderstanding of distributive property and have the student revisit for chosen rudimentary exercises along with remediate the misunderstanding.

Figure 2. Architecture of an Intelligent Tutoring System

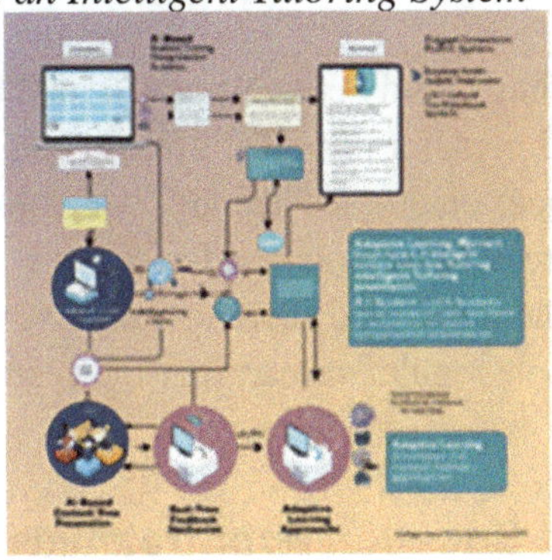

In Figure 2, there is within the system a close loop, which updates the model of the student through learner feedback and feeds back to pedagogical approaches in the tutoring module. Such a feedback loop, in this case, guarantees that instructions are not only responsive to the learner but guided well by the goal.

4.2 Dialogic and Interactive Learning

In some sense, ITS happens to be designed such that they incorporate dialog-based learning. Conversational agents that possess dialogue features, like AutoTutor, have the capacity to converse with learners, presented in a dialogue primarily triggered by the system—hence, the system continues questioning, evaluating the answers, and providing additional hints or explications (Graesser et al., 2005). Incidentally, this is much akin to the Socratic process whereby students are encouraged to bare their mental faculties, which begets cognitive dissonance, ultimately contributing to their education.

NLP (Natural Language Processing) enables ITS to interpret open-ended responses so that students can explain their solutions in natural language instead of just marking variant options. Peacemaker dialogue systems are present to allow deep learning in the context of encouraging elaboration and self-explanation, aspects associated with long term retention (Chi et al., 1994).

4.3 Real-Time Feedback and Metacognitive Support

ITS give immediate feedback aimed at student responses. Again, emphasis on actionable feedback in relation to teaching strategy. Functional feedback is feedback that takes a step further and also informs why a certain error occurred and also provides feedback regarding the why. The units break down step by step, sometimes verifying correctness of a step in a multi-step problem, which is immensely helpful in STEM education.

Metacognitive scaffolding could be incorporated in ITS for making the learner reflect on how best to do things, for instance: "Would you like to practice a similar one?" There would be a focus on queries like this, which would educate the student in metacognition by the creation of patterns. The student would need to assess for himself/herself whether the additional drilling would be beneficial or not. This, with experience, fosters self-regulated learning, the requirement of which is the key to human success.

4.4 Gamification and Engagement Strategies

Gamification is applied to foster motivation in some ITS to increase learner perseverance-achievement milestones, progress bars, points, and stories, which are more effective source for younger children and subjects in which the students tend to show anxiety levels like math or coding.

For instance, Carnegie Learning's MATHia uses visual tracking of progress and multiple measures for attainment according to their accomplishment of assignments. These tools come from Self-Determination Theory principles, i.e., empowerment of autonomy, competence, and relatedness (Deci & Ryan, 2000).

4.5 Benefits for Instructors and Institutions

ITS possess an ability to provide valuable learning analytics for informing instructor decision-making. Dashboards provide granular feedback that can instantly inform instructors about individual students' performance, progress, or even course-level trends based on misconceptions. This information itself will be incorporated into the intervention to craft student-support groups, pace differently, or revise tout court.

In distributed or mass learning system, ITS can scale instruction to personalize without congesting the cost or manpower.

4.6 Limitations and Ethical Issues

Though possessing incredible powers and benefits, ITS only fits into human learning at best. They raise another set of issues in the list of problems which must be solved adequately.

- High Development Expenses: Creating an ITS that is solid in a domain is a significant challenge because it takes an enormous amount of interdisciplinary work and testing.

- Cultural and Language Constraints: ITS are Western standard-based, more or less; these systems are behind the curve in perceiving the level of expectations of the learners and are developed from another learning culture.
- Lack of Emotional Intelligence: Some of the ITS may at times detect the feeling of frustration or the lack of interest but cannot do anything when such feelings are present. This is because no alternative can undertake the empathic and motivational assistance that a human instructor provides.
- Bias in Student Modeling: When an ITS makes a wrong assumption about students' capabilities based on incomplete or skewed data, it can give suboptimal advice, thereby continuing inequality.

Thus, ITS implementation should strictly follow transparency, explainability, and student permission-including showing through precise log records how student data were used in their assistance. Students ought to understand how data warehousing relates to their input; they can contest decisions made and trust that their information is secure in the hands of the collector (Luckin et al., 2016).

5. AUTOMATED FEEDBACK AND EVALUATIONS

It offers a glimpse of the soul of learning-the assessment process-what gauges learning, guides teaching and directs student movement-progresses. Centuries ago, assessment has been more incremental and postponed by using the value of feedback so late that no consideration or adjustment can be made. AI and machine learning are changing this scenario because they provide possibilities for faster, larger, and highly individualized automated tests-doing so much more formative than before. The systems give immediate feedback to learners, assist instructors with spotting patterns in student mastery, and aid administrations with maintaining academic integrity.

This section discusses types, pros and cons of AI-based assessments from the pedagogic and just standpoint.

5.1 Introduction to the AI-Based Assessment Instruments

AI can check a very broad spectrum of student output, ranging from relatively simple mc answers to complex essays or even code. Some of the more recognized tools include:

- Automated Essay Scoring (AES): ETS's e-rater or Turnitin's Revision Assistant are among the automated scoring applications that draw upon natural language processing (NLP) to evaluate grammar, coherence, lexical density, argument structure, and tone (Shermis & Burstein, 2013).

- Code Evaluation Tools: Such tools as HackerRank and Codio may use AI to evaluate coding submissions not only against a correctness criterion but also for their efficiency and organization.
- Speech and Pronunciation Assessors: AI language learning applications, such as Duolingo, analyse the pronunciation, fluency, and vocabulary of students in real time.
- Real-Time Formative Feedback Tools: Examples include Gradescope, which automatically grades mathematics problems and short answer conditions with analysis by a stepwise reason (Piech et al., 2015).

This reduces the burden on teachers while allowing grades to be assigned for thousands of students, thus inhibiting fairness in the assessment process.

5.2 Personalized Real Time Feedback

The best feature that AI-enhanced assessment could offer is instant and specific feedback. The essay author could receive comments on over-particular use of passive voice, suggestions for strengthening transitions, or a breakdown of argument structure-all in seconds-before making adjustments to the draft. This concept truly offers the possibility of formative learning, where the assessment becomes a tool for development rather than a weapon for judgment.

Timely, specific, and actionable feedback-that AI systems give with high reliability-Boud and Molloy (2013) explain. Students are subsequently able to leverage these learning loops in a cycle of iterative improvement as they resubmit and rework based on suggestions from computer systems, thereby boosting their interest and proficiency.

5.3 Insights for Educators through Data

Through data analytics, the understanding student's learning pattern among students and classrooms can be reached by AI-based-Laie.

Every time 80% of the students in that ITS answered a particular concept in geometry in the negative direction.

A coding environment can indicate that more students struggle with loops than syntax.

These results assist teachers to adapt instruction in real time, arrange for remediation classes, or redesign their curriculum. For example, this type of diagnostic precision is a lifesaver for big or distance education classes where one-on-one monitoring is impossible.

Adding analytics dashboards is also a good way since they form transparency and accountability, not just up to showing how students got it wrong, but also hearing why it is wrong. Is it the teaching, the test design, or the learner engagement that is at fault?

5.4 Scalable Assessment and Academic Integrity

With capacity to host mass examinations across considerably large numbers of students simultaneously, this brings about convenience for MOOCs, certifications, and huge enrolment classes. Scalability, however, comes with its problems and challenges concerning cheating and plagiarism.

Plagiarism thus detected by programs like Turnitin is done through semantic analysis and web scraping. New tools such as GPTZero are in development to detect AI-written texts based on sentence complexity, entropy and redundancy (Yu, 2023). Similar, AI-based, online proctoring software can identify suspicious behaviour based on the following: Webcam and screen monitoring; facial detection; and behavioural analytics.

Even though such types of systems would bestow students with the confidence of academic genuineness, they would also bring in a whole range of ethical apprehensions concerning privacy, surveillance, and fairness that require wise resolution (Selwyn, 2019).

5.5 Subjective Vs Issue on Objective Assessment Aspect

Grading essay-type answers is where AI shines, yet even that ability still has limitations regarding more subjective or creative works. For example, AES might misread irony, satire, or culturally determined signals in student writing (Perelman, 2014). Basically, these platforms valorise the formulaic composition over true creativity and thus squelch risk-taking or critical thought.

To counter this, most educators advocate hybrid approaches, whereby AI carries out first-pass marks and feedback, but human teachers will carry out the last judgment on particularly high-stakes or subjective work.

5.6 Ethical and Pedagogical Considerations Meter

The automated test must take into account: Bias: certainly, there is a chance that the system would have been trained on very narrow data sets which, while not being sufficient, are biased against non-native speakers or already disadvantaged groups.

- Transparency: Students would also be entitled to be informed in what ways they were evaluated and to smooth appeals as such.
- Consent: Most important in K–12 contexts, this gathering of student data and algorithmically-based grading must comply with laws like COPPA and FERPA.

What we measure touches assessment beyond measurement, how we determine learning priorities. That should guide the priorities in pedagogy to set AI systems that engender critical thought, creativity, and growth; and not compliance and correctness.

Figure 3. Comparative Study

Aspect	Conventional Test Methods	AI- Based Test Methods
Efficacy	Measures knowledge retention but does not adapt to individual learning methods	Personalized assessments and improved learning outcomes
Consistency	Prone to human errors, biases and inconsistent grading	Ensures unbiased evaluation and automated grading
Influence on Student learning	Encourages rote learning but fosters critical thinking in subjective assessments	Provides real -time feedback and personalized learning paths
Flexibility	Requires manual efforts for question paper creation and grading	Dynamically adjusts difficulty levels based on student performance
Time efficiency	Time consuming	Fast assessment and instant feedback
Scalability	Limited scalability	Highly scalable
Bias and Fairness	Subject to personal biases	Reduces biases but may have algorithmic biases
Suitability	Best for subjective evaluations, creative assessments and interpersonal skill testing	Ideal for objective testing, large-scale exams and personalized learning

The comparisons illustrated in Figure 3 are made from human-led conventional assessments and AI-powered evaluation models against the four critical parameters: speed, homogeneity (consistency), feedback quality, and scalability. Human evaluators surpass at empathy, contextual judgment, and nuanced sensing of student effort but fall behind in the speed of evaluations and consistency. AI systems, on the other hand, offer unmatched efficiency, maintaining a standard of marking and providing real-time analytics. Yet, these systems lack the cultural sensitivity and emotional intuition that human teachers bring to the assessment process. Thus, a few scholars suggest that a perfect assessment model will combine the clinical precision of machine intelligence with the ethical and intuitive teaching of human teachers.

Ethical considerations and shortcomings -AI marking is faster and personalized, but imperfect. Emotionally charged assignments, those laden with cultural nuances, or those requiring individual expressions of thought, appear to be candidates for assigning these AI-marking tools their most difficult tasks. For instance, a poem that utilizes metaphor, irony, or perhaps even local colloquialisms will more than likely be misread or simply go unappreciated by AI trained predominantly on formulaic textbook composition (Perelman, 2014) In the same light, a student may find himself marked down by the AI for providing an answer that seems correct but is unconventional simply because it does not meet the AI's expectations.

Another fundamental concern is bias. Should training datasets for systems that are training their AI tools be biased along the lines of predominantly native English speakers, then such systems could, in essence, disfigure the works of nonnative speakers and reinforce linguistic bias (Selwyn, 2019). In fact, some argue that machine scoring or using undefined rubrics could magnify inequities.

Looking at student privacy, AI test tools sometimes employ behavioural surveillance technologies through measures such as keystroke logging, gaze tracking, and even facial recognition during the tests. Accompanied by the aim of preserving the sanctity of the academic environment, the over-surveillance attitude these measures evoke, thereby raise several consequential questions regarding consent, data processing, and its psychological easing of the students (Buolamwini & Gebru, 2018).

Relatedly, in poorly funded schools, the absence of infrastructure, such as high-speed internet or latest devices, may continually deny students access to the AI system. Without guaranteeing its preferential application in design and implementation, educational systems may tilt towards exacerbating educational inequity (UNESCO, 2021).

6. THE ROLE OF AI IN FACILITATING EDUCATIONAL ACCESSIBILITY

Some age-old issues around accessibility pertain in education worldwide. Most students with disabilities, language differences, inadequate infrastructure, or innovative learning never experience access to high-quality education. In a well-ethical and inclusive design, Artificial Intelligence (AI) gives a marvellous toolset to greatly minimize these barriers and increase educational opportunity. AI can democratize learning for historically underserved students through personalization, automation, multilingualism, and assistive technologies enabling better educational access.

This chapter analyses how AI comes into the enhancement of inclusion and accessibility to education - and hazards of digital exclusion and algorithmic deficiency.
6.1 AI Chatbots and Virtual Assistant Does

The entry point of one of the most widely accessible private uses of AI at the service of students in education has by far been artificial intelligence-powered educational chatbots. These chatbots offer all-day all-night academic and administrative assistance: responding to procedures related to material, scheduling, policies, and more. They have conversational designs devolved by natural language processing (NLP), which will respond in time to relevant, context-sensitive information.

These systems incidentally prove useful for students with learning anxieties, first-generation students, and students being exposed to unfamiliar academic systems. For some examples, the chatbot at Georgia State University reduced "summer melt" for incoming students considerably through answers to often-unknow questions that had previously gone unattended (Page & Gehlbach, 2017).

6.1 Functions of AI Chatbots

Figure 4. Functionality of AI Chatbots

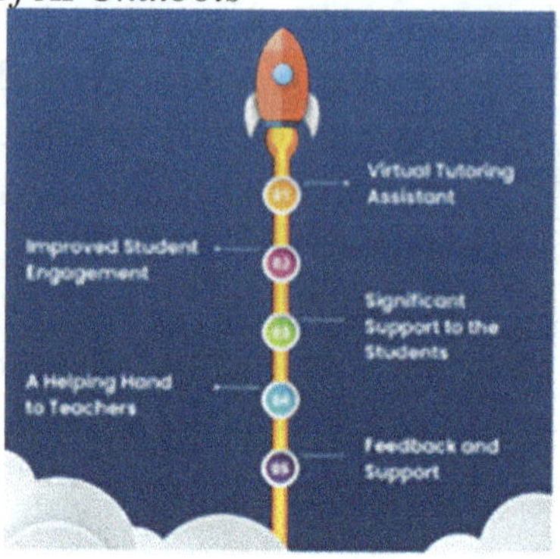

Figure 4 illustrates the general schematic diagram of the internal architecture of an AI chatbot. In short, this user query would be analysed by the language-understanding component at the very start, following which it is fired through a dialog manager to the knowledge base, where the response is computed under the supervision of the student context. The response shape will be built, maybe as an extra question or a refer, simultaneously while the system adjusts its learning model in relation to that specific interaction. The feedback loop of continuous improvement therefore gives the incremental boost of the system in terms of heightened accuracy and consistency and improved responsiveness. But enhancing the multilingual ability and also voice-and-vision recognition would be an added advantage for the performance of these bots. These bots will have a quite engaging and inclusive learning experience for the disabled or multilingual students while understanding either a language or knowledge disparity.

6.2 Technologies Assistive to Disable Students

These are mostly technologies aimed at providing any kind of assistance in learning to visually impaired, hearing-impaired, motor-impaired, and cognitively impaired individuals due to the immense impact they have on implementing this technology.

- Text-to-speech and speech-to-text systems enable dyslexics, mobility, or manuscript-impaired students to be able to utilize these systems.
- Tracking modules, including facial recognition and eye tracking, are able to monitor the attention of non-verbal or orally impaired students (Zhou et al., 2019).
- Predictive keyboards and gesture control enable motor function-impaired users to operate on digital devices as effectively as possible.

Deep learning empowers Microsoft Immersive Reader and Seeing AI to transform text images and environmental consciousness into accessible media in classroom environments and all other physical and digital settings.

6.3 Multilingual and Culturally Responsive AI

Language ranks among the most significant challenges in global education. In this case, the AI translation software such as Google Translate and Microsoft Translator is applicable, because such AI dubbing platforms can provide a live translation of course content, classroom interactions, and user interfaces. Such technologies need to operate through formal and informal learning channels in multilingual environments.

Culturally adapted AI also localizes examples and idioms"; as well as contents into a known context for a student. Thus, understanding, interest, and confidence are increased, especially with indigenous or remote students (UNESCO, 2021). Multilingual pre-trained NLP models also provide space for the phenomenon of skewness between languages and allow for consideration of a variety of non-Western sentence structures and grammar by the AI.

6.4 Voice and Vision Interfaces

Low-literacy, visual, and physically disabled students' near-posterity AI requires voice and vision as interfaces: non-text. Some of what these voice-enabled devices could do, like in homes where Amazon Alexa and the Google Assistant will reside,

- Reading their homework
- Responding to questions based on their curriculum
- Informing them about reading or translating sentences

To support this, image-recognition software has made it possible for the visually impaired students to read signage around them, compute mathematically from pictures, or identify the equipment they possess in their laboratories.

Such multimodal I/0 systems follow the UDL (Universal Design for Learning) path that favors flexible learning experiences to suit numerous learners (CAST, 2018).

6.5 Offline and Low-Bandwidth AI Tools

Availability is not just a student's skill; it is also infrastructure-based: the ubiquitous lack of fixed broadband connections in the majority of poor communities, particularly rural communities, makes cloud apps useless. As such, some platforms incorporate edge AI to locally process data without traversing cloud servers.

A prime example is EkStep, which is creating offline AI-powered learning apps for ultra-low-cost mobile phones at designated basic levels of literacy and numeracy (Natarajan et al., 2020). Such instruments assist educators in lesson planning based on learning objectives and where they are operating.

6.6 Ethical Challenges in Accessible AI

If inclusion comes through AI, the reverse argument may be possible if the technology does not deliver.

In such a scenario, accent identification by speech recognition technology may mishear hence destroying the fate of education for students from one or the other linguistic background.

Facial recognition technology would jigsaw puzzle students from darker skin tone, or facial features of another ethnicity (Buolamwini & Gebru, 2018).

Data-driven accessibility efforts could be leaving behind students who are unable to afford new hardware or update their internet connectivity.

Therefore, it is necessary that such an accessibility AI has along with it:

- Have plans for end-users.
- Test its performance gap or bias.
- Operate on low specifications and offline.
- Collaborate with human teachers rather than opting for full automation.

7. CHALLENGES AND ETHICAL ISSUES

The increasing face of Artificial Intelligence (AI) in the learning environment has provoked a lot of controversy not only regarding its promise, but also regarding its danger. AI holds the promise of personalization, scalability, and improved decision-making, yet these advantages have introduced non-traditional issues regarding inclusion, bias, transparency, surveillance, and consent. If such systems were actually to function in an ethical manner, they would threaten to reproduce inequalities, violate the autonomy of learners, and intrude upon basic rights in a very systematic manner.

This part also examines the ethics and phenomenology of the more urgent issues that plague AI in education: algorithmic bias, surveillance culture, data privacy, the role of the teacher, and infrastructural inequality. Algorithmic Bias and Fairness 7.1 An artificial intelligence (AI) system is not more just than a data set it was trained on. Data sets have embedded within them past imbalances, such as majority language habits, or provincial standards for testing; and therefore unwittingly, AI models may even continue to discriminate (Benjamin, 2019).

Machine essay-scoring algorithms have devalued nonnative language, even if the case's argument was logically compliant (Perelman, 2014). Since splits in social class cross with other qualities, the disconnection of AI systems would also generate discrimination for students who would be chastised as "at risk" for sheer deficiencies on the measure-settlements-profiling, low expectations, or weak interventions may also ensue (Knox, 2020).

It thus means:

- Diversify training datasets
- Implement fairness auditing procedures
- Be transparent regarding model logic and feature selection
- Prompt interdisciplinary participation-including that of educators and social scientists-into the development process of AI

Privacy, Consent, and Data Ethics 7.2 AI at school is therefore an artificial intelligence that inevitably accumulates tiny details and particulars; clickstream data, rate typing, testing, photographs taken, etc. The data basically pertains to personalization and validity checking but poses the following inquiries:

- Who actually owns the data?
- What is storage time?
- Are students (particularly children) ever brought completely up to speed on what is being tracked?

Legislation like FERPA, GDPR, and COPPA attempts to shield students from this. These legislations do not carry out self-regulation; in fact, most of the educational devices do not even contain well-defined, easy-to-understand privacy policies (UNESCO, 2021). More alarmingly, a considerable number of them have privacy policies that contain data-sharing provisions clauses for third parties, and that too, most frequently without asking any sort of approved consent. Schools need to shift towards those models: open consent; anonymizing stored data; opt-out; and informing all stakeholders about data.

7.1 Surveillance and Student Autonomy

The surveillance element of so-called proctoring software under which students are monitored through webcams, screen activity, facial-recognition, and monitoring of bodily movement during exams was intended to maintain academic integrity, yet has been transformed into excessive student monitoring, generating anxiety and distrust (Selwyn, 2019).

For instance, putting a neurodivergent student's behavior under the category of being “suspicious” when actually it is quite innocent. And there's also the lesser accuracy of facial-recognition technology in darker-skinned individuals (Buolamwini & Gebru, 2018), with such a mistake possibly leading to an unjust accusation.

On the other hand, surveillance culture in educational contexts tends to erode instead of maintaining intrinsic motivation. Students who are always under surveillance will be less motivated to risk learning or try things out within developmental learning contexts.

Institutions must free the respect of autonomy and the imposition of integrity on the following basis:

- No alternative provision for AI proctoring
- Make AI surveillance optional (technically feasible)

Notify students of the surveillance possibilities and its auditing Teacher Deskill and Marginalization of the LAAI Lastly, on the aspect of pedagogy, assessment, comment, and delivery of content, the AI system is poised to perform diverse roles. Work amortization does not de-skill teachers or make them feel replaceable, although they are (Holmes et al., 2019). The tasks of mentoring, emotional guidance, and cultural translation cannot be readily replicated or replaced by machines. Teachers will be pushed to the periphery of their work and devalued when institutions value cost and efficiency over possibilities for automation. In addition, trust in pedagogic processes is undermined with transparent technologies of AI displaying no hint of any rationale.

The more effective model is teacher-AI collaboration where teachers are provided dashboards, suggestions, or co-design privileges-but pedagogical control stays with them.

7.2 Infrastructure and Digital Divide

More fundamental but potentially most disruptive is the infrastructure divide. Students at under-resourced schools, rural districts, or either one of these typically do not have:

- Regular Internet access
- Recent hardware
- Private and secure online spaces

Artificial Intelligence will be embedded in the lowest levels of connectivity and digital literacy among people in most of the world (UNESCO, 2021). As such, one would anticipate something conceived to be an inclusive innovation to turn out to be an actual expansion of the digital divide. To this purpose, the policymaker must:

- Redirect resources towards devices access and broadband infrastructure enhancement
- Encourage Edge computing or software with offline usage capability
- Develop AI programs for access and low bandwidth consumption8. AI Education Best Practices to Safeguard Data Privacy

8. BEST PRACTICES TO ENSURE DATA PRIVACY IN AI- DRIVEN EDUCATION

With the integration of AI machines into day-to-day processes in classrooms and institutions, the quantity and sensitivity of data gathered have exponentially increased. Educational AI systems put together huge arrays to personalize learning and measure outcomes, from keystroke histories and learning gains to behaviour indicators and even biometric features. However, this enhanced vision for data use requires commitments to able practices for privacy protection, retention of consent, and institutional responsibility; innovations that do not include these compromises risk eroding the very confidence upon which it stands.

This therefore lists some evidence-based practices that maintain data privacy in environments with AI support for developers, educators, administrators, and policymakers at large.

While we point to opportunities for learning with AI, problems in data governance and protection arise in some areas. The privacy issues arising out of data used in AI and the governance of schools are often highly complicated. There is mass provision of learner data-the behavioural logs, biometric signals, performance patterns, and device activity profiles-will all be considered very pertinent for personalized learning, automated assessment, and better deployment of the Curriculum. But into these possibilities come some very sobering concerns, such as challenging consent, monitoring, algorithmic profiling, and even students' rights. Poorly managed data can put students in immense danger for privacy issues, discrimination, and psychological effects.

All that is left are the best, most ethical, socially responsible, and legally defensible best practices for data privacy management in AI-shared learning environments concerning those so very basic concerns of transparency, security, compliance, and student agency.

8.1 Data Minimization and Purpose Limitation

According to the principle of data minimization, the institution could only collect data for specified purposes that would have to be defined in advance. The GDPR states that the intended purposes for which data may be collected are limited to minus¢~merely the general educational requirements of Eye-tracking of pupils on web-based exam tests

- Typing behaviour
- Mouse activity
- Device location or device metadata

To keep students in AI-based learning confidential, developers must:

- Publicize the purposes of data collection.
- Stop collecting behavioural and biometric data unless pedagogical reasons exist.
- Disable any recording capabilities as default until users decide to opt in.

Additional privacy threats are introduced by unconnected information, unless they are educationally justified, and even that introduces an additional risk of misuse in contravention of such justification.

8.2 Informed Consent and Age-Appropriate Privacy Notices

This means that the consent was informed, willingly provided, and understood. On the other hand, elementary and secondary students willingly provide their information with AI tools without being informed of their data' purposes, storage, or forwarding. Terms of Service are of no use and merely make matters worse with unclear opt-outs.

The best practices are recommended as follows:

- Utilizing clear notice on privacy in language children understand (Livingstone & Third, 2017)
- All data-greedy components must be constructed as opt-in
- Guarantee of parental consent in K-12 settings as mandated by U.S. COPPA
- Continuous notice to users of what and why it's being collected

Students, as much as is practicable, should possess as much control and say over their data as feasible including the control to delete it or refuse to authorize its usage for any non-instructional analysis.

8.3 Compliance with International and Domestic Legislative Frameworks

The AI learning tools need to meet a humongous amount of ethical and legal requirements:

- GDPR (EU): Transparency model, right to be forgotten, and portability of data.
- FERPA (U.S.): Safeguards privacy of students' educational records.
- COPPA (U.S.): Regulates information gathering from children below age 13.
- DPDP Act (India 2023): Demands consent and data fiduciary responsibility.

The leaders of those institutions need to make sure that vendor agreements, internal policies, and tech rollouts adhere to these standards even in cases where the third-party applications being employed are such as chatbots, LMS integrations, or analytics tools (UNESCO, 2021).

8.4 Safe Keeping and Access Control

The data driven by AI is extremely attractive to hackers and third parties, especially in the educational community. This is where intellectual property meets financial aid data and student identifying information. Hence, extremely strict and strict security controls such as:

- Encryption in transit and storage
- Job-role-based access control limiting exposure to sensitive data

- Multi-factor authentication of system administrators and staff
- Regular penetration testing and incident response drill

These should also be made contingent for suppliers as well as a red-lined copy of the third-party processing agreements.

8.5 Explainability and Transparency of the Algorithms

Teachers and students must both possess some insight into the AI system's decision-making, especially in high-stakes applications such as education assessment, admissions, or performance forecasting. This means that such systems must be:

- Explainable: Transparent reason for the output.
- Traceable: Auditable record of data and model modifications.
- Auditable: Records available for inspection by education regulators.

For instance, if a student was labelled "at-risk," he and his teacher should be able to look at what behaviour or scores resulted in the label (Selwyn, 2019). Without explainability, error and bias will not be corrected.

8.6 Anonymization and Ethical Data Use Research

By default, student information needs to be anonymized (e.g., name, email, or IP address obfuscated) when such information is used for research, product design, or reporting-outwards to others. This is strictly essential for:

- Huge learning analytics studies
- EdTech product design
- Institutional benchmarking or funding reports

Additionally, the AI developers should also be adhering to ethical research guidelines such as getting Institutional Review Board (IRB) approval or observing UNESCO's ethics guidelines on AI (UNESCO, 2021).

8.7 Facilitating Student Data Literacy and Autonomy

Students and teachers may know what are their rights to privacy and how data are being used, yet compliance is still maintained; therefore, institutions must embed digital privacy literacy in the curriculum that involves:

- Type of data AI collects
- How to designate privacy levels
- How to and when to reject or refuse AI decision-making power over them

The agency of the student is most significant. Granting controlled access to students for their own data builds trust in a responsible and ethical learning setting that promotes learning and readiness for the future in a meaningful future (Livingstone et al., 2020).9. The Future of AI in Education for Instruction

From the very outset, advancing Artificial Intelligence would alter the premises of instructional paradigm-building, policy-making, infrastructure, and equity considerations. Future classrooms would more probably be intelligent environments, with real-time personalization, human-machine interaction, and inclusive design. Technologies and their ethical development, however, concerning cross-disciplinary collaboration, would have to be in place for such a vision to emerge.

9. THE FUTURE OF AI IN EDUCATION

According to the plans, as new and creative AI solution comes out into the market, education would have been prone to much deeper changes-transformation of instruction, policy, infrastructure, and equity. Learning environments of the future will probably become intelligent ecosystems designed for real-time personalization, human-machine collaboration, and inclusive design. Addressing some of the complex techno-ethical issues within such an ecosystem will, however, require collaboration across disciplines.

9.1 Hyper-Personalization and Autonomy of Learners

The future would bring hyper-personalization through AI: designing learning experiences that are not just tailored to the learner's ability level but according to emotional, cognitive, and context-based signals coming from the circumstances of that learning experience: what's going on in their facial expressions, the tone in their voice, or typing speed.

Further, within this welfare state, students will gain more control over their learning trajectories as AI permits individualized models, intelligent dashboards, and open learner models for monitoring progress, personal target setting, and dynamic feedback, fostering agency and growth in metacognition. This emphasis will serve to transform students from passive consumers into active designers of their learning paths.

9.2 Artificial Intelligence in Furthering Assisting and Designing Learning

In the near future, AI will stand as a whopping co-pilot to the teacher, from grading to registering attendance, not only for administrative purposes but also with lesson plan preparation and differentiation, design of formative assessments, etc. AI platforms can retrieve classroom data and make recommendations for effective intervention; profile students based on compatible learning styles; or create activities aligned with curriculum objectives, in real-time (Holmes et al., 2019).

Such systems will not replace teachers themselves but instead enhance their effectiveness and capacities in ways that allow them to concentrate on the more creative domains of emotional support and one-on-one mentoring.

9.3 Intelligent Institutional Systems and Policy Planning

However, AI would also help with strategic planning at governmental and institutional levels. In fact, using learning analytics and predictive modelling, school districts and universities could predict dropout probabilities, evaluate the effect of programs, and optimize resource allocation via AI.

Projections at the national level in policies simulated by AI from ministries of education would enable ministries to foresee workforce trends, identify curriculum shortfalls, and understand equity across regions in student performance and access. An example is the "AI in Education" framework developed by UNESCO (UNESCO, 2021) for enabling responsible use of AI for evidence-based policymaking, with technology serving the public good rather than commercial ends.

9.4 Trends in Multilingual, Multimodal, and Inclusive AI

Increasing globalization in education will see AI facilitating multilingual learners through real-time translation by AI, culturally relevant content, and dialect-aware chatbots, which all allow for learning in much the same mother languages- reducing cognitive load and maximizing understanding.

In addition, multimodal AI regards text, speech, vision, gesture, and touch that would accommodate different learning styles. For disabled learners, AI would provide screen readers, eye-tracking input, and predictive text functionalities, the level of accessibility will be ranked with the WCAG- that is, Web Content Accessibility Guidelines.

9.5 Synergizing With Innovative Technologies: AR, VR, and Blockchain

The conjunction of AI with all other innovative technologies would bring in entirely new standards of education:

- AR/VR-directed experiential learning environments-like historical simulations, virtual labs, or interactive anatomy courses-would be achieved by AI.
- Then again, blockchain ensures state-proof and verifiable academic qualifications with decentralized learning portfolios.
- Edge computing and the IoT will be AI models even far out into low-connectivity areas and be the means whereby offline learning contexts come into being instead of relying on cloud servers.

Such integrative promises are anticipated to render robust yet scalable and equitable learning solutions for all learners; however, only on the learning design considerations of ethics, access, and pedagogical relevance.

10. CONCLUSION

Education of the future will be transformed by Data Science and Artificial Intelligence. Though intelligent tutoring systems can only engage students in conversation as humans do, learning to manipulate the possibility of encountering artificial intelligence is beneficial. Adaptive learning systems build individualized content applicable to a unique learner aside from integrating assessment and institutional planning instruments powered by AI, which introduces those but does not stop there. Technology should, however, have in place solid pedagogical, ethical, and regulatory frameworks.

This chapter has provided an exploration into ways AI technologies are affecting the learning landscape. It began by presenting a theoretical framework based on Constructivism, Bloom's Taxonomy, Cognitive Load Theory, TPACK, and the SAMR model-offering a lens through which one might judge the pedagogical alignment of AI tools. The later sections then represented a view of AI in personalized learning, intelligent tutoring, automated testing, and inclusive education with sample case studies and comparative schema.

Truly, though promising, AI may bring about threats sufficiently clear to merit consideration. The more subtle questions under scrutiny regard algorithmic bias and student surveillance; the more controversial issues include student privacy and replacing skilled teachers with machines. So unchecked, these may widen inequities in the system or reduce education to a package of measures. Even more, digital dependence denies students hardware connectivity or technical assistance.

As we move forward, AI in education needs not replace instructors or standardize students but to learn to have their education systems become more flexible, responsive, and humanized. An aid to education—rather than a decision-maker—is there to strengthen teachers while valuing diversity in learners and promoting equity instead of undermining it.

This multidisciplinary approach will move toward achieving that goal by cutting across educational, computer scientific, ethical, legal, and psychological paradigms. Not just in technological capacity must institutions make investment; they also need to invest in digital literacy, privacy governance, and culturally responsive design. More than that, innovation must be apportioned in the public interest, and algorithmic transparency guaranteed through the law over data rights. Finally, learners will be in a position to use critical and creative intelligence to adopt AI tools with insentient awareness of enormous potential and limitations in them.

By contrast, AI is not a panacea in itself but a tool. The gap it creates or closes in education, whether it lends learning new robustness or weakness, will rely on the choices made at present. With thoughtful design, equal policies, responsible stewardship, AI can be a transformative partner in forging more equitable, adaptive and learner-centered education systems.

REFERENCES

Anderson, L. W., & Krathwohl, D. R. (2001). *A taxonomy for learning, teaching, and assessing: A revision of Bloom's taxonomy of educational objectives*. Longman.

Arnold, K. E., & Pistilli, M. D. (2012). Course Signals at Purdue: Using learning analytics to increase student success. *Proceedings of the 2nd International Conference on Learning Analytics and Knowledge*, 267–270. DOI: 10.1145/2330601.2330666

Benjamin, R. (2019). Race after technology: Abolitionist tools for the new Jim code. *Polity*.

Boud, D., & Molloy, E. (Eds.). (2013). *Feedback in higher and professional education: Understanding it and doing it well*. Routledge.

Buolamwini, J., & Gebru, T. (2018). Gender shades: Intersectional accuracy disparities in commercial gender classification. *Proceedings of Machine Learning Research*, *81*, 1–15.

CAST. (2018). *Universal Design for Learning Guidelines version 2.2*. http://udlguidelines.cast.org

Chi, M. T. H., Bassok, M., Lewis, M. W., Reimann, P., & Glaser, R. (1994). Self-explanations: How students study and use examples in learning to solve problems. *Cognitive Science*, *18*(2), 145–182.

Conati, C., & Kardan, S. (2013). Student modeling: Supporting personalized instruction, from problem-solving to exploratory open-ended activities. *AI Magazine*, *34*(3), 13–26. DOI: 10.1609/aimag.v34i3.2483

Deci, E. L., & Ryan, R. M. (2000). The "what" and "why" of goal pursuits: Human needs and the self-determination of behavior. *Psychological Inquiry*, *11*(4), 227–268. DOI: 10.1207/S15327965PLI1104_01

Fosnot, C. T. (Ed.). (2013). *Constructivism: Theory, perspectives, and practice* (2nd ed.). Teachers College Press.

Garcia, M., & Patel, R. (2021). Adaptive learning outcomes in middle school mathematics. *Journal of Educational Technology*, *47*(3), 145–161.

Graesser, A. C., Chipman, P., Haynes, B. C., & Olney, A. (2005). AutoTutor: An intelligent tutoring system with mixed-initiative dialogue. *IEEE Transactions on Education*, *48*(4), 612–618. DOI: 10.1109/TE.2005.856149

Holmes, W., Bialik, M., & Fadel, C. (2019). *Artificial Intelligence in Education: Promises and Implications for Teaching and Learning*. Center for Curriculum Redesign.

Kalyuga, S. (2011). Cognitive load theory: How many types of load does it really need? *Educational Psychology Review, 23*(1), 1–19. DOI: 10.1007/s10648-010-9150-7

Knox, J. (2020). Artificial intelligence and education in China. *Learning, Media and Technology, 45*(3), 298–311. DOI: 10.1080/17439884.2020.1754236

Livingstone, S., Stoilova, M., & Nandagiri, R. (2020). *Data and privacy literacy: The role of the school in educating children in a datafied society*. OECD Education Working Paper No. 224.

Livingstone, S., & Third, A. (2017). Children and young people's rights in the digital age: An emerging agenda. *New Media & Society, 19*(5), 657–670. DOI: 10.1177/1461444816686318

Luckin, R., Holmes, W., Griffiths, M., & Forcier, L. B. (2016). *Intelligence Unleashed: An Argument for AI in Education*. Pearson Education.

Mishra, P., & Koehler, M. J. (2006). Technological pedagogical content knowledge: A framework for teacher knowledge. *Teachers College Record, 108*(6), 1017–1054. DOI: 10.1111/j.1467-9620.2006.00684.x

Natarajan, U., Jha, V., & Awasthi, P. (2020). *India's learning transformation: Using AI for equitable education*. World Bank EdTech Blog.

Page, L. C., & Gehlbach, H. (2017). How an artificially intelligent virtual assistant helps students navigate the road to college. *AERA Open, 3*(4), 1–12. DOI: 10.1177/2332858417749220

Pane, J. F., Steiner, E. D., Baird, M. D., & Hamilton, L. S. (2014). *Continued progress: Promising evidence on personalized learning*. RAND Corporation.

Perelman, L. (2014). When "the state of the art" is counting words. In Shermis, M. D., & Burstein, J. (Eds.), *Handbook of Automated Essay Evaluation: Current Applications and New Directions* (pp. 163–181). Routledge.

Piech, C., Huang, J., Nguyen, A., Phulsuksombati, M., Sahami, M., & Guibas, L. (2015). Learning program embeddings to propagate feedback on student code. *Proceedings of the 32nd International Conference on Machine Learning*, 87–95.

Puentedura, R. R. (2006). *Transformation, technology, and education: The SAMR model*. Retrieved from https://hippasus.com/resources/sweden2010/SAMR_TPCK_Intro.pdf

Selwyn, N. (2019). Should robots replace teachers? AI and the future of education. *Polity.*

Shermis, M. D., & Burstein, J. (Eds.). (2013). *Handbook of Automated Essay Evaluation: Current Applications and New Directions.* Routledge. DOI: 10.4324/9780203122761

Sweller, J. (1988). Cognitive load during problem solving: Effects on learning. *Cognitive Science, 12*(2), 257–285. DOI: 10.1207/s15516709cog1202_4

UNESCO. (2021). *AI and education: Guidance for policymakers.* UNESCO Publishing.

Vygotsky, L. S. (1978). *Mind in society: The development of higher psychological processes.* Harvard University Press.

Woolf, B. P. (2010). *Building Intelligent Interactive Tutors: Student-Centered Strategies for Revolutionizing E-learning.* Morgan Kaufmann.

Yu, E. (2023). Detecting AI-generated text: Evaluating the reliability of current models. *Journal of AI Ethics, 5*(1), 22–34.

Zhou, J., Yu, H., & Xu, B. (2019). An eye-tracking study on the usability of educational apps for children with autism. *Behaviour & Information Technology, 38*(1), 1–13.

Chapter 12
Balancing AI and Pedagogy:
The Future of Technology in Education

Manoj Kumar P. A.
https://orcid.org/0009-0004-0877-0533
Christ University, India

ABSTRACT

Education receives transformational changes through artificial intelligence elements we could not have predicted. The discussion now proceeds to show how existing smart systems transform established teaching practices and modify educational student procedures. The public can occasionally witness AI working through education setups that adapt lessons to individual students and chat-based tutoring services and predictive analytics programs which help early detection of academic issues. Such technology systems provide immediate feedback while alerting teachers about students needing help leading to an inevitable transformation of classroom environments. The present educational tools offer promising prospects to advance education into a different future framework. Natural language processing brings interactive experiences to lessons while virtual and augmented reality technologies present virtual simulations such as diverse environments.

MISSION STATEMENT

Our primary aim here is to sketch a balanced view of using an AI-powered learning system—a look at both its clear benefits and its less obvious pitfalls. We want to offer educators, administrators, and policymakers' insights that, gener-

DOI: 10.4018/979-8-3373-2185-1.ch012

ally speaking, help them make better choices, even if things aren't always crystal clear. Often, we try to bridge what theory suggests with what actually happens in practice while also keeping a close eye on the ethical side and social layers of this technology. It's worth noting, as seen in discussions about educational missions that call for clear alignment among all parties involved (Holmes et al., 2023), that such nuance is essential. When we place our analysis within this broader context, we not only focus on things like operational efficiency and improved knowledge—but also stress that ethical guidelines must shape our tech advances to lessen potential socio-economic gaps (Allioui et al., 2023). All in all, our hands-on approach, with its mix of practical concerns and ethical reflections, aims to add a genuine voice to the lively and ever-changing debate in this dynamic field.

INTRODUCTION: THE AI REVOLUTION IN EDUCATION

AI is shaking up education by bringing learning to be more personal, flexible and, all in all, more efficient. However, AI is now part and parcel of evolving education with educational advancements that have traditionally built upon the progress of print publishing, becoming then the internet (Selwyn, 2019). Although in many classrooms AI tools may be viewed as neat add ons, they're changing just how teachers structure lessons and, in some cases, the reworking of entire courses (Ooi et al., 2025). The systems can handle wild has of data, programming the learning for each of them in ways that can enhance engagement and results, which can simply be better (Barger et al., 2024). Close examination shows that AI can completely change the way of education not just at school but also in the outside world.

Introduction to AI in Education

Today, it might seem that including automatic work for admin work and better results for the students is a blend of different methods. AI has an effect on how we learn, and this chapter floats back over the history of learning tech so that AI feels like a recent twist in a long tale. Then, it explores what fuels AI into classrooms, including surveys on numerous AI tools and their benefits. Whether the jump is direct or not, trends in the old chalk boards to today's digital learning spaces make way to say that AI among other educational innovations is the newest for example, a process that never ends and is still ongoing. AI is now present in classrooms and virtual classrooms implementing tasks such as automated grading, smart tutoring systems and even identifying lessons suitable to suit various student requirements. It then moves along to actual uses of real-world cases where current AI setups are changing teaching practices in the strangest of ways. A few driving forces regarding the above phenomena are: the need for more scalable, personalised learning systems, the development of better and better machine learning algorithms, and the necessity to oversee better educational tasks. Finally, this chapter unpacks these factors, where most of them reflect on what such these factors could mean for future of education and suggest whether the promise or the risks of AI, by integrating each of these factors, will potentially make a big transformation in education as a matter of fact (Setyaningsih et al., 2024) .

Core Components of AI-Powered Learning Systems

An AI learning system can be no more than a small unimportant part of a larger computing setup or sometimes, just a part of an integral network to retain users. This AI is also revamping the educational novel by constituting the intelligent, responsive, adaptive learning environment and data based learning strategies (Siddiqui et al., 2025). As a matter of fact, you can say that for all systems the core few pieces serve as a material hidden framework that holds it up, just like any buildings sturdy beams. These elements put together provide a ride that appears more enjoyable: individualized paths for each learner, a little end to arduous paperwork, and an apparent increase in student involvement (Jabbour J et al., 2025). We bring deep, exploratory dives into the data driven processes and how the user interfaces help natural and approachable interactions. In brief, the resulting look under the hood will allow us, generally speaking, to see more of what tech driven programs can do for education and concede more to better teaching and learning results.

Adaptive Learning

AI validates itself as a life saviour of adaptive learning systems with its ability to whip up a personalized study that suits each student's own needs . And these platforms simply constantly active during which they keep track of students replies, conduct, and study info and adjust lessons very quickly. They mash data in real time to keep ideas still and bring new ones and keep learners engaged. For example, names like Knewton and DreamBox show how these tools can change lesson difficulty, create a second road to study, and provide instant feedback - thus ensuring that every student is at a point of difficulty that really matches (Luckin et al., 2018). These systems aren't just about sharpening cognitive skills—these systems can sense about how learners feel and what motivates learners, really making a space for more inclusive, more effective educational environment . In general, current studies evidence that to address heterogeneous learning demands and promote personalised outcomes in different environments, it does not rely exclusively on AI, but rather on the fusion of AI with adaptive learning (Bahroun et al., 2023).

Natural Language Processing (NLP)

NLP really surprise you with the ways that you can built an AI system that can pick up on what people say – spoken or written. In schools, these tools have leaped to action, providing tutoring sets ups that match folks' experience and in turn enhance learning. Essay graders, which speed up waiting times, unique needs, and Q&A apps which respond quickly. Most recent studies can suggest that such tech is usually more personalized learning.at least, it generally improves outcomes overall (Kamalov F et al., 2023). At the same time, deploying ethical and practical headaches that in most circumstances need to be sorted out about this kind of NLP stuff in a way that these systems aid in actualizing a learning space that is engaging and supportive (Hassija et al., 2023).Using AI-based analytics really changes how we consider student performance. As a result, we can spot who early on about students who might be slipping behind academically. Smart predictive models that consist of the mixture of earlier warning signals are possible on the basis of academic records, behaviour trends, and engagement levels. This is a heads-up to begin stepping in before any dropout becomes a real issue (Mukkala et al., 2025). AI technology enables Platforms utilizing these such as BrightSpace Insights, Blackboard Predict and others to provide This information is delivered in a technical and practical way. For educators, AI driven learning analytics open a better opportunity to choose the students who need additional help so that they modify their strategies for the special. case. The ever changing field of educational technology is most often a case of highlight how important predictive. When that's the case, the analytics are for what they can be doing to boost academic outcomes and how schools can be navigating. the unpredictable challenges of modern education.

Computer Vision

AI has been woven into many of the everyday methods of teaching in modern educational spaces. Today most of the schools rely on automatic control of online exams – AI systems built with NLP surprisingly surprise you by detection what are you saying – verbal or written. In schools, these tools are in full effect, enabling tutoring setups which cater to what folks' needs are, essay graders that slim down waiting times and Q&A apps that answer quickly. A trend, and recent studies have proven such tech normally increases outcomes, more generally, and yields more personalized learning (Kamalov F et al., 2023). The ethical and practical headaches that come with deploying this kind of NLP stuff in most cases have to be dealt with, so that these systems really do give rise to a learning space which is engaging and supportive (Hassija et al., 2023).

AI analytics based really opens up on student performance in a way that shakes us away from how we looked at it, toward early signs of someone falling behind academically. Today predictive school models rely on old academic records combined with behaviour trends and engagement levels that once they are mixed together generate early warning signals (heads up) to intervene before any dropout actually happens (Mukkala et al., 2025). Helping platforms such as Brightspace Insights, Blackboard Predict and some others provide actionable insights on retention and success rates (Siemens & Long, 2011) that are both technical and practical. But when AI-driven learning analytics come into play, educators get a better shot at identifying students who don't seem to be keeping up, and, as a result, would be able to adapt how they teach according to each case. This ever shifting field of educational technology tends to show how much predictive analytics matters when it comes to advancing academic results and the rocks and holes an institution is to traverse in today's unpredictable education landscape.

In fact, even resorts to Facial checks and use to measure how technology students are engaged (Raca & Dillenbourg, 2014). Simultaneously, new tools like Microsoft HoloLens and Google Expeditions present a mix of augmented and virtual reality enriched with user base below computer vision tricks to make immersive lessons based on what used to be an amalgamation. It isn't just increasing interactivity, but these technologies seem to actually assist students in understanding on a more profound level (Dede et al., 2017). That is, by allowing teachers to have real time insights and provide feedback that matches each learner's needs, adding computer vision (Gligorea et al, 2023). As the tech world shifts so fast, it is necessary to consider not only how effective but what the ethical problems they may induce (Kamalov et al., 2023).

Automated Assessment

Loads of tedious work is being cut out of the grading game by AI. Now it can do more than basic multiple choice and short answer tests, and in the ways conventional methods found hard to shake. These automated tools do so in many cases helping turn grading fair and consistent and easing the educators overall burden on the overall work of the educator (Balfour, 2013). For instance, Gradescope (Piech et al., 2015) offers students systems that power their feedback on a near-instant basis, and are based on machine learning: a convincing sign that teaching and tech are converging. In addition, AI becomes involved in monitoring the student's progress against certain learning objectives and thus paves the way for a more tailored learning experience (Shute & Ventura, 2013). When these come together, they announce a new era of education, more personalized, scalable, and more efficient while serving a diversity of learner needs. Although challenges such as data privacy, algorithmic bias, and some accessibility issues must be carefully considered to implement (Cooper, 2023)

Transformative Applications of AI in Education

Through artificial intelligence, education receives transformational changes as it creates personalized teaching strategies for individual students. Multiple research suggests that AI introduces new learning pathways which create personal tutoring systems to synchronize with students' individual learning speeds and learning behaviour's An investigation reveals that AI supports institutional teachers as well as schools to build accessible learning spaces which include everyone. Educational systems experience more efficient operation and improved student participation because of this technology modernization (Henriette van Rensburg et al., 2024). The integration of AI into education has resulted in flexible teaching procedures which demonstrate the fundamental connection between artificial intelligence and modern teaching and learning methods.

PERSONALIZED LEARNING PATHWAYS

Table 1. Personalised Learning Pathways

Personalized Learning Pathway Features	Commercial Products Available	Key Features
Individual Learning Pace Optimization	**Khan Academy** (Khanmigo AI)	AI-driven adaptive lessons that adjust to student speed
Dynamic Content Adaptation	**Coursera** (Coursera Plus)	Personalized course recommendations based on progress and interests
Identifying and Addressing Knowledge Gaps	**Edmentum Exact Path**	Diagnostic assessments to tailor instruction to student needs
Accommodating Different Learning Styles	**DreamBox Learning**	Adaptive math platform supporting visual, auditory, and kinaesthetic learning
Tracking Progress and Achieving Milestones	**Duolingo**	AI-driven language learning with progress tracking and milestone achievements
AI Learning Roadmap	**Socratic by Google**	AI-powered tutoring that guides topic progression using visual explanations
Real-time Feedback Mechanisms	**Quizlet AI Tutor**	Instant feedback and AI-powered explanations for learning reinforcement

continued on following page

Table 1. Continued

Personalized Learning Pathway Features	Commercial Products Available	Key Features
Cognitive Modeling of Student Understanding	**Carnegie Learning MATHia**	AI-driven cognitive modelling to personalize math instruction
Adaptive Problem Generation for Assessment	**ALEKS (McGraw-Hill)**	AI-generated problems that adapt to student skill level
AI-Powered Plagiarism Detection	**Turnitin**	AI-based originality checks and academic integrity monitoring
Multi-modal Interaction Capabilities	**Lingvist**	AI-driven personalized vocabulary learning using speech, text, and images
Scaffolded Learning Support	**Smart Sparrow (Pearson)**	Adaptive learning pathways that adjust based on student responses

Enhancing Education Through AI Personalization

AI technology changes traditional education methods since it customizes teaching materials to fulfil the distinct requirements of each learner. Education technology uses advanced methods for understanding student performance by monitoring exam scores alongside assignments together with interactive activities which seems to track student learning gaps in a casual manner. The system operates through data analysis which results in immediate adjustments to lessons that integrate algorithm monitoring with pacing control and skill assessment functionality (Luckin et al., 2016). The content delivery mechanism of AI systems relies on individual student progress along with their level of participation so the system selects materials that optimize educational outcomes. The system collects student test results along with in-class assignments as well as observing student interactions which reveals the learning challenges faced by each student (Chen et al., 2020). The newest software solutions now combine three learning styles through visual, auditory, and hands-on options which creates an engaging educational experience according to Maloy (2021). Educational goals get easier to change as educational dashboard analytics in real time links teachers directly with students to plan and modify academic intentions according to Kaliisa et al (2022). AI systems develop comprehensive instruction sequences that establish proper steps toward constant student learning advancement. Commercial products with student-centred learning features demonstrate how AI transforms education into flexible teaching methods which enhance personalization.

Intelligent Tutoring Systems (ITS)

It is almost certain that AI tutoring systems are shaking up the way students receive help. For one example, the Intelligence Tutoring System provides immediate, one on one support and immediate feedback that many believe helps boost learning a great deal. Both modern systems and smart algorithms are used in modern systems where student work is examined now and given feedback straight away during sessions . In addition, they produce a pretty detailed picture of a student's understanding of the material and track that understanding to predict points in which more bumps might appear later (Susnjak et al., 2022). In fact, some of these tools even whip up quizzes and assessments that shuffle to on the fly to match each students' skills, keeping the challenges fresh and engagement high . AI is also increasing learning – it can help identify academic dishonesty using things like Turnitin and GPTZero, which helps maintain an assessment's credibility you know? In these tutoring setups, the students get help with text, speech, and visuals (Habibzadeh, 2023), and the difficulty of these tutoring setups gradually varies as the student fairs well or not (Johnston et al., 2024). Such systems don't do simply tutor, though: they generally doctor up the features that demonstrate AI's real capability in the classroom. Even the sometimes odd style shifts only become surprising in the sense of being enchanted by the fusion of technology and teaching. This growing process of intelligent tutoring is mainly interesting and suitable for further research and for jumping forward in education in most cases.

Table 2. ITS Systems Available

Intelligent Tutoring System Features	Commercially Available Products	Key Features
Real-time Feedback Mechanisms	**Carnegie Learning MATHia**	AI provides instant, contextualized feedback to enhance retention and comprehension
Cognitive Modelling of Student Understanding	**ALEKS (McGraw-Hill)**	Tracks learner progress and predicts difficulties using AI-driven cognitive modelling
Adaptive Problem Generation for Assessment	**Smart Sparrow (Pearson)**	Customizes problems and quizzes based on student proficiency levels
Multi-modal Interaction Capabilities	**Socratic by Google**	AI-driven tutoring using text, speech, and visual explanations for immersive learning
Scaffolded Learning Support	**DreamBox Learning**	Gradually increases task complexity based on student performance

The Educational Impact of AI

Today's change in education relies on artificial intelligence (AI) tool that provides this artificial learning systems through smart interactive tutoring systems, but with customized techniques and training. To the extent that AI allows schools to quietly change learning as they shift to program is that it actually fit the bill of wide swaths of student needs, which many finds strategic. The role of AI in changing the education is becoming more, and its presence is increasing in the field of education for more inclusive practices accommodating to various learning styles and preference (Gligorea et al., 2023). The growing AI helps continue to reshape education to also include more inclusive ways of educating that to various kinds of kinds and preferences. For the most part, the incorporation of generative AI and machine learning in the educational framework is a matter of providing educators with some handy new tools that is indicative of a subtle paradigm shift in how knowledge is dispensed and digested (Ooi et al., 2025).

AI-Powered Career Guidance

Picking a career in this day and age is not an easy task as work market changes so fast and tech is ever changing and employers are always modifying that they require. In general, AI is mostly leveraging oceans of worldwide jobs data to come up with suggestions that actually work. These recommendations are based on the functioning of machine learning models, natural language processing and big data crunching to give an idea about what are the future prospects of work (Chan et al., 2023) (Kamalov et al., 2023). What AI does is bring these modern tools together and using them, it makes career advice very personal a lot more personal than you've ever seen it, but it is detailed enough so people can actually plan their future professional self in uncertain times. Since employment situations are as tangled as possible and the need for flexible, individual-driven solutions is growing these days, one cannot imagine carving out better career paths without AI-powered methods.

Global Job Market Analysis

AI systems expand upon a vast churning of labour market statistics with diversity, captured from multiple sources. Bits of job adverts, in-depth business reports, and even the stats of the labour force are gathered up and mashed together to predict changing employment trends more and more precisely. These systems also review the skills that are in demand today and the salary forecasts for different parts of the country to decide which career moves might suit them the most. For example, take LinkedIn's Economic Graph. An impressive amount of data —over 900 million professional profiles, about 58 million company records and around 39,000 unique ability data sets gleaned in its extremely large user community and corporate databases. For example, the research in McKinsey & Company generally argue that AI analytics help identify new skill gaps and understand how tech driven job losses relate to the existing pressing demand in upskilling and retraining workers (Manyika et al., 2017). In short, these shared layers help us together create a sense of how our global labour approach is increasingly imbued with the anxieties of our global climate in the lasting vein of our ever changing terrain (Leaver T et al., 2023).

Personalized Career Recommendations

AI career advisor pulls in a sound practical skill check, broad educational overview, and this actually very targeted work matching to offer suggestions for every person. And some of its prediction models are real deep dived into user profiles using some pretty interesting Natural Language Processing models, which compare the application data to what the market needs today (Lokam et al., 2025). The system generally does this by pulling from massive reams of data and cutting edge AI tricks, usually giving insights that lean on what industries have been pursuing as well as what people can actually make happen. By creating this setup, users can not only determine the potential career path for them, but also gauge roughly the kind of skills positions require in order to make better decisions in their work lives . These days AI is a big part of bridging skill gaps and making the decisions, which is a good reason that personalized career advice is an important strategic tool in both education and professional growth (Mehlan, 2025).

Skill Gap Identification and Personalized Learning Pathways

IMapper AI connects the learning centres with a workplace need it would be unlikely otherwise. Typically, this crunches data and uses machine learning to discover where someone's qualifications aren't sufficient to meet what jobs require and steers people to follow some kind of customized education path in today's dog eat dog market. Rather than following a fixed set of steps, it offers the framework of how to actually make your skills current, and then (almost step by step) offers the resources needed to bridge the gaps between your current skills and the actual needs of the job. Digital learning platforms are integrated with its system to provide targeted resources for users to fill their own shortcomings in their own skills. One such example would be Google's Career Certificates Program. As turn pros they have an AI that doesn't simply tell your based on generic advice instead they choose training options that reflect what the market wants to see that fits to your own patterns and preferences (Google certification). As per the World Economic Forum's

Future of Jobs 2020 even, workers tend to learn new skills at a rate of about 50 per cent faster on such AI-enhanced career coaching platforms compared to old school reskilling (Hirani et al., 2024). This is often how this turn of events happens—a mix of schools and tech companies working together—and sometimes messy, yes, but in ways that bring education at least pretty close to catching up with the yet always changing requirements of job market (Dama Rševičius et al., 2024

Resume Optimization and Interview Preparation

AI tools, which use Applicant Tracking Systems to line up resumes, and which also provide a practice interview that goes way beyond the dry style of the usual interview — with a very hands-on approach to the way people answer and the way they speak — help job seekers. For instance, VMock provides almost immediate feedback on the resume, in a way of a prompt advice that usually works in favour of the users, and usually increases their chances of being pursued in the actually busy job market (VMock, 2023). HireVue's system satisfies by looking at video interviews that dive deep, communication and determining whether the candidate is good / right for the job role (HireVue, Knowledge centre). Interestingly, research—especially at the heart referenced by Raghavan et al. (2021) in MIT Sloan Management Review—finds that while interview coaching with AI can sometimes have over 40% higher job placement rates. To that, using immersive virtual reality setups for interview prep have studied to enhance the impression of the practice, and candidates feel more ready for real interviews.

Long-Term Career Path Forecasting

AI is now used as an essential progress tracking tool, scanning up the path of people with comparable skills that climb up the ladder. Sometimes it doesn't dig into what role a given person has taken as a result, but it does spot recurring patterns in promotions plus lateral jobs between other roles, possibly even discovering trends where they aren't immediately transparent. For instance, LinkedIn's Career Explorer brings together technical skills with a broad range of professional job roles and it's not at all unusual for users to jump between jobs or even base decisions on solid insights. According to a study by at Gartner, the use of AI for mapping career paths typically increases long term planning efficiency by over 60% and sets the ground for more strategic moves. It does not only simplifying the daily hunt of new opportunities but is taking advantage of the generative AI innovation that has been working on the improvement of productivity and perfection in every sector (Naqbi et al., 2024). There's also now a strong push to blend in creative checks, and the insights of other fields, including that of Artificial Intelligence in Education (AIEd), which brings up that career forecasting is most reliable thought of in terms of a lot wider professional image (Bond et al., 2024).

AI-Driven Career Guidance

It is therefore that with career guidance from AI, there are a plethora of advantages which include, and predominantly, the attraction of it to organizations. Having said that there are three major problems to solve: the system often processes the data in the skewed manner; secondly, the workings of the algorithms are not really clear and last but not the least, we have to preserve the user privacy. By introducing the multitude of biases that come with old hiring practices into AI recommendations, these career guidance systems continue to be biased in perpetuating long standing inequalities in the job market A recent study from the Stanford Institute for Human Centered AI, cited by Zhang et al. (2022) also generally confirms the finding of the researchers that making AI more explicable really helps ensure that these career guidance systems work fairly and responsibly. Additionally, new findings (Thorne, 2024) state that in order to trim out illogical acting of AI, it needs to be known how it makes its conclusions. This type of openness not only corrects the errors and nudge away those biases, but it also builds trust, and improves user engagement, and suddenly, it's not only more reliable but also more effective (Chan et al., 2023), as companies grapple with messy task of integrating AI into career counselling, keeping these issues front and center is key to creating fair and inclusive paths for everyone looking for professional guidance.

AI as a Game-Changer for Career Guidance

In the present day, students and professionals rely on smart tools—predictive analytics, machine learning, and natural language processing incubated with AI—to make data-driven and scientific moves in their careers. All of these are not just new trendy things from an education perspective; it constantly changes the direction that career guidance should be going in, in a way that fits with an education shift where education and learning are both geared towards matching learning with personal goals and needs (Kamalov et al., 2023). Today, amid our society's need for the system to be more fluid, flexible and able to quickly change from time to time, the role AI plays in connecting the schooling to the job market has become very important (Chan et al., 2023). Furthermore, employers now search for people who can easily adapt to change, and here AI shows off its knack for sifting through giant heaps of data and transforming it into practical insights (Kamalov et al., 2023). In short, you can't overstate AI's power as a game changer in mapping out career paths, clearing the way for new innovations that tweak how we approach both our job trajectories and academic outcomes (Chan et al., 2023).

Table 3. Predictive Career Pathway Mapping Using AI

Aspect	Description	Examples
Global Job Market Analysis	AI analyses job postings, industry trends, and labour market data to predict future workforce needs.	LinkedIn Economic Graph
Personalized Career Recommendations	AI assesses individual skills, education, and interests to suggest the best-fit career paths.	IBM Watson Career Coach
Skill Gap Identification & Learning Pathways	AI detects skill gaps and recommends relevant courses/training programs.	Google Career Certificates, Coursera
Resume Optimization & Interview Preparation	AI helps optimize resumes for ATS and provides real-time interview coaching.	VMock, HireVue
Career Progression Forecasting	AI predicts long-term career growth based on industry trends and similar professional profiles.	LinkedIn Career Explorer
Challenges & Ethical Considerations	AI may reinforce biases in hiring trends, requiring fairness and explainability in recommendations.	Explainable AI (XAI)

AI-ENHANCED MIXED REALITY LEARNING ENVIRONMENTS

Mixed reality is about bringing the physical and digital together in ways that change the way that a student defines learning. Instead of the traditional methods, the classrooms now use innovative tools like holographic tutors, virtual science lab, vivid historical reenactments and real time language translation without students even being aware of how they were sucked in, absorbing information over and over again differently. For instance, these smart tools have often been revealed to increase memory and, even, generate an activist learning that deepens children in the subject matter (Dritsas et al., 2025). When the AI powered MR apps are incorporated with everyday teaching occasionally, they are fitting with pedagogical ideas that intend to make learning spaces inclusive and adaptable for various student needs (Wei et al., 2024). And in the end, although this mix of innovations adds some tech flair, it lays a natural groundwork for a more hands-on, interactive experience that better matches today's educational demands, albeit in a flow that can sometimes feel a bit out of order.

Holographic AI Tutors for Tailored Support

It's real time holographic AI tutors, that quickly and quietly mould their method to suit every pupils' style and tempo. Using sophisticated language tools, they incorporate sophisticated tools that understands the questions of learner, including generation of automatic responses and changes to course material in real time to improve learning outcomes. For example, Microsoft's HoloLens 2 is a great example of previous tech that creates interest when displaying 3D and catches on when those ideas become hard — so clear — through clear visuals . According to research from the Stanford HCI Lab on students using these tutors, in most cases students using these tutors only see around a 30 percent increase in problem solving skills compared to peers who continue with traditional method (Gong et al., 2021). Usually, such a type of prompt, goal-adjusted instruction is imperative, as it guarantees that not only lessons are given, but the content is given with interactive visual bits and engaging elements in the service of the students, keeping their attention and subtly repeating key ideas to stress them in an obvious context. Moreover this approach disposes of one of the traditional dependence on personal teaching what makes quality teaching available to more people .

Immersive Historical Reenactments

AI and mixed reality let students plunge straight into history, making them feel the past both mentally and emotionally. Instead of following a set textbook route, learners now meet real historical figures and wander through ancient scenes—they even get to experience landmark events like the D-Day invasion or the signing of the U.S. Constitution, a point highlighted by TimeLooper which is firm working AR and VR technologies . Often, research such as that by Wang et al. (2021) in the Journal of Educational Technology & Society shows that when learners get hands-on with immersive simulations, they usually boost their historical empathy and memory retention by 40% . When students are dropped right into these pivotal moments, their engagement shoots up; they start chatting about and thinking over the causes and effects more critically. This way of learning, which lets people "live" history rather than just study it, sparks deeper reflection on the messy, complex nature of the past (Kourtesis, 2024).

Virtual Science Labs with AI Safety Oversight

Virtual labs allow learners to experiment in a safe, almost real world environment—essentially you are able to do your own experiment without all the usual variations. Artificial Intelligence (AI) helps the labs out by manage experiments, give instantaneous feedback and do complex scientific work in the traditional lab that would prove difficult. In protecting digital spaces where the high risk experiments can be carried out, Labster AI utilizes a prominent role AI plays in reshaping education and safety as highlighted by the recent surveys of its role in recasting education (Reddy, 2024). Lifting the learning experience has less to do with avoiding the pitfalls of traditional labs and more contribution to a safer learning experience: this mix of tech and teaching puts hands on skills first and cuts out as much risk as realistically possible (Varnosfaderani et al., 2024). As AI evolves, keeping a watchful eye on these virtual setups is more crucial than ever to make sure experiments take place ethically and safely in these increasingly sophisticated learning environments.

AI IN EDUCATION

The research by research by (Keistin et al., 2025) states that virtual science lab using AI can raise student's score by as much as 25% higher than their traditional counterpart . That's a neat example of smart tech improving learning, since virtual labs generally avoid the usual associated risks of chemical experiments or taking care of delicate specimens. Generally speaking, near instant response is provided via AI and that 'instant response' yields in adjustments as people go and interaction with the material in real time. Plus, the system will give out experiments not only to local learners, but to remote students across the globe as well, giving a remote rich selection of students the chance to stretch into more advanced scientific exploration, no matter where they live. Merger of AI in classroom has most of us employ our unified mastery to maximize the gratification and balance it up in parallel by making learning personalized also which is really necessary in our increasingly connected, digital worlds (Vorobyeva et al., 2025).

Real-time Language Translation in International Classrooms

AI powered real time translation is changing the way students interact, going beyond class room norms. Now mixed-language students can chat in the real world with not a barrier between them. Headsets with speech recognizers and language processors pack all that so that whatever's said or written is translated much as that happens spontaneously and inclusively. Real time translation capabilities are used as part of Meta's Quest Pro that ensures language barrier does not affect international students . The MIT Media Lab's research shows most cases where such tech can increase understanding by a good 50% (Song et al., 2023). This increased understanding has made a huge contribution to the expansion of education for students to be able to fully participate in group work and hands on projects without any interruption. In addition, this system promotes teamwork among the students who speak different languages and cultures through cultural exchange in unexpected yet in daily ways. With the technology of real time translation in effect– new languages are more available and interaction is more personal, words may repeat with different words or sentence patterns may shift slightly. In sum, all this tech has created a dynamic such that this tech can be integrated into modern classrooms and one that allows a flow of ideas just as freely as communication (Ooi et al., 2023).

Haptic Feedback for Practical Skill Development

Students get substantial hands-on preparation through virtual objects that Haptic technology and AI confirm. Practitioners across multiple disciplines especially medicine and engineering benefit strongly from this advanced technology. Using AI technology FundamentalVR provides surgeons in mixed-reality training with a realistic sense of touch when they handle simulated objects. According to Johns Hopkins research many medical students excel at surgery practice when they use AI-driven haptic systems). Learners can practice realistic hand-eye coordination without concerns of medical errors in a safe environment due to simulation training. Healthcare staff and engineers handling risky activities achieve fewer errors when this advanced method is used. AI produces quick responses that enhance student learning efficiency and cuts down their training time according to Chengoden (2023) and colleagues. By combining haptic feedback with AI technology training and skill practice can be made much better and more practical (Ullah et al., 2023).

AI-Driven Mixed Reality Innovations

Haptic training systems along with virtual science labs and holographic AI tutors let students understand and practice their classes better at the same time. AI data selection enables developers to create dynamic learning environments that adjust to many student needs and revive educational content that textbooks alone cannot deliver. Adaptive learning platforms merge AI and mixed reality which makes education more interactive and brings students around the world diverse learning material safely and efficiently. The educational system adopts AI-powered MR innovations which creates demand that teachers should expand their AI skills and explore prompt engineering training (Familoni et al., 2024) (Walter, 2024). The purpose of these procedures ensures that the latest technology delivers better educational outcomes and helps students think more critically. Students require personalized learning today because the introduction of technology demands they understand AI and MR systems.. This gradual move toward more customized educational experiences is pretty critical, positioning students to navigate an increasingly tech-driven world where knowing your way around AI and MR isn't just a bonus—it's essential. All in all, AI-powered mixed reality stands as an exciting frontier in edtech, continually reshaping how knowledge is delivered and absorbed, often in delightfully unexpected ways.

AI-Driven Content Creation and Academic Integrity

AI in modern education is not just about one thing but it combines two big tasks. It starts off by jazzing up the content creation and then it comes up with the adaptive learning material that adapts to the learner's pace (Gligorea et al., 2023). At the same time, it is a discrete watchdog of academic integrity that keeps an eye on and detects anything that is academic misconduct. These intelligent systems are generally sophisticated in their algorithms that create the lessons according to one's requirement and thwart cheating to support a beautifully woven and safe environment for learning. In an abstract sense, this combo (fresh educational content, tailored to the audience, and an inherent guard against misconduct) really exemplifies how the AI can transform the learning environment – making it engaging and not what happens in the realm of ethics.

AI's Effects on Academic Integrity

From detection of improper content usage to verification of real originality (the combination of plagiarism protection and fraud protection), academic standards all depend on it — a tangled mix of preventing plagiarism and also of preventing fraud so they lead to ethical standards. Although these two issues seem apart, in practice they reinforce each other to ensure that student work is truly unique. As of late however, artificial intelligence has found its place by offering novel ways to tackle the task of content creation with its recent emergence, however, this base of equilibrium has been disturbed because of the unfortunate possibility artificial intelligence brings along with it of unwanted or even as a possibility intentional plagiarism. According to some, in general, we could say that AI tools can help foster more knowledge on how content is produced (as indicated in (Afroogh et al., 2024), but they are afraid of possible abuses who could confuse authenticity. Thus, institutions must weigh traditional ethical standards against new, innovative practices that create this situation.

Table 4. AI Driver MR Innovation

AI-Driven MR Innovation	Description	Examples	Impact	References
Holographic AI Tutors	AI-powered holographic tutors provide real-time, personalized guidance.	Microsoft HoloLens 2	Adaptive learning, engages students visually, reduces need for one-on-one tutoring	Microsoft (2025), Stanford HCI Lab (2021)
Immersive Historical Reenactments	AI-driven MR allows students to relive historical events in a virtual setting.	TimeLooper, VR history apps	Increases historical empathy, enhances knowledge retention, encourages critical thinking	TimeLooper (2023), Wang et al. (2021)
Virtual Science Labs with AI Safety	AI-powered virtual labs allow students to conduct experiments safely in MR.	Google's Labster, Virtual Chemistry Labs	Eliminates safety risks, AI provides instant feedback, accessible worldwide	Google AI (2022), Harvard (2023)
Real-time Language Translation	AI-driven MR provides real-time translation for multilingual classrooms.	Meta Quest Pro, AI NLP tools	Breaks language barriers, enhances collaboration, improves language learning	Leong, (2024), Meta (2023)
Haptic Feedback for Skill Development	AI-enhanced MR with haptic feedback provides hands-on experience for technical training.	FundamentalVR (surgical training)	Enhances realism in training, reduces errors in high-risk fields, AI-driven skill assessment	Johns Hopkins (2025), FundamentalXR (2025)

AI-POWERED CONTENT GENERATION AND PERSONALIZATION

A revamp in learning is done by AI by automatically generating content that fits each student's individual needs. Its not stuck to a specific formula—instead it harness nifty language tools like Natural Language Processing and Machine Learning, as well as some adaptive algorithms, to whip up the lessons that will grab their interest. For instance, OpenAI with its ChatGPT and GPT 4 platforms, now comes up with tailored lesson plans, full learning modules along with created quizzes. It also benefits educational materials and reduces the load of the teachers Fütterer et al. (2024). As stated, a study from the University of Illinois even says that AI is more effective when it comes to content creation than other traditional teaching methods and the engagement of students with this method increases by an average of 35% at the most (Illinois EdTech Lab, 2022). Considering that the idea is to mix AI with education, it is fair to say that it enables customizing the learning experiences while also that entire learning journey and performance in general (Gligorea et al., 2023).

A wide mix of school materials sprays out from this system—textbooks, assessments, even some multimedia bits that manage to make learning a little more alive. The system changes dynamically showing you different content when you progress. It changes on the fly; the content of course shifts as each student advances on average meaning that what you're looking at just seems right for you. Additionally, there is a nice touch: it is multilingual. It's an arrangement that enables more students across the board to get in; it conveys, if not tongue in cheek, a real commitment to inclusivity. According to some recent studies, these systems might even promote active learning and make a learner more adaptable and creative, a point mentioned in areas such as management where some amount of creativity works well for a person (Leelavathi et al., 2024). Ultimately, this approach not only simplifies the entire educational procedure but also equips students with such an ability that enables them to handle the unpredictable jerks of today's workforce (Chan et al., 2024).

AI-Generated Interactive and Multimedia Learning Resources

Artificial intelligence is transforming the way we learn, even more than we might imagine. Today's educational tools throw lively video clips and immersive simulations with game like interfaces, very often on the fly. One such real example of this shift in action is Knewton (Pearson AI), which provides personalized learning by continuously reviewing student progress and changing the lessons provided in the process (Pearson, 2023). According to Harvard EdTech, research generally shows that interactive content powered by AI can increase student retention by around 40% and this is also the highest for visual or hands on learners (Harvard 2022). Additionally, there has also been a call for evidence based guidelines that will help to ethically integrate such technologies and effectively into classrooms (Chan et al., 2023). In different educational setting, the role of AI is looking very important such that not only can change how students can absorb information but also may change a way how teachers can teach in a new paradigm instead of traditional ways and help to close the gap between traditional education and demanding ways (Alawida et al., 2023).

AI in Plagiarism Detection and Academic Integrity Enforcement

AI is good at generating content and paradoxically, it manages to identify copied content and machine parts as well as contract cheating, which honestly is a serious issue for would be academically honest people. Using smart algorithms they dig in at text patterns, and spot recurring segments — which are trails that generally speaking sometimes will hint to copyright snags. A good example is Turnitin—it goes through submissions to see if a text strikes some machine based tones or some level of similarity to some past work thus prevent plagiarism in schools, colleges making the standards level high . The latter is pretty often presented in recent studies, which say that if you use AI to catch plagiarism, you get not just speed but engage in broader conversations regarding who owns a piece of writing is and what can be considered original work (Qadhi et al., 2024). In general, interdisciplinary engagement of AI tools with the academic ethics shows the need of updating the ethical guidelines perpetually to assist in the intelligent use of AI in higher education (Rudolph et al.,2024).

A study at the Cambridge AI Ethics Lab in 2022 discovered something interesting: when universities, on the other hand, got hands on, academics compliance increased between 50% and this increase helped reduce levels of dishonest work by a noticeable amount. It turns out that overall that matches a fair bit up with wider chatter about the role of AI in education, since so many more conversations about generative AI recently (Bahroun et al., 2023) have similar findings. GAI tech is now making an entry not only to jazz up assessments but also to shape more personalized learning experiences and by and large, load the whole system with a more open and clear-cut approach to teaching (Kamalov F et al., 2023). With each passing day, AI's impact on the education system makes its way out to the open, but it is essential that we see not just the number side of complying to academic standards but also the holistic views reflecting those ethical angles and long run consequences of high jacking the student integrity and entire learning. But when we take all these factors and put them into place, decisionmakers can use its potential without the possible negatives of AI undercutting the benefits, smoothing the bumpy road to AI integration into higher education.

AI-Driven Authorship Verification and Fraud Prevention

Authorship checks rely often on AI that looks at the peculiarities of how something is written and on the technical details of language to test a dodgy academic submission. These systems are used by universities to vet research papers and theses, online test for example, helping to keep academic work trustworthy, said. Crossref is an interesting case with a system based on smart algorithms that can detect modified or fake research . According to Stanford NLP Group, their research shows that these tools are now at around 92 percent accuracy in detecting that a given piece of student work is solid or ghostwritten. Overall speaking, as we watch AI continue to move forward there is a distinct need to shift our methods when it comes to supporting our education system as well as ethical standards, when it comes to stopping authorship fraud.

AI in Real-Time Feedback and Ethical Writing Assistance

Students stay honest thanks to AI that quickly catches mistakes in the citation, mistakes in the original content or messed up ideas. These smart writing tools not only sharpen what a student puts on paper, they also ensure that the work is authentic—the written work has to be done on one's own, because it's not worth the prize if it is not genuine. For example, Grammarly and Scribbr AI, give almost instantaneous feedback, finding any potential plagiarism, strange citation errors and words that are difficult to read . The Journal of Learning Analytics (JLA) study generally shows that making use of AI writing assistants could increase writing quality and reduce unintended plagiarism. The result in this tends to support the notion that AI is an actual asset in education, rather than just a fancy toy (Song et al., 2023), helping the students improve their work, and to remain true to the ethical standards of academic work. Such advances in real time feedback relate to broader debates on how schools should responsibly use AI for learning, where these tools are supposed to augment learning journeys while preserving ethics in the view . Overall, incorporating AI into writing support represents a significant positive move towards the development of both writing skills and ethical learning among learners which promotes thoughtful academicism.

AI TOOLS IN EDUCATION

When you put AI in schools, you aren't just giving them a neat extra, but you really change how students learn. Teaching through its ways is made up of balance and spontaneity as well as attention to making things right. It seems that some research even shows that when they are used, these tools tailor the lessons to the person's need, making the person more engaged, and even enhancing grades using smart tutoring and smart delivery of the content (Bahroun et al., 2023). With good care, institutions can deploy AI to provide powerful benefits, keeping the slipups in check, such as use of computer generated material that could be considered a matter of academic fairness (e.g., Leaver et al., 2023). Generally speaking, the accountable use of artificial intelligence creates an environment that is both creative as well as morally ethically aware in which positive impacts are realized while limiting the likelihood of negative results. This seems necessary, that teachers, administrators, everyone keeps rethinking, refining their AI plans to make learning better, with ethical guidelines kept front and centre.

Table 5. AI-Driven Content Creation and Academic Integrity

AI Application	Description	Examples	Impact	References
AI-Powered Content Generation	AI automates the creation of textbooks, lesson plans, quizzes, and study materials.	OpenAI's ChatGPT, GPT-4, AI-generated lesson plans	Reduces educator workload, enhances accessibility, supports real-time content adaptation	OpenAI (2023), Illinois college of Eduction (2024)
Interactive & Multimedia Learning	AI generates adaptive learning platforms with videos, simulations, and gamification.	Knewton (Pearson AI), AI-driven gamified learning	Increases student engagement, improves retention, personalizes learning experiences	Pearson, Harvard EdTech (2021)
AI-Enhanced Plagiarism Detection	AI tools identify copied, paraphrased, or AI-generated content to uphold academic integrity.	Turnitin AI Detection, Grammarly's plagiarism checker	Ensures originality, detects misconduct, prevents AI-generated fraud	Turnitin (2023), Originality.AI (2025)
AI-Driven Authorship Verification	AI analyzes writing style and metadata to verify authenticity in research papers and online exams.	Crossref's AI authorship tool, Stanford NLP-based verification	Detects contract cheating, strengthens research ethics, prevents impersonation in exams	Borrego, (2023), Stanford NLP Group (n,d)
Real-Time Writing Feedback & Ethical Guidance	AI provides instant feedback on citations, originality, and readability.	Grammarly AI, Scribbr AI	Helps students improve academic writing, reduces unintentional plagiarism, enhances citation accuracy	Grammarly (2024), Rancano, G.(2024)

FUTURE DIRECTIONS AND EMERGING TECHNOLOGIES IN AI FOR EDUCATION

Quantum Computing Applications in Education

Education technology is getting a fresh boost from quantum computing — the technology is promising clear promise for completely reshaping the way we deal with data and solving complex problems, as well as using AI training methods. Related to this is the possibility of getting this method of student data processing to speed up quite a bit once you start integrating this with classical computing and start adding the modern adaptive learning tricks in there, sometimes in really unexpected ways. Three areas that IBM's Quantum AI Lab is focusing on are ways of enhancing overall education systems, customizing learning according to individual's requirements and taking care of complex assessment involving multiple variables. In general, this work shows how Quantum tools can change in academia (IBM,).

According to a Massachusetts Institute of Technology study, the learning speed for quantum boosted AI models is even able to increase adaptive learning speeds by approximately 300% compared to classical systems (Pasupuleti, 2025). Apart from this it means that the education can change dynamically, change the content versus real time performance, and provide a personalized learning experience. With a little thought about the bigger picture, the use of AI powered simulations is greatly enhanced especially in the STEM subjects. And these are the improvements that allow for more interactive, almost immersive modules, so that educators can play around with various teaching strategies. The system supports rapid pattern analysis in the system, therefore, in evaluating the learning of the student quickly and the teacher can adapt according to the diverse needs of the learners (Thangavel et al., 2025).

The implementation of Emotional AI Systems

This emotional AI, or affective computing, means that teachers can experience student emotions in real time and, just as quickly, peek into their commitment, stress and other learning hurdles. Because of its ability to pick up on numerous feelings, educators can develop personalized learning plans, and it catches disengagement before the work is even begun. For example, to make sure that instructors at the University of Cambridge could know how their students are doing in online classes, the school once tested a sort of AI tool that could spot confusion or frustration (Cambridge AI Lab); . In most cases, research in the Journal of Educational Psychology finds that AI tutors with a touch of emotional smarts can really boost student motivation —by up to 40 per cent in online and hybrid setups (Gligorea et al., 2023)

AI-Powered Mixed Reality for Education

Thanks to the advances in AI, modern IT systems are converging parts of VR and AR into what we nowadays call as mixed reality (MR) environments. These are not places to learn to run drills off of a rote memory; rather, it's an opportunity to explore a digital environment while history is highlighted in a live environment in ways you'd never know about otherwise. At times, students are allowed to leap into AI driven Microsoft HoloLens 2 classrooms, utilizing 3D models that are heavy from science and history that in a rather hands on way lead to better mastery of the topic (Microsoft,). Overall, the Stanford XR Lab research concludes that learners in MR classrooms generally retain close to 60% more subject knowledge in STEM subjects than their non MR classmates (Shihab et al., 2023). Finally, all in all, integrating AI into education seems to enhance how well, students remember and understand what they lean, that counts for a huge leap into teaching (Stanford documents).

Brain-Computer Interfaces (BCI) for Learning

The educational interfaces based on the brain signal give people a nice way of improving mental skills and also making learning faster and more custom. For example, these systems, referred to as brain-computer interfaces, are powered by cutting edge AI and process brain signals in real time, and as per the individual's requirements they turn those brain signals into learning materials that cater every individual's need – so, you see, it's so that the learning becomes very personalized. In order to bring this idea to life, fewer pioneers, including Neuralink and Facebook Reality Labs, are operating, such as linking brain signals to educational data and providing instantaneous insights when students are having their sessions . Also pertaining to BCIs, researchers have even proven to Harvard Medical School that BCIs can aid retention of information, specifically in students who experience cognitive challenges, with retention rates typically increasing by as much as 50% (Harvard, 2023). Moving on to the whole immersive twist, the Metaverse combines virtual reality with AI in a very playful (yet effective) dimension, allowing for novel perspectives in the perspective of an educational approach (Chengoden et al., 2023). As such, the combination of brain tech in conjunction with learning appears to be transforming the norm, indicating the means to additional research in the field of educational technology and its innovative implementations (Dwivedi et al., 2022).

Cross-Institutional Learning Networks

Unexpected ways by which AI technology connects both educators and students all over the world are changing. These systems go far beyond merely associating names to the matches of courses, mentors and real-world opportunities to each student based on his unique characteristics. The tech even often draws in data from a combination of universities, research clusters, and any other holes of learning to create an ad hoc network that isn't too fixed or systematic. For example, they should take Coursera's AI Matching. Students have access to top notch educational material all around the world and they are able to receive course suggestions that are in line with their academic aspirations (Coursera). The World Economic Forum's research generally shows that this can boost teamwork by about 70% and in the process lead to deeper knowledge and a type of interdisciplinary insight that is critical to leaning in today (WEF,). At the same time, the notion of cross institutional learning is moving. Gradually, new tech such as generative AI and IoT are getting wedded into the system; and are in fact, playing a key role in nuances of better educational experiences and outcomes .

Table 6. Future Directions and Emerging Technologies in AI for Education

Emerging AI Technology	Description	Examples	Impact	References
Quantum Computing Applications	Quantum AI can optimize learning models, process vast educational data, and enhance adaptive learning.	IBM Quantum AI, MIT's Quantum AI for Education	Real-time curriculum adaptation, faster learning analytics, advanced problem-solving	IBM (2023), MIT (2023)
Emotional AI & Student Well-being	AI detects student emotions (stress, confusion, engagement) and adjusts teaching strategies.	Cambridge AI Lab's emotion recognition tools	Personalized learning, early intervention for mental health support, enhanced student motivation	Cambridge AI Lab (n,d), JEP (2022)
Mixed Reality (MR) Learning Environments	AI-driven MR creates immersive experiences (holographic tutors, VR labs, historical simulations).	Microsoft HoloLens 2, Stanford XR Lab's MR experiments	Engaging learning, hands-on skill training, accessibility to advanced labs	Microsoft (2024), Stanford (n,d)
Brain-Computer Interfaces (BCI)	AI-powered BCIs analyze brain activity to adjust content for better engagement and learning.	Neuralink's BCI for education, Facebook Reality Labs	Hyper-personalized learning, support for cognitive disabilities, direct neural feedback	Parik (2024),)
Cross-Institutional AI Learning Networks	AI connects global students, educators, and research centers for optimized collaboration.	Coursera AI Matching, WEF's AI-driven educational networks	Expands global access to education, interdisciplinary learning, enhanced research partnerships	Sands, E. G (2020), WEF (2024)

THE FUTURE OF AI IN EDUCATION

Educational tech is moving beyond prima facie automation to a the personalized learning, and the creation of rudimentary emotional understanding and a kind of richer interactive set up. Education will likely be a big part of the next wave of changes in quantum AI and emotional AI, and mixed reality (MR) apps, brain-computer interfaces (BCIs), and even at the global level in worldwide learning networks (Keng-Ooi B et al., 2023). At the same time, the potential privacy issues, biases in the AI decision making and roadblocks with regard to access in our schooling systems (Bahroun et al, 2023) are vital aspects that should be scrutinized side by side with all these exciting trends. Schools and universities are sometimes required to implement rigorous policies and adaptable governance structures that permit AI-driven program (Ooi et al., 2025; Bahroun et al., 2023). Through the education perspective, AI serves a promising picture in which it allows for a wide range of people to benefit from tailor made learning, and assists in equalizing the educational playing field (Bahroun et al., 2023).

Innovative Assessment Methods: Evaluating Learning in the AI Era

Tests and exams is now changed with AI. From no longer grading a paper or an answer, today's methods watch learners constantly, measure skills in action and even track learners' progress in absorbing new concepts on a daily basis. This shift includes the immediate feedback and tests those changes on the fly and the practical tools that can help assess what students know. Today, some systems now have artificial intelligence running constant evaluations rather than the periodic tests that may not relate that much to the growth of a student. Several of these continuous approaches involve different forms of learning analytics, and AI is taking a more prominent role in creating closed feedback loops. Taking Open Learning Initiative (OLI), Carnegie Mellon University for instance, they use AI to study student engagement and tweak lessons on the spot (Carnegie Mellon,). Harvard (2022) reports that research from Harvard Graduate School of Education usually shows that such assessments keep and increase student retention rates by about 35% than the traditional exam methods. Daily assessments can make high stakes tests less stressful: They tailor the content immediately to how kids do — a feature that not only helps them learn over the long haul, but keeps the learning active (and, let's face it, more like what you think of as human). Then there's competency-based assessment. Rather than, for instance, testing how long a child sits in class, it tests that a child will have truly learned essential skills. Students do not progress to the next topic until they have proven themselves to be proficient in the previous topic, as we see at Western Governors University (WGU). Even the Journal of Competency-Based Education suggests that using this method could save students' study time and likely speed up the degree process by 38 percent compared to a traditional course structure (JCBE).

Portfolio-Based Evaluation

AI assessments store more than just student records — instead, they package together projects with academic studies and live work that abstracts any fixed formula. These systems observe how students grow — and whether they engage in amusingly unpredictable blending of subjects in the same portfolio — using cunning, occasionally startling algorithms. For instance, digital portfolios based on this technology can monitor not only how well you solve problems but also the speed at which you close on projects at the Massachusetts Institute of Technology

(MIT, 2023) (MIT, 2022). and Prather et al. (2023) show, based on a study, AI driven portfolio assessment can typically provide a more holistic view of student work by 40% in comparison to other traditional exam methods. Overall, this shift towards AI kits with portfolio based on AI Affinity describes one of the trends of adaptive learning approaches in which assessments should incorporate the variety of skills commonly referred to in recent literature (Song et al., 2023).

Continuous Evaluation Systems

Knowing that AI real time powered assessments are taking over to be a substitute for the old manual clunky routine of periodic test, I wouldn't mind it. In order to avoid expressions that would be overused, you can write: Today, schools can use a mix of very fine grained learning data, daily 'checks' of student behaviours, and AI feedback loops to monitor student progress in a way that feels immediate and continuous. For instance, Carnegie Mellon's Open Learning Initiative employs smart system monitoring similar to classroom time for instructors to observe how students do on material and why they may need to spend more or less time on portions of content, and this watch is often made all the quicker through quick content tweaks to meet changing needs (Carnegie Mellon,). Harvard Graduate School of Education also researches that this AI backed ongoing check enhances student retention rates by about 35% than conventional exams (Harvard,). Moreover, other views from recent literature suggest (Kuluşaklı, (2025). that, in general, it seems that continuous assessment methods can actually improve participation in the learning process and increase the engagement of students even when the method employed may not be purposeful each time.

Competency-Based Assessment

The idea of a competency based education system is becoming a possibility as the process of integrating artificial intelligence is happening. AI, in the mix, means students aren't condemned to simply logging hours while they keep their fingers crossed for the opportunity to demonstrate that they've learned something – frequently in ways that more nearly match their own development speed. As far as it is generally speaking, this method of teaching relies on real needs of a single student and does not focus only on his strengths, but on the parts where the man may require more assistance, even though it can also utilize the strengths. According to (Husain, 2024), when learning becomes more personal, it attracts more focus and a certain degree of flexibility which is very important in today's quickly changing educational landscape. More often than not, tailoring such a learning experience not only avoids being outpaced by modern methods but makes education itself more relevant and practical. But, to our surprise, it is actually AI that turns out to play quite an important role here; it's not just a tool, but a game changer that changes the way we teach and that our students' needs will change, and the requirements for the future workforce in the future (Gligorea et al., 2023).

Competency-Based Education

Real education seems fundamental to the teaching of students who thrive by setting their own pace. The whole process changes when learners are able to learn the essential skills at their own pace. For example, Western Governors University has tied AI into a system of checking competencies instead of using these old school grading scales . In other words, they get a chance to show what they really know as opposed to earning a grade. The research noted that, in a vast majority of cases, those utilizing such AI based learning methods complete their degrees almost 28% faster than someone pursuing in a traditional system (Perkins et al., 2024). This organization provides the learners chattiness to study on their own tempo, blending personal touch and contempory techniques. But when it comes to this done by doing school, most often the process of ticking off grades is replaced by the actual mastering topics, which can be much more effective in deepening actual understanding. This innovative method verifies the skills of graduates who tend to come out ready for work, ready for the challenge of today's job market (Ortega-Ochoa et al., 2023). On the other hand, these systems also incorporate some recurring feedback loops that seem to fine tune each student's journey, in line with recent the theories of how creating emotional connection and delivering personalized pointers in learning reflects in learning success.

Assessment Methods

Evaluation methods for AI powered education are robust and play a huge role in the success of AI powered education by establishing a baseline for robust quality of learning and learning outcomes. Assessments can be formative, summative, or adaptive and each has their own merits; they serve to check student progress and how well the curriculum holds up. Most of these systems enable teachers pin data informed insights on to tailor learning that has both engagement and achievement (Kaur et al., 2025). For instance, adaptive assessments alter the difficulty of questions in real time based on how students respond, which is a snazzy approach to prove that AI and a learning system can be wed as something delicate but realistically responsive (Sumartono et al., 2025). With schools beginning to integrate AI into their evaluation mix more and more because of the IoT, understanding how these advanced tools apply to one another plays a pretty big role in producing greater educational outcomes while helping to address the varied needs of learners. In the end, building a complete table of assessment methods not only makes innovations effective, but also provides the base for uninterrupted, sometimes high wave, changes in the role of teaching and learning in the 21st century.

Table 7. Assessment Methods Using AI

Assessment Method	Description	Examples	Impact	References
Continuous Evaluation Systems	AI-powered real-time tracking of student progress, replacing traditional periodic exams.	Carnegie Mellon's Open Learning Initiative (OLI)	Reduces test anxiety, improves knowledge retention, and enables adaptive learning.	Carnegie Mellon (2024), Harvard (2023)
Competency-Based Assessment	Students progress upon mastery rather than fixed timelines, ensuring skill-based learning.	Western Governors University's AI-driven CBE model	Personalized learning speeds, faster degree completion, industry-aligned education.	WGU (n.d),
Portfolio-Based Evaluation	AI tracks student projects, research, and problem-solving for holistic assessment.	MIT's AI-assisted digital portfolios	Encourages creativity, interdisciplinary work, and better university/job applications.	MIT (n.d)
Skill Mastery Tracking	AI monitors micro-skills and competencies, guiding personalized learning.	Duolingo's AI-driven adaptive learning	Identifies strengths, personalizes pathways, and ensures efficient learning.	Duolingo (2023)
Real-World Application Measurement	AI evaluates problem-solving and decision-making in real-world simulations.	Harvard Business School's AI-driven case studies	Enhances workforce readiness, bridges academia-industry gap, improves critical thinking.	HBS (n.d),)

EMERGING TECHNOLOGIES OF AI

The first thing to be explored for quickly changing tech in education is both an unusual and resourceful take. It is not a rigid plan with a fast look at new digital tools with a sort of hands on plan of how to implement AI powered education systems. The resources tie together recent research with real world ideas to provide a set of practical guidelines for the school principal and administrator who, more often than not, are obligated to provide efficiency while promoting ethics. Throughout is repeated tools, frameworks and strategies almost as a refrain, showing that the effective implementation of AI is not just about performance but also delivering to a variety of learner needs . (Opesemowo, 2024). In a broad sense, it forces us to remember in a slightly odd style how putting innovative ideas to work can lead to both ethical puzzles and challenges that are hard to predict.

Integration of Emerging Technologies

The era of such advancements in education is about to start, which promises to make learning experience revolutionary through adapting methods and individualizing the learning to every student. Instead, these innovations combine smart tech like AI and machine learning – those buzzwords you've come to know and love – with practical approaches which quickly sort through data and establish learning path based on the principles of engagement and custom fit. Here it is a mix: of adaptive learning systems personalized to actual time modifications, of tutoring setups that imitate one on one lessons and of AI powered feedback loops which seem to enhance the ways teachers connect with students as well as the ways learners show up, no matter what setting. When incorporating the use of these new tools, educators face some very important ethical issues (data privacy, ensuring all learners, and specifically those that require extra assistance, feel included) as they battle to include them in lessons (Opesemowo, 2024). In its totality, when you view these factors synchronically they are all indicators that infusing fresh technology into education isn't merely support for what we already do, but rather, transforming the way of teaching and expanding the whole arena of learning.

The Role of Quantum Computing in Education

Quantum computers are pretty strong—they are just able to process real time data in a fashion that we have not seen before, on a scale, in things like adaptive learning algorithms (Boixo et al., 2018). On the whole, the power they grant allows educators to go to bat for challenging assignments such as planning course schedules, replaying curriculum minutiae and analyzing learning data (Montanaro, 2016). While quantum computing tends to speed up AI driven simulations, it does give researchers in many instances a bit more precise prediction as to how students learn when they're experimenting with new ways to prevent the knowledge from getting stale while the students learn it (Allioui et al., 2023). Overall, these advancements point towards the changing use of quantum technology for informing the educational scenario by developing a more enriching and interesting learning mechanism.

Bio-Responsive Learning Systems

AI coupled with EEG headsets kicks the process into gear and begins to use neurofeedback to determine how focused someone is and the system adjusts the education material according to the person's needs (Li et al., 2025). Wearable sensors that detect minor changes in heart rate, eye movement, or even some sign of bodily stress have also been used by people and, when you consider it, provide a means of personalizing a learning experience. Especially loaded with emotion reading tools, AI tutors glance at every sign from facial cues, to voice tone, and every kind of biological hint they can detect and, in most cases, they are able to show immediate emotional reassurance as they adjust speed of engagement in real time . In addition to this building a richer and more effective learning environment, in most occasions this kind of back and forth indicates how significant the bio sensitive and biocompatible tech is for tailoring education according to a large part of the population's needs and suggests the potential of bio responsive learning systems to play within our current educational frameworks (Aydin, 2023).

Emotional AI and Its Educational Applications

The capacity to rapidly detect students' emotional states through AI driven sentiment analysis, hence identify weakness of disengagement or increased enthusiasm allows us to adapt the learning strategies on time to time. Similarly, chatbots combined with virtual counselors are looking for signs of stress and burnout and ultimately helping each student with mental wellness just for them . In reality, this forward thinking approach actually unites the vibe of education and emotional health in one classroom. A serious boost, too, is given to feedback, as many AI tools will allow teachers to investigate class interaction by examining nuanced trends in engagement (Demszky et al . 2023). First, these insights nudge instructional methods in the right direction, as well as shape a reduced educational experience in which emotional smarts and academic skills are blended together for better student outcomes .

The Transformative Impact of Mixed Reality Learning Environments

New ways to understand tough ideas flow from mixed reality coupled with AI mentors. Ok, so it isn't just about dry instruction, sometimes you find yourself in recreated historical scenes to which you cannot resist but be drawn into the meteoric historically event no matter how unalive and boring they seem . As Huang et al. (2015) says, these are the bits of knowledge in which you are assured that it will stick in your head just in case you are done reading a textbook. Such virtual and AI run science labs also take another twist in that students can experiment in a safe environment of virtual labs that could not only simulate physical labs but also guide experiments in real time, thus innovating while saving cost . In addition, the tech's natural ability to give live transcription as well as translate speech will remove language barriers making diverse learners chat and collaborate . In general, mixed reality learning space reveals how we can reshape the education into a more dynamic and accessible that can create a revolutionary change in delivering the quality learning, (Malone et al., 2025).

PRACTICAL IMPLEMENTATION FRAMEWORK

This section is a mix of abstract ideas and hands on step by step advice for educators, administrators, and policy makers trying to integrate AI into our daily learning spaces. Those airy, conceptual insights are coupled with clear, if sometimes repetitive, directions educational leaders can use to wend their way through the messy process of merging new tech into classrooms (Limpinan et al., 2025). More often than not, it identifies a course that is reasonably practicable, not just for enhancing the way teaching is carried out but also in taking on the crucial problems and much of the chances that AI may have for education (A Tatnall, 2022). The chapter lays out a series of specific tactics — and, yes, echoes certain of the key ideas — to arm educators with the tools to build a richer, more dynamic learning sphere in which AI actually has a role.

Clear Guidelines for Implementing AI Systems

As Luckin et al. (2016) noted, institutions really need to take a hard look at where their students might be falling short, who makes up faculty in terms of capability, and how well students are understanding what they are learning before rolling out any AI tools. Selecting the right AI system is not simply to select a flexible system that users can easily use; it needs to be an AI system that fits in (Roll & Wylie, 2016) with the many styles of how teachers teach. As Chen et al. (2020) explain in general, that means the best way to get AI to work is to wove these systems into what's already there — your learning management platforms, content hubs, classroom technology — so that, in the end, things don't shut down or break altogether. Additionally, it's critical to establish precise rules for responsible use of generative AI, reconciling the advantages with the ethical problems which could emerge within student–teacher relations as mentioned in (Chan CKY et al., 2023). Liable for making use of new innovations of AI effectively, securing scholarly ethics, and enhancing the learning adventure, such guide can additionally pass to proceed with a direction in a direction that drives in direction of more intimate and pliable homeroom environments that certainly take advantage of what synthetic intelligence can give (Gligorea et al., 2023).

Strategies for Risk Assessment and Mitigation

In order to lock down student information, universities and schools must sync their data safeguards with a few other privacy standards, such as the GDPR, FERPA, and so forth. In the speed of our ever changing digital world, breaches can now very rapidly expose Sensitive details (Selbst et al., 2017; (Alowais et al., 2023), hence this is extremely important to patch those vulnerabilities. Another must is testing AI models with robust bias checks; in many instances, catching discrimination early ensures that AI models give all these groups of students a fair shot at quality learning (Binns, 2018; Owan et al., 2023). Currently AI is no substitute for human educators: AI should serve as the sidekick to them, not take their place, as it still doesn't notice the little emotional and social cues that make a classroom (in both learning and socialization sense). But AI can't spell out all the teaching principles; its real value lies in supporting the old ways of interacting with people – reminding us that at the end of it all, education is about the personal interactions.

Effective Resource Allocation for AI Adoption

In terms of schools, there is a need to chart out a spending plan of investment in AI tech, development of the staff, and projects to expand student access (Renz et al., 2020). Hence, in institutions where positive AI outcomes depend entirely on how well one uses it, a solid AI training to teaching and administrative teams becomes extremely crucial. Equally important is to build a solid digital setup combining these AI tools in an efficient manner right into daily learning and administration (so the schools can really use the AI possibility; (Bočková et al., 2025). Also, AI projects should be tied to clear, measurable goals that reflect their own institutional ambitions and which put each resource in the right place with a sharp focus on student success (Barnes et al., 2024). Taken as a whole, this approach to layered smart money management of AI adoption in education keeps schools nimble, first and foremost, and also able to improve continuously as education continues to evolve.

Metrics for Success and Evaluation Criteria

It can be judged based on three things: performance of students, the extent of participation, and how well information lingers in the time (Chen et al., 2021). For instance, surveys are quite handy. They allow creating AI tools that strive to achieve what educators and users call for. You see, this kind of checking keeps bringing it to our focus that we need to keep modulating these benchmarks and keep the learning system in motion. Become a step absent from this part, where institutions are applauded to customarily study their AI connected costs to spot how those costs impact authorized learning outcomes and each day advancements – a cushioned that is particularly basic for estimating speculations and getting the best esteem out of the tech (Hwang et al., 2020). It is only logical to use all round broad measures, which not only capture immediate impact in a class room but also look at long term and measurable aspects of development (Hassija et al., 2023). By all means, the amalgamation of these distinct evaluation methods can certainly bring enlightenment on whether AI is realised in the right manner or not in our educational context.

CONCLUSION

There is no doubt now that we are in a new era where I-powered learning tools are pushing us into something that combines huge promise with a healthy dose of hurdles, shaping our education future in ways we're just coming to know. For instance, as leaders in the education sector, they need to embrace this change, making smart, well thought out choices for the use of AI, while also thinking about the ethics so that the improvements build on it, rather than replacing the old instructional methods (Leaver). This chapter goes into the details of how AI will be used in schools with both theory and practical applications. Its focus is on benefits, the tricky challenges that rise up, and it even includes some practical tips about how to make AI work for education . On balance, the discussion interweaves solid research with the business of practice, providing others ready if not impecable, stream of insights for folding AI into their teaching approaches. The result? This should be a smoother, richer learning experience that also assumes the role of looking for those ethical dilemmas that sometimes come up .

KEY TAKEAWAYS

AI is quietly making itself an enabler of personalized and adaptive learning that matches the style of every student, engages way more, and lets them easily grasp the idea (Dewi et al., 2023). Instead of monotone and uniform courses, these high tech platforms provide almost instantaneous feedback to assist students in sorting out their learning hurdles more efficiently and may even include automated nudges . Digital learning tools driven by AI frequently assist with bridging education gaps, especially ones that are difficult to span. They often break the barriers of remote or under resourced students from accessing good instruction (Dewi et al., 2023). These systems ensure that, blended in, is language translation, speech recognition, and many assistive features, so that there will be support for the learners in all their different backgrounds and abilities. On occasion the flow might seem a bit off beat, but it truly is a big boost to greater equity. But all these encouraging developments come with several challenges and ethical issues to attend to. The hazy and imperfect ethical workplace aspects of this situation must be considered, generally speaking, as smarter learning solutions then become the norm

Long-Term Achievement

Companies will need to implement strategic rollout plans in order to gain and sustain the competitive advantage. Bringing AI into play in schools isn't a clean, linear process; it starts with trying loads of new AI tricks and then flowing into many training sessions over long periods until teachers really understand how these systems work. Trainers, students, even the administrative staff, everyone does here. In general, the collaboration always between AI developers, educators and policy-makers sometimes results in drawing ethical rules and testing the systems over and over to ensure they fit properly in educational settings. According to recent studies (Bahroun et al., 2023), (Chan et al., 2023), such, hands-on approach also increases the possibility of sustained success while also constructing a more customized learning experience to complement what already is the education structure. In most cases, this is a collaborative, somewhat messy and chaotic due effort that actually fits into the needs of today's classroom, and more often than not prepares teachers and students in the midst of it for whatever the ever changing tech scene throws our way, and makes our school initiatives worthwhile in the long run.

Future Outlook

Soon education is about to take a twist, you might soon find that virtual reality, augmented reality, even mixed reality will be mixed with smart AI to create the best sort of hands on learning experience . The 'flashy tech' is not the whole deal, envision well being programs which team up with programs which monitor how you feel, a moody tracker, as they say of how student health and wellness is checked (Wei et al ., 2024). both students and teachers will occasionally do so across different schools in a global AI network and create unexpected communities that eliminate traditional borders . However, when it comes to testing, these same rules might change, as AI driven assessments could demonstrate real world problem solving and practical understanding – things covered and captured that standardized tests routinely fail .

FINAL THOUGHTS

In schools, AI is a genuine help, not a substitute for teachers. It helps subordinate sub lessons and aid in the admin work of teaching and it helps students to get better results. 'Normally when you're getting AI into the mix it's a very careful, sometimes messy, process, it's something that you have to deal with ethical issues of, it's trying to keep pace with tech developments that are moving very quickly,' says Ooi B et al. (2023). Schools that use AI correctly transform into modern, dynamic learning venues for the purposes of both academic trajectories and personal development through creative, individually designed programs (Michel-Villarreal et al., 2023). In most cases, a shift towards a trend that is more interactive and responsive in nature to learning points to a tendency that how a class of everyday insight along with technical know how can really make a difference.

Unique Contributions of This Chapter

This chapter discusses how new technologies, especially his new term of 'AI', are shaping education in unanticipated ways, creating opportunities and solving questions surrounding its integration. Rather than merely listing challenges, it casually lays out a practical guide to walking an actual path to improved education practices via AI powered learning system (a roadmap to set up AI powered learning systems basically). In this part, fresh, cutting-edge research is brought together with insights from earlier works (from the findings of the role that generative AI plays as a game changer in different educational settings (Naqbi et al., 2024) to constitute useful patchwork resource for educators, policymakers and administrators. Most times these groups are finding themselves meandering through this complex, at times messy unknown garden that AI has thrown them into, as evidenced by what we see in today's movement of changing AI applications and altering classroom methods (Prather et al., 2023). All in all, the chapter points out, in its own meandering way, the distinct contributions AI can offer – from boosting learning outcomes to opening up fairer opportunities in a variety of settings.

Accelerated AI Models

Pairing quantum computing with AI dominated simulations really soars. Together, the combination allows models to quickly run through enormous datasets and, usually, improve their capacity to predict how much students absorbed of the material . Legacy AI systems receive quantum tech boost to kick the computational muscle, trimming for trending student engagement that was impossible before . These analyses could eventually make adjustment to teaching behaviour — on the fly — seem compelling to educators given the patterns in learning behaviour they reveal. Usually, mixing AI along with quantum computing can radically alter educational practices; it makes a combination between old and new time-honoured teaching techniques . This synergy here offers an exciting new way to teach: setting the scene for active learning and deep learning creates the roads to better academic performance. Ultimately, by using these advanced AI models, a more personalized learning experience could be obtained, which would enhance individual outcomes, which are a very important considering that we are experiencing rapid changes in the technological world. In the long run, these advanced AI models could be used to have a more personalized learning experience and thus maximize the individual outcomes—a necessity with our technological landscape as it is improving at lighting speed.

Integration With Existing Infrastructure

Making education with artificial intelligence is not just about installing new technology but inserting a new piece into the existing mechanism. There are two things that schools need from their classroom tools, digital content archives, and their LMS so that those things 'talk' to each other; so to speak (Chen et al., 2020) and that doesn't happen by accident (Ooi et al., 2023). This type of integration helps ensuring a smooth interaction of the whole educational setup as well as enhancing the delivery of lessons. From the general perspective of how fast generative AI is evolving, schools and universities are pushed to review their existing technological frameworks, allowing new opportunities as well as academic values (Michel-Villarreal et al., 2023). Additionally, when educators let these systems freely share information, even if it's about changing the way they did things, they are more likely to find themselves in interesting, more innovative, and more engaging learning spaces (Ooi et al, 2025). Consequently, strategic planning becomes of necessity as it takes care of the messiness of the 'AI tech + established digital infrastructures' which makes for a tough process to merge, and thus build an even stronger education mission (Chen et al., 2020).

STRATEGIES FOR RISK ASSESSMENT AND MITIGATION

Data Privacy and Security Compliance

Using AI in education means having a careful, all-around plan that adheres to real world rules, such as the General Data Protection Regulation (GDPR) and the Family Educational Rights and Privacy Act (FERPA), very important factors in keeping student sensitive information secure (Selbst et al., 2017). In addition to legal responsibility these rules create a relationship of trust with students and teachers, for most of the cases they prescribe exactly how personal educational details are collected, stored and managed (Layode et al., 2024). Failure to comply with such standards by schools would lead to legal and reputational problems, which will hinder the educational benefits that AI is claimed to bring (Mustikawati et al., 2024). However, as tech continues to lace itself into classrooms, maintaining a firm grip on the importance of data privacy is important so as not to achieve AI innovative perks by sacrificing individual rights and good data practices (Layode et al., 2024).

Bias and Fairness Auditing

AI models are put through quite a bit of testing to and find any hidden bias that could mess up every kid's right to learn. That bias is able to get in and change the output in school outcomes, and maintain the inequalities (Binns, 2018). We have to set up fairness audits (a mixture of hands-on reviews on how AI decides something in a classroom, most of the times checking on both the positive and the pitfalls) (Ivanov et al., 2024). Those who weigh out what works and what does not with these tools tend to see clearer pictures of the risks and rewards in these tools, more preferably nudging our education spaces become more welcoming for all learners (Ayeni et al., 2024). Binns (2018) points out that in order to take a proactive stance in spotting and fixing these issues it is not just about tech, but retaining value of equity and justice in our schools as well. That's why we keep working on these bias and fairness checks to the extent that the itself of AI can be a very positive element in the education space..

Minimizing Over-Reliance on AI

AI in classrooms is a noticeable boost to education, but one must keep in mind that technology alike should act as a supplementary, rather than a core, factor to enhance the genuine care of teachers that foster deep emotional and social bonds (Holmes et al., 2021). According to generally accepted studies, real life interaction is critical to critical thinking and social skills, and those smarter than our machines are a hard thing to create (Walter, 2024). As kids delve deeper into custom made AI lessons, the problem is that they are learning to rely too much on such systems and in some cases it may be robbing them of the opportunity to build up personal skills (Yenduri et al., 2024). But teachers are still out on the front lines, guiding the monolingual learner slowly, gently, between the old and the new; introducing the tech tools carefully, in balance, thoughtfully (Walter, 2024). Schools that manage to guard this mix, shelter both the true spirit of learning and the likes of empathy, teamwork, and mentorship along with new tech trends (Holmes et al., 2021). Overall, although this forward thinking blend, with its flaws, possesses the potential to establish a broader comprehensive educational system that views AI more as an assistant instead of a replacement, more importantly, one that takes into account the potential and shortcomings of AI and respects the special contribution of the human teacher to the student's development; and to take advantage of these ideas in the future.

EFFECTIVE RESOURCE ALLOCATION FOR AI ADOPTION

Budget Planning

Many schools today face the challenge of needing to hand out solid training for teachers and give fair access to students today — even as they spend money by buying cool new AI tools (Renz et al., 2020). Popping up everywhere—from the classroom to the background—AI aims to make school teaching and running of schools' smoother. Indeed, if the funding is not monitored closely, these gadgets might inadvertently contribute to the widening of the socio-economic gap between students (Ooi et al., 2023) But this is not the only payday of new challenges: how do personalized learning and smart tutoring benefit from generative AI, which does not seem to slow down (Kamalov et al., 2023)? Externalities beget externalities, and the end result is a successful budget plan that pays for the latest AI gizmos (and persuades parents to pay for the right bandwidth), but also sets aside adequate monies for comprehensive teacher training so that all students will get their share of the benefit of these new innovations.

AI Training for Educators

Focusing on recent studies that emphasize the need for professional development (Zawacki-Richter et al., 2019), it is shown that teachers and school administrators really need to keep up with new tech. Most of the time, because AI in classrooms is quite evolving so fast, teachers are then given the burden of learning both how these tools work and what the deeper teaching effect will be (Gligorea et al., 2023). In my opinion, without mixing AI into everyday teaching what we have is just a mere limited educational experience (Ooi B et al., 2025). With generative AI changing the way that personalized learning occurs so swiftly, it has become quite apparent that training for teachers has to be targeted in order for these tools to actually work well and end up helping students (Zawacki Richter et al., 2019). In general words, continuous professional development in terms of AI literacy should be a positive addend as opposed to a necessity for instructors who are searching for elevating student engagement and reports (Gligorea et al., 2023).

Infrastructure Readiness

For successful rollout of AI driven tools for learning, schools require a strong digital backbone to support them. By upgrading the setup of your classroom you will have fast internet, reliable cloud services, and interactive devices (Luckin, 2017) doing so means more than replacing old technology, it is the basis for learning that is relevant to each student. According to recent reviews, recent reviews generally show that adaptive systems rely heavily on such key components to enable AI to caters to individual learning needs (Bond M et al., 2024). In most cases, the right digital components can add to student engagement and retention and provide the teachers useful data for piloting their methods (Luckin, 2017). In fact, school premises with strong general infrastructure even suggest better student performance (Gligorea et al., 2023). Basically, investing in this sort of tech setup is not a side note, it is a must do strategic play if schools want to be able to keep up with the always changing upshot concerning AI in education.

Learning Outcome Improvements

When it comes to AI in schools, many things get checked, including how much students themselves score, how engaged with schoolwork they are, and how good what they are taught is kept in mind. Continually, research is indicating that employing generative AI promotes personalized learning (Ooi et al., 2023), bringing about an environment wherein students are drawn in more profoundly and have more noteworthy outcomes in general. However, the most recent studies in many of these cases also indicate that in some way teachers can depend on AI to design tailored assessments for various learning forms, thus preparing an atmosphere that promotes long term retention (Bahroun et al., 2023). By leaving schools to examine these bits more casually yet thoroughly, then they can really tease out what AI does; They don't just pump-up grades but they keep in line with other teaching goals and ethical line as well. Overall, redefining this check as this kind of mixed up overlapping check when it comes to using AI is what helps in setting up a systematic if not always ordered framework to understand and improve the experience of the students' learning journey .

Teacher and Student Satisfaction Surveys

Education plays a big role in feedback. As Baker and Inventado (2014) note, it ensures that AI systems follow the goals of schools as a whole and the requirements of individual teachers and students. An effective method to assess if the teaching methods are working and what needs to be improved is through surveys of satisfaction, both carried out by teachers and by the students . As long as schools allow themselves the time to sort through all of this feedback, the schools themselves become much smarter sources of feedback from both schools and learners and are better able to make choices grounded in what it is that learners and educators actually say about what is right for the learning process (Brennan et al., 2004). However, these institutions can lean on insights from such surveys and cook up strategies that not just augment the learning experience, but also ensure the tech they use remains to be flexible and react with what the users need in specific . With that, opinions from both sides of the classroom are offset, and education leaders get the opportunity to experiment and implement teaching styles and practices that improve student outcomes on a massive level (Brennan et al., 2004). All in all, this method of feedback must keep in mind that checking in and updating is crucial to keep the teachers and students' voices talking about modern education.

Cost-Benefit Analysis

t some point, schools must take a fresh look at how much they spent on AI and how that expense played out when it came to learning for students and operating for the schools (Hwang et al., 2020). Unlike numerical calculations alone, these reviews give a sneak peak on the true ROI which has more significant relevance as new perceptions about AI keep springing up in the educational circles. As Kamalov et al., (2023) says, quite a few times, are sayings by people, the fact that when AI is set up with care, it actually increases the overall learning experience. Nevertheless, it is worth appreciating that the same technologies could also be a bit challenging in academic integrity, and maybe prone to bias (Rasul et al., 2023). For the most part, the cost benefit doesn't just involve money, but also how these systems influence learning outcomes, manage the teacher workload, and line up with large system objectives (Hwang et al., 2020). In the end, it allows schools to keep a watch on all of these pieces, and align spending with true progress in teaching and student success in an elusive academic future.

REFERENCES

Afroogh, S., Atkinson, D., Chen, K., & Dhurandhar, A. (2024). The global landscape of academic guidelines for generative AI and large language models. *arXiv preprint*. http://arxiv.org/abs/2406.18842

Al Naqbi, H., Bahroun, Z., & Ahmed, V. (2024). Enhancing work productivity through generative artificial intelligence: A comprehensive literature review. *Sustainability*, *16*(3), 1166. DOI: 10.3390/su16031166

Alawida, M., Mejri, S., Mehmood, A., Chikhaoui, B., & Abiodun, O. I. (2023). A comprehensive study of ChatGPT: Advancements, limitations, and ethical considerations in natural language processing and cybersecurity. *Information (Basel)*, *14*(8), 462. DOI: 10.3390/info14080462

Allioui, H., & Mourdi, Y. (2023). Exploring the full potentials of IoT for better financial growth and stability: A comprehensive survey. *Sensors (Basel)*, *23*(19), 8015. DOI: 10.3390/s23198015

Alowais, S. A., Alghamdi, S. S., Alsuhebany, N., Alqahtani, T., Alshaya, A., Almohareb, S. N., Aldairem, A., Alrashed, M., Bin Saleh, K., Badreldin, H. A., Al Yami, M. S., Al Harbi, S. A., & Albekairy, A. M. (2023). Revolutionizing healthcare: The role of artificial intelligence in clinical practice. *BMC Medical Education*, *23*, 689. DOI: 10.1186/s12909-023-04698-z

Aydin, L. (2023). A review of the current state of bioprinting technology. *MedLiber Regenerative Medicine*, *1*(123), 23–43.

Ayeni, O. O., Al Hamad, N. M., Chisom, O. N., Osawaru, B., & Adewusi, O. E. (2024). AI in education: A review of personalized learning and educational technology. *GSC Advanced Research and Reviews*, *18*(2), 261–271. DOI: 10.30574/gscarr.2024.18.2.0062

Bahroun, Z., Anane, C., Ahmed, V., & Zacca, A. (2023). Transforming education: A comprehensive review of generative artificial intelligence in educational settings through bibliometric and content analysis. *Sustainability*, *15*(17), 12983. DOI: 10.3390/su151712983

Baker, R. S., & Inventado, P. B. (2014). Educational data mining and learning analytics. In Lárusson, J. A., & White, B. (Eds.), *Learning Analytics: From Research to Practice* (pp. 61–75). Springer. DOI: 10.1007/978-1-4614-3305-7_4

Balalle, H., & Pannilage, S. (2025). Reassessing academic integrity in the age of AI: A systematic literature review on AI and academic integrity. *Social Sciences & Humanities Open, 11*, 101299. DOI: 10.1016/j.ssaho.2025.101299

Balfour, S. P. (2013). Assessing writing in MOOCs: Automated essay scoring and Calibrated Peer Review™. *Research & Practice in Assessment, 8*, 40–48.

Barger, V. A., Chennamaneni, P. R., Dahl, A. J., & Peltier, J. W. (2024). A How-To-Guide For Bringing Artificial Intelligence Into Life In Your Marketing Curriculum: A Blueprint For Student Learning And Success. *Marketing Education Review, 35*(2), 99–108. DOI: 10.1080/10528008.2024.2430259

Barnes, E., Hutson, J., & Perry, K. (2024). Enhancing adult learner success in higher education through decision tree models: A machine learning approach. In *Forum for Education Studies* (Vol. 2, No. 3).

Binns, R. (2018). Fairness in machine learning: Lessons from political philosophy. In S. A. Friedler & C. Wilson (Eds.), *Proceedings of the 1st Conference on Fairness, Accountability and Transparency* (pp. 149-159). PMLR. https://proceedings.mlr.press/v81/binns18a.html.

Bočková, K., Procházka, D. A., & Bartoš, P. (2025). The role of artificial intelligence in managing scientific research projects funded by KEGA and VEGA grant schemes. *Journal of Ecohumanism, 4*(1), 1448–1476.

Boixo, S., Isakov, S. V., Smelyanskiy, V. N., Babbush, R., Ding, N., Jiang, Z., Bremner, M. J., Martinis, J. M., & Neven, H. (2018). Characterizing quantum supremacy in near-term devices. *Nature Physics, 14*(6), 595–600. DOI: 10.1038/s41567-018-0124-x

Bond, M., Khosravi, H., de Laat, M., Bergdahl, N., Negrea, V., Oxley, E., Pham, P., Chong, S. W., Siemens, G., Gašević, D., & Rienties, B. (2024). A meta-systematic review of artificial intelligence in higher education: A call for increased ethics, collaboration, and rigor. *International Journal of Educational Technology in Higher Education, 21*, 26. DOI: 10.1186/s41239-023-00436-z

Borrego, Á., Ardanuy, J., & Arguimbau, L. (2023). Crossref as a bibliographic discovery tool in the arts and humanities. *Quantitative Science Studies, 4*(1), 91–104. DOI: 10.1162/qss_a_00240

Brennan, R. L. (2004). *Generalizability theory*. Springer.

Carnegie Mellon University. (n.d.). *Open Learning Initiative*. The Simon Initiative. https://www.cmu.edu/simon/open-simon/toolkit/tools/learning-tools/oli.html

Chan, C. K. Y., & Colloton, T. (2024). *Generative AI in higher education*. Routledge. DOI: 10.4324/9781003459026

Chan, C. K. Y., & Hu, W. (2023). Students' voices on generative AI: Perceptions, benefits, and challenges in higher education. *International Journal of Educational Technology in Higher Education*, *20*, 43. DOI: 10.1186/s41239-023-00411-8

Chan, C. K. Y., & Lee, K. K. W. (2023). The AI generation gap: Are Gen Z students more interested in adopting generative AI such as ChatGPT in teaching and learning than their Gen X and millennial generation teachers? *Smart Learning Environments*, *10*, 25. DOI: 10.1186/s40561-023-00269-3

Chen, L., Chen, P., & Lin, Z. (2020). Artificial intelligence in education: A review. *IEEE Access : Practical Innovations, Open Solutions*, *8*, 75264–75278.

Cheng, N., Broadbent, G., & Chappell, W. (2025, August). *Cognitive loop via in-situ optimization: Self-adaptive reasoning for science*. Microsoft Research. https://www.microsoft.com/en-us/research/publication/cognitive-loop-via-in-situ-optimization-self-adaptive-reasoning-for-science/

Chengoden, R., Victor, N., Huynh-The, T., Yenduri, G., Jhaveri, R. H., Alazab, M., Bhattacharya, S., Hegde, P., Maddikunta, P. K. R., & Gadekallu, T. R. (2023). Metaverse for healthcare: A survey on potential applications, challenges, and future directions. *IEEE Access : Practical Innovations, Open Solutions*, *11*, 12765–12795. DOI: 10.1109/access.2023.3241628

Cooper, G. (2023). Examining science education in ChatGPT: An exploratory study of generative artificial intelligence. *Journal of Science Education and Technology*, *32*(4), 444–452. DOI: 10.1007/s10956-023-10039-y

Damaševičius, R., & Sidekerskienė, T. (2024). Virtual worlds for learning in metaverse: A narrative review. *Sustainability*, *16*(5), 2032. DOI: 10.3390/su16052032

Demszky, D., Liu, J., Hill, H. C., Jurafsky, D., & Piech, C. (2023). Can automated feedback improve teachers' uptake of student ideas? Evidence from a randomized controlled trial in a large-scale online course. *Educational Evaluation and Policy Analysis*, *45*(2), 293–317. DOI: 10.3102/01623737231169270

Dewi, N. P. J. L., Moybeka, A. M. S., Mushthoza, D. A., & Syariatin. (2023). Artificial intelligence and English classroom: The implications of AI toward EFL students' motivation. *Research Gate*. https://core.ac.uk/download/588483975.pdf

Dritsas, E., & Trigka, M. (2025). Methodological and technological advancements in e-learning. *Information (Basel)*, *16*(1), 48.

Dunn, S. (2023). *The era of quantum AI: A new dawn for data science*. IBM Community. https://community.ibm.com/community/user/blogs/scott-dunn/2023/04/27/the-era-of-quantum-ai-a-new-dawn-for-data-science

Duolingo. (2023). *Duolingo Max uses OpenAI's GPT-4 for new learning features*. Duolingo Blog. https://blog.duolingo.com/duolingo-max/

Dwivedi, Y. K., Hughes, L., Clark, E., Rana, N. P., Kumar, V., & Das, A. P. (2022). Metaverse: A new realm of the internet. *International Journal of Information Management*, *66*, 102548.

Dwivedi, Y. K., Hughes, L., Wang, Y., Alalwan, A. A., Ahn, S. J., Balakrishnan, J., Barta, S., Belk, R., Berger, B., Bojovic, S., Chau, K. W., Chen, L., Davison, R. M., Diba, H., Harrigan, P., Heikkilä, M., Hoehle, H., Hughes, D. L., Ismagilova, E., & Williams, M. D. (2022). Metaverse marketing: How the metaverse will shape the future of consumer research and practice. *Psychology and Marketing*, *40*(3), 750–776. DOI: 10.1002/mar.21767

Familoni, B. T., & Onyebuchi, N. C. (2024). Augmented and virtual reality in U.S. education: A review: Analyzing the impact, effectiveness, and future prospects of AR/VR tools in enhancing learning experiences. *International Journal of Applied Research in Social Sciences*, *6*(4), 642–663. DOI: 10.51594/ijarss.v6i4.1043

Feijo, S., & Ouellette, K. (2023). *What will the future of education look like in a world with generative AI?* MIT Open Learning. https://openlearning.mit.edu/news/what-will-future-education-look-world-generative-ai

Fundamental, X. R. (2025). *Immersive technology to accelerate human excellence*. https://www.fundamentalxr.com/

Fütterer, T., Fischer, C., Alekseeva, A., Chen, X., Tate, T., Warschauer, M., & Gerjets, P. (2023). ChatGPT in education: Global reactions to AI innovations. *Scientific Reports*, *13*, 15310. DOI: 10.1038/s41598-023-42227-6

Gartner. (2024). Understand and exploit generative AI with Gartner's new Impact Radar. https://www.gartner.com/en/articles/understand-and-exploit-gen-ai-with-gartner-s-new-impact-radar

Gartner. (n.d.). Career pathing should be like satellite navigation. https://www.gartner.com/en/human-resources/trends/career-pathing-should-be-like-satellite-navigation

Gligorea, I., Cioca, M., Oancea, R., Gorski, A. T., Gorski, H., & Tudorache, P. (2023). Adaptive learning using artificial intelligence in e-learning: A literature review. *Education Sciences*, *13*(12), 1216. DOI: 10.3390/educsci13121216

Gong, J., Han, T., Guo, S., Li, J., Zha, S., Zhang, L., Tian, F., Wang, Q., & Rui, Y. (2021). HoloBoard: A large-format immersive teaching board based on pseudo HoloGraphics. In *Proceedings of the 34th Annual ACM Symposium on User Interface Software and Technology (UIST 2021)* (pp. 441–456). ACM. https://doi.org/DOI: 10.1145/3472749.3474761

Google. (n.d.). Google certified courses online | Grow with Google India. https://grow.google/intl/en_in/certificates

Google AI. (2022). *2022 AI Principles Progress

Grammarly. (2024, May 7). *What is AI? Artificial intelligence explained*. Grammarly Blog. https://www.grammarly.com/blog/ai/what-is-ai/

Habibzadeh, F. (2023). GPTZero performance in identifying artificial intelligence-generated medical texts: A preliminary study. *Journal of Korean Medical Science*, *38*(38). Advance online publication. DOI: 10.3346/jkms.2023.38.e319

Harvard Business Publishing. (n.d.). *Applications of artificial intelligence and machine learning*. Harvard Business Publishing Education. https://hbsp.harvard.edu/catalog/collections/applications-of-ai-and-machine-learning

Harvard Business School Digital Initiative. (2021.). *Knewton personalizes learning with the power of AI*. Harvard Business School. https://d3.harvard.edu/platform-digit/submission/knewton-personalizes-learning-with-the-power-of-ai/

Hassija, V., Chamola, V., Mahapatra, A., Singal, A., Goel, D., Huang, K., Scardapane, S., Spinelli, I., Mahmud, M., & Hussain, A. (2023). Interpreting black-box models: A review on explainable artificial intelligence. *Cognitive Computation*, *16*(1), 45–74. DOI: 10.1007/s12559-023-10179-8

Hirani, R., Noruzi, K., Khuram, H., Hussaini, A. S., Aifuwa, E., Ely, K., Lewis, J. M., Zakrzewski, J., Donner, B., Boucher, J., & Kassab, K. (2024). Artificial intelligence and healthcare: A journey through history, present innovations, and future possibilities. *Life (Chicago, Ill.)*, *14*(5), 557. DOI: 10.3390/life14050557

HireVue. (n.d.). Knowledge Center. https://www.hirevue.com/knowledge-center

Holmes, W., Bialik, M., & Fadel, C. (2021). *Artificial intelligence in education: Promises and implications for teaching and learning*. Center for Curriculum Redesign.

Holmes, W., Iniesto, F., Anastopoulou, S., & Boticario, J. (2023). Stakeholder Perspectives on the Ethics of AI in Distance-Based Higher Education. *International Review of Research in Open and Distance Learning*, *24*, 96–117. DOI: 10.19173/irrodl.v24i2.6089

Husain, A. (2024). Potentials of ChatGPT in computer programming: Insights from programming instructors. *Journal of Information Technology Education: Research, 23*, 002. https://doi.org/DOI: 10.28945/5240

Hwang, G. J., Xie, H., Wah, B. W., & Gašević, D. (2020). Vision, challenges, roles and research issues of Artificial Intelligence in Education. *Computers and Education: Artificial Intelligence*, *1*, 100001. Advance online publication. DOI: 10.1016/j.caeai.2020.100001

Ivanov, S., Soliman, M., Tuomi, A., Alkathiri, N. A., & Al-Alawi, A. N. (2024). Drivers of generative AI adoption in higher education through the lens of the Theory of Planned Behavior. *Technology in Society*, *77*, 102521. DOI: 10.1016/j.techsoc.2024.102521

Jabbour, J., Kleinbard, K., Miller, O., Haussman, R. C., & Reddi, V. (2025). SocratiQ: A generative AI-powered learning companion for personalized education and broader accessibility. *arXiv preprint, abs/2502.00341*.

Johnston, H., Wells, R., Shanks, E., Boey, T., & Parsons, B. (2024). Student perspectives on the use of generative artificial intelligence technologies in higher education. *International Journal for Educational Integrity*, *20*(2), 1–21. DOI: 10.1007/s40979-024-00149-4

Kaliisa, R., & Dolonen, J. A. (2022). CADA: a teacher-facing learning analytics dashboard to foster teachers' awareness of students' participation and discourse patterns in online discussions. *Technology, Knowledge and Learning*, 1–22. Advance online publication. DOI: 10.1007/s10758-022-09598-7

Kamalov, F., Santandreu Calonge, D., & Gurrib, I. (2023). New era of artificial intelligence in education: Towards a sustainable multifaceted revolution. *Sustainability*, *15*(16), 12451. DOI: 10.3390/su151612451

Kestin, G., Miller, K., & Klales, A. (2025). AI tutoring outperforms in-class active learning: An RCT introducing a novel research-based design in an authentic educational setting. *Scientific Reports*, *15*, 17458. DOI: 10.1038/s41598-025-97652-6

Kourtesis, P. (2024). A comprehensive review of multimodal XR applications, risks, and ethical challenges in the metaverse. *Multimodal Technologies and Interaction*, *8*(11), 98. DOI: 10.3390/mti8110098

Kuluşaklı, E. (2025). Student Engagement and Flexibility in Distance Learning in Higher Education. *SAGE Open, 15*(1). (Original work published 2025).DOI: 10.1177/21582440251329979

Layode, O., Ndidi, H. N., Adeleke, G. S., Udeh, E. O., & Labake, T. T. (2024). Data privacy and security challenges in environmental research: Approaches to safeguarding sensitive information. *International Journal of Applied Research in Social Sciences*, *6*(8), 1087–1098.

Leaver, T., & Srdarov, S. (2023). ChatGPT isn't magic. *M/C Journal, 26*(5). DOI: 10.5204/mcj.3004

Leelavathi, R., & Surendhranatha, R. C. (2024). ChatGPT in the classroom: Navigating the generative AI wave in management education. *Journal of Research in Innovative Teaching & Learning*, *17*(3), 402–418. DOI: 10.1108/jrit-01-2024-0017

Leong, J., Pataranutaporn, P., Danry, V., Perteneder, F., Mao, Y., & Maes, P. (2024). Putting things into context: Generative AI-enabled context personalization for vocabulary learning improves learning motivation. In *Proceedings of the CHI Conference on Human Factors in Computing Systems* (CHI '24), May 11–16, 2024, Honolulu, HI, USA (pp. 1–15). ACM. DOI: 10.1145/3544548.3581039

Li, Y., Tian, C., Xu, L., Pei, L., Huang, X., & Wang, X. (2025). EEG-Guided Adaptive Learning: A New Neuroeducational Approach to the Facilitation of Cognitive Control in ADHD Children. *Child: Care, Health and Development*, *51*(4), e70113. DOI: 10.1111/cch.70113

Limpinan, P., Yindeemak, A., Pasmala, R., Nammanee, M., & Jantakoon, T. (2025). A bibliometric analysis of artificial intelligence for multimedia in education by dimensions AI. *Higher Education Studies*, *15*(1), 12–28.

Lokam, G. V., Patil, P. S., Kukade, A. S., Dhule, A. N., & Kothiwale, R. A. (2025). AI-based career guidance system. *International Journal of Creative Research Thoughts*, *13*(5), 1–6. https://www.ijcrt.org/papers/IJCRT2505326.pdf

Luckin, R., Holmes, W., Griffiths, M., & Forcier, L. B. (2018). *Machine learning and human intelligence: The future of education for the 21st century*. UCL Institute of Education Press.

Maleki Varnosfaderani, S., & Forouzanfar, M. (2024). The role of AI in hospitals and clinics: Transforming healthcare in the 21st century. *Bioengineering (Basel, Switzerland)*, *11*(4), 337. DOI: 10.3390/bioengineering11040337

Malone, B. (2025). *Ethical considerations in instructional design enhanced by artificial intelligence: A phenomenological inquiry*. Appalachian State University Digital Collections.

Maloy, R. W., Verock-O'Loughlin, R.-E. A., Edwards, S. A., Trust, T., & Woolf, B. P. (2021). *Transforming learning with new technologies* (4th ed.). Pearson.

Manyika, J., Lund, S., Chui, M., Bughin, J., Woetzel, J., Batra, P., Sanghvi, S., Ko, R., & Saurabh, S. (2017). *Jobs lost, jobs gained: Workforce transitions in a time of automation* (McKinsey Global Institute)*. McKinsey & Company.

Massachusetts Institute of Technology. (n.d.). *Creative portfolios*. MIT Admissions. https://mitadmissions.org/apply/firstyear/portfolios-additional-material/

Mehlan, R., Hess, C., Stierstorfer, Q., & Schaaff, K. (2025). Personalized knowledge transfer through generative AI: Contextualizing learning to individual career goals. *arXiv*. /arXiv.2508.04070.DOI: 10.48550

Meotti, M., & Magliozzi, D. (2023,). *Using artificial intelligence to navigate the new challenges of college and career*. Harvard ALI Social Impact Review. https://www.sir.advancedleadership.harvard.edu/articles/using-artificial-intelligence-to-navigate-the-new-challenges-of-college-and-career

Michel-Villarreal, R., Vilalta-Perdomo, E. L., Salinas-Navarro, D. E., Thierry-Aguilera, R., & Gerardou, F. S. (2023). Challenges and opportunities of generative AI for higher education as explained by ChatGPT. *Education Sciences*, *13*(9), 856. DOI: 10.3390/educsci13090856

Microsoft Corporation. (2024). *HoloLens 2 capabilities and solutions*. Microsoft Learn. https://learn.microsoft.com/en-us/hololens/hololens-commercial-features

Montanaro, A. (2016). *Quantum algorithms: An overview. npj Quantum Information*, *2*(1), Article 15023. .DOI: 10.1038/npjqi.2015.23

Mukkala, P. R., Vuyyuru, T., Ramana, B. S., Murthy, M., Rao, A. S., & Al Said, N. (2025). Integrating ICT with artificial intelligence for transformative education. *Journal of Information Systems Engineering & Management*, *10*(1).

Mustikawati, I. F., Mahmudah, S., Fitriyanti, L., Yuliana, Y., & Utami, R. A. (2024). The impact of telemedicine adoption, AI diagnostics, and patient data privacy on healthcare accessibility and quality in 2024. *Global International Journal of Innovative Research*, *2*(6), 1435–1448.

Myers, C., & Patil, S. (2025, June 20). *Fault lines in health care AI – Part one: The high stakes of AI in medicine*. Johns Hopkins Carey Business School. https://carey.jhu.edu/articles/fault-lines-health-care-ai-part-one-high-stakes-ai-medicine

Office of Communications, College of Education. (2024, October 24). *AI in schools: Pros and cons*. University of Illinois College of Education. https://education.illinois.edu/about/news-events/news/article/2024/10/24/ai-in-schools--pros-and-cons

Online, H. (2023, April 19). *The benefits and limitations of generative AI: Harvard experts answer your questions*. https://www.harvardonline.harvard.edu/blog/benefits-limitations-generative-ai

Ooi, K. B., Koohang, A., Aw, E. C. X., Cham, T. H., Cobanoglu, C., Dennis, C., & Tan, G. W. H. (2025). Unveiling the potential of generative artificial intelligence: A multidimensional journey into the future. *Industrial Management & Data Systems*, *125*(2), 417–432. DOI: 10.1108/IMDS-10-2023-0703

Ooi, K. B., Tan, G. W. H., Al-Emran, M., Al-Sharafi, M. A., Căpă înă, A., Chakraborty, A., Dwivedi, Y. K., Huang, S., Kar, A. K., Khorana, S., Lyu, T., Lv, Z., Paul, J., Pandey, N., Sahu, G. P., Shareef, M. A., Viglia, G., & Wong, L. W. (2023). The potential of generative artificial intelligence across disciplines: Perspectives and future directions. *Journal of Computer Information Systems*, *64*(3), 314–337. DOI: 10.1080/08874417.2023.2261010

Open, A. I. (2025). *Teaching with AI: Part A7*. https://openai.com/index/teaching-with-ai

Opesemowo, O. A. G. (2024). Artificial intelligence in mathematics education. In *Advances in information quality and management* (pp. 1524-1547). IGI Global. https://doi.org/DOI: 10.4018/978-1-6684-7366-5.ch084

Ortega-Ochoa, E., Arguedas, M., & Daradoumis, T. (2023). Empathic pedagogical conversational agents: A systematic literature review. *British Journal of Educational Technology*, *55*(2), 886–909. DOI: 10.1111/bjet.13413

Owan, V. J., Abang, K. B., Idika, D. O., Etta, E. O., & Bassey, B. A. (2023). Exploring the potential of artificial intelligence tools in educational measurement and assessment. *Eurasia Journal of Mathematics, Science and Technology Education*, *19*(9), em2307. Advance online publication. DOI: 10.29333/ejmste/13428

Parikh, P. M., & Venniyoor, A. (2024). Neuralink and Brain-Computer Interface-Exciting Times for Artificial Intelligence. *South Asian Journal of Cancer*, *13*(1), 63–65. DOI: 10.1055/s-0043-1774729

Pasupuleti, M. K. (2025). Next-generation extended reality (XR): A unified framework for integrating AR, VR, and AI-driven immersive technologies. *IEEE Transactions on Visualization and Computer Graphics*.

Perkins, M., & Roe, J. (2024). Academic publisher guidelines on AI usage: A ChatGPT supported thematic analysis. *F1000 Research*, *12*, 1398. DOI: 10.12688/f1000research.142411.2

Piech, C., Huang, J., Nguyen, A., Phulsuksombati, M., Sahami, M., & Guibas, L. (2015). Learning program embeddings to propagate feedback on student code. In *Proceedings of the 32nd International Conference on Machine Learning* (pp. 1093-1102). PMLR.

Prather, J., Denny, P., Leinonen, J., Becker, B. A., Albluwi, I., Craig, M., Keuning, H., Kiesler, N., Kohn, T., Leinonen, J., MacNeil, S., Petersen, A., Pettit, R., Reeves, B. N., & Zingaro, D. (2023, October). The robots are here: Navigating the generative AI revolution in computing education. In *Proceedings of the 2023 Conference on Innovation and Technology in Computer Science Education* V. 2 (pp. 108-121). ACM. https://doi.org/DOI: 10.1145/3623762.3633499

Qadhi, S., Alduais, A., Chaaban, Y., & Khraisheh, M. (2024). Generative AI, research ethics, and higher education research: Insights from a scientometric analysis. *Information (Basel)*, *15*(6), 325. DOI: 10.3390/info15060325

Raca, M., Tormey, R., & Dillenbourg, P. (2014). Sleepers' lag-study on motion and attention. In *Proceedings of the Fourth International Conference on Learning Analytics and Knowledge* (pp. 36-43). ACM.

Raghavan, M., Barocas, S., Kleinberg, J., & Levy, K. (2020). Mitigating bias in algorithmic hiring: Evaluating claims and practices. In *Proceedings of the 2020 Conference on Fairness, Accountability, and Transparency (FAT '20)** (pp. 469–481). Association for Computing Machinery. DOI: 10.1145/3351095.3372828

Rancano, G. (2024, June 10). *Originality AI review: AI detector and more*. Scribbr. Retrieved August 12, 2025, from https://www.scribbr.com/ai-tools/originality-ai-review/

Rasul, T., Nair, S., Kalendra, D. R., Robin, M., de Oliveira Santini, F., Ladeira, W. J., Sun, M., Day, I., Rather, R. A., & Heathcote, L. (2023). The role of ChatGPT in higher education: Benefits, challenges, and future research directions. *Journal of Applied Learning & Teaching*, *6*(1), 41–56. DOI: 10.37074/jalt.2023.6.1.29

Reddy, S. (2024). Generative AI in healthcare: An implementation science-informed translational path on application, integration, and governance. *Implementation Science : IS*, *19*, 21. DOI: 10.1186/s13012-024-01357-9

Renz, A., & Hilbig, R. (2020). Prerequisites for artificial intelligence in further education: Identification of drivers, barriers, and business models of educational technology companies. *International Journal of Educational Technology in Higher Education*, *17*, 14. Advance online publication. DOI: 10.1186/s41239-020-00193-3

IBM Research. (2023, April). *Human-Centered Responsible Artificial Intelligence: Current & Future Trends for CHI 2023. CHI 2023 Proceedings*

Ruan, S., & Davis, G. M. (2021). *EnglishBot: An AI-Powered Conversational System for Second Language Learning*. Stanford University. https://hci.stanford.edu/research/smartprimer/pdfs/EnglishBot_0224.pdf

Rudolph, J., Mohamed Ismail, F. M., & Popenici, Ş. (2024). Higher education's generative artificial intelligence paradox: The meaning of chatbot mania. *Journal of University Teaching and Learning Practice, 21*(1), 03. https://doi.org/DOI: 10.53761/54fs5e77

Sands, E. G., & Sorba, M. (2020). Coursera launches CourseMatch: A machine learning solution that automatically matches a University's on-campus courses to courses on Coursera. *Coursera Blog*. https://blog.coursera.org/coursera-launches-coursematch/

Selbst, A. D., & Powles, J. (2017). Meaningful information and the right to explanation. *International Data Privacy Law*, *7*(4), 233–242. DOI: 10.1093/idpl/ipx022

Selwyn, N. (2019). *Should robots replace teachers? AI and the future of education*. Polity Press.

Setyaningsih, E., Asrori, M., Ngadiso, N., Sumardi, S., Zainnuri, H., & Hariyanti, Y. (2024). Exploring high school EFL teachers' experiences with Magic School AI in lesson planning: Benefits and insights. *Voices of English Language Education Society*, *8*(3), 766–781. DOI: 10.29408/veles.v8i3.27700

Shihab, S. R., Sultana, N., & Samad, A. (2023). Pedagogy designing with augmented reality: A paradigm shift in educational approaches. *Interdiciplinary Journal and Hummanity*, *2*(11), 1–14.

Shute, V. J., & Ventura, M. (2013). *Stealth assessment: Measuring and supporting learning in video games*. MIT Press.

Siddiqui, M. T., Mansoori, M. V., Siddiqui, M. A., & Yadav, A. (2025). AI-enabled pedagogy: Advancing education through innovative teaching tools and the AI-TEACH model. *Journal of Informatics Education and Research*, *5*(1), 45–62.

Siemens, G., & Long, P. (2011). Penetrating the fog: Analytics in learning and education. *EDUCAUSE Review*, *46*(5), 31–40.

Song, C., & Song, Y. (2023). Enhancing academic writing skills and motivation: Assessing the efficacy of ChatGPT in AI-assisted language learning for EFL students. *Frontiers in Psychology*, *14*, 1260843. DOI: 10.3389/fpsyg.2023.1260843

Stanford, N. L. P. Group. (n.d.). *Coreference resolution*. Stanford CoreNLP. https://stanfordnlp.github.io/CoreNLP/coref.html

Stanford University. (n.d.). *Virtual Human Interaction Lab*. Stanford University. https://vhil.stanford.edu/

Sumartono, S., Ayu, W., Sumartono, P., Akbar, W., & Rafsanjani, H. (2025). Transforming education: The impact of artificial intelligence on learning and pedagogical practices. In *Proceedings of the International Seminar Enrichment of Career by Knowledge of Language and Literature* (pp. 234-245).

Susnjak, T., Ramaswami, G. S., & Mathrani, A. (2022). Learning analytics dashboard: A tool for providing actionable insights to learners. *International Journal of Educational Technology in Higher Education, 19*(1), 12. DOI: 10.1186/s41239-021-00313-7

Tatnall, A. (2022). Editorial for EAIT issue 5, 2022. *Education and Information Technologies, 27*(9), 5811–5824.

TechCrunch. (2016, 11 Mei). *Startup Battlefield: Timelooper at Disrupt NY 2016*. YouTube.

Thangavel, S., Sharmila, K., & Sufina, K. (2025). Revolutionizing education through augmented reality (AR) and virtual reality (VR): Innovations, challenges, and future prospects. *Asian Journal of Interdisciplinary Research, 8*(1), 125–140.

The News Desk. (2025, August 20). *Meta breaks language barriers with AI voice translation*. https://mediabrief.com/meta-breaks-language-barriers-with-ai-voice-translation/

Thorne, S. L. (2024). Generative artificial intelligence, co-evolution, and language education. *Modern Language Journal, 108*(3), 567–572. DOI: 10.1111/modl.12932

Turnitin. (n.d.). *AI checker solutions: Ensure academic integrity*. Turnitin. https://www.turnitin.com/solutions/topics/ai-writing/

Ullah, H., Manickam, S., Obaidat, M., Laghari, S. U. A., & Uddin, M. (2023). Exploring the potential of metaverse technology in healthcare: Applications, challenges, and future directions. *IEEE Access : Practical Innovations, Open Solutions, 11*, 69686–69707. DOI: 10.1109/access.2023.3286696

University of Cambridge. (2023, July). *Designing for the future: How a unique AI course is reframing professional learning*. Cambridge Advance Online. https://advanceonline.cam.ac.uk/blog/designing-for-the-future-how-a-unique-ai-course-is-reframing-professional

University of Cambridge. (n.d.). *Cambridge is shaping AI for everyone*. University of Cambridge. https://www.cam.ac.uk/ai

VMock. (n.d.). Career acceleration platform powered by artificial intelligence. https://www.vmock.com/

Vorobyeva, K. I., Belous, S., Savchenko, N. V., Smirnova, L. M., Nikitina, S. A., & Zhdanov, S. P. (2025). Personalized learning through AI: Pedagogical approaches and critical insights. *Contemporary Educational Technology*, *17*(2), ep574. DOI: 10.30935/cedtech/16108

Walter, Y. (2024). Embracing the future of artificial intelligence in the classroom: The relevance of AI literacy, prompt engineering, and critical thinking in modern education. *International Journal of Educational Technology in Higher Education*, *21*, 18. DOI: 10.1186/s41239-024-00448-3

Wang, Y., Liu, C., & Tu, Y.-F. (2021). Factors affecting the adoption of AI-based applications in education: A case study of Chinese higher education institutions. *Journal of Educational Technology & Society*, *24*(3), 116–129. https://www.jstor.org/stable/27032860

Wang, Y., Su, Z., Zhang, N., Xing, R., Liu, D., Luan, T. H., & Shen, X. (2022). A survey on metaverse: Fundamentals, security, and privacy. *IEEE Communications Surveys and Tutorials*, *25*(1), 319–352. DOI: 10.1109/comst.2022.3202047

Wei, X., Wang, L., Lee, L. K., & Liu, R. (2024). Multiple generative AI pedagogical agents in augmented reality environments: A study on implementing the 5E model in science education. *Journal of Educational Computing Research*, *62*(4), 912–935.

Wen, B., van Rensburg, H., O'Neill, S., & Attwood, T. (2024). Autism and neurodiversity in the workplace: A scoping review of key trends, employer roles, interventions and supports. *Journal of Vocational Rehabilitation*, *60*(1), 121–140. DOI: 10.3233/JVR-230060

Western Governors University. (n.d.). *Competency-based education: A new way to learn*. WGU. https://www.wgu.edu/about/story/cbe.html

Whiles, G. (2025, August 26). *Grammarly plagiarism checker review*. Originality.AI. https://originality.ai/blog/grammarly-plagiarism-checker-review

World Economic Forum. (2024). *Shaping the future of learning: The role of AI in Education 4.0* [Insight report]. World Economic Forum. https://www3.weforum.org/docs/WEF_Shaping_the_Future_of_Learning_2024.pdf

Yenduri, G., Ramalingam, M., Selvi, G. C., Supriya, Y., Srivastava, G., Maddikunta, P. K. R., Raj, G. D., Jhaveri, R. H., Prabadevi, B., Wang, W., Vasilakos, A. V., & Gadekallu, T. R. (2024). GPT (generative pre-trained transformer)—A comprehensive review on enabling technologies, potential applications, emerging challenges, and future directions. *IEEE Access : Practical Innovations, Open Solutions, 12*, 54608–54649. DOI: 10.1109/access.2024.3389497

Zawacki-Richter, O., Marín, V. I., Bond, M., & Gouverneur, F. (2019). Systematic review of research on artificial intelligence applications in higher education – where are the educators? *International Journal of Educational Technology in Higher Education, 16*(1), 39. DOI: 10.1186/s41239-019-0171-0

Chapter 13 Innovative Frameworks for LMS Integration in Public Education: Balancing Local Needs with Global Standards

Justin Joy
https://orcid.org/0000-0002-6482-1057
Christ University, India

Helen Josephine V. L.
Christ University, India

Shibu K. Mani
Christ University, India

Jude Sebastian
Christ University, India

ABSTRACT

India has made significant progress in using digital technology in education, with Learning Management Systemsplaying a key role. LMS offer scalable platforms for content delivery, assessment, and engagement, enhancing both teaching and learning. They enable personalized learning, simplify administrative tasks, and bridge the digital divide, improving accessibility across geographies. One such initiative, eVidya, provides digital content to school students. This study explores the role of LMS in public education and the challenges of integrating them into government schools, balancing local needs with global standards. The paper analyzes LMS

DOI: 10.4018/979-8-3373-2185-1.ch013

evolution, key features, and benchmarks, with a detailed review of India's DIKSHA system and comparisons with international platforms like Google Classroom, Canvas, Moodle, and Schoology. It looks at country-specific LMS solutions from the US, Europe Australlia and Asia. The research proposes the Integrated eVidya-LMS Implementation Framework for Karnataka's schools, highlighting the potential benefits for India's digital education landscape.

INTRODUCTION

Digital transformation has become a global phenomenon across sectors such as education, healthcare, agriculture, and business, driven by advancements in affordable hardware, widespread internet access, and catalysts like the COVID-19 pandemic. Education forms the backbone of a nation's development, making the adoption of technology in this sector crucial. Integrating digital technologies at not just higher education but also at the school level is essential, particularly in government schools across Indian states, to ensure equitable access to quality education and foster holistic growth (Al-Fadhli, 2018). The implementation of Learning Management Systems (LMS) in Indian schools is crucial for modernizing education and bridging the digital divide. LMS offers flexible, scalable platforms for delivering quality content, enabling personalized learning, and fostering student-teacher engagement. It facilitates access to resources irrespective of geographical constraints, addressing disparities in urban and rural education. LMS also supports teacher training, streamlines administrative tasks, and integrates technology into pedagogy, aligning education with global standards. Public education systems, particularly in developing regions like India, integrating LMS has been slow due to challenges like inadequate infrastructure, digital illiteracy, and socio-economic disparities. Karnataka, known for its progressive education policies, faces unique challenges such as uneven internet access in rural areas, limited teacher training in digital tools, and a lack of localized content aligned with the state curriculum. Addressing these issues requires an innovative LMS framework tailored to Karnataka's needs while adhering to global educational standards. This paper proposes innovative frameworks for integrating Learning Management Systems in public education, addressing local needs while aligning with global standards to enhance accessibility, inclusivity, and quality in government schools.

Problem Statement

The lack of a contextualized framework for integrating eVidya and LMS in Karnataka's government schools limits effective digital content delivery, inclusivity, and alignment with the state's diverse educational needs.

Objective

This research aims to develop a context-specific framework for the concurrent implementation of eVidya and LMS in government schools in Karnataka.

Background Study

Learning Management Systems (LMS) play a vital role in enhancing the quality and accessibility of education. LMS platforms provide flexible learning opportunities, enabling students to access resources anytime and anywhere, breaking geographical barriers (Bates, 2015). They also offer personalized learning experiences by adapting content to individual needs, thereby increasing student engagement and performance (Garrison & Kanuka, 2004). Furthermore, LMS platforms streamline administrative tasks, allowing teachers to focus more on instructional quality (Anderson & Dron, 2017). By facilitating collaboration and tracking student progress through analytics, LMS contributes significantly to improving educational outcomes.

Figure 1. Criteria for Effective LMS

Fig 1. highlights essential benchmarks for an effective LMS. It emphasizes security to ensure data protection, and access, making it easy for users to log in and access content. Course design, development, and integration focus on structuring and creating educational material efficiently. Course monitoring tracks student prog-

ress, while assessment design focuses on creating evaluative measures. The system promotes collaboration and communication among users and offers productivity tools to enhance learning efficiency. Lastly, ease of use ensures that the platform remains intuitive and user-friendly for all users (Koller, Ng, Do, & Chen, 2013).

CASE STUDIES ON LMS FOR SCHOOL EDUCATION

National LMS Portal – DIKSHA

The eVidya scheme (PM eVidya) is an initiative by the Indian government to unify and enhance digital learning platforms under the "One Nation, One Digital Platform" vision. It offers multi-mode access through TV channels, radio, and online platforms, targeting students across diverse regions, including those with limited connectivity. Key components include DIKSHA, SWAYAM, and television channels for multilingual, inclusive education. DIKSHA (Digital Infrastructure for Knowledge Sharing) is a government initiative launched on 5th September 2017 to provide accessible and interactive digital learning for students, teachers, and parents. It supports teachers, students, and parents by offering interactive resources in multiple regional languages, ensuring inclusivity and bridging the digital divide. . DIKSHA supports diverse content formats and ensures inclusive education through its user-friendly and multilingual approach. Available in 18 languages and as a mobile app, it offers location and class-based learning resources. Students can scan QR codes in textbooks for additional materials, revise lessons, and practice problems with feedback. Teachers benefit from lesson plans, worksheets, professional development courses, and digital assessments. Parents can track classroom activities and assist with learning outside school hours

International Public LMS – Google Classroom, Edmodo

The evolving landscape of education has led to the widespread adoption of Learning Management Systems (LMS) that facilitate the digitalization of learning, offering a seamless way to manage, deliver, and track educational content. These systems are designed to enhance teaching and learning experiences by providing tools for creating, distributing, and assessing assignments, fostering collaboration, and offering personalized learning paths. Among the leading LMS platforms, Google Classroom, Canvas LMS, Edmodo, Moodle, and Schoology have gained global recognition for their user-friendly features, integration capabilities, and scalability. Each of these platforms brings unique advantages, catering to various educational environments, from K-12 to higher education, across national and international contexts. This section explores the features, strengths, and scope of these LMS platforms, emphasizing their impact on modern education and their role in enhancing learning

Google Classroom is a free, web-based learning management system (LMS) designed to help educators create, distribute, and manage assignments efficiently. It integrates with Google Workspace, allowing teachers to use tools like Google Docs, Drive, and Sheets. Classroom simplifies communication between teachers, students, and parents, and offers a paperless workflow with grading features and real-time feedback. It's accessible on various devices and supports asynchronous and synchronous learning (Google Classroom, 2024).

Canvas LMS is a modern, cloud-based learning management system widely used in K-12 and higher education. Renowned for its intuitive interface and flexibility, it supports blended, online, and hybrid learning environments. Canvas offers tools for creating, sharing, and grading assignments, along with built-in video conferencing and discussion forums. It integrates seamlessly with third-party applications like Google Workspace, Zoom, and Microsoft Teams. Canvas provides robust analytics, enabling educators to monitor student progress and engagement. Accessible on multiple devices through its mobile app, Canvas ensures learning anytime, anywhere. Its user-centric design and extensive customization options make it a preferred choice for educators and institutions globally.

Edmodo is a global LMS designed to facilitate communication, collaboration, and content sharing between teachers, students, and parents. It provides tools for assignments, quizzes, and grade tracking, along with a discussion forum for collaborative learning. Edmodo supports secure interactions and can be used to create personalized learning paths, making it ideal for K-12 schools. It's available as a mobile app, enhancing its accessibility (Edmodo, 2024).

Moodle (Modular Object-Oriented Dynamic Learning Environment) is a free, open-source learning management system (LMS) widely used in education. Designed for flexibility and scalability, Moodle supports online and blended learning by providing tools for course creation, assignments, quizzes, and collaborative activities like forums and wikis. It is customizable with a vast range of plugins, supporting adaptive learning, SCORM compliance, and multilingual capabilities. Moodle offers analytics for tracking progress and performance, ensuring data-driven insights. With a mobile-friendly interface, it enables learning on-the-go. Its open-source nature makes it a cost-effective solution for schools and universities, empowering educators to design personalized and engaging learning experiences.

Schoology is an international versatile learning management system (LMS) designed for K-12 and higher education. It facilitates seamless collaboration between students, teachers, and parents, offering tools to manage assignments, assessments, and grades effectively. The platform provides a user-friendly interface, enabling educators to create engaging courses, conduct quizzes, and share resources. Schoology supports integration with popular tools like Google Drive and Microsoft Office, enhancing its functionality. It also includes features for parent-teacher communication, real-time feedback, and progress tracking. With a mobile-friendly design and support for blended and remote learning, Schoology promotes personalized education and fosters an interactive and inclusive learning environment.

Table 1. Comparative analysis national LMS portal and online portals

Feature	National LMS (e.g., eVidya, DIKSHA)	International LMS (e.g., Google Classroom, Edmodo)
Target Audience	Primarily students and teachers in Indian schools	Global schools and international curricula
Content	India-specific content aligned with NCERT/CBSE, regional languages	Multilingual content, supports diverse global curricula
Integration	Limited integration with third-party tools	Extensive integration with EdTech tools and APIs
Technology Infrastructure	Cloud-based with regional hosting	Cloud-first, globally distributed hosting and CDN
Access	Offline access supported in some cases	Strong offline and mobile-first access
Cost	Freely available or subsidized	Freemium or paid tiers with advanced features
Teacher Enablement	Training workshops organized periodically	Self-paced global certifications and 24/7 online support
Analytics	Basic dashboards for monitoring student progress	Advanced analytics, AI-based personalization
Cybersecurity	Standard security protocols	Advanced global security standards (e.g., GDPR-compliance)
User Experience	Moderate due to region-specific challenges	High due to global design standards
Scalability	Moderate scalability for regional needs	High scalability to accommodate global usage
Adoption	Mandatory adoption in many government schools	Voluntary adoption; widely used globally

Table 1 shows the comparative analysis table contrasts the features of national LMS portals, like eVidya and DIKSHA, with online LMS portals, such as Google Classroom and Edmodo, for school education systems. It examines critical aspects such as content, accessibility, scalability, technology infrastructure, and cost (UNESCO, 2024).

- National LMS portals focus on India-specific curricula, support regional languages, and aim at wider government-driven adoption, often free or subsidized. They cater to regional needs but have moderate scalability and user experience.

- Online LMS portals are globally accessible, support diverse curricula, and provide advanced features like AI-driven analytics, extensive integration, and robust cybersecurity. They are mostly freemium or paid, with global scalability and high user experience standards.

This analysis emphasizes the trade-offs between localization and global functionality, showcasing the strengths and challenges of each LMS category in improving the digital education experience.

International Country wise LMS Portal

Each country develops its own educational information system tailored to suit its unique culture and stakeholders. These systems are carefully planned, designed, analyzed, and implemented to meet the specific needs of their populations. By considering local educational requirements, cultural contexts, and the involvement of various stakeholders, these systems ensure an effective and efficient approach to managing educational processes, enhancing communication, and supporting personalized learning experiences (Liaw & Huang, 2007), (Martin, Sun, & Westine, 2019). The careful customization of these systems reflects each country's commitment to fostering a strong, data-driven educational framework that aligns with its values and goals (Mtebe & Raphael, 2018). Notable systems include the Estonian Education Information System (EHIS), which integrates educational data across Estonia, ensuring efficient school management and monitoring of student performance. Similarly, PowerSchool in the US, SIMS in the UK, EduRec in Singapore, e-Education in South Korea, Wilma in Finland, and Edumate in Australia all offer tailored solutions for better school administration, personalized learning, and improved educational outcomes.

Estonian Education Information System (EHIS)

The Estonian Education Information System (EHIS) was piloted in 2004 and became fully operational and mandatory for all schools by January 1, 2005. This state-run, web-based database provides live, individual-based data on education, covering all levels, from kindergarten to universities and hobby schools. EHIS tracks detailed information, such as student performance, exam results, teacher qualifications, and teaching hours. Connected to X-Road, EHIS integrates with other databases for comprehensive data sharing, like retrieving student residency information from the population register or supporting health insurance eligibility.

Schools also connect their management systems to EHIS for seamless reporting and data access. All schools in Estonia utilize "e-school solutions" (e-Estonia, 2025), including digital learning materials and web-based school management software. The Ministry of Education and Research, alongside private companies, offers a wide range of online tools. One such tool, the "e-schoolbag" (e-Koolikott), is an online portal that provides digital learning resources for both teachers and students at various educational levels (OECD, 2025).

Estonian Education Information System (EHIS) in Estonia offers several key advantages. Its real-time data updates ensure the accuracy and consistency of information, such as student registration, by utilizing unique identification numbers. EHIS also connects to other state databases, offering comprehensive insights without redundant data entry. The system supports detailed analyses of educational impacts, including linking educational data to income levels. EHIS fosters evidence-based decision-making by providing public access to aggregated data, empowering citizens and policymakers alike. Furthermore, its well-defined governance structure facilitates efficient development and user feedback integration, ensuring continual improvement. OECD (2025). EHIS faces challenges like underutilization for evidence-based decision-making, limited stakeholder involvement in development, and slow adoption of advanced analytics (OECD, 2025). Public data displays, like school cards, oversimplify school performance, focusing on grades over holistic development. Errors arise from manual data entry, and some schools delay updates, reducing data accuracy despite built-in consistency checks to prevent manipulation.

US – PowerSchool

PowerSchool is a widely used K-12 education management system in the United States. It offers a centralized platform for managing student information, including grades, attendance, assignments, and assessments. The system integrates with various educational tools, allowing teachers to communicate with parents and students efficiently. PowerSchool's real-time data analytics helps administrators track student performance and optimize educational strategies (PowerSchool, 2025). Its mobile app provides easy access to academic information for parents and students, fostering improved communication and engagement in the educational process.

UK – SIMS (School Information Management System)

SIMS is a comprehensive education information system used across the UK to streamline school management tasks. It enables schools to track student attendance, grades, behavior, and assessments, providing a holistic view of student progress. SIMS integrates various data sources, ensuring accurate reporting for teachers, administrators, and parents (SIMS, 2025). It supports personalized learning by helping educators identify strengths and weaknesses in students' performance. The system enhances communication between stakeholders and improves school administration efficiency, contributing to a more organized and data-driven educational environment.

Singapore – EduRec

EduRec is Singapore's education records management system, used by the Ministry of Education to collect and manage data across the country's educational institutions. The system integrates various aspects of education, including student performance, attendance, and academic progress. EduRec supports data-driven decision-making by providing real-time insights to educators, helping them tailor instruction to meet students' needs (Ministry of Education, Singapore, 2025). It facilitates communication between schools, parents, and students, improving collaboration and transparency in the learning process. By centralizing education data, EduRec enhances the effectiveness and efficiency of Singapore's education system.

South Korea – e-Education System

South Korea's e-Education System is a robust digital platform that integrates various educational technologies to improve the quality of teaching and learning. It provides students with access to online content, interactive tools, and assessments, enabling personalized learning experiences (South Korea Ministry of Education, 2025). The system also supports virtual classrooms, real-time feedback, and communication between students and teachers. e-Education enhances the efficiency of administrative tasks and allows schools to collect and analyze student data for better academic support. The platform is part of South Korea's efforts to create a modern, technology-driven education system that promotes innovation and equity.

Finland – Wilma

Wilma is an online communication platform used in Finnish schools to manage student information and foster collaboration between students, parents, and educators. It allows students to track their grades, assignments, and attendance, while parents can monitor their child's academic progress (Wilma, 2025). Teachers can use Wilma to provide feedback, send announcements, and share learning materials. The system supports personalized learning by offering data on student performance and enabling targeted interventions. Wilma is an integral part of Finland's education system, enhancing transparency, engagement, and communication within the school community.

Australia – Edumate

Edumate is an education management system used in Australia to support schools in managing student data, timetables, assessments, and grades. The system offers features such as attendance tracking, report generation, and communication tools for parents and teachers. Edumate helps educators streamline administrative tasks, allowing them to focus on improving teaching and learning outcomes (Edumate, 2025). It supports personalized learning by providing detailed insights into student progress and performance. With its user-friendly interface and mobile access, Edumate fosters better communication and collaboration among students, parents, and school staff, contributing to an efficient and transparent education system.

Comparative Analysis of Country-Wise LMS/ EIS with India's DIKSHA System

The comparative analysis in Table 2 examines various Education Information Systems (EIS) and Learning Management Systems (LMS) across different countries, such as Estonia, the US, the UK, Singapore, South Korea, Finland, and Australia, in comparison with India's DIKSHA platform. This comparison highlights key features, goals, and target audiences to understand their effectiveness in addressing educational needs.

Table 2. Comparative Analysis of Country-Wise LMS/EIS with India's DIKSHA System

Education Information System	Country	Key Features	Target Audience	Purpose/Goal	Comparison with DIKSHA
Estonian Education Information System (EHIS)	Estonia	Centralized platform for student data, academic performance tracking, school management	Schools, Teachers, Students	Efficient management of educational data, performance monitoring, and school operations	DIKSHA provides localized, region-specific educational content, whereas EHIS offers a broader national-level data system.
PowerSchool	United States	Comprehensive student information system, grading, attendance tracking, communication tools	Schools, Teachers, Parents	Improve administrative tasks, student performance tracking, and communication between stakeholders	DIKSHA has a focus on learning resources and tools for teachers, but PowerSchool offers advanced administrative tools.
SIMS (School Information Management System)	United Kingdom	Attendance management, reporting, assessment tracking, financial records	Schools, Teachers, Administrators	Streamline school operations, improve assessment, attendance and financial management	SIMS focuses more on financial management and administration, while DIKSHA prioritizes content delivery and teaching support.
EduRec	Singapore	Data management for student enrolment, grades, performance analysis	Schools, Teachers, Parents	Optimize school administration, enhance learning and assessment practices	DIKSHA provides more interactive learning tools but lacks features like data analysis on performance.
e-Education	South Korea	Online learning management, school scheduling, student performance analytics	Schools, Teachers, Students	Facilitate online learning, integrate real-time student data, and improve administrative efficiency	DIKSHA has strong offline and localized learning support, whereas e-Education emphasizes real-time analytics and scheduling.

continued on following page

Table 2. Continued

Education Information System	Country	Key Features	Target Audience	Purpose/Goal	Comparison with DIKSHA
Wilma	Finland	Digital platform for student data, communication, and reporting	Teachers, Students, Parents	Promote transparent communication, track academic performance, and simplify school administration	DIKSHA emphasizes digital content and language accessibility, while Wilma includes comprehensive communication tools.
Edumate	Australia	School management, timetabling, assessment, financial and reporting tools	Schools, Teachers, Administrators	Improve administrative tasks, optimize timetabling, and enhance educational outcomes	DIKSHA lacks complex scheduling features like Edumate but excels in supporting curriculum-based learning in local languages.

DIKSHA primarily serves the Indian context by focusing on curriculum-based learning, localized language support, and tools for teachers and students. In contrast, international EIS platforms like PowerSchool and SIMS offer broader administrative features, such as financial management and advanced student performance tracking. While DIKSHA provides valuable resources for teachers and students, international systems often provide a more holistic administrative approach, supporting both learning management and school operations comprehensively.

The gap between DIKSHA and other country LMS platforms lies in the level of integration and customization. While platforms like PowerSchool, SIMS, and EHIS offer comprehensive data management, performance analytics, and advanced tools for school administrators, DIKSHA primarily focuses on accessible, interactive learning content for teachers and students. Other systems provide better integration across multiple stakeholders (such as parents, teachers, and administrators) and enable data sharing across multiple schools within the same state, whereas DIKSHA is still developing in terms of these capabilities. There is a need to develop a context-specific framework for the concurrent implementation of eVidya and Learning Management Systems (LMS) in government schools in Karnataka. This framework would address the unique challenges faced by these schools, such as infrastructure gaps and diverse learner needs, while ensuring seamless integration of digital learning tools. The goal is to improve the quality of education, streamline administration, and enhance student engagement.

PROPOSED INTEGRATED EVIDYA-LMS IMPLEMENTATION FRAMEWORK (IEV-LMS)

The proposed integrated eVidya-LMS Implementation framework constitutes 5-layers to ensure the effective integration of eVidya and Learning Management Systems (LMS) in Karnataka's government schools, focusing on access, personalization, and monitoring. Figure 1 shows the proposed integrated e-Vidya LMS implementation framework.

Figure 2. Proposed integrated e-Vidya LMS implementation framework

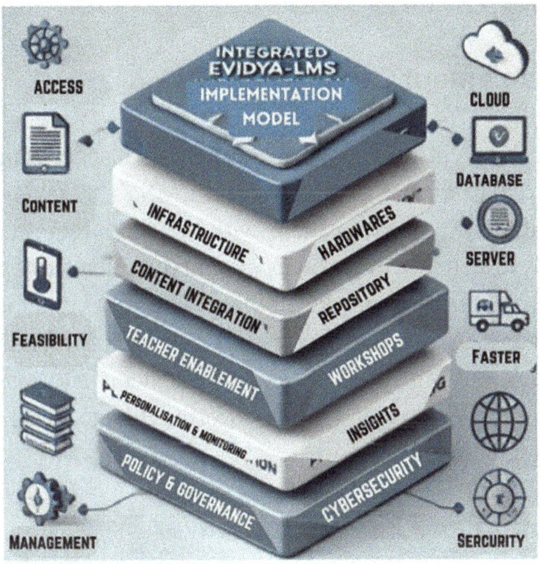

1. Infrastructure Layer

The Infrastructure layer is foundational for the successful integration of eVidya and LMS in Karnataka's government schools. It focuses on providing essential hardware, including smart devices, eVidya kiosks, and LMS-ready computers, ensuring that all schools are equipped for digital learning. Reliable internet connectivity and uninterrupted electricity supply are vital components. Partnerships with local vendors ensure regular maintenance, guaranteeing sustainability. This layer forms the backbone of the model, enabling seamless access to digital education tools, while addressing the challenges of physical infrastructure and connectivity in remote and rural schools.

2. Content Integration Layer

The Content Integration layer ensures seamless alignment between eVidya's digital content repository and the Learning Management System (LMS). It focuses on integrating eVidya's diverse learning materials into the LMS course structure, making it accessible for both students and teachers. This integration facilitates smooth data sharing for assignments, feedback, and other learning activities. The layer also emphasizes the development of multimedia-enriched, inclusive content to cater to various learning needs, ensuring that the resources are accessible to all students, regardless of language or learning ability, thereby fostering a comprehensive and engaging learning experience.

3. Teacher Enablement Layer

The Teacher Enablement layer addresses the need for teacher training and capacity-building for the concurrent use of eVidya and LMS. This layer aims to enhance teachers' digital literacy, equipping them with the skills required to navigate and utilize digital tools effectively. It involves conducting blended teaching programs, digital workshops, and professional development initiatives that focus on improving instructional strategies. Teachers are trained to leverage LMS analytics for tracking student engagement, customizing learning experiences, and making data-driven decisions, ultimately ensuring that digital platforms enhance teaching effectiveness and student learning outcomes.

4. Personalization and Monitoring Layer

The Personalization & Monitoring layer utilizes data analytics to create adaptive, individualized learning pathways for students. By analyzing student engagement and performance, this layer enables personalized interventions to cater to diverse learning needs. Real-time monitoring tools, such as AI-powered dashboards, provide teachers with actionable insights into student progress. Integrated reports from both eVidya and LMS offer a comprehensive view of student performance, enabling timely feedback. This layer's focus on personalization ensures that each student receives tailored support, while continuous monitoring facilitates prompt corrective measures to address learning gaps and optimize educational outcomes.

5. Policy and Governance Layer

The Policy & Governance layer ensures that the implementation of eVidya and LMS is supported by robust governance structures and clear policy frameworks.

This layer focuses on data privacy, cybersecurity, and compliance with educational standards to protect student and institutional data. It involves establishing policies for content regulation, digital resource management, and cybersecurity protocols. Stakeholder feedback loops are created to monitor the effectiveness of the system and incorporate improvements. Regular assessments and performance metrics are used to drive continuous enhancement of the digital education ecosystem, ensuring that it remains secure, efficient, and responsive to the evolving educational landscape.

Features of Integrated e-Vidya LMS Implementation Framework

The Integrated eVidya-LMS Implementation Model offers several key advantages, including a scalable, sustainable framework for digital education in Karnataka's government schools. By focusing on infrastructure, content integration, teacher enablement, personalization, and governance, the model ensures comprehensive support for students and educators. Key features include seamless data sharing between eVidya and LMS, personalized learning experiences, real-time monitoring of student progress, and enhanced teacher training. The model promotes inclusive education through multimedia content and adaptive learning, while maintaining data privacy and cybersecurity. Ultimately, it ensures an accessible, efficient, and secure digital learning environment for all.

CONCLUSION

The research emphasizes the crucial role of Learning Management Systems (LMS) in transforming education, particularly through the integration of national and international platforms. By analyzing various global LMS solutions, such as Google Classroom, Moodle, and EHIS, alongside India's DIKSHA system, the study identifies both strengths and gaps in the current landscape. Notably, the lack of multi-stakeholder integration and cross-school connectivity in DIKSHA has been highlighted as a critical area for development. The proposed Integrated eVidya-LMS Implementation Framework (IeV-LMS) offers a comprehensive, context-specific solution for Karnataka's government schools, focusing on infrastructure, content integration, teacher enablement, personalization, and robust policy governance. This framework is designed to address the unique challenges of scaling digital education in India. By combining technological advancements with localized strategies, IeV-LMS promises to enhance accessibility, improve teacher-student engagement, and support personalized learning, ultimately contributing to more effective and inclusive education for the future.

CONFLICT OF INTEREST STATEMENT

We have no known conflict of interest to disclose.

FUNDING

There was funding involved for this research. The funding was sponsored by ICSSR (Indian Council of Social Science Research) for a major research project titled "Development and Evaluation of a framework for implementation of LMS in Gov't Schools in Karnataka as an extension of E-Vidya" for the time period January 2024 till January 2026.

ACKNOWLEDGMENT

The authors wish to acknowledge the funding and guidance of ICSSR (Indian Council of Social Science Research) to conduct this study and implement these insights in the Government Schools in State of Karnataka, India as part of their funded project.

REFERENCES

Al-Fadhli, S. (2018). The role of learning management systems in education. *International Journal of Educational Technology*, *15*(2), 15–29.

Anderson, T., & Dron, J. (2017). Integrating LMS to enhance educational efficiency. *Journal of Educational Technology & Society*, *20*(4), 50–64.

Bates, A. W. (2015). *Teaching in a digital age: Guidelines for designing teaching and learning*. Tony Bates Associates Ltd.

DIKSHA. (2025, May 3). *DIKSHA portal overview*. https://diksha.gov.in/

Estonia. (2025, May 3). *Education*. https://e-estonia.com/solutions/education/

Edmodo. (2024, September 30). *Edmodo features*. https://www.edmodo.com/

Edumate. (2025, May 3). *Edumate: School management system*. https://www.edumate.com.au

Garrison, D. R., & Kanuka, H. (2004). Blended learning: Uncovering its transformative potential in higher education. *The Internet and Higher Education*, *7*(2), 95–105. DOI: 10.1016/j.iheduc.2004.02.001

Google Classroom. (2024, September 30). *Google Classroom documentation*. https://classroom.google.com/

Koller, D., Ng, A., Do, C., & Chen, Z. (2013). Learning analytics and educational performance: A study of LMS data. *Learning Analytics Journal*, *1*(1), 12–22.

Liaw, S. S., & Huang, H. M. (2007). Development of a web-based collaborative learning system for promoting critical thinking. *Journal of Educational Technology & Society*, *10*(2), 124–136.

Martin, F., Sun, T., & Westine, C. (2019). The impact of LMS on personalized learning. *Journal of Distance Education*, *35*(3), 25–40.

Ministry of Education. India. (2025, May 3). *eVidya initiative*. https://www.education.gov.in/

Ministry of Education. Singapore. (2025, May 3). *EduRec: Education records management system*. https://www.moe.gov.sg

Mtebe, J. S., & Raphael, C. M. (2018). Investigating the challenges and factors influencing the adoption of Learning Management Systems in higher education. *International Journal of Education and Development Using Information and Communication Technology*, *14*(3), 61–74.

OECD. (2025, May 3). Case study: The Estonian Education Information System (EHIS). In *Strengthening the governance of skills systems: Lessons from six OECD countries*. OECD Publishing., DOI: 10.1787/298d6678

PowerSchool. (2025, May 3). *PowerSchool: The leading education technology platform*. https://www.powerschool.com

SIMS. (2025, May 3). *SIMS: Streamline your school management*. https://www.sims.co.uk

South Korea Ministry of Education. (2025, May 3). *e-Education: Online education and student management system*. http://www.moe.go.kr

UNESCO. (2024, December 5). *LMS development and video interactivity*. https://www.unesco.org/en/articles/lms-development-and-video-interactivity

Wilma. (2025, May 3). *Wilma: Online communication and student management platform*. https://www.wilma.com

Chapter 14 Blockchain for Credentialing and Academic Record-Keeping

Subashini Babu
https://orcid.org/0000-0003-1177-5082
Department of Data Science and Business Systems, School of Computing, SRM Institute of Science and Technology, India

Anna Anbumozhi
https://orcid.org/0009-0004-1128-5467
Department of Data Science and Business Systems, School of Computing, SRM Institute of Science and Technology, India

Praveenkumar S.
https://orcid.org/0009-0009-4830-5237
Department of Data Science and Business Systems, School of Computing, SRM Institute of Science and Technology, India

Vasudevan N.
https://orcid.org/0000-0002-4362-8063
Department of Data Science and Business Systems, School of Computing, SRM Institute of Science and Technology, India

Venkatesh Kaliamoorthy
Department of Networking and Communications, School of Computing, SRM Institute of Science and Technology, India

DOI: 10.4018/979-8-3373-2185-1.ch014

ABSTRACT

In the digital era, ensuring the security, authenticity, and accessibility of academic credentials is crucial. Traditional credentialing and academic record-keeping systems suffer from inefficiencies, security vulnerabilities, and verification issues. Blockchain technology offers a decentralized, tamper-proof, and transparent solution to these challenges. This chapter explores blockchain's potential in academic credentialing, examining its benefits, challenges, and real-world applications. Academic institutions currently rely on centralized authorities, which can be inefficient and susceptible to fraud. Blockchain provides an immutable ledger that enables secure issuance, decentralized verification, and fraud prevention. By leveraging cryptographic security and smart contracts, institutions can issue digital diplomas and certificates that are instantly verifiable, eliminating the need for intermediary verification. Blockchain also enhances lifelong learning records by allowing students to consolidate academic achievements into a single digital identity. This improves global mobility.

1. INTRODUCTION

In our constantly accelerating, digital world of work, education is adjusting at a similar pace to the industries it serves. Colleges and learning institutions are facing a new sort of conundrum: How to securely save and gain access to academic records in ways that render them tamper-proof, easily shareable and trusted across borders? Single-use paper diplomas and even digital PDF representations can't keep up — they can be lost, faked or may take weeks to verify (Sharma & Dwivedi, 2024).

Here, blockchain appears as a disruptive new means to do credentialing and academic record-keeping. Blockchain technology, initially conceived to underpin cryptocurrencies such as Bitcoin, is now all grown up, with many cool things in store for how we store and verify educational records. Think of a world where a student can graduate and own a digital, verifiable diploma on a secure blockchain the second that person finishes school. Do not request transcripts (Lizcano et al., 2020). No months-long waiting to confirm what your degrees are worth when applying for jobs outside the country. Employers and universities could attest to the legitimacy of a credential with just a few clicks and never have to phone an issuing institution again.

This is not some far-off dream — it's already happening today in some of the most innovative schools and in some of the most ambitious educational projects. But what is it about blockchain that makes it such a game-changer? (Raj et al., 2015).

Fundamentally, the blockchain provides decentralization, immutability, security, and transparency. These notions fit the requirements of credentialing systems, which require trust, resistance against fraud, and easy access. Unlike a typical database that is centralized under the management of a single organization, blockchain networks distribute trust across multiple stakeholders. Individual records are secure, making it very difficult for a single agent to modify or delete them or to create a fake record (Hasan et al., 2009).

Furthermore, the blockchain allows students to have self-sovereign identities — digital identities that are owned and controlled by the student. Here, learners themselves are the real stewards of their academic pasts, with the ability to pass on their verified credentials directly to employers, universities, and other outside entities without having to route them through intermediaries bogged down by bureaucracy. Nevertheless, as exciting as the potential of blockchain in education is, there are also challenges. Issues such as privacy considerations, interoperability across blockchain systems, scalability, and the legal status of blockchain records must be addressed before it can achieve widespread adoption.

While blockchain's potential in credentialing is recognized, current literature lacks a holistic framework that addresses not only technical feasibility but also the policy, governance, privacy, and adoption roadmap required for mainstream implementation. This chapter seeks to bridge that gap by offering a multi-dimensional analysis of blockchain's applicability, challenges, and future pathways in academic credentialing.

2. FUNDAMENTALS OF BLOCKCHAIN TECHNOLOGY

2.0 Background on Digital Credentialing Technologies

Before the adoption of blockchain, digital credentialing efforts were often based on centralized repositories and badge systems such as Mozilla Open Badges and proprietary Learning Management Systems (LMS). While these systems offered basic digitization, they suffered from limited interoperability, a lack of verification standards, and a high risk of single-point failure. Blockchain introduces a paradigm shift by enabling decentralization, tamper-proof records, and user-controlled sharing through self-sovereign identity models.

2.1 What is Blockchain?

At its heart, blockchain is a special kind of database — but it's unlike the traditional databases you might be familiar with. Imagine a digital ledger that records transactions (Zook & Blankenship, 2018).

Now imagine that this ledger is:

- **Shared** across thousands of computers worldwide.
- **Publicly visible** (in most cases), meaning anyone can see the records.
- **Immutable** — once information is recorded, it cannot be altered without consensus from the entire network (Kim et al., 2021).

Every entry (or transaction) is grouped into a block. Each block contains:

- A list of transactions or records,
- A timestamp,
- A reference (hash) to the previous block.

These blocks are cryptographically linked to form a chain — hence the name blockchain.

The result? A tamper-resistant history of data, maintained not by a single entity, but by a distributed network of participants.

Figure.1 depicts the fundamental principles of blockchain technology, how transactions are formed, authenticated, and incorporated into a chain of blocks via consensus protocols such as Proof of Work. The header of each block includes cryptographic items that provide security and unalterability. The blocks are arranged in a linear chain, and a network of nodes is distributed, holding an agreement-based replica of the blockchain. Such a decentralized approach provides transparency, integrity, and immunity to tampering.

Figure 1. Fundamentals of Blockchain

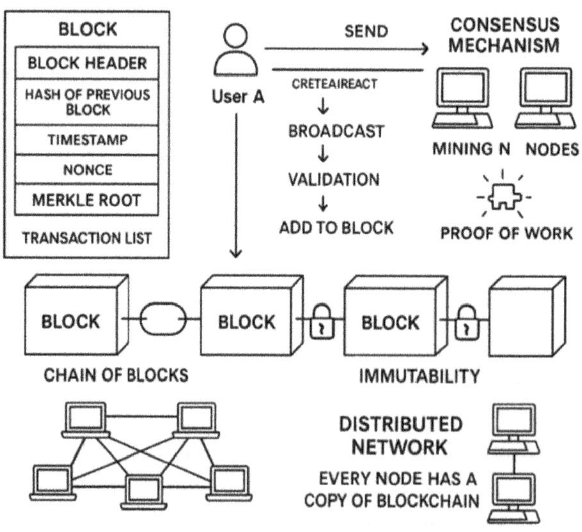

2.2 Key Concepts of Blockchain

2.2.1 Blocks and Hashes

Each block is like a page in a ledger. Once it's full of transactions, it's sealed with a special fingerprint called a hash.

- Hash = A unique digital signature generated by running the block's content through a cryptographic function.
- If even a tiny piece of data inside the block changes, the hash will change — immediately alerting everyone that something's wrong.

Analogy:

Think of it like a tamper-evident seal on a bottle — if someone tries to open it, you'll know.

2.2.2 Consensus Mechanisms

Blockchains need a way to agree on the state of the ledger across all participants. This is called consensus (Xiao et al., 2020).

There are several methods:

- **Proof of Work (PoW)** — Used by Bitcoin. Requires solving complex mathematical problems to validate blocks.
- **Proof of Stake (PoS)** — Validators "stake" their coins as collateral for good behavior.
- **Practical Byzantine Fault Tolerance (PBFT)** — Used in permissioned blockchains where participants are known.Nodes achieve consensus by rounds of communication to withstand faulty or malicious nodes. It's appropriate for private blockchains.
- **Delegated Proof of Stake (DPoS)** -- Voters elect a few delegates who validate blocks in their place. It supports high scalability and speedy transaction processing.
- **Proof of Authority (PoA)**-A handful of trusted validators are authorized to generate new blocks. It's centralised but provides high throughput.

In education blockchains (which usually involve known parties like universities), faster and more energy-efficient consensus methods (like PBFT or PoS) are preferred.

2.2.3 Public vs Private Blockchains

Table 1.

Aspect	Public Blockchain	Private Blockchain
Access	Open to anyone	Restricted to invited members
Example	Bitcoin, Ethereum	Hyperledger Fabric, Corda
Speed and Scalability	Slower	Faster
Use Case	Open diplomas, lifelong learning records	University consortiums, internal records

In education, private or consortium blockchains are often used because they offer more control over privacy and participation. Figure 2 depicts the key components of Blockchain

Figure 2. Key Components of Blockchain

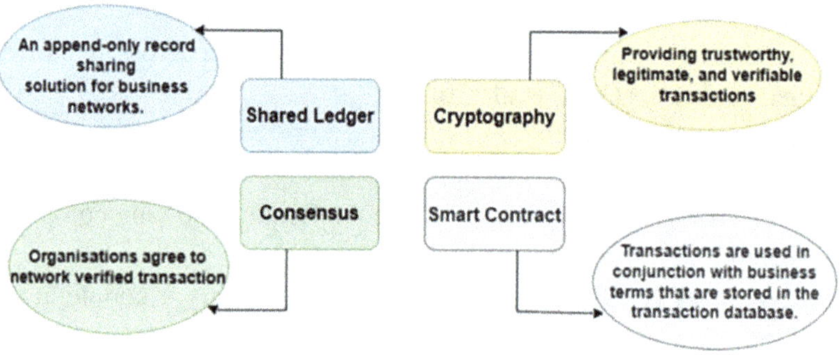

2.2.4 Smart Contracts

Smart contracts are self-executing agreements written in code. They automatically perform actions when predefined conditions are met (Governatori et al., 2018).

In credentialing, smart contracts can:

- Issue a diploma once a student completes the required courses.
- Notify employers when a student's credentials are updated.
- Manage revocation (e.g., retract a certificate if a mistake is discovered).

Example: Upon graduation, a smart contract could automatically mint a digital diploma and send it to the student's digital wallet.

2.3 Why Blockchain Matters for Credentialing

When you think about traditional certificates, you realize:

- They can be forged.
- They require tedious manual verification.
- They're controlled by issuing institutions, not the students.

Blockchain flips this model by enabling:

- **Verifiability without trust** — Anyone can independently verify if a diploma is genuine.
- **Student ownership** — Credentials live with the student, not locked away in a university vault.
- **Global portability** — No more reissuing, translating, or notarizing degrees across borders.

3. BARRIERS IN THE CONVENTIONAL CREDENTIALING MECHANISM

Education has evolved by leaps and bounds in terms of accessibility, but the tools to issue, store, and verify academic credentials have not evolved at the same rate (Canty et al., 2025). Institutions are still overwhelmingly reliant on paper diplomas, physical transcripts, and cumbersome, outdated manual verification methods as depicted in Figure 3. Many of these systems, which were designed and implemented decades ago, are now failing dramatically in an era that is digital and global.

3.1 Risk of Fraud and Forgery

The fraud of academic credentials is an epidemic that jeopardizes the integrity of educational systems. The proliferation of diploma mills—illegitimate enterprises that sell credentials in return for payment—has become more sophisticated, making it difficult for employers, education providers, and even official government entities to differentiate between false and genuine qualifications. There have been high-profile cases of professionals found to be using fraudulent degrees, including MBAs from non-existent schools. Fake certificates are also widely sold online, often appearing to come from prestigious but entirely fictitious universities (Silaghi & Popescu, 2025). This widespread issue undermines trust in valid academic qualifications and devalues the hard work of students who have legitimately earned their degrees.

3.2 Manual, Slow, and Expensive Verification

The academic credential verification process can be unwieldy and time-consuming. When students apply for jobs or further education, confirmation may involve phone calls, faxed transcripts, certified copies, and notaries—all of which can take weeks or even months. This becomes an even greater burden for international or cross-border students, where the bureaucratic processes are both time-consuming and costly. These delays hinder career progression and educational mobility and create bottlenecks for institutions and employers trying to make timely decisions.

3.3 Non-Interoperability of Institutions

The lack of interoperability between institutions is another serious concern. Most universities and schools operate isolated databases that don't talk to each other, use inconsistent data formats, and lack a common framework for sharing digital credentials (Eaton & Carmichael, 2023). This fragmentation creates data silos, making it hard to build a connected global education system. As a result, students often struggle to transfer credits, continue studies across different regions, or combine learning experiences from multiple institutions.

Figure 3. Issues in Traditional Credentialing Systems

3.4 Centralized Control and Ownership

Legacy credentialing systems often put full control of academic records in the hands of institutions or examination boards. Students usually have limited control over how their credentials are shared or accessed, and must go through administrative gatekeepers—sometimes paying fees—just to access their own records. This centralized model diminishes student autonomy and creates inefficiencies when sharing achievements across various platforms and stakeholders.

3.5 Privacy and Data Breaches

Educational institutions are increasingly targeted by cyberattacks due to the concentration of sensitive student data—such as grades, addresses, social security numbers, and financial information. Data breaches have already impacted universities in the U.S., U.K., and Asia, with compromised records sometimes showing up on the dark web. These breaches expose individuals and institutions to identity theft, financial fraud, and serious reputational damage. A more secure, decentralized method of storing credentials is urgently needed to protect student privacy in the digital age.

3.6 No Support for Lifelong Learning Records

Today's learners don't follow a straight path through one university. They participate in MOOCs, bootcamps, professional certifications, micro-credentials, and informal learning programs. Traditional credentialing systems, however, aren't built to capture or validate these diverse, ongoing learning experiences. This becomes a major problem in a fast-changing job market, where skills can quickly become outdated and continuous learning is essential. Without a flexible and reliable way to document lifelong learning, individuals struggle to prove their evolving skills to employers and institutions.

Altogether, these challenges highlighted in Table 3.1 provides the urgent need for a new kind of credentialing system—one that's secure, interoperable, student-focused, and truly designed for the modern educational and professional landscape.

Table 2. Challenges and its Impact

Challenge	Impact
Fraud and forgery	Undermines trust in education
Manual, slow verification	Delays opportunities, increases costs
Lack of interoperability	Limits global mobility and collaboration
Centralized control	Disempowers students
Privacy and security risks	Exposes sensitive student data to breaches
No lifelong learning record-keeping	Fails to recognize dynamic, modern learning paths

4. BLOCKCHAIN SOLUTIONS FOR ACADEMIC RECORD-KEEPING

As we've explored in earlier discussions, traditional systems for managing academic credentials are increasingly falling behind in a world that demands speed, security, and global accessibility. These conventional approaches face numerous challenges — from credential fraud and administrative inefficiencies to a lack of standardization and the disempowerment of students over their own data.

Blockchain technology, with its foundational principles of decentralization, transparency, immutability, and security, offers a groundbreaking alternative. It has the potential to revolutionize how academic records are issued, stored, verified, and shared, transforming the education landscape into a more trustworthy and interconnected system.

4.1 Securing Academic Credentials Against Fraud

One of blockchain's most compelling features is its immutability — once data is written to the blockchain, it cannot be altered or deleted without consensus from the entire network. This characteristic makes it exceptionally effective in protecting academic records from fraud.

Imagine a future where every diploma, certificate, or academic achievement is issued as a tamper-proof entry on a blockchain. In this scenario, any employer, university, or government agency can instantly verify the authenticity of a credential by checking the blockchain. There's no need to trust printed documents or rely on time-consuming manual verifications via phone or email (Lamming et al., 2000).

Attempting to forge or manipulate a credential becomes nearly impossible, as any inconsistency would be immediately flagged against the blockchain's permanent record. Institutions that issue fraudulent or duplicate credentials without authorization would also be exposed, increasing accountability across the board.

This technology strengthens the reputation of educational institutions and restores public trust in academic qualifications. Students benefit from this integrity by being able to showcase their accomplishments confidently, knowing that their credentials carry indisputable proof of authenticity wherever they go.

4.2 Accelerating Verification Processes

Verification of academic credentials is often slow and tedious. Whether a student is applying for a job, enrolling in further education, or migrating internationally, the process typically involves submitting documents, waiting for administrative approval, and relying on institutions to respond — which can take weeks or even months.

Blockchain completely changes this by offering instant verification. Once a credential is recorded on a blockchain, it becomes publicly verifiable (to the extent permitted) through a digital link or a QR code. Students can share their credentials securely and immediately, without intermediaries.

For example, a graduate applying for a position abroad could simply provide a blockchain link to their credential, enabling the hiring manager to verify it within seconds. Similarly, when transferring between universities, verified academic histories can be checked instantly, bypassing the delays typically caused by manual transcript evaluations (Awaji & Solaiman, 2022).

This streamlining reduces administrative overhead for institutions, accelerates hiring and admissions processes for employers and universities, and spares students the frustration of delays and red tape.

4.3 Enabling Interoperability Across Borders

One of the most transformative benefits of blockchain is its ability to foster interoperability between different educational systems. Today, students moving between countries or institutions often have to deal with a patchwork of incompatible formats, policies, and validation procedures.

Blockchain can unify this fragmented landscape by using shared, standardized data formats and making credentials accessible via a global, decentralized network. Whether a student studies in Asia and applies to a university in Europe or earns a micro-credential in the U.S. to apply for work in Africa, blockchain ensures their credentials are universally accessible, verifiable, and trustworthy.

This level of interoperability supports a more mobile student population, encourages global collaboration in education, and opens the door to new hybrid learning models that span continents. With blockchain, a student's academic journey becomes portable and persistent, unhindered by borders or institutional silos.

4.4 Empowering Students with Ownership of Their Credentials

Traditionally, educational institutions hold the authority over academic records. Students often need to formally request their own transcripts or certificates, sometimes paying fees or waiting days to receive them (Fekete & Kiss, 2023). This setup gives institutions control over information that ultimately belongs to the student.

Blockchain fundamentally shifts this dynamic by enabling student ownership of credentials. This concept aligns with the principles of self-sovereign identity (SSI), which advocate for learner-controlled, decentralized management of personal data and credentials (Grech et al., 2021). When an institution issues a blockchain-based credential, it is not only secure but also self-sovereign — meaning that students can store it in a personal digital wallet.

With this approach, students no longer need to rely on institutions to access or share their credentials. They can manage their academic achievements directly, deciding when, where, and with whom to share them — all without requiring re-authorization or assistance.

This decentralization aligns with broader digital trends that empower individuals to control their own data. Even if an issuing university were to close, merge, or change systems, students would still retain uninterrupted access to their records. In this way, blockchain upholds the principle that learners should own their educational histories — not merely have access to them.

Figure 4. Blockchain Solution for Academic Record Keeping

4.5 Enhancing Data Privacy and Security

While blockchain is often associated with transparency, it also supports robust privacy protections through advanced cryptographic techniques.

One such method is the use of zero-knowledge proofs, which allow one party to prove to another that a statement is true — without revealing the underlying data. Another approach is selective disclosure, where the student can choose to share only specific parts of their record with a verifier.

For example, a job applicant could verify possession of a certain degree without revealing grades or unrelated credentials. This ensures that students retain control over their personal information and only share what's necessary for a particular purpose.

Additionally, because blockchain operates on a decentralized network, it avoids the single-point vulnerabilities of centralized databases. Instead of all data being stored in one location — a tempting target for hackers — information is distributed across many nodes, significantly reducing the risk of data breaches and unauthorized access.

By combining verifiability with privacy and robust security, blockchain strikes a powerful balance that traditional systems have long struggled to achieve.

4.6 Supporting Lifelong Learning and Micro-Credentials

Education is no longer a one-time event in early adulthood — it is a lifelong journey. Professionals continually upgrade their skills through short courses, online learning platforms, workshops, certifications, and informal learning experiences.

However, traditional credentialing systems are designed to recognize only formal degrees, often overlooking smaller or non-traditional learning achievements (Werquin, 2012). Blockchain offers a solution by providing an infrastructure that can record micro-credentials and non-degree learning just as securely as a full diploma.

With blockchain, every workshop attended, course completed, or badge earned can be documented immutably. Over time, these records build a comprehensive learning portfolio that reflects a person's evolving skillset.

This kind of dynamic, blockchain-based academic record allows individuals to present a richer and more nuanced narrative of their competencies. It supports new models of credentialing that are modular, flexible, and personalized, meeting the demands of a rapidly changing job market and continuous learning culture.

4.7 Real-World Initiatives and Early Success Stories

Blockchain in education is no longer a futuristic idea — it is already being implemented in various parts of the world, with promising results.

- The Massachusetts Institute of Technology (MIT) has issued blockchain-based diplomas that allow graduates to instantly share verified digital credentials with employers or other institutions.
- The University of Nicosia in Cyprus has similarly adopted blockchain to publish academic certificates for its students, enhancing verification and eliminating the need for paper-based records.
- The European Commission's Europass initiative is working to integrate blockchain into a broader digital credentialing system across Europe, creating a standardized and decentralized method for issuing and verifying educational qualifications.
- The Velocity Network Foundation, a global nonprofit, is developing a blockchain-based system for career credentials and workforce mobility, aiming to build a trustworthy digital ecosystem for employment records.
- In India, the National Academic Depository (NAD) is experimenting with blockchain-linked services to verify university-issued degrees across institutions.
- Similarly, in South Africa and Kenya, pilot initiatives have demonstrated how blockchain can address verification gaps for transnational student mobility.

These real-world initiatives, as depicted in Figure.4 demonstrate that blockchain is not merely a theoretical solution — it is actively reshaping how academic records are issued, verified, and shared. These pioneers show the potential for scalability and adoption on a global scale.

Blockchain technology provides a holistic solution to many of the long-standing issues plaguing traditional academic record-keeping. It:

- Prevents fraud through immutability,
- Speeds up verification through instant access,
- Supports cross-border recognition through interoperability,
- Empowers students through self-ownership,
- Preserves privacy through cryptography,
- Secures data through decentralization,
- And supports the modern learner through the recognition of lifelong learning.

Together, these features pave the way for a more trustworthy, efficient, and inclusive academic ecosystem — one where credentials are portable, secure, and fully under the student's control. As global adoption grows, blockchain has the potential to redefine how we think about education and achievement in the 21st century.

5. DESIGNING BLOCKCHAIN-BASED ACADEMIC RECORD SYSTEMS

Blockchain holds tremendous promise for revolutionizing the way academic credentials are managed, but realizing its full potential requires careful design choices (Ayub Khan et al., 2021). Universities, governments, and educational consortia must make a series of important decisions about architecture, standards, governance, and user experience. Here, we walk through how to design effective blockchain-based systems for academic record-keeping, step by step — not only the technology itself, but also the ecosystems and policies that will make such systems succeed in the real world.

5.1 Defining the Purpose and Scope

The first and most critical step is to define why the blockchain is being used and what problem it is intended to solve. Educational institutions must articulate whether the system is designed primarily for issuing degrees, managing professional certifications, verifying micro-credentials, or all of the above.

Clarity of purpose ensures that design choices remain aligned with user needs.

For instance, a platform focused on full degree verification may emphasize robustness and immutability, while a micro-credential system for online courses may prioritize flexibility and scalability.Moreover, it is essential to decide whether the system will serve a single institution, a national education system, or a broader international audience. Each scenario brings different technical and governance implications.

5.2 Choosing Between Public and Private Blockchains

One of the earliest architectural choices is whether to build the system on a public blockchain, a private blockchain, or a permissioned consortium blockchain.

Public blockchains, such as Ethereum, offer maximum transparency and decentralization but often face challenges related to scalability, transaction costs, and privacy regulations (Subashini et al., 2024).

Private blockchains, on the other hand, provide greater control and efficiency, though they may sacrifice some elements of trustlessness. Permissioned blockchains strike a balance, allowing only vetted institutions to participate in validating transactions while maintaining a level of decentralization and interoperability.The choice should depend on factors like trust requirements, legal compliance, scalability needs, and the cultural context of the educational ecosystem.

5.3 Credential Standards and Data Structures

To ensure that blockchain-based academic records are usable and verifiable across different platforms and jurisdictions, it is vital to adopt or align with emerging global standards for digital credentials.

Two important standards deserve special attention:

- **W3C Verifiable Credentials**: A flexible data model for expressing statements about a subject that can be cryptographically verified.
- **Open Badges (by IMS Global)**: A widely adopted standard for recognizing learning achievements in a structured, machine-readable format.

Designers must create credential templates that include key information such as:

- Student identifiers (with privacy protections)
- Issuer details
- Description of achievement
- Date of issuance
- Expiration (if applicable)
- Digital signatures

By adhering to these standards, systems ensure that their records are not siloed but are interoperable across institutions, employers, and jurisdictions.

5.4 Smart Contracts for Credential Issuance and Revocation

Smart contracts — self-executing programs that run on the blockchain — play a vital role in automating the issuance and management of academic records.

When a student completes a degree or certification:

- A smart contract can automatically verify the fulfillment of requirements.
- It can then trigger the issuance of a verifiable credential recorded on the blockchain.
- Students receive digital proofs that can be shared or stored in their digital wallets.

Smart contracts can also handle revocations. For example, suppose a credential was issued in error or a certification expires. In that case, the issuing institution can update the blockchain to reflect this without erasing the original record — ensuring transparency and accountability. Careful coding and security auditing of smart contracts are essential, as vulnerabilities can seriously affect a system of trust.

Below is a sample smart contract written in Solidity (the most commonly used language for Ethereum-based blockchains). This contract illustrates the issuance and revocation of academic credentials.

Sample Smart Contract

```
pragma solidity ^0.8.0;
// Institution Setup & Access Control
contract AcademicCredential {
    address public institution;
    modifier onlyInstitution() {
        require(msg.sender == institution, "Only institution
can perform this action");
        _;
    }
    constructor() {
        institution = msg.sender; // Institution is the con-
tract deployer
    }
        // Credential Structure
    struct Credential {
        string studentName;
        string course;
        uint256 dateIssued;
        bool isRevoked;
    }
    mapping(address => Credential) public credentials;
    // Events for Transparency
    event CredentialIssued(address indexed student, string
course);
    event CredentialRevoked(address indexed student);
    // Credential Issuance Function
    function issueCredential(
        address _student,
        string memory _studentName,
        string memory _course
    ) public onlyInstitution {
```

```
        require(bytes(credentials[_student].course).length
== 0, "Credential already issued");
        credentials[_student] = Credential({
            studentName: _studentName,
            course: _course,
            dateIssued: block.timestamp,
            isRevoked: false
        });
        emit CredentialIssued(_student, _course);
    }
    // Credential Revocation Function
    function revokeCredential(address _student) public only-
Institution {
        require(bytes(credentials[_student].course).length >
0, "Credential does not exist");
        require(!credentials[_student].isRevoked, "Creden-
tial already revoked");
        credentials[_student].isRevoked = true;
        emit CredentialRevoked(_student);
    }
  // Public Credential Viewer
    function viewCredential(address _student) public view
returns (
        string memory studentName,
        string memory course,
        uint256 dateIssued,
        bool isRevoked
    ) {
        Credential memory cred = credentials[_student];
        return (cred.studentName, cred.course, cred.dateIs-
sued, cred.isRevoked);    }}
```

Explanation:

- **Institution Setup** – Defines who controls the contract and access restrictions.
- **Credential Structure** – Outlines what a credential includes.
- **Events** – Log actions on the blockchain (e.g., issuing or revoking a credential).
- **Issuance Function** – Automatically issues a credential based on inputs.
- **Revocation Function** – Allows the institution to revoke an existing credential.

- **Viewer Function** – Lets anyone (like employers) view the credential's status.

5.5 Privacy by Design: Protecting Student Data

While blockchain is inherently transparent, academic systems must ensure compliance with privacy regulations like GDPR, HIPAA, or local education laws. Protecting students' sensitive data is non-negotiable.

Rather than storing full academic records directly on-chain, best practices recommend:

- Storing only cryptographic hashes of credentials on the blockchain.
- Keeping the actual data off-chain in secure, controlled environments.
- Using privacy-preserving technologies such as zero-knowledge proofs or selective disclosure protocols to allow verifications without revealing unnecessary personal details.

Such strategies preserve the verifiability benefits of blockchain without compromising individual rights to privacy.

5.6 User Experience: Making Blockchain Invisible

A successful blockchain credentialing system must offer a user experience that is simple, intuitive, and accessible, even for users who have no technical knowledge of blockchain.Students, employers, and administrators should be able to:

- Request, receive, and verify credentials through friendly interfaces.
- Store credentials easily in digital wallets (mobile apps, web-based platforms).
- Share verifications via email links, QR codes, or integrated portals.

The underlying blockchain complexity should be hidden from everyday users. Good design focuses on user needs first, using blockchain as a silent enabler rather than a visible burden.

5.7 Governance: Building Trust Across Institutions

Blockchain's decentralized nature requires thoughtful governance. Educational credentialing systems must answer questions such as:

- Who is authorized to issue credentials?
- How are nodes or validators selected?

- How are disputes resolved?
- How are updates to standards or protocols managed?

Some systems create governance councils made up of universities, accreditation bodies, and even student representatives. Mustafa et al. (Islam et al., 2025) propose a comprehensive blockchain governance framework integrating legal, ethical, and operational protocols for large-scale public deployments. Others adopt consortium models where multiple trusted parties share control. Without good governance, even the best technical architecture can fail. Governance builds the human trust necessary to complement technological trust.

5.8 Integration with Existing Systems

Finally, blockchain-based credentialing platforms must integrate smoothly with universities' existing student information systems (SIS), learning management systems (LMS), and administration portals.

Rather than replacing everything overnight, systems should provide APIs, plugins, and middleware that allow institutions to gradually extend their current operations into blockchain environments.This approach eases adoption, minimizes disruption, and allows institutions to build confidence over time.

Designing blockchain-based academic record-keeping systems is not merely a technological exercise (Lemieux, 2019). It requires holistic thinking that integrates technical architecture, legal compliance, data privacy, user experience, and governance frameworks.By addressing these areas thoughtfully, educational institutions can build powerful systems that restore trust in academic achievements, empower lifelong learners, and connect the world's educational ecosystems in ways never before possible.

6. REAL-WORLD IMPLEMENTATIONS AND CASE STUDIES

Although the idea of blockchain for keeping academic records may still seem like science fiction to some, forward-thinking institutions and organizations globally have already started making it a reality. Their early experiments provide useful lessons, expose practical issues, and show the revolutionary potential of decentralized credentialing systems.

6.1 MIT's Digital Diplomas Initiative

In 2017, the Massachusetts Institute of Technology (MIT) broke ground by becoming among the first institutions of higher education to offer blockchain-based diplomas.

Through its Blockcerts platform, built in partnership with Learning Machine (now Hyland Credentials), MIT allowed graduates to receive paper diplomas in the conventional way, as well as secure digital certificates held on the Bitcoin blockchain.

Students accessed their digital diplomas via a dedicated mobile app. These credentials were:

- Tamper-proof
- Easily shareable
- Immediately verifiable by institutions or employers without having to approach MIT itself.

The pilot project of MIT was successful in demonstrating how blockchain could give students ownership of their accomplishments while drastically streamlining verification procedures. It also generated interest in the larger academic community, leading other universities to consider using similar models.

6.2 The University of Nicosia: A Blockchain Trailblazer

The University of Nicosia (UNIC) in Cyprus is commonly considered to be the first university in the world to implement blockchain credentials on a full institutional basis (Silaghi & Popescu, 2025). As early as 2014, UNIC started issuing certificates for its courses in digital currency based on blockchain technology. Seeing the broader potential, UNIC subsequently applied blockchain issuance to diplomas in a variety of fields. Their objectives were:

- To ensure global verifiability of their certificates
- Streamlining administrative workload on alumni services
- Leading the way in blockchain education and adoption

UNIC's activities showed that blockchain was not an experiment in theory but could be successfully integrated into actual academic processes.

6.3 European Blockchain Services Infrastructure (EBSI)

In Europe, the vision of applying blockchain to education scaled to continental proportions with the European Blockchain Services Infrastructure (EBSI), a project of the European Commission (Baniata & Kertesz, 2022). EBSI plans to develop cross-border digital services based on blockchain, and issuing and verifying educational credentials is one of its prime use cases.Participating countries envision a future where European citizens can:

- Move freely across borders
- Carry their academic achievements with them in digital wallets
- Instantly prove their qualifications when seeking employment or pursuing further education abroad

By developing a common framework for blockchain credentials, EBSI addresses both technological and regulatory challenges, setting the stage for a trusted, interoperable ecosystem across the European Union.

6.4 Sony Global Education: Building a Platform for Learning Histories

Sony, working in partnership with IBM, has dabbled with blockchain-based models to create and store learning histories in a distributed way. Sony's commitment signals that giant technology firms look beyond blockchain as a niche novelty for education but regard it as fundamental infrastructure for the future digital economy (Tapscott & Kaplan, 2019).

Their work seeks to:

- Store various forms of learning across different institutions in a common ledger
- Enable people to control a complete and tamper-evident record of their learning experience
- Facilitate institutions and employers to rapidly and reliably verify learning histories

6.5 Learning Machine and Blockcerts: A Decentralized Ecosystem

Outside of individual institutions, such as Blockcerts, have become ecosystem enablers. Blockcerts is an open blockchain standard for credentials, initially developed with MIT funding, and built to be completely decentralized — enabling any issuer, learner, or verifier to join without the need for a central authority (Capece et al., 2020).

The Blockcerts platform facilitates:

- Creation and issuance of credentials, signing
- Private storage of credentials in individual digital wallets
- Public verification via blockchain anchors

Its open-source mentality has spurred use by universities, technical schools, and professional certification agencies globally, leveling the field of access to blockchain credentialing.

6.6 Key Lessons from Early Implementations

Though these examples in action show vast potential, they expose pragmatic challenges with which newcomers must be ready to cope.

First, institutional adoption is essential. Without leadership endorsement and clear internal messaging, blockchain initiatives are likely to be misinterpreted or underutilized.

Second, user experience is critical. Systems need to be intuitive, particularly for non-technical users, or else adoption rates decline.

Third, interoperability is not a given. Even with standards such as Blockcerts or W3C Verifiable Credentials, careful integration effort is required to achieve compatibility between different institutions and national systems.

Lastly, scalability is still something to consider. Some initial pilots functioned beautifully at tiny scale but ran into issues when scaled up to thousands or tens of thousands of people.

These findings inform future initiatives toward more lasting, user-empowering designs.

6.7 A Vision of the Future: Global Academic Mobility

Picture a near future in which all learners — high school students, college graduates, or lifelong learners — have a digital backpack containing verified credentials.

Such blockchain-anchored records would be:

- Recognized across borders
- Instantly shareable with employers
- Resilient against institutional closures or data loss

- Privacy-respecting, placing individuals fully in control of their information

Such a world would incredibly increase educational access, employment prospects, and individual autonomy — making possible a genuinely global learning society.

The real-world applications we have seen in this chapter preview this vision. Each success story, each innovation, and even each misstep add to an expanding body of knowledge about how blockchain can enable education systems to meet the challenges of the 21st century.

Real-world applications show that blockchain credentialing is no longer a fantasy or a test in the lab (Li et al., 2023). Universities, governments, and tech firms worldwide are already proving its viability and benefits. As it gains traction, early movers' lessons will be crucial in defining systems that are more inclusive, secure, interoperable, and learner-focused.

7.CHALLENGES AND BARRIERS TO ADOPTION

As promising as blockchain-based credentialing systems are, widespread adoption across the educational landscape faces several formidable hurdles.

While early pilots demonstrate feasibility and enthusiasm is growing, real-world conditions — ranging from technological complexity to regulatory concerns — create significant barriers. Understanding these challenges is critical not only for avoiding pitfalls but for designing systems that can achieve lasting success.

7.1 Technological Complexity

Blockchain technology, though maturing, remains highly technical and complex for many educational institutions.

Universities and schools, whose core expertise lies in pedagogy and research rather than distributed ledger systems, may find blockchain daunting for several reasons:

- Integration with existing systems (like Student Information Systems or Learning Management Systems) often requires specialized middleware and APIs.
- Smart contract development demands deep technical expertise, especially to ensure security and legal compliance.
- Choice of blockchain platforms (public, private, or consortium) can be confusing without clear technical guidelines.

Without sufficient technical capacity or the support of strong technology partners, institutions risk implementing systems that are unreliable, insecure, or difficult to maintain.

7.2 Legal and Regulatory Uncertainty

Education is a highly regulated domain. The immutable nature of blockchain records (Funk et al., 2018) — one of the technology's greatest strengths — can conflict with legal requirements around:

- The Right to Be Forgotten (GDPR Article 17)
- Student Data Privacy (such as the U.S. FERPA regulations)
- Accreditation and Credential Validation Laws in different jurisdictions
- Zeide and Nissenbaum (Zeide & Nissenbaum, 2018) argue that learner privacy risks in digital education systems are often underestimated, particularly when data control shifts from institutions to platforms without transparent oversight.

If a student demands that their personal data be deleted, but that data has already been recorded on an immutable blockchain, how should an institution respond?

Strategies like on-chain hashing (storing only encrypted representations) help, but many institutions remain wary. Additionally, the lack of clear regulatory frameworks around blockchain usage in education creates hesitation, especially among risk-averse administrators and legal departments (Mustafa et al., 2025).

7.3 Financial and Resource Constraints

Launching a blockchain credentialing project is not cheap. Costs arise from:

- Hiring or contracting blockchain development expertise
- Conducting thorough security audits
- Training staff and administrators on the new system
- Maintaining and upgrading the platform over time

For many universities — especially smaller or public institutions operating under tight budgets — such costs can be prohibitive without external funding or clear economic justification. Moreover, blockchain projects may compete internally with other pressing digital transformation priorities, such as upgrading online learning environments or cybersecurity defenses. Without a strong financial case or sustainable funding model, blockchain initiatives risk being seen as luxurious experiments rather than essential infrastructure.

7.4 Resistance to Change

Education, by its very nature, is considered to be a field rooted in tradition.

Academic institutions, particularly prestigious ones, tend to be conservative about adopting radically new technologies, for good reasons:

- Protecting the integrity and reputation of their degrees
- Avoiding disruption to critical student services
- Preserving established accreditation processes

Stakeholders — faculty, registrars, alumni offices, and even students themselves — may resist blockchain adoption if they perceive it as risky, unnecessary, or burdensome. Change management thus becomes a critical factor. Successful adoption often requires strong leadership, clear communication of benefits, gradual rollout strategies, and active engagement with all stakeholders (Leape et al., 2006).

7.5 Scalability and Performance Concerns

While blockchain can manage credentials securely, concerns about scalability persist.

Public blockchains, especially those using proof-of-work consensus mechanisms, have limitations in transaction throughput and speed. Issues include:

- High transaction fees (gas fees) on platforms like Ethereum during network congestion
- Latency in recording and confirming transactions
- Storage and retrieval inefficiencies when dealing with massive numbers of credentials

Emerging solutions — such as layer-2 scaling technologies, proof-of-stake blockchains, or permissioned networks — offer promise. But these add new layers of technical and operational complexity that institutions must carefully navigate.

7.6 Interoperability Challenges

An isolated blockchain-based credential system offers little value if it cannot communicate with others. True educational mobility demands that records issued by one institution can be verified and accepted by others across borders, sectors, and platforms.

However, the global landscape remains fragmented:

- Different institutions adopt different standards (Blockcerts, W3C Verifiable Credentials, proprietary models) (Zeide & Nissenbaum, 2018)
- Different blockchains (Ethereum, Hyperledger, private chains) create compatibility barriers (Alam et al., 2021).
- Varying credential taxonomies and metadata structures complicate cross-institutional recognition

Without deliberate efforts to promote open standards and interoperability, blockchain credentialing risks creating new digital silos rather than solving the old ones.

7.7 Cultural and Ethical Considerations

Finally, blockchain-based credentialing raises important cultural and ethical questions:

- Should individuals truly "own" their credentials, even when issued by an institution?
- Could blockchain systems reinforce existing inequities if only well-funded universities adopt them first?
- How do we ensure that blockchain does not become a tool for surveillance, exclusion, or data commodification under the guise of innovation?

Cultural values about education, privacy, authority, and technology vary widely around the world. Designers of blockchain systems must tread carefully, building inclusive, respectful, and context-sensitive solutions. Ethical design is not an optional feature. It is a foundation for trust and legitimacy. Blockchain has the potential to revolutionize academic credentialing, but the path to widespread adoption is neither smooth nor automatic.

Technological, legal, financial, cultural, and organizational challenges must be thoughtfully addressed.

Institutions that succeed in this transformation will be those that:

- Build deep technical capacity or partner wisely
- Engage stakeholders transparently
- Align blockchain systems with legal and ethical standards
- Focus on usability and real-world interoperability

7.8 Policy Alignment and Accreditation Frameworks

Blockchain credentialing systems must align with regional and national policies around education, data governance, and accreditation. For example, many countries have Qualification Frameworks (e.g., EQF in Europe, NQF in India) that define learning outcomes, levels, and competencies. Blockchain solutions must map credentials onto these frameworks to gain legitimacy. Furthermore, integration with digital identity initiatives like India's Aadhaar, Estonia's eID, or the EU's eIDAS can enhance verification and compliance.

8. STRATEGIC ROADMAP FOR INSTITUTIONS: FROM PILOTS TO MAINSTREAM ADOPTION

As universities and educational institutions begin to explore the possibilities of blockchain for credentialing, it's crucial to take a structured, strategic approach to ensure success. Moving from pilot projects to full-scale adoption requires careful planning, clear objectives, and an ongoing commitment to improvement (Vreugdenhil et al., 2012). This chapter outlines a strategic roadmap that institutions can follow, from the initial exploration phase to a sustainable, institution-wide implementation of blockchain credentialing.

8.1 Phase 1: Exploration and Understanding

The first step in any blockchain adoption journey is exploration and understanding. Institutions must assess their current systems, define clear objectives, and determine whether blockchain technology aligns with their goals. This phase involves several key activities:

8.1.1 Building Awareness and Education

Start by fostering internal awareness about the potential of blockchain in education. This includes educating key stakeholders — from administrators to faculty members to technical teams — about the fundamental concepts of blockchain, its benefits, and its challenges. Hosting workshops, webinars, or bringing in external experts can help demystify the technology.

8.1.2 Defining Use Cases and Objectives

Not all institutions will use blockchain in the same way. For some, it might be about issuing secure, verifiable degrees, while for others, it could involve managing the full spectrum of learning achievements, including microcredentials and certificates. Therefore, defining the specific use case and setting clear, measurable objectives is essential. Key questions to ask include:

- What problem is blockchain solving? (e.g., reducing fraud, improving student mobility, enhancing data privacy)
- What are the long-term benefits of using blockchain for credentialing?
- How will success be measured?

This phase may also involve consulting with external partners who have already implemented blockchain credentialing systems to understand best practices and challenges.

8.2 Phase 2: Planning and Design

8.2.1 Selecting the Right Blockchain Platform

Choosing the appropriate blockchain platform is one of the most critical decisions. Institutions must assess several factors:

- **Public vs. Private Blockchains**: Public blockchains (like Ethereum) are decentralized and transparent, but they can be costly and slow. Private blockchains or consortium blockchains (such as Hyperledger or Corda) might offer more control and scalability but may lack decentralization.
- **Scalability**: Will the platform be able to handle large volumes of credentials as the institution grows? Scalability is a key consideration when choosing a blockchain platform.
- **Security**: Ensuring the security of student data is paramount. Institutions must evaluate the security features of the chosen blockchain and ensure it meets the necessary compliance standards for data privacy.

8.2.2 Designing User-Friendly Systems

The system must be designed with users in mind — students, administrators, and employers. A user-centric design will ensure that blockchain credentials are easy to access, verify, and manage. Some considerations include:

- Developing a simple, intuitive interface for students to access and share their credentials
- Providing clear instructions on how to verify credentials for employers and other institutions
- Offering mobile compatibility, as many students and employers prefer to access credentials via their smartphones.

8.2.3 Collaboration with Stakeholders

This phase also involves working closely with internal stakeholders (such as registrars, IT teams, and faculty members) and external stakeholders (employers, other educational institutions, and regulatory bodies). Collaboration ensures that all parties have a clear understanding of how the system will work and how it will integrate with existing workflows.

8.3 Phase 3: Pilot Implementation

8.3.1 Defining the Scope of the Pilot

The pilot should focus on a specific group of users or departments to minimize risk and make troubleshooting easier. For example, the pilot could start with a small cohort of graduates or a particular program, such as a certificate course, to test the blockchain credentialing process. The key objectives of the pilot phase should be to:

- Test the usability and functionality of the system
- Ensure compatibility with existing systems (e.g., SIS, LMS)
- Collect feedback from stakeholders (students, faculty, employers)

8.3.2 Iterative Testing and Improvement

As the pilot progresses, **feedback loops** should be established to gather insights from users. Continuous testing and improvement during this phase are crucial for ironing out any technical issues, refining the user experience, and making necessary adjustments before the full-scale implementation.

8.3.3 Evaluating Success

Once the pilot phase is complete, it's time to evaluate its success. Key performance indicators (KPIs) such as user adoption rates, system performance, feedback from users, and the time required for verification processes can help assess the effectiveness of the blockchain solution. If the pilot is successful, the institution can proceed to the next phase. If issues arise, further testing and adjustments will be needed before moving forward.

8.4 Phase 4: Full-Scale Implementation

8.4.1 Scaling the System

Scaling involves expanding the blockchain system to include all academic programs, courses, and departments. As Alammary (Alammary, 2024) emphasizes, building sustainable, scalable blockchain infrastructure requires modular architecture and cross-institutional collaboration across different jurisdictions. The IT team will need to ensure the platform can handle the increased data and user load while maintaining performance and security. It may also be necessary to integrate the blockchain system with other institutional platforms to ensure seamless workflows.

8.4.2 Ensuring Institutional Buy-In

Full-scale implementation requires the commitment of institutional leadership. Administrators must ensure that the necessary resources are allocated, and that the adoption of blockchain is communicated clearly to all stakeholders. Faculty and staff must be properly trained to manage the system and assist students with any issues they encounter.

8.4.3 Communication and Training

Effective communication is essential during this phase. Institutions should develop training programs for staff and students to ensure smooth adoption. Clear documentation and guidance on how to use the blockchain system, how to issue and verify credentials, and how to address potential issues will help prevent confusion and frustration.

8.5 Phase 5: Ongoing Maintenance and Evaluation

After the full-scale implementation, the work doesn't stop. Blockchain systems require continuous monitoring, maintenance, and evaluation (Zhang et al., 2020).

8.5.1 Monitoring System Performance

Regular audits and performance reviews are essential to ensure that the system is functioning optimally. Monitoring tools can help detect issues such as network slowdowns, security breaches, or user experience problems, allowing for quick corrective actions.

8.5.2 Ongoing Improvements

Blockchain technology is evolving rapidly. Institutions should stay abreast of technological advancements, regulatory changes, and industry trends to ensure their system remains cutting-edge. Continuous updates, system optimizations, and new feature rollouts will help maintain the system's relevance and effectiveness.

8.5.3 Gathering Feedback

Regularly soliciting feedback from students, faculty, and employers can provide valuable insights into areas for improvement (Shah et al., 2015). Ongoing user feedback ensures that the system evolves based on real-world needs, rather than remaining static.

9. THE FUTURE OF BLOCKCHAIN IN EDUCATION

Blockchain technology, though still in its early stages of adoption in education, holds the promise of radically reshaping how institutions manage academic credentials, student records, and even learning itself. As the technology matures, its potential applications within education extend far beyond the confines of credentialing. Here it takes a deep dive into the future of blockchain in education, exploring how it will evolve, the innovative ways it could be used, and the long-term impact it may have on the educational landscape.

9.1 The Expanding Role of Blockchain in Education

Looking ahead, the role of blockchain will likely expand from simply issuing verifiable academic credentials to encompassing a wide range of educational processes. Already, we see the early stages of blockchain systems used for student records, diplomas, and course certifications. (Legris et al., 2003) But as the technology becomes more widely accepted, it will play an increasingly critical role in areas such as:

- **Student Data Ownership and Control**: One of blockchain's most profound promises is to give students control over their own educational data. In the future, students may hold digital wallets that store their entire educational history — not just their diplomas, but also grades, projects, skills, and achievements. Students will have the freedom to share or withhold access to their data at their discretion, which could reshape how personal information is managed and shared within the education sector.
- **Microcredentialing and Lifelong Learning**: With the rise of microcredentials and stackable credentials, blockchain will make it easier to track and verify smaller, more frequent achievements. These could range from completing a course to earning a specific skill or even contributing to an academic publication. Over time, these microcredentials could replace or supplement traditional degrees, creating a more flexible, personalized education path that reflects real-world achievements.
- **Decentralized Learning Platforms**: Blockchain could give rise to decentralized educational platforms where content creation, accreditation, and verification are distributed across the network rather than being controlled by a central authority. This could democratize education by reducing barriers to entry, particularly in countries or communities with limited access to traditional institutions.
- **Transparent and Fairer Funding**: Blockchain's transparency and immutability could transform how educational funding is allocated. Institutions could use blockchain to track and manage funding more transparently, ensuring that scholarships, grants, and loans are allocated efficiently and fairly. Furthermore, blockchain could be used for decentralized education funding models, where donors and institutions can track exactly how funds are used in real time.

9.2 Blockchain and Inter-Institutional Collaboration

Education today is increasingly global. Students often transfer between institutions, pursue joint degrees, or engage in study abroad programs. Blockchain could make inter-institutional collaboration far more seamless by providing a universal framework for academic records that is recognized and accepted globally (Alammary, 2024). Imagine a scenario where a student can take courses across different universities in different countries and have all their learning achievements securely recorded and verified on a single, immutable blockchain.

This global interoperability of credentials would eliminate the current issues of credential verification across borders, where universities may face delays and inefficiencies in confirming a student's academic history (Grech et al., 2021).

Blockchain's immutable and transparent nature ensures that once a credential is recorded, it can be verified instantly by any institution, employer, or regulatory body, regardless of location.

This shift would pave the way for a truly global education system, enabling students to navigate seamlessly between institutions, employers, and governments across the world, without the traditional barriers that exist today.

9.3 A Paradigm Shift in Academic Recognition

Beyond the administrative functions of blockchain, the technology could usher in a paradigm shift in how academic achievement is recognized (Ramasamy & Khan, 2024). In the future, a student's record could be more than just a list of grades or degrees; it could be a dynamic, comprehensive portfolio of their learning journey, including:

- **Skills Acquired**: Blockchain could track the development of both hard and soft skills over time. Employers may look at these skill portfolios, which could be far more accurate and personalized than traditional resumes or CVs.
- **Experiential Learning**: Many educational systems are already moving towards incorporating experiential learning — where students learn through real-world, practical experiences. Blockchain could securely store records of this learning, whether it's internships, volunteer work, research projects, or fieldwork, providing a more holistic picture of a student's education.
- **Recognition of Prior Learning**: Blockchain could also play a key role in the recognition of prior learning. Individuals with non-traditional educational backgrounds, such as those who have gained skills through work experience, online courses, or self-study, could have their learning achievements securely recorded and verified. This would make it easier for them to gain credit toward formal qualifications, thus promoting lifelong learning and more equitable educational pathways.

9.4 The Integration of Blockchain with Emerging Technologies

As blockchain becomes more integrated into educational systems, its true potential will be realized when combined with other emerging technologies such as artificial intelligence (AI), big data, and the Internet of Things (IoT) (Atlam et al., 2020). Here's how these technologies could converge:

- **AI and Blockchain for Personalized Learning**: Blockchain can serve as a secure repository for AI-driven insights about a student's learning habits and preferences.
- **Big Data and Blockchain for Predictive Analytics**: By combining blockchain with big data analytics, institutions can track student progress more accurately and predict academic outcomes.
- **IoT and Blockchain for Real-Time Learning**: In future educational environments, smart classrooms equipped with IoT devices (like wearables, sensors, and interactive tools) will collect vast amounts of data about student engagement, participation, and learning outcomes.

9.5 Addressing Challenges to Full-Scale Adoption

While the potential for blockchain in education is immense, the challenges discussed in earlier chapters — such as regulatory hurdles, technological limitations, and resistance to change — must be addressed for the vision of blockchain in education to become a reality. This means:

- **Developing clear legal frameworks** that ensure student data privacy while promoting the benefits of decentralization and immutability.
- **Simplifying the technology** so that institutions of all sizes and resources can adopt it without requiring deep technical expertise.
- **Encouraging global cooperation** among educational institutions, governments, and blockchain developers to create common standards that promote interoperability and security.

9.6 The Future of Blockchain-Verified Credentials

The day may come when a blockchain-verified credential is as universally recognized as a traditional diploma, but with even more credibility (Poikaryil et al., 2024). As blockchain adoption grows, employers will increasingly turn to decentralized credential verification platforms to streamline the hiring process. Instead of relying on outdated and error-prone methods, employers will be able to instantly access verified records, ensuring that what applicants claim is accurate and up-to-date.

10. CASE STUDIES: SUCCESS STORIES OF BLOCKCHAIN IN EDUCATION

Blockchain technology is already making waves in the education sector, with institutions around the world experimenting with and implementing blockchain solutions for credentialing, student records, and more.

10.1 Case Study 1: MIT - Digital Diplomas

The Massachusetts Institute of Technology (MIT) has been a pioneer in adopting blockchain technology for credentialing (Rauthan et al., 2021). In 2017, MIT launched a pilot program called Blockcerts, allowing graduates to receive their diplomas in the form of blockchain-based, verifiable certificates. These digital diplomas are secure, tamper-proof, and can be easily shared with employers or other institutions. The success of this program has led to its expansion, and MIT continues to explore new ways of using blockchain to verify academic credentials.

10.2 Case Study 2: The University of Nicosia - Blockchain for Degrees

The University of Nicosia in Cyprus was one of the first universities to offer blockchain-verified degrees. Since 2014, it has been issuing digital diplomas and transcripts on the blockchain (Roshanzade, 2023). The university uses the Blockcerts framework to ensure that students' academic achievements are secure and easily verifiable by employers. This initiative has been a success, with both local and international employers recognizing the ease and security of blockchain-based credentials.

10.3 Case Study 3: Sony Global Education - Blockchain for Learning Records

Sony Global Education, in collaboration with IBM, developed a blockchain-based platform that allows students to securely store their learning achievements, including grades and academic history (Hameed et al., 2019). This platform aims to offer a more transparent, immutable way of storing educational records, ensuring that all stakeholders — including students, employers, and institutions — can access verifiable data. The platform is being piloted in various educational systems, helping shape the future of decentralized academic record-keeping.

10.4 Case Study 4: Tertiary Education Commission of New Zealand - Blockchain for Microcredentials

In New Zealand, the Tertiary Education Commission has been working with blockchain technology to issue microcredentials (Selvaratnam & Sankey, 2021). These are digital credentials awarded for specific skills or knowledge acquired outside of traditional degrees. The blockchain ensures that these microcredentials are securely issued and verified, providing students with portable, verifiable proof of their skills. This initiative is seen as a significant step toward recognizing alternative learning pathways in the workforce.

10.5 Case Study 5: APRU (Asia-Pacific Rim Universities) - Blockchain for Regional Collaboration

APRU, a consortium of universities in the Asia-Pacific region, is experimenting with blockchain to enable cross-institutional credential verification (Yang et al., 2025). By using blockchain, the group aims to create a seamless way for students to transfer credits and verify academic achievements across borders. This collaboration enhances student mobility, helping to eliminate the friction in credit transfers and recognition of qualifications.

REFERENCES

Alam, S., Asim, M., Shuaib, M., & Khan, M. U. S. (2021). Blockchain-based initiatives: Current state and challenges. *Computer Networks*, *198*, 108395. DOI: 10.1016/j.comnet.2021.108395

Alammary, A. S. (2024). Building a sustainable digital infrastructure for higher education: A blockchain-based solution for cross-institutional enrollment. *Sustainability (Basel)*, *17*(1), 194. DOI: 10.3390/su17010194

Alammary, A. S. (2024). Building a sustainable digital infrastructure for higher education: A blockchain-based solution for cross-institutional enrollment. *Sustainability (Basel)*, *17*(1), 194. DOI: 10.3390/su17010194

Atlam, H. F., Alenezi, A., Alharthi, A., Walters, R. J., & Wills, G. B. (2020). A review of blockchain in internet of things and AI. *Big Data and Cognitive Computing*, *4*(4), 28. DOI: 10.3390/bdcc4040028

Awaji, B., & Solaiman, E. (2022). Design, implementation, and evaluation of blockchain-based trusted achievement record system for students in higher education. *arXiv preprint arXiv:2204.12547.* DOI: 10.5220/0011044200003182

Ayub Khan, A., Rahman, M. S., Alam, M. M., Rehman, S. U., & Kim, J. M. (2021). Educational blockchain: A secure degree attestation and verification traceability architecture for higher education commission. *Applied Sciences (Basel, Switzerland)*, *11*(22), 10917. DOI: 10.3390/app112210917

Baniata, H., & Kertesz, A. (2022). Prifob: A privacy-aware fog-enhanced blockchain-based system for global accreditation and credential verification. *Journal of Network and Computer Applications*, *205*, 103440. DOI: 10.1016/j.jnca.2022.103440

Canty, R. B., Bao, S., Coley, C. W., Li, S., Manson, A. L., Wang, S., Caffrey, D. R., Church, G. M., Dorr, B. M., Friedler, S. A., Gromski, P. S., Hall, D., Hazen, S. P., Hinkson, I. V., Klavs, F., Krzyzanowski, P. M., Lawrence, C., Lee, D. H., Li, R., & McGill, C. M. (2025). Science acceleration and accessibility with self-driving labs. *Nature Communications*, *16*(1), 3856. DOI: 10.1038/s41467-025-59231-1 PMID: 40274856

Capece, G., Levialdi Ghiron, N., & Pasquale, F. (2020). Blockchain technology: Redefining trust for digital certificates. *Sustainability (Basel)*, *12*(21), 8952. DOI: 10.3390/su12218952

Eaton, S. E., & Carmichael, J. J. (2023). Fake degrees and credential fraud, contract cheating, and paper mills: Overview and historical perspectives. In *Fake degrees and fraudulent credentials in higher education* (pp. 1–22).

Fekete, D. L., & Kiss, A. (2023). Toward building smart contract-based higher education systems using zero-knowledge Ethereum virtual machine. *Electronics (Basel), 12*(3), 664. DOI: 10.3390/electronics12030664

Funk, E., Meyer, H. S., Gilbert, J. H. V., & Oandasan, I. F. (2018). Blockchain technology: A data framework to improve validity, trust, and accountability of information exchange in health professions education. *Academic Medicine, 93*(12), 1791–1794. DOI: 10.1097/ACM.0000000000002326 PMID: 29901658

Governatori, G., Idelberger, F., Milosevic, Z., Riveret, R., Sartor, G., & Xu, X. (2018). On legal contracts, imperative and declarative smart contracts, and blockchain systems. *Artificial Intelligence and Law, 26*(4), 377–409. DOI: 10.1007/s10506-018-9223-3

Grech, A., Sood, I., & Ariño, L. (2021). Blockchain, self-sovereign identity and digital credentials: Promise versus praxis in education. *Frontiers in Blockchain, 4*, 616779. DOI: 10.3389/fbloc.2021.616779

Grech, A., Sood, I., & Ariño, L. (2021). Blockchain, self-sovereign identity and digital credentials: Promise versus praxis in education. *Frontiers in Blockchain, 4*, 616779. DOI: 10.3389/fbloc.2021.616779

Hameed, B., Yasin, M., & Khan, R. (2019). A review of blockchain based educational projects. *International Journal of Advanced Computer Science and Applications, 10*(10). Advance online publication. DOI: 10.14569/IJACSA.2019.0101065

Hasan, R., Sion, R., & Winslett, M. (2009). Preventing history forgery with secure provenance. [TOS]. *ACM Transactions on Storage, 5*(4), 1–43. DOI: 10.1145/1629080.1629082

Islam, R., Rahman, M. M., Rehman, S. U., Gumaei, A., & Hossain, M. S. (2025). Decentralized trust framework for smart cities: A blockchain-enabled cybersecurity and data integrity model. *Scientific Reports, 15*(1), 23454. DOI: 10.1038/s41598-025-06405-y PMID: 40603417

Kim, Y., Back, J., & Kim, J. (2021). A tamper-resistant algorithm using blockchain for the digital tachograph. *Electronics (Basel), 10*(5), 581. DOI: 10.3390/electronics10050581

Lamming, M., Bowers, J., Light, A., Mariani, J., & Blomberg, J. (2000). Satchel: Providing access to any document, any time, anywhere. [TOCHI]. *ACM Transactions on Computer-Human Interaction*, *7*(3), 322–352. DOI: 10.1145/355324.355326

Leape, L. L., Rogers, G., Hanna, D., Griswold, P., Federico, F., Fenn, C. A., Bates, D. W., & Kirle, L. (2006). Developing and implementing new safe practices: Voluntary adoption through statewide collaboratives. *BMJ Quality & Safety*, *15*(4), 289–295. DOI: 10.1136/qshc.2005.017632 PMID: 16885255

Legris, P., Ingham, J., & Collerette, P. (2003). Why do people use information technology? A critical review of the technology acceptance model. *Information & Management*, *40*(3), 191–204. DOI: 10.1016/S0378-7206(01)00143-4

Lemieux, V. L. (2019). Blockchain and public record keeping: Of temples, prisons, and the (re) configuration of power. *Frontiers in Blockchain*, *2*, 5. DOI: 10.3389/fbloc.2019.00005

Li, Z. Z., Wang, Q., Qiao, S., Zhang, L., & Chen, X. (2023). Enhancing blockchain adoption through tailored software engineering: An industrial-grounded study in education credentialing. *Distributed Ledger Technologies: Research and Practice*, *2*(4), 1–24. DOI: 10.1145/3632532

Lizcano, D., Lara, J. A., White, B., & Aljawarneh, S. (2020). Blockchain-based approach to create a model of trust in open and ubiquitous higher education. *Journal of Computing in Higher Education*, *32*(1), 109–134. DOI: 10.1007/s12528-019-09209-y

Mustafa, G., Rehman, S. U., Khan, I. U., Khattak, H. A., & Kim, K. (2025). Blockchain-based governance models in e-government: A comprehensive framework for legal, technical, ethical and security considerations. *International Journal of Law and Management*, *67*(1), 37–55. DOI: 10.1108/IJLMA-08-2023-0172

Poikaryil, O. B., Azeem, M., Khan, S., & Ahmad, I. (2024). Transformative fusion: Leveraging blockchain and AI for educational data analytics in modern education systems. In *Blockchain and AI in shaping the modern education system* (pp. 182–208). CRC Press.

Raj, P., Deka, G. C., & Chinnasamy, C. (2015). High-performance big-data analytics. In *Computing systems and approaches* (Vol. 1). Springer.

Ramasamy, L. K., & Khan, F. (2024). Blockchain-based e-learning platform: Transforming education through decentralization. In *Blockchain for global education* (pp. 103–123). Springer Nature Switzerland. DOI: 10.1007/978-3-031-52123-2_6

Rauthan, J. S., Reddy, G. J., & Agarwal, P. (2021). Blockchain and the digital credentialing for education system. In *Proceedings of Integrated Intelligence Enable Networks and Computing: IIENC 2020*. Springer Singapore. DOI: 10.1007/978-981-33-6307-6_90

Roshanzade, T. (2023). A qualitative study of investigating the adoption of blockchain technology in higher education.

Selvaratnam, R., & Sankey, M. (2021). The state of micro-credentials implementation and practice in Australasian higher education. *Open Praxis*, *13*(2), 228–238. DOI: 10.5944/openpraxis.13.2.130

Shah, M., Grebennikov, L., & Nair, C. S. (2015). A decade of study on employer feedback on the quality of university graduates. *Quality Assurance in Education*, *23*(3), 262–278. DOI: 10.1108/QAE-04-2014-0018

Sharma, S., & Dwivedi, R. (2024). A survey on blockchain deployment for biometric systems. *IET Blockchain*, *4*(2), 124–151. DOI: 10.1049/blc2.12063

Silaghi, D. L., & Popescu, D. E. (2025). A systematic review of blockchain-based initiatives in comparison to best practices used in higher education institutions. *Computers*, *14*(4), 141. DOI: 10.3390/computers14040141

Silaghi, D. L., & Popescu, D. E. (2025). A systematic review of blockchain-based initiatives in comparison to best practices used in higher education institutions. *Computers*, *14*(4), 141. DOI: 10.3390/computers14040141

Subashini, B., Shanthi, P., & Venkatesh, K. (2024). Blockchain-enabled quality assurance and traceability in the Indian confectionery market. In *2024 International Conference on Innovative Computing, Intelligent Communication and Smart Electrical Systems (ICSES)* (pp. 1–6). IEEE. DOI: 10.1109/ICSES63760.2024.10910618

Tapscott, D., & Kaplan, A. (2019). *Blockchain revolution in education and lifelong learning*. Blockchain Research Institute–IBM Institute for Business Value.

Vreugdenhil, H., Taljaard, S., & Slinger, J. H. (2012). Pilot projects and their diffusion: A case study of integrated coastal management in South Africa. *International Journal of Sustainable Development*, *15*(1–2), 148–172. DOI: 10.1504/IJSD.2012.044039

Werquin, P. (2012). The missing link to connect education and employment: Recognition of non-formal and informal learning outcomes. *Journal of Education and Work*, *25*(3), 259–278. DOI: 10.1080/13639080.2012.687574

Xiao, Y., Zhang, N., Lou, W., & Hou, Y. T. (2020). A survey of distributed consensus protocols for blockchain networks. *IEEE Communications Surveys and Tutorials, 22*(2), 1432–1465. DOI: 10.1109/COMST.2020.2969706

Yang, L., Zhang, Y., Liu, W., & Chen, X. (2025). Interoperability of the metaverse: A digital ecosystem perspective review. *IEEE Engineering Management Review, 53*(3), 29–54. DOI: 10.1109/EMR.2025.3564923

Zeide, E., & Nissenbaum, H. (2018). Learner privacy in MOOCs and virtual education. *Theory and Research in Education, 16*(3), 280–307. DOI: 10.1177/1477878518815340

Zeide, E., & Nissenbaum, H. (2018). Learner privacy in MOOCs and virtual education. *Theory and Research in Education, 16*(3), 280–307. DOI: 10.1177/1477878518815340

Zhang, A., Man, J., Sun, Q., & Liu, Y. (2020). Blockchain-based life cycle assessment: An implementation framework and system architecture. *Resources, Conservation and Recycling, 152*, 104512. DOI: 10.1016/j.resconrec.2019.104512

Zook, M. A., & Blankenship, J. (2018). New spaces of disruption? The failures of Bitcoin and the rhetorical power of algorithmic governance. *Geoforum, 96*, 248–255. DOI: 10.1016/j.geoforum.2018.08.023

Chapter 15
Privacy-Preserving Data Sharing Technologies

Bhargavi Konda
https://orcid.org/0009-0001-4704-1526
University of the Cumberlands, USA

Akhila Reddy Yadulla
https://orcid.org/0009-0005-6377-6265
University of the Cumberlands, USA

Mounica Yenugula
https://orcid.org/0009-0002-3259-4563
University of the Cumberlands, USA

Vinay Kumar Kasula
https://orcid.org/0009-0001-1131-3059
University of the Cumberlands, USA

ABSTRACT

The quick advancement of big data sharing increases the importance of protecting data privacy. Differential privacy appeared in 2006 to become the fundamental privacy-preserving data mining and publication method. Various technologies, including federated learning, homomorphic encryption, and secure multi-party computation, have introduced new solutions for safeguarding data privacy during recent technological developments. Differential privacy is experiencing a comparison test in current technology markets because Google and Apple have integrated it into new products. This chapter begin by examining the differential privacy systems used in traditional centralized data models and their usage in data mining and publish-

DOI: 10.4018/979-8-3373-2185-1.ch015

ing processes. The chapter investigates modern developments in local differential privacy by examining randomized response Bloom filters and statistical inference tools related to crowdsourcing systems.

I. INTRODUCTION

The digital era brings extensive attention from academic institutions, governments, and enterprises to safeguard privacy, especially because huge volumes of sensitive data are regularly shared and generated daily. The management of extensive personal information databases belongs to governments alongside enterprise collection and analysis of behavioral data from users, which includes location data, consumer patterns, and social interaction records. Cloud environment users face constrained access to their stored personal data, which drives extensive privacy violation apprehension. Centered data storage and processing systems generate one major risk point that facilitates privacy infringements on a large scale. Bangkok demands powerful data protection methods and proper laws to guarantee security while maximizing the social value and economic potential of user information.

Privacy research originated from the development of privacy protection techniques through anonymization methods. The concept of private disclosure control invented by Dalenius ignited the development of k-anonymity, together with other algorithms designed to stop data re-identification through equivalence class grouping (Loukides & Lomax, 2021). The research community added three models to privacy protection, including l-diversity, t-closeness, and (\u03b1, k)-anonymity to cope with different adversary background knowledge restrictions. The methods offered limited protection when adversaries possessed broad knowledge of associated external information (Li et al., 2006; Zhou & Pei,2011; Tu et al., 2018).

The year 2006 marked a significant achievement, with differential privacy (DP) being introduced by Dwork (Zhu et al., 2017). DP establishes a rigorous mathematical system that protects privacy by ensuring that data respondents remain anonymous even when their information is added or removed from query inputs. The addition of precise noise to data enables resistance against inference attacks during situations where adversaries have extensive knowledge of the data. DP strengthened its position as a fundamental technology for data protection that major tech companies currently employ in their operational implementations.

1.1. Advancements in Differential Privacy

Various commercial systems currently use Differential Privacy, which demonstrates its practical application benefits. Apple uses DP within its iOS platform to protect QuickType and Safari Suggestions through its implementation (Caruso, 2024; Pochintesta, 2012). Chrome users benefit from the implementation of DP, which enables Google to obtain telemetry information without exposing their identities (Munir et al., 2024). The smartphone data collection at Samsung runs with DP implementation for user privacy protection (Khandelwal et al., 2024).

The research field of DP has undergone two main developments.

- Centralized Differential Privacy (CDP):

CDP depends on an authorized data curator to function, and researchers extensively use it to process secure data aggregation query systems and data publishing activities. The latest CDP research strives to optimize noise addition systems as a method for improving data utility and privacy protection levels. Research teams have created new dataset processing methods that make high-dimensional information simpler to manage, thus leading to its practical use in healthcare analytics and financial modeling. CDP exists as a distributed system solution for multiple organizations to collaborate securely with their privacy-protected data (He et al., 2014; Dwork & Roth, 2014; Goryczka et al., 2013).

- Local Differential Privacy (LDP):

LDP provides end-to-end data protection through the direct application of noise at the source, making privacy features operational before data transmission occurs. A large number of industries now use this model for tasks including crowd-sourcing, stream data analysis, and edge computing implementations. The application of different privacy-preserving models includes Google Chrome telemetry data collection and frequency mining activities in Apple analytics systems. Adaptive noise calibration techniques in LDP have improved both privacy robustness and utility, according to recent research (Erlingsson et al., 2014; Thakurta et al., 2017; Kulynych et al., 2024; Wang & Xu, 2023).

1.2. Emerging Trends and Applications

The introduction of differential privacy into modern technologies enables solutions for modern privacy needs. DP within federated learning allows multiple users to maintain their privacy during distributed model updates while training collaborative machine learning models (Triastcyn, & Faltings, 2019; Vaijainthymala, 2024). Blockchain systems implement DP to provide both transaction viewability and data confidentiality, thus resolving privacy challenges that occur in decentralized systems (Zhou et al., 2023). Edge computing applications, together with the Internet of Things (IoT), use DP as a data protection tool for analyzing distributed sensor information without compromising privacy (Alwarafy et al., 2020). DP, alongside artificial intelligence (AI) techniques, forms a new trend in processing sensitive data throughout medical diagnosis and financial risk assessment operations. The integration of DP into artificial intelligence models ensures untraceable individual input, which solves problems of privacy breaches and adversarial attacks in AI systems (Krishnamoorthy, 2024; Triastcyn & Faltings, 2019).

1.3. Challenges and Future Directions

The introduction of differential privacy into modern technologies enables solutions for modern privacy needs. DP in federated learning makes it possible for clients to collaborate on model training without revealing specific information from their datasets during distributed update processes(Triastcyn & Faltings, 2019; Vaijainthymala, 2024). Blockchain systems deploy DP as a method to provide transaction visibility while safeguarding confidential data to preserve privacy during decentralized operations (Zhou et al., 2023). Edge computing applications, together with the Internet of Things (IoT), use DP as a data protection tool for analyzing distributed sensor information without compromising privacy (Alwarafy et al., 2020). DP, alongside artificial intelligence (AI) techniques, forms a new trend in processing sensitive data throughout medical diagnosis and financial risk assessment operations. By integrating DP with AI systems, the model operations become undetectable, which prevents both adversarial attacks and privacy disclosure (Krishnamoorthy, 2024; Triastcyn & Faltings, 2019).

II. DIFFERENTIAL PRIVACY MODELS: ADVANCEMENTS AND CORE CONCEPTS

Differential privacy (DP) has become the dominant paradigm in data processing, allowing data to be used for research and other analytical purposes. This approach primarily addresses those issues with the possibility of sharing sensitive data with adversaries and the drive to conduct research on the data. The two most prevalent models of DP are the Centralized Trusted Curator Model and the Local Differential Privacy (LDP) Model. The Centralized Trusted Curator Model is one of the two models of differential privacy that is widely used in various applications. The model assumes the existence of a trusted third-party data curator, who is the person responsible for collecting and managing raw data. The mere idea of privacy in this model is to add random noise to the results of data queries or any analyses made on the data, resulting in the privacy differential being enforced before the data is released. This method is frequently employed in instances where the custodian is somebody who can be trusted, and the most important thing is just the analysis of the data and not the sharing of raw data.

Basic Points:

- Raw data is kept in one place and is mostly run by the curator.
- Data inquiries or outputs are made by adding noise.
- It is highly useful because the original data is still available for internal users to analyze it by themselves.

Example Mechanism: Laplace Mechanism The Laplace mechanism is an algorithm used to ensure that the resultant distribution of the outputs of the data queries is similar to that of the original one, as proven by the following statement:$A(D) = f(D) + Y, Y \sim Lap(\Delta f/\epsilon)$

where $f(D)$ is the query function, and Δf is the sensitivity.

2.1. Local Differential Privacy (LDP) Model

With this local model, there's no need to rely on a trusted curator. It uses privacy-preserving technology right on the user's device before any data gets collected. This means that only altered (noised) data is sent to the data collector, keeping individual privacy safe right from the start.

Key Features:

- Noise is added to the user's device before any data is collected.
- Raw data stays on the user's device and never leaves.
- This approach lowers risks tied to central storage but might lead to less useful data.

Example Mechanism: Randomized Response. One effective way to maintain privacy is with randomized response, a simple yet powerful tool in local differential privacy (LDP). Here's how it works: Participants tackle sensitive survey questions by flipping a coin:

- Heads: Answer honestly.
- Tails: Give a random answer.

This method provides a cover while still allowing for accurate collective statistics.

2.2. Core Definitions in Differential Privacy

Definition 1: (ε, δ)-Differential Privacy

A randomized algorithm FFF satisfies (ϵ, δ) -DP if, for all adjacent datasets DDD and D′D'D′, and any possible output RRR:

$$Pr(F(D) \in R) \leq e\epsilon Pr(F(D') \in R) + \delta$$

Here:

- ϵ controls the privacy level: smaller values mean stronger privacy.
- δ accounts for the probability of a privacy breach.

Definition 2: (ε, δ)-Local Differential Privacy

In LDP, the definition applies to individual data points. For user inputs v_1 and v_2:

$$Pr\left(F\left(v_1\right) \in R\right) \leq e^{\epsilon} Pr\left(F\left(v_2\right) \in R\right) + \delta$$

This ensures minimal information leakage about user inputs.

2.3. Sensitivity and Noise Mechanisms

Sensitivity Definition:
The sensitivity Δf of a function f is the maximum difference in function output between two adjacent datasets:

$$\Delta f = \max_{D, D'} \| \ f(D) - f(D') \ \|_1$$

Example Mechanisms:

- Laplace Mechanism: Adds Laplace noise proportional to sensitivity Δf\Delta fΔf.
- Exponential Mechanism: Used for categorical outputs, selecting outputs based on their utility scores.
- Gaussian Mechanism: Adds Gaussian noise, often used for approximate differential privacy.

Table 1. Comparison of Centralized and Local Models

Feature	Centralized Model	Local Model
Trust Requirement	A trusted third party is required	No trusted party is needed
Noise Application	At the query/output stage	At the data collection stage
Data Utility	High (access to raw data)	Moderate (due to noise added)
Storage Risk	High (centralized storage)	Low (data never leaves the user)

2.4. Applications and Real-World Use Cases

1. Centralized Model Applications:
   a. Keep your data private and still request the data you need to operate (for example, Google uses RAPPOR technology to protect telemetry info).
   b. Only communicating diversified (de-identified) data to healthcare institutions so they can analyze the information without making it easier for anyone to trace back the original patient (like how we can learn from the movement of a crowd while not seeing who in particular is actually within the crowd).
2. Local Model Applications:
   a. When people submit their predictions on the next iPhone's features (i.e., Apple's predictive typing feature in iOS).
   b. While privacy is ensured (as those interferences are resolved using differential

2.5. Challenges and Future Directions

First of all, it should be pointed out that although both models have made a significant contribution to privacy protection, there are still a few challenges that are on the cards:

- The foremost task is to set the right amount of the privacy-utility ratio: More noise is generally equal to less utility.
- Scalability is a very important point: It is very necessary that we maintain an efficient process when we deal with data in large quantities.
- ·The next point to deal with is how we should get real-world adoption: Our challenge, hence, must be to implant privacy in those industries that are really interested in it.

Future Directions:

- Striving for hybrid models, which are a mixture of both centralized and local strategies.
- Putting a lot of effort into the development of systems that can handle datasets with high power loads.
- Utilizing state-of-the-art techniques like deep learning while keeping the promise of

III. RESEARCH DIRECTIONS IN DIFFERENTIAL PRIVACY

3.1. Differential Privacy for Data Mining and Data Publishing

The arrival of the Internet and the large-scale increase of data in the digital age have inspired data protection (DP) to be at the forefront of the difference in privacy conservation techniques in data mining and data publication. Differential privacy tries to ensure that the inclusion or exclusion of a single data point does not significantly affect the output of any analysis, thus providing a formal privacy guarantee. The main principle behind the difference in privacy is that the production of any analysis should be statistically uninterrupted, even when there is sensitive information in the dataset. This idea is mathematically formalized through the following privacy situation:

$$Pr[M(D) \in S] \leq e\epsilon \times Pr[M(D') \in S]$$

Where:

- $M(D)$ is the mechanism applied to the dataset D.
- ϵ is the privacy budget or parameter controlling the noise added to the data.
- S is any possible outcome of the mechanism.
- D' is the dataset identical to D except for one record.

The parameter ϵ governs the privacy-utility trade-off: a smaller ϵ implies better privacy but lower data utility as more noise is introduced.

3.1.1. Challenges with Early Privacy Control Methods:

Early privacy mechanisms, such as ke-inflammatory, L-wiseness, and T-closure, were widely used for the protection of sensitive data. However, they have many limitations:

- Dependence on a reliable third party (TTP): Methods like K-Nemation require a central authority to handle and ensure anonymity. This introduces a risk, as third parties can be compromised.
- Religion for background knowledge attacks: Attackers accessible to accessory information can still de-nausea.
- Guarantee of formal secrecy deficiency: Techniques like K-Nemation include strong, quantitative privacy, which makes them susceptible to attacks.

Despite theoretical benefits, these methods do not guarantee strong privacy security in modern contexts where data curators can be compromised. This is particularly important as large-scale data collectors, such as social media platforms and government agencies, manage sensitive data.

3.1.2. Recent Advances in Centralized DP Models:

The centralized DP model depends on a reliable data curator to collect and publish data while preserving privacy. In this approach, to prevent the leakage of sensitive information, a noise function (often based on the latest or Gauss distribution) is applied to the data before publishing. Centralized DPs include notable progress:

- Median Mechanism:By focusing on statistical mediators, the mechanism allows for more accurate queries while maintaining differences in privacy. This approach is more efficient than previous methods, allowing a larger number of questions under the same privacy budget (Roth &Roughgarden, 2010).
- Histogram Publication (DPCube algorithm):The proposed DPCube, an algorithm based on K-D trees, is used to customize questions for histogram data. The DPCube allows the data to be divided into high-dimensional locations, enhancing the guarantee of privacy by improving query efficiency (Xiao et al., 2012).
- Wavelet Change: Engel& Eibl (2015) and Ngui et al. (2013) introduced wavelet-based techniques for data aggregation. By changing the data into a wavelet domain, these methods help reduce the noise added to the data during the aggregation process, preserving data utility while maintaining privacy.
- GrathyQureed Methods: Chan et al. (2011) proposed a hierarchical query system that reduces the amount of noise in the results. By structuring the queries hierarchically, they ensure that low noise is added to the data, which makes the results more accurate while maintaining the guarantee of strong privacy. Despite these advances, the centralized DP remains insecure about privacy violations, especially because a reliable curator holds and processes sensitive data.

3.2. Local Differential Privacy (LDP) for Data Collection and Analysis

In 2013, Duchi et al. (2013) introduced Local Differential Privacy (LDP), a privacy model that shifts the responsibility for privacy protection from a central authority to individual data sources. This eliminates the need for a trusted third-party curator and ensures that privacy is maintained right at the source of data collection. The key principle behind LDP is that the privacy mechanism is applied directly at the user's end so that only "noised" data is shared with data collectors.

3.2.1. LDP Mechanisms and Applications:

The LDP mechanism hinders the data at the end of the user by introducing noise, ensuring that the original data cannot be rebuilt even by someone who has access to a large amount of other data.

1. Google Chrome's wrappers (randomly random secrecy-protection ordinance response): Google's rapport system LDP is one of the most famous applications of LDP (Ye & Hu, 2020). It uses random response techniques for the protection of client-side data, especially classified data such as use figures, frequency calculations, and histograms. The rapper employs two different secrecy mechanisms:
    a. Permanent random response (PRR): This mechanism adds frequent noise to each individual reaction, ensuring that the information shared with the server is replaced in such a way that prevents any estimates of individual data values. B. Immediate random reaction (IRR): Unlike PRR, IRR adds temporary noise that is removed after a single use, providing privacy for one-time reactions. In addition to the noise, the bloom filter is used to compress data, which shows further uncertainty and helps resist attacks such as set membership conclusions. Rapor privacy-utility allows fine control over business, allowing privacy managers to adjust the level of noise according to the sensitivity of the data.
2. Stream frequent items with LDPMINER: For applications that include real-time data processing, LDPMINER has been developed to mine continuous items on streaming data with a differential privacy guarantee (Qin et al., 2016). The process operates in two stages:
    a. Succinct Histogram (SH) Sampling using the algorithm: This phase identifies potentially frequent objects in the data stream.
    b. Recognition using Rappor: After samples of the SHE algorithm, wrappers are used to refine frequency estimates by adding noise, ensuring that the privacy of individual objects is protected.

This two-step process enables the LDP miner to handle dynamic data currents while preserving privacy and maintaining high accuracy in constant detection.

3. Use of LDP of Apple: Apple has been a pioneer in the large-scale deployment of LDP techniques, which integrates them into its products such as macOS and iOS. Apple employs several privacy-protection techniques to ensure that the data is safely collected:
   a. Local sampling: Before sending to the Apple server, the user gives a sample of data from the user's device.
   b. Hash Encryption: The data is encrypted locally before transmission to prevent unauthorized users from accessing it.
   c. Noise disturbances: The noise is added to the data to prevent exact values from being rebuilt. Apple's implementation enables the extraction of total data from large datasets, ensuring the privacy of individual users. Theoretical analysis of LDP mechanisms, such as those used in wrappers, ensures that even with noisy data, meaningful population-level insights can be achieved.

3.3. Theoretical Foundation of LDP:

The differential privacy definition applied to LDP can be mathematically described as:

$$Pr[M(D) \in S] \leq e^{\epsilon} \times Pr[M(D') \in S]$$

Where M represents the mechanism, the dataset, and ϵ controls the privacy of the data. A small ϵ provides more privacy but reduces the utility of the data as more noise is added. The randomness initiated by the LDP mechanism ensures that individual data points cannot be understood even with access to large versions of data, even individual data points.

IV. EMERGING CHALLENGES AND FUTURE DIRECTIONS IN DIFFERENTIAL PRIVACY

With the surge in decentralized data environments—ranging from smartphones and IoT devices to edge computing systems—Federated Learning (FL) has emerged as a critical paradigm for privacy-preserving machine learning. FL enables multiple clients to collaboratively train a global model without sharing raw data, thereby reducing data transmission costs and enhancing confidentiality. However, even without direct data exchange, model updates can leak sensitive information through gradient inversion or membership inference attacks. To mitigate such risks, Differential Privacy (DP) has been integrated into FL pipelines, offering a formal, mathematical privacy guarantee.

4.1. Mechanisms of Differential Privacy in Federated Learning

Federated learning has emerged as a popular paradigm for decentralized machine learning, where data is distributed across devices. Unlike traditional centralized learning, the federated learning models allow the model to be trained on local devices without updating the model. This approach has been adopted widely because of its privacy-protection nature and the ability to reduce communication costs. However, the integration of differences in federated learning presents many unique challenges. In federated learning, the privacy of individual data points must be maintained while ensuring that the collected model is useful. One of the major challenges is the close trade between model accuracy and privacy protection. Adding direct noise to the model update is a common approach to implementing DP, but it can significantly reduce the accuracy of the global model, especially with limited data or low updates.

The DP mechanism can be formally applied to federal learning by adding noise to gradients or model parameters during the aggregation phase. A common method for adding noise to gradients is through Gaussian noise or Laplacian noise. Federated learning may be represented by a guarantee of privacy:

$$Pr[M(\theta) \in S] \leq e^{\epsilon} \times Pr[M(\theta') \in S]$$

where the model represents parameters after the noise is added to $M(\theta)$ Gradients. ϵ Privacy is budgeted, and the strength of noise is controlled. θ are model parameters for the original and modified updates, respectively.

4.1.1. Technical Challenges and Trade-offs

While DP enhances privacy, it introduces several technical limitations in federated settings:

- Utility Loss: The injected noise can degrade model accuracy, especially in cases of high privacy demands (small ϵ) or limited data availability.
- Computational Overhead: Implementing DP-SGD requires gradient clipping and noise generation, increasing client-side resource demands and battery consumption.
- Non-IID Data Distribution: Real-world FL scenarios often involve non-identically and independently distributed (non-IID) data across clients.

Uniform noise calibration becomes suboptimal, necessitating personalized privacy budgets or adaptive mechanisms.

- Communication Complexity: Adding DP also increases the volume of messages and metadata exchanged, further stressing bandwidth-constrained environments.

4.1.2. Comparative Technologies and Integrative Architectures

To overcome the limitations of using DP in isolation, researchers have explored hybrid privacy-preserving architectures:

- Homomorphic Encryption (HE): HE allows arithmetic operations on encrypted data. In FL, it can encrypt model updates such that the server aggregates them without decryption. However, HE introduces substantial computational overhead and may not scale well on edge devices.
- Secure Multi-Party Computation (SMPC): SMPC allows multiple parties to compute a joint function over their inputs while keeping them private. Applied in FL, SMPC ensures that no individual client can infer others' model updates. Unlike DP, SMPC does not introduce noise but comes with higher communication latency.
- Federated Analytics with DP + SMPC: This architecture uses SMPC to aggregate encrypted updates and DP to ensure no individual update can be inferred from the output. This combination offers both computational privacy (via SMPC) and statistical privacy (via DP), balancing security and utility.

4.1.3. Use Cases and Applications

Concrete implementations of DP-enabled FL are already being explored across domains:

- Healthcare: Institutions collaboratively train models on sensitive patient data (e.g., predicting disease risk) without compromising individual privacy (e.g., Google's FL+DP framework on diabetes prediction).
- Finance: Banks leverage FL to detect fraud by training on user transaction patterns, where privacy guarantees are enforced using DP and SMPC.
- Smartphones and Edge Devices: Mobile OS platforms (e.g., Apple's Siri, Google Gboard) utilize FL and DP to improve user personalization without uploading personal data to central servers.

4.1.4. Research Outlook and Future Directions

While DP in FL is a promising step toward privacy-preserving AI, its full potential will be realized through integration with cutting-edge cryptographic tools like HE and SMPC. Future work should focus on:

- Adaptive Noise Scaling: Dynamic adjustment of noise levels based on data sensitivity and model convergence rates.
- Personalized Privacy Budgets: Tailoring ϵ\epsilonϵ per user or device to account for varying data sensitivity.
- Efficient DP on Edge: Lightweight DP protocols for resource-constrained devices in edge environments.
- Legal Compliance Frameworks: Mapping DP implementations to comply with international regulations such as GDPR, HIPAA, and the EU Data Governance Act—particularly under the "right to be forgotten" and auditability requirements.

4.2. Differential Privacy for Data Sharing in Blockchain

The blockchain technique, which ensures decentralization and irreversibility, has been combined with differences to enable safe data sharing. In a blockchain setting, several sides can share data without the need to rely on a central authority, thus maintaining privacy in the distributed network. However, the combination of DP and blockchain shows additional complications due to the transparency and irreversibility of blockchain networks. In a specific blockchain landscape, when sensitive data is stored or shared through a public account book, the data must be preserved against unauthorized access. Differential privacy provides a mechanism to ensure that sensitive data shared on the blockchain cannot be exploited or reverse-engineered. It can be particularly useful in healthcare, finance, or any domain where private information needs to be exchanged in decentralized networks.

4.2.1. Key Challenges:

- Cost and efficiency of transactions: Blockchain networks, especially those that employ proof-of-work (PoW), incur significant computational costs. Applying the difference on top of its top can increase the cost of transactions, as noise should be added to each transaction to preserve privacy.
- Privacy versus transparency: The decentralized nature of blockchain is designed to promote transparency. However, applying the DP to the transaction

reduces the amount of information available, which can affect the transparency and audits of the blockchain system.

- Smart Contracts and DP: Integrating differential privacy in smart contracts requires additional work to ensure that the execution of contracts does not compromise privacy. In particular, the DP mechanism should be applied in such a way that the privacy of individual users or transactions is preserved while still being able to function correctly in smart contracts.

The research in this region focuses on developing the DP mechanism that corresponds to the specific requirements of blockchain platforms. A potential solution is the use of zero-knowledge proof (zkps) with DP. ZKPS can allow a party to prove that they know a piece of information without disclosing themselves. When combined with DP, ZKP can ensure that sensitive information is not leaked when providing transparency and verification in blockchain transactions.

4.3. Differential Privacy in Privacy-Preserving Machine Learning

As machine learning models become rapidly sophisticated, the need for privacy-preservation mechanisms in their training processes is becoming more important. The learned model does not reveal information about any individual data points that have been applied to discriminatory privacy to ensure that machine learning has been applied. This has developed privacy-protection machine learning (PPML) techniques that use DPs to protect the privacy of training data. A major application of DP in machine learning is during the training of models on sensitive data, such as in healthcare, where trained models on patient data should not highlight information about individual patients. Many approaches have been developed to include DP in machine learning models:

1. Differential private stochastic gradient descent (DP-SGD): DP-SGD is an extension of the widely used stochastic gradient descent (SGD) algorithm, which adds noise to gradients during training. The noise is calibrated based on the sensitivity of the gradients to ensure discriminatory privacy. The mechanism can be described mathematically:

$$DP - SGD\left(g_t \right) = \frac{g_t}{clip\left(g_t, C\right)} + N(0, \sigma^2)$$

where g_t represents the gradient at the time step t,C is the clipping bound,σ is the noise scale parameter, and$N(0, \sigma^2)$ is the Gaussian noise added.

1. Private Federated Learning: In Federated Learning, where data is distributed on many devices, DP is used to ensure that individual updates from each device do not leak sensitive information. During the local update, confidentiality is ensured by adding noise to gradients and ensuring that only collected noise for model aggregation and noise information is sent to the central server. The integration of the DP in the machine learning model enables its application in a sensitive domain, but the model remains challenged by the balance between accuracy and the guarantee of privacy.

4.4. Research instructions and open problems

1. Privacy-use business improves: DP is one of the most pressing issues in the field of DP, which is a balance between privacy and utility. In many scenarios, obtaining strict privacy can lead to significant erosion of utility, making it difficult to apply DP in real-world applications. New methods are being developed to achieve a better balance, such as adaptive noise joint techniques that adjust based on data characteristics.
2. Difference in Edge Computing Privacy: Edge Computing, where data is processed close to the source (e.g., on devices such as smartphones, IoT devices, and sensors), presents unique challenges for privacy. Due to limited computational resources on the edge, the privacy-preservation mechanisms need to be mild and efficient while still ensuring a guarantee of strong privacy. Research is focusing on light DP protocols that can be executed on resources.
3. Combination of DP with other privacy-conservation techniques: Future research can focus on a combination of DP with other secure multi-party computation (SMPC) and other secrecy encryption techniques like Homomorphic Encryption (HE) by taking advantage of the strength of these techniques
4. Differential Privacy (DP) has become a foundational technique for privacy-preserving data analysis and machine learning. As its adoption broadens across decentralized and distributed systems, new challenges arise concerning accuracy, scalability, and regulatory compliance. This article investigates emerging research directions, focusing on hybrid privacy-preserving architectures and their implications in federated learning, blockchain, and edge computing. It further explores the integration of DP with Secure Multi-Party Computation (SMPC), Homomorphic Encryption (HE), and the alignment of DP with international privacy regulations such as GDPR, HIPAA, and the EU Data Governance Act.

DP offers mathematically grounded guarantees against individual data leakage by introducing calibrated noise into statistical queries or learning processes. Its application in contemporarysystems—particularly decentralized and distributed architectures—requires novel adaptations to ensure utility, computational efficiency, and legal compliance.

- Hybrid Architectures: DP with Federated Learning and SMPC: In federated learning (FL), model training occurs locally on user devices, minimizing raw data exposure. However, the addition of DP noise often leads to degraded model accuracy, especially under non-IID data distributions. To address this, recent research advocates hybrid architectures combining FL with SMPC and HE. In such systems, encrypted gradient updates are aggregated using SMPC, and DP noise is applied post-aggregation to balance privacy and model fidelity. These integrative designs enhance resilience against inference attacks while preserving model utility, enabling privacy-preserving federated analytics.
- Performance, Scalability, and Privacy Trade-offs: A central research challenge lies in optimizing the trade-off between privacy guarantees and system performance. The use of DP in edge and resource-constrained environments, such as IoT and mobile devices, necessitates lightweight DP protocols and adaptive noise mechanisms. Approaches such as dynamic clipping bounds, personalized privacy budgets, and sparsification techniques are being investigated to reduce communication and computation overheads while maintaining acceptable utility.
- Differential Privacy in Blockchain Systems: Blockchain's inherent transparency and immutability pose significant obstacles for privacy preservation. Applying DP in public ledgers introduces complexity, as noise must be carefully introduced without compromising auditability. Moreover, DP's application in smart contracts requires runtime compatibility and resistance to indirect data leakage. Combining DP with cryptographic techniques such as Zero-Knowledge Proofs (ZKPs) provides promising pathways to reconcile transparency with privacy in decentralized environments.
- Legal and Ethical Considerations: The deployment of DP in decentralized contexts must consider compliance with privacy legislation. Under the General Data Protection Regulation (GDPR), DP supports data minimization and anonymization mandates, although compatibility with "right to erasure" provisions remains an open question. In healthcare applications governed by HIPAA, DP enables secure model training on sensitive patient data. The EU Data Governance Act introduces additional data sovereignty requirements, emphasizing transparency and user control. Ethically, DP-based systems must ensure fairness, prevent disproportionate impacts across demographic groups, and provide verifiable privacy guarantees.

V. COMPARATIVE ANALYSIS OF PRIVACY-PRESERVING MECHANISMS

While a wide array of privacy-preserving methods—such as Differential Privacy (DP), Homomorphic Encryption (HE), Secure Multi-Party Computation (SMPC), and Zero-Knowledge Proofs (ZKPs)—have been proposed and explored in decentralized learning and blockchain systems, a critical evaluation of their relative strengths, limitations, and readiness for deployment is essential to guide practical adoption and future research.

5.1. Critical Discussion

- Differential Privacy (DP) is the most widely adopted technique due to its mathematical rigor and relatively low computational requirements. However, its core limitation is the trade-off between utility and privacy, especially in non-IID federated settings or when applied naively without adaptive mechanisms.
- Homomorphic Encryption (HE) offers strong confidentiality guarantees by enabling computation on encrypted data. Despite this, its computational overhead is substantial, limiting its feasibility on edge devices or latency-sensitive applications. HE is better suited for centralized or hybrid cloud-edge setups with sufficient computational resources.
- Secure Multi-Party Computation (SMPC) ensures full cryptographic privacy without adding noise, making it appealing where exact computations are critical. Its major drawback is communication complexity and synchronization requirements, which hinder scalability in highly dynamic or large-scale environments.
- Zero-Knowledge Proofs (ZKPs) combined with DP present a novel solution to the privacy-transparency conflict in blockchain applications. They allow proof of data validity without revealing the data itself. However, ZKP integration remains computationally intensive and is still in its early stages of standardization and deployment.

Table 2. Comparison Across Key Dimensions

Technique	Privacy Guarantee	Computational Overhead	Communication Overhead	Scalability	Deployment Maturity	Use Case Suitability
Differential Privacy (DP)	Statistical; protects against individual inference	Low to moderate	Minimal	High (with trade-off)	Mature (e.g., Apple, Google)	FL on mobile/edge, healthcare analytics
Homomorphic Encryption (HE)	Strong computational privacy	High	Low (after encryption)	Moderate	Experimental for real-time systems	Aggregated model updates, financial data sharing
Secure Multi-Party Computation (SMPC)	Cryptographic; no data leakage	Moderate	High	Limited (latency-sensitive)	Growing; used in collaborative AI	Collaborative healthcare, inter-bank analytics
ZKPs with DP	Verification without data exposure	High	Moderate	Moderate	Emerging (blockchain pilot use)	Smart contracts, verifiable DP on-chain

5.2. Use Case-Driven Suitability

- DP is preferred in resource-constrained, user-facing applications like smartphone personalization (e.g., Google Gboard).
- HE is favored in financial systems where sensitive data needs to be aggregated securely.
- SMPC finds its strength in multi-institutional collaborations, such as federated clinical research.
- ZKPs are best suited for blockchain ecosystems demanding both transparency and privacy, such as decentralized identity verification and auditable smart contracts.

VI. CONCLUSION

Differential privacy (DP) has emerged as a cornerstone technique to ensure data privacy, enabling valuable data analysis, and its applications expand to various domains such as data mining, machine learning, federated learning, blockchain, and age computing. As the concerns of privacy continue to increase, especially in the data-rich environment, DP provides a guarantee of strong privacy without compromising the utility of data, although its integration in real-world systems presents several challenges. In the context of data mining and publication, the DP mechanisms have evolved from theoretical constructions to practical solutions with notable contributions, such as medium mechanisms, DPCUBE, and wavelet changes. This progress has greatly improved the efficiency and privacy guarantee of the centralized DP system. However, centralized approaches are unsafe for privacy violations, mainly due to their dependence on a reliable third-party curator, which highlights the requirement for more secure, decentralized options. The introduction of local difference secrecy (LDP) has addressed several boundaries inherent in the centralized model. The use of LDP mechanisms, such as the Rappor of Google Chrome and the LDP of Apple, has achieved significant traction due to their ability to analyze data without centralizing sensitive information. This paradigm change ensures that privacy protection is directly applied to the end user, which is an important step towards increasing privacy-conservation technologies in real-world applications. LDP has shown immense potential in both the Internet application and the age computing environment, where the user data is spread and decentralized. However, despite this progress, there are many challenges in applying for a DP in LA.

In addition, privacy-conservation machine learning has seen adequate progress with the development of techniques such as differentiated private stochastic gradients (DP-SGD), which enables the training of machine learning models on sensitive data while maintaining privacy. However, as the area moves forward, the privacy-use business is a significant obstacle. Adding noise to ensure privacy often results in a decrease in model accuracy, which can limit the purpose of DP in some important areas, such as healthcare or finance, where high accuracy is paramount. DP Edge faces additional challenges in edge computing due to the device's resource transactions. The mild implementation of the DP protocol in such an environment is an active area of research, focusing on designing scalable and efficient mechanisms that maintain secrecy without overwhelming the limited computational resources available on edge equipment. Future research on different privacy issues should focus on overcoming these challenges. This involves the development of mechanisms that improve the balance between privacy and utility, especially in federal learning and edge computing environments. Another important direction is the discovery of hybrid privacy-growing technologies that connect the DP with other cryptographic techniques, such as Homomorphic Encryption and Secure Multi-Party Computation (SMPC). By taking advantage of the strength of these technologies, it is possible to create a stronger privacy-preservation system that can handle diverse, large-scale data applications more effectively. Additionally, as more data-sharing platforms and decentralized systems emerge, different privacy measures must continue to develop to handle the specific requirements of these new paradigms. DP combination with blocks.

Finally, while the difference in privacy has made significant progress in enabling the safety of sensitive data and captivity-conservation data analysis, scalability, computational efficiency, and significant work in addressing the business is yet to be done. As the area moves forward, the differences from the innovations in decentralized data systems, machine learning, and federated learning will be further enhanced by the usefulness of privacy techniques. Researchers and physicians should continue to detect new solutions that will ensure rapid data-manual privacy protection in the world, empowering individuals and organizations to share and analyze data without compromising privacy. Continuous advancement of different privacy not only promises to preserve privacy but also to promote confidence in the data-sharing ecosystem, from healthcare and finance to IOT and beyond.

Future Research Instructions:

- Increased privacy-use balance: checking the adaptive noise mechanism and dynamic privacy budget that can be accommodated based on the nature of data and queries.
- Federated and Edge Computing Integration: Developing light, efficient DP methods that are suited to a resource-composed environment.
- Blockchain and DP coordination: Finding ways to include differential privacy in the blockchain network without compromising transparency and verification.
- Hybrid privacy model: a combination of DP with other secrecy-enhancing techniques like SMPC to create strong and scalable privacy-conservation solutions for large-scale data applications.

As these research fields come out, the future of different privacy will shape the next generation of privacy-conservation technologies, which will enable a safe, more secure digital ecosystem.

REFERENCES

Alwarafy, A., Al-Thelaya, K. A., Abdallah, M., Schneider, J., & Hamdi, M. (2020). A Survey on Security and Privacy Issues in Edge Computing-Assisted Internet of Things. arXiv preprint arXiv:2008.03252. https://arxiv.org/abs/2008.03252

Caruso, A. (2024). *Forensic Analysis of Mobile Spyware: Investigating Security, Vulnerabilities, and Detection Challenges in Android and iOS Platforms* (Doctoral dissertation, Politecnico di Torino).

Chan, T.-H. H., Shi, E., & Song, D. (2011). *Private and continual release of statistics.* In *Proceedings of the 39th International Colloquium Conference on Automata, Languages, and Programming (ICALP'11)* (pp. 405–417). Springer. https://doi.org/ DOI: 10.1007/978-3-642-22006-7_34

Duchi, J. C., Jordan, M. I., & Wainwright, M. J. (2013, October). Local privacy and statistical minimax rates. In *2013 IEEE 54th annual symposium on foundations of computer science* (pp. 429-438). IEEE.

Dwork, C., & Roth, A. (2014). The Algorithmic Foundations of Differential Privacy. *Foundations and Trends® in Theoretical Computer Science*, 9(3–4), 211–407. https://doi.org/DOI: 10.1561/0400000042

Engel, D., & Eibl, G. (2015). Wavelet-based multiresolution smart meter privacy. *IEEE Transactions on Smart Grid*, *8*(4), 1710–1721. DOI: 10.1109/TSG.2015.2504395

Erlingsson, Ú., Pihur, V., & Korolova, A. (2014). RAPPOR: Randomized Aggregatable Privacy-Preserving Ordinal Response. *Proceedings of the 2014 ACM SIGSAC Conference on Computer and Communications Security*, 1054–1067. https://doi.org/ DOI: 10.1145/2660267.2660348

Goryczka, S., Xiong, L., & Li, J. (2013). Differentially Private Federated Data Publishing. *Proceedings of the 6th ACM Conference on Security and Privacy in Wireless and Mobile Networks*, 3–14. https://doi.org/DOI: 10.1145/2462096.2462098

He, X., Machanavajjhala, A., Ding, B., & Chen, Y. (2014). Blowfish Privacy: Tuning Privacy-Utility Trade-offs Using Policies. *Proceedings of the 2014 ACM SIGMOD International Conference on Management of Data*, 1447–1458. https://doi.org/DOI: 10.1145/2588555.2588581

Khandelwal, R., Nayak, A., Chung, P., Fawaz, K., Bianchi, A., Celik, Z. B., & Hussain, S. R. (2024). Unpacking privacy labels: A measurement and developer perspective on google's data safety section. In *33rd USENIX Security Symposium (USENIX Security 24)* (pp. 2831-2848).

Krishnamoorthy, M. V. (2024). Data Obfuscation through Latent Space Projection (LSP) for Privacy-Preserving AI Governance: Case Studies in Medical Diagnosis and Finance Fraud Detection. arXiv preprint arXiv:2410.17459. https://arxiv.org/abs/2410.17459

Kulynych, B., Gomez, J. F., Kaissis, G., Calmon, F. du P., & Troncoso, C. (2024). Attack-Aware Noise Calibration for Differential Privacy. *arXiv Preprint arXiv:2407.02191*. https://arxiv.org/abs/2407.02191

Li, N., Li, T., & Venkatasubramanian, S. (2006, April). t-closeness: Privacy beyond k-anonymity and l-diversity. In *2007 IEEE 23rd international conference on data engineering* (pp. 106-115). IEEE.

Loukides, G., & Lomax, N. (2021). Privacy-preserving data publishing through anonymization, statistical disclosure control, and de-identification.

Munir, S., Kollnig, K., Shuba, A., & Shafiq, Z. (2024). Google's Chrome Antitrust Paradox. *arXiv preprint arXiv:2406.11856.*

Ngui, W. K., Leong, M. S., Hee, L. M., & Abdelrhman, A. M. (2013). Wavelet analysis: Mother wavelet selection methods. *Applied Mechanics and Materials*, *393*, 953–958. DOI: 10.4028/www.scientific.net/AMM.393.953

Pochintesta, E. (2012). Comparison Of Apple's Ios 5 And Android For Mobile Applications Development: A Developer's Perspective.

Qin, Z., Yang, Y., Yu, T., Khalil, I., Xiao, X., & Ren, K. (2016, October). Heavy hitter estimation over set-valued data with local differential privacy. In *Proceedings of the 2016 ACM SIGSAC conference on computer and communications security* (pp. 192-203). DOI: 10.1145/2976749.2978409

Roth, A., & Roughgarden, T. (2010, June). Interactive privacy via the median mechanism. In *Proceedings of the forty-second ACM symposium on Theory of Computing* (pp. 765-774). DOI: 10.1145/1806689.1806794

Thakurta, A., Evans, D., & Vadhan, S. (2017). Learning with Privacy at Scale. *Apple Machine Learning Research.* https://machinelearning.apple.com/research/learning-with-privacy-at-scale

Triastcyn, A., & Faltings, B. (2019). Federated Learning with Bayesian Differential Privacy. arXiv preprint arXiv:1911.10071. https://arxiv.org/abs/1911.10071 DOI: 10.1109/BigData47090.2019.9005465

Triastcyn, A., & Faltings, B. (2019). Federated Learning with Bayesian Differential Privacy. arXiv preprint arXiv:1911.10071. https://arxiv.org/abs/1911.10071 DOI: 10.1109/BigData47090.2019.9005465

Tu, Z., Zhao, K., Xu, F., Li, Y., Su, L., & Jin, D. (2018). Protecting trajectory from semantic attack considering ${k}$-anonymity, ${l}$-diversity, and ${t}$-closeness. *IEEE Transactions on Network and Service Management*, *16*(1), 264–278. DOI: 10.1109/TNSM.2018.2877790

Vaijainthymala Krishnamoorthy, M. (2024). Data Obfuscation through Latent Space Projection (LSP) for Privacy-Preserving AI Governance: Case Studies in Medical Diagnosis and Finance Fraud Detection. arXiv preprint arXiv:2410.17459. https://arxiv.org/abs/2410.17459

Wang, Y., & Xu, W. (2023). APLDP: Adaptive Personalized Local Differential Privacy Data Collection. *Computers & Security*, *129*, 102927. DOI: 10.1016/j.cose.2023.102927

Xiao, Y., Xiong, L., Fan, L., & Goryczka, S. (2012). DPCube: Differentially private histogram release through multidimensional partitioning. *arXiv preprint arXiv:1202.5358*

Ye, Q., & Hu, H. (2020, January). Local differential privacy: Tools, challenges, and opportunities. In *International Conference on Web Information Systems Engineering* (pp. 13-23). Singapore: Springer Singapore. DOI: 10.1007/978-981-15-3281-8_2

Zhou, B., & Pei, J. (2011). The k-anonymity and l-diversity approaches for privacy preservation in social networks against neighborhood attacks. *Knowledge and Information Systems*, *28*(1), 47–77. DOI: 10.1007/s10115-010-0311-2

Zhou, W., Zhang, D., Han, G., Zhu, W., & Wang, X. (2023). A Blockchain-Based Privacy-Preserving and Fair Data Transaction Model in IoT. *Applied Sciences (Basel, Switzerland)*, *13*(22), 12389. DOI: 10.3390/app132212389

Zhu, T., Li, G., Zhou, W., & Philip, S. Y. (2017). *Differential privacy and applications*. Springer International Publishing. DOI: 10.1007/978-3-319-62004-6

Chapter 16
Evaluation and Improvement of Artificial Intelligence and Data Science-Based Salt and Pepper Noise Reduction Techniques

Devadatta Das
https://orcid.org/0000-0002-4913-7433
Haldia Institute of Technology, India

Animesh Samanta
Haldia Institute of Technology, India

Sabyasachi Samanta
https://orcid.org/0000-0001-8858-4132
Haldia Institute of Technology, India

ABSTRACT

Detecting and removing impulse noise remains a difficult task in image processing, especially for Salt and Pepper Noise (SAPN) and Random Valued Impulse Noise (RVIN). SAPN impacts pixels with intensities between '0' and '255', but RVIN introduces arbitrary pixel values between '0' and '255', resulting in stray dots that are difficult to remove. Recent advances in AI and data science are critical in tackling these difficulties, allowing for personalised and adaptable learning experiences via platforms such as virtual assistants and intelligent tutoring systems. This work

DOI: 10.4018/979-8-3373-2185-1.ch016

focusses on recent advances in picture restoration for impulse noise-affected images, including surveying and analysing approaches using metrics like PSNR and SSIM. Qualitative assessments compare visual outcomes across standard test images, highlighting the importance of this research in domains such as healthcare and astronomy, with hopeful implications for future academics and enthusiasts alike.

1. INTRODUCTION

In today's world, images perform significant role. In this world, there are many types of noise that can be present in any image. In image processing, noise is very difficult problem that are faced by everyone by the image. Image noise is the unintentional alteration of an image's color or brightness. Also we can say it is the phase of electronic noise. Image sensor and circuitry of a scanner or digital camera can produce the image noise. So here, we discuss about Salt-and-pepper noise and Random valued impulse noise. Salt-and-pepper noise is a frame of noise, it can be seen on images for sometimes. In this type of noise, the value of some pixels became maximum and minimum value in the grade of 0-255. Black and white points are represented by Salt-and-pepper noise. We can say that salt-and-pepper noise is a type of impulse noise (Erkan et al., 2020). It is being in natural images. Certain suggested filters can eliminate noise caused by salt and pepper that are median filter (MF) and adaptive median filter (AMF), those two methods are most popular for removing salt-and-pepper noise (Alanazi et al., 2023). After discussing Salt-and-pepper noise, now we discuss about Random valued impulse noise. Random valued impulse noise change the value of the pixels randomly. Any intensity pixel value are presented in Random valued impulse noise. It is tabulated into two parts, static and dynamic. Impulse noise are removed by some other median filters (Wu et al., 2020). Adaptive learning platforms improve student engagement and comprehension by customising instructional materials to each learner's needs (Jiao et al., 2023). Furthermore, gamification combined with AI creates engaging and dynamic learning environments (Korus & Huang, 2016). Education becomes more effective and data-driven when instructors use data science tools, especially learning analytics, to monitor student progress, spot learning trends, and improve teaching methods (Kumar et al., n.d.). Digital image processing technology includes transforming picture impulses into digital signals, a process that computers carry out and is hence also known as computer technique for picture processing (Wang, 2024).

2. REVIEW OF SOME PROPOSED TECHNIQUES

2.1 NON-LOCAL ADAPTIVE MEAN FILTER (NAMF)

In this section, we went over the NAMF method for eliminating pepper and salt noise. We can say that NAMF is transmitted filter for removing Salt-and-pepper noise. There are two stages in NAMF, (1) Salt-and-pepper noise detection, (2) Salt-and-pepper noise correction. Details of those techniques are discussed in below.

(1) Salt-and-pepper noise detection

In detection part, we have to say that in defected image, the salt pixel value is equal to the maximum gray value 255 and the pepper pixel value is equal to the minimum value 0. Now, let P be an initial 8-bit gray level image, the size of the image is C X D, and $p_{a,b}$ be the value of gray of the pixel at (a, b) location. Let Q be a noisy image and $q_{a,b}$ represent the location of the pixel. Let R be an indicator matrix, r(a, b) = 1 meant $q_{a,b}$ is noisy pixel applicant, r(a, b) = 0 meant $q_{a,b}$ is noiseless. $q_{a,b}$ is infected by Salt-and-pepper noise, i.e., 0 or 255. So we can say easily q_{min} = 0 and q_{max} = 255. So from this condition, we can say that the image is detected by Salt-and-pepper noise,

r(a, b) = 1, $q_{a,b}$ = 0 or 255

r(a, b) = 0, otherwise

(2) Salt and pepper noise correction

The noisy pixels are replaced in two steps. Let S be the primarily replaced image, s resemble the final output image. So at first we will have to use the mean value of $T_{i,j}$ for replacing the noisy pixels. At next, the three neighboring pixels of S are selected. Now we use the non-local-mean (NLM) method for again replacing the noisy pixels. After performing the NLM method, we get $s_{a,b}$. We can perform fast implementation of NLM method that is based calculation of piece interval using addition of lines that promote NAMF technique.

Advantage

(i) NAMF accepts non-local-mean method that is based on Salt-and-pepper noise.
(ii) NAMF is better than PSNR and SSIM at the time of calculating the experimental result.

Disadvantage

(i) NAMF is resembling at the time of processing to the most state-of-the-art techniques.
(ii) NAMF can constraint more analyzing, when noise level is high.

2.2 CELLULAR AUTOMATA

In this section, we have to see a new technique for removing Salt-and-pepper noise, which is Cellular automata. Cellular automata is known as limited grid (Yang et al., 2020). In Cellular automata, there are many cells that are present on there. The value of each and every cell is subjected on its former value and also hanged with the value of its neighbors (González-Hidalgo et al., 2021). Five different tuples represent the Cellular automata. To decrease Salt-and-pepper noise from an image, we use Cellular automata. We take an effective filter that is veiled on 25 neighborhood pixels. And also take the median value of the neighborhood values, x_{med} rearranged the pixel values. At first we take a 5 x 5 matrix and the size of the pixels are determined with the size of the neighborhood pixels. For Cellular automata, we take four deviation values, that values are x_{med}, x_{std}, $x_{\min}$=0, $x_{\max}$=255. Where x_{std} means the standard deviation value of the neighborhood cells.

Here, we can reviewed the noise detection and correction technique by Cellular automata that are discussed in below.

(1) Noise detection

At first we have to check the values of each and every cell with larger and equal to $x_{\max}$ and also with smaller and equal to $x_{\min}$. If the value of cells are smaller than $x_{\min}$ and also larger than $x_{\min}$ then we can say that the pixels are noisy.

(2) Noise correction

At first we have to check the value of the cells in Cellular automata. If the values are smooth then the neighborhood cells changed that values by the new value.

Advantage

(i) It is simple technique for removing Salt-and-pepper noise.
(ii) It is powerful technique.

Disadvantage

(i) There are need some progress.

2.3 Effecting and removal of Salt-and-pepper noise by using RGB color image, MF etc.

In this section, we have to study the effect of Salt-and-pepper noise and removing the noise from RGB color image. RGB color model is represented by the combination of three colors, Red, Green and Blue. RGB color image is attacked by noise, because image is seized by some sensing devices and communication noise is carried, at that time, the optical condition of an image is narrowed. By using median filter, we can remove Salt-and-pepper noise easily. It is working by progressing the image pixel by pixel, each value is changed by their median value of neighboring pixels. Median filter is used for removing Salt-and-pepper noise. It can work by provoking the image. Each value is changed with its median value with the value of the neighboring pixels. PSNR means Peak Signal Noise Ratio, it uses a model of mathematical equation. By using PSNR, we can measure the amount of noise that is decreased (Balasubramanian et al., 2016). Condense algorithms are analyzed by PSNR. We can calculate PSNR by this formula that are shown in below.

$$PSNR = 20*\log10\ (255 / RMSE)$$

(1) Noise detection

So at first, we achieve the origin RGB image. The noise ratio is altered when Salt-and-pepper noise is added in the image. We have to compose the columns of RGB. Now, we have to find the color combination with maximum iteration and minimum iteration. Then we can detect the noisy pixels with maximum and minimum instinct.

(2) Noise correction

We attain the RGB image. Now, we have to perform the measurement of the image. Then red, green and blue color channels are collected particularly. Median filter is applied, noise is caught in red, by using median filter, and we can remove the noise from red. From this way, we can detect noise in green and then blue, we can use mean filter and remove the noise. After completing the whole process, we get a noise free image.

Advantage

(i) A lofty condition Salt-and-pepper noise correction and rejection are supplied by median filter because PSNR gives the steep value.

(ii) Median filter remove a noise easily.

Disadvantage

(i) PSNR is subsided when noise ratio is enhanced.
(ii) In noise correction, the property of median filter is reduced when noise ratio is in advance way.

2.4 Quartile based noise reduction approach

Quartile means dividing a set of data into 4 different parts, we can say temporarily that twenty five percent of the data become smaller than the first quartile, twenty five percent would be the first and second quartile, twenty five percent would be the second and third quartile, and also we can say that twenty five percent become larger than the third quartile. Quartile based is one of the common technique for removing Salt-and-pepper noise. This method is used for better resolution of an image. It's working procedure veiled on nature of the pixel between the Salt-and-pepper values that is based on quartile. In this approach, we take 3 X 3 pixel block, each and every pixel is actuated from the top left corner to the right bottom corner (Wang et al., 2018).

In this method, we reviewed the noise correction approach that are discussed in below.

At first we have to take 3 X 3 matrix of an image, and the input image estimate three quartiles, a1, a2, a3 assess for the distinct involution in the matrix of 3 X 3. Then assimilate the center position of the image matrix that is involutes with a1, a2 and a3. If first quartile is greater than the center pixel then the position of the center pixel is changed by third quartile (a3). If the center pixel is smaller than or equal with first and third quartile then the position of the center pixel is changed by second quartile (a2). If the center pixel is greater than third quartile then the position of the center pixel is changed by first quartile (a1).

Advantage

(i) In quartile technique, a large group of pixel is divided into three or four parts.
(ii) It is simple technique.

Disadvantage

(i) It is time consuming.
(ii) In high noise density, the output would be not good.

2.5 Detail aware filter

In this section, we have to review some filters for removing Salt-and-pepper noise. That are discussed in below.

(a) Switching filters

It use the switching process for choosing the optimum output in the step of noise exposing and noise emendation. In this step, at first we have to check the center pixel and to identify that the pixel is noisy or not. And then identify the neighboring corrupted pixel, those pixels are noisy, from that pixels, noise are removed by using four Laplacian Convolution Kernels (Erkan & Kilicman, 2016).

(b) Decision filters

In this method, non-noisy pixels are fixed, but noisy pixels are changed. Noisy pixels are removed by Kriging Interpolation Value. Corrupted pixels are interweaved from un-corrupted pixels with narrow neighborhood.

(c) Noise adaptive fuzzy switching median filter (NAFSMF)

It is mixed with adaptive median filter and fuzzy switching median filter. There are two stages in NAFSMF, noise detection and noise correction. In noise detection stage, noisy image is localized for describing the noisy pixels. In noise correction, fuzzy rule is applied for removing the noise. By using fuzzy rule, at first the luminance difference would be calculated and then perform fuzzy derivation and fuzzy smoothing.

By using those filters, Salt-and-pepper noise can be removed.

Advantage

(i) Those filters work well when noise density is high.
(ii) NAFSMF is better than switching median filter.

Disadvantage

(i) In NAFSMF, when we calculate the luminance difference, then time is consumed.
(ii) NAFSMF is complex method.

2.6 Fuzzy decision based median filter

This technique is used for removing impulse noise. This median filter requires two stages, noise detection and noise correction that are discussed in below.

(1) Noise detection

In noise detection procedure, we take two intensities that are 0 and 255. These intensities helps us for detecting the noisy pixels (Yu & Hou, 2018). For marking the noisy pixels, we have to create a binary mask detect (x, y). Now we have to check, that the binary mask is true or false. If true then the pixels are non-noisy, else the pixels are noisy.

(2) Noise correction

In correction part, we have to use a square filtering window, the dimensions of the window is odd (Wang et al., 2018). In the window, first four pixels are defined by f(x, y). We have to identify the local information Pd(x, y). Then calculate the median pixel at the location of (x, y) and the find the luminance difference. Ld(x, y). Noisy pixels would be arranged to 255. Local information is used for taking a variable of fuzzy input. And also we have to take the thresholds values. And then we can removed the noise from the noisy pixel.

Advantage

(i) By using this technique, we have to found the local exception.
(ii) It works well at high noise density.

Disadvantage

(i) Here, fuzzy rules are applied for regulating the parameters.
(ii) It attentive all the direction of encircling the worked pixel.

2.7 Fixed valued Impulse noise removal techniques

In this section, we reviewed some filtering technique for removing impulse noise. There are two types of image filtering, spatial domain filtering and Frequency domain filtering. Median filters are improved from few years, Simple median filter (SMF), Adaptive median filter (AMF), Decision based median filter (DBMF), Decision based untrimmed median filter (DBUTMF), Edge preserving median filter (Jiao et al., 2023). Here we have to discuss SMF, DBMF and DBUTMF that are given below.

(1) Simple median filter (SMF)

At first we take a 3 X 3 block of pixels. And then check each and every pixel, that the pixel is noisy or noise free. If we detect a noisy pixel then we define the median value of that 3 X 3 pixel block and then remove the pixel by the median value. After changing the noisy pixel, previous process would be repeated until noisy pixels would become noise free.

(2) Decision based median filter (DBMF)

We have to take a 3 X 3 matrix, and the center pixel is marked, and then check the center pixel is noisy or not. If the center pixel quibbles between 0 and 255, then it would be noise free, otherwise it would be noisy. If center pixel became noisy then we have to calculate the median value of the center pixel. If median value is uniformed to 0 and 255 then noisy pixel can be changed by the median value. Then the previous step would be repeated.

(3) Decision based untrimmed median filter (DBUTMF)

We take a 3 X 3 window and select the center. If the value of the center is quibbled between 0 and 255 then it is not noisy. If the value of the center is sufficient with 0 and 255 then it is noisy. Then calculate the median value of the center and replace the noisy pixel by the median value, and the previous step would be repeated.

Advantage

(i) All techniques are simple and easy to use.
(ii) Those techniques are used from many years because from those techniques, noise can be removed easily.

Disadvantage

(i) After calculating the median value and replacing the center pixel, then the whole process repeated, so it is time consuming.
(ii) If the noise percentage would become 90%, then those techniques are not working in better way.

2.8 Edge preserving fuzzy filter

By using this technique, we can remove the impulse noise from an image. Impulse noise means the original value of the pixel would be changed in a range between

0 and 255. This method is more powerful with lower false alarm (FA) and miss detection (MD) values. For data clustering, we have to use Fuzzy C-Means (FCM) (Vivekanandam, 2021).

(1) Impulse noise detection

Detection process would be done in two step. In first step, we have to detect the noise on globular way and then collect the notification from a corrupted image.

(2) Impulse noise correction

At first we have to derogate the rates of false alarm and miss detection. We have to conserved the edges and also recognize the elevated kind of image at the end of the user.

Advantage

(i) Edges are conserved.
(ii) The performance is better than other technique so the estimation time is less.

Disadvantage

(i) It is used only for impulse noise correction.

2.9 Hybrid median filter

From this technique, impulse noise can be removed. It is prosper statement of median filter. Impulse noise is removed by this filter widely. Here, median value of the noisy pixel is calculated and also we have to calculate the median value of the neighboring pixel. And then we add the median value of neighboring pixel to the aboriginal value. Also we can say Hybrid median filter is other form of non-filtering (Chen & Meng, 2022). When edges are conserved then impulse noise is removed easily because it is non-straight group in the matrix. In this technique, two different median values are used, median value of the center pixel and median value of the neighboring pixel (Elad et al., 2023). The final result would be two median value and the original pixel value.

Advantage

(i) It is better than median filter.
(ii) Noisy image can be rectify by using this filter.

Disadvantage

(i) Estimation cost is steep.
(ii) It is non-direct filtering method.

2.10 Boundary edges of filter

By using this technique, we remove a steep impulse noise. It performs in better way in boundaries (Thanh et al., 2021). Here, edges are cited. When pixel is working and the size of the matrix is extended in maximal, then it includes 0s and 1s and the combination of both (Jin et al., 2017). If the combination of 0s and 1s are shown then we have to know that there would be a high impulse noise. The combination is smoothen. Here we can take a 4 X 4 block of pixels. That are 1s or 0s. Then the size of the block would be advanced, i.e. 5 X 5. Then detect the noisy pixels and change the pixels with the value of the median. In correction part, we have to use the adaptive median filter. The size of the AMF would be increased.

Advantage

(i) It is used in MRI image.
(ii) It can remove the high impulse noise.

Disadvantage

(i) Here, the block size would be increased.
(ii) It is complex technique.

Here in Table 1, we compared the PSNR values with the different filter with respect to 10% to 80% Salt and pepper noise density. Different filters are used in different way, at first we used AMF filter for removing Salt and pepper noise, by using AMF, and we got values with respect to 10% to 80% noise density. Then we used SMF, AWMF, NAMF and DBA. So all filters gave the result, but here, NAMF gives the better result with respect to 10% to 80% noise density. By using NAMF, we got the higher PSNR values. We know, if the value of PSNR would become high, then the quality of the image would be good. So here, NAMF is better than other filters for removing Salt and pepper noise.

Table 1. Comparison of PSNR (db) for different filters at expansive grade in noise density with respect to 10% to 80% Salt and Pepper Noise

Filters	10%	20%	30%	40%	50%	60%	70%	80%
AMF	34.15	33.12	32.05	31.45	29.25	28.45	26.24	24.23
SMF	32.12	31.55	31.12	30.44	28.14	25.12	23.45	21.41
AWMF	32.16	31.41	30.44	29.13	28.56	27.40	26.66	25.77
NAMF	41.32	39.18	37.12	34.13	32.50	29.32	28.60	7.57
DBA	35.23	33.12	31.05	29.12	27.56	24.11	22.50	20.65

Figure 1. Image output using 10% to 80% Salt and Pepper Noise

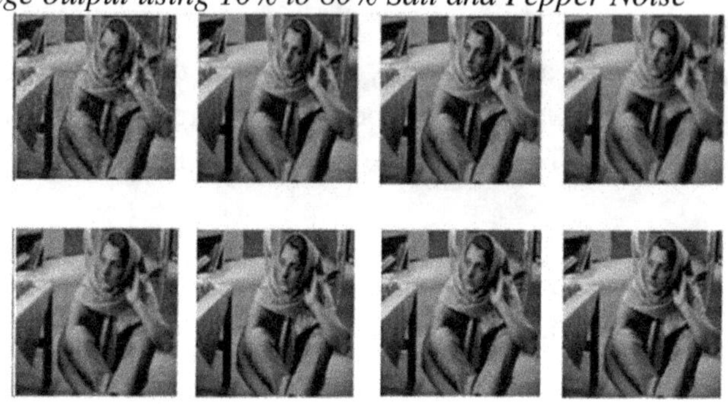

Here in Table 2, we compared the SSIM values with different filter with respect to 10% to 80% Salt and pepper noise density. We used the same filters that are used on table 1. We used AMF, SMF, AWMF, NAMF and DBA. At first we used AMF, we got the result. Then we used SMF, AWMF, NAMF and DBA. Here, NAMF gave the better result with respect to 10% to 80% noise density. We know, if the value of SSIM would become closer with 1, then the image quality would be good. So here, NAMF gave the SSIM values with respect to 10% to 80% noise density and that values are closer with 1. So NAMF is better than the other filters.

Table 2. Comparison of SSIM values of some filters for at expansive grade in noise density with respect to 10% to 80% Salt and pepper noise

Filters	**10%**	**20%**	**30%**	**40%**	**50%**	**60%**	**70%**	**80%**
AMF	0.7744	0.7556	0.7224	0.6955	0.6638	0.6212	0.5970	0.5860
SMF	0.3683	0.3785	0.3942	0.4156	0.4229	0.3955	0.3641	0.3439
AWMF	0.9644	0.9442	0.9222	0.8965	0.8445	0.8113	0.7847	0.7652

continued on following page

Table 2. Continued

Filters	10%	20%	30%	40%	50%	60%	70%	80%
NAMF	0.9932	0.9754	0.9432	0.9147	0.8813	0.8511	0.8364	0.8150
DBA	0.8234	0.7845	0.7532	0.7064	0.6579	0.6364	0.6099	0.5748

Figure 2. Image (LENA) output using 10% to 80% Salt and Pepper Noise

Here in Table 3, we compared the PSNR values by using the different filters on different way with respect to 10% TO 80% Random valued impulse noise density. That filters are used in this type of noise which are DBMF, SMF, NAFSM, FSM, AFSM. So at first we used DBMF, we got a result. Then we used SMF, NAFSM, FSM and AFSM. AFSM gave the better result than other filters. AFSM gives the high PSNR values that is better than the other filters. We have to define in Table1, that if the PSNR value would become high then we can say that the quality of the image would be good. So here, AFSM is better for removing impulse noise.

Figure 3. Image (LENA) output using 10% to 80% Random valued impulse noise

Table 3. Comparison of PSNR (db) of some filters for at expansive grade in noise density with respect to 10% to 80% Random valued impulse noise

Filters	10%	20%	30%	40%	50%	60%	70%	80%
DBMF	0.4123	0.7845	0.8415	0.9641	1.1421	1.3654	1.5678	2.1321
SMF	0.0015	0.0017	0.0016	0.0014	0.0013	0.0012	0.0013	0.0014
NAFSM	0.9190	0.8945	0.8632	0.8336	0.8264	0.8036	0.7910	0.7784
FSM	0.9117	0.8811	0.8439	0.8149	0.7863	0.7514	0.7438	0.7214
AFSM	0.9476	0.9226	0.9165	0.8961	0.8840	0.8712	0.8695	0.8457

Here in Table 4, we compared the SSIM value with respect to 10% to 80% Random valued impulse noise density. We used the same filters that are used in Table 3. At first we used DBMF, we got the result. Then we used SMF, NAFSM, FSM and AFSM. Here, AFSM gave the better result than the other filters. We have to define in Table 2, that if the value of SSIM is closer with 1 then we can say that the image quality would be good. Here, AFSM gave the value that would be closer with 1. So AFSM is better than the other filters for removing impulse noise.

Figure 4. Image output using 10% to 80% Random valued impulse noise

Table 4. Comparison of SSIM values of some filters for at expansive grade in noise density with respect to 10% to 80% Random valued impulse noise

Filters	10%	20%	30%	40%	50%	60%	70%	80%
DBMF	33.51	32.46	31.11	30.31	29.10	27.74	24.33	21.32
SMF	58.65	51.36	46.12	40.38	35.61	30.77	26.45	20.39
NAFSM	37.06	34.52	32.02	31.25	30.53	28.66	25.31	22.36

continued on following page

Table 4. Continued

Filters	10%	20%	30%	40%	50%	60%	70%	80%
FSM	36.12	34.09	32.47	30.21	28.65	27.85	24.33	21.39
AFSM	40.08	39.16	37.17	35.39	33.84	30.33	27.37	23.69

Once pertinent digital photos have been obtained, Later image processing, which includes coding processing and compression, becomes crucial. This comprises coding techniques such model-based and neural network coding processing, arranging all operational data, and compressing relevant data. Following picture restoration, the image is transformed, and then pertinent sections are segmented using image analysis. Following the quantification of the image's geographical features, image equipment and presentation are finally realised. Picture registration is carried out after picture reconstruction. This procedure includes coding, restoration, augmentation, and denoising of images. With the support of numerous outside variables and developments in artificial intelligence technology, the reproducibility of digital image processing technology has significantly increased over time. When compared to traditional image processing technology, digital image processing technology has a number of unique application properties.

3. CONCLUSION

In this paper, our investigation digs into the complex state of image noise, particularly focusing on two widespread types: salt and pepper noise, and impulse noise. Our commencement involved an exhaustive review of various scholarly works, through which we gleaned insights into diverse image noise filters. The synthesis of these filters from the referenced papers enabled us to comprehend their nuanced mechanisms for noise elimination. Furthermore, we conducted a comparative analysis, scrutinizing the Peak Signal-to-Noise Ratio (PSNR) and Structural Similarity Index (SSIM) values across different filters to gauge their efficacy in noise reduction. As we chart our trajectory forward, our commitment extends to an expansive exploration of contemporary literature. Our future endeavors aspire to not only assimilate a broader spectrum of research but also to innovate and implement advanced techniques for image noise reduction, thereby contributing to the evolving landscape of image processing and enhancement. In the field of image processing, segmentation helps in picture analysis, research, and recognition by somewhat reducing the complexity of image processing. Currently, only basic region and edge segmentation techniques are available, indicating that digital picture technology is still in its infancy.

REFERENCES

Alanazi, T. M., Berriri, K., Albekairi, M., Ben Atitallah, A., Sahbani, A., & Kaaniche, K. (2023). New Real-Time High-Density Impulsive Noise Removal Method Applied to Medical Images. In Diagnostics (Vol. 13, Issue 10, p. 1709). MDPI AG. DOI: 10.3390/diagnostics13101709

Balasubramanian, G., Chilambuchelvan, A., Vijayan, S., & Gowrison, G. (2016). Probabilistic decision based filter to remove impulse noise using patch else trimmed median. In AEU - International Journal of Electronics and Communications (Vol. 70, Issue 4, pp. 471–481). Elsevier BV. DOI: 10.1016/j.aeue.2016.01.013

Elad, M., Kawar, B., & Vaksman, G. (2023). Image Denoising: The Deep Learning Revolution and Beyond — A Survey Paper — (Version 1). arXiv. DOI: 10.48550/ARXIV.2301.03362

Erkan, U., & Kilicman, A. (2016). Two new methods for removing salt-and-pepper noise from digital images. In ScienceAsia (Vol. 42, Issue 1, p. 28). Science Society of Thailand. DOI: 10.2306/scienceasia1513-1874.2016.42.028

Erkan, U., Thanh, D. N. H., Enginoglu, S., & Memis, S. (2020). Improved Adaptive Weighted Mean Filter for Salt-and-Pepper Noise Removal. In 2020 International Conference on Electrical, Communication, and Computer Engineering (ICECCE). 2020 International Conference on Electrical, Communication, and Computer Engineering (ICECCE). IEEE. DOI: 10.1109/ICECCE49384.2020.9179351

Esakkirajan, S., Veerakumar, T., Subramanyam, A. N., & PremChand, C. H. (2011). Removal of High Density Salt and Pepper Noise Through Modified Decision Based Unsymmetric Trimmed Median Filter. In IEEE Signal Processing Letters (Vol. 18, Issue 5, pp. 287–290). Institute of Electrical and Electronics Engineers (IEEE). DOI: 10.1109/LSP.2011.2122333

Fromont, E., Prado, A., & Robardet, C. (2009). Constraint-based Subspace Clustering. In Proceedings of the 2009 SIAM International Conference on Data Mining. Proceedings of the 2009 SIAM International Conference on Data Mining. Society for Industrial and Applied Mathematics. DOI: 10.1137/1.9781611972795.3

González-Hidalgo, M., Massanet, S., Mir, A., & Ruiz-Aguilera, D. (2021). Impulsive Noise Removal with an Adaptive Weighted Arithmetic Mean Operator for Any Noise Density. In Applied Sciences (Vol. 11, Issue 2, p. 560). MDPI AG. DOI: 10.3390/app11020560

Han, K. (2020). Personalized News Recommendation and Simulation Based on Improved Collaborative Filtering Algorithm. In Wang, W. (Ed.), *Complexity* (Vol. 2020, pp. 1–12). Hindawi Limited., DOI: 10.1155/2020/8834908

Huang, K., & Zhu, H. (2021). Image Noise Removal Method Based on Improved Nonlocal Mean Algorithm. In Cherifi, H. (Ed.), *Complexity* (Vol. 2021, pp. 1–10). Hindawi Limited., DOI: 10.1155/2021/5578788

Jiao, S., Shi, J., Wang, Y., & Wang, R. (2023). A novel image noise reduction method for composite multistable stochastic resonance systems. In Heliyon (Vol. 9, Issue 3, p. e14431). Elsevier BV. DOI: 10.1016/j.heliyon.2023.e14431

Jin, Q., Grama, I., Kervrann, C., & Liu, Q. (2017). Nonlocal Means and Optimal Weights for Noise Removal. In SIAM Journal on Imaging Sciences (Vol. 10, Issue 4, pp. 1878–1920). Society for Industrial & Applied Mathematics (SIAM). DOI: 10.1137/16M1080781

Korus, P., & Huang, J. (2016). Multi-Scale Fusion for Improved Localization of Malicious Tampering in Digital Images. In IEEE Transactions on Image Processing (Vol. 25, Issue 3, pp. 1312–1326). Institute of Electrical and Electronics Engineers (IEEE). DOI: 10.1109/TIP.2016.2518870

Kumar, S. S., Taheri, F., & Islam, M. R. (n.d.). Artificial Intelligence and Image Processing Approaches in Damage Assessment and Material Evaluation. In *International Conference on Computational Intelligence for Modelling, Control and Automation and International Conference on Intelligent Agents, Web Technologies and Internet Commerce (CIMCA-IAWTIC'06)* (Vol. 1, pp. 307–313). IEEE. DOI: 10.1109/CIMCA.2005.1631284

Meng, G. (2022). Application of Digital Image Processing Technology in the Remote Interactive Art Teaching System. In Chen, C.-L. (Ed.), *Security and Communication Networks* (Vol. 2022, pp. 1–12). Hindawi Limited., DOI: 10.1155/2022/6419117

Nader, J. A., Z., & Zahran, B. (2017). Analysis of Color Image Filtering Methods. In International Journal of Computer Applications (Vol. 174, Issue 8, pp. 12–17). Foundation of Computer Science. DOI: 10.5120/ijca2017915449

Shao, S., & Zhang, K. (2020). An Improved Multisensor Self-Adaptive Weighted Fusion Algorithm Based on Discrete Kalman Filtering. In *Complexity* (Vol. 2020, pp. 1–9). Hindawi Limited., DOI: 10.1155/2020/9673764

Song, S., Dai, X., Huang, Z., & Gong, D. (2020). Load Parameter Identification for Parallel Robot Manipulator Based on Extended Kalman Filter. In Wang, N. (Ed.), *Complexity* (Vol. 2020, pp. 1–12). Hindawi Limited., DOI: 10.1155/2020/8816374

Thanh, D. N. H., Prasath, V. B. S., Dvoenko, S., & Hieu, L. M. (2021). An adaptive image inpainting method based on euler's elastica with adaptive parameters estimation and the discrete gradient method. In *Signal Processing* (Vol. 178, p. 107797). Elsevier BV., DOI: 10.1016/j.sigpro.2020.107797

Vivekanandam, B. (2021). Unstructured Noise Removal for Industrial Sensor Imaging Unit by Hybrid Adaptive Median Algorithm. In Journal of Innovative Image Processing (Vol. 3, Issue 4, pp. 284–297). Inventive Research Organization. DOI: 10.36548/jiip.2021.4.001

Wang, J. (2024). Research on Development of Generative Artificial Intelligence. In Frontiers in Computing and Intelligent Systems (Vol. 8, Issue 1, pp. 69–74). Darcy & Roy Press Co. Ltd. DOI: 10.54097/d24rqq11

Wang, L., Chen, Y., Lin, F., Chen, Y., Yu, F., & Cai, Z. (2018). Impulse Noise Denoising Using Total Variation with Overlapping Group Sparsity and Lp-Pseudo-Norm Shrinkage. In Applied Sciences (Vol. 8, Issue 11, p. 2317). MDPI AG. DOI: 10.3390/app8112317

Wu, H., He, Y., Chen, Y., Li, S., & Peng, Z. (2020). Seismic Acoustic Impedance Inversion Using Mixed Second-Order Fractional ATpV Regularization. In IEEE Access (Vol. 8, pp. 3442–3452). Institute of Electrical and Electronics Engineers (IEEE). DOI: 10.1109/ACCESS.2019.2962552

Yang, J.-H., Zhao, X.-L., Ji, T.-Y., Ma, T.-H., & Huang, T.-Z. (2020). Low-rank tensor train for tensor robust principal component analysis. In *Applied Mathematics and Computation* (Vol. 367, p. 124783). Elsevier BV., DOI: 10.1016/j.amc.2019.124783

Yu, L., & Hou, J. (2018). Large-Screen Interactive Imaging System with Switching Federated Filter Method Based on 3D Sensor. In Complexity (Vol. 2018, pp. 1–11). Hindawi Limited. DOI: 10.1155/2018/8730281

Zagorchev, L., & Goshtasby, A. (2006). A comparative study of transformation functions for nonrigid image registration. In IEEE Transactions on Image Processing (Vol. 15, Issue 3, pp. 529–538). Institute of Electrical and Electronics Engineers (IEEE). DOI: 10.1109/TIP.2005.863114

Zhai, G., & Min, X. (2020). Perceptual image quality assessment: a survey. In Science China Information Sciences (Vol. 63, Issue 11). Springer Science and Business Media LLC. DOI: 10.1007/s11432-019-2757-1

Compilation of References

Abisoye, A. (2023). AI literacy in STEM education: Policy strategies for preparing the future workforce. *Journal of Frontiers in Multidisciplinary Research*, *4*(1), 17–24. DOI: 10.54660/JFMR.2023.4.1.17-24

Acikgoz, Y., Davison, K., Ezerins, M., & Laske, M. (2020). Justice perceptions of artificial intelligence in selection. *International Journal of Selection and Assessment*, *28*(4), 399–416. Advance online publication. DOI: 10.1111/ijsa.12306

Adeoye, M. A., Prastikawati, E. F., & Riwayatiningsih, R. (2025). Beyond Traditional Testing: Exploring the Efficacy of Adaptive Assessments in Shaping Future Learners. *Journal of Nonformal Education*, *11*(1), 153–169. DOI: 10.15294/jone.v11i1.19934

Afroogh, S., Atkinson, D., Chen, K., & Dhurandhar, A. (2024). The global landscape of academic guidelines for generative AI and large language models. *arXiv preprint*. http://arxiv.org/abs/2406.18842

Ahmed, R. R., Akbar, W., Aijaz, M., Channar, Z. A., Ahmed, F., & Parmar, V. (2023). The role of green innovation on environmental and organizational performance: Moderation of human resource practices and management commitment. *Heliyon*, *9*(1), e12679. Advance online publication. DOI: 10.1016/j.heliyon.2022.e12679 PMID: 36660461

AI in Education Statistics. (2025). *AI in education statistics*. https://www.aiprm.com/ai-in-education-statistics/

Akpan, I. J., Kobara, Y. M., Owolabi, J., Akpan, A. A., & Offodile, O. F. (2025). Conversational and generative artificial intelligence and human–chatbot interaction in education and research. *International Transactions in Operational Research*, *32*(3), 1251–1281. DOI: 10.1111/itor.13522

Al Naqbi, H., Bahroun, Z., & Ahmed, V. (2024). Enhancing work productivity through generative artificial intelligence: A comprehensive literature review. *Sustainability, 16*(3), 1166. DOI: 10.3390/su16031166

Alammary, A. S. (2024). Building a sustainable digital infrastructure for higher education: A blockchain-based solution for cross-institutional enrollment. *Sustainability (Basel), 17*(1), 194. DOI: 10.3390/su17010194

Alam, S., Asim, M., Shuaib, M., & Khan, M. U. S. (2021). Blockchain-based initiatives: Current state and challenges. *Computer Networks, 198*, 108395. DOI: 10.1016/j.comnet.2021.108395

Alanazi, T. M., Berriri, K., Albekairi, M., Ben Atitallah, A., Sahbani, A., & Kaaniche, K. (2023). New Real-Time High-Density Impulsive Noise Removal Method Applied to Medical Images. In Diagnostics (Vol. 13, Issue 10, p. 1709). MDPI AG. DOI: 10.3390/diagnostics13101709

Alasmari, T. (2024). Acceptance factors of generative AI in EFL teaching: A pedagogical perspective. https://core.ac.uk/download/628120355.pdf

Alawida, M., Mejri, S., Mehmood, A., Chikhaoui, B., & Abiodun, O. I. (2023). A comprehensive study of ChatGPT: Advancements, limitations, and ethical considerations in natural language processing and cybersecurity. *Information (Basel), 14*(8), 462. DOI: 10.3390/info14080462

Albreiki, B., Zaki, N., & Alashwal, H. (2021). A systematic literature review of student' performance prediction using machine learning techniques. *Education Sciences, 11*(9), 552. DOI: 10.3390/educsci11090552

Alenezi, A. (2024). Evaluating the effectiveness of AI-powered adaptive learning systems in secondary schools. *International Journal on Studies in Education, 6*(4), 686–700. DOI: 10.46328/ijonse.264

Alexander, B., Asino, T. I., & Bai, J. Y. H. (2024). The manifesto for teaching and learning in a time of generative AI: A critical collective stance to better navigate the future. https://core.ac.uk/download/636730349.pdf

Al-Fadhli, S. (2018). The role of learning management systems in education. *International Journal of Educational Technology, 15*(2), 15–29.

Alhamadi, A. A., & Alhamadi, A. A. (2024). Analyzing The Effect Of Learning Management Systems Powered By Artificial Intelligence On Teaching And Learning In Higher Education. *Journal Of Data Acquisition And Processing, 39*(1), 87–98.

Ali, A., Hingle, A., & Johri, A. (2024). Generative artificial intelligence in higher education: Evidence from an analysis of institutional policies and guidelines. https://arxiv.org/abs/2402.01659

Ali, O., Murray, P. A., Momin, M., Dwivedi, Y. K., & Malik, T. (2024). The effects of artificial intelligence applications in educational settings: Challenges and strategies. *Technological Forecasting and Social Change*, *199*, 123076. Advance online publication. DOI: 10.1016/j.techfore.2023.123076

Allen, I. E., & Seaman, J. (2016). *Online report card: Tracking online education in the United States*. Babson Survey Research Group.

Allioui, H., & Mourdi, Y. (2023). Exploring the full potentials of IoT for better financial growth and stability: A comprehensive survey. *Sensors (Basel)*, *23*(19), 8015. DOI: 10.3390/s23198015

Alonso-Fernández, C., Calvo-Morata, A., Freire, M., Martínez-Ortiz, I., & Fernández-Manjón, B. (2019). Applications of data science to game learning analytics data: A systematic literature review. *Computers & Education*, *141*, 103612. DOI: 10.1016/j.compedu.2019.103612

Alotaibi, N. S., & Alshehri, A. H. (2023). Prospers and obstacles in using artificial intelligence in Saudi Arabia Higher Education institutions—The potential of AI-based learning outcomes. *Sustainability (Basel)*, *15*(13), 10723. DOI: 10.3390/su151310723

Alowais, S. A., Alghamdi, S. S., Alsuhebany, N., Alqahtani, T., Alshaya, A., Almohareb, S. N., Aldairem, A., Alrashed, M., Bin Saleh, K., Badreldin, H. A., Al Yami, M. S., Al Harbi, S. A., & Albekairy, A. M. (2023). Revolutionizing healthcare: The role of artificial intelligence in clinical practice. *BMC Medical Education*, *23*, 689. DOI: 10.1186/s12909-023-04698-z

Alpaydin, E. (2010). *Introduction to machine learning*. The MIT.

Alshahrani, B. T., Pileggi, S. F., & Karimi, F. (2024). A Social Perspective on AI in the Higher Education System: A Semisystematic Literature Review. In *Electronics (Switzerland)* (Vol. 13, Issue 8). Multidisciplinary Digital Publishing Institute (MDPI). DOI: 10.3390/electronics13081572

Alshammari, M. T. (2025). An Investigation into ChatGPT-Enhanced Adaptive E-learning Systems. *TEM Journal*, *14*(1), 503–510. DOI: 10.18421/TEM141-45

Altinay, Z., Altinay, F., Tlili, A., & Vatankhah, S. (2025). “Keep your friends close, but your enemies closer:” ChatGPT in tourism and hospitality. *Journal of Hospitality and Tourism Technology*, *16*(2), 213–228. DOI: 10.1108/JHTT-03-2024-0139

Alwarafy, A., Al-Thelaya, K. A., Abdallah, M., Schneider, J., & Hamdi, M. (2020). A Survey on Security and Privacy Issues in Edge Computing-Assisted Internet of Things. arXiv preprint arXiv:2008.03252. https://arxiv.org/abs/2008.03252

Alzen, J. L., Langdon, L. S., & Otero, V. K. (2018). A logistic regression investigation of the relationship between the Learning Assistant model and failure rates in introductory STEM courses. *International Journal of STEM Education*, *5*(1), 56. DOI: 10.1186/s40594-018-0152-1 PMID: 30631745

Amos, C., Holmes, G., & Strutton, D. (2008). Exploring the relationship between celebrity endorser effects and advertising effectiveness: A quantitative synthesis of effect size. *International Journal of Advertising*, *27*(2), 209–234. DOI: 10.1080/02650487.2008.11073052

Anderson, L. W., & Krathwohl, D. R. (2001). *A taxonomy for learning, teaching, and assessing: A revision of Bloom's taxonomy of educational objectives*. Longman.

Anderson, T., & Dron, J. (2017). Integrating LMS to enhance educational efficiency. *Journal of Educational Technology & Society*, *20*(4), 50–64.

Anggoro, S., Fitriati, A., Thoe, N. K., Talib, C. A., & Mareza, L. (2024). Differentiated instruction based on multiple intelligences as promising joyful and meaningful learning. *Int J Eval & Res Educ ISSN*, *2252*(8822), 1195. DOI: 10.11591/ijere.v13i2.24791

Apisuksakul, K., Pimdee, P., & Sukkamart, A. (2024). Blended and collaboration-based learning management model to enhance mobile website user experience (UX) design skills. https://core.ac.uk/download/620884859.pdf

Appleton, J. J., Christenson, S. L., & Furlong, M. J. (2008). Student engagement with school: Critical conceptual and methodological issues of the construct. *Psychology in the Schools*, *45*(5), 369–386. DOI: 10.1002/pits.20303

Arnold, K. E., & Pistilli, M. D. (2012). Course Signals at Purdue: Using learning analytics to increase student success. *Proceedings of the 2nd International Conference on Learning Analytics and Knowledge*, 267–270. DOI: 10.1145/2330601.2330666

Asad, M. M., & Ajaz, A. (2024). Impact of ChatGPT and generative AI on lifelong learning and upskilling learners in higher education: Unveiling the challenges and opportunities globally. *The International Journal of Information and Learning Technology*, *41*(5), 507–523. DOI: 10.1108/IJILT-06-2024-0103

Asperis, R. (2025). Education in the world of AI. In *Preprints*.

Atkinson-Toal, A., & Guo, C. (2024). Generative artificial intelligence (AI) education policies of UK universities. *Enhancing Teaching and Learning in Higher Education*, *2*, 70–94. DOI: 10.62512/etlhe.20

Atlam, H. F., Alenezi, A., Alharthi, A., Walters, R. J., & Wills, G. B. (2020). A review of blockchain in internet of things and AI. *Big Data and Cognitive Computing*, *4*(4), 28. DOI: 10.3390/bdcc4040028

Awad, M., & Khanna, R. (2015). *Efficient learning machines theories, concepts, and applications for engineers and system designers*. A.

Awaji, B., & Solaiman, E. (2022). Design, implementation, and evaluation of blockchain-based trusted achievement record system for students in higher education. *arXiv preprint arXiv:2204.12547*. DOI: 10.5220/0011044200003182

Aydin, L. (2023). A review of the current state of bioprinting technology. *MedLiber Regenerative Medicine*, *1*(123), 23–43.

Ayeni, O. O., Al Hamad, N. M., Chisom, O. N., Osawaru, B., & Adewusi, O. E. (2024). AI in education: A review of personalized learning and educational technology. *GSC Advanced Research and Reviews*, *18*(2), 261–271. DOI: 10.30574/gscarr.2024.18.2.0062

Ayub Khan, A., Rahman, M. S., Alam, M. M., Rehman, S. U., & Kim, J. M. (2021). Educational blockchain: A secure degree attestation and verification traceability architecture for higher education commission. *Applied Sciences (Basel, Switzerland)*, *11*(22), 10917. DOI: 10.3390/app112210917

Azzam, A., & Charles, T. (2025). K-12 STEM Teachers' Experiences with Artificial Intelligence. *TEM Journal, 14*(1).

Babu, C. S., Yuvansankar, M., & Tharuneshwaran, K. (2025). Personalized Learning and Student Engagement: Leveraging AI for Enhanced Learning Experiences in Distance Education. In *AI and Learning Analytics in Distance Learning* (pp. 73-102). IGI Global Scientific Publishing.

Bachhal, P., Ahuja, S., & Gargrish, S. (2021). Educational data mining: A review. *Journal of Physics: Conference Series*, *1950*(1), 012022. DOI: 10.1088/1742-6596/1950/1/012022

Bada, S. O., & Olusegun, S. (2015). Constructivism learning theory: A paradigm for teaching and learning. *Journal of Research & Method in Education*, *5*(6), 66–70. DOI: 10.9790/7388-05616670

Badawy, W., Helal, M. M. I., Hashim, A., Zinhom, H., & Shaban, M. (2025). Ethical boundaries and data-sharing practices in AI-enhanced nursing: An Arab perspective. *International Nursing Review*, *72*(1), e70013. DOI: 10.1111/inr.70013 PMID: 40070199

Bahroun, Z., Anane, C., Ahmed, V., & Zacca, A. (2023). Transforming education: A comprehensive review of generative artificial intelligence in educational settings through bibliometric and content analysis. *Sustainability*, *15*(17), 12983. DOI: 10.3390/su151712983

Baillifard, A., Gabella, M., Lavenex, P. B., & Martarelli, C. S. (2023). Implementing learning principles with a personal AI tutor: A case study. *arXiv preprint arXiv:2309*.13060. /arXiv.2309.13060DOI: 10.48550

Baker, R. S., Hawn, A., & Lee, S. (2023). Algorithmic bias: The state of the situation and policy recommendations. https://www.oecd.org/en/publications/oecd-digital-education-outlook-2023_c74f03de-en/full-report/algorithmic-bias-the-state-of-the-situation-and-policy-recommendations

Baker, R., & Siemens, G. (2014). Educational data mining and learning analytics. .DOI: 10.1017/CBO9781139519526.016

Baker, R. S., Gowda, S. M., Wixon, M., Kalka, J., Wagner, A. Z., Salvi, A., Aleven, V., Kusbit, G. W., Ocumpaugh, J., & Rossi, L. (2012). Towards Sensor-Free Affect Detection in Cognitive Tutor Algebra. *International Conference on Educational Data Mining*, Chania, Greece.

Baker, R. S., & Inventado, P. B. (2014). Educational data mining and learning analytics. In Lárusson, J. A., & White, B. (Eds.), *Learning Analytics: From Research to Practice* (pp. 61–75). Springer. DOI: 10.1007/978-1-4614-3305-7_4

Balalle, H., & Pannilage, S. (2025). Reassessing academic integrity in the age of AI: A systematic literature review on AI and academic integrity. *Social Sciences & Humanities Open*, *11*, 101299. DOI: 10.1016/j.ssaho.2025.101299

Balasubramaniam, N., Kauppinen, M., Rannisto, A., Hiekkanen, K., & Kujala, S. (2023). Transparency and explainability of AI systems: From ethical guidelines to requirements. *Information and Software Technology*, *159*, 107197. DOI: 10.1016/j.infsof.2023.107197

Balasubramanian, G., Chilambuchelvan, A., Vijayan, S., & Gowrison, G. (2016). Probabilistic decision based filter to remove impulse noise using patch else trimmed median. In AEU - International Journal of Electronics and Communications (Vol. 70, Issue 4, pp. 471–481). Elsevier BV. DOI: 10.1016/j.aeue.2016.01.013

Balfour, S. P. (2013). Assessing writing in MOOCs: Automated essay scoring and Calibrated Peer Review™. *Research & Practice in Assessment*, *8*, 40–48.

Banada, M. (2025). AI powered attendance system for class rooms using face recognition. *Indian Scientific Journal of Research in Engineering and Management*, *7*(1), 1–9. Advance online publication. DOI: 10.55041/IJSREM40676

Baniata, H., & Kertesz, A. (2022). Prifob: A privacy-aware fog-enhanced blockchain-based system for global accreditation and credential verification. *Journal of Network and Computer Applications*, *205*, 103440. DOI: 10.1016/j.jnca.2022.103440

Banik, B. G., & Gullapelly, A. (2025). AI-Powered Gamification and Interactive Learning Tools for Enhancing Student Engagement. In *Driving Quality Education Through AI and Data Science* (pp. 283–310). IGI Global Scientific Publishing. DOI: 10.4018/979-8-3693-8292-9.ch013

Barger, V. A., Chennamaneni, P. R., Dahl, A. J., & Peltier, J. W. (2024). A How-To-Guide For Bringing Artificial Intelligence Into Life In Your Marketing Curriculum: A Blueprint For Student Learning And Success. *Marketing Education Review*, *35*(2), 99–108. DOI: 10.1080/10528008.2024.2430259

Barnard, J. (1997). T*he World Wide Web and Higher Education. The Promise of Virtual Universities and Online Libraries*, *37*(3), 30–35.

Barnes, E., Hutson, J., & Perry, K. (2024). Enhancing adult learner success in higher education through decision tree models: A machine learning approach. In *Forum for Education Studies* (Vol. 2, No. 3).

Barnes, E., & Hutson, J. (2024). Navigating the ethical terrain of AI in higher education: Strategies for mitigating bias and promoting fairness. *Forum Edu. Stud.*, *2*(2), 1229. DOI: 10.59400/fes.v2i2.1229

Basri, W. S. (2024). Effectiveness of AI-powered Tutoring Systems in Enhancing Learning Outcomes. *Eurasian Journal of Educational Research (EJER)*, (110).

Bastomi, B., Mujahid, A. Z., Asmuni Asmuni and Sibron, A., Audina, M., & Harto, K. (2024). Bringing artificial Intelligence (AI) in teaching and learning process. TOFEDU: The Future of Education Journal, 3(5), 1825–1831.

Bates, A. W. (2015). *Teaching in a digital age: Guidelines for designing teaching and learning*. Tony Bates Associates Ltd.

Benjamin, R. (2019). Race after technology: Abolitionist tools for the new Jim code. *Polity*.

Bernard, R. M., Abrami, P. C., Borokhovski, E., Wade, C. A., Tamim, R. M., Surkes, M. A., & Bethel, E. C. (2009). A Meta-Analysis of Three Types of Interaction Treatments in Distance Education. *Review of Educational Research, 79*(3), 1243–1289. DOI: 10.3102/0034654309333844

Bernard, R. M., Abrami, P. C., Lou, Y., Borokhovski, E., Wade, A., Wozney, L., Wallet, P. A., Fiset, M., & Huang, B. (2004). How Does Distance Education Compare With Classroom Instruction? A Meta-Analysis of the Empirical Literature. *Review of Educational Research, 74*(3), 379–439. DOI: 10.3102/00346543074003379

Bhagat, S., & Kim, D. J. (2020). Higher Education Amidst COVID-19: Challenges and Silver Lining. *Information Systems Management, 37*(4), 366–371. DOI: 10.1080/10580530.2020.1824040

Bhardwaj, S., & Sharma, I. (2025). Exploring the Effects of AI-Powered Personalized Classroom Management Strategies. In *AI Applications and Strategies in Teacher Education* (pp. 21–42). IGI Global.

Bhatia, A., Bhatia, P., & Sood, D. (2024). Leveraging AI to transform online higher education: Focusing on personalized learning, assessment, and student engagement. *International Journal of Management and Humanities, 11*(1), 111-119.

Bian, Q., Ling, X., & Yan, S. (2024). Bridging the algorithmic divide. *Education as Change*, •••, 28.

Billingsley, B., Billingsley, B., & Clarke, S. (2024). Big questions and interdisciplinary learning: Issue 1. https://core.ac.uk/download/617176985.pdf

Binns, R. (2018). Fairness in machine learning: Lessons from political philosophy. In S. A. Friedler & C. Wilson (Eds.), *Proceedings of the 1st Conference on Fairness, Accountability and Transparency* (pp. 149-159). PMLR. https://proceedings.mlr.press/v81/binns18a.html.

Bishop, C. M. (2016). *Pattern recognition and machine learning*. Springer.

Bixler, K., & Ceballos, M. (2025). Principals Leading AI in Schools for Instructional Leadership: A Conceptual Model for Principal AI Use. *Leadership and Policy in Schools, 24*(1), 137–154. DOI: 10.1080/15700763.2024.2428297

Blonder, R., & Feldman-Maggor, Y. (2024). AI for chemistry teaching: Responsible AI and ethical considerations. *Chemistry Teacher International : Best Practices in Chemistry Education, 6*(4), 385–395. DOI: 10.1515/cti-2024-0014

Bluemink, J., & Järvelä, S. (2004). Face-to-face encounters as contextual support for Web-based discussions in a teacher education course. *The Internet and Higher Education*, *7*(3), 199–215. DOI: 10.1016/j.iheduc.2004.06.006

Bočková, K., Procházka, D. A., & Bartoš, P. (2025). The role of artificial intelligence in managing scientific research projects funded by KEGA and VEGA grant schemes. *Journal of Ecohumanism*, *4*(1), 1448–1476.

Boixo, S., Isakov, S. V., Smelyanskiy, V. N., Babbush, R., Ding, N., Jiang, Z., Bremner, M. J., Martinis, J. M., & Neven, H. (2018). Characterizing quantum supremacy in near-term devices. *Nature Physics*, *14*(6), 595–600. DOI: 10.1038/s41567-018-0124-x

Bond, M., Khosravi, H., de Laat, M., Bergdahl, N., Negrea, V., Oxley, E., Pham, P., Chong, S. W., Siemens, G., Gašević, D., & Rienties, B. (2024). A meta-systematic review of artificial intelligence in higher education: A call for increased ethics, collaboration, and rigor. *International Journal of Educational Technology in Higher Education*, *21*, 26. DOI: 10.1186/s41239-023-00436-z

Bond, M., Zawacki-Richter, O., & Nichols, M. (2019). Revisiting five decades of educational technology research: A content and authorship analysis of the British Journal of Educational Technology. *British Journal of Educational Technology*, *50*(1), 12–63. DOI: 10.1111/bjet.12730

Borrego, Á., Ardanuy, J., & Arguimbau, L. (2023). Crossref as a bibliographic discovery tool in the arts and humanities. *Quantitative Science Studies*, *4*(1), 91–104. DOI: 10.1162/qss_a_00240

Boud, D., & Molloy, E. (Eds.). (2013). *Feedback in higher and professional education: Understanding it and doing it well*. Routledge.

Bowen, R. S., & Cooper, M. M. (2022). Grading on a Curve as a Systemic Issue of Equity in Chemistry Education. *Journal of Chemical Education*, *99*(1), 185–194. DOI: 10.1021/acs.jchemed.1c00369

Brennan, R. L. (2004). *Generalizability theory*. Springer.

Buckingham Shum, S., & Ferguson, R. (2012). Social Learning Analytics. *Journal of Educational Technology & Society*, *15*(3), 3–26. https://www.jstor.org/stable/jeductechsoci.15.3.3

Bulut, O., Beiting-Parrish, M., Casabianca, J. M., Slater, S. C., Jiao, H., Song, D., . . . Morilova, P. (2024). The rise of artificial intelligence in educational measurement: Opportunities and ethical challenges. *arXiv preprint arXiv:2406*.18900. https://doi.org/DOI: 10.59863/MIQL7785

Buolamwini, J., & Gebru, T. (2018). Gender shades: Intersectional accuracy disparities in commercial gender classification. *Proceedings of Machine Learning Research*, *81*, 1–15.

Bura, C., & Myakala, P. K. (2024). *Advancing Transformative Education: Generative AI as a Catalyst for Equity and Innovation*. https://arxiv.org/abs/2411.15971

Canavesi, A., Passerini, K., & Ravarini, A. (2024). From users to allies: Exploring educator and generative AI roles in shaping the future of higher education. https://core.ac.uk/download/620769088.pdf

Canning, E. A., Muenks, K., Green, D. J., & Murphy, M. C. (2019). STEM faculty who believe ability is fixed have larger racial achievement gaps and inspire less student motivation in their classes. *Science Advances*, *5*(2), eaau4734. Advance online publication. DOI: 10.1126/sciadv.aau4734 PMID: 30793027

Canty, R. B., Bao, S., Coley, C. W., Li, S., Manson, A. L., Wang, S., Caffrey, D. R., Church, G. M., Dorr, B. M., Friedler, S. A., Gromski, P. S., Hall, D., Hazen, S. P., Hinkson, I. V., Klavs, F., Krzyzanowski, P. M., Lawrence, C., Lee, D. H., Li, R., & McGill, C. M. (2025). Science acceleration and accessibility with self-driving labs. *Nature Communications*, *16*(1), 3856. DOI: 10.1038/s41467-025-59231-1 PMID: 40274856

Capece, G., Levialdi Ghiron, N., & Pasquale, F. (2020). Blockchain technology: Redefining trust for digital certificates. *Sustainability (Basel)*, *12*(21), 8952. DOI: 10.3390/su12218952

Carnegie Mellon University. (n.d.). *Open Learning Initiative*. The Simon Initiative. https://www.cmu.edu/simon/open-simon/toolkit/tools/learning-tools/oli.html

Caruso, A. (2024). *Forensic Analysis of Mobile Spyware: Investigating Security, Vulnerabilities, and Detection Challenges in Android and iOS Platforms* (Doctoral dissertation, Politecnico di Torino).

Casey, J. R., Russell, A., & Courey, A. J. (2023). Participation in high-structure general chemistry course increases student sense of belonging and persistence to organic chemistry. *Journal of Chemical Education*, *100*(8), 2860–2872. DOI: 10.1021/acs.jchemed.2c01253 PMID: 37577453

CAST. (2018). *Universal Design for Learning Guidelines version 2.2*. http://udlguidelines.cast.org

Castelli, F. R., & Sarvary, M. A. (2021). Why students do not turn on their video cameras during online classes and an equitable and inclusive plan to encourage them to do so. *Ecology and Evolution*, *11*(8), 3565–3576. DOI: 10.1002/ece3.7123 PMID: 33898009

Celik, I., Dindar, M., Muukkonen, H., & Järvelä, S. (2022). The promises and challenges of artificial intelligence for teachers: A systematic review of research. *TechTrends*, *66*(4), 616–630. DOI: 10.1007/s11528-022-00715-y

Chananagari Prabhakar, R. R. (2024). Privacy-preserving AI database systems in education analytics. *International Journal of Multidisciplinary Research and Growth*, *5*(6), 1626–1629. DOI: 10.54660/.IJMRGE.2024.5.6.1626-1629

Chan, C. K. Y. (2023). A comprehensive AI policy education framework for university teaching and learning. *International Journal of Educational Technology in Higher Education*, *20*(1), 38. DOI: 10.1186/s41239-023-00408-3

Chan, C. K. Y., & Colloton, T. (2024). *Generative AI in higher education*. Routledge. DOI: 10.4324/9781003459026

Chan, C. K. Y., & Hu, W. (2023). Students' voices on generative AI: Perceptions, benefits, and challenges in higher education. *International Journal of Educational Technology in Higher Education*, *20*(1), 43. DOI: 10.1186/s41239-023-00411-8

Chan, C. K. Y., & Lee, K. K. W. (2023). The AI generation gap: Are Gen Z students more interested in adopting generative AI such as ChatGPT in teaching and learning than their Gen X and millennial generation teachers? *Smart Learning Environments*, *10*, 25. DOI: 10.1186/s40561-023-00269-3

Chandler, K. (2016). Using Breakout Rooms in Synchronous Online Tutorials. *Journal of Perspectives in Applied Academic Practice*, *4*(3). Advance online publication. DOI: 10.14297/jpaap.v4i3.216

Chan, T.-H. H., Shi, E., & Song, D. (2011). *Private and continual release of statistics*. In *Proceedings of the 39th International Colloquium Conference on Automata, Languages, and Programming (ICALP'11)* (pp. 405–417). Springer. https://doi.org/ DOI: 10.1007/978-3-642-22006-7_34

Chembe, C., Nasilele, N. B., & Msendo, R. (2023). The fuss about artificial intelligence in education sector: Should we worry? *Zictjournal*, *7*(2), 30–35. DOI: 10.33260/zictjournal.v7i2.269

Chen, A., Zhang, Y., Jia, J., Liang, M., Cha, Y., & Lim, C. P. (2025). A systematic review and Meta-analysis of AI-enabled assessment in language learning: Design, implementation, and effectiveness. *Journal of Computer Assisted Learning*, *41*(1), e13064. DOI: 10.1111/jcal.13064

Cheng, N., Broadbent, G., & Chappell, W. (2025, August). *Cognitive loop via in-situ optimization: Self-adaptive reasoning for science*. Microsoft Research. https://www.microsoft.com/en-us/research/publication/cognitive-loop-via-in-situ-optimization-self-adaptive-reasoning-for-science/

Chengoden, R., Victor, N., Huynh-The, T., Yenduri, G., Jhaveri, R. H., Alazab, M., Bhattacharya, S., Hegde, P., Maddikunta, P. K. R., & Gadekallu, T. R. (2023). Metaverse for healthcare: A survey on potential applications, challenges, and future directions. *IEEE Access : Practical Innovations, Open Solutions*, *11*, 12765–12795. DOI: 10.1109/access.2023.3241628

Chen, L., Chen, P., & Lin, Z. (2020). Artificial intelligence in education: A review. *IEEE Access : Practical Innovations, Open Solutions*, *8*, 75264–75278.

Chen, L., Chen, P., & Lin, Z. (2020). Artificial Intelligence in Education: A Review. *IEEE Access : Practical Innovations, Open Solutions*, *8*, 75264–75278. DOI: 10.1109/ACCESS.2020.2988510

Chen, X., Xie, H., Zou, D., & Hwang, G. J. (2020). Application and theory gaps during the rise of artificial intelligence in education. *Computers and Education: Artificial Intelligence*, *1*, 100002. DOI: 10.1016/j.caeai.2020.100002

Chi, M. T. H., Bassok, M., Lewis, M. W., Reimann, P., & Glaser, R. (1994). Self-explanations: How students study and use examples in learning to solve problems. *Cognitive Science*, *18*(2), 145–182.

Chu, T. H., Chao, C. M., Liu, H. H., & Chen, D. F. (2022). Developing an Extended Theory of UTAUT 2 Model to Explore Factors Influencing Taiwanese Consumer Adoption of Intelligent Elevators. *SAGE Open*, *12*(4),. Advance online publication. DOI: 10.1177/21582440221142209

Cioci, G. (2025). AI in the class: Uses, doubts, challenges and perceptions of a sample of teachers from different nationalities. EDUC. *Science and Society*, *2*, 38–55.

Clark, R. E. (2000). Evaluating Distance Education. *Strategies and Cautions*, *1*(1), 3–16.

Conati, C., & Kardan, S. (2013). Student modeling: Supporting personalized instruction, from problem-solving to exploratory open-ended activities. *AI Magazine*, *34*(3), 13–26. DOI: 10.1609/aimag.v34i3.2483

Conrad, K. (2024). A blueprint for an AI bill of rights for education. Critical AI, 2(1).

Conrad, D. L. (2002). Engagement, Excitement, Anxiety, and Fear: Learners' Experiences of Starting an Online Course. *American Journal of Distance Education, 16*(4), 205–226. DOI: 10.1207/S15389286AJDE1604_2

Cooper, G. (2023). Examining science education in ChatGPT: An exploratory study of generative artificial intelligence. *Journal of Science Education and Technology, 32*(4), 444–452. DOI: 10.1007/s10956-023-10039-y

Crawford, K., & Paglen, T. (2021). Correction to: Excavating AI: the politics of images in machine learning training sets. *AI & Society, 36*(4), 1399. DOI: 10.1007/s00146-021-01301-1

Crossley, S. A., Allen, D., & McNamara, D. S. (2011). Text simplification and comprehensible input: A case for an intuitive approach. *Language Teaching Research, 16*(1), 89–108. DOI: 10.1177/1362168811423456

Cui, G., Lockee, B., & Meng, C. (2013). Building modern online social presence: A review of social presence theory and its instructional design implications for future trends. *Education and Information Technologies, 18*(4), 661–685. DOI: 10.1007/s10639-012-9192-1

Cukurova, M., Hertz, B., & Kralj, L. Saltidou, & et al. (2024). Professional development for teachers in the age of AI. https://core.ac.uk/download/603246853.pdf

Dahl, J. E., & Mørch, A. (2025). A theoretical and empirical analysis of tensions between learning objects and constructivism. *Education and Information Technologies*, 1–50. DOI: 10.1007/s10639-025-13636-z

Dairo, A. O., & Szűcs, K. (2025). Adaptive learning engine for driving marketing channel performance: A machine learning approach. *Journal of Research in Interactive Marketing, 19*(6), 952–968. Advance online publication. DOI: 10.1108/JRIM-02-2024-0098

Damaševičius, R., & Sidekerskienė, T. (2024). Virtual worlds for learning in metaverse: A narrative review. *Sustainability, 16*(5), 2032. DOI: 10.3390/su16052032

Dang, S., Quach, S., & Roberts, R. E. (2025). How time fuels AI device adoption: A contextual model enriched by machine learning. *Technological Forecasting and Social Change, 212*, 123975. DOI: 10.1016/j.techfore.2025.123975

Deci, E. L., & Ryan, R. M. (2000). The "what" and "why" of goal pursuits: Human needs and the self-determination of behavior. *Psychological Inquiry, 11*(4), 227–268. DOI: 10.1207/S15327965PLI1104_01

Deci, E. L., & Ryan, R. M. (2013). *Intrinsic motivation and self-determination in human behavior*. Springer Science & Business Media.

DeMonbrun, M., Finelli, C. J., Prince, M., Shekhar, P., Henderon, C., & Waters, C. (2017). Creating an Instrument to Measure Student Response to Instructional Practices. *Journal of Engineering Education, 106*(2), 273–298. DOI: 10.1002/jee.20162

Demszky, D., Liu, J., Hill, H. C., Jurafsky, D., & Piech, C. (2023). Can automated feedback improve teachers' uptake of student ideas? Evidence from a randomized controlled trial in a large-scale online course. *Educational Evaluation and Policy Analysis, 45*(2), 293–317. DOI: 10.3102/01623737231169270

DeNoyelles, A., Zydney, J. M., & Chen, B. (2014). *Strategies for creating a community of inquiry through online asynchronous discussions.* 10(1).

Dewi, N. P. J. L., Moybeka, A. M. S., Mushthoza, D. A., & Syariatin. (2023). Artificial intelligence and English classroom: The implications of AI toward EFL students' motivation. *Research Gate*. https://core.ac.uk/download/588483975.pdf

DIKSHA. (2025, May 3). *DIKSHA portal overview*. https://diksha.gov.in/

Dimitriadou, E., & Lanitis, A. (2023). A critical evaluation, challenges, and future perspectives of using artificial intelligence and emerging technologies in smart classrooms. *Smart Learning Environments, 10*(1), 12. DOI: 10.1186/s40561-023-00231-3 PMID: 40478141

Ding, N. (2025). Ethical considerations in the application of artificial intelligence in education. *International Journal of Education and Humanities, 19*(1), 178–182. DOI: 10.54097/78e6gr15

Dixson, M. D. (2015). Measuring Student Engagement in the Online Course: The Online Student Engagement Scale (OSE). *Online Learning : the Official Journal of the Online Learning Consortium, 19*(4). Advance online publication. DOI: 10.24059/olj.v19i4.561

Dong, L., Tang, X., & Wang, X. (2025). Examining the Effect of Artificial Intelligence in Relation to Students' Academic Achievement in the Classroom: A Meta-Analysis. *Computers and Education: Artificial Intelligence, 100400*, 100400. Advance online publication. DOI: 10.1016/j.caeai.2025.100400

Dritsas, E., & Trigka, M. (2025). Methodological and technological advancements in e-learning. *Information (Basel), 16*(1), 48.

Du Plooy, E., Casteleijn, D., & Franzsen, D. (2024). Personalized adaptive learning in higher education: A scoping review of key characteristics and impact on academic performance and engagement. *Heliyon, 10*(21), e39630. Advance online publication. DOI: 10.1016/j.heliyon.2024.e39630 PMID: 39524879

Duchi, J. C., Jordan, M. I., & Wainwright, M. J. (2013, October). Local privacy and statistical minimax rates. In *2013 IEEE 54th annual symposium on foundations of computer science* (pp. 429-438). IEEE.

Dumbuya, E. (2023). Personalized Learning through Artificial Intelligence: Revolutionizing Education. *Available at SSRN* 5023248.

Dunn, S. (2023). *The era of quantum AI: A new dawn for data science*. IBM Community. https://community.ibm.com/community/user/blogs/scott-dunn/2023/04/27/the-era-of-quantum-ai-a-new-dawn-for-data-science

Duolingo. (2023). *Duolingo Max uses OpenAI's GPT-4 for new learning features*. Duolingo Blog. https://blog.duolingo.com/duolingo-max/

Dushyant Nimavat, K. K., & Bajaj, S. D. A. S. B. S. N. (2023). Ethical considerations in using artificial intelligence to improve Teaching and learning. *Tuijin Jishu, 44*(4), 1031–1038. DOI: 10.52783/tjjpt.v44.i4.966

Dutton, J., Dutton, M., & Perry, J. (2019). How do online students differ from lecture students? *Online Learning : the Official Journal of the Online Learning Consortium, 6*(1). Advance online publication. DOI: 10.24059/olj.v6i1.1869

Du, X., Yang, J., Hung, J. L., & Shelton, B. (2020). Educational data mining: A systematic review of research and emerging trends. *Information Discovery and Delivery, 48*(4), 225–236. DOI: 10.1108/IDD-09-2019-0070

Dwahdh, L., & Alshraifin, N. (2025). The impact of computerized adaptive test termination rules on accuracy across different ability estimation methods. *Eurasia Journal of Mathematics, Science and Technology Education, 21*(1), em2571. DOI: 10.29333/ejmste/15897

Dwivedi, Y. K. (2025). Generative Artificial Intelligence (GenAI) in entrepreneurial education and practice: Emerging insights, the GAIN Framework, and research agenda. *The International Entrepreneurship and Management Journal, 21*(1), 1–21. DOI: 10.1007/s11365-025-01089-2

Dwivedi, Y. K., Hughes, L., Clark, E., Rana, N. P., Kumar, V., & Das, A. P. (2022). Metaverse: A new realm of the internet. *International Journal of Information Management, 66*, 102548.

Dwivedi, Y. K., Hughes, L., Wang, Y., Alalwan, A. A., Ahn, S. J., Balakrishnan, J., Barta, S., Belk, R., Berger, B., Bojovic, S., Chau, K. W., Chen, L., Davison, R. M., Diba, H., Harrigan, P., Heikkilä, M., Hoehle, H., Hughes, D. L., Ismagilova, E., & Williams, M. D. (2022). Metaverse marketing: How the metaverse will shape the future of consumer research and practice. *Psychology and Marketing*, *40*(3), 750–776. DOI: 10.1002/mar.21767

Dwork, C., & Roth, A. (2014). The Algorithmic Foundations of Differential Privacy. *Foundations and Trends® in Theoretical Computer Science*, 9(3–4), 211–407. https://doi.org/DOI: 10.1561/0400000042

Eaton, S. E., & Carmichael, J. J. (2023). Fake degrees and credential fraud, contract cheating, and paper mills: Overview and historical perspectives. In *Fake degrees and fraudulent credentials in higher education* (pp. 1–22).

Ebem, D. U., Ikegwu, A. C., Ezugwu, C. J., Ikpo, C. V., & Ogbunude, F. O. (2024). Machine Learning-Based Real-Time Feedback Assessment System for Student Performance *Prediction in Tertiary Institution*s.

Eberlein, T., Kampmeier, J., Minderhout, V., Moog, R. S., Platt, T., Varma-Nelson, P., & White, H. B. (2008). Pedagogies of engagement in science: A comparison of PBL, POGIL, and PLTL. *Biochemistry and Molecular Biology Education*, *36*(4), 262–273. DOI: 10.1002/bmb.20204 PMID: 19381266

Edmodo. (2024, September 30). *Edmodo features*. https://www.edmodo.com/

Edumate. (2025, May 3). *Edumate: School management system*. https://www.edumate.com.au

Elad, M., Kawar, B., & Vaksman, G. (2023). Image Denoising: The Deep Learning Revolution and Beyond — A Survey Paper — (Version 1). arXiv. DOI: 10.48550/ARXIV.2301.03362

Ellikkal, A., & Rajamohan, S. (2024). *AI-enabled personalized learning: empowering management students for improving engagement and academic performance*. Vilakshan-XIMB Journal of Management.

Elsayed, A. M., Kholikov, A., Abdullayeva, I., Al-Farouni, M., & Wodajo, M. R. (2024). Teacher support in AI-assisted exams: An experimental study to inspect the effects on demotivation, anxiety management in exams, L2 learning experience, and academic success. *Language Testing in Asia*, *14*(1), 53. DOI: 10.1186/s40468-024-00328-7

Eltahir, M. E., & Babiker, F. M. E. (2024). The influence of artificial intelligence tools on student performance in e-learning environments: Case study. *Electronic Journal of e-Learning*, *22*(9), 91–110. DOI: 10.34190/ejel.22.9.3639

Engel, D., & Eibl, G. (2015). Wavelet-based multiresolution smart meter privacy. *IEEE Transactions on Smart Grid*, *8*(4), 1710–1721. DOI: 10.1109/TSG.2015.2504395

Erkan, U., & Kilicman, A. (2016). Two new methods for removing salt-and-pepper noise from digital images. In ScienceAsia (Vol. 42, Issue 1, p. 28). Science Society of Thailand. DOI: 10.2306/scienceasia1513-1874.2016.42.028

Erkan, U., Thanh, D. N. H., Enginoglu, S., & Memis, S. (2020). Improved Adaptive Weighted Mean Filter for Salt-and-Pepper Noise Removal. In 2020 International Conference on Electrical, Communication, and Computer Engineering (ICECCE). 2020 International Conference on Electrical, Communication, and Computer Engineering (ICECCE). IEEE. DOI: 10.1109/ICECCE49384.2020.9179351

Erlingsson, Ú., Pihur, V., & Korolova, A. (2014). RAPPOR: Randomized Aggregatable Privacy-Preserving Ordinal Response. *Proceedings of the 2014 ACM SIGSAC Conference on Computer and Communications Security*, 1054–1067. https://doi.org/ DOI: 10.1145/2660267.2660348

Ersozlu, Z., Taheri, S., & Koch, I. (2024). A review of machine learning methods used for educational data. *Education and Information Technologies*, *29*(16), 22125–22145. DOI: 10.1007/s10639-024-12704-0

Ertl, B., Fischer, F., & Mandl, H. (2006). Conceptual and socio-cognitive support for collaborative learning in videoconferencing environments. *Computers & Education*, *47*(3), 298–315. DOI: 10.1016/j.compedu.2004.11.001

Esakkirajan, S., Veerakumar, T., Subramanyam, A. N., & PremChand, C. H. (2011). Removal of High Density Salt and Pepper Noise Through Modified Decision Based Unsymmetric Trimmed Median Filter. In IEEE Signal Processing Letters (Vol. 18, Issue 5, pp. 287–290). Institute of Electrical and Electronics Engineers (IEEE). DOI: 10.1109/LSP.2011.2122333

Estonia. (2025, May 3). *Education*. https://e-estonia.com/solutions/education/

Eynon, R. (2023). The ethics of AI in education: Challenges and opportunities. *Journal of Educational Technology & Society*, *26*(1), 45–58.

Eynon, R., & Geniets, A. (2016). The digital skills paradox: How do digitally excluded youth develop skills to use the internet? *Learning, Media and Technology*, *41*(3), 463–479. DOI: 10.1080/17439884.2014.1002845

Fadli Mappisabbi, A. M., Amirullah, N., & Batti', S. (2024). Leveraging data and artificial intelligence for innovative educational management practices. *Ijmre-ITB, 2*(2), 182–192. DOI: 10.54066/ijmre-itb.v2i2.1788

Familoni, B. T., & Onyebuchi, N. C. (2024). Augmented and virtual reality in U.S. education: A review: Analyzing the impact, effectiveness, and future prospects of AR/VR tools in enhancing learning experiences. *International Journal of Applied Research in Social Sciences, 6*(4), 642–663. DOI: 10.51594/ijarss.v6i4.1043

Farooqi, M. T. K., Amanat, I., & Awan, S. M. (2024). Ethical considerations and challenges in the integration of artificial intelligence in education: A systematic review. *JEMS: A Journal of Emergency Medical Services, 3*(4), 35–50. DOI: 10.69565/jems.v3i4.314

Fauziddin, M., Adha, T. R., Arifiyanti, N., Indriyani, F., Rizki, L. M., Wulandary, V., & Reddy, V. S. V. (2025). The impact of AI on the future of education in Indonesia. *Educ. J. Ilm. Pendidik, 3*(1), 11–16. DOI: 10.70437/educative.v3i1.828

Feijo, S., & Ouellette, K. (2023). *What will the future of education look like in a world with generative AI?* MIT Open Learning. https://openlearning.mit.edu/news/what-will-future-education-look-world-generative-ai

Fekete, D. L., & Kiss, A. (2023). Toward building smart contract-based higher education systems using zero-knowledge Ethereum virtual machine. *Electronics (Basel), 12*(3), 664. DOI: 10.3390/electronics12030664

Fiock, H. (2020). Designing a Community of Inquiry in Online Courses. *International Review of Research in Open and Distance Learning, 21*(1), 134–152. DOI: 10.19173/irrodl.v20i5.3985

Fitas, R. (2025). Inclusive Education with AI: Supporting Special Needs and Tackling Language Barriers. *arXiv preprint arXiv:2504.14120*. DOI: 10.2139/ssrn.5366398

Fitria, T. N. (2021). Artificial Intelligence (AI) in Education: Using AI Tools for Teaching and Learning Process. *Proceedings of the National Seminar on Business, Economics, Social Sciences, and Technology, 1*(1), 1–10. https://prosiding.stie-aas.ac.id/index.php/prosenas/article/view/106

Fitzpatrick, K. K., Darcy, A., & Vierhile, M. (2017). Delivering Cognitive Behavior Therapy to Young Adults With Symptoms of Depression and Anxiety Using a Fully Automated Conversational Agent (Woebot): A Randomized Controlled Trial. *JMIR Mental Health, 4*(2), e19. DOI: 10.2196/mental.7785 PMID: 28588005

Flener-Lovitt, C., Bailey, K., & Han, R. (2020). Using Structured Teams to Develop Social Presence in Asynchronous Chemistry Courses. *Journal of Chemical Education, 97*(9), 2519–2525. DOI: 10.1021/acs.jchemed.0c00765

Floridi, L., Cowls, J., Beltrametti, M., Chatila, R., Chazerand, P., Dignum, V., Luetge, C., Madelin, R., Pagallo, U., Rossi, F., Schafer, B., Valcke, P., & Vayena, E. (2018). AI4People—An Ethical Framework for a Good AI Society: Opportunities, Risks, Principles, and Recommendations. *Minds and Machines, 28*(4), 689–707. DOI: 10.1007/s11023-018-9482-5 PMID: 30930541

Fodouop Kouam, A. W. (2024). The effectiveness of intelligent tutoring systems in supporting students with varying levels of programming experience. *Discover Education, 3*(1), 1–13. DOI: 10.1007/s44217-024-00385-3

Folorunso, A., & Olanipekun, K. (2024). A policy framework on AI usage in developing countries and its impact. *Global J. Eng. Technol. Adv., 21*(1), 154–166. DOI: 10.30574/gjeta.2024.21.1.0192

Fosnot, C. T. (Ed.). (2013). *Constructivism: Theory, perspectives, and practice* (2nd ed.). Teachers College Press.

Fredricks, J. A., Blumenfeld, P. C., & Paris, A. H. (2004). School Engagement: Potential of the Concept, State of the Evidence. *Review of Educational Research, 74*(1), 59–109. DOI: 10.3102/00346543074001059

Fromont, E., Prado, A., & Robardet, C. (2009). Constraint-based Subspace Clustering. In Proceedings of the 2009 SIAM International Conference on Data Mining. Proceedings of the 2009 SIAM International Conference on Data Mining. Society for Industrial and Applied Mathematics. DOI: 10.1137/1.9781611972795.3

Fu, Y., & Weng, Z. (2024). Navigating the ethical terrain of AI in education: A systematic review on framing responsible human-centered AI practices. *Computers and Education: Artificial Intelligence*, 100306.

Fulfer, K. D., Wachter, E., Muzyka, J. L., Demoranville, L. T., Fieberg, J. E., Haile, J. D., Scott, D., Song, Y., Workman, J. M., & Young, K. J. (2020). #StayCentred: Maintaining Personal Education at Centre College During COVID-19. *Journal of Chemical Education, 97*(9), 2783–2787. DOI: 10.1021/acs.jchemed.0c00726

Fundamental, X. R. (2025). *Immersive technology to accelerate human excellence*. https://www.fundamentalxr.com/

Fung, F. M., & Lam, Y. (2020). How COVID-19 Disrupted Our "Flipped" Freshman Organic Chemistry Course: Insights Gained from Singapore. *Journal of Chemical Education, 97*(9), 2573–2580. DOI: 10.1021/acs.jchemed.0c00590

Funk, E., Meyer, H. S., Gilbert, J. H. V., & Oandasan, I. F. (2018). Blockchain technology: A data framework to improve validity, trust, and accountability of information exchange in health professions education. *Academic Medicine*, *93*(12), 1791–1794. DOI: 10.1097/ACM.0000000000002326 PMID: 29901658

Furlong, M. J., & Christenson, S. L. (2008). Engaging students with school and academics: A relevant construct for all students. *Psychology in the Schools*, *45*(5), 365–368. DOI: 10.1002/pits.20302

Fütterer, T., Fischer, C., Alekseeva, A., Chen, X., Tate, T., Warschauer, M., & Gerjets, P. (2023). ChatGPT in education: Global reactions to AI innovations. *Scientific Reports*, *13*, 15310. DOI: 10.1038/s41598-023-42227-6

Garcia Brustenga, G., Fuertes Alpiste, M., & Molas Castells, N. (2018). Briefing paper: chatbots in education (1st ed.). eLearn Center. Universitat Oberta de Catalunya. DOI: 10.7238/elc.chatbots.2018

Garcia Peñalvo, F. J., Alier, M., Pereira, J., & Casany, M. J. (2024). Safe, transparent, and ethical artificial intelligence. Int. J. Educ. Res. Innov., 22, 1–21.

Garcia, M., & Patel, R. (2021). Adaptive learning outcomes in middle school mathematics. *Journal of Educational Technology*, *47*(3), 145–161.

Gardner, H. (1993). Multiple Intelligences. New York: Basic Books, Hons of Learning Harper Collins Publ. Inc.

Garrison, D. R., Anderson, T., & Archer, W. (1999). Critical Inquiry in a Text-Based Environment: Computer Conferencing in Higher Education. *The Internet and Higher Education*, *2*(2–3), 87–105. DOI: 10.1016/S1096-7516(00)00016-6

Garrison, D. R., & Kanuka, H. (2004). Blended learning: Uncovering its transformative potential in higher education. *The Internet and Higher Education*, *7*(2), 95–105. DOI: 10.1016/j.iheduc.2004.02.001

Gartner. (2024). Understand and exploit generative AI with Gartner's new Impact Radar. https://www.gartner.com/en/articles/understand-and-exploit-gen-ai-with-gartner-s-new-impact-radar

Gartner. (n.d.). Career pathing should be like satellite navigation. https://www.gartner.com/en/human-resources/trends/career-pathing-should-be-like-satellite-navigation

Gašević, D., Dawson, S., Rogers, T., & Gasevic, D. (2016). Learning analytics should not promote one size fits all: The effects of instructional conditions in predicting academic success. *The Internet and Higher Education*, *28*, 68–84. DOI: 10.1016/j.iheduc.2015.10.002

Gavira Durón, N., & Jiménez-Preciado, A. L. (2025). Exploring the role of AI in higher education: A natural language processing analysis of emerging trends and discourses. *The TQM Journal.* Advance online publication. DOI: 10.1108/TQM-10-2024-0376

Geiselhofer, M., Gorman, A., & Hsu, H.-P. (2024). Preliminary study on pre-service teachers' applications and perceptions of generative artificial intelligence for lesson planning. https://core.ac.uk/download/621114994.pdf

Gemmel, P. M., Goetz, M. K., James, N. M., Jesse, K. A., & Ratliff, B. J. (2020). Collaborative Learning in Chemistry: Impact of COVID-19. *Journal of Chemical Education*, *97*(9), 2899–2904. DOI: 10.1021/acs.jchemed.0c00713

Gerardou, F. S., Michel-Villarreal, R., & Salinas-Navarro, D. E. Thierry-Aguilera, & et al. (2023). Challenges and opportunities of generative AI for higher education as explained by ChatGPT. https://core.ac.uk/download/586151541.pdf

Gherhe , V., imon, S., & Para, I. (2021). Analysing Students' Reasons for Keeping Their Webcams on or off during Online Classes. *Sustainability (Basel)*, *13*(6), 3203. DOI: 10.3390/su13063203

Giesbers, B., Rienties, B., Tempelaar, D., & Gijselaers, W. (2013). Investigating the relations between motivation, tool use, participation, and performance in an e-learning course using web-videoconferencing. *Computers in Human Behavior*, *29*(1), 285–292. DOI: 10.1016/j.chb.2012.09.005

Gillies, D. (2008). Student perspectives on videoconferencing in teacher education at a distance. *Distance Education*, *29*(1), 107–118. DOI: 10.1080/01587910802004878

Giri, A. (2025). Revolutionizing Student Evaluation: The Power of AI Powered Assessment. In *Improving Student Assessment With Emerging AI Tools* (pp. 333-362). IGI Global Scientific Publishing.

Gligorea, I., Cioca, M., Oancea, R., Gorski, A. T , Gorski, H., & Tudorache, P. (2023). Adaptive learning using artificial intelligence in e-learning: A literature review. *Education Sciences*, *13*(12), 1216. DOI: 10.3390/educsci13121216

Gong, J., Han, T., Guo, S., Li, J., Zha, S., Zhang, L., Tian, F., Wang, Q., & Rui, Y. (2021). HoloBoard: A large-format immersive teaching board based on pseudo HoloGraphics. In *Proceedings of the 34th Annual ACM Symposium on User Interface Software and Technology (UIST 2021)* (pp. 441–456). ACM. https://doi.org/DOI: 10.1145/3472749.3474761

González-Hidalgo, M., Massanet, S., Mir, A., & Ruiz-Aguilera, D. (2021). Impulsive Noise Removal with an Adaptive Weighted Arithmetic Mean Operator for Any Noise Density. In Applied Sciences (Vol. 11, Issue 2, p. 560). MDPI AG. DOI: 10.3390/app11020560

Goodfellow, I., Bengio, Y., & Courville, A. (2016). *Deep learning* (1st ed.). MIT Press.

Google AI. (2022). *2022 AI Principles Progress

Google Classroom. (2024, September 30). *Google Classroom documentation*. https://classroom.google.com/

Google. (n.d.). Google certified courses online | Grow with Google India. https://grow.google/intl/en_in/certificates

Goryczka, S., Xiong, L., & Li, J. (2013). Differentially Private Federated Data Publishing. *Proceedings of the 6th ACM Conference on Security and Privacy in Wireless and Mobile Networks*, 3–14. https://doi.org/DOI: 10.1145/2462096.2462098

Governatori, G., Idelberger, F., Milosevic, Z., Riveret, R., Sartor, G., & Xu, X. (2018). On legal contracts, imperative and declarative smart contracts, and blockchain systems. *Artificial Intelligence and Law*, *26*(4), 377–409. DOI: 10.1007/s10506-018-9223-3

Graesser, A. C., Chipman, P., Haynes, B. C., & Olney, A. (2005). AutoTutor: An intelligent tutoring system with mixed-initiative dialogue. *IEEE Transactions on Education*, *48*(4), 612–618. DOI: 10.1109/TE.2005.856149

Grammarly. (2024, May 7). *What is AI? Artificial intelligence explained*. Grammarly Blog. https://www.grammarly.com/blog/ai/what-is-ai/

Gray, K., Slavotinek, J., Dimaguila, G. L., & Choo, D. (2022). Artificial intelligence education for the health workforce: Expert survey of approaches and needs. *JMIR Medical Education*, *8*(2), e35223. DOI: 10.2196/35223 PMID: 35249885

Grech, A., Sood, I., & Ariño, L. (2021). Blockchain, self-sovereign identity and digital credentials: Promise versus praxis in education. *Frontiers in Blockchain*, *4*, 616779. DOI: 10.3389/fbloc.2021.616779

Guettala, M., Bourekkache, S., Kazar, O., & Harous, S. (2024). Generative Artificial Intelligence in Education: Advancing Adaptive and Personalized Learning. *Acta Informatica Pragensia*, *13*(3), 460–489. DOI: 10.18267/j.aip.235

Guizzardi, R., Amaral, G., Guizzardi, G., & Mylopoulos, J. (2020). Ethical Requirements for AI Systems. In Goutte, C., & Zhu, X. (Eds.), *Advances in Artificial Intelligence* (pp. 251–256). Springer International Publishing. DOI: 10.1007/978-3-030-47358-7_24

Gupta, S., & Jaiswal, R. (2025). A deep learning-based hybrid PLS-SEM-ANN approach for predicting factors improving AI-driven decision-making proficiency for future leaders. *Journal of International Education in Business*. DOI: 10.1108/JIEB-05-2024-0058

Gupta, S., Jaiswal, R., & Gupta, S. K. (2024). Digital nomads: a systematic literature review and future research agenda. *Tourism Review*. DOI: 10.1108/TR-12-2023-0869

Gupta, S., & Jaiswal, R. (2024a). How can we improve AI competencies for tomorrow's leaders: Insights from multi-stakeholders' interaction. *International Journal of Management Education*, *22*(3), 101070. DOI: 10.1016/j.ijme.2024.101070

Gupta, S., & Jaiswal, R. (2024b). How can we improve Hospitality Excellence for Sustainable Development using machine learning. *Journal of Hospitality & Tourism Education*, 1–13. DOI: 10.1080/10963758.2024.2420267

Habibzadeh, F. (2023). GPTZero performance in identifying artificial intelligence-generated medical texts: A preliminary study. *Journal of Korean Medical Science*, *38*(38). Advance online publication. DOI: 10.3346/jkms.2023.38.e319

Halkiopoulos, C., & Gkintoni, E. (2024). Leveraging AI in E-Learning: Personalized Learning and Adaptive Assessment through Cognitive Neuropsychology—A Systematic Analysis. *Electronics (Basel)*, *13*(18), 3762. DOI: 10.3390/electronics13183762

Hameed, B., Yasin, M., & Khan, R. (2019). A review of blockchain based educational projects. *International Journal of Advanced Computer Science and Applications*, *10*(10). Advance online publication. DOI: 10.14569/IJACSA.2019.0101065

Han, K. (2020). Personalized News Recommendation and Simulation Based on Improved Collaborative Filtering Algorithm. In Wang, W. (Ed.), *Complexity* (Vol. 2020, pp. 1–12). Hindawi Limited., DOI: 10.1155/2020/8834908

Hanson, U. Y. O. K., Okonkwo, C. A., & Orakwe, C. U. (2024). Implementing AI-enhanced learning analytics to improve educational outcomes using psychological insights. *Journal of Educational Technology Innovations*.

Hardaker, G., & Glenn, L. E. (2025). Artificial intelligence for personalized learning: A systematic literature review. *International Journal of Information and Learning Technology*, *42*(1), 1–14. DOI: 10.1108/IJILT-07-2024-0160

Hare, R., & Tang, Y. (2024, October). Ontology-driven Reinforcement Learning for Personalized Student Support. In *2024 IEEE International Conference on Systems, Man, and Cybernetics (SMC)* (pp. 2555-2560). IEEE. DOI: 10.1109/SMC54092.2024.10832036

Harvard Business Publishing. (n.d.). *Applications of artificial intelligence and machine learning*. Harvard Business Publishing Education. https://hbsp.harvard.edu/catalog/collections/applications-of-ai-and-machine-learning

Harvard Business School Digital Initiative. (2021.). *Knewton personalizes learning with the power of AI*. Harvard Business School. https://d3.harvard.edu/platform-digit/submission/knewton-personalizes-learning-with-the-power-of-ai/

Hasan, R., Sion, R., & Winslett, M. (2009). Preventing history forgery with secure provenance. [TOS]. *ACM Transactions on Storage*, *5*(4), 1–43. DOI: 10.1145/1629080.1629082

Hashim, A., Akeel, W., & Khalaf, A. (2020). Student performance prediction model based on supervised machine learning algorithms. *IOP Conference Series. Materials Science and Engineering*, *928*(3), 032019. DOI: 10.1088/1757-899X/928/3/032019

Hassija, V., Chamola, V., Mahapatra, A., Singal, A., Goel, D., Huang, K., Scardapane, S., Spinelli, I., Mahmud, M., & Hussain, A. (2023). Interpreting black-box models: A review on explainable artificial intelligence. *Cognitive Computation*, *16*(1), 45–74. DOI: 10.1007/s12559-023-10179-8

Hastie, T., Tibshirani, R., & Friedman, J. (2009). *Elements of statistical learning: Data mining, inference, and prediction* (2nd ed., Vol. 2). Springer. DOI: 10.1007/978-0-387-84858-7

Hefnawi, A. (2025). Shifting the narrative: From technocentric to purpose-driven artificial intelligence in education. *Management in Education*. Advance online publication. DOI: 10.1177/08920206251322644

Henrie, C. R., Halverson, L. R., & Graham, C. R. (2015). Measuring student engagement in technology-mediated learning: A review. *Computers & Education*, *90*, 36–53. DOI: 10.1016/j.compedu.2015.09.005

Herath, D., Dinuwan, C., Ihalagedara, C., & Ambegoda, T. (2024). Enhancing Educational Outcomes Through AI Powered Learning Strategy Recommendation System. *International Journal of Advanced Computer Science and Applications*, *15*(10). Advance online publication. DOI: 10.14569/IJACSA.2024.0151075

Hernandez, M., Canals, J., & Paredes, S. (2023). The impact of real-time feedback on student engagement: A systematic review. *Journal of Educational Technology & Society*, *26*(2), 45–58. https://www.jstor.org/stable/26473042

He, X., Machanavajjhala, A., Ding, B., & Chen, Y. (2014). Blowfish Privacy: Tuning Privacy-Utility Trade-offs Using Policies. *Proceedings of the 2014 ACM SIGMOD International Conference on Management of Data*, 1447–1458. https://doi.org/DOI: 10.1145/2588555.2588581

He, Z., Zhang, Q., & Zhang, M. (2022). Real-time emotion recognition for classroom engagement monitoring using facial expression and physiological data. *Computers in Human Behavior, 120*, 106740. DOI: 10.1016/j.chb.2021.106740

Hilbert, S., Coors, S., Kraus, E. B., Bischl, B., Frei, M., Lindl, A., Wild, J., Krauss, S., Goretzko, D., & Stachl, C. (2021). *Machine Learning for the Educational Sciences*. . io/3hnr6.DOI: 10.31234/osf.io/3hnr6_v1

Hirani, R., Noruzi, K., Khuram, H., Hussaini, A. S., Aifuwa, E., Ely, K., Lewis, J. M., Zakrzewski, J., Donner, B., Boucher, J., & Kassab, K. (2024). Artificial intelligence and healthcare: A journey through history, present innovations, and future possibilities. *Life (Chicago, Ill.)*, *14*(5), 557. DOI: 10.3390/life14050557

HireVue. (n.d.). Knowledge Center. https://www.hirevue.com/knowledge-center

Holmes, W., Bialik, M., & Fadel, C. (2019). *Artificial Intelligence in Education: Promises and Implications for Teaching and Learning*. Center for Curriculum Redesign.

Holmes, W., Bialik, M., & Fadel, C. (2021). *Artificial intelligence in education: Promises and implications for teaching and learning*. Center for Curriculum Redesign.

Holmes, W., Iniesto, F., Anastopoulou, S., & Boticario, J. (2023). Stakeholder Perspectives on the Ethics of AI in Distance-Based Higher Education. *International Review of Research in Open and Distance Learning*, *24*, 96–117. DOI: 10.19173/irrodl.v24i2.6089

Holmes, W., Porayska-Pomsta, K., Holstein, K., Sutherland, E., Baker, T., Shum, S. B., Santos, O. C., Rodrigo, M. T., Cukurova, M., Bittencourt, I. I., & Koedinger, K. R. (2022). Ethics of AI in education: Towards a community-wide framework. *International Journal of Artificial Intelligence in Education*, *32*(3), 504–526. DOI: 10.1007/s40593-021-00239-1

Hsu, C., & Yeh, C. (2020). Mining the student dropout in higher education. *ASTM International Journal of Testing and Evaluation*, *48*(6), 4563–4575. DOI: 10.1520/JTE20180021

Huang, L., Zhang, Y., & Liu, X. (2023). Detecting classroom engagement using computer vision: A review. *Education and Information Technologies, 28*(5), 5791–5806. DOI: 10.1007/s10639-022-10761-9

Hu, S. (2024). The effect of artificial intelligence-assisted personalized learning on student learning outcomes: A meta-analysis based on 31 empirical research papers. *Science Insights Education Frontiers, 24*(1), 3873–3894. DOI: 10.15354/sief.24.re395

Husain, A. (2024). Potentials of ChatGPT in computer programming: Insights from programming instructors. *Journal of Information Technology Education: Research, 23*, 002. https://doi.org/DOI: 10.28945/5240

Hussain, S., & Khan, M. Q. (2023). Student-performulator: Predicting students' academic performance at secondary and intermediate levels using machine learning. *Annals of Data Science, 10*(3), 637–655. DOI: 10.1007/s40745-021-00341-0 PMID: 38624826

Huynh-The, T., Pham, Q.-V., Pham, X.-Q., Nguyen, T. T., Han, Z., & Kim, D.-S. (2023). Artificial intelligence for the metaverse: A survey. *Engineering Applications of Artificial Intelligence, 117*, 105581. DOI: 10.1016/j.engappai.2022.105581

Huynh, V. W., & Gillen-O'Neel, C. (2016). Discrimination and sleep: The protective role of school belonging. *Youth & Society, 48*(5), 649–672. DOI: 10.1177/0044118X13506720

Hwang, G. J., Xie, H., Wah, B. W., & Gašević, D. (2020). Vision, challenges, roles and research issues of Artificial Intelligence in Education. *Computers and Education: Artificial Intelligence, 1*, 100001. Advance online publication. DOI: 10.1016/j.caeai.2020.100001

IBM Research. (2023, April). *Human-Centered Responsible Artificial Intelligence: Current & Future Trends for CHI 2023. CHI 2023 Proceedings*

Ifenthaler, D., Majumdar, R., Gorissen, P., Judge, M., Mishra, S., Raffaghelli, J., & Shimada, A. (2024). Artificial intelligence in education: Implications for policymakers, researchers, and practitioners. *Technology, Knowledge and Learning,* 1-18. DOI: 10.1007/s10758-024-09747-0

Ifenthaler, D., & Yau, J. Y. K. (2020). Utilising learning analytics to support study success in higher education: A systematic review. *Educational Technology Research and Development, 68*(4), 1961–1990. DOI: 10.1007/s11423-020-09788-z

Ihichr, A., Oustous, O., El Idrissi, Y. E. B., & Lahcen, A. A. (2024). A Systematic Review on Assessment in Adaptive Learning: Theories, Algorithms and Techniques. *International Journal of Advanced Computer Science and Applications, 15*(7). Advance online publication. DOI: 10.14569/IJACSA.2024.0150785

Ikegwu, A. C., Nweke, H. F., Anikwe, C. V., Alo, U. R., & Okonkwo, O. R. (2022). Big data analytics for data-driven industry: A review of data sources, tools, challenges, solutions, and research directions. *Cluster Computing, 25*(5), 3343–3387. DOI: 10.1007/s10586-022-03568-5

Imjai, N., Promma, W., Visedsun, N., Usman, B., & Aujirapongpan, S. (2025). Fraud detection skills of Thai Gen Z accountants: The roles of digital competency, data science literacy and diagnostic skills. *International Journal of Information Management Data Insights, 5*(1), 100308. DOI: 10.1016/j.jjimei.2024.100308

Inkster, B., Sarda, S., & Subramanian, V. (2018). An empathy-driven, conversational artificial intelligence agent (Wysa) for digital mental well-being: Real-world data evaluation mixed-methods study. *JMIR mHealth and uHealth, 6*(11), e12106. Advance online publication. DOI: 10.2196/12106 PMID: 30470676

Islam, R., Rahman, M. M., Rehman, S. U., Gumaei, A., & Hossain, M. S. (2025). Decentralized trust framework for smart cities: A blockchain-enabled cybersecurity and data integrity model. *Scientific Reports, 15*(1), 23454. DOI: 10.1038/s41598-025-06405-y PMID: 40603417

Issah, I., Appiah, O., Appiahene, P., & Inusah, F. (2023). A systematic review of the literature on machine learning application of determining the attributes influencing academic performance. *Decision Analytics Journal, 7*, 100204. DOI: 10.1016/j.dajour.2023.100204

Ivanov, S., Soliman, M., Tuomi, A., Alkathiri, N. A., & Al-Alawi, A. N. (2024). Drivers of generative AI adoption in higher education through the lens of the Theory of Planned Behavior. *Technology in Society, 77*, 102521. DOI: 10.1016/j.techsoc.2024.102521

Jabbour, J., Kleinbard, K., Miller, O., Haussman, R. C., & Reddi, V. (2025). SocratiQ: A generative AI-powered learning companion for personalized education and broader accessibility. *arXiv preprint, abs/2502.00341.*

Jaiswal, R. (2024). An Investigation into How Artificial Intelligence (AI) has Enhanced Quality Engineering. In *Contemporary Digital Transformation and Organizational Effectiveness in Business 4.0* (pp. 121-129). Apple Academic Press.

Jaiswal, R. (2025). A Retrospection of Business Intelligence in the Era of Big Data Analytics and Artificial Intelligence for Fintech. *Advanced Digital Technologies in Financial and Business Management: Unleashing the Power of Artificial Intelligence, Machine Learning, Blockchain, and the Internet of Things*, 15.

Jaiswal, R., Gupta, S., & Tiwari, A. K. (2022a). Delineation of blockchain technology in finance: A scientometric view. *Annals of financial economics, 17*(4), 2250025. DOI: 10.1142/S2010495222500257

Jaiswal, R., Gupta, S., & Tiwari, A. K. (2025). Environmental, social and governance-type investing: a multi-stakeholder machine learning analysis. *Management Decision*. DOI: 10.1108/MD-04-2024-0930

Jaiswal, R., Gupta, S.K., & Gupta, S. (2024b). Current trends and future research agenda on climate-resilient infrastructure in developing sustainable tourist destinations. *Achieving sustainable transformation in tourism and hospitality sectors*, 16-35. DOI: 10.4018/979-8-3693-3390-7.ch002

Jaiswal, R. (2023). Being Agile: Transcendent Solutions to Enduring Problems in the Age of COVID-19. *MDIM Journal of Management Review and Practice., 1*(2), 96–106. DOI: 10.1177/mjmrp.231200388

Jaiswal, R., & Gupta, S. (2023). Global research trends on blockchain technology in finance: Past, present and future. *International Journal of Electronic Finance, 14*(3). Advance online publication. DOI: 10.1504/IJEF.2025.10059748

Jaiswal, R., & Gupta, S. (2024). Money talks, happiness walks: Dissecting the secrets of global bliss with machine learning. *Journal of Chinese Economic and Business Studies, 22*(1), 111–158. DOI: 10.1080/14765284.2023.2245277

Jaiswal, R., Gupta, S., & Gupta, S. K. (2025). The impending disruption of digital nomadism: Opportunities, challenges, and research agenda. *World Leisure Journal, 67*(1), 74–104. DOI: 10.1080/16078055.2024.2346091

Jaiswal, R., Gupta, S., & Tiwari, A. K. (2023). Dissecting the compensation conundrum: A machine learning-based prognostication of key determinants in a complex labor market. *Management Decision, 61*(8), 2322–2353. DOI: 10.1108/MD-07-2022-0976

Jaiswal, R., Gupta, S., & Tiwari, A. K. (2024a). Big data and machine learning-based decision support system to reshape the vaticination of insurance claims. *Technological Forecasting and Social Change, 209*, 123829. DOI: 10.1016/j.techfore.2024.123829

Jaiswal, R., Gupta, S., & Tiwari, A. K. (2024d). Decoding mood of the Twitterverse on ESG investing: Opinion mining and key themes using machine learning. *Management Research Review*, *47*(8), 1221–1252. DOI: 10.1108/MRR-07-2023-0526

Jaiswal, R., Khan, M. I. A., & Kumar, M. (2024c). Charting the course: Exploring the changing terrain of online shopping and future directions for research. *International Journal of Electronic Business*, *19*(1), 56–79. DOI: 10.1504/IJEB.2024.135653

Jaiswal, R., & Kumar, D. (2023). Quality Education for Sustainable Development Goals: Past, Present and Future. *National Journal of Education*, *18*(2), 127–141.

Jaiswal, R., Kumar, D., & Sharma, V. D. (2022b). Bibliometric retrospection of the literature on India's export promotion program (1964–2022). *BHU Management Review*, *9*(2), 36–53.

Jamal, A., Jaiswal, R., Sayyad, S., Pandit, P., & Sayyad, F. (2022). A Comprehensive Survey of Various Machine Learning Techniques to Counter Security Issues Related to Mobile Malwares. *International Journal of Next-Generation Computing*, *13*(3). Advance online publication. DOI: 10.47164/ijngc.v13i3.807

Jamieson, M. V. (2020). Keeping a Learning Community and Academic Integrity Intact after a Mid-Term Shift to Online Learning in Chemical Engineering Design During the COVID-19 Pandemic. *Journal of Chemical Education*, *97*(9), 2768–2772. DOI: 10.1021/acs.jchemed.0c00785

Japkowicz, N., & Shah, M. (2011). *Evaluating learning algorithms: A classification perspective*. Evaluating Learning Algorithms. A Classification Perspective. DOI: 10.1017/CBO9780511921803

Jasrai, L. (2025). Extending UTAUT model to examine the usages of ChatGPT among Indian students in higher education: A structural equation modelling approach. *The TQM Journal*. Advance online publication. DOI: 10.1108/TQM-12-2024-0498

Jayasundara, J. M. P. V. K., Gilbert, T., Kersten, S., & Meng, L. (2022). How UK HE STEM Students Were Motivated to Switch Their Cameras on: A Study of the Development of Compassionate Communications in Task-focused Online Group Meetings. *Education Sciences*, *12*(5), 317. DOI: 10.3390/educsci12050317

Jiang, H., Li, M., Witte, P., Geertman, S., & Pan, H. (2025). Urban Chatter: Exploring the potential of ChatGPT-like and generative AI in enhancing planning support. *Cities (London, England)*, *158*, 105701. DOI: 10.1016/j.cities.2025.105701

Jiao, S., Shi, J., Wang, Y., & Wang, R. (2023). A novel image noise reduction method for composite multistable stochastic resonance systems. In Heliyon (Vol. 9, Issue 3, p. e14431). Elsevier BV. DOI: 10.1016/j.heliyon.2023.e14431

Jin, Q., Grama, I., Kervrann, C., & Liu, Q. (2017). Nonlocal Means and Optimal Weights for Noise Removal. In SIAM Journal on Imaging Sciences (Vol. 10, Issue 4, pp. 1878–1920). Society for Industrial & Applied Mathematics (SIAM). DOI: 10.1137/16M1080781

Jin, G., & Bierma, T. J. (2011). Guided-Inquiry Learning in Environmental Health. *Journal of Environmental Health, 73*(6), 80–85. PMID: 21306099

Johnston, H., Wells, R., Shanks, E., Boey, T., & Parsons, B. (2024). Student perspectives on the use of generative artificial intelligence technologies in higher education. *International Journal for Educational Integrity, 20*(2), 1–21. DOI: 10.1007/s40979-024-00149-4

Kaelbling, L. P., Littman, M. L., & Moore, A. W. (1996). Reinforcement learning: A survey. *Journal of Artificial Intelligence Research, 4*, 237–285. DOI: 10.1613/jair.301

Kakina, A. (2025). Artificial Intelligence for functional literacy development. Eurasian Science Review, 2(Special Issue).

Kaldaras, L., Wang, K. D., Nardo, J. E., Price, A., Perkins, K., Wieman, C., & Salehi, S. (2024). Employing technology-enhanced feedback and scaffolding to support the development of deep science understanding using computer simulations. *International Journal of STEM Education, 11*(1), 30. DOI: 10.1186/s40594-024-00490-7

Kaliisa, R., & Dolonen, J. A. (2022). CADA: a teacher-facing learning analytics dashboard to foster teachers' awareness of students' participation and discourse patterns in online discussions. *Technology, Knowledge and Learning*, 1–22. Advance online publication. DOI: 10.1007/s10758-022-09598-7

Kalyuga, S. (2011). Cognitive load theory: How many types of load does it really need? *Educational Psychology Review, 23*(1), 1–19. DOI: 10.1007/s10648-010-9150-7

Kamali, J., Alpat, M. F., & Bozkurt, A. (2024). AI ethics as a complex and multifaceted challenge: Decoding educators' AI ethics alignment through the lens of activity theory. *International Journal of Educational Technology in Higher Education, 21*(1), 1–20. DOI: 10.1186/s41239-024-00496-9

Kamalov, F., Santandreu Calonge, D., & Gurrib, I. (2023). New era of artificial intelligence in education: Towards a sustainable multifaceted revolution. *Sustainability, 15*(16), 12451. DOI: 10.3390/su151612451

Kanchon, M. K. H., Sadman, M., Nabila, K. F., Tarannum, R., & Khan, R. (2024). Enhancing Personalized learning: AI-driven identification of learning styles and content modification strategies. *International Journal of Cognitive Computing in Engineering, 5*, 269–278. DOI: 10.1016/j.ijcce.2024.06.002

Karran, A. J., Charland, P., Martineau, J. T., de Arana, A., Lesage, A. M., Senecal, S., & Leger, P.

Karweit, N. (1989). Time and Learning: A Review. In *School and Classroom Organization* (pp. 69–95). L. Erlbaum Associates.

Kayyali, M. (2025). The Impact of Personalized Learning on Student Engagement and Achievement in STEAM. In *Integrating Personalized Learning Methods Into STEAM Education* (pp. 51–78). IGI Global Scientific Publishing. DOI: 10.4018/979-8-3693-7718-5.ch003

Keiding, T. B., & Qvortrup, A. (2014). Feedback as real-time constructions. *E-Learning and Digital Media*, *11*(2), 191–203. DOI: 10.2304/elea.2014.11.2.191

Kerimbayev, N., Umirzakova, Z., Shadiev, R., & Jotsov, V. (2023). A student-centered approach using modern technologies in distance learning: A systematic review of the literature. *Smart Learning Environments*, *10*(1), 61. DOI: 10.1186/s40561-023-00280-8

Kerr, S., O'Rourke, S., & Lynch, A. (2020). Real-time AI-driven feedback in personalized learning: Applications and challenges. *International Journal of Artificial Intelligence in Education*, *30*(4), 432–450. DOI: 10.1007/s40593-020-00208-4

Kestin, G., Miller, K., & Klales, A. (2025). AI tutoring outperforms in-class active learning: An RCT introducing a novel research-based design in an authentic educational setting. *Scientific Reports*, *15*, 17458. DOI: 10.1038/s41598-025-97652-6

Khalaf, A., Dahr, J. M., Najm, I. A., Kamel, M. B. M., Hashim, A. S., Akeel, W. A., & Humadi, M. A. (2021). Supervised learning algorithms in educational data mining: A systematic review. *Southeast Europe Journal of Soft Computing*, *10*, 55–70. DOI: 10.21533/scjournal.v10i1.199

Khalil, M., Shakya, R., & Liu, Q. (2025, April). Towards Privacy-Preserving Data-Driven Education: The Potential of Federated Learning. In *2025 International Conference on New Trends in Computing Sciences (ICTCS)* (pp. 113–118). IEEE. DOI: 10.1109/ICTCS65341.2025.10989403

Khan, A. (2024). Exploring the Role of Machine Learning in Enhancing Student Engagement and Performance. *Journal of AI Integration in Education*, *1*(2), 24–35.

Khan, A., & Ghosh, S. K. (2021). Student performance analysis and prediction in classroom learning: A review of educational data mining studies. *Education and Information Technologies*, *26*(1), 205–240. DOI: 10.1007/s10639-020-10230-3

Khandelwal, R., Nayak, A., Chung, P., Fawaz, K., Bianchi, A., Celik, Z. B., & Hussain, S. R. (2024). Unpacking privacy labels: A measurement and developer perspective on google's data safety section. In *33rd USENIX Security Symposium (USENIX Security 24)* (pp. 2831-2848).

Khan, S., Mazhar, T., Shahzad, T., Khan, M. A., Rehman, A. U., Saeed, M. M., & Hamam, H. (2025). Harnessing AI for sustainable higher education: Ethical considerations, operational efficiency, and future directions. *Discover Sustainability*, *6*(1), 23. DOI: 10.1007/s43621-025-00809-6

Khlaif, Z., Odeh, A., & Bsharat, T. R. (2024). Generative AI-powered adaptive assessment. In *Power of Persuasive Educational Technologies in Enhancing Learning* (pp. 157–176). IGI Global. DOI: 10.4018/979-8-3693-6397-3.ch007

Kim, Y., Back, J., & Kim, J. (2021). A tamper-resistant algorithm using blockchain for the digital tachograph. *Electronics (Basel)*, *10*(5), 581. DOI: 10.3390/electronics10050581

Kinder, A., Briese, F. J., Jacobs, M., Dern, N., Glodny, N., Jacobs, S., & Leßmann, S. (2025). Effects of adaptive feedback generated by a large language model: A case study in teacher education. *Computers and Education: Artificial Intelligence*, *8*, 100349. DOI: 10.1016/j.caeai.2024.100349

Knox, J. (2020). Artificial intelligence and education in China. *Learning, Media and Technology*, *45*(3), 298–311. DOI: 10.1080/17439884.2020.1754236

Koch, I. (2013). *Analysis of multivariate and high-dimensional data*. Cambridge University Press. DOI: 10.1017/CBO9781139025805

Koebe, P. (2025). How digital technologies and AI contribute to achieving the health-related SDGs. *International Journal of Information Management Data Insights*, *5*(1), 100298. DOI: 10.1016/j.jjimei.2024.100298

Koller, D., Ng, A., Do, C., & Chen, Z. (2013). Learning analytics and educational performance: A study of LMS data. *Learning Analytics Journal*, *1*(1), 12–22.

Korus, P., & Huang, J. (2016). Multi-Scale Fusion for Improved Localization of Malicious Tampering in Digital Images. In IEEE Transactions on Image Processing (Vol. 25, Issue 3, pp. 1312–1326). Institute of Electrical and Electronics Engineers (IEEE). DOI: 10.1109/TIP.2016.2518870

Kourtesis, P. (2024). A comprehensive review of multimodal XR applications, risks, and ethical challenges in the metaverse. *Multimodal Technologies and Interaction*, *8*(11), 98. DOI: 10.3390/mti8110098

Krishnamoorthy, M. V. (2024). Data Obfuscation through Latent Space Projection (LSP) for Privacy-Preserving AI Governance: Case Studies in Medical Diagnosis and Finance Fraud Detection. arXiv preprint arXiv:2410.17459. https://arxiv.org/abs/2410.17459

Krishnamoorthy, R., Srivastava, M., & Khanna, D. (2025). AI in higher education: Tapping educators' perspective. *International Journal of System Assurance Engineering and Management*, •••, 1–13. DOI: 10.1007/s13198-024-02657-5

Krstić, L., Aleksić, V., & Krstić, M. (2022). Artificial Intelligence in Education. *RE:view*, 223–228. Advance online publication. DOI: 10.46793/TIE22.223K

Kuh, G. D. (2001). Assessing What Really Matters to Student Learning Inside The National Survey of Student Engagement. *Change*, *33*(3), 10–17. DOI: 10.1080/00091380109601795

Kuluşaklı, E. (2025). Student Engagement and Flexibility in Distance Learning in Higher Education. *SAGE Open, 15*(1). (Original work published 2025).DOI: 10.1177/21582440251329979

Kulynych, B., Gomez, J. F., Kaissis, G., Calmon, F. du P., & Troncoso, C. (2024). Attack-Aware Noise Calibration for Differential Privacy. *arXiv Preprint arXiv:2407.02191*. https://arxiv.org/abs/2407.02191

Kumar, R. (2024). *Case Based Scenario Questions. Latest insights.* https://www.oecd.org/en/topics/sub-issues/artificial-intelligence-and-education-and-skills.html

Kumar, P., Saxena, C., & Baber, H. (2021). Learner-content interaction in e-learning-the moderating role of perceived harm of COVID-19 in assessing the satisfaction of learners. *Smart Learning Environments*, *8*(1), 5. Advance online publication. DOI: 10.1186/s40561-021-00149-8 PMID: 40477398

Kumar, S. S., Taheri, F., & Islam, M. R. (n.d.). Artificial Intelligence and Image Processing Approaches in Damage Assessment and Material Evaluation. In *International Conference on Computational Intelligence for Modelling, Control and Automation and International Conference on Intelligent Agents, Web Technologies and Internet Commerce (CIMCA-IAWTIC'06)* (Vol. 1, pp. 307–313). IEEE. DOI: 10.1109/CIMCA.2005.1631284

Kumar, S., Billa, L. V. L., Bhimineni, O., Jaiswal, R., & Bisht, A. (2022). Implementation of ICT Tools in A Vocational Skill Development Program. *International Journal of Next-Generation Computing*, *13*(3). Advance online publication. DOI: 10.47164/ijngc.v13i3.729

Kumar, T. K., & Tummala, D. S. (2023). Artificial intelligence-based real-time facial emotion monitoring system. *Proceedings of the International Conference on Computer, Communication and Electronics Engineering*, 1–5. DOI: 10.1109/ICCCE58854.2023.10246038

Lakshmi, K., Khan, S., Kumar, P. A., Wagh, V., & Vasanti, G. (2024). AI-Powered Learning Analytics: Transforming Educational Outcomes Through ICT Integration. *Library of Progress-Library Science, Information Technology & Computer, 44*(3).

Lamming, M., Bowers, J., Light, A., Mariani, J., & Blomberg, J. (2000). Satchel: Providing access to any document, any time, anywhere. [TOCHI]. *ACM Transactions on Computer-Human Interaction*, *7*(3), 322–352. DOI: 10.1145/355324.355326

Langove, S. A., & Khan, A. (2024). Automated Grading and Feedback Systems: Reducing Teacher Workload and Improving Student Performance. *Journal of Asian Development Studies*, *13*(4), 202–212. DOI: 10.62345/jads.2024.13.4.16

Lan, Z., & Tsao, H.-J. (2025). The relationship between classroom learning engagement of secondary vocational school students and psychological factors based on video analysis technology. *WSEAS Transactions on Information Science and Applications*, *22*(14), 146–152. Advance online publication. DOI: 10.37394/23209.2025.22.14

Laun, M., & Wolff, F. (2025). Chatbots in education: Hype or help? A meta-analysis. *Learning and Individual Differences*, *119*, 102646. Advance online publication. DOI: 10.1016/j.lindif.2025.102646

Layode, O., Ndidi, H. N., Adeleke, G. S., Udeh, E. O., & Labake, T. T. (2024). Data privacy and security challenges in environmental research: Approaches to safeguarding sensitive information. *International Journal of Applied Research in Social Sciences*, *6*(8), 1087–1098.

Leape, L. L., Rogers, G., Hanna, D., Griswold, P., Federico, F., Fenn, C. A., Bates, D. W., & Kirle, L. (2006). Developing and implementing new safe practices: Voluntary adoption through statewide collaboratives. *BMJ Quality & Safety*, *15*(4), 289–295. DOI: 10.1136/qshc.2005.017632 PMID: 16885255

Leaver, T., & Srdarov, S. (2023). ChatGPT isn't magic. *M/C Journal, 26*(5). DOI: 10.5204/mcj.3004

Leelavathi, R., & Surendhranatha, R. C. (2024). ChatGPT in the classroom: Navigating the generative AI wave in management education. *Journal of Research in Innovative Teaching & Learning*, *17*(3), 402–418. DOI: 10.1108/jrit-01-2024-0017

Legris, P., Ingham, J., & Collerette, P. (2003). Why do people use information technology? A critical review of the technology acceptance model. *Information & Management, 40*(3), 191–204. DOI: 10.1016/S0378-7206(01)00143-4

Leite, H. (2025). Artificial intelligence in higher education: Research notes from a longitudinal study. *Technological Forecasting and Social Change, 215*, 124115. DOI: 10.1016/j.techfore.2025.124115

Lemieux, V. L. (2019). Blockchain and public record keeping: Of temples, prisons, and the (re) configuration of power. *Frontiers in Blockchain, 2*, 5. DOI: 10.3389/fbloc.2019.00005

Leong, J., Pataranutaporn, P., Danry, V., Perteneder, F., Mao, Y., & Maes, P. (2024). Putting things into context: Generative AI-enabled context personalization for vocabulary learning improves learning motivation. In *Proceedings of the CHI Conference on Human Factors in Computing Systems* (CHI '24), May 11–16, 2024, Honolulu, HI, USA (pp. 1–15). ACM. DOI: 10.1145/3544548.3581039

Letjani, K. P., Kurniawan, K., & Muthaiyah, S. (2025). Adoption of chatgpt in educational institutions in Botswana: A customer perspective. *Asia Pacific Management Review, 30*(1), 100346. DOI: 10.1016/j.apmrv.2024.100346

Li, N., Li, T., & Venkatasubramanian, S. (2006, April). t-closeness: Privacy beyond k-anonymity and l-diversity. In *2007 IEEE 23rd international conference on data engineering* (pp. 106-115). IEEE.

Li, N., Romera Rodriguez, G., Xu, Y., Bhatt, P., Nguyen, H. A., Serpi, A., Tsai, C., & Carroll, J. M. (2022). Picturing One's Self: Camera Use in Zoom Classes during the COVID-19 Pandemic. *Proceedings of the Ninth ACM Conference on Learning @ Scale*, 151–162. DOI: 10.1145/3491140.3528284

Liang, Z. C., Cheng, T., King Luen, D., Japashov, N., & Hiae, T. (2024). *Empowering Industry 5.0: Nurturing STEM Tertiary Education and Careers Through Additional Mathematics* (pp. 124–155). DOI: 10.4018/979-8-3693-2814-9.ch005

Liaw, S. S., & Huang, H. M. (2007). Development of a web-based collaborative learning system for promoting critical thinking. *Journal of Educational Technology & Society, 10*(2), 124–136.

Limpinan, P., Yindeemak, A., Pasmala, R., Nammanee, M., & Jantakoon, T. (2025). A bibliometric analysis of artificial intelligence for multimedia in education by dimensions AI. *Higher Education Studies, 15*(1), 12–28.

Lin, H. (2022). Influences of artificial intelligence in education on teaching effectiveness: The mediating effect of teachers' perceptions of educational technology. *International Journal of Emerging Technologies in Learning*, *17*(24), 144–156. DOI: 10.3991/ijet.v17i24.36037

Lin, H., & Chen, Q. (2024). Artificial intelligence (AI)-integrated educational applications and college students' creativity and academic emotions: Students and teachers' perceptions and attitudes. *BMC Psychology*, *12*(1), 487. DOI: 10.1186/s40359-024-01979-0 PMID: 39285268

Lin, M. P.-C., Liu, A. L., Poitras, E., Chang, M., & Chang, D. H. (2024). An Exploratory Study on the Efficacy and Inclusivity of AI Technologies in Diverse Learning Environments. *Sustainability (Basel)*, *16*(20), 8992. DOI: 10.3390/su16208992

Liu, Z., Yin, S. X., Lin, G., & Chen, N. F. (2024). Personality-aware student simulation for conversational intelligent tutoring systems. *arXiv preprint arXiv:2404.06762.* DOI: 10.18653/v1/2024.emnlp-main.37

Livingstone, S., Stoilova, M., & Nandagiri, R. (2020). *Data and privacy literacy: The role of the school in educating children in a datafied society.* OECD Education Working Paper No. 224.

Livingstone, S., & Third, A. (2017). Children and young people's rights in the digital age: An emerging agenda. *New Media & Society*, *19*(5), 657–670. DOI: 10.1177/1461444816686318

Li, Y., Tian, C., Xu, L., Pei, L., Huang, X., & Wang, X. (2025). EEG-Guided Adaptive Learning: A New Neuroeducational Approach to the Facilitation of Cognitive Control in ADHD Children. *Child: Care, Health and Development*, *51*(4), e70113. DOI: 10.1111/cch.70113

Li, Y., Zhang, X., & Liu, H. (2022). A review of the ethical implications of computer vision in educational settings. *Ethics and Information Technology*, *24*(2), 153–166. DOI: 10.1007/s10676-021-09550-5

Li, Z. Z., Wang, Q., Qiao, S., Zhang, L., & Chen, X. (2023). Enhancing blockchain adoption through tailored software engineering: An industrial-grounded study in education credentialing. *Distributed Ledger Technologies: Research and Practice*, *2*(4), 1–24. DOI: 10.1145/3632532

Li, Z., Chen, L., & Wu, C. (2023). Emotion recognition and attention analysis for student engagement in classrooms: A multimodal approach. *Journal of Educational Psychology*, *115*(4), 586–599. DOI: 10.1037/edu0000532

Lizcano, D., Lara, J. A., White, B., & Aljawarneh, S. (2020). Blockchain-based approach to create a model of trust in open and ubiquitous higher education. *Journal of Computing in Higher Education, 32*(1), 109–134. DOI: 10.1007/s12528-019-09209-y

Łodzikowski, K., Foltz, P. W., & Behrens, J. T. (2024). Generative AI and Its Educational Implications. In D. Kourkoulou, A.-O. (Olnancy) Tzirides, B. Cope, & M. Kalantzis (Eds.), *Trust and Inclusion in AI-Mediated Education: Where Human Learning Meets Learning Machines* (pp. 35–57). Springer Nature Switzerland. DOI: 10.1007/978-3-031-64487-0_2

Lokam, G. V., Patil, P. S., Kukade, A. S., Dhule, A. N., & Kothiwale, R. A. (2025). AI-based career guidance system. *International Journal of Creative Research Thoughts, 13*(5), 1–6. https://www.ijcrt.org/papers/IJCRT2505326.pdf

Loukides, G., & Lomax, N. (2021). Privacy-preserving data publishing through anonymization, statistical disclosure control, and de-identification.

Luckin, R. (2020). *AI for school teachers*. Routledge.

Luckin, R., Holmes, W., & Forcier, L. B. (2022). The future of AI in education: 13 things we can do to prepare. *Educational Researcher, 51*(4), 267–275.

Luckin, R., Holmes, W., Griffiths, M., & Forcier, L. B. (2016). *Intelligence Unleashed: An Argument for AI in Education*. Pearson Education.

Luckin, R., Holmes, W., Griffiths, M., & Forcier, L. B. (2018). *Machine learning and human intelligence: The future of education for the 21st century*. UCL Institute of Education Press.

Lund, B. D., Wang, T., Mannuru, N. R., Nie, B., Shimray, S., & Wang, Z. (2023). ChatGPT and a new academic reality: Artificial Intelligence-written research papers and the ethics of the large language models in scholarly publishing. *Journal of the Association for Information Science and Technology, 74*(5), 570–581. DOI: 10.1002/asi.24750

Luo, J., Zheng, C., Yin, J., & Teo, H. H. (2025). Design and assessment of AI-based learning tools in higher education: A systematic review. *International Journal of Educational Technology in Higher Education, 22*(1), 42. DOI: 10.1186/s41239-025-00540-2

Machado, A., Tenório, K., Santos, M. M., Barros, A. P., Rodrigues, L., Mello, R. F., Paiva, R., & Dermeval, D. (2025). Workload perception in educational resource recommendation supported by artificial intelligence: A controlled experiment with teachers. *Smart Learning Environments, 12*(1), 20. DOI: 10.1186/s40561-025-00373-6

Machkour, M., El Jihaoui, M., Lamalif, L., Faris, S., & Mansouri, K. (2025, February). Toward an adaptive learning assessment pathway. In *Frontiers in Education* (Vol. 10, p. 1498233). Frontiers Media SA. DOI: 10.3389/feduc.2025.1498233

Maleki Varnosfaderani, S., & Forouzanfar, M. (2024). The role of AI in hospitals and clinics: Transforming healthcare in the 21st century. *Bioengineering (Basel, Switzerland), 11*(4), 337. DOI: 10.3390/bioengineering11040337

Malone, B. (2025). *Ethical considerations in instructional design enhanced by artificial intelligence: A phenomenological inquiry*. Appalachian State University Digital Collections.

Maloy, R. W., Verock-O'Loughlin, R.-E. A., Edwards, S. A., Trust, T., & Woolf, B. P. (2021). *Transforming learning with new technologies* (4th ed.). Pearson.

Manyika, J., Lund, S., Chui, M., Bughin, J., Woetzel, J., Batra, P., Sanghvi, S., Ko, R., & Saurabh, S. (2017). *Jobs lost, jobs gained: Workforce transitions in a time of automation* (McKinsey Global Institute)*. McKinsey & Company.

Marin, A. R., & Jiménez, O. R. (2024). Advancing education through AI-powered learning strategies and teaching techniques. In *ICERI2024 Proceedings* (pp. 10381-10388). IATED.

Maroju, P. K., & Aragani, V. M. (2025). Predictive Analytics in Education: Early Intervention and Proactive Support With Gen AI Cloud. In *Smart Education and Sustainable Learning Environments in Smart Cities* (pp. 317–332). IGI Global Scientific Publishing. DOI: 10.4018/979-8-3693-7723-9.ch019

Marouf, M., Alchilibi, H., Sakr, D. K., Alkhayyat, A., & Pateriya, N. (2024). AI in real-time student performance monitoring using IoE. *Advances in Computational Intelligence and Robotics, 19*, 275–288. Advance online publication. DOI: 10.4018/979-8-3693-7367-5.ch019

Martin, F., & Bolliger, D. U. (2018). Engagement Matters: Student Perceptions on the Importance of Engagement Strategies in the Online Learning Environment. *Online Learning : the Official Journal of the Online Learning Consortium, 22*(1). Advance online publication. DOI: 10.24059/olj.v22i1.1092

Martin, F., Sun, T., & Westine, C. (2019). The impact of LMS on personalized learning. *Journal of Distance Education, 35*(3), 25–40.

Massachusetts Institute of Technology. (n.d.). *Creative portfolios*. MIT Admissions. https://mitadmissions.org/apply/firstyear/portfolios-additional-material/

Medaglia, R., Gil-Garcia, J. R., & Pardo, T. A. (2023). Artificial Intelligence in government: Taking stock and moving forward. *Social Science Computer Review*, *41*(1), 123–140. DOI: 10.1177/08944393211034087

Meng, G. (2022). Application of Digital Image Processing Technology in the Remote Interactive Art Teaching System. In Chen, C.-L. (Ed.), *Security and Communication Networks* (Vol. 2022, pp. 1–12). Hindawi Limited., DOI: 10.1155/2022/6419117

Meotti, M., & Magliozzi, D. (2023,). *Using artificial intelligence to navigate the new challenges of college and career*. Harvard ALI Social Impact Review. https://www.sir.advancedleadership.harvard.edu/articles/using-artificial-intelligence-to-navigate-the-new-challenges-of-college-and-career

Merino-Campos, C. (2025). The Impact of Artificial Intelligence on Personalized Learning in Higher Education: A Systematic Review. *Trends in Higher Education*, *4*(2), 17. DOI: 10.3390/higheredu4020017

Mhlanga, D. (2023). Open AI in Education, the Responsible and Ethical Use of ChatGPT Towards Lifelong Learning. SSRN *Electronic Journal*. DOI: 10.2139/ssrn.4354422

Michel-Villarreal, R., Vilalta-Perdomo, E. L., Salinas-Navarro, D. E., Thierry-Aguilera, R., & Gerardou, F. S. (2023). Challenges and opportunities of generative AI for higher education as explained by ChatGPT. *Education Sciences*, *13*(9), 856. DOI: 10.3390/educsci13090856

Microsoft Corporation. (2024). *HoloLens 2 capabilities and solutions*. Microsoft Learn. https://learn.microsoft.com/en-us/hololens/hololens-commercial-features

Ministry of Education. India. (2025, May 3). *eVidya initiative*. https://www.education.gov.in/

Ministry of Education. Singapore. (2025, May 3). *EduRec: Education records management system*. https://www.moe.gov.sg

Mirdad, K., Daeli, O. P. M., Septiani, N., Ekawati, A., & Rusilowati, U. (2024). Optimizing student engagement and performance usingai-enabled educational tools. *Journal of Computer Science and Technology Application*, *1*(1), 53–60.

Mishra, P., & Koehler, M. J. (2006). Technological pedagogical content knowledge: A framework for teacher knowledge. *Teachers College Record*, *108*(6), 1017–1054. DOI: 10.1111/j.1467-9620.2006.00684.x

Mogwe, A. W. (2018). Real-Time concept feedback in lectures for Botho University students. *International Journal of Advanced Computer Science and Applications*, *9*(6). Advance online publication. DOI: 10.14569/IJACSA.2018.090635

Montanaro, A. (2016). *Quantum algorithms: An overview. npj Quantum Information, 2*(1), Article 15023. .DOI: 10.1038/npjqi.2015.23

Moore, M. G. (1989). Editorial: Three types of interaction. *American Journal of Distance Education*, *3*(2), 1–7. DOI: 10.1080/08923648909526659

Mori, Y., Nakamura, Y., & Ohta, K. (2022). The integration of cognitive load and eye-tracking for real-time classroom attention analysis. *Journal of Learning Analytics*, *9*(1), 34–49. DOI: 10.18608/jla.2022.0901

Mtebe, J. S., & Raphael, C. M. (2018). Investigating the challenges and factors influencing the adoption of Learning Management Systems in higher education. *International Journal of Education and Development Using Information and Communication Technology*, *14*(3), 61–74.

Muhammad Hani Bayan, F. (2024). The ethics of AI: Navigating the moral dilemmas of artificial intelligence. *Arab Journal for Scientific Publishing*, *7*(66), 1–11. DOI: 10.36571/ajsp661

Mukkala, P. R., Vuyyuru, T., Ramana, B. S., Murthy, M., Rao, A. S., & Al Said, N. (2025). Integrating ICT with artificial intelligence for transformative education. *Journal of Information Systems Engineering & Management*, *10*(1).

Munir, S., Kollnig, K., Shuba, A., & Shafiq, Z. (2024). Google's Chrome Antitrust Paradox. *arXiv preprint arXiv:2406.11856.*

Murugesan, G., Jaiswal, R., Kshatri, S. S., & Bhonsle, D. (2022). Developing machine learning based framework for the network traffic prediction. *International Journal of Next-Generation Computing*, *13*(3). Advance online publication. DOI: 10.47164/ijngc.v13i3.787

Murwanenda, R., Budirahardjo, R., Setyorini, D., Prijatmoko, D., & Handayani, A. T. W. (2024). Korelasi pola asuh orang tua terhadap kejadian Early Childhood Caries pada anak usia 36 sampai 71 bulan: Studi cross-sectional. *Jurnal Kedokteran Gigi Universitas Padjadjaran*, *36*(2), 141–148. DOI: 10.24198/jkg.v36i2.50330

Mustafa, G., Rehman, S. U., Khan, I. U., Khattak, H. A., & Kim, K. (2025). Blockchain-based governance models in e-government: A comprehensive framework for legal, technical, ethical and security considerations. *International Journal of Law and Management*, *67*(1), 37–55. DOI: 10.1108/IJLMA-08-2023-0172

Mustikawati, I. F., Mahmudah, S., Fitriyanti, L., Yuliana, Y., & Utami, R. A. (2024). The impact of telemedicine adoption, AI diagnostics, and patient data privacy on healthcare accessibility and quality in 2024. *Global International Journal of Innovative Research*, *2*(6), 1435–1448.

Mvondo, G. F. N., Niu, B., & Eivazinezhad, S. (2025). Exploring the ethical use of LLM chatbots in higher education. *Journal of Business Research*, *200*, 115575. Advance online publication. DOI: 10.1016/j.jbusres.2025.115575

Myers, C., & Patil, S. (2025, June 20). *Fault lines in health care AI – Part one: The high stakes of AI in medicine*. Johns Hopkins Carey Business School. https://carey.jhu.edu/articles/fault-lines-health-care-ai-part-one-high-stakes-ai-medicine

Myers, T., Monypenny, R., & Trevathan, J. (2012). Overcoming the glassy-eyed nod: An application of process-oriented guided inquiry learning techniques in information technology. *Journal of Learning Design*, *5*(1), 12–22. DOI: 10.5204/jld.v5i1.97

Myllykoski-Laine, S., Lahdenperä, J., Nikander, L., & Postareff, L. (2023). Students' experiences of the development of generic competences in the Finnish higher education context – the role of the teaching-learning environment and approaches to learning. *European Journal of Higher Education*, *13*(4), 448–467. DOI: 10.1080/21568235.2022.2058975

Nader, J. A., Z., & Zahran, B. (2017). Analysis of Color Image Filtering Methods. In International Journal of Computer Applications (Vol. 174, Issue 8, pp. 12–17). Foundation of Computer Science. DOI: 10.5120/ijca2017915449

Nagtegaal, R. (2021). The impact of using algorithms for managerial decisions on public employees' procedural justice. *Government Information Quarterly*, *38*(1), 101536. DOI: 10.1016/j.giq.2020.101536

Natarajan, U., Jha, V., & Awasthi, P. (2020). *India's learning transformation: Using AI for equitable education*. World Bank EdTech Blog.

National Science Board. (2018). Science & Engineering Indicators 2018. *National Science Foundation*. Retrieved from https://www.nsf.gov/statistics/2018/nsb20181/report/sections/elementary-and-secondary-mathematics-and-science-education/instructional-technology-and-digital-learning

Neophytou, R., Liasidou, S., Pipyros, K., & Christofi, A. (2025). Artificial intelligence driven adaptive learning methods in sustainable tourism education. *Worldwide Hospitality and Tourism Themes*, *17*(1), 120–131. DOI: 10.1108/WHATT-12-2024-0308

Ngui, W. K., Leong, M. S., Hee, L. M., & Abdelrhman, A. M. (2013). Wavelet analysis: Mother wavelet selection methods. *Applied Mechanics and Materials, 393*, 953–958. DOI: 10.4028/www.scientific.net/AMM.393.953

Nguyen, K. A., Borrego, M., Finelli, C. J., DeMonbrun, M., Crockett, C., Tharayil, S., Shekhar, P., Waters, C., & Rosenberg, R. (2021). Instructor strategies to aid implementation of active learning: A systematic literature review. *International Journal of STEM Education, 8*(1), 9. DOI: 10.1186/s40594-021-00270-7

Nuangchalerm, P. (2023). AI-driven learning analytics in STEM education. *International Journal of Research in STEM Education, 5*(2), 77–84. DOI: 10.33830/ijrse.v5i2.1596

Nwoko, H. (2024). *Mom Blames Character.AI for Her Teen' Death-What Parents Should Know A new lawsuit brings attention to the potential dangers of this AI platform.* https://www.parents.com/

OECD. (2025, May 3). Case study: The Estonian Education Information System (EHIS). In *Strengthening the governance of skills systems: Lessons from six OECD countries.* OECD Publishing., DOI: 10.1787/298d6678

Office of Communications, College of Education. (2024, October 24). *AI in schools: Pros and cons.* University of Illinois College of Education. https://education.illinois.edu/about/news-events/news/article/2024/10/24/ai-in-schools--pros-and-cons

Ogbu Eke, E. (2024). Assessing the readiness and attitudes of Nigerian teacher educators towards adoption of artificial intelligence in educational settings. J. Educ. Technol. Online Learn., 7(4-ICETOL 2024 Special), 473–487.

Oh, S. H., & Sanfilippo, M. (2024). University governance for responsible AI. *Proceedings of the ALISE Annual Conference.*

Onesi-Ozigagun, O., Ololade, Y. J., Eyo-Udo, N. L., & Ogundipe, D. O. (2024). Revolutionizing education through AI: A comprehensive review of enhancing learning experiences. *International Journal of Applied Research in Social Sciences, 6*(4), 589–607. DOI: 10.51594/ijarss.v6i4.1011

Online, H. (2023, April 19). *The benefits and limitations of generative AI: Harvard experts answer your questions.* https://www.harvardonline.harvard.edu/blog/benefits-limitations-generative-ai

Ooi, K. B., Koohang, A., Aw, E. C. X., Cham, T. H., Cobanoglu, C., Dennis, C., & Tan, G. W. H. (2025). Unveiling the potential of generative artificial intelligence: A multidimensional journey into the future. *Industrial Management & Data Systems, 125*(2), 417–432. DOI: 10.1108/IMDS-10-2023-0703

Ooi, K.-B., Tan, G. W.-H., Al-Emran, M., Al-Sharafi, M. A., Capatina, A., Chakraborty, A., Dwivedi, Y. K., Huang, T.-L., Kar, A. K., Lee, V.-H., Loh, X.-M., Micu, A., Mikalef, P., Mogaji, E., Pandey, N., Raman, R., Rana, N. P., Sarker, P., Sharma, A., & Wong, L.-W. (2025). The Potential of Generative Artificial Intelligence Across Disciplines: Perspectives and Future Directions. *Journal of Computer Information Systems*, *65*(1), 76–107. DOI: 10.1080/08874417.2023.2261010

Open, A. I. (2025). *Teaching with AI: Part A7*. https://openai.com/index/teaching-with-ai

Opesemowo, O. A. G. (2024). Artificial intelligence in mathematics education. In *Advances in information quality and management* (pp. 1524-1547). IGI Global. https://doi.org/DOI: 10.4018/978-1-6684-7366-5.ch084

Ortega-Ochoa, E., Arguedas, M., & Daradoumis, T. (2023). Empathic pedagogical conversational agents: A systematic literature review. *British Journal of Educational Technology*, *55*(2), 886–909. DOI: 10.1111/bjet.13413

Oshrat, Y., Aumann, Y., Hollander, T., Maksimov, O., Ostroumov, A., Shechtman, N., & Kraus, S. (2022a). *Efficient Customer Service Combining Human Operators and Virtual Agents*. https://arxiv.org/abs/2209.05226

Ouyang, F., Wu, M., Zheng, L., Zhang, L., & Jiao, P. (2023). Integration of artificial intelligence performance prediction and learning analytics to improve student learning in an online engineering course. *International Journal of Educational Technology in Higher Education*, *20*(1), 4. DOI: 10.1186/s41239-022-00372-4 PMID: 36683653

Owan, V. J., Abang, K. B., Idika, D. O., Etta, E. O., & Bassey, B. A. (2023). Exploring the potential of artificial intelligence tools in educational measurement and assessment. *Eurasia Journal of Mathematics, Science and Technology Education*, *19*(9), em2307. Advance online publication. DOI: 10.29333/ejmste/13428

Page, L. C., & Gehlbach, H. (2017). How an artificially intelligent virtual assistant helps students navigate the road to college. *AERA Open*, *3*(4), 1–12. DOI: 10.1177/2332858417749220

Pane, J. F., Steiner, E. D., Baird, M. D., & Hamilton, L. S. (2014). *Continued progress: Promising evidence on personalized learning*. RAND Corporation.

Parikh, P. M., & Venniyoor, A. (2024). Neuralink and Brain-Computer Interface-Exciting Times for Artificial Intelligence. *South Asian Journal of Cancer*, *13*(1), 63–65. DOI: 10.1055/s-0043-1774729

Parker, A. (1999). Interaction in Distance Education. *The Critical Conversation*, *12*, 13–17.

Parsad, B. (2008). *Distance Education at Degree-Granting Postsecondary Institutions: 2006–07 (National Center for Education Statistics, Institute of Education Sciences).* US Department of Education.

Pasupuleti, M. K. (2025). Next-generation extended reality (XR): A unified framework for integrating AR, VR, and AI-driven immersive technologies. *IEEE Transactions on Visualization and Computer Graphics.*

Pektaş, H. M., Karamustafaoğlu, O., & Çelik, H. (2025). The Role of Educational Data Mining and Artificial Intelligence Supported Learning Analytics on Conceptual Change: New Approaches to Differentiated Instruction. *Journal of Science Education and Technology*, 1–26. DOI: 10.1007/s10956-025-10214-3

Pereira, A., Costa, A., & Silva, F. (2020). Automated technologies for measuring cognitive load and attention in educational settings: A critical review. *Journal of Educational Computing Research, 57*(5), 1250–1272. DOI: 10.1177/0735633120905724

Perelman, L. (2014). When "the state of the art" is counting words. In Shermis, M. D., & Burstein, J. (Eds.), *Handbook of Automated Essay Evaluation: Current Applications and New Directions* (pp. 163–181). Routledge.

Perets, E. A., Chabeda, D., Gong, A. Z., Huang, X., Fung, T. S., Ng, K. Y., Bathgate, M., & Yan, E. C. Y. (2020). Impact of the Emergency Transition to Remote Teaching on Student Engagement in a Non-STEM Undergraduate Chemistry Course in the Time of COVID-19. *Journal of Chemical Education, 97*(9), 2439–2447. DOI: 10.1021/acs.jchemed.0c00879

Perkins, M., & Roe, J. (2024). Academic publisher guidelines on AI usage: A ChatGPT supported thematic analysis. *F1000 Research, 12*, 1398. DOI: 10.12688/f1000research.142411.2

Phelan, D., Maguire, H., & Finnegan, C. (2025). Scoping Review of Universal Design for Learning Principles Embedded in Subjects in Secondary Education. *European Journal of Education, 60*(1), e70016. DOI: 10.1111/ejed.70016

Picard, R. W., Vyzas, E., & Healey, J. (2020). Toward machine emotional intelligence: Analysis of affective physiological state. *IEEE Transactions on Pattern Analysis and Machine Intelligence, 22*(12), 1174–1191. DOI: 10.1109/34.903103

Piech, C., Huang, J., Nguyen, A., Phulsuksombati, M., Sahami, M., & Guibas, L. (2015). Learning program embeddings to propagate feedback on student code. *Proceedings of the 32nd International Conference on Machine Learning*, 87–95.

Pillai, R., Sivathanu, B., Metri, B., & Kaushik, N. (2023). Students' adoption of AI-based teacher-bots (T-bots) for learning in higher education. *Information Technology & People*. Advance online publication. DOI: 10.1108/ITP-02-2021-0152

Pochintesta, E. (2012). Comparison Of Apple's Ios 5 And Android For Mobile Applications Development: A Developer's Perspective.

Poikaryil, O. B., Azeem, M., Khan, S., & Ahmad, I. (2024). Transformative fusion: Leveraging blockchain and AI for educational data analytics in modern education systems. In *Blockchain and AI in shaping the modern education system* (pp. 182–208). CRC Press.

PowerSchool. (2025, May 3). *PowerSchool: The leading education technology platform*. https://www.powerschool.com

Prakash, J., Swathiramya, R., Balambigai, G., Menaha, R., & Abhirami, J. S. (2024). AI-driven real-time feedback system for enhanced student support: Leveraging sentiment analysis and machine learning algorithms. *International Journal of Computational and Experimental Science and Engineering*. DOI: 10.22399/ijcesen.780

Prakhar, P., Gupta, S., & Jaiswal, R. (2025a). Battery technology and charging infrastructure for EVs: a resource-based and dynamic capability view of entrepreneurial opportunities. *Information Discovery and Delivery*. DOI: 10.1108/IDD-09-2024-0143

Prakhar, P., Jaiswal, R., & Gupta, S. (2024a). Entrepreneurship in the electric vehicle sector: Past, present and future directions. *Parikalpana: KIIT Journal of Management, 20*(1), 5-26. DOI: 10.23862/kiit-parikalpana/2024/v20/i1/225089

Prakhar, P., Jabeen, F., Jaiswal, R., Gupta, S., Piccardi, P., & Jose, S. (2025b). Mapping the electric vehicle adoption scholarship for sustainability: An integrated theoretical framework and future research directions. *Management of Environmental Quality, 36*(1), 249–276. DOI: 10.1108/MEQ-04-2024-0153

Prakhar, P., Jaiswal, R., Gupta, S., & Tiwari, A. K. (2024c). Electric vehicles in transition: Opportunities, challenges, and research agenda–A systematic literature review. *Journal of Environmental Management, 372*, 123415. DOI: 10.1016/j.jenvman.2024.123415 PMID: 39581008

Prakhar, P., Jaiswal, R., & Khan, M. I. A. (2024b). Bibliometric perspectives on sustainable tourism and future research agenda. In *Managing Tourism and Hospitality Sectors for Sustainable Global Transformation* (pp. 1–16). IGI Global. DOI: 10.4018/979-8-3693-6260-0.ch001

Pratama, M. P., Sampelolo, R., & Lura, H. (2023). Revolutionizing education: harnessing the power of artificial intelligence for personalized learning. *Klasikal: Journal of Education, Language Teaching and Science, 5*(2), 350-357.

Prather, J., Denny, P., Leinonen, J., Becker, B. A., Albluwi, I., Craig, M., Keuning, H., Kiesler, N., Kohn, T., Leinonen, J., MacNeil, S., Petersen, A., Pettit, R., Reeves, B. N., & Zingaro, D. (2023, October). The robots are here: Navigating the generative AI revolution in computing education. In *Proceedings of the 2023 Conference on Innovation and Technology in Computer Science Education* V. 2 (pp. 108-121). ACM. https://doi.org/DOI: 10.1145/3623762.3633499

Priyadharsini, V., & Mary, R. S. (2024). Universal Design for Learning (UDL) in Inclusive Education: Accelerating Learning for All. *Shanlax International Journal of Arts. Science and Humanities, 11*(4), 145–150. DOI: 10.34293/sijash.v11i4.7489

Puentedura, R. R. (2006). *Transformation, technology, and education: The SAMR model.* Retrieved from https://hippasus.com/resources/sweden2010/SAMR_TPCK_Intro.pdf

Qadhi, S., Alduais, A., Chaaban, Y., & Khraisheh, M. (2024). Generative AI, research ethics, and higher education research: Insights from a scientometric analysis. *Information (Basel), 15*(6), 325. DOI: 10.3390/info15060325

Qin, Z., Yang, Y., Yu, T., Khalil, I., Xiao, X., & Ren, K. (2016, October). Heavy hitter estimation over set-valued data with local differential privacy. In *Proceedings of the 2016 ACM SIGSAC conference on computer and communications security* (pp. 192-203). DOI: 10.1145/2976749.2978409

Raca, M., Tormey, R., & Dillenbourg, P. (2014). Sleepers' lag-study on motion and attention. In *Proceedings of the Fourth International Conference on Learning Analytics and Knowledge* (pp. 36-43). ACM.

Raghavan, M., Barocas, S., Kleinberg, J., & Levy, K. (2020). Mitigating bias in algorithmic hiring: Evaluating claims and practices. In *Proceedings of the 2020 Conference on Fairness, Accountability, and Transparency (FAT '20)** (pp. 469–481). Association for Computing Machinery. DOI: 10.1145/3351095.3372828

Rahate, V., Mehta, A. K., Deshpande, S., Jawarkar, P., Disawal, V., & Sarge, P. (2025). Impact of AI-Driven Learning Management Systems on Institutional Efficiency and Student Engagement. *Metallurgical and Materials Engineering, 31*(2), 98–103. DOI: 10.63278/1341

Rajan, S., & Niranjan, L. R. (2025). The double-edged sword of ChatGPT: Fostering and hindering creativity in postgraduate academics in Bengaluru. *International Journal of Educational Management, 39*(2), 317–337. DOI: 10.1108/IJEM-03-2024-0181

Raj, P., Deka, G. C., & Chinnasamy, C. (2015). High-performance big-data analytics. In *Computing systems and approaches* (Vol. 1). Springer.

Raker, J. R., Dood, A. J., Srinivasan, S., & Murphy, K. L. (2021). Pedagogies of engagement use in postsecondary chemistry education in the United States: Results from a national survey. *Chemistry Education Research and Practice*, *22*(1), 30–42. DOI: 10.1039/D0RP00125B

Ramasamy, L. K., & Khan, F. (2024). Blockchain-based e-learning platform: Transforming education through decentralization. In *Blockchain for global education* (pp. 103–123). Springer Nature Switzerland. DOI: 10.1007/978-3-031-52123-2_6

Rana, N. P., Pillai, R., Sivathanu, B., & Malik, N. (2024). Assessing the nexus of Generative AI adoption, ethical considerations and organizational performance. *Technovation, 135*, 103064. DOI: 10.1016/j.technovation.2024.103064

Rancano, G. (2024, June 10). *Originality AI review: AI detector and more*. Scribbr. Retrieved August 12, 2025, from https://www.scribbr.com/ai-tools/originality-ai-review/

Raslan, G. (2024, March). The impact of the zone of proximal development concept (scaffolding) on the students' problem-solving skills and learning outcomes. *In BUiD Doctoral Research Conference 2023*: Multidisciplinary Studies (pp. 59–66). Cham: Springer Nature Switzerland. DOI: 10.1007/978-3-031-56121-4_6

Rasul, T., Nair, S., Kalendra, D. R., Robin, M., de Oliveira Santini, F., Ladeira, W. J., Sun, M., Day, I., Rather, R. A., & Heathcote, L. (2023). The role of ChatGPT in higher education: Benefits, challenges, and future research directions. *Journal of Applied Learning & Teaching*, *6*(1), 41–56. DOI: 10.37074/jalt.2023.6.1.29

Rauthan, J. S., Reddy, G. J., & Agarwal, P. (2021). Blockchain and the digital credentialing for education system. In *Proceedings of Integrated Intelligence Enable Networks and Computing: IIENC 2020.* Springer Singapore. DOI: 10.1007/978-981-33-6307-6_90

Ravichandran, K. (2024). Identifying Learning Difficulties at an Early Stage in Education with the Help of Artificial Intelligence Models and Predictive Analytics. *International Research Journal of Multidisciplinary Scope*, *5*(4), 1455–1461. DOI: 10.47857/irjms.2024.v05i04.01821

Reddy, S. (2024). Generative AI in healthcare: An implementation science-informed translational path on application, integration, and governance. *Implementation Science : IS, 19*, 21. DOI: 10.1186/s13012-024-01357-9

Reethika, A., & Priya, P. K. (2024). Using ai-powered predictive analytics tools to identify students falling behind or dropping out. In *Innovation in the University 4.0 System based on Smart Technologies* (pp. 101–115). Chapman and Hall/CRC. DOI: 10.1201/9781003425809-7

Reiserer, M., Ertl, B., & Mandl, H. (2023). Fostering Collaborative Knowledge Construction in Desktop Video-conferencing. Effects of Content Schemes and Cooperation Scripts in Peer Teaching Settings. In G. Stahl, Computer Support for Collaborative Learning (1st ed., pp. 379–388). *Routledge*. DOI: 10.4324/9781315045467-55

Rekha, K., Gopal, K., Satheeskumar, D., Anand, U. A., Doss, D. S. S., & Elayaperumal, S. (2024, May). Ai-Powered Personalized Learning System Design: Student Engagement and Performance Tracking System. In *2024 4th International Conference on Advance Computing and Innovative Technologies in Engineering (ICACITE)* (pp. 1125-1130). IEEE.

Renz, A., & Hilbig, R. (2020). Prerequisites for artificial intelligence in further education: Identification of drivers, barriers, and business models of educational technology companies. *International Journal of Educational Technology in Higher Education, 17*, 14. Advance online publication. DOI: 10.1186/s41239-020-00193-3

Reschly, A. L., & Christenson, S. L. (Eds.). (2022). *Handbook of Research on Student Engagement*. Springer International Publishing., DOI: 10.1007/978-3-031-07853-8

Resnick, M. (2024). Generative AI and Creative Learning: Concerns, Opportunities, and Choices. *An MIT Exploration of Generative AI*. DOI: 10.21428/e4baedd9.cf3e35e5

Richardson, J. C., Arbaugh, J. B., Cleveland-Innes, M., Ice, P., Swan, K. P., & Garrison, D. R. (2012). Using the Community of Inquiry Framework to Inform Effective Instructional Design. In Moller, L., & Huett, J. (Eds.), *The Next Generation of Distance Education* (pp. 97–125)., DOI: 10.1007/978-1-4614-1785-9_7

Rillo, A. G., Martínez-Carrillo, B. E., Castillo-Cardiel, J. A., & Rementería-Salinas, J. M. (2020). Constructivism: *An interpretation from medical education. IOSR J Res Method Educ, 10*(3), 13. https://www.iosrjournals.org/iosr-jrme/papers/Vol-10%20Issue-3/Series-7/A1003070112.pdf

Roberts, L. N., Solomon, F. N., & Cummings, R. (2024). Navigating the AI landscape. In *Advances in Educational Technologies and Instructional Design* (pp. 268–285). IGI Global.

Rodriguez, J.-M. G., Hunter, K. H., Scharlott, L. J., & Becker, N. M. (2020). A Review of Research on Process Oriented Guided Inquiry Learning: Implications for Research and Practice. *Journal of Chemical Education*, *97*(10), 3506–3520. DOI: 10.1021/acs.jchemed.0c00355

Ronas, S. M. S., Almonte, J. C. R., Arca, J. B., & Padron, R. P. (2023). The new norm of learning: Implementing learner-centered education with technology students. *International Journal of Multidisciplinary: Applied Business and Education Research*, *4*(4), 1278–1286. DOI: 10.11594/ijmaber.04.04.23

Roshanzade, T. (2023). A qualitative study of investigating the adoption of blockchain technology in higher education.

Roth, A., & Roughgarden, T. (2010, June). Interactive privacy via the median mechanism. In *Proceedings of the forty-second ACM symposium on Theory of Computing* (pp. 765-774). DOI: 10.1145/1806689.1806794

Ruan, S., & Davis, G. M. (2021). *EnglishBot: An AI-Powered Conversational System for Second Language Learning*. Stanford University. https://hci.stanford.edu/research/smartprimer/pdfs/EnglishBot_0224.pdf

Rudolph, J., Mohamed Ismail, F. M., & Popenici, Ş. (2024). Higher education's generative artificial intelligence paradox: The meaning of chatbot mania. *Journal of University Teaching and Learning Practice, 21*(1), 03. https://doi.org/DOI: 10.53761/54fs5e77

Runhaar, T. P. (2024). *Secure AI-Enhanced Student Engagement Analysis* (Bachelor's thesis, University of Twente).

Sa'idah, S. (2025). A review on EEG-based multimodal learning for emotion recognition. *Artificial Intelligence Review*, *58*(5), 131. Advance online publication. DOI: 10.1007/s10462-025-11126-9

Saborío-Taylor, S., & Rojas-Ramírez, F. (2024). Universal design for learning and artificial intelligence in the digital era: Fostering inclusion and autonomous learning. *International Journal of Professional Development. Learners and Learning*, *6*(2), ep2408. Advance online publication. DOI: 10.30935/ijpdll/14694

Safdar, U., Shafi, S., & Junaid, M. (2025). The impact of AI-driven gamification on student engagement and academic performance in English language teaching. *Indus Journal of Social Sciences*, *3*(1), 646–656. DOI: 10.59075/ijss.v3i1.758

Sain, Z. H., Aziz, A. L., & Lawal, U. S. (2024). Ethics of AI integration in higher education: Exploring moral dimensions. [JAIEM]. *Journal of Asian Islamic Educational Management*, *2*(1), 1–10. DOI: 10.53889/jaiem.v2i1.431

Sajja, R., Sermet, Y., Cikmaz, M., Cwiertny, D., & Demir, I. (2024). Artificial intelligence-enabled intelligent assistant for personalized and adaptive learning in higher education. *Information (Basel)*, *15*(10), 596. DOI: 10.3390/info15100596

Saleem, S., Aziz, M. U., Iqbal, M. J., & Abbas, S. (2025). AI in Education: Personalized Learning Systems and Their Impact on Student Performance and Engagement. *The Critical Review of Social Sciences Studies*, *3*(1), 2445–2459. DOI: 10.59075/c35qa453

Salha, S., Mousa, A., & Khayat, S. (2025). Artificial Intelligence in Education (AIED) Policies in School Context: A Mixed Approach Research. *Leadership and Policy in Schools*, *24*(1), 27–45. DOI: 10.1080/15700763.2024.2443675

Sanchez, J. (2024). The impact of artificial intelligence on teachers performance: Automatization of paperwork and enhancing of mediation. In *EDULEARN24 Proceedings* (pp. 7274–7278). IATED. DOI: 10.21125/edulearn.2024.1717

Sands, E. G., & Sorba, M. (2020). Coursera launches CourseMatch: A machine learning solution that automatically matches a University's on-campus courses to courses on Coursera. *Coursera Blog*. https://blog.coursera.org/coursera-launches-coursematch/

Schwartz, H. (2020). *Remote Learning Is Here to Stay: Results from the First American School District Panel Survey*. RAND Corporation., DOI: 10.7249/RRA956-1

Schwenck, C. M., & Pryor, J. D. (2021). Student perspectives on camera usage to engage and connect in foundational education classes: It's time to turn your cameras on. *International Journal of Educational Research Open*, *2*, 100079. DOI: 10.1016/j.ijedro.2021.100079

Selbst, A. D., & Powles, J. (2017). Meaningful information and the right to explanation. *International Data Privacy Law*, *7*(4), 233–242. DOI: 10.1093/idpl/ipx022

Selco, J. I., & Habbak, M. (2021). STEM Students' Perceptions on Emergency Online Learning during the COVID-19 Pandemic: Challenges and Successes. *Education Sciences*, *11*(12), 799. DOI: 10.3390/educsci11120799

Selvarajah, K., ElKott, N., Babu, P. R., & Patel, D. (2024). Enhancing classroom engagement through AI-powered emotional, head pose, and gaze tracking: A novel approach to responsive teaching. *International Multidisciplinary Research Journal*, *31*, 1–8. Advance online publication. DOI: 10.47722/imrj.2001.31

Selvaratnam, R., & Venaruzzo, L. (2024). Governance of artificial intelligence and data in Australasian higher education: A snapshot of policy and practice. ASCILITE Publications, 1–7.

Selvaratnam, R., & Sankey, M. (2021). The state of micro-credentials implementation and practice in Australasian higher education. *Open Praxis*, *13*(2), 228–238. DOI: 10.5944/openpraxis.13.2.130

Selwyn, N. (2019). Should robots replace teachers? AI and the future of education. *Polity*.

Selwyn, N. (2021). *Should robots replace teachers? AI and the future of education*. Polity Press.

Selwyn, N. (2022). The future of AI in education: Critical perspectives. *Learning, Media and Technology*, *47*(1), 1–15.

Serra, A. (2025). AI lawyering skills trainers: Transforming legal education with generative AI. https://core.ac.uk/download/635940326.pdf

Setyaningsih, E., Asrori, M., Ngadiso, N., Sumardi, S., Zainnuri, H., & Hariyanti, Y. (2024). Exploring high school EFL teachers' experiences with Magic School AI in lesson planning: Benefits and insights. *Voices of English Language Education Society*, *8*(3), 766–781. DOI: 10.29408/veles.v8i3.27700

Shah, M., Grebennikov, L., & Nair, C. S. (2015). A decade of study on employer feedback on the quality of university graduates. *Quality Assurance in Education*, *23*(3), 262–278. DOI: 10.1108/QAE-04-2014-0018

Shahzad, T., Mazhar, T., Tariq, M. U., Ahmad, W., Ouahada, K., & Hamam, H. (2025). A comprehensive review of large language models: Issues and solutions in learning environments. *Discover Sustainability*, *6*(1), 27. Advance online publication. DOI: 10.1007/s43621-025-00815-8

Sharma, S., & Dwivedi, R. (2024). A survey on blockchain deployment for biometric systems. *IET Blockchain*, *4*(2), 124–151. DOI: 10.1049/blc2.12063

Shete, S. G., Koshti, P., & Pujari, V. I. (2024, April). The Impact of AI-Powered Personalization on Academic Performance in Students. In *2024 5th International Conference on Recent Trends in Computer Science and Technology (ICRTCST)* (pp. 295-301). IEEE. DOI: 10.1109/ICRTCST61793.2024.10578480

Shezad, F., Goswami, R., Shaheen, A., & Khan, I. (2025). AI in Teacher Training and Professional Development: A Tool for Continuous Learning and Skill Enhancement. *Review of Education. Administration & Law*, *8*(1), 179–191. DOI: 10.47067/real.v8i1.416

Shihab, S. R., Sultana, N., & Samad, A. (2023). Pedagogy designing with augmented reality: A paradigm shift in educational approaches. *Interdiciplinary Journal and Hummanity*, *2*(11), 1–14.

Shin, D. (2021). The effects of explainability and causability on perception, trust, and acceptance: Implications for explainable AI. *International Journal of Human-Computer Studies*, *146*, 102551. DOI: 10.1016/j.ijhcs.2020.102551

Shin, D., & Park, Y. J. (2019). Role of fairness, Accountability, and transparency in algorithmic affordance. *Computers in Human Behavior*, *98*, 277–284. DOI: 10.1016/j.chb.2019.04.019

Shoaib, M., Sayed, N., Singh, J., Shafi, J., Khan, S., & Ali, F. (2024). AI student success predictor: Enhancing personalized learning in campus management systems. *Computers in Human Behavior*, *158*, 108301. DOI: 10.1016/j.chb.2024.108301

Shockley, K. M., Gabriel, A. S., Robertson, D., Rosen, C. C., Chawla, N., Ganster, M. L., & Ezerins, M. E. (2021). The fatiguing effects of camera use in virtual meetings: A within-person field experiment. *The Journal of Applied Psychology*, *106*(8), 1137–1155. DOI: 10.1037/apl0000948 PMID: 34423999

Shrestha, A. K., Barthwal, A., Campbell, M., Shouli, A., Syed, S., Joshi, S., & Vassileva, J. (2024). Navigating AI to unpack youth privacy concerns: An in-depth exploration and systematic review. *arXiv preprint arXiv:2412*.16369.DOI: 10.1109/IEMCON62851.2024.11093125

Shute, V. J., & Ventura, M. (2013). *Stealth assessment: Measuring and supporting learning in video games*. MIT Press.

Siddiqui, M. T., Mansoori, M. V., Siddiqui, M. A., & Yadav, A. (2025). AI-enabled pedagogy: Advancing education through innovative teaching tools and the AI-TEACH model. *Journal of Informatics Education and Research*, *5*(1), 45–62.

Siddiqui, N., Khalid, M. A., Ahmed, A., Aleem, A., Irfan, M., Ahmad, W., & Muslim, F. B. (2023). An AI-based classroom monitoring system leveraging computer vision and machine learning. *IEEE International Conference on Building and Communicating Technology*. DOI: 10.1109/IBCAST59916.2023.10713048

Siemens, G., & Long, P. (2011). Penetrating the fog: Analytics in learning and education. *EDUCAUSE Review*, *46*(5), 31–40.

Silaghi, D. L., & Popescu, D. E. (2025). A systematic review of blockchain-based initiatives in comparison to best practices used in higher education institutions. *Computers*, *14*(4), 141. DOI: 10.3390/computers14040141

Silva, G., Godwin, G., & Jayanagara, O. (2024). The Impact of AI on Personalized Learning and Educational Analytics. *International Transactions on Education Technology*, *3*(1), 36–46. DOI: 10.33050/itee.v3i1.669

SIMS. (2025, May 3). *SIMS: Streamline your school management.* https://www.sims.co.uk

Singh, R. (2018). *AI and Chatbots in Education: What Does The FutureHold?* Chatbot Magazine. https://chatbotsmagazine.com/ai-and-chatbots-in-education-what-does-the-futurehold-9772f5c13960

Singhal, M. K. (2020). Facilitating Virtual Medicinal Chemistry Active Learning Assignments Using Advanced Zoom Features during COVID-19 Campus Closure. *Journal of Chemical Education*, *97*(9), 2711–2714. DOI: 10.1021/acs.jchemed.0c00675

Singh, S., Jaiswal, R., Gupta, S., & Kumar, C. (2024). What we know and what should we know about the future of blockchain in finance. *F1000 Research*, *13*, 1051. DOI: 10.12688/f1000research.153215.1 PMID: 40520947

Smith, D., & Hullinger, J. (2024). *TIME100 CLIMATE 2024 Photo-Illustration by TIME (Source Image: Courtesy David Smith) TIME100 CLIMATE 2024.* https://time.com/7172491/david-smith/?utm_source=chatgpt.com

Smith, P. L., & Dillon, C. L. (2009). *Comparing distance learning and classroom learning: Conceptual considerations.* 13(2), 6–23. DOI: 10.1080/08923649909527020

Smith, C. (2021). Real-time emotion detection in classroom environments: Exploring the gaps in multimodal feedback. *International Journal of Human-Computer Studies*, *151*, 102580. DOI: 10.1016/j.ijhcs.2021.102580

Sobin, C., Subheesh, N. P., & Ali, J. (2023). In-class student emotion and engagement detection system (iSEEDS): An AI-based approach for responsive teaching. *IEEE Global Engineering Education Conference (EDUCON).* DOI: 10.1109/EDUCON54358.2023.10125254

Söderlund, M., & Oikarinen, E. L. (2021). Service encounters with virtual agents: An examination of perceived humanness as a source of customer satisfaction. *European Journal of Marketing*, *55*(13), 94–121. DOI: 10.1108/EJM-09-2019-0748

Song, C., & Song, Y. (2023). Enhancing academic writing skills and motivation: Assessing the efficacy of ChatGPT in AI-assisted language learning for EFL students. *Frontiers in Psychology, 14*, 1260843. DOI: 10.3389/fpsyg.2023.1260843

Song, L., Singleton, E. S., Hill, J. R., & Koh, M. H. (2004). Improving online learning: Student perceptions of useful and challenging characteristics. *The Internet and Higher Education*, *7*(1), 59–70. DOI: 10.1016/j.iheduc.2003.11.003

South Korea Ministry of Education. (2025, May 3). *e-Education: Online education and student management system.* http://www.moe.go.kr

Srivastava, M., Iranmanesh, R., Cui, Y., Gopinath, D., Sumner, E. S., Silva, A., & Sadigh, D. (2025, March). Shared Autonomy for Proximal Teaching. *In 2025, 20th ACM/IEEE International Conference on Human-Robot Interaction (HRI)* (pp. 232-241). IEEE. DOI: 10.48550/arXiv.2502.19899

Stahl, B. C., & Eke, D. (2024). The ethics of ChatGPT – Exploring the ethical issues of an emerging technology. *International Journal of Information Management, 74*, 102700. DOI: 10.1016/j.ijinfomgt.2023.102700

Stanford University. (n.d.). *Virtual Human Interaction Lab.* Stanford University. https://vhil.stanford.edu/

Stanford, N. L. P. Group. (n.d.). *Coreference resolution.* Stanford CoreNLP. https://stanfordnlp.github.io/CoreNLP/coref.html

Strielkowski, W., Grebennikova, V., Lisovskiy, A., Rakhimova, G., & Vasileva, T. (2024). AI-Driven adaptive learning for sustainable educational transformation. *Sustainable Development*. Advance online publication. DOI: 10.1002/sd.3221

Subashini, B., Shanthi, P., & Venkatesh, K. (2024). Blockchain-enabled quality assurance and traceability in the Indian confectionery market. In *2024 International Conference on Innovative Computing, Intelligent Communication and Smart Electrical Systems (ICSES)* (pp. 1–6). IEEE. DOI: 10.1109/ICSES63760.2024.10910618

Sumartono, S., Ayu, W., Sumartono, P., Akbar, W., & Rafsanjani, H. (2025). Transforming education: The impact of artificial intelligence on learning and pedagogical practices. In *Proceedings of the International Seminar Enrichment of Career by Knowledge of Language and Literature* (pp. 234-245).

Sumathy, V., & Navamani, G. (2024). AI-Driven Personalized Learning: Enhancing Student Success through Adaptive Technologies. *Library of Progress-Library Science, Information Technology & Computer, 44*(3).

Support the Guardian Fund independent journalism with $15 per month Support us Housing Real estate listing gaffe exposes widespread use of AI in Australian industry-and potential risks. (n.d.). https://www.theguardian.com/australia-news/2024/nov/12/real-estate-listing-gaffe-exposes-widespread-use-of-ai-in-australian-industry-and-potenti

Susnjak, T., Ramaswami, G. S., & Mathrani, A. (2022). Learning analytics dashboard: A tool for providing actionable insights to learners. *International Journal of Educational Technology in Higher Education*, *19*(1), 12. DOI: 10.1186/s41239-021-00313-7

Swan, K., & Ice, P. (2010). The community of inquiry framework ten years later: Introduction to the special issue. *The Internet and Higher Education*, *13*(1–2), 1–4. DOI: 10.1016/j.iheduc.2009.11.003

Sweller, J. (1988). Cognitive load during problem solving: Effects on learning. *Cognitive Science*, *12*(2), 257–285. DOI: 10.1207/s15516709cog1202_4

Tabora, L. A. T., Ampatuan, D. S. I. S., Castaneda, M. A. C., Galinato, E. J. U., & Zulueta, E. E. M. (2024, June). The Impact of Artificial Intelligence (AI) Systems on the Personalized Learning Outcomes for Senior High School Students: A Systematic Review. *In Proceedings of the 2024 10th International Conference on Frontiers of Educational Technologies* (pp. 67-74). DOI: 10.1145/3678392.3678393

Talbot, R. M., Hartley, L. M., Matzetta, K., & Wee, B. S. (2015). Transforming Undergraduate Science Education With Learning Assistants: Student Satisfaction in Large-Enrollment Courses. *Journal of College Science Teaching*, *44*(5), 24–30. DOI: 10.1080/0047231X.2015.12454809

Tanner, K. D. (2013). Structure Matters: Twenty-One Teaching Strategies to Promote Student Engagement and Cultivate Classroom Equity. *CBE Life Sciences Education*, *12*(3), 322–331. DOI: 10.1187/cbe.13-06-0115 PMID: 24006379

Tan, X., Cheng, G., & Ling, M. H. (2024). Artificial intelligence in teaching and teacher professional development: A systematic review. *Computers and Education: Artificial Intelligence*, *100355*. Advance online publication. DOI: 10.1016/j.caeai.2024.100355

Tapscott, D., & Kaplan, A. (2019). *Blockchain revolution in education and lifelong learning*. Blockchain Research Institute–IBM Institute for Business Value.

Tariq, M. U. (2025). AI and Work-Life Balance: Transforming Employee Wellbeing in the Modern Workplace. In Ahmed, E., Babar, A., Samad, A., Ahmed, R., & Beydoun, G. (Eds.), *Strengthening Human Relations in Organizations With AI* (pp. 85–110). IGI Global Scientific Publishing. DOI: 10.4018/979-8-3693-6507-6.ch004

Tariq, M. U. (2025). AI-Enhanced Project-Based Learning: Revolutionizing Commerce Education With Generative AI. In ElSayary, A. (Ed.), *Prompt Engineering and Generative AI Applications for Teaching and Learning* (pp. 125–142). IGI Global Scientific Publishing. DOI: 10.4018/979-8-3693-7332-3.ch008

Tariq, M. U. (2025). Harnessing the Power of GANs and Meta-Learning for Few-Shot Image Generation. In Simaiya, S., Lilhore, U., Sharma, Y., & Kumar, S. (Eds.), *Exploring Generative Adversarial Networks and Meta-Learning Synergies* (pp. 301–324). IGI Global Scientific Publishing. DOI: 10.4018/979-8-3693-7575-4.ch012

Tariq, M. U. (2025). Leveraging Artificial Intelligence to Enhance Diversity and Drive Business Innovation. In Margaretha van der Poll, H., Andrew van der Poll, J., & Ngwakwe, C. (Eds.), *Diversity, AI, and Sustainability for Financial Growth* (pp. 79–96). IGI Global Scientific Publishing. DOI: 10.4018/979-8-3693-6011-8.ch004

Tariq, M. U. (2025). Smart Forecasting With AI: Revolutionizing Energy Consumption and Storage. In Derbali, A. (Ed.), *Integrating Artificial Intelligence Into the Energy Sector* (pp. 165–184). IGI Global Scientific Publishing. DOI: 10.4018/979-8-3693-7112-1.ch009

Tatnall, A. (2022). Editorial for EAIT issue 5, 2022. *Education and Information Technologies*, *27*(9), 5811–5824.

Tavakoli, A., Kumar, S., Boukhechba, M., & Heydarian, A. (2021). *Driver State and Behavior Detection Through Smart Wearables*. DOI: 10.1109/IV48863.2021.9575431

TechCrunch. (2016, 11 Mei). *Startup Battlefield: Timelooper at Disrupt NY 2016*. YouTube.

Thakurta, A., Evans, D., & Vadhan, S. (2017). Learning with Privacy at Scale. *Apple Machine Learning Research*. https://machinelearning.apple.com/research/learning-with-privacy-at-scale

Thangavel, S., Sharmila, K., & Sufina, K. (2025). Revolutionizing education through augmented reality (AR) and virtual reality (VR): Innovations, challenges, and future prospects. *Asian Journal of Interdisciplinary Research*, *8*(1), 125–140.

Thanh, D. N. H., Prasath, V. B. S., Dvoenko, S., & Hieu, L. M. (2021). An adaptive image inpainting method based on euler's elastica with adaptive parameters estimation and the discrete gradient method. In *Signal Processing* (Vol. 178, p. 107797). Elsevier BV., DOI: 10.1016/j.sigpro.2020.107797

Tharayil, S., Borrego, M., Prince, M., Nguyen, K. A., Shekhar, P., Finelli, C. J., & Waters, C. (2018). Strategies to mitigate student resistance to active learning. *International Journal of STEM Education*, *5*(1), 7. DOI: 10.1186/s40594-018-0102-y PMID: 30631697

The News Desk. (2025, August 20). *Meta breaks language barriers with AI voice translation*. https://mediabrief.com/meta-breaks-language-barriers-with-ai-voice-translation/

Thorne, S. L. (2024). Generative artificial intelligence, co-evolution, and language education. *Modern Language Journal*, *108*(3), 567–572. DOI: 10.1111/modl.12932

Thüs, D., Malone, S., & Brünken, R. (2024). Exploring generative AI in higher education: A RAG system to enhance student engagement with scientific literature. *Frontiers in Psychology*, *15*, 1474892. DOI: 10.3389/fpsyg.2024.1474892 PMID: 39463458

Trabelsi, Z., Alnajjar, F., Parambil, M., Gochoo, M. E., & Ali, L. (2023). Real-time attention monitoring system for classroom: A deep learning approach for student's behavior recognition. *Big Data and Cognitive Computing*, *7*(1), 48. DOI: 10.3390/bdcc7010048

Trang, N. T. Q., National Academy of Public Administration Vietnam, Thi Thu, P., & National Academy of Public Administration Vietnam. (2024). The role of AI in improving student learning outcomes: Evidence in Vietnam. INTERNATIONAL JOURNAL OF MULTIDISCIPLINARY RESEARCH AND ANALYSIS, 07(06).

Triastcyn, A., & Faltings, B. (2019). Federated Learning with Bayesian Differential Privacy. arXiv preprint arXiv:1911.10071. https://arxiv.org/abs/1911.10071 DOI: 10.1109/BigData47090.2019.9005465

Trindade, M. A., Edirisinghe, G. S., & Luo, L. (2025). Teaching mathematical concepts in management with generative artificial intelligence: The power of human oversight in AI-driven learning. *International Journal of Management Education*, *23*(2), 101104. DOI: 10.1016/j.ijme.2024.101104

Turnitin. (n.d.). *AI checker solutions: Ensure academic integrity*. Turnitin. https://www.turnitin.com/solutions/topics/ai-writing/

Tu, Z., Zhao, K., Xu, F., Li, Y., Su, L., & Jin, D. (2018). Protecting trajectory from semantic attack considering ${k}$-anonymity, ${l}$-diversity, and ${t}$-closeness. *IEEE Transactions on Network and Service Management, 16*(1), 264–278. DOI: 10.1109/TNSM.2018.2877790

Twenge, J. M., & Campbell, W. K. (2019). Media Use Is Linked to Lower Psychological Well-Being: Evidence from Three Datasets. *The Psychiatric Quarterly, 90*(2), 311–331. DOI: 10.1007/s11126-019-09630-7 PMID: 30859387

Ullah, H., Manickam, S., Obaidat, M., Laghari, S. U. A., & Uddin, M. (2023). Exploring the potential of metaverse technology in healthcare: Applications, challenges, and future directions. *IEEE Access : Practical Innovations, Open Solutions, 11*, 69686–69707. DOI: 10.1109/access.2023.3286696

UNESCO. (2021). *AI and education: Guidance for policymakers*. UNESCO Publishing.

UNESCO. (2023), *Global Education Monitorin (GEM) Report 2020 Press release*. https://www.unesco.org/en/articles/global-education-monitoring-gem-report-2020

UNESCO. (2024, December 5). *LMS development and video interactivity*. https://www.unesco.org/en/articles/lms-development-and-video-interactivity

University of Cambridge. (2023, July). *Designing for the future: How a unique AI course is reframing professional learning*. Cambridge Advance Online. https://advanceonline.cam.ac.uk/blog/designing-for-the-future-how-a-unique-ai-course-is-reframing-professional

University of Cambridge. (n.d.). *Cambridge is shaping AI for everyone*. University of Cambridge. https://www.cam.ac.uk/ai

Vaijainthymala Krishnamoorthy, M. (2024). Data Obfuscation through Latent Space Projection (LSP) for Privacy-Preserving AI Governance: Case Studies in Medical Diagnosis and Finance Fraud Detection. arXiv preprint arXiv:2410.17459. https://arxiv.org/abs/2410.17459

Val, O. O. (2024). The role of Artificial Intelligence (AI) in enhancing cybersecurity for educational technologies in US public schools. *Asian J. Res. Com. Sci., 17*(11), 114–133. DOI: 10.9734/ajrcos/2024/v17i11523

van Bussel, M. J. P., Odekerken–Schröder, G. J., Ou, C., Swart, R. R., & Jacobs, M. J. G. (2022). Analyzing the determinants to accept a virtual assistant and use cases among cancer patients: A mixed methods study. *BMC Health Services Research, 22*(1), 890. Advance online publication. DOI: 10.1186/s12913-022-08189-7 PMID: 35804356

Van Dusen, B., & Nissen, J. (2020). Associations between learning assistants, passing introductory physics, and equity: A quantitative critical race theory investigation. *Physical Review. Physics Education Research, 16*(1), 010117. DOI: 10.1103/PhysRevPhysEducRes.16.010117

Van Heuvelen, K. M., Daub, G. W., & Ryswyk, H. V. (2020). Emergency Remote Instruction during the COVID-19 Pandemic Reshapes Collaborative Learning in General Chemistry. *Journal of Chemical Education, 97*(9), 2884–2888. DOI: 10.1021/acs.jchemed.0c00691

Vashishth, T. K., Sharma, V., Sharma, K. K., Kumar, B., Panwar, R., & Chaudhary, S. (2024). AI-driven learning analytics for personalized feedback and assessment in higher education. In *Using traditional design methods to enhance AI-driven decision making* (pp. 206–230). IGI Global Scientific Publishing. DOI: 10.4018/979-8-3693-0639-0.ch009

Verma, S., Kashive, N., & Gupta, A. (2025). Examining predictors of generative-AI acceptance and usage in academic research: A sequential mixed-methods approach. *Benchmarking*. Advance online publication. DOI: 10.1108/BIJ-07-2024-0564

Veytia Bucheli, M. G., Gómez-Galán, J., Cáceres Mesa, M. L., & López Catalán, L. (2024). Digital Technologies as enablers of universal design for learning: Higher education students' perceptions in the context of SDG4. *Discover Sustainability, 5*(1), 1–29. DOI: 10.1007/s43621-024-00699-0

Vivekanandam, B. (2021). Unstructured Noise Removal for Industrial Sensor Imaging Unit by Hybrid Adaptive Median Algorithm. In Journal of Innovative Image Processing (Vol. 3, Issue 4, pp. 284–297). Inventive Research Organization. DOI: 10.36548/jiip.2021.4.001

VMock. (n.d.). Career acceleration platform powered by artificial intelligence. https://www.vmock.com/

Vonderwell, S., & Zachariah, S. (2005). Factors that Influence Participation In Online Learning. *Journal of Research on Technology in Education, 38*(2), 213–230. DOI: 10.1080/15391523.2005.10782457

Vorobyeva, K. I., Belous, S., Savchenko, N. V., Smirnova, L. M., Nikitina, S. A., & Zhdanov, S.

Vorobyeva, K. I., Belous, S., Savchenko, N. V., Smirnova, L. M., Nikitina, S. A., & Zhdanov, S. P. (2025). Personalized learning through AI: Pedagogical approaches and critical insights. *Contemporary Educational Technology, 17*(2), ep574. DOI: 10.30935/cedtech/16108

Vreugdenhil, H., Taljaard, S., & Slinger, J. H. (2012). Pilot projects and their diffusion: A case study of integrated coastal management in South Africa. *International Journal of Sustainable Development, 15*(1–2), 148–172. DOI: 10.1504/IJSD.2012.044039

Vygotsky, L. S. (1978). *Mind in society: The development of higher psychological processes.* Harvard University Press.

Wadhwa, R., Rabby, F., Bansal, R., & Hundekari, S. (2024). Drivers and Impact of Artificial Intelligence on Student Engagement. In *AI algorithms and ChatGPT for student engagement in online learning* (pp. 161–170). IGI Global. DOI: 10.4018/979-8-3693-4268-8.ch011

Walter, Y. (2024). Embracing the future of artificial intelligence in the classroom: The relevance of AI literacy, prompt engineering, and critical thinking in modern education. *International Journal of Educational Technology in Higher Education, 21*, 18. DOI: 10.1186/s41239-024-00448-3

Walton Family Foundation. (2024). AI Chatbots in Schools. https://www.waltonfamily foundation.org/learning/the-value-of-ai-in-todays-classrooms

Wan Ismail, W. S., Awang, N. A., & Mohd Pauzi, N. (2023). An overview of the use of artificial intelligence (AI) tools in higher education. *International Journal on E-Learning and Higher Education, 19*(3), 27–40. DOI: 10.24191/ijelhe.v19n3.1932

Wan, F., Li, Z., Chen, Y. F., & Lei, C. F. (2024). Charting the Course in the Digital Transformation: Navigating the Intersection of the Hospitality Industry and Education. *Journal of Hospitality & Tourism Education*, 1–14. DOI: 10.1080/10963758.2024.2433067

Wang, J. (2024). Research on Development of Generative Artificial Intelligence. In Frontiers in Computing and Intelligent Systems (Vol. 8, Issue 1, pp. 69–74). Darcy & Roy Press Co. Ltd. DOI: 10.54097/d24rqq11

Wang, L., Chen, Y., Lin, F., Chen, Y., Yu, F., & Cai, Z. (2018). Impulse Noise Denoising Using Total Variation with Overlapping Group Sparsity and Lp-Pseudo-Norm Shrinkage. In Applied Sciences (Vol. 8, Issue 11, p. 2317). MDPI AG. DOI: 10.3390/app8112317

Wang, L., Li, S., & Chen, Y. (2024). Early Adaptation of Assessments Using Generative Artificial Intelligence and the Impact on Student Learning: A Case Study. *African Journal of Inter/Multidisciplinary Studies, 6*(1), 1-12. DOI: 10.51415/ajims.v6i1.1532

Wang, H., Dang, A., Wu, Z., & Mac, S. (2023). *Generative AI in Higher Education: Seeing ChatGPT Through Universities' Policies*. Resources, and Guidelines. DOI: 10.1016/j.caeai.2024.100326

Wang, H., Long, T., Yin, L., Zhang, W., Xia, W., Hong, Q., & Yu, Y. (2023, August). Gmocat: A graph-enhanced multi-objective method for computerized adaptive testing. In *Proceedings of the 29th ACM SIGKDD Conference on Knowledge Discovery and Data Mining* (pp. 2279-2289). DOI: 10.1145/3580305.3599367

Wang, L., Li, Y., & Zhang, Y. (2021). Eye-tracking and gaze-based analysis of student attention in classroom settings. *Educational Psychology Review*, *33*(1), 179–196. DOI: 10.1007/s10648-020-09571-3

Wang, M., Liu, X., & Yu, J. (2023). Real-time emotion detection in classroom environments for enhancing student engagement. *Journal of Educational Technology & Society*, *26*(3), 80–94. DOI: 10.1177/0261977X22114265

Wang, S., Wang, F., Zhu, Z., Wang, J., Tran, T., & Du, Z. (2024). Artificial intelligence in education: A systematic literature review. *Expert Systems with Applications*, *252*, 124167. DOI: 10.1016/j.eswa.2024.124167

Wang, Y., Liu, C., & Tu, Y.-F. (2021). Factors affecting the adoption of AI-based applications in education: A case study of Chinese higher education institutions. *Journal of Educational Technology & Society*, *24*(3), 116–129. https://www.jstor.org/stable/27032860

Wang, Y., Su, Z., Zhang, N., Xing, R., Liu, D., Luan, T. H., & Shen, X. (2022). A survey on metaverse: Fundamentals, security, and privacy. *IEEE Communications Surveys and Tutorials*, *25*(1), 319–352. DOI: 10.1109/comst.2022.3202047

Wang, Y., & Xu, W. (2023). APLDP: Adaptive Personalized Local Differential Privacy Data Collection. *Computers & Security*, *129*, 102927. DOI: 10.1016/j.cose.2023.102927

Wei, X., Wang, L., Lee, L. K., & Liu, R. (2024). Multiple generative AI pedagogical agents in augmented reality environments: A study on implementing the 5E model in science education. *Journal of Educational Computing Research*, *62*(4), 912–935.

Wen, B., van Rensburg, H., O'Neill, S., & Attwood, T. (2024). Autism and neurodiversity in the workplace: A scoping review of key trends, employer roles, interventions and supports. *Journal of Vocational Rehabilitation*, *60*(1), 121–140. DOI: 10.3233/JVR-230060

Wenzel, T. (2020). Collaborative Group Learning in Remotely Taught Analytical Chemistry Courses. *Journal of Chemical Education*, *97*(9), 2715–2718. DOI: 10.1021/acs.jchemed.0c00520

Werquin, P. (2012). The missing link to connect education and employment: Recognition of non-formal and informal learning outcomes. *Journal of Education and Work*, *25*(3), 259–278. DOI: 10.1080/13639080.2012.687574

Wester, E. R., Walsh, L. L., Arango-Caro, S., & Callis-Duehl, K. L. (2021). Student Engagement Declines in STEM Undergraduates during COVID-19–Driven Remote Learning. *Journal of Microbiology & Biology Education*, 22(1), ev22i1.2385. DOI: 10.1128/jmbe.v22i1.2385

Western Governors University. (n.d.). *Competency-based education: A new way to learn*. WGU. https://www.wgu.edu/about/story/cbe.html

Whiles, G. (2025, August 26). *Grammarly plagiarism checker review*. Originality. AI. https://originality.ai/blog/grammarly-plagiarism-checker-review

Wiboolyasarin, W., Wiboolyasarin, K., Tiranant, P., Jinowat, N., & Boonyakitanont, P. (2025). AI-driven chatbots in second language education: A systematic review of their efficacy and pedagogical implications. In *Ampersand* (Vol. 14). Elsevier Ltd. DOI: 10.1016/j.amper.2025.100224

Wijekumar, K. K., Lei, P., Rice, M., Beerwinkle, A., Zhang, S., & Meyer, B. J. (2024). A web-based intelligent tutoring system for reading comprehension delivered to fifth-grade students attending high-poverty schools: Results from a replication efficacy study. *Journal of Educational Psychology*, *116*(8), 1333–1351. Advance online publication. DOI: 10.1037/edu0000878

Williamson, B. (2021). The social life of AI in education. *Learning, Media and Technology*, *46*(3), 306–319.

Williamson, B., & Eynon, R. (2020). Historical threads, missing links, and future directions in AI in education. *Learning, Media and Technology*, *45*(3), 223–235. DOI: 10.1080/17439884.2020.1798995

Wilma. (2025, May 3). *Wilma: Online communication and student management platform*. https://www.wilma.com

Wise, A. F., Saghafian, M., & Padmanabhan, P. (2012). Towards more precise design guidance: Specifying and testing the functions of assigned student roles in online discussions. *Educational Technology Research and Development*, *60*(1), 55–82. DOI: 10.1007/s11423-011-9212-7

Wong, J. M. S., Tang, W. K. W., & Li, K. C. (2025). Digital transformation in higher education: Tertiary students' perspectives on online learning and its implications for the future. *International Journal of Innovation and Learning*, *37*(5), 1–18. DOI: 10.1504/IJIL.2025.144600

Woodbury, J., Arneson, J. B., & Offerdahl, E. G. (2022). Adapting Team-Based Learning for an Online Biochemistry Course. *Journal of Chemical Education*, *99*(8), 2964–2971. DOI: 10.1021/acs.jchemed.2c00259

Woolf, B. P. (2010). *Building Intelligent Interactive Tutors: Student-Centered Strategies for Revolutionizing E-learning*. Morgan Kaufmann.

World Economic Forum. (2024). *Shaping the future of learning: The role of AI in Education 4.0* [Insight report]. World Economic Forum. https://www3.weforum.org/docs/WEF_Shaping_the_Future_of_Learning_2024.pdf

Wu, H., He, Y., Chen, Y., Li, S., & Peng, Z. (2020). Seismic Acoustic Impedance Inversion Using Mixed Second-Order Fractional ATpV Regularization. In IEEE Access (Vol. 8, pp. 3442–3452). Institute of Electrical and Electronics Engineers (IEEE). DOI: 10.1109/ACCESS.2019.2962552

Wu, J. (2024). Modeling Personalized Smart Teaching for Learner Needs. *Applied Mathematics and Nonlinear Sciences.*, *9*(1), 1–18. DOI: 10.2478/amns-2024-1384

Xiao, Y., Xiong, L., Fan, L., & Goryczka, S. (2012). DPCube: Differentially private histogram release through multidimensional partitioning. *arXiv preprint arXiv:1202.5358*

Xiao, Y., Zhang, N., Lou, W., & Hou, Y. T. (2020). A survey of distributed consensus protocols for blockchain networks. *IEEE Communications Surveys and Tutorials*, *22*(2), 1432–1465. DOI: 10.1109/COMST.2020.2969706

Xia, Q., Weng, X., Ouyang, F., Lin, T. J., & Chiu, T. K. (2024). A scoping review on how generative artificial intelligence transforms assessment in higher education. *International Journal of Educational Technology in Higher Education*, *21*(1), 40. DOI: 10.1186/s41239-024-00468-z

Xie, X., Yang, D., & Wang, F. (2021). Multimodal emotion detection systems in education: A survey. *Computers & Education*, *164*, 104105. DOI: 10.1016/j.compedu.2020.104105

Xu, X., Zhao, F., & Lee, W. (2020). Emotion recognition in classroom environments: A comparative study using facial expression and speech. *Journal of Educational Psychology*, *112*(6), 1056–1067. DOI: 10.1037/edu0000402

Xu, Z. (2024). AI in education: Enhancing learning experiences and student outcomes. *Applied and Computational Engineering*, *51*(1), 104–111. DOI: 10.54254/2755-2721/51/20241187

Yakhina, R., Grigorieva, K., Batrova, N., & Lukoyanova, M. (2024). AI-Powered Tools For Enhancing Engagement And Academic Performance Of Engineering Students. In *INTED2024 Proceedings* (pp. 2990-2996). IATED. DOI: 10.21125/inted.2024.0809

Yamamoto, K., Thomas, E. C., & Karns, E. A. (1969). School-related attitudes in middleschool-age students. *American Educational Research Journal*, *6*(2), 191–206. DOI: 10.3102/00028312006002191

Yang, Z. Q., Cao, J., Li, X., Wang, K., Zheng, X., Poon, K. C. F., & Lai, D. (2024, June). DMP_AI: An AI-Aided K-12 System for Teaching and Learning in Diverse Schools. In *International Conference on Blended Learning* (pp. 117-130). Singapore: Springer Nature Singapore. DOI: 10.1007/978-981-97-4442-8_9

Yang, J.-H., Zhao, X.-L., Ji, T.-Y., Ma, T.-H., & Huang, T.-Z. (2020). Low-rank tensor train for tensor robust principal component analysis. In *Applied Mathematics and Computation* (Vol. 367, p. 124783). Elsevier BV., DOI: 10.1016/j.amc.2019.124783

Yang, L., Zhang, Y., Liu, W., & Chen, X. (2025). Interoperability of the metaverse: A digital ecosystem perspective review. *IEEE Engineering Management Review*, *53*(3), 29–54. DOI: 10.1109/EMR.2025.3564923

Yang, S., & Evans, C. (2019). Opportunities and challenges in using AI chatbots in higher education. *ACM International Conference Proceeding Series*, 79–83. DOI: 10.1145/3371647.3371659

Yang, Y., Chen, J., & Zhuang, X. (2025). Self-determination theory and the influence of social support, self-regulated learning, and flow experience on student learning engagement in self-directed e-learning. *Frontiers in Psychology*, *16*, 1545980. DOI: 10.3389/fpsyg.2025.1545980 PMID: 40207130

Yaseen, H., Mohammad, A. S., Ashal, N., Abusaimeh, H., Ali, A., & Sharabati, A.-A. A. (2025). The Impact of Adaptive Learning Technologies, Personalized Feedback, and Interactive AI Tools on Student Engagement: *The Moderating Role of Digital Literacy. Sustainability (Basel)*, *17*(3), 1133. DOI: 10.3390/su17031133

Ye, Q., & Hu, H. (2020, January). Local differential privacy: Tools, challenges, and opportunities. In *International Conference on Web Information Systems Engineering* (pp. 13-23). Singapore: Springer Singapore. DOI: 10.1007/978-981-15-3281-8_2

Yenduri, G., Ramalingam, M., Selvi, G. C., Supriya, Y., Srivastava, G., Maddikunta, P. K. R., Raj, G. D., Jhaveri, R. H., Prabadevi, B., Wang, W., Vasilakos, A. V., & Gadekallu, T. R. (2024). GPT (generative pre-trained transformer)—A comprehensive review on enabling technologies, potential applications, emerging challenges, and future directions. *IEEE Access : Practical Innovations, Open Solutions, 12*, 54608–54649. DOI: 10.1109/access.2024.3389497

Yim, I. H. Y., & Wegerif, R. (2024). *Teachers' perceptions, attitudes, and acceptance of artificial intelligence (AI) educational learning tools: An exploratory study on AI literacy for young students*. Future in Educational Research.

Yu, L., & Hou, J. (2018). Large-Screen Interactive Imaging System with Switching Federated Filter Method Based on 3D Sensor. In Complexity (Vol. 2018, pp. 1–11). Hindawi Limited. DOI: 10.1155/2018/8730281

Yu, E. (2023). Detecting AI-generated text: Evaluating the reliability of current models. *Journal of AI Ethics*, *5*(1), 22–34.

Yusuf, A., Pervin, N., Román-González, M., & Noor, N. M. (2024). Generative AI in education and research: A systematic mapping review. In *Review of Education* (Vol. 12, Issue 2). John Wiley and Sons Inc. DOI: 10.1002/rev3.3489

Zagorchev, L., & Goshtasby, A. (2006). A comparative study of transformation functions for nonrigid image registration. In IEEE Transactions on Image Processing (Vol. 15, Issue 3, pp. 529–538). Institute of Electrical and Electronics Engineers (IEEE). DOI: 10.1109/TIP.2005.863114

Zapata, L. I. V., Acosta Enriquez, B. G., Montes Ninaquispe, J. C., Ruiz Carrillo, J. A., Villarreal Gonzales, L. S., Morales, J. A., & Sevilla Angelaths, M. A. (2024). Employment of generative artificial intelligence in classroom environments to improve financial education in secondary school students. *Acad. J. Interdiscip. Stud.*, *13*(3), 121. DOI: 10.36941/ajis-2024-0069

Zawacki-Richter, O., Marín, V. I., Bond, M., & Gouverneur, F. (2019). Systematic review of research on artificial intelligence applications in higher education – where are the educators? *International Journal of Educational Technology in Higher Education*, *16*(1), 39. DOI: 10.1186/s41239-019-0171-0

Zawacki-Richter, O., Marín, V. I., Bond, M., & Gouverneur, F. (2020). Systematic review of research on artificial intelligence applications in higher education. *International Journal of Educational Technology in Higher Education*, *17*(1), 1–27.

Zeide, E., & Nissenbaum, H. (2018). Learner privacy in MOOCs and virtual education. *Theory and Research in Education*, *16*(3), 280–307. DOI: 10.1177/1477878518815340

Zhai, G., & Min, X. (2020). Perceptual image quality assessment: a survey. In Science China Information Sciences (Vol. 63, Issue 11). Springer Science and Business Media LLC. DOI: 10.1007/s11432-019-2757-1

Zhang, A., Man, J., Sun, Q., & Liu, Y. (2020). Blockchain-based life cycle assessment: An implementation framework and system architecture. *Resources, Conservation and Recycling*, *152*, 104512. DOI: 10.1016/j.resconrec.2019.104512

Zhang, J., & Zhang, Z. (2024). AI in teacher education: Unlocking new dimensions in teaching support, inclusive learning, and digital literacy. *Journal of Computer Assisted Learning*, *40*(4), 1871–1885. DOI: 10.1111/jcal.12988

Zhang, K., & Aslan, A. B. (2021). AI technologies for education: Recent research & future directions. *Computers and Education: Artificial Intelligence*, *2*, 100025. DOI: 10.1016/j.caeai.2021.100025

Zhang, Y. (2025). Study on comprehensive management of online learning resources for digital education and teaching reform. *International Journal of Networking and Virtual Organisations*, *32*(1-4), 36–48. DOI: 10.1504/IJNVO.2025.145364

Zhou, B., & Pei, J. (2011). The k-anonymity and l-diversity approaches for privacy preservation in social networks against neighborhood attacks. *Knowledge and Information Systems*, *28*(1), 47–77. DOI: 10.1007/s10115-010-0311-2

Zhou, J., Yu, H., & Xu, B. (2019). An eye-tracking study on the usability of educational apps for children with autism. *Behaviour & Information Technology*, *38*(1), 1–13.

Zhou, S., Li, Y., & Zhao, Z. (2021). Computer vision and artificial intelligence for detecting student engagement in the classroom: A review. *Journal of Educational Technology Systems*, *49*(3), 348–369. DOI: 10.1177/00472395211041703

Zhou, W., Zhang, D., Han, G., Zhu, W., & Wang, X. (2023). A Blockchain-Based Privacy-Preserving and Fair Data Transaction Model in IoT. *Applied Sciences (Basel, Switzerland)*, *13*(22), 12389. DOI: 10.3390/app132212389

Zhu, T., Li, G., Zhou, W., & Philip, S. Y. (2017). *Differential privacy and applications*. Springer International Publishing. DOI: 10.1007/978-3-319-62004-6

Zook, M. A., & Blankenship, J. (2018). New spaces of disruption? The failures of Bitcoin and the rhetorical power of algorithmic governance. *Geoforum*, *96*, 248–255. DOI: 10.1016/j.geoforum.2018.08.023

Zulfiqar, S., Sarwar, B., Huo, C., Zhao, X., & ul Mahasbi, H. (2025). AI-powered education: Driving entrepreneurial spirit among university students. *International Journal of Management Education*, *23*(2), 101106. DOI: 10.1016/j.ijme.2024.101106

About the Contributors

Jeffrey Moore is Professor of Management and disability intelligence researcher at Anderson University, South Carolina. Raised in France, he earned his PhD from the University of Nice Sophia-Antipolis (IAE). His work focuses on transforming organizational cultures through complexity leadership and employing people with disabilities. He leads Anderson University's research team, partnering with Walgreens and Sephora on disability employment practices. He has authored book chapters (2017, 2019, 2023) and published in AMLE, JMD, and ODJ. Dr. Moore was keynote at Handong Global University–UNAI (2022, South Korea) on enterprises embracing disability inclusion. Awards include Best Paper (2019 Dutch HRM Network) and AOM's Outstanding Scholar-Practitioner Collaboration (2015). For 20 years, he has worked with manufacturing firms and distribution centers, uniquely collaborating with Walgreens, Sephora, and Dollar Tree on inclusive teams.

Sharad Gupta is a seasoned educator and corporate trainer with over two decades of experience in academia, research, and professional development. He is currently pursuing a Ph.D. focused on Blockchain-enabled Employee Life Cycle Frameworks at CHRIST (Deemed to be University), India. He holds an e-Diploma in CORe from Harvard Business School, along with advanced degrees in Education (M.Ed.), Commerce (M.Com.), and an MBA in Marketing and Finance. Dr. Gupta serves as an Assistant Professor at CHRIST (Deemed to be University), Pune Lavasa Campus, where he specializes in Human Resource Management, Leadership Development, and Corporate Strategy. He has held key administrative roles, including Convener of the Institution Innovation Council, fostering innovation and entrepreneurial growth. With international teaching experience in Malaysia and the Maldives, he has guided MBA, Ph.D., and Professional Doctorate students across culturally diverse environments. Dr. Gupta has co-authored several books, including Innovative Pedagogy: A Beginner's Guide to Modern Teaching Strategies and WealthWise: Lessons from India's Warren Buffett. His research contributions extend to journals and conferences, focusing on HR analytics, AI in education, and blockchain applications. Recognized for his expertise in instructional design, Dr. Gupta has developed e-learning modules, designed corporate training programs, and managed digital learning platforms during his tenure with leading organizations like Bajaj Housing Finance and ICICI Bank. He brings a unique blend of academic rigor and industry acumen, making impactful contributions to both fields. Dr. Gupta continues to innovate in education and research, bridging the gap between academic theories and real-world applications, and inspiring the next generation of learners and leaders.

Manjari Sharma is an Associate Professor at CHRIST (Deemed to be University), Pune Lavasa Campus, India. She earned her Ph.D. in Economic Administration and Financial Management from the University of Rajasthan, India, in 2014. She also holds an MBA in Finance and Marketing and an M.Com. in Economic Administration and Financial Management. With over 15 years of experience in academia across diverse geographical locations, including India, Malaysia, and the Maldives, Dr. Sharma has contributed extensively to education and research. Her areas of expertise include Managerial Economics, Securities Analysis, Portfolio Management, Financial Modeling, and Design Thinking. She has guided numerous undergraduate, postgraduate, and doctoral students, emphasizing practical applications and innovative pedagogies. Dr. Sharma has co-authored multiple books, such as Innovative Pedagogy: A Beginner's Guide to Modern Teaching Strategies and WealthWise: Lessons from India's Warren Buffett. She has published widely on topics like AI in education, stock market behavior, and sustainable business practices, contributing to journals and presenting at international conferences. In addition to her academic pursuits, Dr. Sharma has held several administrative roles, including Campus Level Coordinator for Immersion and Exchange Programs, Research Committee Member, and Co-Convener for International Conferences. Her commitment to interdisciplinary research, experiential learning, and global academic collaboration has significantly influenced her teaching and research methodologies. Dr. Sharma continues to innovate in higher education, bridging the gap between theory and practice, and is dedicated to mentoring the next generation of scholars and professionals.

Ajay Garg, a name associated with researches and innovations, a name that tasted success in everything it looked upon. Born on 2nd Feb 1987, Ajay has seen quite a feat in his career at an early stage and setting a model for so many aspirants of success in their life. His one of the greatest achievements was the development of the Magic Technology that was highly appreciated by former President of India, Late Dr. A.P.J Abdul Kalam and getting his appreciation itself means a world.

Ajay is a research scholar and has published various research papers at national and international conferences. Also he has bagged many awards and won many technical competitions during his academic phase. He has worked with ETH Research Lab as a Research Assistant to Padmabhushan Dr. Vijay Bhatkar (father of India's first Super Computer). He has been an active volunteer for Honey Bee Network and SRISTI. Also he is a creator of the Techpedia under the leadership of Padmashree Dr. Anil Gupta (Professor, IIM Ahmedabad). Ajay has joined his hands with Dr. Ganesh Natarajan(Former Vice Chairman & CEO- Zensar Technologies) for a social cause in an NGO for nurturing India's best talent award by awarding innovative projects of students and creating a product based startups. He has been a mentor for multiple startups. Presently, he is associated with Big 4, Ernest and Young as a Manager, FRSM.

Helen Josephine V L is an Associate Professor specializing in Business Analytics at the School of Business and Management, Christ University, Bangalore. With over 27 years of combined academic and industry experience, she began her career as a software engineer, working in reputed companies across India and Singapore. She transitioned to academia after 12 years in the software industry and has since accumulated 15 years of teaching experience in engineering colleges and universities. Dr. Helen holds an MCA from St. Joseph's College, Bharathidasan University, and M.Phil and Ph.D. degrees from Bharathiar University. She also completed MBA – Operations and supply chain management at Pondicherry University. Her teaching expertise spans a wide range of subjects, including Business Analytics, and Data Science courses, Machine Learning, Deep Learning, Cloud Computing, Internet of Things, She is also proficient in various programming languages, such as Python, R, Java, C++, and more. Dr. Helen's research focuses on applying artificial intelligence, machine learning, and natural language processing to solve real-world business problems, with particular interest in recommender systems and sentiment analysis. An active researcher, Dr. Helen has more than 20 publications in Web of Science and Scopus indexed journals, and she has authored several book chapters. She has published nine patents in the fields of AI and IoT and serves as a Ph.D. supervisor under Visvesvaraya Technological University and Christ University. She has been involved in multiple projects, including a 20-lakh ICSSR project, and is a reviewer for several prestigious journals. Dr. Helen's extensive industry and academic background make her a key contributor to both education and research.

***

Kanaga Prasath B is currently pursuing Bachelor's Degree in Adhi College of Engineering and Technology Kancheepuram.

Arnold Z. Catipay is an educator, curator, and academic librarian committed to advancing inclusive and joyful learning. He currently serves as the Head Librarian and also holds a teaching position at Sultan Kudarat State University, where he combines academic librarianship and instruction to promote access to quality education and lifelong learning. Mr. Catipay has completed the academic requirements for the Doctor of Philosophy in Technology Education Management at the University of Southern Mindanao – Kidapawan City Campus. He holds a Master in Library Science, major in Library and Information Management Science, from Universidad de Zamboanga, and a Bachelor of Secondary Education, major in Library Science, from Notre Dame University – Cotabato City. A member of the Philippine Librarians Association, he has also served as Director of American Spaces Jolo and as Regional Sending Coordinator for the Kennedy-Lugar Youth Exchange and Study (YES) Program – Sulu Chapter. He is a passionate advocate of literacy and community engagement, and the founder of Tuklas BookLAT and Bangka ng mga Pangarap—mobile storytelling caravans that bring books and read-aloud sessions to underprivileged and remote communities.

Donald A. Cogo is an Assistant Professor at Sultan Kudarat State University, specializing in Filipino language and literature. He has completed the academic requirements for a Doctor of Philosophy in Education, major in Filipino, at the University of Southern Mindanao. He also holds a Master of Arts in Education, major in Filipino, from St. Michael's College, Iligan City, and a Bachelor of Secondary Education, major in Filipino, from Sultan Kudarat State University. A licensed professional teacher, Cogo is also a literary writer whose works have been featured in various journals, including Kusina ng Talinhaga. His research contributions have been recognized and registered with the Intellectual Property Office of the Philippines (IPOPHIL) as a co-author. Beyond academia, he serves as the provincial coordinator of Samahan ng mga Guro at Iba Pang Propesyonal sa Wika Inc. (SAGIP-WIKA). Passionate about preserving and promoting Filipino literature, he actively engages in community initiatives, conducting workshops for aspiring writers and delivering lectures on the significance of Filipino cultural narratives.

Anusga G. is an Asst.professor with the Department of Computer Science and Engineering at AIML, Sreenidhi Institute of Science and Technology, Hyderabad, Telangana, India.

Oindrilla Ghosh is a Research Scholar hailing from the School of Law at Christ (Deemed to be University) Bangalore, India, who focuses her research on the health of tribal communities. Her work includes total 20 publications on Neuroscience on Organizational Behavior at IGI Global and also Environmental Disasters that are indexed in SCOPUS and Web of Sciences conference proceedings. She completed her early education at Loreto Day School, Bowbazar, and achieved distinction in her undergraduate (B.A/LL.B) and postgraduate (LL.M) studies at Calcutta University. Having served as an Assistant Professor of Law at Kingston Law College, Barasat, Kolkata, Ghosh has actively participated in numerous National Conferences, International Conferences, UN Global Summits, webinars, and seminars organized by prestigious academic institutions. Her expertise lies in health perspectives, environmental studies, human behavior, and related areas. Additionally, she has conducted various workshops and lectures in educational institutions, and is engaged with NGO's to help the needy

Pawan Kr. Goel is an accomplished academician and researcher with 19.5 years of experience, is an Associate Professor at Raj Kumar Goel Institute of Technology, Ghaziabad. He holds a Ph.D. in Computer Science Engineering and is UGC NET qualified. His expertise spans various domains, including wireless sensor networks, cloud computing, and artificial intelligence. Dr. Goel has published extensively in prestigious journals and conferences, with notable papers on topics such as cybersecurity, IoT, and machine learning. He is an active member of numerous professional bodies, including the IEEE, Computer Society of India and the International Association of Engineers. Recognized for his contributions, he has received several awards and certificates of appreciation. Dr. Goel is dedicated to fostering industry-academia collaborations and has organized numerous workshops and seminars. He is also involved in various training programs, MOOCs, and NPTEL certifications, contributing significantly to the advancement of education and research in his field.

Shashank Gupta is an impact-driven software professional in data science and machine learning in the Fintech industry. He aspires to solve real-world problems using state-of-the-art techniques like machine learning, deep learning, and data science, and perform at his best level to showcase the potential in the workplace for collective betterment. He has been working as Director at Morgan Stanley since 2019 and has prior experience working with Dell and Chegg India. He holds a Diploma in Artificial Intelligence and Machine Learning (DAIML) from the University of Hyderabad (UoH) and a Master of Computer Application (MCA) from GLA University. His interest lies in finance, machine learning, risk management, compliance, and governance..

Ila Gupta, has completed a Master of Technology (M.Tech.) in VLSI Design and hold a Bachelor of Education (B.Ed.) degree. Currently, she is working as an Assistant Teacher in the Basic Education Department. With a strong academic background in both advanced technology and education, she is passionate about combining technical knowledge with effective teaching methodologies to create an engaging and impactful learning environment for students. Her goal is to contribute positively to the education sector by inspiring young learners and supporting their academic growth.

Rachana Jaiswal is an Assistant Professor in the Department of Business Management, School of Management, HNB Garhwal (A Central) University, Srinagar, Uttarakhand, India. Prior to joining HNB Garhwal University in 2012, she held academic positions at the Central University of Jharkhand (CUJ) and the University of Pune. She holds a Ph.D. (2022), is UGC-JRF qualified (2011), and holds an MBA (2011) from the University of Pune and an M.Com (2008) from Banaras Hindu University (BHU). She is currently pursuing the final stage of the CMA qualification. Dr. Jaiswal has guided over 60 postgraduate students and is presently supervising three Ph.D. scholars. She has authored more than 35 research papers and 30 book chapters in reputed journals and edited volumes, and has received ten best paper awards. She has also presented over 80 research papers at national and international conferences. Her research interests lie at the intersection of finance, human capital, and applied machine learning.

Helen Josephine V.L. is an Associate Professor at Christ University, Bangalore, and Co-Investigator of an ICSSR (Indian Council for Social Science Research) funded project that informed her chapter in this book. She has over 31 publications in Scopus/Web of Science journals, more than 10 patents in IoT and AI, and several book chapters. Her research focuses on machine learning and NLP in business, particularly recommender systems. A visiting researcher at Anderson University, USA, she actively mentors scholars and contributes to boards, journal reviews, and national and international forums.

Justin Joy, Associate Professor at the School of Business and Management, Bangalore Campus, brings a wealth of expertise in the fields of technology integration and educational innovation. His research primarily focuses on enhancing learning management systems and advancing automation in academic settings. Notable funded research includes the development of a framework for implementing Learning Management Systems in Karnataka's government schools, sponsored by ICSSR, India. Dr. Joy has contributed extensively to academic literature, with articles published in esteemed journals and book chapters. He holds multiple patents, including innovations in IoT-enabled systems and real-time engagement monitoring. His consultancy work spans LMS implementation, faculty development, and timetable management, showcasing his commitment to practical educational solutions. Dr. Joy is also an active speaker, having delivered keynote addresses on ethics in AI and conducted various training programs, including a prominent leadership workshop and several faculty development initiatives. His multifaceted contributions reflect his dedication to advancing both technology and education.

Vinay Kumar Kasula has a Master's in Technology from Osmania University, followed by a second Master's from Northwest Missouri State University. His academic journey has been driven by a deep-rooted interest in research and advanced technologies. This passion led him to pursue and complete a Ph.D. at the University of the Cumberlands, where he graduated in 2024, focusing on areas including Blockchain, Artificial Intelligence, Deep Learning, Machine Learning, Data Analytics, and Cybersecurity. With over a decade of industry experience, currently as a Senior Systems Analyst, he has applied and expanded his expertise in these domains, continually exploring and integrating innovative solutions to meet evolving technological challenges. This blend of education, research, and practical experience fueled his commitment to advancements in these cutting-edge fields.

Bhargavi Konda works as a senior systems analyst in the human resources information systems department for a healthcare company. She mainly works with data analysis and generates reports for various departments in the organization. She has been one of the major contributors in maintaining employee records, supporting all HR departments, and especially working with payroll operations from her team. She earned her master's degree from Osmania University (2001-2004). She received the gold medal and Star Student of the Year awards for her outstanding performance. She was placed in an IT consulting company right after her master's, and she worked as an Oracle technical consultant from 2004 to 2012. In that period, she was awarded the Outstanding Trainer award for her commitment and dedication. She has experience implementing applications in the banking and manufacturing sectors. She was passionate about higher studies, so she started to pursue a Ph.D. in IT in 2019. She earned a Ph.D. degree in Information Technology in the year 2024 from the University of the Cumberlands. She is excited to work on many journals and publications in the future and wants to continue her research.

Binod Kumar is a graduate student known for his academic excellence, with his total 15 scholarly works indexed in Scopus database on Neuroscience in Organizational Behavior, Neuromarketing and AI Applications on Wildlife Conservation. Hailing from Ranchi, Jharkhand in India, Binod is currently pursuing a

Master of Laws (LL.M) at the prestigious Radha Govind University. His passion for technology and innovation along with climate changes is evident through his high academic performance and numerous projects. Binod has a keen interest in artificial intelligence, machine learning, neuropsychology, climate changes and disaster management, fields in which he has undertaken several research projects. He is particularly fascinated by the potential of AI to solve real-world problems and is dedicated to learning and applying new techniques in these areas. He volunteers at local NGOs, teaching underprivileged children basic computer skills. With a strong foundation in law and a commitment to making a positive impact, Binod Kumar is poised to become a future leader in the legal industry.

Zokir Mamadiyarov is a professor working in the Department of Finance and Tourism at Termez University of Economics and Service, Termez, Uzbekistan.

Shibu K. Mani is a Professor in Civil Engineering at the School of Engineering and Technology, CHRIST (Deemed to be University), Bengaluru, India. With over 20 years of experience in the field of Disaster and Safety Science, his research interests focus on interdisciplinary approaches to Safety and Disaster Management, emphasizing safety, disaster recovery, and governance. He is particularly dedicated to community-based disaster risk reduction. Dr. Mani has authored more than 25 journal publications, many of which address critical issues and case studies in disaster management. He is also the Co-Investigator of the funded ICSSR (Indian Council for Social Science Research) Project that enabled the insights for the chapter written for this book.

Ajay Krishna Manoj, Data Scientist with 6+ years of experience in converting raw data into actionable insights. Extensively applied statistical techniques/machine learning algorithms, LLMs and now Generative AI to solve real-world business problems in E-Commerce. Driven by the joy of testing hypotheses and interpreting data.

Grace Joy T. Millendez is professor, coach and mentor whose specialization is in the field of information technology. She finished her Master in Information Technology at Notre Dame of Marbel University, Koronadal City. Being a moderator, she combines her skills and ability in teaching and molding the minds and intelligences of today's genre. She serves as the Gender and Development Coordinator of Sultan Kudarat State University-Kalamansig Campus. She was also one of the members of the Committee on crafting of the policies and guidelines for the Childminding and Breastfeeding Facility official handbook of the said university.

Rajasshrie Pillai completed her Post-doctoral degree from IIT Kharagpur and PhD in management. She is a Professor at Chandragupt Institute of Business Management, Panta. She is a life member of the National HRD Network(NHRDN), India, and the Indian Society of Training and Development (ISTD). Her research interests are technology adoption, human resource management, and consumer behaviour. Her research has been published in journals such as: Information Technology and People, International Journal of Hospitality Management, Journal of Retailing and Consumer Services, Production Planning and Control, Journal of Business Research and Technovation. She has rich experience of twenty years in teaching, research, and administration.

Ramya R. completed her B.E and M.E degree in Computer science and engineering. She had 14 years of teaching experience in various Engineering colleges. She did PhD in computer science and engineering and published many articles and book chapters in her domain. She specialises in edge computing, cloud computing, Machine learning, artificial intelligence, Quality of services and resource management.

Ravikumar R. Natarajan is an experienced academician with over 12+ years of teaching and research expertise across institutions in India, the UAE, and the Maldives. He currently serves as an Assistant Professor at Marwadi University, Rajkot, specializing in Machine Learning, Recommender Systems, and AI-driven applications in healthcare and security. He holds a Ph.D. in Machine Learning and Recommender Systems from Amity University, Jaipur, a Master of Engineering in CSE from VMRF University, Salem, and a Bachelor of Engineering in CSE from Anna University. He also has a MiniMBA from the Swiss eLearning Institute. Dr. Ravikumar has authored more than 8+ multiple SCIE/Scopus-indexed journal articles, 25+ IEEE/Springer conference papers, and co-authored a book on Artificial Intelligence. He has also published 9 patents and contributed 10+ book chapters in emerging domains such as Federated Learning, Blockchain, and Digital Twins for IGI Global, Wiley and Springer publisher. He actively mentors students through initiatives like the Research Activities Club (RAC) and Student Research Internship Training (SRIT), promoting innovation and research culture.

Pallavi Rajan is a student with the Department of Computer Science and Engineering at AIML, Sreenidhi Institute of Science and Technology, Hyderabad, Telangana, India.

Feruza Ruzimova is working in the Department of Pedagogy and Psychology, Urgench State University, Urgench, Uzbekistan

Aarthi S is a dedicated Assistant Professor in Computer Science with over six years of teaching experience. She is currently pursuing her Ph.D. at Marwadi University, Gujarat, and holds an M.Phil. and MCA from Bharathiar University, Tamil Nadu. Throughout her academic career, Aarthi has specialized in programming languages such as C++, Java, and C, and contributed to research in recommender systems and AI-related data privacy. She has published journal articles, contributed to book chapters, and actively participated in technical workshops. Known for her student mentorship and engagement in academic events, Aarthi remains committed to fostering innovation and excellence in computer science education.

Fahad Salendab is a scholar and leader in the field of higher education, holding a Ph.D. in Educational Administration. As a Licensed Professional Teacher and Associate Professor, he has dedicated his career to advancing the quality of education through research, teaching, and leadership. A multi-awarded faculty member, Dr. Salendab is recognized for his outstanding contributions to education, research, and institutional development. He is a registered author with the National Book Development Board (NBDB). His commitment to research is further reflected in his role as an Associate Member of the DOST–National Research Council of the Philippines, where he collaborates on initiatives that address critical issues in education and development. He also serves as an editorial board member for various national and international research journals, contributing to the advancement of scholarly publishing and peer-reviewed academic discourse. As an active participant in accreditation processes, Dr. Salendab ensures the continuous improvement of academic programs, demonstrating his dedication to quality assurance and institutional growth.

N Santhoshi is an Asst.professor with the Department of Computer Science and Engineering at AIML, Sreenidhi Institute of Science and Technology, Hyderabad, Telangana, India.

Jude Sebastian is a research assistant at Christ University and works for the ICSSR project that was inspirational in generating the insights for the submitted chapter. He has a post graduation from Cochin University, Kerala, India.

Brijesh Sivathanu, Ph.D.in Business Management and Administration is working as a Professor in the School of Business and Management, Christ University, Bengaluru, Karnataka, India. He is a life member of All India Management Association (AIMA), Computer Society of India (CSI), Indian Society for Technology Education (ISTE), Indian Commerce Association (ICA), Indian Science Congress Association (ISCA) and Analytics Society of India (ASI). His current research interests include marketing, business analytics, information systems, technology adoption, emerging technologies such as GenAI, AI, IoT and its applications across various industries. His research work has been published in international journals of repute indexed in ABDC, SSCI, SCI, WoS and Scopus. He features in the elite list of the top 2% of scientists worldwide in Business and Management for the third consecutive year in succession (2022, 2023, and 2024), as recognized by Stanford University and Elsevier. He has as a rich work experience of more than two decades in teaching, research and administration.

Praveen Kumar T presently joined MAHE School of Business, Dubai Campus, UAE as Assistant Professor and was working as an Associate Professor in the School of Business and Management, Christ (Deemed to be University), Bangalore. Graduated with BTech in Textile Technology (University rank holder) and ME(QEM) (University rank holder) From CEG, and holds a Master's and Doctorate in Management. He has academic and corporate experience of 15 years. He has presented 25 papers at national and international conferences and participated in 20 FDPs. Published more than 20 Research articles in Indexed Journals. Having expertise in Research, Data analytics, Innovative teaching andragogy and Outcome based education implementation. Acting as a consultant for NAAC, NBA and AACSB and other international accreditation process implementation for various engineering and management institutions

Venkat T is a professor and Head of the Department of Computer Science and Engineering at AIML, Sreenidhi Institute of Science and Technology, Hyderabad, Telangana, India.

Muhammad Usman Tariq has more than 16+ year's experience in industry and academia. He has authored more than 200+ research articles, 110+ case studies, 150+ book chapters and several books other than 4 patents. He is founder and CEO of The Case HQ, a unique repository for courses, narrative and video case studies. He has been working as a consultant and trainer for industries representing six sigma, quality, health and safety, environmental systems, project management, and information security standards. His work has encompassed sectors in aviation, manufacturing, food, hospitality, education, finance, research, software and transportation. He has diverse and significant experience working with accreditation agencies of ABET, ACBSP, AACSB, WASC, CAA, EFQM and NCEAC. Additionally, Dr. Tariq has operational experience in incubators, research labs, government research projects, private sector startups, program creation and management at various industrial and academic levels. He is Certified Higher Education Teacher from Harvard University, USA, Certified Online Educator from

HMBSU, Certified Six Sigma Master Black Belt and has been awarded PFHEA, SFSEDA, SMIEEE, and CMBE.

Athyul Thomas VS is a third-year B.Tech Information Technology student at Sathyabama Institute of Science and Technology with a CGPA of 8.89. Thomas VS has received the Scholarship-Merit for Academic Excellence. Thomas VS's research interests include V2X communication, 5G, DSRC, IEEE 802.11bd, and Neuro-Symbolic Federated Learning. Thomas VS had worked on smart voting systems using facial recognition and AI-powered platforms for learning disability detection.

Akhila Reddy Yadulla holds an MS in Computer Science from Northwestern Polytechnic University in 2016, an MS in Information Technology Management from Campbellsville University in 2019, and a Ph.D. in Information Technology from the University of the Cumberlands in 2024. She is an accomplished Senior Software Engineer with over eight years of experience in Java full-stack development and expertise in the Software Development Life Cycle. Dr. Yadulla is proficient in Java, Spring Boot, Hibernate, RESTful APIs, Angular, React, Microservices, SQL/NoSQL databases, DevOps, and Agile methodologies. Her research focuses on Cybersecurity, Artificial Intelligence, Data Science, Big Data, Blockchain Technologies, Amazon Web Services, and Machine Learning. She combines deep technical knowledge, advanced problem-solving skills, and AI-driven innovative solutions in cutting-edge technologies. Notably, she led a team in developing a secure and scalable microservices architecture for significant telecommunication and banking platforms, resulting in a major increase in system performance.

Mounica Yenugula is a skilled IT professional with a strong academic background and an experienced Cloud Engineer. She holds a Ph.D. in Information Technology from the University of Cumberlands, where her research focused on critical security and trust issues in cloud environments. Her academic journey began with a Bachelor of Technology in Electronics and Communication Engineering from Koneru Lakshmaih University and continued with a Master of Science in Electrical Engineering from California State University, Los Angeles. As a certified Cloud Engineer, Mounica has successfully implemented cloud solutions within the financial sector, driving digital transformation. Her active involvement in the Women in IT community and her role as a judge for the Globee Awards demonstrate her commitment to industry advancement and innovation.

Index

E

F

G

I

L

N

P

R

S

T

www.ingramcontent.com/pod-product-compliance
Lightning Source LLC
LaVergne TN
LVHW081330021026
849161LV00008BA/1823